Occupational Health Law

Occupational Health Law

Fourth Edition

Diana M. Kloss

LLB (London), LLM (Tulane), Barrister (Gray's Inn), Hon FFoM,
Honorary Senior Lecturer in Occupational Health Law, University of Manchester,
Part-time Chairman of Employment Tribunals

Blackwell
Science

Published by Blackwell Science,
a Blackwell Publishing company

Editorial offices:
Blackwell Science Ltd, 9600 Garsington Road, Oxford OX4 2DQ, UK
   Tel: +44 (0) 1865 776868
Blackwell Publishing Inc., 350 Main Street, Malden, MA 02148-5020, USA
   Tel: +1 781 388 8250
Blackwell Science Asia Pty, 550 Swanston Street, Carlton, Victoria 3053, Australia
   Tel: +61 (0)3 8359 1011

First edition published 1989 by BSP Professional Books
Second edition published 1994 by Blackwell Science
Third edition published 1998 by Blackwell Science
Fourth edition published 2005 by Blackwell Publishing

Library of Congress Cataloging-in-Publication Data
is available

ISBN 0-632-06497-8

A catalogue record for this title is available from the British Library

Set in 10/12 pt Palatino
by DP Photosetting, Aylesbury, Bucks
Printed and bound in Great Britain
by TJ International, Padstow, Cornwall

The publisher's policy is to use permanent paper from mills that operate a sustainable forestry policy, and which has been manufactured from pulp processed using acid-free and elementary chlorine-free practices. Furthermore, the publisher ensures that the text paper and cover board used have met acceptable environmental accreditation standards.

For further information on Blackwell Publishing, visit our website:
www.blackwellpublishing.com

Contents

Preface to the Fourth Edition

It is six years since the publication of the third edition, and it has been a period of enormous change in the field of occupational health. The importance of trying to reduce the costs of health care has led the Government to look closely at the need for prevention in respect of work-related disease, and to consider how occupational health cover might be extended to more workers, especially those in small and medium-sized enterprises. The Health and Safety Executive, which in the past tended to concentrate mainly on workplace accidents, has been directing its attention more and more towards health issues, in particular to stress.

The involvement of the European Union has continued, especially in the field of health and safety law and laws against discrimination at work, and the incorporation into UK law of the European Convention on Human Rights has raised many novel issues for our courts. There has been an inexorable rise in the number of actions brought in civil courts for personal injury, leading to increases in employers' liability insurance. There have been important changes in civil procedure brought about by the Woolf reforms and significant developments in the law of data protection and freedom of information.

Perhaps the most significant development for occupational health professionals has been the Disability Discrimination Act, giving them a new role, but also creating some difficult ethical problems. In 2004 the Act was extended to millions more workers, including employees of small businesses and the emergency services.

In preceding editions of this book I tried to thank those who had assisted me, but the list has now become too long to mention everyone. I should like, however, to acknowledge Professor Tim Lee, now Emeritus Professor of Occupational Medicine in the University of Manchester, who first gave me the idea for the book, and his successors, Professor Nicola Cherry and Professor Raymond Agius. Dr Susan Robson, Professor Margot Brazier and Mrs Maureen Mulholland have been towers of strength and Richard Miles, my publisher, has shown unending patience.

These years have been for me also a time of change. I was delighted to be made an Honorary Fellow of the Faculty of Occupational Medicine and an Honorary Life Member of the Association of Local Authority Medical Advisers. I became a member of the Industrial Injuries Advisory Council. Dr John Ballard and his team in the AtWork Partnership have involved me in a number of new enterprises. I retired from my full-time post in the University of Manchester but was made an Honorary Senior Lecturer in Occupational Health Law. And I became the proud grandmother of Samantha and Amelia. This edition, like the others, is dedicated to the grandfather they will never know, my late husband, Günther Kloss.

I have tried to incorporate developments up to the end of 2004. Where 'he', 'his', etc. are used, these should be taken to represent both genders.

Diana Kloss
Manchester

Abbreviations

ABPI	Association of the British Pharmaceutical Industry
ACAS	Advisory, Conciliation and Arbitration Service
ACDP	Advisory Committee on Dangerous Pathogens
AD	Appointed Doctor
AFOM	Associate Member of the Faculty of Occupational Medicine of the Royal College of Physicians
AML	Additional maternity leave
BAT	Best available technique
BMA	British Medical Association
CEN	Comité Européen de la Normalisation
CENELEC	Comité Européen de la Normalisation Electronique
CHIP	Chemicals (Hazard Information and Packaging for Supply) Regulations 2002
COPD	Chronic obstructive pulmonary disease
COREC	Central Office for Research Ethics Committees
COSHH	Control of Substances Hazardous to Health (Regulations and Approved Code of Practice) 2002
CPR	Civil Procedure Rules
CRE	Commission for Racial Equality
CRHCP	Council for the Regulation of Healthcare Professions
DDA	Disability Discrimination Act 1995
DDP	Dismissal and disciplinary procedures
DH	Department of Health
DPA	Data Protection Act 1998
DRC	Disability Rights Commission
DSS	Department of Social Security
DWP	Department of Work and Pensions
EAGA	Expert Advisory Group on AIDS
EAV	Exposure action value
EC	European Community
ECJ	European Court of Justice
ECSC	European Coal and Steel Community
EMA	Employment Medical Adviser
EMAS	Employment Medical Advisory Service
ENA	Employment Nursing Adviser (renamed HM Inspector of Health and Safety (Occupational Health) in 1998
EOC	Equal Opportunities Commission
EPA	Equal Pay Act 1970
EPCA	Employment Protection (Consolidation) Act 1978

ERA	Employment Rights Act 1996
ESAW	European Statistics on Accidents at Work
EU	European Union
EURATOM	European Atomic Energy Community
FOIA	Freedom of Information Act 2000
FSA	Financial Services Authority
GAIC	Genetic and Insurance Committee
GMC	General Medical Council
GP	General Practitioner
HAVS	Hand-arm vibration syndrome
HELA	HSE/Local Authority Enforcement Liaison Committee
HGC	Human Genetics Commission
HSC	Health and Safety Commission
HSE	Health and Safety Executive
HSWA	Health and Safety at Work Act 1974
IIAC	Industrial Injuries Advisory Council
ILO	International Labour Organisation
IPPC	Integrated pollution prevention and control
ME	Myalgic encephalomyelitis (chronic fatigue syndrome)
MEL	Maximum exposure limit
MFOM	Member of the Faculty of Occupational Medicine of the Royal College of Physicians
MS	Multiple sclerosis
MSP	Maternity Suspension Pay
NHS	National Health Service
NI	National Insurance
NIOSH	National Institute for Occupational Safety and Health (USA)
NMC	Nursing and Midwifery Council
OES	Occupational exposure standard
Ofsted	Office for Standards in Education
OH	Occupational health
OHAC	Occupational Health Advisory Committee
OTC	Over the counter
PIN	Provisional Improvement Notice
POM	Prescription only medicine
PPE	Personal protective equipment
PUWER	Provision and Use of Work Equipment Regulations 1992
RCN	Royal College of Nursing
REA	Reduced earnings allowance
RIDDOR	Reporting of Injuries, Diseases and Dangerous Occurrences Regulations 1995
RMO	Regional Medical Officer
RSI	Repetitive strain injury
SAHW	Safe and Healthy Working
SDA	Sex Discrimination Act 1975 and 1986
SMEs	Small and medium-sized enterprises
SMP	Statutory Maternity Pay

SSP	Statutory sick pay
THOR	The Health and Occupation Reporting Network
UKAP	United Kingdom Panel for Health Care Workers Infected with Blood-borne Viruses
UKCC	United Kingdom Central Council (for Nurses, Midwives and Health Visitors)
VWF	Vibration white finger
WEL	Workplace exposure limit
WRULD	Work related upper limb disorder
WSA	Worker safety adviser

Table of Cases

Table of Statutes

Table of Statutory Instruments

General Introduction

Law and ethics

Doctors and nurses are subject to the law and to the courts. As professionals, they are also ruled by ethical principles which may impose more onerous duties. In the United Kingdom the regulation of the professions is delegated by Parliament to professional bodies, like the General Medical Council (GMC) for doctors (Medical Act 1983), and the Nursing and Midwifery Council (NMC) (formerly the United Kingdom Central Council for Nursing, Midwifery and Health Visiting (UKCC)) for nurses, midwives and health visitors (Nurses, Midwives and Health Visitors Act 1997). The decision whether an individual has behaved so disgracefully that he or she is unfit to continue as a doctor or nurse is granted to committees of these bodies. Appeals by the health professional to the courts were in the past only likely to succeed if the professional conduct committee failed to hold a fair hearing, or reached a decision which the judges considered so glaringly unreasonable that it must be beyond the committee's remit. Mr Singh, a senior nurse, was struck off the register of nurses in 1984 because he had given intravenous injections without a Certificate of Competence from his employing health authority (*Singh* v. *UKCC*). He had not contravened any legal provision, nor had any patient been injured. The decision of the Professional Conduct Committee of the then UKCC reflected the concern of the nursing profession that nurses should not accept delegated tasks from a doctor without proper training (the Certificate of Competence was regarded at the time as necessary proof of such training). A High Court judge refused to interfere:

> 'Whether on the facts proved the conduct of the appellant amounted to misconduct is a matter for the members of his profession, and an appellate tribunal would be very slow indeed to substitute its own opinion for that of experienced members of the profession ...'

It can fairly be said that in recent years the professional bodies have lost much of the confidence which the general public once placed in them. A series of careless, incompetent and occasionally criminal doctors have been allowed to continue in practice without the professional body taking any action. One prime example was the eventual disclosure of excessive mortality of children undergoing certain types of heart surgery at Bristol Royal Infirmary. It came to light only through the actions of a 'whistleblower' anaesthetist who had to move to Australia because of the opprobrium to which he was subjected. Dr Roylance, the Chief Executive, was struck off the medical register by the General Medical Council because of his management failures, which were held to amount to serious professional misconduct. This was upheld by the Privy Council (*Roylance* v. *General Medical Council* (1999)). Legislation has now created a Council for the Regulation of Healthcare Professions (CRHCP), set up under the National Health Service Reform and Healthcare Professions Act 2002, with power to ask for a review of decisions thought to be too lenient.

In *CRHCP* v. *Nursing and Midwifery Council and Truscott* (2004) Stephen Truscott was a paediatric nurse employed as a staff nurse. It was alleged that while on duty he had downloaded sexually explicit material on a computer. He admitted the charge of misconduct. The Nursing and Midwifery Council Professional Conduct Committee imposed a caution that would remain on his record for five years. The CRHCP protested that this penalty was unduly lenient and nothing short of removal from the register would be appropriate. They appealed to the High Court under the new procedure, but the court refused to interfere. The pornography was adult and not criminal. Truscott had already been dismissed. The power of the court to interfere was for the protection of members of the public, rather than the punishment of the individual.

In a similar case involving a doctor, the court held that it had power to hear an appeal against the GMC Professional Conduct Committee's ruling that a GP was not guilty of conducting a sexual relationship with one of his patients. The decision had been reached without hearing important relevant evidence, for example from the doctor's partners who had been ready to give evidence (*CRHCP* v. *GMC and Dr Ruscillo* (2004)). The Professional Conduct Committee should consider the case a second time, this time with all the relevant evidence available.

English law is found in the decisions of courts, in Acts of Parliament, and in statutory regulations made by authority of Parliament. Ethical rules are more difficult to discover. Both the medical and nursing professions now publish guidance to their members in fairly general terms. The GMC publishes a series of advisory booklets on ethics under the heading *Duties of a Doctor*. The Nursing and Midwifery Council has produced a Code of Professional Conduct (2002). The Faculty of Occupational Medicine of the Royal College of Physicians in 1993 published revised advice on ethics for doctors practising in occupational health. This has been re-issued with a supplement in 1997 and in 2004 is again under review. In 2001 a further publication, *Good Medical Practice for Occupational Physicians*, was produced. None of these codes is directly binding in law: they are an indication to the professions of the attitudes of other professionals who may be called upon to sit in judgment on their professional practice. This is not to underestimate their importance. The loss of the right to practise one's skills is a sanction greatly to be feared.

It is important to realise that neither the British Medical Association (BMA) nor the Royal College of Nursing (RCN) has any statutory function. They are 'trade unions' whose job is to represent their members. Nevertheless, both bodies are active in ethical debate. Disagreement is possible. The GMC has ruled that a doctor may break the confidence of a child too young to be able to appreciate his medical condition and therefore to give consent to treatment. The BMA, on the other hand, has argued that even a child's secrets must be respected, lest he be deterred from seeking help. In 1993 the BMA published a comprehensive survey of medical ethics, *Medical Ethics Today* (2nd edition 2004).

The RCN in its turn has produced the *Code of Professional Practice for Occupational Health Nurses* (1987).

Law and ethics may conflict. The law says that confidence dies with the individual, but many professionals consider it unethical to reveal clinical details after the patient's death. The law allows the testing of anonymous samples of blood, such that the donor of the sample cannot be told of any defect. Is this ethically sound? The Helsinki Declaration on experiments on human subjects states that experimental treatment of a therapeutic nature, if approved by an ethics committee, does not always require the subject's consent. English law permits no such exception to the need for informed consent. Lawyers are not competent to advise on ethics, but the courts will not sanction unlawful behaviour simply because it is regarded as ethical, just as the professions will not approve unethical behaviour simply because it is lawful. Fortunately, in most cases law and ethics agree.

There are now international ethical principles established in the field of occupational medicine. The International Commission on Occupational Health in 1992 published the *International Code of Ethics for Occupational Health Professionals*. This gives three basic principles:

(1) Occupational health practice must be performed according to the highest professional standards and ethical principles. Occupational health professionals must serve the health and social well-being of the workers, individually and collectively. They also contribute to environmental and community health.

(2) The obligations of occupational health professionals include protecting the life and the health of the worker, respecting human dignity and promoting the highest ethical principles in occupational health policies and programmes. Integrity in professional conduct, impartiality and the protection of the confidentiality of health data and of the privacy of workers are part of these obligations.

(3) Occupational health professionals are experts who must enjoy full professional independence in the execution of their functions. They must acquire and maintain the competence necessary for their duties and require conditions which allow them to carry out their tasks according to good practice and professional ethics.

This is bland and uncontroversial. General comments which may be made are to note the emphasis on prevention and health promotion, the expansion of the role of occupational health professionals into the field of environmental protection of the wider community and the need for 'a programme of professional audit of their own activities in order to ensure that appropriate standards have been set, that they are being met and that deficiencies, if any, are detected and corrected'.

The sources of English law

In modern times, law is found in statute and in precedent. Because English law has never been brought together into one code, the judges are still competent to make legal rules without reference to Parliament. This law, made by the judiciary, case by case, brick on brick, is known as the common law. Much of the law of contract and tort (civil liability for unlawful acts) is still in this form. Criminal law, on the other hand, is nearly all enacted in statute. Judges, therefore, fulfil two functions in our system: they declare and develop the common law, and they interpret the meaning of Acts of Parliament.

As in the medical profession, the opinion of those at the top of the hierarchy is more respected than that of juniors. So, decisions of the Judicial Committee of the House of Lords, the highest court, are binding on all other courts. Decisions of the Court of Appeal are binding on all courts other than the House of Lords. Decisions of the Employment Appeal Tribunal are binding on employment tribunals. But even the most senior judges must yield to the will of elected representatives of the people. In our unwritten constitution, Parliament can overturn every judgment by a simple statute.

Parliament has no time to consider every detail of complex legislation. Its practice is to establish broad principles in a parent Act, giving power to a delegate, often a Minister, to make regulations which will be laid before it, and in a few cases will need its affirmative approval. The Health and Safety at Work Act 1974 provides that an employer must do that which is reasonably practicable to ensure that his employees are reasonably safe; delegated legislation in the form of statutory instruments made under the authority of the Act lays down detailed provision for safety representatives, first aid, substances hazardous to health and so on.

Legislation, both primary and delegated, carries binding legal sanctions. It tends to be interpreted literally by English courts. A statute which talks about 'employees' will not apply to self-employed contractors. Laws which give compensation for 'accidental injury' will not cover cases where an employee has contracted a disease over a long period of exposure. If legislation is subject to decades of this literal approach, it becomes over-complex and impenetrably obscure.

Draftsmen strive to express themselves more and more clearly, but tend to lose the policy in a plethora of technical vocabulary. Within the last 20 years, especially in the field of employment law, it has become popular to attach Codes of Practice to Acts of Parliament, to which the Act directs courts and tribunals to refer as an aid to interpretation. Though these Codes are not in themselves the law, to fail to follow their advice will be *prima facie* evidence of a breach of the law. Examples are Approved Codes of Practice under the Health and Safety at Work Act and the ACAS Codes under a number of employment statutes. Amendment of a Code is simpler than altering legislation and judges can be more flexible in their interpretation.

Criminal and civil law

The criminal law is concerned with the punishment of those who offend against society as a whole. Criminal prosecutions are brought by public officials such as the Crown Prosecution Service (Procurator Fiscal in Scotland) and the Health and

Safety Executive. The defendant has to bear the costs of his defence, unless he qualifies for legal aid. If a defendant is convicted, he will be sentenced to some form of penalty, like a fine, imprisonment or community service. The money paid in fines goes to the courts, not to the victims of crime.

Compensation is a function of the civil law. The claimant (pursuer in Scotland), the individual harmed by an unlawful act, sues in the civil courts or tribunals for damages to make up for what he has suffered. He may also ask for a court order, like an injunction (interdict in Scotland), directing the defendant to return to legality, breach of which will be a contempt of court. The claimant has to finance his own civil action, unless poor enough to qualify for legal aid. Up to now, the English and Scots legal professions have set their face against contingent fees which are paid to the lawyer out of any damages awarded to his client. However, it is now possible for a solicitor or barrister to represent his client on a conditional fee basis, that is that he will waive his fee if he is unsuccessful, and solicitors and barristers are able to charge a higher fee if successful in litigation. The winner of an action in the civil courts will almost always obtain an order that the loser must pay his costs. For this reason, claimants who employ lawyers on a conditional fee basis have to take out insurance to cover the defendant's costs if they are unsuccessful.

The separation of punishment and compensation is not absolute. Criminal courts are empowered to order the convicted criminal to pay small amounts of compensation. Victims of violent crime can claim compensation, financed by taxation, from the Criminal Injuries Compensation Board. Those who flout an injunction granted by a civil court may be jailed for contempt. Also, many incidents give rise to both civil and criminal proceedings. For example, a company fails to provide protection for employees working with asbestos. It is prosecuted, convicted and fined in the criminal court for breach of regulations made under the Health and Safety at Work Act, a criminal statute. One of the employees concerned is diagnosed as suffering from lung cancer and asbestosis. He claims a disablement pension from the Department of Work and Pensions and sues his employer in a civil court for damages for the torts of negligence and breach of statutory duty. The criminal penalty will be paid by the company, but the compensation will be paid by insurance, state-administered in the case of the pension and privately organised in the case of the award of damages.

The geographical extent of the law

The United Kingdom consists of England, Wales, Scotland and Northern Ireland. England and Wales have the same law, but Scotland has a separate legal system and different procedures. As a general rule, Acts of the Westminster Parliament relating to health and safety, employment law and equal opportunities apply throughout Great Britain (which includes Scotland but excludes Northern Ireland). Northern Ireland is at present governed directly from Westminster. Legislation is usually extended to the Province by statutory instrument. Scotland and Wales now have devolved administrations and the Scottish Parliament has power to make law in a number of important fields, including health and education.

The Health and Safety at Work Act (Application outside Great Britain) Order 1995 extends the application of the Health and Safety at Work Act to offshore oil and gas installations, pipeline work, offshore construction, diving operations, etc. Safety statutes do not otherwise protect those who work abroad: they will have to rely on local regulations. A national of any Member State of the European Union must be allowed to work in any other Member State and will be entitled to the same social security benefits as the 'locals'. Medical and nursing qualifications obtained in any Member State must be recognised in all other Member States.

Employment laws, including health and safety laws, protect those who work in Great Britain. Unfair dismissal under section 94 Employment Rights Act 1996 has been held not to extend to a security adviser at an RAF base on Ascension Island, even though he was a British citizen, domiciled in England, working for a British company and receiving his wages in a bank account in England (*Lawson* v. *Serco* (2004)). His employment was wholly outside GB. The decision would have been different had he normally worked in GB but been dismissed during a temporary tour of duty abroad. The anti-discrimination legislation does not apply where the employee does his work wholly outside GB, but if the employee does at least part of his work in GB, or the work is undertaken for the purposes of the employer's establishment in GB and the employee was ordinarily resident in GB at the time of recruitment or at some time during the employee's work, he will be protected (Equal Opportunities (Employment Legislation) (Territorial Limits) Regulations 1999).

An action for damages for a breach of contract (including a contract of employment) may be brought in domestic courts against an employer with a place of business here, wherever the employee works. There are special, and highly complicated, rules about the jurisdiction of courts in the European Union, which are outside the scope of this book. The law which the court will apply will be that chosen by the parties in their agreement. Where they have not made a choice, it will be the law of the place where the employee habitually works. A choice of law other than that of England, Scotland or Northern Ireland cannot deprive an employee of his rights under the law of Great Britain if he habitually works in this country (Contracts (Applicable Law) Act 1990).

Where a worker injured abroad seeks compensation from his British employer, who is unwilling to defend the case here, the UK court might decide to refuse to entertain the case because the foreign court is more appropriate. In one case of an industrial accident which occurred in Scotland, the English court decided that the injured workman must sue in the Scottish court, because all the witnesses were in Scotland (*MacShannon* v. *Rockware Glass* (1978)). But in *Connelly* v. *RTZ* (1997), an English worker who had been injured whilst working in Namibia for a British company was permitted to sue in the English court because legal aid was available here.

Following the Connelly case, a number of workers who were resident in South Africa brought actions in the English courts for compensation for the damage caused to them by working in the asbestos mines in South Africa for a local subsidiary of a British parent company, Cape plc. More than 3000 claimants eventually became involved. The employer argued that England was not an appropriate forum, because the claimants were all South Africans, spoke little

English, had suffered the damage (mainly mesothelioma and asbestosis) in South Africa, and because all the evidence was in South Africa. The claimants submitted that without legal aid (which was not available to them in South Africa) they could not practically continue with their suits. In England there was also the possibility of using conditional fee arrangements with the lawyers. The House of Lords held that, though South Africa was the natural forum, this was a case where that was outweighed by the interests of justice. At the time of writing, millions of pounds have been paid in settlements to the South African workers (*Lubbe* v. *Cape plc* (2000)).

The law of the European Union

There are a number of European Community treaties: the European Atomic Energy Community (Euratom) Treaty, the Treaty of Rome, the Maastricht Treaty, the Treaty of Amsterdam and the Nice Treaty. The European Coal and Steel Community expired in 2002. The treaty which founded the European Economic Community, the Treaty of Rome, in 1958 sought to create a common market between the Member States by providing for the free movement of goods, persons, services and capital and restraining anti-competitive measures like monopolies and restrictive practices. It was incorporated into United Kingdom law by the European Communities Act 1972. The following 25 countries are now members of the Union: Belgium, France, Italy, Luxembourg, Netherlands, Germany, Denmark, Eire, United Kingdom, Greece, Spain, Portugal, Austria, Finland, Sweden, Cyprus, Czech Republic, Estonia, Hungary, Latvia, Lithuania, Malta, Poland, Slovakia and Slovenia. The Rome treaty was substantially amended by the Single European Act (1986) and more recently by the Treaty on European Union agreed at Maastricht in 1992. Further important changes were made in 1999 in the Treaty of Amsterdam, and in the Treaty of Nice in 2003. Further changes will probably be made as a result of the Treaty of Accession of ten new Member States, which came into force on 1 May 2004. A proposal for a written constitution for the European Union is causing dissension, especially in the United Kingdom. Because the European Union has no separate legal existence, the term 'European Community' is still in use.

The power to make new laws is given to the Council of Ministers and to the European Commission. Each Member State sends one Minister to the Council meetings. Sometimes the meeting is of Foreign Ministers, sometimes of Agriculture Ministers, and so on. The bureaucracy of the Community is the European Commission which is situated in Brussels. The judicial power is conferred on the Court of Justice of the European Community (ECJ) in Luxembourg. Each Member State has one judge on the court. Its principal task is to interpret the treaties and secondary legislation made with their authority. A Court of First Instance was created in 1988 to relieve the burden on the European Court. It deals *inter alia* with disputes involving employees of the European institutions, cases brought by individuals against Community institutions and decisions concerning the Community trade mark. Where the European Court makes a ruling on Community law, the courts of Member States must recognise and enforce it, and there is no appeal from its decisions.

The directly elected European Parliament at first had mainly a consultative and debating function, and its powers still fall short of a full legislative role, though the Maastricht treaty gave it a power of veto in limited areas. Today, the European Parliament exercises substantial powers of a legislative, budgetary and supervisory nature. The strengthening of a co-decision procedure in the Treaties of Amsterdam and Nice obliges the Council to submit proposed legislation to the Parliament on three occasions. Where amendments are made by the Parliament, the Council can reject or modify these only by unanimous vote.

Secondary legislation takes the form of regulations, directives and decisions. Regulations are mandatory. They have the force of law throughout the Community without the need to be ratified by the legislatures of the Member States. Directives are 'binding as to the result to be achieved', but leave the choice of method to the states concerned. They therefore require domestic implementing legislation. The Consumer Protection Act 1987 was passed to give effect to the principles laid down in the Product Liability Directive. It is not unknown for states to drag their feet. More than once the United Kingdom has been taken to the European Court by the Commission for failure to implement a directive. In *Marshall* v. *Southampton HA* (1986), the ECJ held that an individual employed by a Government could sue that Government under the provisions of an unimplemented directive as though it had been implemented, a privilege not available to non-Government employees. Employment in the National Health Service was held to be Government service. The European Court further developed the law in *Francovitch* v. *Italy* (1990) when it held that an individual may in some circumstances sue a Government for damages for failure to enact a directive within the specified period.

Decisions are rulings given by the Commission in individual cases and may be addressed to a state, an organisation or an individual. They are binding only on the individual addressed. Recommendations are persuasive, but not legally binding. Salvatore Grimaldi was born in Italy, but had worked for a long period in mining and construction in Belgium. He was diagnosed as suffering from an osteo-articular or angioneurotic impairment of the hand (Dupuytren's contraction), which he claimed was an occupational disease caused by the use of a pneumatic drill. This was not a prescribed disease under Belgian law, and Grimaldi was refused social security compensation. He appealed to the European Court.

The European Commission had made recommendations in 1962 and 1966 setting out a 'European schedule of occupational disease', including 'illness for over-exertion of the peritendonous tissue', and calling on Member States to introduce legislation granting compensation to those workers affected by such diseases and also to those able to prove that their disease was caused by work but unable to take advantage of domestic law because the disease was not prescribed. The European Court held that recommendations could not confer rights directly on individuals, but should be taken into consideration by national courts when interpreting domestic legislation, e.g. in cases of ambiguity (*Grimaldi* v. *Fonds des Maladies Professionelles* (1990)). A further recommendation in 1990 called on Member States to adopt the schedule, and this was repeated in 2003.

The European Treaties and laws made thereunder deal primarily with matters relating to the establishment of free trade. Much of our law is unaffected by a

European dimension. The EC Treaty is not concerned with the law of theft, the grounds for divorce, the validity of wills or the need to obtain the consent of a patient to medical treatment. But a free market demands that no enterprise should be able to obtain an unfair advantage by ignoring essential safety measures imposed by law on its competitors. Every producer must start from the same baseline. Member States are unwilling to pass laws to protect the health of workers or the community which demand costly expenditure, if other States are permitted to maintain nineteenth century practices.

The EC Treaty anticipated the need to deal with social as well as economic problems: 'Member States agree upon the need to promote improved working conditions and an improved standard of living for workers ...'. Article 137 provided that the Commission had the task of promoting close cooperation between Member States in the social field, particularly in matters relating to employment, labour law and working conditions, basic and advanced vocational training, social security, prevention of occupational accidents and diseases, occupational hygiene, and the right of association and collective bargaining between employers and workers. In 1997, the Treaty of Amsterdam made further important changes to permit the United Kingdom to accede to the European Social Charter which it had rejected at the negotiations in Maastricht in 1991.

In 1974, an Advisory Committee on Safety, Hygiene and Health Protection was established to assist the Commission. It has had a significant influence on the development of policy. A series of Action Programmes on Safety and Health at Work have been adopted. The Committee reports annually.

The adoption of directives to implement its initiatives was hampered by the necessity to obtain unanimity among Member States. It was possible for only one State to veto any measure in the Council of Ministers. In 1987, however, the Single European Act came into operation. The countries of Europe agreed to establish a truly common market, with the abolition of all barriers to trade, by 1992. The resultant amendments to the Treaty of Rome included Article 138. Under this Article, it is now possible to adopt directives laying down minimum health and safety standards which exceed recognised standards in Member States. Qualified majority voting gives larger nations more votes than smaller ones, but allows even one of the 'Big Four' (France, Germany, Italy and the United Kingdom) to have legislation forced on it by the other Member States.

Similar principles apply to the enactment of directives in the field of consumer safety (Article 95). The EC Council may by a qualified majority approve standards for electrical and other goods. In this area, the standards are both minimum and maximum, lest states attempt to protect the home producer by keeping out goods which do not conform to unnecessarily high standards. The long-term solution is to establish European standards to replace those of the individual countries, and European organisations have been created to bring this about: Comité Européen de la Normalisation (CEN) and Comité Européen de la Normalisation Electronique (CENELEC) (for electrical apparatus).

The Single European Act (Article 157) for the first time included specific provisions allowing the Council of Ministers to legislate by a qualified majority in the area of environmental protection by, for example, setting minimum standards for toxic emissions into the atmosphere and water purity. States are permitted to set higher standards for themselves, unless this conflicts with the free market. In *EC Commission* v. *Denmark* (1989) a Danish law that beer and soft drinks could only be marketed in reusable containers for which a deposit must be charged was upheld by the European Court, even though it to some extent discriminated against foreign producers, because it reduced the quantity of litter damaging the environment.

The pace of change has been considerably expedited by the new system. Between 1970 and 1985 only six health and safety at work Directives were adopted by the European Council. In July 1987, however, a third Action Programme on safety, health and hygiene at work was adopted. A long list of measures was proposed by the Commission, including 15 new Directives. By 1989 a 'Framework' Directive for the Introduction of Measures to Encourage Improvements in Safety of Health of Workers was approved by the Council of Ministers. This has been enacted into UK law by the Management of Health and Safety at Work Regulations (1992, amended 1999) which require employers to assess risks to employees, provide them with health surveillance, give them information and training and appoint competent persons to supervise a safe system of work.

Shortly after, five 'Daughter Directives' containing more specific provisions about health, safety and welfare provision in the workplace (heating, lighting, ventilation, cleanliness and so on), machinery and work equipment safety, personal protective equipment, visual display units and the handling of heavy loads were passed. These are now incorporated into UK law as the Workplace (Health, Safety and Welfare) Regulations 1992, Provision and Use of Work Equipment Regulations 1992, Personal Protective Equipment at Work Regulations 1992, Health and Safety (Display Screen Equipment) Regulations 1992 and Manual Handling Operations Regulations 1992. All these regulations are discussed in detail in Chapter 5, and are regularly reviewed and sometimes updated.

In 1994 a European Agency for Safety and Health at Work was established in Spain. It is charged with the following tasks:

(1)   to collect and disseminate technical, scientific and economic information in Member States to identify existing national priorities and programmes;
(2)   to collect technical, scientific and economic information on research into safety and health at work and on other research activities and to disseminate the results of that research;
(3)   to promote and support co-operation and exchange of information and experience among Member States including information on training programmes;
(4)   to organise conferences and seminars and exchanges of experts;
(5)   to supply European Union bodies and Member States with technical, scientific and economic information in order to enable them to formulate and implement policies;
(6)   to establish a network for the provision of information;
(7)   to collect and make available information on safety and health from and to countries outside the European Union and international organisations;
(8)   to provide technical, scientific and economic information on methods and tools for implementing preventive activities, paying particular attention to the problems of small and medium sized organisations; and

(9)   to contribute to the development of European Union action programmes relating to the protection of health and safety at work.

Further developments have been the creation of a Committee of Senior Labour Inspectors (1995), a Scientific Committee for Occupational Exposure Limits to Chemical Agents (1995) and a Major Accident Hazards Bureau (1996). Information on the causal relationships between diseases and exposures in the workplace was published by the Commission in 1997 (*Information notices on diagnosis of occupational diseases*) and a recommendation in 2003 called on all Member States to introduce into their national laws measures to help to prevent these diseases and to compensate the victims. This recommendation placed emphasis on the need for Member States to make their statistics on occupational diseases compatible with the European schedule, so that information on the causative agent or factor, the medical diagnosis and the gender of the patient is available for each case of occupational disease. A Communication from the Commission entitled *Adapting to change in work and society: a new Community strategy on health and safety at work 2002–2006* attaches particular importance to the prevention of occupational diseases. Member States are encouraged to set national targets.

The importance of statistics was reflected in research done by the European Agency which led to a report in 2000 providing a comprehensive overview of the occupational health and safety situation in the European Union. The accession of ten new Member States, many with industries which have lacked investment resources for 50 years or more, will no doubt significantly alter the profile of the average European enterprise.

The Commission's strategy acknowledged that its legal framework is complex and unclear and promised simplification and rationalisation through consolidation of directives and a single report on their implementation. At the same time, it will try to improve the application of the existing law, notably through the European Union Senior Labour Inspectors Committee.

Although the safety of workers has been an important part of European Community policy since the foundation of the Coal and Steel Community in 1951, and the Treaty of Rome provided specifically for equal pay for men and women at work (see Chapter 9), the use of Community law to lay down minimum rights for workers in other areas is far more controversial. Article 95 permits legislation on working conditions if it is necessary to ensure the effective functioning of the common market, and measures to protect workers affected by collective redundancies, transfer of the undertaking in which they are employed and the insolvency of their employer have been enacted under this power.

Conflict arose between the majority of European governments who regarded the protection of the worker as an important aim for social legislation, and the free marketeers in the UK government who preferred to allow market forces to determine workers' rights unfettered by what they regarded as artificial barriers to economic growth.

In December 1989 11 Member States signed a Community Charter of Fundamental Social Rights of Workers (the Social Charter). This was largely a declaration of policy, without direct legal effect. The UK government stood alone in refusing to agree to the principle that workers' rights should be enshrined in

European law, and did not sign the Charter. The Charter's provisions are expressed in general aspirational terms. It deals with minimum wages, working hours and holidays, rights of association and the right to negotiate and conclude collective agreements.

At the meeting of governments at Maastricht in December 1991, the majority of Member States agreed that they wished to adopt further measures to pursue the aims of the Social Charter. Again, the UK government was in a minority of one. The compromise eventually reached (the Maastricht Protocol) was that all 12 Member States agreed that 11 states (all except the UK) might have recourse to the institutions, procedures and mechanisms of the Treaty of Rome for the purposes of taking the acts and decisions necessary to give effect to the new agreement. The UK government would not participate in this process, though it would not interfere with the 11, and it would continue to comply with pre-Maastricht legislation.

The political and social problems created by this two-tier system were many. In particular, its implementation was thought to result in the British worker becoming the poor man of Europe, with significantly lower wage rates and reduced legal protection against exploitation by the employer, although increased trade through the production of more competitive goods increased general prosperity. There were signs that multi-national companies looked favourably at siting their plants in the UK to take advantage of lower rates of pay.

The legal problems were formidable. It was not easy to differentiate between the various types of legislation. Take, for example, the Working Time Directive, which created minimum daily and weekly rest periods and annual paid holidays of a minimum length. If, as the Commission argued, this was as a health and safety measure it could be passed by a qualified majority without the consent of the UK government and must then be enacted into UK law. If it were to be classified as a 'workers' rights' measure, it might either fall within what is now Article 95, in which case it could only become law if all the Member States agreed, or alternatively (but less likely) it could be regarded as an attempt to implement the Social Charter falling within the Maastricht Protocol and therefore not involving the UK at all.

This issue was litigated in the European Court in 1996. In *United Kingdom* v. *EU Council* the European Court held that 'working environment', 'safety' and 'health' in what is now Article 138 of the EC Treaty should be interpreted liberally to embrace all factors (physical or otherwise) capable of affecting the health and safety of the worker in his working environment. Legislation on rest periods, holidays and night working was held to be relevant to health, defined by the World Health Organisation as 'a state of complete physical, mental and social well-being and not merely the absence of disease or infirmity'. Thus, the Working Time Directive is mandatory on the United Kingdom.

The Social Charter and the Maastricht Protocol emphasised the principle of subsidiarity, namely that the Community must recognise the differing social structures and the diversity of national practices of the Member States, and legislate only where it is necessary to achieve the objectives of the treaties. There can be no Community-wide minimum fair wage, because of the many differences in cost of living, incidence of taxation and social security etc., but there can be the espousal of the concept of a legally guaranteed fair wage for each individual country. The Labour Government elected in May 1997 adopted the Social Charter for the United Kingdom, and introduced national minimum wage legislation. In the Treaty of Amsterdam 1997 the UK Government agreed to accept qualified majority voting for all Social Charter Directives in the future, and to adopt those Directives already agreed by the other Member States after Maastricht. These are the European Works Council Directive, the Parental Leave Directive, the Part-Time Workers Directive and the Directive on Burden of Proof in Sex Discrimination cases.

The previous Conservative government expressed concern that, at a time when it was pursuing a policy of deregulation on the home front with the aim of freeing industry from petty legal restrictions which deter growth, new and onerous duties were being introduced through membership of the European Community. 'Health and safety legislation could be brought into disrepute by introducing bureaucratic requirements which would not be complied with' (*Review of implementation and enforcement of EC law in the UK* (1993) Department of Trade and Industry). The DTI report recommended the designation of one of the Health and Safety Commissioners as especially concerned, as far as possible, to look after the interests of the small employer. In 2000 a report from the Department of Environment, Transport and the Regions stated that 'a more deeply engrained culture of self-regulation needs to be cultivated, most crucially in the 3.7 million businesses with less than 250 employees'.

The implementation of EC law is for the Member States, who must adjust the European principles to their own domestic institutions, but the essence of the principles must reach the statute book. In particular, the granting of exemptions to the self-employed and small businesses, unless permitted by the Directive, would be a breach of European law for which the government could be condemned by the European Court, though Article 138 directs the Member States to be conscious of the needs of small and medium-sized undertakings. Meanwhile, directives continue to dictate minimum health and safety requirements throughout Europe. Changes in the regulations relating to noise, and new regulations on hand-arm vibration syndrome, are only two examples of new legislation coming directly from Europe.

The European Convention on Human Rights and the Human Rights Act 1998

The Council of Europe was established at the end of World War II, before the European Union. Though several nations are members of both, the two bodies are quite separate. The European Convention on Human Rights and Fundamental Freedoms is a treaty of the Council of Europe, to which the UK is a signatory, in fact one of the founding members. It creates the European Court of Human Rights. The European Court in Luxembourg (the Court of Justice of the European Communities) must not be confused with the European Court of Human Rights in Strasbourg, France. Decisions of the Strasbourg Court are not directly enforceable in the UK, though they carry considerable moral and political influence.

Although the UK was a prime mover in the creation of the Human Rights Convention, the impetus for which was the horror of what had been done to the Jews in Germany under the Third Reich, the British Government for a number of years was of the view that it was unnecessary to give UK citizens the right to petition the Strasbourg court, since everyone knew that the UK was above reproach. In 1966 it was accepted that this was not necessarily the case and that British citizens should be given the right to appeal to the Human Rights Court where they were dissatisfied with the lack of a remedy from the domestic courts, and for 20 years this was the ultimate source of complaint for those who were dissatisfied with British justice. Because there was no internal procedure to challenge a decision as contrary to the Human Rights Convention, a disproportionate number of claims was made to the Human Rights Court by British citizens.

The Labour Government elected in 1997 declared that the UK would incorporate the Convention on Human Rights into UK law and this was done by means of the Human Rights Act 1998, which came into force fully in 2000. The Act preserves the sovereignty of the Westminster and Scottish Parliaments. In the last resort, an Act of Parliament can lawfully deprive British citizens of their rights under the Convention. However, Parliament, and the courts in interpreting legislation, are obliged as far as possible to comply with the Convention. Thus, a decision of the UK Parliament to pass legislation which conflicts with the Convention will be a deliberate decision that the interests of this country override the Human Rights Convention. In such an unlikely case the Strasbourg court and the other members of the Council of Europe might make representations, and there is the possibility that the UK might even be expelled from membership of the Council of Europe. The higher courts are given power by the Act to make a declaration of incompatibility between legislation and the Convention. This happens only rarely, but when it does there is obviously pressure on the legislature to change the law.

The rights under the Convention can only be enforced through UK courts directly against public authorities. These include the civil service, local authorities, NHS bodies and police authorities. Since courts and tribunals are public authorities, they must interpret existing and future legislation, and develop the common law, in conformity with the Convention wherever possible. They must have regard to Strasbourg case law. While the employees of public authorities can sue the employer directly for a breach, employees in the private sector have to take a more roundabout route. For example, an employee claiming unfair dismissal will be able to argue that conduct by the employer which breaches the Convention must by definition be unfair. Also, the Government has a duty to protect its citizens by law from invasions of their human rights by a private employer.

Not all rights under the Convention are absolute, and it provides a number of acceptable reasons for restricting the rights of the citizen. For example, the right to freedom of expression in Article 10 includes the right to wear whatever clothes and hair styles the individual chooses, but the employer is entitled to demand outfits which are decent, do not constitute a health and safety risk, and do not damage the employer's image. The right to freedom of religion and belief in Article 9 may be limited by the employer's reasonable demands. For example, in *X v. United Kingdom* (1981) a Muslim schoolteacher was held not to have the right to take Friday afternoons off to attend the mosque. The employer had offered to set aside a room in the school where he could pray, or alternatively to give him a four day a week contract. In a nominally Christian country those from other faiths must to some extent conform with the prevailing customs. However, employers are expected to do what is reasonably practicable to accommodate them. Legislation has been passed to allow Sikhs not to wear hard hats on construction sites (Construction (Head Protection) Regulations 1989), but the regulations do not apply to other places of work. Although the prohibition of beards for reasons of hygiene may be justified, it would be necessary for an employer to show that suitable protective clothing would not adequately control the risk (see Chapter 9).

The Convention approach is to decide whether a particular qualification of a right is proportionate. The test of proportionality also contains within it its own concept of procedural fairness. An infringement of a qualified right is much less likely to be a proportionate response to a legitimate aim if the person affected by the action was not consulted or not given a right to a hearing.

'Inherent in the whole of the Convention is a search for the fair balance between the demands of the general interest of the community and the requirements of the protection of the individual's rights.' (*Soering* v. *UK* (1989))

There is a 'margin of appreciation', that is each state is allowed a certain freedom to evaluate its public policy decisions. Not all countries will interpret the Convention in exactly the same way. An example would be the law of obscenity which restrains the freedom of expression of publishers. Some countries' laws will be more liberal than others in what they permit.

Convention rights important for OH professionals are Article 5, the right to liberty and security of person, Article 6, the right to a fair trial, Article 8, the right to respect for private and family life, Article 9, freedom of thought, conscience and religion, and Article 10, freedom of expression. There is no freestanding right to complain of discrimination. Article 14 states that the enjoyment of the rights and freedoms set forth in the Convention must be secured without discrimination on any ground such as sex, race, colour, language, religion, political or other opinion, national or social origin, association with a national minority, property, birth or other status. For example, my right to freedom of expression should not depend on whether I am black or white, male or female, a member of the Liberal Democrat or British National Party. My right to a fair trial includes the right to an interpreter if I do not speak English.

Article 8 of the Convention, the right to respect for private and family life, home and correspondence, has given rise to a number of cases both in the Strasbourg and the UK courts. English law up to now, though recognising a duty of confidence, has not developed a general right of privacy. What is the difference? In *Kaye v. Robertson* (1991) Gordon Kaye, a television actor, was badly injured when a hoarding fell on his car in a storm. A photographer without permission took photographs of him lying in his hospital bed after an operation and sold them to a newspaper. The court held that there was no right to privacy. However, in 2003 Naomi Campbell, a model, was photographed in the street leaving a meeting of Narcotics Anonymous and the picture was published in the *Daily Mirror*. The House of Lords held that this was a breach of the duty of confidence by the other member of the group who had notified the press that Naomi was attending the meetings, and that the photographs should not have been published. They discussed the conflict between Article 8 and Article 10, the right of freedom of speech, and held that in this case there was no public interest overriding the claimant's right to have her private life remain private (*Campbell* v. *MGN*). Attempts have been made to persuade UK courts that Article 8 could be used to create a general right of privacy, but they have not so far succeeded. Nevertheless, Article 8 has strengthened the right to have confidential information respected, which is very relevant to occupational health (Chapter 3).

The courts have held that matters in the public domain do not fall within the protection of Article 8. In *X* v. *Y* (2004) the applicant was employed as a development officer for a charity which promoted personal development among young people. His post involved working with young offenders. He was arrested for engaging in consensual sexual activity with another man in a public toilet and was cautioned for an offence under the Sexual Offences Act. He did not reveal this to his employers, but when they discovered it through police checks they dismissed him for gross misconduct. They emphasised that it was not his homosexuality that was in issue, but his deliberate failure to disclose a criminal offence that was relevant to his job. The charity was not a public authority, so no action could be brought for a breach of the Human Rights Act. Nevertheless, the Court of Appeal held that in determining whether the dismissal was fair the tribunal should take into account the Convention. The applicant argued that the dismissal was a breach of Article 8, since at the time of the offence he was off duty and the incident did not involve any of his clients. The court held, however, that as the crime was committed in a public place it could not be regarded as private. In any event, the applicant was guilty of a criminal offence, which is not a private matter. 'The applicant wished to keep the matter private. That does not make it part of his private life or deprive it of its public aspect.' It was held that the dismissal was fair.

Alison Halford was Assistant Chief Constable of Merseyside Police. She failed to achieve further promotion in Merseyside and elsewhere, because, she said, of her gender. Eventually she made a complaint to a tribunal, backed by the Equal Opportunities Commission. She claimed that her telephone calls from her office to her solicitor were intercepted. It was not unlawful in UK domestic law at the time for the employer to listen to his employee's calls on the office telephone. Ms Halford therefore complained to the Strasbourg Court under Article 8 and her complaint was upheld (*Halford* v. *UK* (1997)). She had a reasonable expectation that her calls would not be overheard, since the Chief Constable had assured her that she could make private calls on that phone. Legislation is now in place to permit employers to monitor telecommunications at work, but only when employees have been warned that monitoring is in place. The Regulation of Investigatory Powers Act 2000 permits interception of a communication over a telecommunication system if this is a legitimate business practice. The Telecommunications (Lawful Business Practice) Regulations 2000 authorise businesses to monitor or record communications for good business reasons, e.g. for the purpose of quality control, to prevent or detect crime, to investigate or detect unauthorised use of the telephone, emails, or the Internet. The employer must make all reasonable efforts to inform every person who may use the system that interception may take place. In the case of occupational health communications, it is important that agreement is reached with the employer that these will not be monitored. The Information Commissioner in the draft Part 4 of the Data Protection Code of Practice emphasises this point (Chapter 3).

Evidence given in legal proceedings may be challenged as obtained through an invasion of privacy under the Human Rights Act. Jean Jones was employed by the University of Warwick. She dropped a full cash box with a broken lid on to her right wrist, causing a small cut. She said that she had developed a focal dystonia, and claimed damages in excess of £135,000. The defendant was suspicious of this claim and hired an enquiry agent who obtained access to the claimant's home by posing as a market researcher. He had a hidden camera. The defendant's expert, having seen the films taken in her home, was of the opinion that the claimant had an entirely satisfactory function in her right hand. It was not in dispute that the enquiry agent was guilty of trespass. The issue was whether the illegally obtained films should be admitted in evidence. The claimant argued that they should not be, because they were obtained in breach of Article 8 by invading her home; the defendant argued that they should because there were a true record, not manufactured, and without them the defendant would be denied a fair trial under Article 6. The court agreed to admit the evidence as probative, but ordered the defendant to pay the costs of the litigation to establish the admissibility of the evidence (*Jones* v. *University of Warwick* (2003)).

International Labour Organisation

This was founded in 1919 by those nations who had been the victors in World War I, to bring together representatives of employers' and workers' organisations and also of governments of participating states. It holds international conferences annually in Geneva and acts as a focus for those who strive to raise standards of protection for workers, not merely in the field of health and safety, but in industrial relations in general. Most countries belong to the International Labour Organisation (ILO), which is the oldest and most experienced international body concerned with the establishment of international labour standards.

The ILO adopts Conventions and Recommendations. Ratification of a Convention amounts to an undertaking that its provisions will be given legally binding force by a legislative enactment. Even then, a government may denounce a Convention at a later date, as the British Government has done with laws preventing women workers from being employed at unsocial hours (see Chapter 9). A Recommendation does not have to be ratified, but adoption by a government signifies that the government will in the future be guided by the Recommendation if and when it decides to act. The ILO has produced a Convention and Recommendation relating to the provision of occupational health services (see Chapter 1).

Chapter 1
The Provision of Occupational Health Services

1.1   The development of occupational health services

The origins of occupational health provision lie in the heyday of the Industrial Revolution. Workers in the mills and factories, in common with all except the well-to-do, had no access to medical services because they could not afford them. Some benevolent employers, moved by the suffering of the masses, provided housing and medical services out of their profits; most did not. The nature of this provision was not in any sense connected with work-related disease or injury; it was general medicine for workers and their families such as is today provided by the general practitioner in the National Health Service. Workers still perceive the provision of medical and nursing services at work as a mark of a good and caring employer; it goes together in their minds with decent canteen facilities and a good working environment. On the other hand, now that the NHS gives everyone access to free medical treatment, it may be considered wasteful for there to be duplication of treatment facilities, other than to provide first aid in an emergency. This argument might be more easily sustained if the NHS were not under constant financial pressure. Also, if the provision of physiotherapy at the workplace saves the worker having to take a day off a week to attend the hospital, it may be of financial benefit to the employer and reduce the burden on public funds. Increasingly, employers in the private sector see the health of their key workers as a business asset to be maintained with medical and nursing assistance in the same way as engineers maintain machinery, though in practice regular health surveillance of such workers is often contracted out to private health organisations.

Other developments which contributed to the growth of occupational health (OH) services were various Acts of Parliament passed to give the employee a right to compensation against his employer (beginning with the Workmen's Compensation Act 1897), long since transferred to the Welfare State under the industrial injuries legislation, and to protect the consumer against risks caused by the ill-health of workers in, for example, the food processing and transport industries. The principal motives behind the introduction of medical monitoring by occupational health professionals in response to these measures were to protect the employer against legal action and the public against injury, rather than to care for the welfare of the workers, though the genuine concern for their employees of pioneer companies like Chloride and Pilkington's must also be acknowledged. Other factors were the increase in statutory regulations to protect the munitions

workers during World War I and the need after both World Wars to help the
disabled to find and maintain suitable employment.

    After World War II there were several official reports on provision for occu-
pational health, including the Dale Report in 1951 and the Porritt Report in
1962. The Robens Committee on Health and Safety at Work, reporting in 1972,
stated that in their understanding occupational health included two main elements – occupational medicine, which is a specialised branch of preventive
medicine, and occupational hygiene, which is the province of the chemist and
the engineer engaged in the measurement and physical control of environmental hazards. 'Clearly these two elements must be closely integrated, since
the basis for environmental control must be derived from the medical assessment of risk.' The Committee placed the greatest stress on their fear that the
employment of large numbers of doctors and nurses in the workplace would be
a wasteful duplication of the general practitioner service. They were largely in
agreement with the view of the Government that: 'In the field of occupational
health the working environment is of predominant importance, and it is engineers, chemists and others rather than doctors who have the expertise to
change it.'

    The Health and Safety Commission (HSC) in 1977 produced a wide-ranging
discussion document: *Occupational Health Services – The Way Ahead*. This highlighted the problem of providing services for workers in small organisations. It
explored various ways of promoting cooperation between employers, like the
establishment of group industrial health services (Slough is a well-known
example) to which small companies could subscribe according to the number of
their employees, or the 'leasing' of spare capacity in a large organisation to other
employers in the locality.

    The Health and Safety Executive (HSE) in 1982 published a booklet entitled
Guidelines for Occupational Health Services, which gave practical guidance on the
functions, staffing and operation of OH services. This stressed that each organisation has its own needs. The number of employees, the number of locations, the
number and severity of potential hazards, any statutory requirements for health
surveillance, and the availability of and distance from NHS facilities must all be
taken into account.

    In 1983 the Select Committee on Science and Technology of the House of Lords
chaired by Lord Gregson reviewed the future provision of occupational health
and hygiene services. It defined occupational health as the physical and mental
well-being of the workers and occupational hygiene as the control of physical,
chemical and biological factors in the workplace which may affect the health of the
worker. The Gregson Committee perceived the main aim of an occupational
health service as the promotion of the health and safety of those employed at the
workplace. Occupational medicine was described as 'a branch of preventive
medicine with some therapeutic functions'. No full survey of occupational health
services had ever been undertaken, but what research had been done revealed
that at that time (1976), full-time medical and nursing personnel were concentrated in large industries, as might be expected. Many large companies relied
on part-time medical advisors who might be local general practitioners (GPs). Few
of these had special training in occupational medicine: 87.6 per cent of firms,

employing 36 per cent of the workforce, had no medical service apart from first-aiders (*Occupational Health Services – The Way Ahead* (1977)).

The Committee concluded that more provision was needed in small firms. They put considerable emphasis on preventive medicine:

'Early detection of hazards of work and the timely adoption of preventive measures will not only alleviate individual suffering: they will lighten the financial burden which sickness imposes upon the State. There are also sound business reasons for ensuring that a workforce remains healthy. A healthy worker is a more efficient worker: absenteeism is lower and productivity higher.'

The costs of the service should continue to be borne by the employers in reflection of their general duty under the Health and Safety at Work Act. However, Gregson was not in favour of imposing a legal obligation to provide an occupational health service. The Committee thought that a non-statutory Code of Practice should be drawn up and monitored by the Employment Medical Advisory Service (EMAS). Tax incentives could be conferred on those who implemented the Code, and insurance companies might take it into account in fixing premiums. General practitioners should be encouraged to extend the occupational health side of their activities and to acquire additional qualifications. Occupational health nurses should be the first point of contact between the patient and other sources of referral. Trade unions and employees should be given more opportunity to have a voice in the management of occupational health services.

So far, there has been no significant move towards either a voluntary or a statutory Code of Practice. Meanwhile there have been international developments. As long ago as 1962, the European Commission recommended that a statutory obligation to provide an occupational health service should be introduced at least for large employers (as has been shown, this would not represent much of a change in this country where most large concerns already have such a service). In June 1985, the International Labour Organisation (ILO) adopted a Convention (No. 161) and a supporting Recommendation (No. 171) on Occupational Health Services. The Convention defines occupational health services as:

'services entrusted with essentially preventive functions and responsible for advising the employer, the workers and their representatives in the undertaking on:

(1) the requirements for establishing and maintaining a safe and healthy working environment which will facilitate optimal physical and mental health in relation to work; and
(2) the adaptation of work to the capabilities of workers in the light of their state of physical and mental health.'

It should be noted that the Convention covers occupational hygiene and ergonomic services as well as medical and nursing services. Signatories to it will have to formulate, implement and periodically review a coherent national policy on occupational health services and to develop progressively occupational health services for all workers such as are adequate and appropriate to the specific risks of the undertakings. The UK Government has sought the advice of the HSC on whether the UK should ratify and/or accept Recommendation 171, which is in similar terms to the Convention, but would not, if implemented, carry the same mandatory legal force as the Convention, were the Convention to be adopted here. The HSC has advised that no decision should be taken at this stage.

If this country were to ratify the Convention, legislation would eventually be needed. An additional duty would have to be imposed on employers by amendments to the Health and Safety at Work Act whereby they would be compelled to provide an adequate and appropriate occupational health service, as defined in the legislation, or be guilty of a criminal offence. Further legal provisions would be needed to implement specific requirements. The legislation would not have to come into immediate effect, but would commit us to a process of progressive development.

The Recommendation could be accepted only in part; there would be a moral though not a legal obligation to implement any provisions which had been accepted. However, acceptance of the Recommendation would not require any major changes in our law.

As the Convention is under discussion, it may be worthwhile to examine its structure, especially as it demonstrates the trend of the international community's thinking on occupational health services. Important aspects are as follows:

(1) It employs legal sanctions, rather than the voluntary approach which has so far prevailed in the UK.
(2) It adopts a multidisciplinary approach, regarding the doctor and the nurse as part of a team which also includes the hygienist and the ergonomist.
(3) It contemplates that there shall be recognised qualifications for personnel providing occupational health services.
(4) It requires the involvement of the workers themselves in the management of the service.
(5) It sees the function of the service as essentially preventive; treatment is confined to first aid and emergency treatment.

As has been seen, the movement in occupational health has been away from treatment but towards prevention. If an employer wishes to provide 'private treatment' services in addition to the NHS because he thinks them economically worthwhile he may do so, but this is less important than the identification of work-related hazards and the steps taken to protect the workers against them. A Joint ILO/World Health Organisation Committee in 1950 wrote this:

'Occupational health should aim at the promotion and maintenance of the highest degree of physical, mental and social well-being of workers in all occupations; the prevention among workers of departures from health caused by their working conditions; the protection of workers in their employment from risks resulting from factors adverse to health; the placing and maintenance of the worker in an occupational environment adapted to his physiological and psychological equipment.'

The UK Government's response to the Gregson report was published in 1984 (Select Committee on Science and Technology). It enthusiastically welcomed the conclusion that 'the responsibility for occupational health and hygiene services should lie largely with individual employers'. It doubted whether GPs could provide services as an integral part of primary care without reducing efficiency. The Government made clear its determination not to provide OH services out of public funds.

At the same time, the HSC agreed that there should be a review of the participation of GPs in occupational health practice. The Commission supported the provision of a training and qualification scheme appropriate for doctors working for only a small part of their time in industry. It recognised 'the important role of trained occupational health nurses ... which is frequently misunderstood and ... could be widened in scope'.

In 1986 the HSC issued a statement of policy in response to the Gregson Report. It declined at that stage to formulate a Code of Practice. Instead it has initiated a programme of action. This included:

(1) the preparation of guidelines for employers on such matters as the benefits and availability of OH services;
(2) a publicity campaign especially aimed at small firms about the appropriate use of OH services;
(3) the encouragement of new projects by the Industry Advisory Committees (organisations set up within particular industries, under the aegis of the HSE, to make recommendations to the HSC);
(4) the promotion by the HSE of conferences and seminars for the exchange of practical information about the provision of OH services;
(5) liaison with training bodies to promote the training of OH specialists and make managers more aware of health and safety;
(6) the improvement of co-ordination with the National Health Service;
(7) co-ordination between the organisations involved in the provision of OH services, including larger employers, public and professional bodies, academic departments, group services and independent consultancies.

Many health professionals working in occupational health criticised what they saw as a lack of resolve in the HSC. However, the ILO Convention did have an indirect effect on the law of the United Kingdom, because it was one of the important influences which led to the European Community's Framework Directive, incorporated into UK law in the Management of Health and Safety at Work Regulations 1992 (see Chapter 5).

A research report commissioned by the HSE entitled *Occupational Health Provision at Work* was published in 1993. The three-tier survey was based on 820 private sector and 100 public sector organisations and 912 employees. It was discovered that 65 per cent of private sector establishments had some occupational health measures (defined as any action which could prevent work-related ill-health), as compared to almost 100 per cent in the public sector; 89 per cent of the workforce was employed in establishments which had some occupational health measures; 34 per cent of all employees worked in organisations which employed a doctor, either full-time or part-time, and 53 per cent had access to some health professional. The employee/doctor ratio was 212:1. In just under half of the establishments using health professionals in the private sector there was at least one person with specialist OH qualifications. This rose to 74 per cent in the public sector. When employees were asked to report health problems caused by work, they most frequently mentioned back and other physical strains and stress. Also mentioned were headaches and eye strain, deafness, skin problems and asthma.

In the last 15 years there has been a sea change in the attitude of the government to occupational health. A White Paper, *The Health of the Nation*, was published in 1992. Successive governments since the inauguration of the National Health Service after World War II had come to realise that spending on health care must be contained. The creation of an internal market by separating the authorities who provide health care from those who purchase it was one strategy to try to secure better value for money. Another was to try to encourage the population to take care of its own health. The White Paper demonstrated the government's commitment to preventive medicine. It selected five key areas in which national targets were fixed. These were coronary heart disease and stroke, cancers, mental illness, HIV/AIDS and sexual health, and accidents.

The White Paper emphasised the importance of a healthy workplace and proposed the setting up of a task force to examine and develop activity on health promotion in the workplace. It also encouraged the NHS to set an example to other employers to show what can be achieved. The NHS Management Executive set up a task group of NHS managers, Health Education Authority representatives and professionals to review the way in which the NHS promoted the health of its own employees.

Further important proposals were initiated in 1998. A Green Paper *Our Healthier Nation* proposed a ten-year strategy for occupational health, to be set out in a consultation paper from the HSC. The Occupational Health Strategy Unit within the HSE's Health Directorate, set up in 1996, was charged with the responsibility of developing a national 'vision for occupational health'.

At the same time there was a marked increase in the numbers of regulations governing health and safety at work, particularly those originating in European Community Directives. Many of these were designed to prevent long term injury to health, as compared to the prevention of accidental injury. Health professionals with the necessary training and expertise are especially valuable to employers who need advice on the implementation of the regulations and the provision of health surveillance to ensure that the employees are not suffering adverse effects from their work. Perhaps the most important of these regulations are the Management of Health and Safety at Work Regulations 1992, implementing the EC Framework Directive. These oblige all employers, with minor exceptions, to make a suitable and sufficient assessment of the risks to the health and safety of their employees, and to those not in their employment, arising out of the conduct of their undertakings. Every employer shall ensure that his employees are provided with such health surveillance as is appropriate. The Approved Code of Practice advises that, at least in some instances, this will necessitate the services of 'an Occupational Health Nurse' or medical surveillance by 'an appropriately qualified practitioner'. Taken with the emphasis in the regulations on the need to employ competent persons, it would seem that the employment of health professionals with specialist qualifications in occupational health was at last gaining official recognition. An Occupational Health and Safety Lead Body was established to develop vocational qualifications for health and safety practitioners (including OH physicians and nurses).

Amendments to the Approved Code of Practice accompanying the amended Management Regulations 1999 give guidance on the appointment of competent persons. Paragraph 49 states:

> 'Employers who appoint doctors, nurses or other health professionals to advise them on the effects of work on employee health, or to carry out certain procedures, for example health surveillance, should first check that such providers can offer evidence of a sufficient level of expertise or training in occupational health. Registers of competent practitioners are maintained by several professional bodies, and are often valuable.'

Competence does not necessarily depend on paper qualifications, but may also require an understanding of relevant best practice, an awareness of the limitations of one's own experience and knowledge, and the willingness and ability to supplement existing experience and knowledge, when necessary, by obtaining external help and advice. A British Standard (BS 8800) was published in 1996: Guide to occupational health and safety management systems.

The Health and Safety Commission expressed one of its priorities as the establishment of the key points of attack in improving occupational health and identifying the extent of occupational ill-health, and the taking of appropriate action to exploit the linkages between occupational health and the Government's 'Health of the Nation' initiative.

> 'The assessment and management of health risks – the central requirement of the various regulations – are often more complex or involve greater uncertainty than for occupational safety risks. Targeted guidance on assessment and management, and on selecting expert advice, will be needed by employers and employee representatives, as well as by health and safety inspectors, as an essential tool to ensure effective action.'

The Commission planned to continue to give high priority to epidemiological research. A successful consultant-based scheme for the surveillance of occupational lung disease has been continued, and extended to a number of other work-related diseases. It is now known as THOR (The Health and Occupation Reporting Network) and is administered by the Department of Occupational and Environmental Medicine of the University of Manchester. More attention is being paid to general practitioners, who may fail to identify the connection between a patient's work and his medical condition. The Health and Safety Executive in 1992 produced a booklet on occupational health for family doctors: *Your Patients and their Work*.

In 2000 the Department of the Environment, Transport and the Regions published a Strategy Statement (see Chapter 5). It set out targets for reducing the number of days lost through illness and injury at work. The role of occupational health was seen as central to achieving this reduction. The HSC's report, *An Occupational Health Strategy for Great Britain* (2001), set out a number of objectives. Interested parties will work together to achieve the following targets by 2010:

(1)   a 20% reduction in the incidence of work-related ill-health;
(2)   a 20% reduction in ill-health to members of the public caused by work activity;
(3)   a 30% reduction in the number of work days lost due to work-related ill-health;
(4)   that everyone currently in employment but off work due to ill-health or disability is, where necessary and appropriate, made aware of opportunities for rehabilitation back into work as early as possible; and
(5)   that everyone currently not in employment due to ill-health or disability is, where necessary and appropriate, made aware of and offered opportunities to prepare for and find work.

'We can currently estimate that, in present value terms, the gross benefits to society of reaching three of the headline targets may be between £8.6–21.8 billion by 2010.'

A Partnership Board was set up to oversee the implementation and delivery of the strategy, and responsible to them is a Programme Action Group to facilitate the delivery of each of the strategy's five programmes of work (compliance, continuous improvement, knowledge, skills and support mechanisms). Programme 1 (to improve the law in relation to occupational health and compliance with it) is the most relevant to this book. The aim is to encourage the important work of developing standards, or guidance on best practice, and to support occupational health legislation, as well as enforcing the law when appropriate. The priority areas include:

(1)   improving the law by introducing agreed new and revised health-related legislation and/or guidance and by removing unnecessary legislation;
(2)   increasing the involvement of health and safety representatives;
(3)   increasing fines/sentences and other disincentives to breaches of the law;
(4)   increasing information on the economic benefits of addressing occupational health in order to help promote compliance;
(5)   raising awareness of the law within priority groups (e.g. small firms);
(6)   securing consistent enforcement action on health issues;
(7)   increasing the involvement of interested parties (e.g. trade associations) to produce standards; and
(8)   raising awareness among employers that reasonable adjustments to working arrangements should be made for employees or job seekers who are, or who become, disabled.

Programme 5 (to ensure that appropriate mechanisms are in place to deliver information, advice and other support on occupational health) is also particularly relevant to occupational health professionals. The aim is to give everyone access to the appropriate occupational health support. It will examine 'the feasibility of new legislation on the accessibility and availability of occupational health support' and 'ensure that support is provided by professionally skilled people when appropriate'. One recommendation is to provide occupational health training for primary care teams.

Reference is made in the HSC document to the Occupational Health Advisory Committee Report and Recommendations on improving access to occupational health support (2000). This excellent and comprehensive report should be read by all those concerned with the provision of occupational health services. It makes the point that changing patterns of employment mean that an increasing proportion of the working population are employed in small enterprises where there is no ready access to occupational health advice. The report draws comparisons with the position in other Member States of the European Union, from France where occupational health is very much grounded in occupational medicine to Finland where all employers must have a multi-disciplinary service, 50 per cent of the costs of which can be reimbursed through national sickness insurance.

The Committee reports that in the UK public sector almost half the total workforce has access to some form of occupational health advice, but that the picture is very different in the private sector. There is a decrease in the number of people covered by in-house services. Indications are that smaller companies either do not use occupational health support at all or rely on GPs or nurses, some of whom are not trained in occupational health. EMAS and the HSE and local authority inspectors are a source of information and guidance, but their resources are stretched. Employers of small and medium-sized enterprises (SMEs) have little awareness of occupational health legislation.

Even where OH support is provided by employers, it is often viewed with suspicion by workers who see it as concerned mainly with sickness absence monitoring. 'The fundamental issue is one of recognition that the prevention of work-related ill-health should form an essential aspect of the running of any organisation.' Attention needs to be paid to tackle health inequalities through the workplace. Women, ethnic minorities and the disabled may need different treatment from other workers. There is a need for partnerships at local level. Occupational health support should be linked strategically with NHS and local authority initiatives. One example of such a partnership is the Sheffield Occupational Health Advisory Service which is developing a service to patients through the four Sheffield Primary Care Trust practices. It has created a Manual of Occupational Health in Primary Care. A similar organisation is Health Works in the London East End Borough of Newham.

There is debate about whether a change in employer behaviour can be brought about without new legislation to make the provision of OH support mandatory. Enforcement, however, would be challenging and the patchy availability of OH support would create difficulties in some areas.

The TUC supports the creation of a duty on employers to ensure that employees have access to individual medical advice. An alternative would be legislation to require mandatory self-assessment and auditing by employers, with tax incentives for employers who perform well (a pilot scheme exists in Alberta, Canada).

> 'One of the most effective incentives for individual organisations would be convincing evidence that the costs of ill-health interventions would be outweighed by the benefits.'

A project in South West Water concluded that the cost to the industry of work-related ill-health amounted to £8,650 for each worker affected. It might be that the imposition of a charge for the costs of the treatment of work-related ill-health through the NHS on employers' insurance companies, leading to higher premiums, would make employers more careful. This would, however, be more effective for accidents than for diseases because the latter often take longer to develop and are difficult to attribute to a particular employer.

Information and training are vital. The HSE's campaign *Good Health is Good Business* has been successful in raising awareness of hazards to health in the workplace.

As regards the delivery of OH support there should be a three-tiered approach. The first tier involves the GP, safety representatives, trade unions, trade associations and so on. The second tier is professional advice from, for example, a safety adviser, occupational health nurse with a basic qualification, or occupational hygienist. The top tier is professional advice from a specialist, for example an experienced occupational physician (and, I suggest, an experienced OH nurse practitioner).

There should be more training for GPs in occupational health, certainly where they are contracted to provide OH services to employers without possessing even the basic qualification of the Diploma in Occupational Medicine. Primary care trusts should have available specialist expertise in occupational health and safety. Some larger practices might have a doctor or nurse recognised as an OH specialist. There are insufficient numbers of trained staff to support a national occupational health service provided through the NHS, though that is not necessarily something to be deplored, as a predominantly medically led service could inhibit the development of multi-disciplinary teams.

Worker support and involvement is central.

> 'Employers need to secure the practical and enthusiastic commitment of their workforce to make sure that preventive approaches are actually implemented.'

It is important that they are not only consulted, but also given the opportunity to contribute proactively, especially in the process of risk identification.

In conclusion, there is no one solution that will meet the occupational health support needs of everyone; flexibility is the key to delivery mechanisms.

Following the OHAC Report, a number of research reports have been commissioned by the HSE, including *The evaluation of occupational health advice in primary care* (2004) and *Review of occupational health and safety of Britain's ethnic minorities* (2004).

1.2 The legal obligations of the employer

The law imposes a number of specific obligations on the employer relating to the health of his workers and, more generally, in the Health and Safety at Work Act obliges him to ensure their health and safety so far as is reasonably practicable. So far, there is no specific duty in our law on the employer to provide qualified medical or nursing staff at the place of work. The *Health and Safety (First Aid) Regulations 1981* oblige employers to provide adequate and appropriate first-aid equipment and facilities and an appropriate number of adequately qualified and trained persons to render first aid to his employees. The 1990 Approved Code of Practice recommended by way of a guide that at least one first-aider to every 50 employees was necessary, and more in areas of greater hazard. Revisions in 1997 place less emphasis on numbers than on the degree of hazard, but they are still a useful starting point. These numbers refer to employees present at work together at any time; where there is shift-working first-aiders may be needed for each shift. In high-risk areas like the manufacture of chemicals at least one first-aider trained not only in general principles but also in the particular risks of his employer's business should be available. Where a first-aider is not required, an appointed person must be available whenever employees are at work. This person must be capable of taking charge of a first-aid box and have instructions on how to call for medical assistance. A first-aid room with the necessary staff and equipment is only required when the process is especially dangerous, as on a large construction site or in the manufacture of chemicals, or in an isolated spot. The employer must tell his workers about first-aid facilities and where to find a first-aider. To be qualified as a first-aider under the statute, the employee must have been trained and received a certificate of qualification approved by the HSE.

   Amendments and additions to the Approved Code of Practice came into force in 1990. More guidance is given on appropriate first-aid materials and more extensive provision is made for training and for refresher courses (every three years). Further amendments came into force in 1997 and are likely to be again amended in 2005.

   It will be noted that there is no obligation in these regulations to have a qualified doctor or nurse regularly on the premises, though an employer who has an OH service will not have to comply with the detailed provisions of the Approved Code of Practice if he is in effect providing a service which reaches standards at least as high. However, when workers are employed in especially hazardous processes, like working with asbestos, lead or ionising radiations, statutory regulations may require regular health surveillance, which will demand the presence of medical personnel at least to supervise regular examinations. The introduction of the Control of Substances Hazardous to Health Regulations has substantially increased these requirements, because they not only extend the list of named substances (to include, for example, vinyl chloride monomer and benzene), but also oblige the employer to assess the hazards of all substances with which his employees have contact at work and to introduce regular surveillance where there is a reasonable likelihood that an identifiable disease or adverse health effect may occur from exposure to a hazardous substance (see Chapter 4).

1.3   Who pays?

In some industrial countries, the provision of an occupational health service is regarded as an important part of the Welfare State. In Italy, for example, the prevention of accidents and ill-health at work is one of the functions of the local health authorities. Though the NHS has in the past been seen primarily as a treatment service, preventive medicine has gained in importance, especially as soaring costs have placed intolerable strains on the Exchequer. The policy documents and strategies already discussed in this chapter demonstrate the new commitment to disease prevention and health promotion.

Facilities for the treatment of non-emergency conditions at the workplace can with justification be charged to the employer. He may be willing to pay a doctor, dentist or nurse to treat his workers at the factory so that they do not have to waste working time travelling to the GP's surgery, though this may be resisted by the local GPs if they do more than treat emergencies and minor injuries.

But what of the preventive aspect of occupational medicine? The State provides the Employment Medical Advisory Service, but the numbers of personnel are too small to be able to do more than lead and advise. Where statutory regulations oblige the employer to monitor the health of his workers he is compelled by law to pay the fees of an Appointed Doctor. The small employer will find it difficult to do much more than this, but there is evidence that employees in such enterprises are at greater risk than those in larger organisations. If the provision of an OH service for every employee is to be a practical possibility, either it must be taken over by the NHS or more cost-effective methods must be found.

The Gregson Committee was not enthusiastic about an NHS takeover, principally because it found that the health service did not yet succeed in caring adequately for its own personnel, let alone anyone else's. Since the publication of the first edition of this book, NHS Trusts have improved their occupational health services, but a report of the National Audit Office in 2003 described the provision of OH within the NHS as 'patchy'.

A significant development has been the creation of NHS Plus in 2001, after a surprise announcement by Alan Milburn, then the Secretary of State for Health, at a conference in 2000. NHS Plus is a network of occupational health services based in NHS hospitals. The network provides an OH service to NHS staff, and also sells its services to the private sector. There are over 90 providers around the country offering a wide range of services. This is not part of free statutory NHS provision.

The equivalent organisation in Scotland is Safe and Healthy Working (SAHW), which was launched in 2003, but its remit is wider than NHS Plus, since it gives all kinds of health and safety advice via NHS occupational health and safety services. It is also free, and offers free workplace visits by a generalist health and safety practitioner.

It would seem that the employer must continue to pay, but that costs could be reduced by a number of employers combining together, or a large enterprise offering spare capacity to small local firms. In the 1980s and early 1990s economic theory advised that market forces must be allowed to operate; if it was in the economic interests of employers to provide an OH service, they would eventually do so. Employers needed to be shown how their business could benefit financially if they were to be persuaded to extend medical and nursing services at the workplace.

The Health and Safety Executive has sought to estimate the costs of accidents and ill-health at work. There are over one million accidents resulting in injury every year, and some 1.3 million workers suffering from ill-health caused or made worse by their work have had to take time off. This results in a loss of 24.3 million working days and a cost to the British economy of between £2.9 billion and £4.2 billion. The overall cost of work accidents and work-related ill-health to employers is estimated to be around £2.5 billion a year. This estimation includes the cost of employers' liability insurance and the cost of recruiting and training replacements for injured workers, as well as property loss. This is equal to between 5 per cent and 10 per cent of gross trading profits. It does not include the costs of social security and the NHS, or the personal losses of the victims of accident and disease. Altogether, the total cost to society is estimated as between £14 billion and £18 billion a year (*The costs to Britain of workplace accidents and work-related ill-health in 1995/96* (second edition 1999)).

A further book was published in 1997, including five case studies. The purpose of these studies is to show that 'there is no contradiction between health and safety and profitability'. The HSE's guide *Successful Health and Safety Management* (1997) is based on the principles of loss control and quality management. An important common denominator is the adoption of a total loss control approach which seeks to identify and eliminate risks, whether or not they lead to injury. For example, a patch of leaking oil could lead to slipping, a fire, breakdown of the machinery, or may have no adverse consequences. If patches of oil are eliminated, then there will be no risk, and no loss. One case study concerned a construction site where the costs of accidents amounted to 8.5 per cent of tender price. Many costs were uninsured, including legal costs, expenditure on emergency supplies, overtime working and temporary labour, and loss of expertise and experience.

'The majority of accidents and incidents are not caused by careless workers but by failures in control (either within the organisation or within the particular job) which are the responsibility of management.'

Further examples of the economic benefit of occupational health provision were published by the Health and Safety Commission in 2004, but an HSE survey published in 2003 found that small and medium-sized firms spend up to 15 times more per employee in achieving compliance with work safety regulations (*Costs of compliance with health and safety regulations in SMEs*).

Advice from the Health and Safety Executive on occupational health services (1989) advised that the benefits of such a service are:

(1) compliance with legal responsibilities;
(2) reduced labour turnover and increased efficiency;
(3) less sickness absence and fewer compensation claims through detection of health hazards and adoption of preventive measures;
(4) less waste of employees' work time through provision of on-site first aid and treatment facilities;

(5)   improved general health through introduction of health promotion and
      education programmes;
(6)   a better motivated workforce and higher calibre job applicants through
      showing that the employer cares about the health of its workers.

Most employed people work for employers whose workforce is too small for a
comprehensive in-house occupational health service. But the specific needs of
small and medium-sized firms can be met in a number of ways. A qualified
occupational health nurse can be employed full-time, a part-time visiting doctor
may be appointed, the safety officers can have a key role in introducing and
monitoring measures to control the working environment and in checking on their
adequacy and effectiveness. Some firms become members of a group occupational
health service which provides occupational health facilities on a shared basis to a
number of local firms. Some large organisations with comprehensive in-house
services are prepared to offer facilities to small local firms, and the local hospital
may contract out services through NHS Plus. There are also independent
organisations operating occupational health services on a consultancy basis, and
services provided by private health insurers.

These services may be cost-effective. Several examples are given by the Health
and Safety Executive. The first is an organisation requiring a high level of
employee fitness which has a dispersed workforce of some 2500 people based at
26 sites, some of which are 30 miles or more from headquarters. Medical surveillance is carried out at headquarters by a part-time medical adviser, costing the
employer both overtime payments and travelling expenses. The employment of a
nurse to visit all the sites and refer to headquarters only those employees who
have to see the medical adviser is more than compensated by reductions in
overtime and travelling expenses for the workers. A second example is a chemical
company employing over 1000 people and concerned about absence from work
due to muscle and joint disorders. It arranges for a self-employed physiotherapist
to attend three mornings a week. The employer benefits greatly from the reduction in absences from work from sickness and attending for treatment outside the
workplace. Easy access to the physiotherapy service also assists early treatment
which is often essential to a good outcome. Finally, a company using isocyanates
requires health surveillance of the workforce. EMAS advises the company to
contact a local GP. The GP notices other occupational health problems, such as
skin conditions and stress-related symptoms. This leads to regular workplace
visits, which improve the health status of the workforce and benefit manager/
worker relationships.

The HSE has produced information about the tax and National Insurance
treatment of occupational health support. An employer is able to claim a
deduction against business profits in providing health-related benefits to
employees, provided the expenditure is wholly and exclusively for the purpose of
the business. The benefit of private medical care provided free or cheaply by
employers to employees is subject to tax on the employee. However, the following
benefits are not subject to income tax: medical and other treatment for the consequences of work-related accidents or ill-health, health screening and check-ups,
welfare counselling, equipment and services for disabled workers, employee-only

recreational and sporting facilities. This is as long as the benefits are provided by the employer directly to the employee. If the employee is given money to pay for the benefits he will have to pay income tax.

1.4   The Employment Medical Advisory Service and Appointed Doctors

In 1833 and 1844 the Factory Acts required child workers to be examined by a local surgeon or physician to assess whether they were under the legal minimum working age (nine). The 1855 Factory Act conferred on these Certifying Factory Surgeons the task of certifying that young people were not incapacitated for work and of investigating industrial accidents. The doctor was independent both of the employer and of the employee, though paid by the factory owner. Later in the century, legislation required the Certifying Factory Surgeons also to investigate cases of industrial disease. In addition, employers were compelled to pay Appointed Surgeons to undertake regular medical examination of those working with specified substances like lead and phosphorus. The first full-time Medical Inspector of Factories was appointed in 1898.

Part-time medical practitioners have, therefore, conducted medical examinations in industry for a century. They now operate under the supervision of full-time specialists in occupational medicine, the Employment Medical Advisory Service (EMAS) and are called Appointed Doctors (ADs). Their principal function is to undertake examinations of workers in the workplace and to assess their fitness for work when the employer is bound by statute to carry out regular health surveillance. The ADs are appointed by the Health and Safety Executive through EMAS in respect of a particular company or companies and premises. EMAS is able to ask for evidence of occupational health qualifications and experience when making appointments, though these are not mandatory legal requirements. The ADs are obliged to comply with both the clinical and administrative procedures set by EMAS; they are subject to inspection by Employment Medical Advisers. It is very important that proper clinical records are kept and statistical returns made to EMAS. If the work of the AD is unsatisfactory, his appointment may be revoked without a reason being stated or an explanation given. The employer has to pay fees for medical surveillance required by law.

The functions of EMAS are laid down in section 55 of the Health and Safety at Work Act. It undertakes the following responsibilities:

(1) Advice to the inspectorate on the occupational health aspects of Regulations and Approved Codes of Practice (see Chapter 5).
(2) Regular examinations of persons employed on known hazardous operations.
(3) Other medical examinations, investigations and surveys. An Adviser has power to require an employer to permit him to carry out a medical examination of any employee whose health the Adviser believes may be in danger because of his work.
(4) Advice to the HSE, employers, trade unions and others on the occupational health aspects of poisonous substances, immunological disorders, physical

hazards, dust, and mental stress, including setting standards of exposure to harmful processes and substances.
(5) Research into occupational health.
(6) Advice on the provision of occupational health and first aid services.
(7) Advice on the medical aspects of rehabilitation and training for and placement in employment.

EMAS employs both doctors (EMAs) and nurses (Inspectors of Health and Safety (Occupational Health)) as well as support staff. It also provides the secretariat for two of the Health and Safety Commission's Advisory Committees:

(1) the Occupational Health Advisory Committee (OHAC), covering wide-ranging questions in the field of occupational health
(2) the Advisory Committee on Dangerous Pathogens (ACDP).

1.5 *The occupational health physician*

The British Medical Association (BMA) defines an OH physician as

'a doctor who in relation to any particular workplace takes full medical responsibility for advising those working therein including contractors working on the site on all matters connected directly or indirectly with the work. These may have a bearing on health as it affects work and the effect of work on health including that of the public at large, either in general or as individuals.' (*The Occupational Physician*)

An OH physician must be a registered medical practitioner. He may also be an Associate Member of the Faculty of Occupational Medicine of the Royal College of Physicians (AFOM) or possess a Diploma in Industrial Health. Further experience and a dissertation enables a doctor to apply for membership of the Faculty (MFOM). The MFOM is a career specialist qualification. Specialist training in occupational medicine is prescribed by the Faculty of Occupational Medicine and conforms to the requirements of the European Specialist Medical Qualifications Order 1995. The route to entry on to the Specialist Register of the General Medical Council involves four years training in an approved post and attainment of the AFOM and MFOM. There is as yet no legal requirement that the OH physician should hold any other qualification than ordinary registration. General practitioners often take up a post of OH doctor in an organisation on a part-time basis. Many part-timers are not Associates of the Faculty of Occupational Medicine, though it is possible to qualify for this by a period of experience in industry and an examination.

No formal arrangements exist for training in occupational health for medical students. Occupational medicine is the only medical specialty in Britain in which the cost of training is not defrayed from public funds. Obviously, the Faculty would prefer that a formal occupational health qualification be made a legal requirement, but at present there are insufficient training facilities available for the numbers required. The Faculty has developed a training course for physicians who do not need the full specialist qualification, leading to an examination. This judges basic knowledge and competence in occupational medicine, with the award of a Diploma for successful candidates. It remains quite separate from the AFOM/MFOM which continues to be the route for those wishing to specialise in occupational medicine. It is likely that a court in examining whether an employer had employed a competent doctor to give OH advice would consider the Diploma to be the minimum qualification. A Diploma in Disability Assessment Medicine was created in 1999.

The BMA sets out the duties of an occupational physician as follows:

(1) *The effects of health on capacity to work*
(a) Advice to employees on all health matters relating to their working capacity. Examination of applicants for employment and advice as to their placement.
(b) Immediate treatment of medical and surgical emergencies occurring at the place of employment.
(c) Examinations and continued observation of persons returning to work after absence due to illness or accident, and advice on suitable work.
(d) Health supervision of all employees with special reference to those particularly vulnerable, like the disabled.

(2) *The effects of work on health*
(a) Responsibility for first-aid services.
(b) Periodical examinations and medical supervision of persons exposed to special hazards.
(c) Advice to management regarding the working environment in relation to health, the occurrence and significance of hazards, the health aspects of safety, and statutory requirements in relation to health.
(d) Medical supervision of health and hygiene of staff and facilities, with special reference to canteens, those working on the production of food and drugs for sale and those providing a service to the public.
(e) Health education for employees.
(f) Advice to health and safety committees.
(g) Liaison with other specialists working in the field.

The introduction of revalidation as a requirement for all physicians on the medical register was accompanied by a call from the General Medical Council to each College and Faculty to develop its own principles of Good Medical Practice. The Faculty of Occupational Medicine in 2001 published *Good Medical Practice for Occupational Physicians*. The purpose of this document is to provide a standard against which individual physicians may be judged. It accompanies the Faculty's *Guidance on Ethics for Occupational Physicians* (1999).

'The ethical code of occupational physicians recognises these dual responsibilities [to patients and to employers or third parties]... Nevertheless, the doctor should make care of the individual patient his first concern and this

responsibility takes precedence over other responsibilities, save for the exceptions described by the GMC.'

The document provides a useful list of good clinical practice in occupational
health. This should include:

(1)   making an adequate assessment of the patient's health, based on the clinical
      and occupational history, and clinical signs, an understanding of the work,
      and, if necessary, an appropriate examination of the patient, and any rele-
      vant medical reports and tests;
(2)   making a competent assessment of the interaction between workers and
      their jobs – including occupational factors that may adversely affect their
      health and safety, or that of others; and factors in the individual that may
      pose special difficulties in the safe, effective conduct of their duties and
      fitness for work;
(3)   organising investigations important to the assessment of occupational risks
      or fitness for work;
(4)   providing specific occupational interventions where indicated;
(5)   taking suitable and prompt action when necessary;
(6)   providing patients with the information they need to protect themselves
      against occupational risks;
(7)   apprising the patient of other sources of help and advice (such as the HSE,
      human resource managers and safety representatives);
(8)   referring the patient to their general practitioner when indicated;
(9)   collecting enough information to make a competent assessment of the risks
      from work, including information on groups of workers;
(10) visiting the workplace where appropriate, in order to gain an under-
      standing of the work environment, the nature and demands of the work,
      and the risks to health;
(11) advising on the measures required to control the health and safety risks
      arising from work activities, especially any obligations which are statutory;
(12) advising on health surveillance when indicated (e.g. to protect workers'
      health, to confirm the adequacy of control measures, or to fulfil a statutory
      obligation) and interpreting the findings;
(13) assessing competently patients' capability for work and the options for
      rehabilitation or redeployment in cases considered for ill-health retirement;
(14) encouraging employers to accommodate workers with illness or disability,
      and advising employers and employees on any statutory requirements and
      sources of assistance relating to disability;
(15) encouraging employers not to discriminate unfairly against employees with
      health problems.

Criticisms of the medical profession and of the lax control over physicians exercised by the General Medical Council have led the professional body to create a
scheme for revalidation of professional qualifications. The practice of doctors will
be subject to regular appraisal. The GMC guidance is published in *A Licence to
Practise and Revalidation* (2003). The Faculty of Occupational Medicine in con-

junction with the Society of Occupational Medicine has developed a programme
to assist occupational physicians to obtain revalidation. This requires the physician to collect and submit information about his or her practice over a five-year
cycle. The responsibility for proving competence rests with the individual. It is
competence, not excellence, which is needed. The basic scheme is that doctors
must collect evidence of their compliance with standards set out in a document
published by the Faculty and the Society in 2003: *Standards in Occupational Medical
Practice: Guidance for Appraisal.* In addition, medical appraisal by another doctor
will be required for all NHS consultants and GPs, but not for non-NHS doctors,
though it is recommended. The Society of Occupational Medicine is considering
the development of a generic format of appraisal for occupational physicians and
procedures for occupational physicians to find an appraiser. Appraisal will
benefit doctors by helping them to show that they are giving good medical care,
enabling them to identify and correct weaknesses in their practice, protecting
them against unfounded criticism, and assisting in the collection of appropriate
data to inform the revalidation process. Appraisal in this sense is separate from
appraisal by a manager which is usually from a standpoint of business efficiency.
Management might prefer that the OH doctor did not observe all the ethical
standards, for example those relating to confidentiality.

The Standards document, which is based on *Good Medical Practice for Occupational Physicians* already discussed, refers to knowledge of the law. Occupational
physicians should normally be able to report to managers on occupational health
performance and requirements in ways which are accessible, placing it within a
business framework and also providing the medico-legal context. Occupational
physicians should keep abreast of changes in legislation and Codes of Practice that
affect their practice (and, I would suggest, relevant case law).

Research published by the Health and Safety Executive in 2004 assessed the
competencies of occupational physicians from the customer's perspective (*Competencies of Occupational Physicians*). Readers may be surprised to learn that at the
top of the list of required competencies as rated by their customers is advising on
law and ethics. Training in law was not, however, highly rated by focus group
participants.

1.6   The occupational health nurse

The first recorded occupational health nurse was Philippa Flowerday who was
appointed in 1878 by Colmans of Norwich. She assisted the doctor at the factory
and then visited sick employees and their families in their own homes. Her work
reflected the treatment-based philosophy of the time and also the 'doctor's helper'
attitude to nursing staff. There has been no statutory function for nurses com-
parable to that of the Appointed Doctors, so that OH nursing has been centred
very much round the role of providing first aid in the workplace. The sympathetic
nurse with time to listen and guaranteed confidentiality has also been a popular
source of advice for such sociomedical problems as members of the worker's
family drinking too much, overtiredness caused by stress, menopausal symptoms
and so on. A survey undertaken on behalf of the Royal College of Nursing in 1982

showed that caring for the sick and injured and counselling were the two functions most often mentioned by OH nurses in describing their work.

Because nurses command lower salaries than doctors, employers in times of prosperity were often willing to provide a nurse in the factory for the welfare of their workers. In more straitened times, they have been asking what the nurses can contribute that cannot be done equally well by first-aiders and welfare officers. Treatment is available free from the NHS; why should the employer duplicate it? The occupational health nursing profession is, therefore, having to justify itself by demonstrating that nurses too have an important role to play in a system based on prevention rather than treatment. They find this much easier to do when they can show specialist training and qualifications and when they are able to work independently of the doctor, though under overall medical supervision. In practice, many OH services are managed by nurses, who tend these days to be termed Occupational Health Advisers, with physicians being employed part-time.

The Royal College of Nursing (RCN) was at one time responsible for training occupational health nurses. From August 1988, validation of courses and standards became the responsibility of the National Boards for Nursing, Midwifery and Health Visiting. There were three recognised qualifications. The first was the Occupational Health Practice Nurse Award which was obtained after a practical course open to enrolled and registered nurses which demonstrated how nursing skills are adapted for use in an industrial setting. The Occupational Health Nursing Certificate could be obtained after a period of training, either one academic year full-time or two years (six terms) on day release, and covered all aspects of OH. Only registered nurses could become fully qualified OH nurses. The third qualification was the Occupational Health Nursing Diploma. In the 1990s transitional arrangements were created to enable nurses with at least five years' experience in OH to undertake further training in order to obtain a post-registration graduate qualification in OH nursing. From 31 October 1998 only the qualification of Specialist Practitioner in OH nursing (at first degree level) has been recorded in the NMC Professional Register. None of these qualifications has statutory recognition, so that anyone can work in an OH department without having completed specialist training, though they may not be regarded as competent persons under the health and safety legislation without it, unless working under the supervision of a qualified OH nurse or physician.

The revolutionary changes in nurse education brought about by Project 2000 have had significant effects on the training of occupational health nurses. Courses are validated jointly by the National Boards and the universities and have been upgraded to degree level. The syllabus has been planned using the framework of the Hanasaari model, developed at a conference in Finland. This stresses the need to regard the total environment in which the workplace is set.

Occupational Health Review conducted an up-to-date survey of the work of OH nurses in 1996 with the assistance of the RCN Society of Occupational Health Nursing. The number of OH nurses then employed in the UK was estimated to be about 5000–8000. The majority were women, about 80 per cent full-time; 95 per cent of respondents to the questionnaire had a formal OH qualification, including 10 per cent with a degree. The ratio of OH nurses to employees was three times higher in the private sector than the public sector; 95 per cent of OH nurses worked with a physician in the team. About one in six organisations employed only GPs with no formal OH qualification. Health promotion was a part of more nurses' jobs than any other activity. Most time was taken up with routine health screening. Six out of ten nurses experienced conflict with the physician at least some of the time, and more than eight out of ten had problems with human resources departments and departmental managers. Nine out of ten nurses received at least some encouragement from their employer to undertake continuing professional development.

In 1987 the RCN compiled the *Code of Professional Practice in Occupational Health Nursing* and in 1991 produced a *Guide to Occupational Health Nursing*. The RCN defined the functions of the OH nurse in very much the same terms as the BMA defined the OH physician's role, with the significant addition of the provision of a routine treatment service. In practice, the OH nurse is likely to be spending a significant part of her time in providing and training others in first aid, screening employees, both pre- and post-recruitment, keeping records and generally giving advice. Increasingly, the nurse has been drawn into health education about work-related hazards and about general health, like the importance of a good diet and the dangers of smoking.

The Employment Nursing Advisers are full-time employees of the Health and Safety Executive and part of the Employment Medical Advisory Service. They are key figures in occupational health because many nurses are working on their own and have only EMAS to turn to for advice and information. In recent years, much of their time has been spent in advising employers about the provision and training of first-aiders, who, as has been seen, do not have to be qualified nurses. They were given a new title in 1998: HM Inspectors of Health and Safety (Occupational Health) to stress that they work alongside other inspectors in investigating complaints and possible breaches of the law, and have all the powers of the HSE inspectorate.

In 1993 the HSE published Anna Dorward's study *Managers' perceptions of the role and continuing education needs of occupational health nurses*. Predictably, lay managers had a far more limited perception of the role of the occupational health nurse than did doctor managers or nurse managers: they saw them only as providing treatment for illness and injury at work. Only 50 per cent of lay managers supported nurses taking time off to attend courses. It would seem that the occupational health nursing profession still has a need to sell itself to employers as a vital component in health and safety provision. Training initiatives will have to take into account that the acquisition of more extensive qualifications involves significant sacrifice of time and money for most OH nurses. The English National Board and the Department of Health in 1998 produced *Occupational Health Nursing* to highlight the role of the OH nurse in the workplace. At the time of writing there is a significant shortage of qualified OH nurses, which is reflected in a rise in salaries.

1.7 The inter-disciplinary nature of occupational health

The law is on the whole very unspecific about demarcation between doctors and nurses. There are a number of detailed regulations about the supply and administration of medicines. Prescription only medicines (POMs) may only be supplied through a registered pharmacy on the written prescription of a doctor, dentist, or very exceptionally a specially registered nurse; and no person may administer medicines parenterally (administration by breach of the skin or mucous membrane) unless he is either a doctor or a dentist or acting in accordance with the directions of such a person. However, there are exceptions for OH nurses, to be found in statutory regulations. These exempt from the above requirements the supply or administration of medicines in the course of an occupational health scheme by a registered nurse where the nurse is acting in accordance with the written general instructions of a doctor.

> 'When a doctor signs a general instruction relating to the type of POM a nurse may supply (or in the case of injectables administer), it must be borne in mind that as the doctor is not prescribing for an individual patient, the nurse must exercise professional judgment and discretion when considering which product to administer or supply for the nature of the condition or combination of conditions from which the patient may be suffering.' (RCN: *Occupational Health Nursing Services Handbook* (1991))

Careful records must be kept and the nurse, who should be specifically named in the doctor's authorisation, must never delegate her authority to a first-aider or other nurse (see Chapter 2).

The Prescription Only Medicines (Human Use) Order 1997, Schedule 5, permits registered nurses employed at a place of work to be in possession of controlled drugs (like morphine) for the purpose of administration to persons injured or taken ill at the place of work at which the nurse is employed. The drugs must have been supplied to the nurse by a doctor employed at the place of work for the medical supervision of workers. Security must be efficient and the nurse must keep a register detailing every administration of the drugs. If the drugs are lost or stolen the nurse must report to the police as soon as possible.

Apart from the legislation about medicines, the division between the roles of doctor and nurse in any setting rests essentially on custom and practice. Both professions have something to say about the matter in their ethical rules. The Faculty of Occupational Medicine's *Good Medical Practice* (2001) states:

> 'Delegation involves asking a colleague to provide treatment, care or advice on your behalf. When you delegate in this way you must be sure that the person to whom you delegate is competent to carry out the procedure or provide the therapy or advice involved and where possible account to a statutory regulatory body. If you delegate within the team to someone other than a doctor, you will still be responsible for the overall occupational medical care of the patient.'

The Nursing and Midwifery Council, in its Code of Professional Conduct, states that a nurse should acknowledge any limitations of competence and refuse to perform tasks outside those limitations. This is all very well as a general principle but there are many situations in which members of both professions disagree as to what is proper. It is not practically possible to lay down all the tasks which it is acceptable for a nurse to perform. The OH nurse often works in a team with safety officers and hygienists as well as doctors. Often she is on her own when an emergency arises. The NMC recognises the need for flexibility:

'In an emergency, in or outside the work setting, you have a professional duty to provide care. The care provided would be judged against what could reasonably be expected from someone with your knowledge, skills and abilities when placed in those particular circumstances.' (*Code of Professional Conduct* (2002))

The RCN has advised its members that the role of the OH nurse is not a static one confined by a list of tasks or duties. The nurse must be conscious of the need to observe the NMC Code of Conduct, acquire a basic qualification in OH nursing, acquire appropriate skills and attend periodic retraining. However, nurses are warned that the RCN Indemnity Insurance Scheme excludes cover to those undertaking radiography who are not registered members of the Society of Radiographers. Although a joint committee of the BMA and RCN advised that there should be a procedure for consultation between OH personnel to define their relative responsibilities, there can still be friction. The nurses in particular sometimes find themselves in conflict with safety officers. If the problem proves intractable, the best advice is for the nurse to contact EMAS at the local HSE offices. The Faculty of Occupational Medicine in *Good Medical Practice* (2001) advises that teamwork is an essential part of occupational medical practice:

'You must work constructively within teams and respect the skills and contributions of your colleagues. Working in a team does not change your personal accountability for your professional conduct and the care you provide.'

Doctors and nurses are themselves legally liable for any acts of negligence which cause damage. The OH doctor is only liable for the negligence of the nurse if he was himself negligent in asking her to do something without checking that she was qualified. If they are employees acting in the course of employment, their employer is also vicariously liable for their negligence. It does not follow that, just because an employee is acting in an unauthorised way, he is exceeding the scope of his employment (see Chapter 7).

1.8 The relationship between the occupational health service and the general practitioner

The preventive aspects of the OH specialists need not impinge on the general practitioner's function. If the worker is found to be suffering from some work-related illness, or has an accident at work, the GP should be informed, if the patient gives consent. Treatment is more problematic. The BMA advises that the occupational physician should treat a patient only in co-operation with the patient's GP except in an emergency. If he thinks that the worker should consult his GP, he should urge him to do so. The occupational physician should refer a patient directly to hospital only in consultation or in agreement with the GP. He should not influence or appear to influence any worker in his choice of GP. The RCN advises OH nurses not to undertake specific treatments without the request of the GP in writing, other than treatment for minor injuries and in an emergency. Vaccination and immunisation programmes for workers at risk must be supervised by a registered medical practitioner.

An area of potential conflict is the confirmation that absence from work is due to sickness so that the worker can claim sick leave and sick pay from his employer. This is usually the GP's job and he is only obliged by his contract to give a certificate free of charge after seven days' absence. However, the employer may ask the OH department for their advice as to the fitness of the worker. The employer's motive may be suspicion that the employee is malingering. Frequent or lengthy absence may indicate a serious health problem which may put other workers at risk. The worker's absence may be causing the employer financial problems and other employees may be showing resentment. The BMA advises consultation with the GP (with the employee's consent). If the GP and the OH doctor disagree, and there is the prospect of disciplinary action, the employer may allow the employee within company procedures the right to go 'on appeal' to an independent consultant (see Chapter 8).

Where the occupational physician is also the worker's general practitioner (a not uncommon event), he must be careful to keep the two functions separate. In such cases, it might be preferable to advise the patient to see another doctor in the practice (if there is one). Information about the employee must not be transferred from the OH to the GP records, or *vice versa*, without the employee's consent.

'Wherever possible, a doctor should avoid acting both as occupational health adviser to an individual and as his primary health physician. If this is unavoidable, particular care should be taken to ensure that the patient understands the context of the consultation and agrees to its terms.' (*Good Medical Practice for Occupational Physicians*)

Chapter 2
The Legal Status and Liability of the OH Professional

2.1   *Servants and independent contractors*

In the medical and nursing professions there is a diversity of outlets for professional skills. In examining the status of the occupational health (OH) doctor and nurse, it is necessary first to analyse the various types of occupational health service which exist today. The main distinction to be made is between the OH service which is set up 'in-house' by the employer, and that which is bought in from an outside consultant who is in business on his own account. Most OH professionals who work full-time for one employer are his 'servants' (employees) in the legal sense, whereas the independent OH consultants are usually what lawyers term 'independent contractors'. A further complication is that, for example, a nurse may be employed by a company like BMI which provides OH services to employers, but be lent out to BMI's customers. As regards BMI she is a servant, but when she visits the company to which she is sent to give advice or examinations she is an independent contractor.

The importance of all this is that the law divides contracts to sell one's labour to another into *contracts of service* and *contracts for services*. A junior hospital doctor or a nurse in an NHS hospital is a servant employed by the NHS trust under a contract of service. A general practitioner (GP) in the NHS is a self-employed independent contractor employed by the Health Authority under a contract for services. This is not merely an antiquated conundrum for lawyers: it has vital consequences in practice. The employer is liable vicariously for the negligence of his servant, but not in general of his independent contractor. Many statutory employment protection rights like the right not to be unfairly dismissed are given only to those employed under a contract of service. The employee has PAYE and National Insurance contributions deducted from his wages by his employer; not so the self-employed independent contractor. The self-employed have the benefit of more generous tax allowances under Schedule D rather than Schedule E, but they cannot claim jobseeker's allowance, statutory redundancy payments, or industrial injuries insurance benefits.

How can an individual determine into which category he falls? The courts have laid down various tests, but none is conclusive. It is instructive to see how the parties themselves have labelled their relationship, but courts have sometimes refused to accept this, as in one case where a manual labourer on a building site was told by the foreman that he was 'on the lump' and would not have tax and National Insurance contributions deducted. When he later had an accident on the site, the court held that he was, after all, an employee and was therefore covered by the Construction (Working Places) Regulations 1966 which did not protect self-employed persons (*Ferguson* v. *Dawson* (1976)). In a later case the court, having held that a semi-skilled worker in a factory who had for several years with his agreement been classified as self-employed was in law an employee and could thus complain to an industrial tribunal that he had been unfairly dismissed, sent the papers to the Inland Revenue so that back taxes could be collected (*Young and Woods* v. *West* (1980)). What the law looks for is evidence about the degree of dependence of the employed person. If he is controlled in the performance of his work, is an integral part of the employer's organisation, uses tools and equipment supplied by his employer and cannot provide a substitute to do his job without his employer's permission, he is likely to be an employee under a contract of service. The number of hours worked is not conclusive: many part-time workers are servants rather than independent contractors.

The British Medical Association (BMA) advises that the doctor should be clear whether he is being offered a contract of service or one for services, and that legal advice should be sought on the wording of any draft contract. Strictly speaking, a contract does not need to be in writing to be legally enforceable, but it is easier to prove what has been agreed if there is written evidence. An employer must give a written statement of the basic terms of a contract of employment to his employee within eight weeks of his starting work. This does not apply to independent contractors. It is unlikely that the courts would accept that a full-time doctor or nurse working in-house was anything other than an employee. A nurse working part-time for one company only would probably be in a similar position, but a physician or nurse providing a few hours a week on a sessional basis, especially if he or she visits more than one company, probably falls into the self-employed category.

In *Westminster City Council* v. *Shah* (1985), the Employment Appeal Tribunal upheld the decision of an industrial tribunal that a GP who acted as a locum occupational health physician for the Council for five morning sessions a week was directly employed by the Council. His normal hours of work were fixed, he was paid a fixed fee for each session, irrespective of the amount of work involved, and all his work was done on the Council's premises as they required. On the other hand he was not subject to their disciplinary procedures, he received no holiday pay and he was assessed (wrongly, in the tribunal's opinion) to income tax under Schedule D. The court emphasised that each case had to be looked at on its facts 'in the round'.

'Certainty in this area of the law seems to be a will o' the wisp in whose pursuit there are always dangers.'

In contrast, in *Kapfunde* v. *Abbey National* (1998) a GP acted part-time as a consultant for Abbey National. She assessed pre-employment questionnaires and gave other advice, including undertaking medical examinations of employees and job applicants. She could perform the examinations herself, or employ a locum. She had complete discretion over the way in which she performed any responsibility, including the choice of contractors to provide external blood tests and

X-ray services and payment for them. She sometimes used her own premises and always her own medical bag. She managed her own tax and national insurance affairs. The judge held that she was an independent contractor, not an employee, and that the employer was not therefore vicariously liable for her. The factor which swung the decision was probably that the doctor could appoint a delegate to do the job. It is the essence of a contract of employment that the employee has to perform his duties in person.

If all that the doctor does is to act as an Appointed Doctor (AD) for the purpose of performing statutory tests he is employed by the Crown, even though he will be paid by the employer of the workers and will have a contract with the employer for the payment of his fees. Doctors and nurses employed by the Health and Safety Executive (HSE) are also Crown servants.

2.2   Liability for criminal acts

The special responsibilities imposed by criminal statutes to promote the health and safety of the workers are most often placed on the shoulders of the employer or the occupier of the workplace, rather than on individual employees. The GP who employs nurses and receptionists is, as an employer, subject to prosecution under section 2 of the Health and Safety at Work Act 1974 (HSWA) if he fails to do that which is reasonably practicable to ensure the health, safety and welfare at work of his employees. Since the abolition of the Crown immunity of NHS authorities from prosecution under the HSWA, an NHS Trust can be taken to court for a similar failure.

Prosecutions of individuals rather than employing organisations are sometimes brought under section 7 HSWA which imposes a duty on every *employee* while at work to take reasonable care for the health and safety of himself and of other persons who may be affected by his acts or omissions at work and to co-operate with the employer or any person so far as is necessary to enable him to perform his statutory duties under health and safety legislation. Only if the doctor or nurse is an employee will he be bound by this section. The duty is to take reasonable care, i.e. not to be negligent: the burden of proof of negligence in this section is on the prosecution. A doctor who discovered that a vehicle driver had developed a condition likely to cause him to be a source of danger to other employees or the public might be in breach of this section if, having failed to persuade the driver to tell the employer, he did not inform management that the driver was unfit. The duty of confidence yields to the duty to protect others (see Chapter 3).

There have been a number of instances where the Crown Prosecution Service has brought a prosecution against a health professional for manslaughter where a patient has died through gross negligence. In one case, doctors who prescribed a lethal cocktail of drugs in excessive doses to a prisoner on remand were convicted of manslaughter (see Brahams (1992)). The patient who died had asked for a tranquilliser (see also Chapter 5). There is no record of an occupational physician or nurse being accused of such an offence.

Where the OH professional is incompetent, there may be a prosecution under section 36 HSWA. Where the employer's commission of an offence is due to the act or default of an OH professional, the doctor or nurse is guilty of an offence and may be prosecuted and convicted as well as, or instead of, the employer. In *R* v. *Lockwood* (2001) an occupational hygienist worked as a consultant for a number of clients, including a woodworking factory. As a consultant he was not an employee. An HSE inspector discovered that the level of airborne dust in the factory was well over the legal limit and the employer was in breach of the Control of Substances Hazardous to Health Regulations. The employer had relied on Lockwood's advice. The advice was defective, because the consultant had failed to comply with the standards and procedures recommended by his profession. The HSE decided that a criminal prosecution should be brought, not against the employer, which had reasonably relied on the advice, but against the expert himself. Lockwood was found not to be a competent person, as required by the Management of Health and Safety at Work Regulations. He was fined £1000 and ordered to pay £2000 in costs because, by his default, he had caused the employer to commit an offence under the COSHH Regulations. Although no similar prosecutions have been pursued against OH professionals, the HSE confirms that cases have been considered.

In a similar case in 2004 a health and safety consultant, Christopher Hooper, was fined £3000 plus £750 costs for carrying out inadequate risk assessments of a woodworking machine which led to an employee losing part of a finger. The employer was also prosecuted and fined £5000 plus £837 costs.

2.3   *Liability for negligence*

In the civil law of tort, a duty of care falls on anyone who is placed in a position where he can as a reasonable individual foresee that his actions may cause harm to others. A tort (called delict in Scots law) is a wrongful act or omission, other than a breach of contract, in respect of which damages can be claimed by the victim from the wrongdoer in respect of loss or injury. The duty is to take the care which the reasonable man would have taken in all the circumstances of the case. Who is the reasonable man? He is the average, ordinary man 'on the Clapham omnibus', as one Victorian judge put it. If he holds himself out as having a particular skill, like a doctor, nurse, solicitor or accountant, he is judged by the standard of the reasonable average member of his branch of the profession; if an action is taken in the courts this standard will be explained by expert witnesses drawn from the same profession.

A failure to take reasonable care will not in itself give rise to a civil action for damages: there must also be damage to a plaintiff or plaintiffs. (The law of neg-ligence will be examined more fully in Chapter 7.) An instructive case was that of *Stokes* v. *Guest, Keen and Nettlefold* (1968). Mr Stokes was frequently required in the course of his employment as a tool-setter by GKN to lean over oily machines. He died of scrotal cancer after 15 years' employment. The risk of cancer from mineral oil was established by research from the late 1940s. In 1960, the then Factory Inspectorate published a leaflet advising employers to give warnings to and monitor those who worked with mineral oil. GKN employed Dr Lloyd as a full-time OH physician; although he realised the risk, especially as another employee in the same factory had died of scrotal cancer in 1963, he decided that it was too small to make periodic inspections and warnings necessary. Stokes died in 1966 and it was held that if he had been warned earlier he might have survived.

The judge recognised the dilemma of the OH physician:

'A factory doctor when advising his employers on questions of safety precautions is subject to pressures and has to give weight to considerations which do not apply as between a doctor and his patient and is expected to give, and in this case regularly gave, to his employers advice based partly on medical and partly on economic and administrative considerations. For instance he may consider some precaution medically desirable but hesitate to recommend expanding his department to cope with it, having been refused such expansion before; or there may be questions of frightening workers off the job or of interfering with production.'

Dr Lloyd had seen one man in 1962 who had been advised by a specialist and his GP to cease working with oil; he told him to stay at work to keep up his earnings. He had given a talk to the works council in 1963 about the importance of changing working clothes; he had mentioned scrotal cancer in the talk but it had been omitted from the minutes which were generally distributed because they were read by both sexes! It was held that the doctor was negligent in not warning and testing the workers. As he was an employee, GKN were held vicariously liable for his negligence and had to pay damages to Mr Stokes' widow.

Compare *Brown* v. *Rolls-Royce* (1960) in which an employee contracted dermatitis through contact with machine oil. The employers did not supply barrier cream, about which at the time there was a division of opinion in the medical profession. They relied on their medical officer, Dr Collier, and on his advice barrier cream was not one of the precautions required, though most other employers did supply it. It was decided that there was no negligence, because it had not been proved that barrier cream was an effective precaution against dermatitis in this job.

A number of different points arise from these cases:

(1) They demonstrate the inherent dilemma in the position of the OH professional with duties to both employee and employer, but they also illustrate that the primary duty is to the employee. With respect to the judge in *Stokes*, it is not the job of the doctor or nurse to balance the books. Of course, the OH department must exercise commonsense and tact when dealing with both management and trade unions. There will be some suggested changes to the working environment which will make life more pleasant but are not absolutely necessary, and others which are needed to protect against harm. Therein lies the importance of the expertise of the specialist. He must be able to place information about the likely medical risks (based on his reading of official publications and the results of research published in medical journals) before management so that they can make an informed decision. He should also have some knowledge of possible precautionary measures and their efficacy. If he finds evidence that there is a real risk of injury, it is his duty to communicate it to the employers, however much preventive measures may cost. He cannot thereafter be held responsible if they do not take his advice, though this may eventually be held to be negligence by the managers. In the long run it may prove cheaper to spend money on precautions now than on damages later, quite apart from the human costs.

In a case heard in 1984 James Kellett claimed damages for industrial deafness sustained in the course of his employment in the British Rail Engineering works at Crewe. He was first provided with ear muffs in 1979. His case rested mainly on the argument that he should have been provided with hearing protection at a much earlier date. In a previous decision relating to shipbuilders (*Thompson* v. *Smith's Shiprepairers* (1984)), the court had set the date when the average British employer should have taken precautions against noise-induced hearing loss at about 1963 when a Government report, *Noise and the Worker*, was published. However, in British Rail's employ in the early 1950s was a Divisional Medical Officer at Eastleigh, a Dr Howkins. This exemplary physician wrote to the Chief Medical Officer of BR in 1951 that he had tested samples of ear defenders in the boiler shops and had found them particularly effective. A request from him and from the works committee that the defenders should be provided free of charge was rejected by management because of the cost (1s 3d a pair). In 1955 a proposal from a consultant physician to do research into industrial deafness in the workshops at Swindon was rejected by BR management partly because of fears that it might precipitate claims for damages from the workers. Because of this evidence, the judge in Mr Kellet's case set the date at which BR should have provided ear defenders as 1955, eight years earlier than for industry generally (*Kellet* v. *BR Engineering*). This may not seem so significant until it is appreciated that there were over 2000 claims for industrial deafness made against BR and that the earlier date substantially increased the measure of damages in nearly every case.

(2) They show that the employer is vicariously liable for the negligence of OH professionals as long as they are directly employed. He may also be liable for an independent consultant under the employer's non-delegable duty (Chapter 7), but this is more doubtful. This is one reason why it may be important to ascertain whether there is a contract of service or for services.

(3) They demonstrate how important it is to keep up-to-date, especially with Government publications. Another case, *Burgess* v. *Thorn Consumer Electronics Ltd* (1983), concerned a Guidance Note from the HSE about tenosynovitis. This was received by Thorn at their factory at Bexhill, but the personnel department failed to recognise it as an occupational hazard for the workers. At the factory, there was no specialist OH assistance; the 'surgery' was staffed by first-aiders. It was held that the employer was negligent in not warning Mrs Burgess that if she started having pains in her wrist or arm she should see her doctor immediately. If she had been warned the condition could have been diagnosed before surgery was needed.

(4) The judge in the *Stokes* case summarised the duty of the employer (and the same standard will be applied to doctors and nurses) as follows:

'... the overall test is still the conduct of the reasonable and prudent employer, taking positive thought for the safety of his workers in the light of what he knows or ought to know; where there is a recognised and general practice which has been followed for a substantial period in similar circumstances without mishap, he is entitled to follow it, unless in the light of common sense or newer knowledge it is clearly bad; but, where there is developing knowledge, he must keep reasonably abreast of it and not be too slow to apply it; and where he has in fact greater than average knowledge of the risks, he may be thereby obliged to take more than the average or standard precautions. He must weigh up the risk in terms of the likelihood of injury occurring and the potential consequences if it does; and he must balance against this the probable effec-tiveness of the precautions that can be taken to meet it and the expense and inconvenience they involve. If he is found to have fallen below the standard to be properly expected of a reasonable and prudent employer in these respects, he is negligent.'

Doctors have taken the attitude that when they examine an applicant for a job or for insurance or entry to a pension fund, they are not in a doctor/patient rela-tionship with that person. They see themselves having three forms of contact with patients: the traditional therapeutic relationship, that of the impartial medical examiner reporting to a third party, and that of the research worker. The impli-cation for some doctors is that they are not as strictly bound by ethical duties in the second and third situations.

'The absence of a patient/physician relationship may result in the absence of an unambiguous duty of the physician to uncover disease, disclose medical data to the patient, advise the employee of risks of further exposure, and protect the confidentiality of the information disclosed and the advice given.' (Samuels: Medical Surveillance, *Journal of Occupational Medicine,* Aug. 1986)

In previous editions of this book, I doubted whether this was an accurate reflection of the legal position. My view was supported by the High Court in *Baker* v. *Kaye* (1997). Mr Baker was a television sales executive. He was offered employment by NBC Europe, a subsidiary of General Electric, as director of international sales. The offer, contained in a letter from GE's human resources manager, was to take effect from 1 March, subject to a satisfactory medical report from the company doctor, Dr Kaye. Mr Baker heard of the offer while attending a trade convention in Monte Carlo. On his return he attended Dr Kaye's office for the pre-employment assessment, in the course of which a blood sample was taken. When Dr Kaye received the results of the test, he considered that there was evi-dence of over-indulgence in alcohol. He telephoned the company to ask about the nature of the job, and was told that it was stressful, involving a high degree of responsibility, a great deal of business entertaining and frequent trips abroad. Dr Kaye knew that the company was intolerant of heavy drinking. He arranged to see Mr Baker again and asked about his alcohol consumption. Mr Baker admitted to having drunk slightly more than usual when he was in Monte Carlo. Dr Kaye took a second sample of blood and advised him to consult his GP, who recommended that he abstain from alcohol for several days, after which she would repeat the tests. Meanwhile, Mr Baker, not anticipating any serious problems, resigned from his previous job.

When Dr Kaye received the results of the second test he concluded that Mr Baker had an alcohol problem. He discussed the results with a medical colleague, a consultant gastroenterologist, and with GE's former Medical Officer, both of whom agreed with him. He informed the company that he was unable to recommend Mr Baker (though not, of course, giving the reason) and told Mr Baker of what he had done, and why. Mr Baker did not get the job. Tests taken by his GP after a short period of abstinence showed substantial improvement and after two weeks were within normal limits. A month later Professor McIntyre, a consultant physician, examined Mr Baker and advised that there was no evidence of liver damage.

Mr Baker was now in the position that he had unconditionally resigned from his previous job and had not been appointed to the new one, since the offer of employment had been conditional on the satisfactory report of the OH physician. He sued the physician for negligence, claiming damages for loss of the GE post. The case raised the question of whether a medical practitioner retained by an employer to carry out pre-employment medical assessments of prospective employees owes a duty of care to the prospective employee. It was held that he does. Three features of the relationship were considered of particular importance. The first was that the defendant knew that the plaintiff's employment depended on the assessment, the second that he regarded himself as under a duty of confidentiality towards the patient, and the third that the defendant regarded himself as under a duty to the plaintiff to advise him to seek medical advice if any health problems were disclosed by the examination. There was no conflict between the doctor's duty to the company, and that towards the prospective employee. The duty was to take reasonable care in arriving at a judgment whether or not to recommend the plaintiff for employment, bearing in mind the company's requirements.

Was Dr Kaye negligent? The plaintiff was supported by the expert evidence of Professor McIntyre and of Dr Cockcroft, a consultant in occupational medicine. The defendant called Sir Anthony Dawson, an independent healthcare consultant. It was held that, on the facts, Dr Kaye was not negligent. The judge decided that it was not essential to explore the plaintiff's absenteeism record, because of the high degree of independence enjoyed by senior managers (a more junior employee might be different). He decided that it was not essential to weigh the plaintiff (Mr Baker was 'clinically corpulent'). He decided that a substantial body of reasonable medical opinion would have arrived at the same conclusions as Dr Kaye about the blood tests. Mr Baker lost the action.

The view that a doctor owes a duty of care to a job applicant, at least as regards physical harm, is supported by the decision of the Court of Appeal in *R* v. *Croydon Health Authority* (1997). A radiologist examined a woman who was a job applicant. He negligently failed to report to the occupational physician the evidence of primary pulmonary hypertension disclosed by a pre-employment x-ray. The court held that there was a duty of care imposed by law on the radiologist to the job applicant in relation to the pre-employment assessment.

In a subsequent case in 1998, *Kapfunde* v. *Abbey National*, the Court of Appeal disagreed with the decision in *Baker* v. *Kaye*. Mrs Kapfunde applied for a job with the Abbey National and completed a medical questionnaire disclosing details of her sickness absence record in her previous employment. The questionnaire was reviewed by Dr Daniel, Abbey National's independent occupational health physician, who advised that the applicant's medical history indicated that she was likely to have a higher than average absence level. She suffered from sickle cell anaemia. Mrs Kapfunde, who was not considered for the job, sued the Abbey National as Dr Daniel's employer, arguing that she was negligent. The court held, first, that Dr Daniel was not an employee but an independent contractor, so that Abbey National could not be vicariously liable for her. Secondly, they decided that, in any event, she was not negligent, because she had exercised the skill and care to be expected of a reasonably competent OH physician in the circumstances. Dr Daniel never saw Mrs Kapfunde in person, she merely assessed her questionnaire. The case arose before the Disability Discrimination Act came into force. Now, there might be an argument that Mrs Kapfunde was a disabled person under the Act.

The main interest in the judgment lies in the conclusion that Dr Daniel did not owe Mrs Kapfunde a duty of care. The Court of Appeal drew an analogy with the decision of the House of Lords in *X* v. *Bedfordshire County Council* (1995), where it was held that the psychiatrists who examined children at the request of the local authority in cases of suspected child abuse owed no duty of care to those children or their parents. In later case law, after an appeal to the European Court of Human Rights, the courts have held that the psychiatrist does owe a duty of care to the child, though not to the parents (*JD and Others* v. *East Berkshire Community Health* (2003)). Thus, the authority of the *Kapfunde* decision has been weakened. In addition, the harm suffered by the job applicant was economic only: she did not get the job. It is submitted that had there been physical harm the OH physician could have been liable for a negligent failure to diagnose a physical problem and to warn the job applicant of the need to consult her GP, as in the *Croydon* case above.

In the United States, liability has been imposed on OH doctors who negligently failed to diagnose medical conditions. For example, in *Green* v. *Walker* (1990) an employee was required to undergo annual health checks. The doctor carried out all the tests, found the results to be normal and classified the employee as fit. A year later the employee was diagnosed with lung cancer. It was held that the doctor owed a duty of care to the employee. This has also been applied to pre-employment examinations (*Betesh* v. *United States* (1974)).

'When a doctor conducts a physical examination, the examinee generally assumes that "no news is good news" and relies on the assumption that any serious condition will be revealed.'

The general principle is that the duty of care in negligence arises whenever it can be foreseen that a careless act or omission may harm another. There is no duty to assist a stranger, but if the doctor or nurse as it were creates a relationship by examining or testing an individual a duty will arise at least to perform the examination carefully. In Mrs Sutton's case (next section) a nurse in a Well Woman Clinic who examined a woman for breast cancer and did not refer her to a doctor when she complained of a lump in her breast was held liable for negligence. A doctor using a healthy volunteer for research is not in a therapeutic relationship but he will be liable if he negligently causes damage to the volunteer.

As will be discussed in Chapter 3, there is no blanket obligation in law to give the patient information about himself, but it is likely that courts would hold a doctor negligent if, having discovered in the course of screening that a worker was showing signs of susceptibility to a substance, he did not at least warn the patient to avoid further exposure. Only if the worker's condition were incurable, could not be treated and could not be passed on to others might there be justification for the doctor's silence. In one incident, a part-time occupational health physician passing through the factory chanced to see a worker stripped to the waist. He noticed swelling of glands and other clearly visible symptoms of Hodgkin's disease. He obtained the man's consent to writing a letter to his GP, who in his turn sent him to a consultant who confirmed the diagnosis and commenced immediate treatment. Would the OH physician have been acting negligently if he had not at least advised the man that he should consult his own doctor? What if a doctor acting as an impartial medical examiner for an insurance company discovers such symptoms? Even though the company expressly forbids him to discuss his report with the applicant, it would be negligent (and, as a mere lawyer, I should have thought unethical) for the doctor not to indicate to him that he should seek further medical advice (one possibility is to obtain the applicant's agreement to sending a confidential letter to his GP).

What, then, *is* the difference between the therapeutic and the other relationships? As you would expect, it is the existence or absence of a duty to give treatment. The doctor or nurse who examines an applicant for a job undertakes only to assess his medical suitability. He has no further obligation. He can say: 'I have been asked to examine you by the employer. These are the examinations I propose to do. I shall only perform them with your agreement and I shall only give the results to the employer with your consent. If you refuse consent I cannot write a report about you and in that case I don't think you have much chance of the job, but that is your decision'.

There is no doubt that the OH professional does owe a duty of care to employees in employment and this is discussed in the next section. It is important to note that the duty of *confidence* arises in any situation, pre-employment, in employment, or if the doctor is an independent medical examiner, where the patient confides in the physician. It is not dependent on the presence or absence of a duty of care.

2.4 *Liability to the workers*

Occupational physicians and nurses have a two-fold duty to the work-force. Since they have no contract with the employees (the contract is with the employer) their duty flows only from the law of tort. In the first place, they assume a broad obligation towards all those employed by the employer while at work. The OH doctor or nurse is in one sense like a general practitioner who has accepted patients on to his list. The list comprises all the workers in that part of the workplace over which he has jurisdiction. He only undertakes to care for the workers while they are at work and he does not usually promise to provide treatment other than in an emergency. Lest this be thought so onerous a duty as to deter any from the practice of occupational medicine, remember that the duty is to take reasonable care, the care that an average professional would take in all the circumstances, taking into account available resources and the degree of risk. A doctor who only visits a factory for one afternoon a week cannot be reasonably expected to monitor the health of the entire workforce in every particular. In medical negligence suits, the ability of the doctor to bring evidence that he is supported by the opinion and practice of other doctors even if there is an opposing school of thought is very good evidence that he has acted with reasonable care (*Maynard* v. *W. Midlands RHA* (1985)).

What if the doctor or nurse becomes aware that an employee is suffering from a disease which he may communicate to other workers or is in some other way a danger – a disturbed patient who is threatening violence, or a driver who is taking addictive drugs? The health professional may have a positive duty to breach confidence for the protection of others and may be liable in negligence if he does not do so. Just as the physician had a duty to warn Mr Stokes about the cancer-inducing mineral oil, he might have a duty to tell him (or at least the human resources department) that the man working next to him in the factory is an unpredictable schizophrenic (see Chapter 3).

The American courts have held a doctor liable for not warning a young woman that one of his patients had murderous intentions towards her, which he had confided to the doctor. After she was murdered by the patient, her parents sued the doctor. The court held that he was negligent in not breaking his patient's confidence (*Tarasoff* v. *University of California* (1976)). In English law a doctor is not usually responsible for the wrongful acts of an adult. For example, in *Palmer* v. *Tees NHS Trust* (1998) a mentally ill patient who was receiving out-patient treatment at the defendant hospital brutalised and murdered a little girl. The mother sued the hospital for negligently failing to confine, supervise or otherwise control the patient concerned, but the hospital was held to have owed her no duty of care in the circumstances. There may, however, be a special case where, as in *Tarasoff*, the potential victim is identifiable. In the Canadian case of *Pittman Estate* v. *Bain* (1994) a doctor was held liable to the wife of a patient for failing to warn the patient that he was HIV-positive, with the result that his wife also contracted HIV. Would the answer have been the same had the doctor informed the husband of his HIV status, but knew that the husband was keeping the information from his wife? Would the doctor be under a duty to breach the husband's confidence in order to protect the wife? It is unclear what attitude the English courts would adopt to such a situation. Certainly, our courts would probably not hold a doctor liable for breach of confidence if he did decide to disclose the fact of her husband's HIV status to his wife, because that would be a disclosure in the public interest (Chapter 3).

If a doctor knows that a worker is carrying the HIV virus, is he negligent if he does not reveal it to those with whom the worker comes into contact? The medical evidence is that it is virtually impossible to transmit the virus through normal contact, so that in almost every case it will not constitute negligence if management and fellow-workers are kept in ignorance. Only if there is a real risk of contact with contaminated blood or body fluids which cannot be avoided by standard hygiene procedures employed in every case, as with exposure-prone medical and surgical procedures, should the doctor or nurse consider breaching confidence in the interests of others.

Secondly, the OH professional has a duty of care towards any worker who approaches him for advice or assistance. A careless diagnosis, an inappropriate prescription, a failure to refer someone for specialist advice can all constitute negligence. For example, Mrs Sutton went for a health check to a Well Woman Clinic. She told the nurse who examined her, Nurse Hancock, that she thought she had a lump in her breast. The nurse could not feel it, so she did not refer the matter to a doctor as she ought to have done. It was held that the nurse was negligent because she should not have taken upon herself the role of diagnostician. Her employer, a private health organisation, was held vicariously liable despite her disobedience to instructions: she was still acting in the course of her employment as a nurse. The damages were low in this case because the judge found that all that would have been achieved by an earlier referral was a few more years' life (*Sutton* v. *Population Services* (1981)).

The House of Lords in *Spring* v. *Guardian Assurance* (1994) reviewed the potential liability of referees (not the sporting kind!). The plaintiff was an appointed company representative of the defendants for the purpose of selling their investment products. He was dismissed. He then applied for a job with another company. Under the rules of the regulatory body, LAUTRO, the new employers had to seek a reference from the previous employer. Having received an unfavourable reference, they refused to employ him. The reference was negligently prepared. It stated that Mr Spring was a man 'of little or no integrity and could not be regarded as honest', but this was based on one incident which the employers had failed properly to investigate, and which, if they had, disclosed no dishonesty on Mr Spring's part. The House of Lords, reversing the decision of the Court of Appeal, held that an employer who gave a reference in respect of a former employee owed that employee a duty to take reasonable care and would be liable to him in negligence if the employee suffered damage through failure to take reasonable care.

This case raises very important issues with respect to medical reports. Is a doctor or nurse writing such a report potentially liable in negligence to the subject of the report? Is there a duty of care? A report written by one health professional to another *for the purposes of treatment* is subject to a duty to take reasonable care. A consultant who negligently gives the wrong advice to the patient's GP who in consequence prescribes the wrong drug would be liable to the patient in negligence. Also, a health professional or hygienist who negligently performs screening tests could be held liable to the worker whose early symptoms or overexposure go unmarked. But occupational health reports are mostly not of this kind. They represent the opinion of the OH professional as to the competence and ability of the worker to do a job, and have financial rather than medical consequences. The occupational physician is asked to write a report on the fitness of a pilot but confuses two employees and attaches the alcoholic's report to the pilot's records. In another example, the doctor negligently advises the employer that a worker is fit to work, and therefore malingering when he takes sick leave, because the doctor has failed to make a careful examination and to appreciate the worker's true medical condition. *Spring* v. *Guardian Assurance* is House of Lords authority that a referee can be held liable in negligence for economic loss and was followed in principle in *Baker* v. *Kaye* (above) in that if on the facts in this case the court had held that Dr Kaye had been negligent the plaintiff would have been awarded damages. The later decision of *Kapfunde* v. *Abbey National* (1998) has cast doubt on whether the principle should be applied in a pre-employment context, at least where the doctor has not seen the job applicant, but has given advice only on the basis of a pre-employment questionnaire.

The doctor must also have the employer's interest in mind, because a medical report which is carelessly written in the applicant's favour, resulting in the employer taking on an unreliable employee, might give rise to an action by the employer. For negligence to be established, it would be necessary to show not just that the doctor's assessment of the worker in question was at fault but that there had been a failure to do what a reasonable doctor would have done. An example would be a report of a pre-employment medical examination which stated that an employee with obvious symptoms of a serious heart condition was in the best of health.

Doctors in particular should be warned that it is not merely the content of their writing which needs attention. James Prendergast, an asthmatic, was prescribed Amoxil by his doctor. The writing on the prescription was so illegible that the pharmacist dispensed Daonil. The judge held that both the pharmacist and the doctor were negligent. The doctor had a duty to write clearly and the pharmacist should have checked with him because the dosage prescribed was unusually high for Daonil. The GP was 25 per cent and the pharmacist 75 per cent responsible (*Prendergast* v. *Sam and Dee* (1988)).

2.5 *Duties under the Disability Discrimination Act 1995*

The great majority of complaints of disability discrimination taken to employment tribunals name the employer as the respondent, but the OH professional may also be potentially liable. Section 57 of the DDA provides that any person who knowingly aids another person to do an unlawful act is to be treated as himself doing the same kind of unlawful act. An employee or agent shall be taken to have aided the employer or principal to do the Act. For example, if an organisation's OH nurse or physician knowingly discriminates against disabled applicants for employment, the employer will be primarily responsible, but the OH professional may also be liable, having aided the company to commit the discrimination in question. This was the situation in *London Borough of Hammersmith and Fulham* v. *Farnsworth* (2000) where an applicant for a job as a residential social worker, who had a history of serious depression, was rejected by the employer on the advice of the occupational physician who reported that she was likely to have higher than average sickness absence. Both the local authority and the physician were sued.

The physician was held liable, but the case against her was reversed on appeal on a technicality.

Section 57 provides a defence. A person does not knowingly aid another to do an unlawful act if he or she acts in reliance on a statement made to him or her by that other person. The statement must be to the effect that the discriminatory act would not be unlawful because of any provision of the DDA 1995 and it must be reasonable to rely on that statement. It is difficult to see how such a statement might be made to OH by the employer where the employer's decision is based on OH advice. It might cover an assurance by the employer that health and safety regulations justified the act of discrimination. One problem here is that codes of ethics prevent the OH professional from disclosing clinical details without consent, so that if consent cannot be obtained the decision on whether or not to recommend the disabled person for employment will, in practice, have to be made by the OH doctor or nurse, rather than the manager.

2.6   *Consent to medical treatment*

Every adult is entitled to decide what physical contact he will permit and it is both criminal and tortious to perform any form of medical examination or treatment on him without his consent. The layman describes such an invasion of the person as an assault, but technically an assault is only a threat of physical contact; the unpermitted contact itself is described as a battery. The fact that a patient may need treatment, even life-saving treatment, is irrelevant: the patient must decide.

There are several exceptions. Where the patient is unconscious, emergency treatment of a life-saving nature may be performed without consent. It is not legally necessary to obtain the consent of relatives in such a case. Consent may be implied by conduct: the employee who holds out his arm for blood to be taken need not, strictly speaking, be required to sign a consent form. Children of 16 or over have the right to give consent on their own behalf (Family Law Reform Act 1969) and the parents' views are irrelevant unless the child is physically or mentally handicapped (this is despite the law that full legal independence is only acquired at 18). Treatment of young children can only be performed with the consent of at least one parent, or the local authority if they are in care; older children under 16 may give a valid consent if they can appreciate the nature and consequences of the treatment (*Gillick* v. *West Norfolk and Wisbech AHA* (1985)).

There is no battery if the patient knows the broad nature of the proposed treatment and agrees to it. Suppose that an OH physician undertakes a programme of vaccination at the place of work. He obtains the written consent of each individual worker to give injections of a particular vaccine. He commits no battery, but he may still be held liable in negligence if he has not informed the workers before they agreed to participate of any risks inherent in the vaccine to be administered. This is the doctrine of 'informed consent' and it is part of the law of negligence. Doctors and nurses when obtaining the patient's consent must give them the information which a reasonable doctor or nurse would have given that patient (*Sidaway* v. *Board of Governors of the Bethlem Royal and the Maudsley Hospital* (1985)). That case concerned a woman who alleged that she had not been told about an inherent risk of less than 1 per cent of damage to her spinal cord before she consented to have an operation which, though carefully performed, left her partially paralysed. The evidence was that some surgeons would have told, but that others would have kept silent. Mrs Sidaway's action failed. Only rarely will the courts overrule medical opinion, as in the case of a young man who underwent colorectal surgery without being warned of the small risk of impotence. The judge held that despite evidence that it was not the practice of the medical profession to give warning of this risk, he would nevertheless consider it unreasonable not to do so (*Smith* v. *Tunbridge Wells AHA* (1994)).

In the case of *Bolitho* v. *City and Hackney HA* (1998) the House of Lords held that the standard of care was that of 'responsible, reasonable and respectable' practitioners. After this, medical expert witnesses have to demonstrate the reasonableness of their opinion, rather than relying on an assertion that their eminence dictates that their views must be respected.

The doctrine of informed consent does not entitle the patient to all the facts about his case, merely the material facts about the proposed treatment. The English courts have not adopted the American attitude that the patient must be given every detail, and have left the issue of what should be communicated to the medical profession. It is they, after all, who alone can identify 'the doctor on the Clapham omnibus'. Note that the signing of a consent form of itself is *never* conclusive in these cases. The law puts less store on the form of the agreement than on the reality of the consent.

The consent of an individual to the taking of blood will prevent it from being either a criminal or civil battery, unless he was misled by false information as to the purpose of the test. A routine blood test for other purposes could be used also to test for HIV antibodies without a battery being committed. As to negligence, however, as there is at present no effective treatment leading to a complete cure, and the discovery that an individual is infected with the virus can lead to severe consequences, both financial and emotional, it is probably true that a health professional's duty of care to his patient demands that he tests for HIV only after he has obtained his fully informed consent.

There is some debate about the accuracy of this advice. The GMC has received an opinion that informed consent is not always necessary for HIV tests, and that where a health professional has suffered an injury through e.g. a needlestick injury and has been exposed to the blood or body fluids of a patient who is unconscious or otherwise incompetent, HIV tests may lawfully be performed on blood already obtained from the patient for other purposes. The Nursing and Midwifery Council's advice to its members contradicts this. Without a test case, it is impossible to give a definitive ruling on this dilemma, but caution dictates that consent should be obtained. Where there is a likelihood that the patient is HIV-positive, prophylactic drugs may be administered to the health professional as a precautionary measure. These drugs have been very successful in prolonging the lives of AIDS patients, though it is not yet clear whether the improvement is indefinite. This may be a material factor in influencing the court to approve 'emergency' HIV tests without consent, since the patient who knows of his condition can now be offered treatment.

The testing of anonymous samples, such that the donor cannot be made aware of the result because the tester does not know his identity, is lawful, whether or not it is ethical. Testing of identified samples without the knowledge of the donor is *not* anonymous; the doctor or nurse can identify the samples. It is the latter kind of procedure which could lead to an action in negligence, because the employee has not given informed consent.

It should be noted that when a statute provides for obligatory medical examination of workers it does not mean that they can be examined without their consent. Such statutes commonly provide that the worker has a statutory duty to present himself for a test, e.g. Regulation 34(5) Ionising Radiations Regulations 1999:

> 'An employee ... shall when required by his employer and at the cost of the employer, present himself during his working hours for such medical examination and tests as may be required ... and shall furnish the employment medical adviser or appointed doctor with such information concerning his health as the employment medical adviser or doctor may reasonably require.'

If the employee refuses, the doctor must respect that decision although the employer will then be justified in taking disciplinary action, since the employee will be in breach of the law.

2.7   Liability to the employer

The OH professional will have a contract with the organisation which employs him, so he will have duties both in contract and in tort. If he is employed under a contract of employment, the law implies many obligations into the relationship which form part of the agreement even if nothing has been said or written. The duty of trust and fidelity discussed in Chapter 3 is a good example of an implied term. One other significant duty is to take care in carrying out his job. In a case in 1956 one employee negligently injured another by reversing a vehicle into him on the employer's premises. The employer paid compensation to the injured employee and claimed on his employer's liability policy. Insurance companies have a right of subrogation, i.e. they take over all the rights which the insured person had when they pay out on the policy. Acting in the name of the employer, the insurance company sued the careless driver for all the loss which he had caused his employer by his negligence. The House of Lords decided that negligent employees have a duty to compensate their employer for the damages he has been forced to pay because of their carelessness (*Lister* v. *Romford Ice and Cold Storage* (1956)). After establishing the point of principle, the insurance companies indicated that they would not in future reimburse themselves by pursuing employees, unless there was wilful misconduct or collusion. Also, in the later case of *Morris* v. *Ford Motor Co.* (1973), the Court of Appeal refused to allow an insurance company to sue the driver of a fork-lift truck who had negligently injured the employee of a subcontractor.

Thus, where an employer is insured against liability to his employees caused by the negligence of directly employed OH personnel (as is required by the

Employers' Liability (Compulsory Insurance) Act 1969), it is unlikely that an indemnity will be obtained by the employer's insurance company from the doctor or nurse's protection society or professional indemnity policy. Before 1990 hospital doctors working in the NHS were required by their contracts of employment to take out policies with defence organisations so that the employer could obtain indemnity if the doctor was negligent. This system was abandoned from 1 January 1990 (HC(89)34).

2.8   Liability to the public

The health professional does not have a *legal* duty to provide medical care for those whom he has not accepted as patients. There is no duty in English law to act as a Good Samaritan and go to the aid of someone lying seriously injured in the street, but if you do you will have an obligation to take reasonable care. What if an employee of a subcontractor, or a visiting member of the public, is taken ill or has an accident on the premises where the OH doctor or nurse is at work? The BMA in *The Occupational Physician* (1984) advises that the OH doctor takes full medical responsibility only for those *working* on site, including contractors, but to the extent that he is concerned with the effect of work on health, he is advised that included therein is the health of the public at large, either in general or as individuals.

It is unlikely that a health professional would be held to owe a *legal* duty to the general public. His obligation to the wider community is a moral and ethical duty. In an extreme case, it might oblige him, against the wishes of his employer, to reveal dangers to the public of which they are in ignorance (see Chapter 3). Mostly, of course, the OH professional is unable to do more than advise and warn, but should do whatever is reasonable in all the circumstances of the case.

2.9   Health care workers with blood-borne viruses

HIV

Ill-informed fears about the dangers of contracting AIDS from an HIV-infected health professional, fuelled by worldwide publicity about the Florida dentist who allegedly infected several of his patients, have led to the setting-up by the Department of Health of the UK Advisory Panel for Health Care Workers Infected with Blood-borne Viruses (UKAP). This has a strong occupational health representation. It has now been transferred to the Health Protection Agency. The Expert Advisory Group on AIDS (EAGA) in 1994 produced guidelines for health authorities and health professionals on the management of HIV-infected health care workers, updated in 1998 and 2003. These provide, *inter alia*:

(1)   All health care workers should scrupulously adopt safe working practices to prevent transmission of HIV infection.
(2)   HIV-infected health care workers should not perform exposure-prone pro-

cedures. (These are procedures where there is a risk that injury to the worker may result in exposure of the patient's open tissues to the blood of the worker. They include those where the worker's gloved hands may be in contact with sharp instruments, needle tips or sharp tissues (spicules of bone or teeth) inside a patient's open body cavity, wound or confined anatomical space where the hands or fingertips may not be completely visible at all times.) Where there is doubt, expert advice should be obtained from a specialist occupational physician who may in turn wish to consult UKAP.

(3)   Health care workers have an ethical duty to patients. Those who believe that they may have been exposed to HIV infection in their personal life or in the course of their work must seek appropriate expert medical advice, and, if appropriate, diagnostic HIV antibody testing.

(4)   Infected health care workers who have performed exposure-prone procedures must cease these activities immediately and seek expert occupational health advice. A nominated medical officer in the employing authority should be notified on a strictly confidential basis. If a 'look-back' study (notice to the public together with help-lines and the offer of HIV tests for any patient concerned about possible infection) is being contemplated, the local Director of Public Health must be consulted.

(5)   Physicians who are aware that infected health care workers under their care have not sought or followed advice, and are continuing to perform exposure-prone procedures, have a duty to inform the appropriate professional body and the nominated medical officer.

(6)   Employers must make every effort to arrange suitable alternative employment, or early retirement, for HIV-infected health care workers.

(7)   All patients who have undergone an exposure-prone procedure where the infected health care worker was the sole or main operator should, as far as is practicable, be notified of this (in a look-back study).

   A look-back study is one where patients known to have been treated by a health professional now identified as HIV-positive, where the procedure was exposure prone, are notified and invited to take an HIV test. Because of the immense costs of such exercises and the disturbance caused to members of the public who are needlessly put in fear of having contracted AIDS, the latest advice suggests that a look-back study will not always be necessary when a health care worker is found to be HIV-positive. Much depends on the nature of the exposure-prone procedures undertaken by the health care worker, and evidence about the reliability of his or her infection controls. Advice should be sought from UKAP.

(8)   Employers have a duty to keep information about an HIV-infected worker confidential, unless the individual consents to disclosure, or, in exceptional circumstances, where it is considered that patients need to be told for the purpose of treatment or the prevention of the spread of infection. This duty does not end with the death of the worker (though if AIDS is mentioned on the death certificate, this is a public document to which all have access).

A failure of a professional who knows or suspects that he is HIV-positive to seek medical advice and act on it is regarded as serious professional misconduct by the medical, nursing and dental professions. The GMC removed from the medical register the name of Dr Patrick Ngosa in 1997 for serious professional misconduct. He was a gynaecologist who feared that he had acquired the HIV virus from a woman with whom he had an affair but refused to have a test and continued to work.

An epidemiological overview of the risk of transmission of HIV from health care worker to patient has been commissioned. Thus far, the evidence is that the risk is tiny and that it is more likely that the health professional will contract HIV from the patient.

In 1991 Tameside and Glossop and Trafford Health Authorities sent letters to women known to have been the patients of an obstetrician diagnosed as HIV-positive. Letters were sent to the patients' homes, rather than through their GPs. Several patients alleged that they had suffered psychiatric damage through the method of communication. The Court of Appeal held that the defendants had not been negligent. Following Department of Health guidelines at the time was important evidence that they had taken reasonable care (*AB* v. *Tameside and Glossop Health Authority* (1997)).

The Government has up to now been opposed to the introduction of compulsory testing either of health care workers or patients. The test is unreliable in the first months of the infection, and at best can provide only a 'snapshot' of the individual's HIV status on the day of the test. However, it has instituted a campaign to persuade pregnant women in ante-natal clinics to take tests in order to help prevent transmission of the virus to the unborn child.

Public disquiet about the employment in the UK of nurses from Africa, with a much higher percentage of HIV-positive citizens in their populations than in Europe, led the Government to set up a Working Group to discuss a new health clearance policy for health care workers new to the NHS. The Working Group looked at potential risks posed to patients from health care workers infected with serious communicable diseases, in particular HIV, hepatitis B, hepatitis C and tuberculosis. Because of the need to comply with the race relations legislation and the Human Rights Act, the Working Group recommended that all new entrants to the NHS, whether from the UK or abroad, who were likely to perform exposure-prone procedures (a qualification which excludes most nursing staff and general practitioners) should be tested for blood-borne viruses and TB pre-employment. The draft guidance was published in 2003, but at the time of writing has not been confirmed.

Hepatitis B

Hepatitis B presents different problems from the HIV virus. There is a reliable vaccine, and medical treatment results in most cases having a happy outcome, though it is still a serious disease. There is less social stigma attached to hepatitus B infection than to HIV infection. Nevertheless, it is far more likely that hepatitis B will be transferred in the course of medical, dental or nursing practice. The Department of Health published recommendations in 1993, updated in 2000, and hepatitis B has been added to the remit of UKAP.

The key recommendations are:

(1) All health care workers should follow general infection control guidelines and adopt safe working practices.

(2) All health care workers who perform exposure-prone procedures, and all medical, dental, nursing and midwifery students should be immunised against hepatitis B, unless immunity has been documented. Their response to the vaccine should subsequently be checked.

(3) Health care workers who are hepatitis B e-antigen (HBeAg) positive should not perform exposure-prone procedures in which injury to the worker could result in blood contaminating the patient's tissues. (Dr Gaud, a London surgeon who, realising that he was e-antigen positive, substituted another person's blood for his own for the purposes of a blood test and continued to operate, infecting several patients, was sent to prison and struck off the medical register.)

(4) Health care workers who are hepatitis B surface antigen (HBsAg) positive but who are not HBeAg positive need not be barred from any area of work unless they have been associated with the transmission of hepatitis B to patients whilst HBeAg negative or have a viral load which exceeds 10^3 genome equivalents per ml. All hepatitis B infected health care workers who are e-antigen negative and who perform exposure-prone procedures or clinical duties in renal units must be tested every 12 months for viral load (hepatitis B virus DNA).

(5) Staff whose work involves exposure-prone procedures and who fail to respond to the vaccine should be permitted to continue in their work provided they are not e-antigen positive carriers of the virus and do not have a viral load of more than 10^3 genome equivalents per ml. Inoculation incidents must be treated and followed up.

(6) Health Authorities and Trusts should ensure that members of staff employed or taking up employment or other health care workers contracted to provide a service which involves carrying out exposure-prone procedures are immunised against the hepatitis B virus, that their antibody response is checked and that carriers of the virus who are HBeAg positive or have a high viral load do not undertake such procedures.

(7) Occupational health departments should be involved in developing local procedures for managing hepatitis B-infected health care workers.

(8) Employers should make every effort to provide alternative employment should this be needed.

(9) The UK Advisory Panel is available when specific occupational advice cannot be obtained locally.

Hepatitis B is a notifiable disease and a prescribed industrial disease for health care workers. Benefits are also available under the NHS Injury Benefits Scheme for NHS staff.

Hepatitis C

Hepatitis C is giving rise to increasing cause for concern. There is no preventive vaccine and infection can cause serious liver damage, sometimes many years later. The risk of transmission to the patient from the health care worker, especially in the course of major surgery, is far higher than the risk of HIV transmission. Guidance was published by the Department of Health in 2002. The key recommendations are:

(1)   Those health care workers found to be hepatitis C positive should not be allowed to perform exposure-prone procedures. Those known to be infected must be tested for hepatitis C virus RNA.

(2)   Health care workers who are intending to undertake professional training for a career that relies upon the performance of exposure-prone procedures should be tested for antibodies to hepatitis C virus and, if positive, for hepatitis C virus RNA. Those found to be hepatitis C RNA positive should be restricted from starting such training whilst they are carrying the virus.

(3)   Health care workers who perform exposure-prone procedures and who believe they may have been exposed to hepatitis C infection should promptly seek and follow confidential professional advice (e.g. from an OH physician) on whether they should be tested for hepatitis C. They should cease performing exposure-prone procedures if they are carrying the virus.

(4)   Hepatitis C infected health care workers who have responded successfully to treatment with anti-viral therapy should be allowed to resume exposure-prone procedures or to start professional training for a career that relies upon the performance of exposure-prone procedures. Successful response to treatment is defined as remaining hepatitis C virus RNA negative six months after cessation of treatment. Successfully treated health care workers will be allowed to return to performing exposure-prone procedures at that time. They should be shown still to be virus RNA negative six months later.

(5)   Staff are provided with information and training about measures to reduce the risk of occupational exposure to hepatitis C infection (e.g. safe handling and disposal of sharps and measures to reduce risks during surgical procedures).

There is currently no post-exposure prophylaxis for hepatitis C, though early treatment may prevent chronic infection. Where a patient has been exposed to a health care worker's blood, the ethical and legal duty of the health care worker is to give information to clinicians to enable the patient to be given treatment as soon as possible. Where it is proved that there has been transmission to a patient, a look-back study is advised. UKAP is investigating whether it is necessary to commission a look-back study where no transmission has been identified. Advice should be sought from UKAP. Hepatitis C is a notifiable disease, and falls within the NHS Injury Benefits Scheme and the Industrial Injuries Disablement Benefit Scheme.

Asymptomatic infection with a blood-borne virus at present does not count as a disability under the Disability Discrimination Act, though there are proposals for change to make HIV infection a disability from diagnosis. Now that treatment is available for HIV and hepatitis B and C, it may be thought reasonable to move towards mandatory testing, although it must be recognised that a negative test today is no guarantee that an infection will not be acquired at a later date. Certainly, the testing of students before they begin their careers seems advisable in order to ensure that years of study are not wasted. It is important that the professions provide training flexible enough to allow a student infected with a blood-borne virus with an ambition, say, to qualify as a psychiatrist, to achieve basic professional competence without performing exposure-prone procedures.

2.10 Professional indemnity

Those who work for others rather than themselves often assume that any legal liability falls on the employer alone. This is definitely not the law. The primary liability for negligence lies with the person who commits the negligent act. Sometimes there is no alternative defendant. An independent consultant is the only possible defendant if he makes a careless mistake. If he is in partnership, his partners are also liable. Where the doctor or nurse is an employee, the employer is vicariously liable: they are both responsible. If the employer is in financial difficulty and uninsured, or claims a contribution or indemnity from the employee, or where the plaintiff out of revenge chooses to pursue the employee instead of or as well as the employer, damages and costs may threaten. The OH professional may be involved in a HSWA prosecution in which he may need legal advice and representation (it is not possible to insure against a criminal fine). For these reasons, every professional should be covered by professional liability insurance, despite the lack of a legal obligation to insure. Nursing staff commonly insure through membership of the Royal College of Nursing (RCN) or a trade union, doctors have professional indemnity through the Medical Defence Union or the Medical Protection Society. The latter are not, strictly speaking, insurance companies, because they have a discretion whether to indemnify (*Medical Defence Union* v. *Department of Trade* (1979)). The Faculty of Occupational Medicine's guidance *Good Medical Practice for Occupational Physicians* (2001) advises that in his own interest and that of his patients, the doctor should obtain adequate insurance or professional indemnity cover for any part of his practice not covered by an employer's indemnity scheme.

Nurses are often troubled that they are not covered if they undertake 'extended role' tasks without proper authority. Because essentially the proper role of a nurse rests on custom and practice, it is impossible to lay down a definitive list of nursing tasks. The RCN in its guidance notes for the occupational health nurse advises that each OH department should draw up an agreement about the tasks which the nurse is expected to perform. No nurse should undertake any procedure for which she is not trained and competent to perform. The OH nurse is not covered by RCN indemnity insurance when she undertakes radiography. The RCN is reluctant to draw up lists of duties which could be regarded as a restriction on the development of the OH nurse's role in a true professional sense. On the other hand, OH nurses need to recognise those areas of expertise which rightly belong to other professions, such as medicine, radiography or physiotherapy. The emphasis is on demarcation agreements, especially with doctors who carry the ultimate clinical responsibility, and on training to enable the nurse to extend her role competently.

2.11   The conduct of research

Research on humans is of two kinds: clinical research on ill patients and research on healthy volunteers. In law both need the informed consent of the subjects. As has been seen, this allows a doctor or nurse to withhold information if a reasonable doctor or nurse would have kept silent, as long as the subject knew the broad nature of what was to be done.

Ethical rules are laid down in the Declaration of Helsinki 2000. The Royal College of Physicians produced a third edition of its *Guidelines on the Practice of Ethics Committees* in 1996. The Department of Health produced guidelines for research ethics committees in 1991, updated in 2001. The Helsinki Declaration demands that every subject

> '... must be adequately informed of the aims, methods, sources of funding, any possible conflicts of interest, institutional affiliations of the researcher, the anticipated benefits and the potential risks of the study and the discomfort it may entail ... the doctor should obtain the subject's freely given informed consent, preferably in writing.'

The 2000 amendments to the Declaration insist that therapeutic and non-therapeutic research should be subject to the same controls. The Department of Health guidelines have had to be substantially amended to allow for the changes brought about by the Clinical Trials Regulations 2004. *The Research Governance Framework for Health and Social Care* (2001) indicated a need for review of NHS ethics committees and this has been done under the umbrella of the Central Office for Research Ethics Committees (COREC).

NHS employees who fail to obtain ethics committee approval for a research project would be subject to disciplinary action. The professional bodies would be likely to regard a failure to obtain ethical approval as professional misconduct.

On 1 May 2004 the Medicines for Human Use (Clinical Trials) Regulations came into force in the UK. These implement the European Clinical Trials Directive and are the first comprehensive legislative provisions dealing with research on human beings, rather than animals. The Regulations deal with all kinds of ethics committees, both in the NHS and the universities, and also independent research contractors engaged in pharmaceutical research on healthy volunteers. Research on NHS patients or premises must be referred to an NHS ethics committee.

The College of Physicians in 1986 made the following recommendations relating to research on healthy volunteers:

(1) All research involving healthy volunteers should be approved by an ethics committee.
(2) All studies should be scientifically and ethically justified.
(3) Confidentiality should be maintained (see Chapter 3).
(4) No study on healthy volunteers should involve more than minimal risk and there should be full disclosure of risks.
(5) There should be no financial inducement or any coercion that might persuade a volunteer to take part in a study against his better judgment. Payment should be related to expenses, inconvenience and discomfort, not risk.
(6) The volunteer should be asked to give permission to the researcher for his general practitioner and, if appropriate, 'a company or other medical officer' to be contacted for details of past history. Where appropriate, he should be medically examined and be asked about relevant medical history. He should sign a consent form.
(7) Any significant untoward event occurring during or after a study affecting a volunteer should be communicated to the general practitioner and appropriate medical action taken to safeguard the volunteer's health.
(8) The sponsor, whether this be a commercial organisation, university, NHS or other institution, should agree to pay compensation for any injury caused by participation in a research study without regard to proof of negligence.

Research on healthy volunteers often takes the form of a drug study. The Association of the British Pharmaceutical Industry (ABPI) in 1988 published its *Guidelines for Medical Experiments in Non-Patient Human Volunteers*, revised in 1990. Its recommendations are similar to those in the Royal College of Physicians' report. Where research is proposed on a 'captive audience', e.g. medical students or employees, no-one should be made to feel under obligation to volunteer, nor should they be disadvantaged in any way by not volunteering. Volunteers may be rewarded in cash or in kind, but the amount should be reasonable and related to time, inconvenience and discomfort, not risk. The ABPI operates an *ex gratia* scheme whereby any healthy volunteer in a drug trial mounted by an ABPI member will receive compensation for any injury arising from the trial.

In an occupational health setting it will be necessary also to obtain the agreement and support of the employer, and probably the trade unions. The OH physician must be very careful to ensure that any volunteers have freely consented to take part. He should make clear at the start his role as a research investigator.

'Occupational physicians may be perceived by workers to be part of management and therefore it is particularly important to ensure that informed agreement is given freely and that individuals recognise that they are free to withdraw at any time without detriment. Consent of trades unions to participate in research projects should not be taken to imply the consent of all individuals involved.' (Faculty of Occupational Medicine: *Guidance on Ethics* (1993))

Drugs research using patients is regulated by the Medicines Act 1968. The Committee on Safety of Medicines must license human trials by granting a clinical trial certificate (or exemption from the need to hold such a certificate) and will only do so if satisfied with preliminary research and animal tests. Any adverse reactions must be reported to the committee. This does not apply to non-therapeutic research because it is not regarded as the administration of a medi-cinal product. Contraception is defined as therapeutic.

Epidemiological research using data only is discussed in Chapter 3. In my experience, most occupational health research involves an investigation of data and thus confidentiality is of major importance.

2.12   The rights of OH professionals

Thus far we have examined only those obligations which the law places on doc-tors and nurses working in industry. They will be relieved to read that they also have rights. The relationship with the employer will, as has been explained, rest on a contract. It is advisable to insist on a written agreement, and employees (but not the self-employed) can demand a written statement of pay, hours, holidays, pension and sick pay provision, periods of notice and disciplinary rules and grievance procedures, under the Employment Rights Act 1996. This statement must contain a job title, but not necessarily a job description. If the employee's duties are not spelled out and a dispute arises, there may have to be reference to the job advertisement, what was said at the interview and custom and practice.

The Employment Rights Act 1996 gives the right to complain to an employment tribunal and to claim compensation from the employer to any employee who has been designated to carry out activities in connection with preventing or reducing risks to the health and safety of employees at work and who has been disciplined or dismissed by the employer for carrying out or proposing to carry out such activities (see Chapter 8).

An interesting case was that of *Woodroffe* v. *British Gas* (1985). Miss Woodroffe was a State Registered Nurse who in 1980 entered the employment of British Gas as an OH nurse. She was given a job description which did not make any express reference to taking blood samples or giving talks on health matters to other employees. Shortly after she took up her post, a new Medical Officer was appointed. He thought that she should take blood samples and give health edu-cation talks. Miss Woodroffe explained that these tasks were classified at the time as 'extended role' and that she had not been trained to carry them out. The doctor offered her training which she refused. After a while, he persuaded her to take on these extra responsibilities, which she did with reluctance. The Medical Officer became dissatisfied with her work, including her keeping of records. He instituted an enquiry which he presided over and which recommended her dismissal. She appealed to a higher level of management, and was represented by a member of her professional body, but the appeal was dismissed. A complaint to an industrial tribunal of unfair dismissal, and subsequent appeals to the Employment Appeal Tribunal and the Court of Appeal were also unsuccessful.

Nurses will be interested to note that it was the opinion of the Employment Appeal Tribunal that if Nurse Woodroffe had refused to carry out the additional tasks altogether she could not have been criticised, for they were not tasks which she had been hired to perform. If she had been persuaded to receive specialist training in occupational health the difficulties might have been resolved. There is, however, no legal duty on the employer to give money and time off for further training, so if the doctor or nurse wants this, he or she should negotiate it as part of the contract. The Right to Time Off for Study or Training Regulations 2001 apply only to 16 and 17 year olds.

The employer's duty to take reasonable care for the employee's health and safety applies equally to the occupational health department. The employee is entitled to refuse to put himself in a position of imminent personal danger, as did the bank employee who declined to work in Turkey where he had previously been sentenced to death (*Ottoman Bank* v. *Chakarian* (1930)). Doctors and nurses frequently disregard their own safety to go to the assistance of their patients. One such was Dr Baker. Contractors were cleaning a deep well. They installed a petrol pump on a ledge 29 feet below ground, creating dangerous fumes in a closed space. Two workers were overcome by fumes and were lying down the well unconscious. Dr Baker was urged not to go down but he said: 'There are two men down there. I must see what I can do for them.' He died on the way to hospital. When his widow sought compensation from the contractors, they argued that the doctor had caused his own death by his foolhardiness. The widow submitted that it was reasonable for a doctor to take risks to try to save the lives of workers who had been placed in mortal danger by their employer's lack of care. The Court of Appeal held the defendants liable. 'Bearing in mind that danger invites rescue, the court should not be astute to accept criticism of the rescuer's conduct from the wrong-doer who created the danger.' (*Baker* v. *Hopkins* (1959))

Chapter 3
Medical Records and Confidentiality

3.1 The ownership of records

Many of the legal problems of occupational health (OH) workers involve the maintenance, disclosure, transfer or destruction of records of tests and clinical examinations. Central to all these issues is the question of ownership and the right to control medical records. Any words which are reduced to writing comprise two elements: the physical paper on which the words are written or the computers or floppy disk in which they are recorded, and the information contained therein. In the National Health Service, the medical records of patients clearly belong physically to the Primary Care Trusts (in the case of general practitioner (GP) records) and NHS Trusts (in the case of hospital records) and ultimately, therefore, to the Secretary of State. This is because the contracts of health service personnel provide that patients' records must be made on health service forms. It is also, practically speaking, the most sensible system, because doctors come and go and records must be kept by a permanent central organisation. Only the records of private patients belong to the health professional with whom they have a contract.

Do the same rules apply to the OH records of *employees* of the health authorities? It is probable that these, like all occupational health records, both within and outside the NHS, are physically the property of the employer, because they will be recorded on the employer's paper or computer and held on the employer's premises. In addition, if the doctor or nurse is directly employed under a contract of employment, there is an implied term in the contract that the fruits of the employee produced in the course of employment (and this will extend to patent rights to inventions, and copyrights in written publications, like research findings) belong to the employer.

Doctors and nurses need not feel aggrieved that this is the law, for it does not necessarily follow that the owner of the records has the right of control over the information contained therein. The general practitioner is in control of a patient's records while he continues to have that patient on his list. There is nothing to prevent the occupational health department having an agreement with the employer whereby the health professionals and their staff have exclusive access to OH records. This arrangement, to be watertight, should be incorporated in a written agreement which can form part of the doctor's or nurse's contract, just as many companies have standard contracts with employees about the ownership of inventions. The Faculty of Occupational Medicine recommends that where management has a legal requirement to maintain health records (e.g. under the COSHH Regulations) there should be a clear distinction between such records and clinical medical records. The latter should be under the sole supervision of the occupational health department.

The right to control medical records will carry with it increased responsibilities. First and foremost, there is the duty to take care of the records and ensure that they are only read by authorised personnel. In the days when documents were held in filing cabinets, it was important to keep them locked; nowadays, more sophisticated controls are necessary to keep computer-held data from being made public, especially where a system is shared with other users or there is telephone access. Passwords will have to be built in and security procedures instituted. In particular, visual display units should not be sited where casual passers-by can read them. Where data are held on computer the controller of the data will have duties under the Data Protection Act 1998 (DPA).

The physician may move to another job or may retire. The professionally qualified nurse may be made redundant and replaced only by unqualified first-aiders. The employer may engage the services of a new provider. If the medical records are destroyed this could harm the workers, both individually and as research data which could benefit all. As the records belong to the employer they should be left where they are, but the control be handed over to the new doctor or nurse. The Faculty of Occupational Medicine recommends that

'before agreeing to the transfer of clinical records, the outgoing provider should be satisfied that the new contractors are professionally competent and have arrangements to store and safeguard the records appropriately.'

What if there will be no new health professional? In a case where a business is closing down, the Faculty of Occupational Medicine recommends that if an organisation is to be closed and will cease to exist it will be necessary to ensure that records are transferred with individual consent either to each employee's own doctor or to another medical adviser. Similar advice would presumably be given in a case of closure of an OH department. The doctor or nurse might also consider giving a copy of the results of periodic examinations to the worker himself, failing a national system of such records as exists for ionising radiation workers (National Radiological Protection Board), or they may be offered to the Health and Safety Executive (HSE). The Faculty recommends that in the last resort the physician should destroy his records, other than those where retention is required by statute, but this could be risky advice if, as has been argued, the records are not his property.

3.2 How long should records be kept?

The obvious answer is only as long as is necessary, but how long is that? Occupational diseases may take 20 or more years to develop. Patients died of meso-thelioma decades after their only contact with asbestos while making gas masks during World War II. Occasionally, there is a statutory rule. The Ionising Radiations Regulations 1999 oblige the employer to preserve records of tests on employees exposed to radiation for 50 years. The Control of Substances Hazardous to Health (COSHH) Regulations provide that the health record of health surveillance procedures carried out on employees exposed to hazardous substances shall be kept for at least 40 years from the last entry. Otherwise, common sense must be used. The DH recommends in a circular to health authorities that hospital health records should be held for a minimum of eight years after the conclusion of treatment and GP records for a minimum of ten years. Obstetric records should be kept for at least 25 years, and those relating to mentally disordered persons for at least 20 years. The British Medical Association (BMA) recommends a minimum of ten years after the employee left the employment, but advises that records of significant episodes, exposures or accidents should be preserved beyond that limit. However, it must not be forgotten that the employer has an interest in the preservation of records which he may later need to defend an allegation of negligence. The best course is probably to discuss the matter with the employing organisation, which will be likely to agree to provide extra storage facilities for records which it wants to preserve.

3.3 The duty of confidence

The duty to keep secrets is enshrined in all codes of medical ethics. All health professionals know that it is one of the strictest ethical rules of their various professions that they should not give confidential information about a patient to third parties other than in exceptional cases. If this obligation is breached, doctors or nurses may find themselves before the professional conduct committee of their professional body (the General Medical Council (GMC) for doctors and the Nursing and Midwifery Council (NMC) for nurses, midwives and health visitors) and may even run the risk of being struck off the register, depending on the seriousness of the offence. The law leaves the matter of professional ethics to the professions themselves, so it is from them that guidance must be obtained on what constitutes good professional practice.

There is a legal as well as an ethical duty of confidence. Lawyers sometimes find it difficult to define the legal category into which the duty of confidence falls. For our purposes it is sufficient to state that the duty arises where there is a contract between the confider and the confidant which includes a term (which may be express or implied) that confidence will be kept, or there is a relationship between the parties which implies a duty of confidence.

An example of the first is a contract of employment, and of the second the marital relationship. There is little doubt that a health professional has such a duty, either through contract (doctor and private patient) or through the general duty of fidelity (occupational health physician and worker, NHS practitioner and patient). OH professionals owe a duty of confidence not only to workers in employment but also to job applicants in respect of pre-employment screening, unless the job applicant has consented to personnel having access to pre-employment questionnaires (a questionable practice with which some OH practitioners refuse to cooperate). Therefore, if an OH physician were to reveal to the human resources department without permission the fact that an employee had a drink problem so that she was not considered for promotion, the physician could probably be sued for damages for financial loss. Where the patient suffers only mental distress there is probably no right to damages, but the Law Commission has recommended that damages should be obtainable.

Are there any circumstances in which the physician is entitled to break confidence? The GMC, in its guidelines *Confidentiality: Protecting and Providing Information*, updated in 2004, lists a number of exceptions to the duty of confidence. These are as follows:

(1) The patient or his lawyer gives explicit consent.
(2) The doctor shares information with other health professionals who are part of the health care team concerned with the care of the patient for the purposes of that care.
(3) Parliament requires disclosure, for example of notifiable diseases.
(4) A court of law orders the doctor to disclose information.
(5) Disclosure is made to statutory regulatory bodies for investigation into a health professional's fitness to practise.
(6) Disclosure in the public interest, e.g. to the police about a serious crime.

The Code of Professional Conduct of the NMC (2002) gives this advice:

'To trust another person with private and personal information about yourself is a significant matter. If the person to whom that information is given is a nurse, midwife or health visitor, the patient or client has a right to believe that this information, given in confidence, will only be used for the purposes for which it was given and will not be released to others without their permission.'

The Royal College of Nursing in 2003 produced *Confidentiality: Guidance for Occupational Health Nurses* and in the same year the Department of Health published an NHS Code of Practice on Confidentiality. The Information Commissioner has published *The Use and Disclosure of Health Data* (2002) and a draft Code of Practice (Part 4) (2004) concerning employers' use of health information. All these documents would be taken into account by courts and tribunals in interpreting the law, as, of course, would the Faculty of Occupational Medicine's Code of Ethics, which was updated in 2005.

Secretarial staff who have no code of ethics but may have to be given access to confidential information should be trained in the importance of confidentiality and warned that their jobs are at risk if they wrongly reveal information. In the context of occupational health, it is especially vital to keep clinical records separate from other personnel records. No employee who consults the OH department should be assumed to have impliedly consented to the involvement of anyone outside it, even the welfare officer. Clerical staff must have it explained that they are responsible only to the OH staff for records, which should not normally leave the department. An Appendix to *Guidance on Ethics for Occupational Physicians* produced by the Faculty of Occupational Medicine (1997) sets out a form of words for a medical confidentiality agreement for non-medical personnel.

Social workers may also be regarded as part of the team, especially in general practice, but the GMC advises that patients must be informed if the doctor needs to share identifiable information with anyone employed by another organisation or agency. The code of ethics of the British Association of Social Workers imposes a duty of confidence on its members.

The legal justification for involving other members of the health care team and clerical and social workers is probably that the patient has impliedly consented to disclosure in the normal course of patient care. If this is correct, it means that the patient can withdraw his consent by, for example, ordering the doctor or nurse not to discuss his case with another health professional or social worker. Of course, if the case is one where the 'public interest' is involved, like one of non-accidental injury, disclosure may be justified for that reason. What of the patient who refuses to talk unless he is promised that no record will be kept and no-one else involved? The professional will have to exercise judgment. Imagine an occupational health nurse who, having been sworn to secrecy, is then told that the employee is taking illegal drugs which are affecting her in such a way that she may injure herself and others. The nurse would probably be legally and ethically entitled to report the matter at least to the doctor, if there is one, or, if not, to the employer, but her credibility with the other workers might be seriously damaged. If she does not pass on the information or make a record, later treatment by another acting in ignorance may be prejudiced, and there may be a serious accident. It may be better not in advance to accede to a patient's request that confidence be complete, but to warn that in exceptional circumstances information might have to be passed on.

The Faculty of Occupational Medicine of the Royal College of Physicians in its *Guidance on Ethics for Occupational Physicians* states that access to clinical data should be confined to the OH physician and the OH nurse, although clerical support staff and other members of the OH department may also need to see it.

'Normally, the written informed consent of the individual is required before access to clinical data may be granted to others, whoever they may be and whether professionally qualified or not, e.g. solicitors, insurers, managers, trades union representatives, employment medical advisers, etc.'

It reminds OH physicians that, with regard to their own colleagues and staff, when they are acting as line managers they should not demand any wider access than would be given to other managers.

One situation which regularly causes conflict between the OH and human resources departments is that in which the employer is threatened with legal action by the employee, either for compensation for a work-related injury or for unfair dismissal. If the OH department is known to give information too readily, its standing with the workforce will be irreparably damaged. Judicial guidance on this matter is to be found in the decision of the Court of Appeal in *Dunn* v. *British Coal Corporation* (1993). The employee was a 53-year-old miner who sustained injuries to his neck while working at the coal face, as a result of which he was unable to work as a miner. He sued his employer for damages. His solicitor obtained a report from a consultant orthopaedic surgeon which stated that Dunn had no prior history of neck pain. The employers doubted this medical evidence. They wished to have Dunn medically examined by their own expert, and asked that he should be given access to the plaintiff's hospital records, his GP records and the employer's own occupational physician's notes.

'So far as the latter is concerned, the employer's solicitors took the view, correctly in my opinion, that although these records had been compiled by their own servant or agent the employee was entitled to claim that as between him and the doctor they were confidential.' (Lord Justice Stuart-Smith)

The employee refused consent to disclosure of any records other than those directly related to the accident. The employers asked the court to order the disclosure of all the medical records, because they suspected that the plaintiff at the time of the accident was suffering from a pre-existing medical condition which might have forced him to give up work in any event. This would, of course, substantially reduce any damages he was awarded for loss of earnings.

The court ordered that the action could not proceed until the employee gave consent to the disclosure of all his medical records (including his occupational health records) to his employer's medical expert. The documents would be received by him in confidence and he would have to respect that confidence, except in so far as it was necessary to refer to matters which were relevant to the litigation.

'Thus, for example, the fact that an employee was or had been suffering from some sexually transmitted disease would be quite irrelevant unless it affected his future earning capacity, as might be the case if he was suffering from AIDS.'

The OH records of an employee who is bringing a legal action against his employer, whether in the court or the employment tribunal, should not, therefore, be disclosed to the employer without the consent of the employee or a court order.

An example of such an order arose in *Hanlon* v. *Kirlees Metropolitan Council* (2004). Mr Hanlon was employed by Chubb Security Services, contractors of the Council, to take charge of its CCTV screens. He alleged disability discrimination by the Council, and stated that he had both a physical and mental impairment. Mr Hanlon had been seen by his employer's OH adviser, but was unwilling to consent to his OH records being produced. He argued that to force him to do so was a breach of Article 8 of the Human Rights Act. The employment tribunal held that his right to privacy had to be balanced against the Council's right to a fair trial under Article 6 and ordered him to agree to the disclosure of his OH records. When he refused, the tribunal eventually struck out his application on the ground that his conduct had been unreasonable. This decision was approved by the Employment Appeal Tribunal.

The General Medical Council, in 2004, in a letter to an occupational physician, published on the Society of Occupational Medicine's website, gave this advice:

'The current guidance is based on the view that the relationship between doctors and patients may be damaged if disclosures are made to solicitors without the patient's knowledge or consent . . . It has been our longstanding policy to advise that consent to such disclosures is needed even though the consequences of a refusal may be either that the patient must drop the claim, or the records are disclosed later, at the direction of the court, or under the disclosure rules.'

A consent form for the release of information has been agreed between the BMA and the Law Society.

In 2004 the National Health Service announced its intention to move into a system of 'seamless care' where all health records are held on computer. The Electronic Health Record will be accessible by health professionals and by the patient himself on the Internet. Many healthcare professionals are concerned about whether such a system will adequately protect confidentiality. A parallel development has been the creation of Occupational Health Smart Cards. These are being issued to NHS doctors in training. Once complete, the aim is to extend the use of the cards to all hospital medical staff. The cards will record registration status, Criminal Records Bureau clearance and occupational health and immunisation records required for pre-employment health clearance. The card system is fully encrypted and works on a dual-PIN entry basis. Nobody outside occupational health will have access to personal and confidential OH data. Data is stored securely at a national NHS database centre in Wakefield.

3.4   The consent of the patient

This may, strictly speaking, be given orally, but for the protection of the doctor and the nurse it should always, if possible, be obtained in writing. Where a patient has authorised disclosure to a third party, he may not appreciate that his full medical records over a number of years may be produced, so that the OH physician or nurse should clarify with him the extent to which he is willing to authorise disclosure. However, it would be wrong for a physician to allow the patient to offer misleading evidence by presenting an incomplete picture. The employee who is claiming damages for noise-induced hearing loss and who authorises the doctor to disclose to his solicitors the results of audiograms, while asking him to suppress notes of conversations with the patient about the dangers of his part-time job in a disco, should be told that all matters relevant to deafness must be included, or, alternatively, that no disclosure will be made.

In the occupational setting, the issue will often be one of advising the employer or the trustees of the pension fund whether the employee is fit for work.

'Advice given to management about the results of a medical assessment should generally be confined to advice on ability and limitations of function. Clinical details should be excluded and even when the individual has himself given clinical information to management, the occupational physician should exercise caution before confirming any of it. If a report on the health and fitness for work of an employee is to be communicated to management it is important to ensure that the employee understands the physician's duty to the employer. The contents of the proposed report should be discussed with the employee and consideration should be given to obtaining the signed consent of the employee to be examined in such circumstances.' (Faculty of Occupational Medicine: *Guidance on Ethics* (1993).)

3.5   Relationship with other health professionals

It is a breach of confidence to disclose facts about the patient even to another doctor or nurse, so that if such disclosure is to be made, it must be justified as in the patient's or the public interest or by showing that the patient either expressly or impliedly agreed. Where a patient is in the care of a team of health professionals, it is fairly easy to imply that he is willing to allow all members of the team access to his records. Communication with the patient's general practitioner, or to another occupational physician employed by a different organisation (which may include a company in the same corporate structure but legally separate) should normally be only with his consent, unless there is some special reason why the information should be transferred in the patient's or the public interest. This means that if the employee moves to a different employment he should be asked to give written consent to the transfer of medical records to his new employer. The need for care in such matters is illustrated by one case where an occupational physician routinely notified an employee's GP of the employee's raised blood pressure. Later, the man failed to obtain life assurance, because the insurance company insisted on a medical report from the GP.

3.6   Medical audit

Good medical practice requires that medical practice is audited, and occupational health is not exempt. The General Medical Council regards medical audit as an inherent part of clinical practice. In its 2004 Guidance it states:

'All doctors in clinical practice have a duty to participate in clinical audit.'

Identifiable data may be disclosed provided the doctor is satisfied that the patients in general have been informed that their data may be used for clinical audit, and they have not objected.

'Where clinical audit is to be undertaken by another organisation, information should be anonymised wherever that is practicable.'

In any other case, express consent must be obtained before identifiable data is disclosed.

3.7   Disclosure of information to researchers

It is important for records to be kept of accidents and diseases of workers because the emergence of a pattern can give early warning of the necessity for preventive action. The Declaration of Helsinki, the international ethical code on research on humans, lays down guidelines on the conduct of research which have already been discussed in Chapter 2. Epidemiological research may not necessitate the performance of additional procedures, but merely the collection and analysis of data. The OH professional who does his own research will be in control of his records, but he may be involved in a project in which others ask for access to identifiable patient data. Any research protocol must be well-designed and it should be discussed with an ethics committee before commencement; if one is not available, the researcher may approach the Faculty of Occupational Medicine. All research on NHS patients, in NHS premises, or using NHS records must be approved by an NHS Research Ethics Committee. Remembering that the doctor and nurse are being paid by the employer, permission should also be sought from management. Good industrial relations practice dictates consultation with the trade unions.

In 2000 considerable debate was generated by the GMC's advice to doctors that identifiable information should not be given to the National Cancer Registries or to researchers without the consent of the patient. Epidemiologists were up in arms that this requirement would hinder important research into the causes of disease, and letters were written to the press. A common misunderstanding was that this was dictated by the provisions of the Data Protection Act, but in fact it was the common law of confidence which was the main stumbling block.

Anonymised information cannot be the subject of a duty of confidence. In *R v. Department of Health ex parte Source Informatics Ltd* (2000) the applicant was a data collection company which wished to collect anonymised data from pharmacists about GP's prescribing habits, in order to sell these data commercially. The Court of Appeal held that the proposed scheme did not involve a breach of confidence because the patients' identities would be protected. In practice, however, most epidemiological research data cannot be completely anonymised, since it will be important to know the age, sex, profession and often the postcode, even if the name of the research subject can be replaced by a number. The advice of the GMC made it difficult for researchers to collect data, since clinicians became concerned that they might be found to be in breach of their professional ethics if they collaborated with a research project. Their view was that it was time consuming and impractical to obtain consent from patients in every case.

The Data Protection Act 1998 does not require the consent of the patient to the disclosure of data for the purposes of research. Schedules 2 and 3 permit processing without the consent of the data subject where it is necessary for the purposes of legitimate interests pursued by the controller and where it is necessary for medical purposes (including medical research) and is undertaken by a health professional or a person who owes an equivalent duty of confidentiality.

The common law of confidence does not permit disclosure without consent, but it may be argued that patients give implied consent to the use of their confidential information for research. Unfortunately, this was the argument which was used to justify the retention of body parts of deceased children in Bristol and Liverpool, which led to public inquiries and to the revision of the Human Tissue Act. Implied consent has therefore to some extent been discredited. The Information Commissioner has stated that implied consent is acceptable, but that patients must be made aware of the possibilities. You cannot impliedly consent to something unless you know that it exists. In *Use and Disclosure of Health Information* (2002) the Information Commissioner states: 'In most cases where consent is required in order to satisfy the common law duty of confidence, the Commissioner accepts that implied consent is valid. She does not accept that implied consent is a lesser form of consent. But, because the consent must be informed, patients should be made aware that their data may be used for research purposes designed to better understand and treat their conditions. A poster in the surgery or notice in the local paper is unlikely to be sufficient. She recommends a standard information leaflet, information provided face to face in the course of a consultation, information included with an appointment card, or a letter sent to the patient's home.'

Because of the problems of establishing that the informed consent has been given, even if only implied, the Government was unwilling to rely on the vagaries of the common law and created new regulations which came into force in June 2002 under a power given in section 60 of the Health and Social Care Act 2001. These are the Health Service (Control of Patient Information) Regulations 2002. They permit the processing of confidential personal information without the consent of the patient in the public interest, and have specific provisions relating to neoplasia and communicable diseases. Other confidential patient information may also be processed for medical purposes provided that the processing has been approved by the Secretary of State and, in the case of medical research, by a research ethics committee. The Patient Information Advisory Group is a representative body which advises the Secretary of State about the regulations. They include 'the processing of confidential patient information that relates to the present or past geographical location of patients (including where necessary information from which patients can be identified) which is required for medical research into the locations at which disease or other medical conditions may occur.'

Even without the regulations, it is arguable that epidemiological research is in the public interest, and that consent may therefore be waived. The GMC in its 2004 guidance seems to accept this. It states that disclosure in the public interest may be justified where the records are of such age and/or number that reasonable efforts to trace patients are unlikely to be successful.

3.8   Disclosure in the public interest

'The public interest' is a phrase of venerable antiquity which is employed by the courts to justify invasions of private rights. In English law it is invoked where the security of the State is at risk, or where the welfare of a community, or a part of it, is in jeopardy. Most of the leading cases concern the Government's attempts to gag former employees, or involve commercial concerns who try to protect trade secrets. Who defines the public interest? In the end it must be the judges themselves, and their views will change and develop. For many years the courts have applied a doctrine that 'there is no confidence in an iniquity'. If the patient or client has been guilty of a crime, he cannot seek the protection of the law to help to keep it secret. The patient who confesses that he has just killed his mother cannot complain if the doctor calls the police. Most cases are not as obvious as this. A policeman appears in the occupational health department, asking for information about employees in connection with a burglary during which one of the thieves escaped by jumping off a wall into some bushes. The doctor knows that one particular worker has recently been treated for scratches and cuts which he said were the result of a weekend's gardening. The doctor is under no legal obligation to tell the police anything. Is it in the public interest to be frank, when the employee may be completely innocent? The answer is probably that confidence should be preserved, since there is no imminent danger to others.

The concept of public interest has been widened by the courts in recent years. Mr Evans, a scientist formerly employed by Lion Laboratories, was permitted by the Court of Appeal, against the wishes of his former employer, to publish details in the press of secret technical aspects of the Lion Intoximeter, because the reliability of the device was a matter in which the public were justifiably concerned (*Lion Laboratories* v. *Evans* (1984)). On the other hand, the courts in 1987 granted an injunction against the *News of the World* preventing it from publishing hospital records identifying two NHS doctors who were suffering from AIDS (*X* v. *Y*). 'The public in general and patients in particular are entitled to expect hospital records to be confidential and it is not for any individual to take it upon himself to breach that confidence.' In the latter case there was little actual danger to patients. It is highly unlikely that a health professional will transfer the AIDS virus to his patient in the course of practice. After this case, the GMC and the UKCC issued guidance to members of the professions who are carriers of the virus. They should seek medical advice and act on it. Only if they refuse to take the precautions recommended to them should their medical advisers report the matter to third parties (see Chapter 2).

Another case in which the doctor's duty of confidence was considered by the courts was *W* v. *Egdell* (1990). An independent psychiatrist had been asked by solicitors acting for W, a patient detained in a secure hospital, to examine him with a view to using his report to support an application to a mental health review tribunal for W's discharge or transfer to a regional secure unit. W, diagnosed as a paranoid schizophrenic, had killed five people ten years before. Dr Egdell wished the tribunal to know that he opposed W's application, because he believed him to be a psychopath, but found that his adverse report on W's condition had been suppressed by the solicitors, though they subsequently withdrew the tribunal application. The psychiatrist felt that it was his public duty to communicate his views about W to the authorities, to be kept with his records and be available on any subsequent application. He sent his report, against the wishes of the patient, to the medical director of the hospital and the Home Office. The Court of Appeal dismissed W's action for breach of confidence. Dr Egdell's duty to the public justified his actions.

In *Woolgar* v. *Chief Constable of Sussex Police* (1999) a registered nurse and matron of a nursing home was arrested and interviewed by police following the death of a patient in her care. The police decided not to charge her with a criminal offence but referred the matter to the UKCC, her professional body. Mrs Woolgar sought to prevent the police from sending the tape of her interview to the UKCC, alleging that it was confidential. It was held that if the police come into possession of confidential information which, in their reasonable view, in the interests of public health and safety should be considered by a professional or regulatory body, then the police are free to pass that information to the relevant regulatory body for its consideration. The same would probably apply to a doctor or nurse who revealed confidential information to the GMC or NMC in good faith because of a concern about the conduct of a colleague. The GMC states that where such a referral involves disclosing patient information, the doctor should first seek the patient's consent, wherever practicable. Disclosure of information without consent may be justified, but doctors are advised to contact the GMC or other regulatory body for advice.

Occasionally, a doctor or nurse may be confronted with an employee who knows that his job is endangering his health (for example because he has developed an allergy or is putting too much strain on a damaged joint), but refuses to allow the health professional to alert third parties. In the case of statutory medical examinations, the Appointed Doctor or Employment Medical Adviser will be obliged to tell the employer and the HSE that the employee is unfit. Otherwise, if there is no risk to third parties, both law and ethics probably dictate silence. The worker should be fully informed of the risk that he runs. For the protection of the doctor or nurse, he may be asked to sign a statement that it is at the worker's request that his condition is being kept from management. The Faculty of Occupational Medicine in its *Guidance on Ethics* (1993) states that occupational physicians should appreciate that when advising on the nature or extent of a work-related health risk, they should not presume to decide for others whether or not that risk is acceptable.

The RCN document *Confidentiality in Occupational Health* (2003) gives contrary advice. It gives the example of a nurse who diagnosed occupational asthma in an employee working in a grain store. The employee refused to allow the nurse to give information to managers or his GP because he could not afford to lose the job. The advice given is that the nurse is entitled to disclose the employee's condition to management without his consent in order to protect the worker. The General Medical Council also advises that disclosure of personal information without consent may be justified in the public interest where failure to do so may expose *the patient* or others to risk of death or serious harm.

In these, admittedly rare, cases we find a conflict between the need to protect the worker and worker autonomy. In the area of clinical practice, courts have held that patient autonomy is paramount (this is assuming that the patient is mentally competent to make an informed decision). In *St George's Healthcare NHS Trust* v. *S* (1998) S, who was 36 weeks pregnant, sought to register as a new patient with a GP. She was diagnosed as suffering from eclampsia and advised that she needed urgent medical care without which her life and that of her unborn child were in danger. She refused medical assistance. She was sectioned under the Mental Health Act and transferred to an obstetric unit in a hospital. A High Court judge granted a declaration that she could be treated without her consent, a Caesarean section was performed, and S gave birth to a baby girl. The Court of Appeal held that S had been unlawfully detained, since she was mentally competent, and that the operation should not have been performed. An adult patient of sound mind has an absolute right to refuse any, or all, medical treatment including treatment necessary to save the patient's life, and that right is not diminished by the fact that she is pregnant. However, in *R* v. *Ashworth Hospital Authority ex parte Brady* (2000) force feeding of the Moors murderer Ian Brady was held justified as his hunger strike was a manifestation or symptom of the prisoner's mental disorder, though the High Court held in *Secretary of State for the Home Department* v. *Robb* (1994) that a prisoner of sound mind, but with a personality disorder, should not be force fed.

It is submitted that the public interest justifies a breach of confidence to protect third parties, but not to protect the patient or the worker against himself.

One of the most difficult dilemmas for the doctor or nurse is to be confronted with a state of affairs where he has to choose between competing interests. Suppose that a doctor in the course of a confidential consultation with an employee discovers that the employee is an alcoholic and is likely to be operating machinery while inebriated. If the doctor keeps confidence an accident may happen in which a third party may be injured; if he tells the human resources department that the man is unfit, the employee may be sacked and the rest of the workforce become much more wary of confiding in the doctor in the future.

No-one can give perfect advice on how to deal with such a dilemma, but the following pointers may prove valuable:

(1) The patient may be persuaded of the dangers of the situation and may give permission for the truth to be revealed, or at least be willing to ask for a transfer.
(2) If the employer has enlightened policies, it may be possible for the worker to keep his job in the long term if he successfully undergoes treatment. The occupational health department can prove influential in persuading management to adopt such policies.
(3) Influential professional bodies recognise that in these cases it may be permissible to breach confidence.

The Faculty of Occupational Medicine's *Guidance on Ethics* says this:

'Occasionally, an occupational physician ... may find that an individual is unfit for a job where the safety of other workers or of the public is concerned. He should then take great care to explain fully why he thinks the disclosure of unfitness is necessary. If sufficient time is taken in explanation, there is rarely difficulty in obtaining agreement. When this is not obtained the occupational physician is faced with an ethical dilemma. No firm guidance is possible, and each situation must be considered on its merits. On such occasions it may be useful for the occupational physician to discuss the issue with an experienced colleague. Ultimately, the safety of other workers and the general public must prevail as one of the exceptions to the duty of confidentiality.'

3.9   Legal obligation to disclose information

A number of different statutory provisions compel disclosure of information to a public body. The principal examples relevant especially to occupational health practice are as follows:

(1) The reporting of notifiable infectious diseases (Public Health (Control of Disease) Act 1984 and Public Health (Infectious Diseases) Regulations 1988).
The following diseases must be reported by the doctor to the local public health authority: acute encephalitis, acute meningitis, meningococcal septicaemia, acute poliomyelitis, anthrax, cholera, diphtheria, dysentery, infective jaundice, Lassa fever, leprosy, leptospirosis, malaria, Marburgh disease, measles, mumps, rubella, ophthalmia neonatorum, paratyphoid fever, plague, rabies, relapsing fever, scarlet fever, smallpox, tetanus, tuberculosis, typhus, viral hepatitis, viral haemorrhagic fever, whooping cough, yellow fever and food poisoning.

AIDS is not a notifiable disease, although certain provisions of the Public Health Act have been extended to AIDS, giving power to a magistrate on the application of a local authority to order the compulsory detention of an AIDS sufferer in hospital if he would not take proper precautions to prevent the spread of the virus if allowed to go free. There are special regulations obliging confidence to be preserved in cases of sexually transmitted diseases. The NHS (Venereal Diseases) Regulations 1974 require health authorities to take all necessary steps to secure that any information capable of identifying an individual obtained with respect to persons examined or treated for any sexually transmitted disease shall not be disclosed *except for the purpose of communicating the information to a doctor or someone working under his direction in connection with the treatment of persons suffering from the disease or the prevention of its spread.* It will be seen that, contrary to the practice of hospital sexually transmitted disease clinics, the regulations allow the patient's GP to be notified. It is the general law of confidence which forbids disclosure to the GP without the patient's consent, except in a situation of overriding public interest.

(2) Notification of suspicion of terrorism (Terrorism Act 2000).
It is an offence for any person without reasonable excuse to fail to disclose to the police information which comes to his attention in the course of a trade, profession, business or employment which leads to a belief or suspicion that any other person has financed acts of terrorism.

(3) Notification of accidents and dangerous occurrences at work and of work-related disease (Reporting of Injuries, Diseases and Dangerous Occurrences Regulations (RIDDOR) (1995)).
There have been laws about the notification of accidents in the workplace for many years but it was only in 1980 that one set of regulations applying to all premises where people were employed was introduced. These required reporting by the employer to the local authority or Health and Safety Executive (HSE) not only of major accidents but also of dangerous occurrences, i.e. incidents which could have led to serious injury but by good fortune ended up as 'near-misses'. The introduction in 1983 of the statutory sick pay scheme, which shifted the burden of short-term sick pay from the DSS to the employer, meant that there was no longer an automatic procedure for notifying the Government of minor injuries at work. Also, it was decided that it was important to try to identify the occupational risks of contracting diseases through the collection of accurate statistics. Regulations made in 1985 and up-dated in 1995 which place the duty to report on

the employer or other person in control of work premises require notification of the following:

(1) The death of any person as a result of an accident (including an act of violence) arising out of or in connection with work. Major injuries as a result of an accident arising out of or in connection with work. Major injuries are any fracture, other than to fingers, thumbs or toes; any amputation; dislocation of the shoulder, hip, knee or spine; loss of sight (whether temporary or permanent); any chemical or hot metal burn to the eye, or any penetrating injury to the eye; any injury caused by an electrical shock or electrical burn leading to unconsciousness or requiring resuscitation or admittance to hospital for more than 24 hours; any other injury leading to hypothermia, heat-induced illness or to unconsciousness, requiring resuscitation or requiring admittance to hospital for more than 24 hours; loss of consciousness caused by asphyxia or by exposure to a harmful substance or biological agent; either of the following conditions which result from the absorption of any substance by inhalation, ingestion, or through the skin: acute illness requiring medical treatment or loss of consciousness; acute illness which requires medical treatment where there is reason to believe that this resulted from exposure to a biological agent or its toxins or infected material. Injuries reportable in respect of members of the public are confined to deaths or injuries which cause a person to be taken from the site of the accident to hospital.
(2) Dangerous occurrences. These are listed in Schedule 2 to the regulations. Needlestick injuries to health care workers are reportable.
(3) Minor injuries causing a person to be incapacitated for work for more than three consecutive days (but not falling within the definition of a major injury).
(4) Industrially linked diseases. Schedule 3 to the regulations lists forms of illness in Column 1 with, opposite each of these, a list of occupations or work-processes in Column 2. If an employee contracts a Column 1 disease while working in a Column 2 process it is notifiable. Some examples are mesothelioma, lung cancer or asbestosis contracted while working with asbestos, hepatitis contracted while working with human blood products or body secretions or excretions, bone cancer or blood dyscrasia while working with ionising radiation and hand–arm vibration syndrome while using various hand-held tools or percussive drills or holding material being worked upon by pounding machines in shoe manufacture.

A case of disease in an employee must be reported only if a written diagnosis has been received from a doctor, for example, on a medical certificate. It is very important to note that RIDDOR does not override medical confidentiality. It is commonly assumed that, where a disease is reportable under RIDDOR, a doctor or nurse *must* report it to the employer, whether or not the worker has given consent. This is definitely not the case, as the HSE's own guidance confirms. An occupational health nurse was faced with a demand from a health and safety adviser that she release clinical OH records to him, 'as otherwise you will be in breach of RIDDOR'. She resisted, but had she complied she would have been in breach of her professional obligations as a nurse and would have had no defence.

In any event, without a report in writing from a registered medical practitioner, no duty to report could arise. A diagnosis by a nurse is insufficient. Many reports under RIDDOR arise from the submission of a medical certificate issued by a GP in compliance with rules about sickness absence.

Doctors are asked to use the common descriptions of each disease set out in the regulations so that the employer can easily recognise when a report must be made. If a person receiving training who is not an employee is involved, the training body must report, and the self-employed should report in respect of themselves. Reporting a case of disease does not necessarily signify that it was caused by work. The employer does not have to report if the employee does not work in a listed job even if he knows that he worked in such a job in the past. A controversial proposal to oblige employers to report cases of occupational disease identified during health surveillance, whether or not it appeared in the RIDDOR list, has not yet been implemented because of the wide disparity in the national provision of health surveillance. The omission of noise-induced hearing loss has given rise to criticism.

Note that major injuries and dangerous occurrences must be notified to the local authority environmental health department (responsible for offices, shops, warehouses and residential accommodation) or the Health and Safety Executive by telephone or e-mail, followed by a written report within ten days; minor injuries and industrially-linked diseases are to be notified on the standard form. Records must be kept and the authorities may ask for further information of notified matters (which may include medical records).

If the employer can prove that he had taken reasonable steps to have all notifiable events brought to his notice but that nevertheless he was not aware of the notifiable accident, event or disease he will not be guilty of any offence; for this reason it is important to institute a reliable and comprehensive reporting system among employees. Since 1990 a special supplement to the Employment Department's Labour Force Survey has disclosed just how inaccurate the RIDDOR statistics are. The Health and Safety Commission has estimated that no more than 30 per cent of work-related injuries were being reported before the regulations were overhauled. The danger of failure to report is, of course, that it produces inaccurate statistics which may conceal serious dangers or suggest inappropriate trends. In 2004 the whole system of reporting was under review.

Some employers ask occupational health departments to take responsibility for reporting accidents and disease. This should be resisted, since it may bring the duty of confidentiality of the health professional towards the workers into conflict with his duty to the employer. Do not confuse notifiable diseases under the Public Health Act, where medical confidentiality must be overriden, with reportable diseases under RIDDOR.

3.10   Legal obligation to reply to questions

Sometimes there is an obligation to give information, but only if an official body requests it. The main category of cases falling under this head involves the giving of evidence in the course of legal proceedings, or where legal proceedings are pending. English law does not, unlike some other systems, confer any special privilege on health professionals to refuse to disclose information confided in them by their patients *before* legal proceedings are in prospect. The only statements privileged from disclosure even in the highest courts are those which attract *'legal professional privilege'*, that is either communications between a client and his professional legal adviser or communications between a third party and the client or his lawyer, *where they were made in contemplation of litigation and the dominant purpose was to prepare for litigation.* Thus, a doctor who is asked by solicitors to give expert medical evidence in connection with a claim for compensation and prepares a report for that purpose may find that it is never produced because it is not as favourable as was wished. The privilege here is not that of the doctor, but of the lawyer's client. If an employer instigates an inquiry into an accident at work, partly because he anticipates litigation, but partly because he wishes to make a full investigation to ensure that the incident is not repeated, the subsequent report is not privileged against disclosure, because litigation is not the sole or dominant purpose for which the document was prepared (*Waugh* v. *British Rail* (1980)).

There is no general legal obligation on anyone to answer questions posed by the police, or give them access to medical records, even where they are investigating a serious crime, though if a deliberate lie is told or money is taken for suppressing information a criminal offence may be committed. One exception is the Road Traffic Act which obliges answers to police questions where they are investigating a serious driving offence. Under the Police and Criminal Evidence Act 1984, a search warrant to give the police access to medical or counselling records or samples of human tissue or fluid taken for the purposes of medical treatment may be obtained from a circuit judge but only in exceptional cases. In *R* v. *Cardiff Crown Court, ex parte Kellam* (1993), it was held that the court should not order disclosure of records relating to the times of admission, discharge and leave of patients in a mental hospital, which the police wanted in order to check the movements of a mental patient suspected of murder. There would have been nothing to prevent the trust giving voluntary disclosure (*R* v. *Singleton* (1994)). Singleton was charged with murder. After his arrest he was asked by the police to provide a sample of tooth marks, because the victim had bite marks in her chin. He refused, but his dentist voluntarily gave his dental records to the police. The evidence was held admissible and Singleton was convicted. Had an application been made to the judge for an order to force the dentist to disclose, he might well have refused it. Should a doctor demand a search warrant before giving information to the police? It is probably advisable where there is no element of urgency, but in a case of danger that further crimes may be committed, the courts, the GMC and the NMC all sanction breach of confidence. If a prosecution actually proceeds to trial, a doctor or nurse could be called as a witness and ordered by the judge or the magistrates to answer questions on oath. Professional ethics would not in law justify a refusal to answer, which would constitute a contempt of court, as would a refusal to comply with a search warrant.

The police occasionally assert that they have a right to search a doctor's manual or computer records without a warrant where they have entered premises in order to carry out a lawful arrest or with the permission of the occupier. This is probably true where they have reasonable grounds for believing that they will find evidence of a crime which must be seized in order to prevent it being concealed, lost, altered or destroyed.

Crimes against the health and safety of the workforce are policed by the HSE and the local authorities. These public officials have special powers of enforcement which include the power to demand information and exceed the powers of the police. Section 20 of the Health and Safety at Work Act 1974 (HSWA), discussed in Chapter 5, gives them power in the course of an examination or investigation to inspect and take copies of books and documents without a warrant and without the permission of the occupier, as long as they do so for the purpose of enforcing safety legislation. There is no exemption for medical records, and all documentary records, whether or not required by statute, are included. The inspector may require any person whom he has reasonable cause to believe to be able to give any relevant information, to answer questions and to sign a declaration of the truth of his answers. Such a statement will not be admissible against its maker in any legal proceedings. The privilege against self-incrimination means that in any event the person actually suspected of a crime has the right to remain silent, but section 20 allows the inspector to compel a *witness* to give evidence when he might otherwise decline for fear of reprisal from his employer. An occupational health professional might be ordered to make a statement about the medical condition of a worker. If he declined, he could be prosecuted for a criminal offence under section 33 HSWA.

In addition, the Health and Safety Commission (HSC) has power, with the consent of the Secretary of State (which may be given in general terms), to serve a notice demanding that information be furnished either to the HSC or the HSE of matters needed to carry out their statutory functions. Although this information is not to be disseminated to the public as a whole, it may be given to local authorities and to the police. It may also be disclosed in legal proceedings. (The coming into force of the Freedom of Information Act 2000 (FOIA) in 2005 has led to a review of the dissemination of information by the HSC and HSE, and it is likely that in the future more information will be made public, within the constraints of the FOIA.) The inspectors *shall*, in circumstances where it is necessary to do so for the purpose of keeping persons (or their representatives) employed at any premises adequately informed about matters affecting their health, safety and welfare, give to them or their representatives factual information relating to the premises or anything done therein and information about any action they propose to take.

The Environment and Safety Information Act 1988 imposes a duty on the authorities empowered to issue improvement and prohibition notices under the Health and Safety at Work Act to maintain a register of such notices open to public inspection. An entry may be modified to protect trade secrets or secret manufacturing processes.

In 1992 the Environmental Information Regulations came into force and have now been replaced by 2004 Regulations. Any public authority which holds environmental information must both progressively make the information available to the public by electronic means which are easily accessible and make it available on request. Environmental information relates to the state of the elements of the environment, such as air, water, soil, landscape, factors such as noise, radiation or waste that affect the environment, measures, policies and activities likely to affect the environment, reports on the implementation of environmental legislation, cost-benefit analyses, and the state of human health and safety, including the contamination of the food chain, and conditions of human life, such as cultural sites. There are exemptions similar to those in the FOIA, including national security and public safety, the confidentiality of commercial and industrial information, personal data and the protection of the environment to which the information relates. There is a presumption in favour of disclosure.

A Coroner's Court also has power to order disclosure of medical records or other confidential medical information.

If the employee is dismissed because the employer determines that he is medically unfit, it is possible that the OH physician may be called as a witness and ordered to produce records before an employment tribunal. The same may occur when an employee is suing his employer for negligence or breach of statutory duty in the High Court or County Court, or claiming social security benefits before a social security tribunal. All these have the power to order disclosure and the physician or nurse who disobeys could be punished for contempt of court. However, the judge or tribunal chairman has a discretion about the admission of evidence. In one case the House of Lords refused to order the NSPCC to disclose the name of an informant, lest others be deterred from reporting suspected cruelty (*D* v. *NSPCC* (1978)). Sometimes, the Government withholds information in the interest of national security. This is known as public interest immunity and has been held by the European Court of Human Rights not to be a breach of Article 6 of the Convention which gives the right to a fair trial. The Faculty of Occupational Medicine advises that in civil cases, unless the patient has consented to disclosure, the physician should wait for a formal court order, 'but physicians should not be misled by solicitors who state that an application for a court order has been made'.

3.11   Legal professional privilege

This is an exception both to the right of subject access under the Data Protection Act and the right to know under the Freedom of Information Act. It is a well-established principle that a lawyer cannot be compelled, even by a court of law, to reveal information which has been given to him in confidence by his client, or by a third party like an expert witness, in connection with adversarial litigation. In this regard lawyers have a privilege which health professionals and priests lack. The justification is the right to a fair trial. Those engaged in litigation must be able to confide freely in their lawyers. However, the lawyer is bound by professional Codes of Ethics not to lie to a court. Where the client tells his lawyer that he is guilty of a crime, the lawyer cannot ethically support him in a plea of not guilty, though his suspicions about whether the stolen goods really did fall off the back of a lorry are irrelevant. The defendant must be judged by the court, not his lawyer.

Where solicitors for the employer ask occupational health for a report in relation to actual or pending litigation, these communications are privileged and need not be revealed, although in practice the OH report will be important evidence which the employer will usually voluntarily disclose to the court. Information obtained for purposes other than litigation, such as a report of an investigation into the causes of an accident at work, is not covered by legal professional privilege. In *Waugh* v. *British Rail* (1980) the employer had set up an inquiry into the causes of a railway accident. The report of the inquiry was directed to the company's legal department, and privilege was claimed. It was held that the principal purpose of the report was to discover what had gone wrong, not to defend legal proceedings, so it had to be disclosed.

The privilege also extends to communications between the lawyer and his client made for the purpose of giving or seeking legal advice. The Court of Appeal held in *Three Rivers District Council* v. *Governor of the Bank of England* (2004) that the legal advice privilege does not cover documents passing between a lawyer and an independent third party, even if they are created with the dominant purpose of obtaining legal advice. Even company employees may be regarded as third parties. This might affect OH professionals who are asked by lawyers to give a report on an employee's health (which should not, of course, be given without consent). Unless this is for the dominant purpose of contemplated or actual litigation, the report may not be protected by privilege. The decision was reviewed by the House of Lords, and upheld in part. In practice, most OH reports will be generated through a request from a manager and will not be covered by legal professional privilege. If there is doubt in this complex area, OH professionals are advised to seek independent legal advice. The Scottish title for legal professional privilege is confidentiality of communications, and the law of Scotland differs from English law, though the two concepts have much in common.

General advice from lawyers about policy, for example for dealing with sickness absence, might in the past have been regarded as privileged, but the Information Commissioner advises that public authorities should consider making such advice available to the public under the Freedom of Information Act in order to assist public understanding of decisions made by the authority.

3.12   Pre-trial disclosure in civil proceedings

There is a distinction between pre-action disclosure (before the claim form is issued) and pre-trial disclosure, known as discovery (after the action has commenced but before it has come to court). Pre-action disclosure of medical records is often made as a result of an application under the Civil Procedure Rules, Parts 25.1 and 31.16, in an action for damages for death or personal injury. If a claimant is able to show that it is likely that he may have a case for damages for some injury, he may ask the court for an order against a possible defendant (even before the issue of a claim form). This procedure is not available in employment tribunals, nor is the procedure under Part 31.17 CPR whereby disclosure may be ordered of records in the possession of a third party, like a doctor or a hospital, after the claim form has been issued. The court now has a discretion whether to confine the order to disclosure to a named physician or lawyer nominated by the claimant, rather than the patient in person. This power may be exercised if the medical details are particularly distressing (as where the patient is dying), or very technical.

Where a complaint of unfair dismissal or disability discrimination has been made to an employment tribunal, either party can request an order that the other produce relevant documents for perusal before the hearing. Since the OH professional would not be a party to the unfair dismissal complaint, the only way he could be compelled by the employer to give evidence or produce his medical records without the consent of the employee would be to seek a witness order requiring him to produce them at the hearing. The employer would be unable to show that he had relied upon the detailed medical evidence in making his decision to dismiss unless the employee had previously consented to disclosure. Employers are limited to the evidence known to them at the date of dismissal when they seek to prove that they acted fairly (*Devis* v. *Atkins* (1977) (see further Chapter 8)).

3.13 *Confidential information in the courts*

Courts are not eager to order disclosure of confidential information unless it is necessary in the interests of justice. In a case in 1979, a woman civil servant complained that she had not been promoted because of her sex and her trade union activities; she asked the industrial tribunal to order her employer to produce not only her own confidential records but also those of fellow employees who had been promoted, for comparison. The House of Lords held that the tribunals should, if necessary, censor confidential files before allowing the other party to see them, so that only relevant information is revealed (*Science Research Council* v. *Nassé*). Needless to say, the doctor or nurse should not assume the role of censor, though courts will be sympathetic to requests to hold back records if good reasons are given.

A case which involved occupational health records raised an interesting debate. Mr Nawaz was an employee of the Ford Motor Co. After 18 months' absence from work during which he had provided his employer with certificates from his doctor saying that he was unfit, he was asked to submit to an examination by the employer's OH physician. The latter decided that Nawaz was fit, but the GP continued to certify him as unfit. Nawaz agreed to see a consultant nominated by the employers. The OH physician gave the consultant information about Nawaz and his job; the consultant eventually reported that in his opinion Nawaz should recommence work because he was fit to do so. When the employee continued to refuse, he was dismissed for unauthorised absence. On an application to an industrial tribunal for unfair dismissal, Nawaz asked for disclosure of all his medical records, including the correspondence between Ford's doctor and the consultant and the consultant's report in full. The company objected that the managers who had made the decision to dismiss had never seen those records – they had respected medical confidence and acted on the experts' conclusion that Nawaz was fit. Since the employer's duty under the Employment Protection Act (now re-enacted as the Employment Rights Act) is only to act as a reasonable employer on the available evidence, the issue before the tribunal was not whether

Mr Nawaz was in fact fit for work, but whether it was reasonable for management to act on that assumption, so that detailed medical information was not relevant and should not be produced.

The Employment Appeal Tribunal disagreed. Discovery must be granted if it is necessary to dispose fairly of the action. Even though management are not expected to be able to assess the merits of medical argument, they are not absolved from carrying out, through their medical agent, the proper investigation which is required in any case of dismissal. Nawaz needed to examine the medical correspondence to be sure that the consultant had been properly informed and that his conclusions justified the advice that Nawaz was fit. In other words, it was possible that Ford's doctor through prejudice had written that Nawaz was a well-known malingerer and should not be trusted; only if all the records were produced would it be clear that he had acted fairly (*Ford Motor Co.* v. *Nawaz* (1987)).

The power to order discovery is conferred by law on courts, tribunals and other similar bodies, like the Health Service Commissioner (Ombudsman). The Advisory, Conciliation and Arbitration Service (ACAS) does not have such powers, nor do purely domestic inquiries set up by an employer to investigate any matter. If there is doubt about whether a doctor or nurse is obliged by law to produce confidential records, advice should be sought from the professional organisations.

3.14   Expert witnesses

If the case comes to trial, and most civil cases are settled out of court, often at the eleventh hour, the doctor or nurse may be summoned to appear as a witness. They may be there in one of two capacities. Most commonly, an OH physician or nurse will be called because he has been involved in the examination or treatment of a patient whose health is an issue before the court. In these circumstances, the evidence will be drawn from personal knowledge of the course of the patient's illness (witnesses of fact). In some cases, however, the health professional may be called as an expert witness, not because he has had any clinical contact with the patient prior to the legal proceedings, but because he can advise the court about technical matters not within the judge's competence.

In the former case, if the judge insists, he may be ordered to answer questions and may be punished for contempt if no answer is forthcoming. (When the health professional feels that information about a patient is particularly sensitive, he should ask the judge to exercise his discretion by allowing the information to remain secret; if necessary, the judge may first peruse the evidence in private. The judge will always respect the desire to preserve confidence if the interests of justice permit.) In the latter case, the expert will have become involved after legal proceedings were mooted, so that he will only be summoned to give evidence if he has volunteered to do so and the patient has agreed, and no breach of confidence will arise. The other side will be unable to obtain an order compelling disclosure of an expert medical report which has been rejected by the party who requested it as unfavourable to his case. Such a document is covered by legal professional privilege as a communication made in contemplation of litigation (see above).

Use of expert medical reports is illustrated by the case of a plaintiff, Mr

Brooks, who worked in a cotton spinning mill for 20 years and was eventually diagnosed as suffering from byssinosis. He claimed damages from his employers because, he alleged, they had been negligent in not providing sufficient ventilation. The employers' main defence was that Mr Brooks's symptoms were caused by smoking not by cotton dust and they produced the evidence of confidential medical records held by his GP which showed a diagnosis of bronchitis caused by cigarette smoking. Three consultant physicians brought into the case only after Brooks decided to take legal proceedings and who examined him at his request gave expert evidence for the plaintiff that his disability was to some extent caused by cotton dust. This diagnosis rested crucially on the plaintiff's account of suffering increased breathlessness on Mondays after a break from work (a classic indication of byssinosis). There was no mention of this symptom in the GP's records. The judge accepted the plaintiff's account and gave him damages to compensate for 50 per cent of his disability (the other 50 per cent was held due to cigarettes) (*Brooks* v. *J. and P. Coates Ltd* (1984)). Note that the GP was compelled to produce his records, but that the court could not have compelled the consultants' reports to be produced if the plaintiff had wished to suppress them because they were covered by legal professional privilege.

Because, as has been shown, any records, however private, may end up being read out in open court, it is important not to indulge in jokey comments and to make records as clear as possible. It is also an important protection for the patient who may still be working for the employer after the health professional has moved on to another post.

The Disability Discrimination Act 1995 has made it more likely that an OH professional will be required to give evidence in person, though in the majority of cases only written statements will be required. One important decision involving a medical expert witness was *Kapadia* v. *London Borough of Lambeth* (2000). Mr Kapadia was employed as an accountant. He was suffering from reactive depression and was seeing a counsellor. He was retired on medical grounds in 1997. He complained to an employment tribunal that he had been discriminated against for a reason related to disability. The employment tribunal determined by a majority (the chairman dissenting) that he was not disabled. They rejected expert evidence from both Kapadia's GP and a consultant psychologist that without the counselling sessions there would have been a strong likelihood that Kapadia would have had a complete mental breakdown. The report of the case states that the employer had sought an independent medical opinion and through the applicant's solicitor had arranged for Kapadia to see an OH physician employed in the NHS, that Kapadia had given consent in writing to this examination, and that the doctor had prepared a report, but had declined to give it to the employer because he had been advised that the Access to Medical Reports Act 1988 applied, so that Kapadia had to be allowed to read it first. (In fact the Act did not apply, because he was not a doctor who had been concerned with the clinical care of the patient.) As a result, the doctor did not give evidence in the tribunal.

The Court of Appeal held that the tribunal was wrong in its decision. It should have accepted the medical evidence for the applicant, since it was uncontested. The OH report should have been disclosed by the doctor to the employer and to the tribunal because no further consent was required from the applicant. 'By consenting to being examined on behalf of the employers he was consenting to the disclosure to the employers of a report resulting from that examination.'

In fact, it may be that the information given to the Court of Appeal about the OH doctor's report was inaccurate. The doctor in question states that he did not write a report because Kapadia had not given informed consent and that he attended the tribunal hearing after a witness order had been obtained against him, but that he was not called as a witness.

Expert witnesses are now covered by Part 5 of the Civil Procedure Rules. Their overriding duty is to the court. Courts have power to direct the parties to instruct a single joint expert, to save costs. Employment tribunals have power to direct that expert medical evidence be obtained, and, if necessary, to authorise payment out of public funds.

The expert witness must be independent, objective and unbiased. In *De Keyser* v. *Wilson* (2001) Miss Wilson claimed that she had been constructively dismissed. She said she had a depressive illness which had been caused by stress at work. The employer's view was that her illness had resulted from a number of factors and events in her private life. Miss Wilson agreed to be seen by an OH specialist appointed by the employers. Their representative sent a letter of instructions which set out a number of facts about her, for example the death of her brother which had led to her being hounded by the press, a contested custody case, an adulterous affair, and the criminal conviction of a man described as her lover. The letter invited the consultant to make a critical examination of the GP's assessment that Miss Wilson's illness had been caused by her employment. The tribunal found that the letter of instruction contained material which was irrelevant and abusive. The Employment Appeal Tribunal directed that the case should be allowed to proceed, but that another expert should be appointed, to be instructed in more objective terms. These could refer in general to the possibility that life factors were more important to her depression than work, but should not be so specific as the previous instructions.

The expert must not usurp the judicial function: he is there to advise. In *Abadeh* v. *British Telecommunications plc* (2001) Mr Abadeh received a sudden blast of high-pitched high volume noise through his headset. This resulted in permanent hearing loss, tinnitus and post traumatic stress disorder. The tribunal heard evidence from BT's regional medical officer that his impairments were not enough to have a substantial impact on his ability to carry out normal day-to-day activities and that in her opinion he was not disabled. The tribunal accepted this evidence, but the Employment Appeal Tribunal held that they had been over-influenced by the regional medical officer's assessment and had in effect adopted it instead of making their own. The medical report should deal with the doctor's diagnosis of the impairment, the doctor's observation of the applicant carrying out day-to-day activities and the ease with which he was able to perform those functions, together with any relevant opinion as to prognosis and the effect of medication, but the decision on whether he was disabled was for the tribunal, not the doctor. The tribunal was also at fault in totally disregarding the fact that Abadeh had been assessed as 18 per cent disabled for the purposes of industrial injuries benefit. Although the legislation was different, this was clearly relevant evidence for the tribunal to take into account, though the weight to be given to it was for them to decide.

When giving evidence, the witness should be careful to avoid speculation and should stick to the facts. If he does not understand a question he should ask for it to be repeated. If he does not know the answer to a question he should say so. Remember that it will often be the job of the lawyer for the other side to cast doubt on the medical evidence and that this can be done by making a witness angry and flustered.

3.15 The patient's right to know

Where it is the patient who is demanding his own records, confidentiality is irrelevant, because it is the *patient's* confidence which the law protects. The right of subject access should be given, and not merely to encourage the paranoid. A case reported in the BMA's *News Review* concerned Helen Mann, a young woman who moved home and transferred to a new GP. When she visited her new doctor for the first time he began to discuss her addiction to drugs which appeared on her records. As she had never taken any illegal drug, she was totally nonplussed. Investigation revealed that a heroin addict of about the same age had been using her name. It was only by proving that she was abroad at the time the counterfeit Helen had been seen that she persuaded the doctors to amend the notes. No real harm had been done, but if the patient had not changed doctors she might have been refused jobs, mortgages or insurance because of a bad medical report without ever knowing the source of her lack of success.

The right to receive information is as valuable as the right to see medical reports and records. In the following situations the patient has a legal right to be told details and/or to see his own medical records:

(1) Where the patient is being asked to give consent to an examination or procedure, he must be given sufficient information to enable him to give an informed consent. The doctor must satisfy the *Sidaway* test (see Chapter 2), i.e. he must tell the patient what a reasonable physician would have told him in all the circumstances of the case.

(2) Where the patient must be given information to warn him or her of the need for treatment. For example, if an occupational physician institutes cytological smear testing of female employees and finds any adverse signs, he will be liable in negligence if he does not take reasonable care to notify the employee concerned of the need for further investigation.

(3) There is a right of access to a health record conferred by the Data Protection Act 1998. This extends to information held on computer, but also manually, such as letters, X-rays, tape recordings, photographs, video recordings. For a full account see the section on computer records and data protection later in this chapter. Where a patient is dead, the Data Protection Act does not apply, but the Access to Health Records Act 1990 gives the right of access to the patient's personal representative and any person who may have a claim arising out of the patient's death.

(4) The Access to Medical Reports Act 1988 gives patients the right to see copies of medical reports requested from their doctors for employment or insurance purposes (on payment of a reasonable fee). The Act refers to 'a report relating to the physical or mental health of the individual prepared by a medical practitioner *who is or has been responsible for the clinical care of the individual'*. 'Care' includes examination, investigation and diagnosis for the purposes of, or in connection with, any form of medical treatment. On its face, this excludes reports of independent medical examinations and pre-employment screening by the occupational physician (a pre-employment report by the GP or consultant treating the job applicant would fall squarely within the provisions of the Act). More doubtful will be reports by OH physicians on existing workers, since in some cases but not others there will have been a clinical care relationship with an individual worker. Surely it would be invidious to single out a minority of the workers: in my view, it would seem good practice to comply with the Act in all cases.

This legislation gives patients a chance to correct errors (or, if the doctor is unwilling to amend the report, to attach to it a statement of the patient's views), and to withdraw consent to reports being sent if they object to them. A doctor who has been notified that a patient desires access to his report before it is sent to the employer or insurance company will have to wait 21 days. If the patient has not by then taken steps to arrange access, the doctor can supply the report without the patient seeing it. Copies of medical reports supplied for employment or insurance purposes must be retained for at least six months and must be available on request to the person to whom the report relates if application is made within six months of the report having been supplied.

The doctor will be able to withhold all or part of a report from his patient if it would in his opinion be likely to cause serious harm to his physical or mental health or the physical or mental health of others, would indicate the intentions of the practitioner in respect of the individual, or would reveal the identity of or information about another person without that person's consent (except a health professional involved in the care of the individual). It would be impossible to withhold a complete report from a patient without notifying him that it contains sensitive material which is deemed unsuitable for him to see. In fact, the Act obliges the doctor to inform the patient if all or part of a report is withheld. The Act provides that a complaint of a breach of the Act may be made to the County or Sheriff Court, which may order the employer, insurance company or doctor to comply.

Both the Access to Medical Reports Act and the Data Protection Act provide that any term or condition of a contract is void in so far as it purports to require an individual to supply a copy of a medical report or record or to produce to any other person such a report or record. Employers who put a term in the contract of employment stating that employees must provide copies of their GP reports or records if required to do so, can be told that the employee has no duty to comply.

(5) Statutory regulations sometimes direct that individuals must be given information about themselves. Examples in the field of health and safety at work are those relating to the control of lead and ionising radiations, and also the COSHH Regulations. The pattern of these regulations is to impose a legal requirement on both employer and employee to undertake regular testing by doctors appointed by the Employment Medical Advisory Service (EMAS). The detailed record of these tests identified by the name of the individual worker is a confidential document which should not be disclosed to the employer or the general practitioner without the consent of the individual, although it must be made available for inspection by EMAS. The law requires that the Appointed Doctor inform the individual of his fitness to work with the dangerous substance, and notify the employer that he has undertaken the necessary examinations. The outcome of the examination may only be made known to the employer if the employee consents, but the employer and EMAS *must* be notified of persons certified as unfit, or fit only under specified conditions. Group results without individual identification can be given to the employer and to other interested parties when relevant to the provision and/or effectiveness of preventive measures.

The Work in Compressed Air Regulations 1996 are even more wide-ranging. The compressed air contractor must appoint a contract medical adviser, who may be the appointed doctor. Medical surveillance must take place at least every 12 months. The employer shall ensure that a health record is maintained (which must be kept for at least 40 years), and that employees are given a copy after they have ceased to work on the project. The regulations also oblige employers to provide facilities for medical treatment of those working with compressed air.

The Faculty of Occupational Medicine recommends that the individual has the right to be informed of the findings of any clinical examination, whether or not required by statute, but that these should not be disclosed to a third party (including his own doctor) without the individual's informed consent.

It may be important for worker representatives to be told about possible hazards. Though they should not be given access to the medical record of an individual without his consent, section 28 of the Health and Safety at Work Act allows the HSE to reveal information to employees or their representatives which is necessary to keep them adequately informed about matters affecting their health, safety and welfare. There is nothing in section 28 which excludes the disclosure of confidential medical information, though in practice it would be most unlikely that identifiable patient information would be revealed by this method. Section 28 also permits an inspector to furnish any person who appears to him likely to be a party to civil proceedings with a written statement of relevant facts observed by him in the course of the exercise of his statutory powers. The Safety Representatives and Safety Committees Regulations 1977 provide that safety representatives shall be entitled to inspect any document which the employer is required by safety legislation to keep, except a document consisting of or relating to any health record of an identifiable individual.

3.16 *Computer records and data protection*

Medical records consisting of the results of regular tests and examinations are increasingly being computerised. The law of evidence makes computer printouts admissible evidence in both criminal and civil courts. In some instances, it is *real* evidence, that is primary evidence of what actually occurred. One example was *R v. Spiby* (1990) where the Court of Appeal held that a printout from a computerised machine used to monitor telephone calls and record the numbers to which the calls were made and the duration of the calls, was admissible as real evidence. In other examples, computer printouts are hearsay evidence, that is they record what the operator put into the machine, without the operator being available to give evidence himself as to the accuracy of the records. The law of evidence allows many exceptions to the rule that hearsay evidence is not admissible in legal proceedings. Section 69 of the Police and Criminal Evidence Act 1986 provides that statements in documents produced by a computer are admissible in criminal proceedings as evidence of any fact stated therein as long as there are no reasonable grounds for believing that the statement is inaccurate because of improper use of the computer, and there is evidence that at all material times the computer was operating properly. A certificate is required from a person in a responsible position relating to the operation of the computer. Hilda Shepherd was convicted of theft from Marks and Spencer of items of clothing and food. The store detective gave evidence in court that the till rolls, which were linked to a central computer, showed no trace of the unique product code for the clothing found in Hilda's car nor was there any group of prices matching the items of food she said she had purchased. The detective described how the tills operated, what the central computer did, and stated that there was no evidence of malfunction on the relevant day. Mrs Shepherd's conviction was upheld by the House of Lords (*R v. Shepherd* (1993)). Hearsay evidence is admissible in civil proceedings (Civil Evidence Act 1995), and the Police and Criminal Evidence Act does not apply. Nonetheless, judges have a discretion as to what weight to give to evidence of any kind. It is advisable to use software which restricts the operator's power to alter entries at a later date, so that it can be proved that the evidence has not been tampered with after something has gone wrong.

Legal controls over those holding data on computer were first introduced in the UK by the Data Protection Act 1984, which arose from a Council of Europe Convention of 1981. It was replaced by the Data Protection Act 1998, implementing a European Union Directive of 1995. The Act controls the holding of personal data, defined as data which relate to a living individual who can be identified either from those data or from other information which is in the possession of, or is likely to come into the possession of, the data controller. Information on a computer listed according to numbers is personal data if the controller holds a list of the names of the individuals to which the numbers correspond, or can obtain such a list. It includes any expression of opinion about the individual and any indication of the intentions of the data controller or any other person in respect of the individual. Data means information which is processed by means of equipment operating automatically in response to instructions given for that purpose (computer data), or which is recorded as part of a 'relevant filing system', or forms part of an 'accessible record'. Accessible records are health records, educational records and accessible public records, that is housing and social services records held by a local authority. Accessible records may be held in any form, either on computer, or in a filing cabinet, or a mixture of both. The definition of a health record is in section 68(2):

'any record which (a) consists of information relating to the physical or mental health or condition of an individual, and (b) has been made by or on behalf of a health professional in connection with the care of that individual.'

Thus, a medical record which includes letters from a consultant, GP notes, reports from a physiotherapist, X-rays, results of blood tests and so on is covered by the Data Protection Act, whether or not the information is held in whole or in part on computer. The list of health professionals includes doctors, nurses, dentists, physiotherapists, speech therapists, opticians, pharmacists and even music therapists. It is likely that a DNA or fingerprint database falls within the Act, since these constitute information about an individual. Certainly written reports about the results of drugs and alcohol tests fall within its scope, as do reports about genetic tests.

Since the Act refers to health professionals connected with the care of an individual, rather than *clinical* care, it is submitted that it must apply to occupational health records. Care is not defined in the Act, but it would be difficult for an OH professional to argue that he or she is not concerned with the care of workers.

The definition of a relevant filing system is:

'any set of information relating to individuals to the extent that, although the information is not processed by means of equipment operating automatically in response to instructions given for that purpose, the set is structured, either by reference to individuals or by reference to criteria relating to individuals, in such a way that specific information relating to a particular individual is readily accessible.'

This definition was examined for the first time by the court in *Durant* v. *Financial Services Authority* (2003). Michael Durant was a customer of Barclays Bank. There had been litigation between them, which he lost, in 1993. He complained to the Financial Services Authority (FSA), which conducted an investigation. He asked the FSA for disclosure of documents relating to him held both on computer and in manual files. The FSA refused access to the manual files on two grounds, first that they did not contain personal data within the Act and second that they did not form part of a manual filing system. The documents in question related to Mr Durant's claim against the bank and were filed mainly under his name.

Mr Durant argued that any letter or document which mentioned his name was data which related to him, but the Court of Appeal disagreed. 'Mere mention of a data subject in a document held by a data controller does not necessarily amount to personal data.' It should be information which is biographical, and which has the data subject as its focus, rather than some other person with whom he may have been involved, as in this case Barclays Bank. Personal data covers the name of an individual, his address and telephone number, his hobbies, his employment, his religion, his HIV status and his bad back, but not documents generated by the FSA arising from his complaint, which concerned Barclays Bank rather than Mr Durant.

The definition of a relevant filing system was also restrictively interpreted. The purpose of the definition was to limit disclosure to manual data that could be easily accessed (apart from health, education, social work and housing records where all data must be disclosed).

> 'That requires a filing system so referenced or indexed that it enables the data controller's employee responsible to identify at the outset of his search with reasonable certainty and speed the file or files in which the specific data relating to the person requesting the information is located and to locate the relevant information about him within the file or files, without having to make a manual search of them.'

A file of papers with a name on the front filed according to date is not included, but a named file arranged under clearly designated sub-sections like education, history of employment, earnings, sickness absence and holidays may be. After the Durant decision, some employers are refusing to disclose information in manual personnel files. It will be in their interest from this point of view, though not perhaps that of efficiency, to keep them as unstructured as possible.

The Freedom of Information Act 2000 (FOIA) has added to the Data Protection Act (DPA) definition of personal data. The FOIA gives a right to request information from public authorities, however it is held, with exemptions. Even if personal data are in unstructured manual form, and therefore not covered by the DPA, where held by a public authority they may be accessible under the FOIA. However, where individuals request information about themselves, the FOIA does not apply. Personal information about others will often also be exempt because disclosure would be a breach of the data protection principles or the data are exempt from subject access under the DPA.

The DPA imposes duties on the data controller, that is a person who (either alone or jointly or in common with other persons) determines the purposes for which and the manner in which any personal data are, or are to be, processed. In my view occupational health records are (or should be) in the control of the head of the OH department, rather than the employer, despite the undoubted fact that they are the property of the employer. The Act deals with control, not ownership. This issue has not so far been litigated. The duties imposed by the Act are:

(1) *The duty to notify the Information Commissioner of the holding of personal data.* The controller must give a description of the categories of data, the purpose or purposes for which they are collected and processed and a description of the recipient or recipients to whom the data controller may wish to disclose the data. A fee of £35 (at the time of writing) is payable and notification must be renewed every year. Notification is only mandatory for data held on computer. It is a criminal offence to process data without notification. Processing means obtaining, recording or holding the information or data or carrying out any operation or set of operations on the information or data, including organisation, adaptation or alteration of the information or data, retrieval, consultation or use of the information or data, disclosure of the information by transmission, dissemination or otherwise making available, or the alignment, combination, blocking, erasure or destruction of the information or data.

(2) *The duty to observe the data protection principles.* These are:

(a) Personal data shall be processed fairly and lawfully.
(b) Personal data shall be obtained only for one or more specified lawful purposes, and shall not be further processed in any manner incompatible with that purpose or those purposes.
(c) Personal data shall be adequate, relevant and not excessive in relation to the purpose or purposes for which they are processed.
(d) Personal data shall be accurate and, where necessary, kept up to date.
(e) Personal data processed for any purpose or purposes shall not be kept longer than is necessary for that purpose or those purposes.
(f) Personal data shall be processed in accordance with the rights of data subjects under this Act.
(g) Appropriate technical and organisational measures shall be taken against unauthorised or unlawful processing of personal data and against accidental loss of, destruction of, or damage to, personal data.
(h) Personal data shall not be transferred to a country or territory outside the European Economic Area unless that country or territory ensures an adequate level of protection for the rights and freedoms of data subjects in relation to the processing of personal data.

The Faculty of Occupational Medicine recommends that as a precautionary measure a regular updated copy of computer records should be taken and kept in a separate and secure location. No unauthorised software should be used on the system to prevent the risk of computer viruses being introduced which can corrupt information. A policy statement detailing procedures for security and confidentiality should be prepared, and all staff with access to the occupational health unit should receive training and sign the policy statement to acknowledge their responsibilities.

There are special rules about sensitive data. Sensitive personal data means personal data consisting of information as to:

(a) the racial or ethnic origin of the data subject;
(b) his political opinions;
(c) his religious or other beliefs;
(d) whether he is a member of a trade union;
(e) his physical or mental health or condition;
(f) his sexual life;
(g) the commission or alleged commission by him of any offence; or
(h) any proceedings for any offence committed or alleged to have been committed by him, the disposal of such proceedings or the sentence of any court in such proceedings.

The most important data protection principle is the first, that personal data shall be processed fairly and lawfully and, in particular, shall not be processed unless at least one of the conditions in Schedule 2 is met, and in the case of sensitive personal data, at least one of the conditions in Schedule 3 is also met. Schedule 2 contains a number of conditions, including that the data subject has given consent to the processing, that the processing is necessary for compliance with a legal obligation to which the data controller is subject (as, for example, the health and safety legislation), or that the processing is necessary for the administration of justice or for the purposes of legitimate interests pursued by the data controller or by the third party or parties to whom the data is disclosed, except where the processing is unwarranted in any particular case by reason of prejudice to the rights and freedoms or legitimate interests of the data subject.

Schedule 3 contains an even longer list, of which the most important conditions for the OH professional are that the data subject has given explicit consent, that the processing is necessary for the purposes of exercising or performing any right or obligation which is conferred or imposed by law on the data controller in connection with employment (as, for example, the administration of statutory sick pay), or that the processing is necessary to protect the vital interests of the data subject or another person and either the consent of the data subject cannot be obtained or, where a third party is at risk, the consent of the data subject has been unreasonably withheld. Further conditions are that the processing is necessary for the purpose of or in connection with legal proceedings, including prospective legal proceedings, that it is necessary for the administration of justice, or that it is necessary for medical purposes and is undertaken by a health professional or a person who owes a duty of confidentiality equivalent to that of a health professional (for example a clerical assistant in the OH department whose contract of employment incorporates a duty of confidence). 'Medical purposes' includes the purposes of preventative medicine, medical diagnosis, medical research, the provision of care and treatment and the management of healthcare services.

It is vital to note that the DPA permits processing of sensitive data *without consent* if one of the other conditions applies. It does not, however, replace or remove the common law duty of confidentiality which, as we have seen, requires express or implied consent to be given to the disclosure of information other than in exceptional circumstances. The common law is stricter than the statute and the data controller must comply with both. Data must be processed lawfully and that includes in compliance with the common law, which has been discussed earlier in the chapter, and which has been incorporated by reference into the statute.

(3) *The duty to allow the data subject access to data about himself (section 7).* Remember that there is a right of access to a health record in whatever form it is held, computer or manual, or a mixture of both, and that a health record is defined by section 68 as any record relating to physical or mental health or condition made by or on behalf of a health professional. When is a record 'made' by a health professional? Certainly when he enters data into the computer, or writes a report, but what if he merely adds a letter to a file of documents? He may reply to a letter of referral from management and staple the reply to the referral. Is the management letter part of the health record even though not written by a health professional? This will be important when a worker requests access to his OH records and the manager directs that his letter should not be disclosed. There is no case law on this point, but it can be argued that to impose an obligation to give access to an OH report without including the letter to which it replies is to defeat the purpose of the Act. Photocopying the letter would, presumably, count as making a record. It seems absurd that the incorporation of the original in the file might not be covered by the Act. The worker might be able to obtain the manager's letter by asking for a copy of his personnel file, but would be unable to access that file unless it is on computer or in a relevant filing system.

The DPA repeals and replaces the Access to Health Records Act 1990, except with respect to the health records of the deceased, since the DPA relates only to data about living individuals. All records must be disclosed, whenever made, and information must be communicated in an intelligible form.

An individual is entitled to be informed by the data controller whether personal data about him are being processed, and to receive a copy of the data within a reasonable time (usually 40 days). The data subject must make his request in writing and must pay a small fee, currently £10 for computer data and £50 for data including manual data. The data controller is entitled to check whether the applicant is in fact the data subject, or someone acting with his authority.

There are special rules about medical and social work records in statutory regulations. The order relating to medical records (Data Protection (Subject Access Modification) (Health) Order 2000) applies to personal data consisting of information as to the physical or mental health or condition of the data subject. Subject access may be refused if it would in the health professional's opinion be likely to cause serious harm to the physical or mental health or condition of the data subject or any other person.

It would seem that the protection of the physical or mental health of the health professional might be a reason for withholding information (where, for example, the patient is a mentally disturbed 'stalker' who might attack the doctor if he read what had been written about him).

The other principal exemption to the right of subject access is where compliance would disclose information relating to a third party who can be identified from that information. This is covered by section 7 Data Protection Act. Where a data controller cannot comply with a request for data without disclosing information relating to another individual who can be identified from that information (including identifying him as the source of information sought by the request), he is not obliged to comply with the request unless:

(1) the other individual has consented to the disclosure of the information to the person making the request; or
(2) it is reasonable in the circumstances to comply with the request without the consent of the other individual; or
(3) the information is contained in a health record and the other individual is a health professional who has compiled or contributed to the health record or has been involved in the care of the data subject in his capacity as a health professional.

This provision had to be included in the DPA because of the decision of the European Court of Human Rights in *Gaskin* v. *UK* (1989). Gaskin had been in the care of Liverpool City Council for most of his childhood, and had been placed with a number of foster parents. He alleged that he had been the victim of child abuse, and asked for his social work records. Many of the documents had been compiled by third parties such as doctors, and when the authority asked for their consent to disclosure they refused it. The local authority refused disclosure, because they never as a matter of principle gave that information without consent. The Strasbourg Court held that such a blanket exemption was a breach of Article 8 of the European Human Rights Convention. The court had to have the power to decide that access should be granted where a contributor fails to answer or withholds consent.

This dilemma is likely to arise in OH practice where a worker asks for access to his OH records and they are found to contain information from managers or fellow workers. The first step is to see whether information can be redacted in order to render those individuals anonymous, 'whether by the omission of names or other identifying particulars or otherwise'. If this is impracticable, the OH professional should ask the third party for permission to disclose. Although, strictly speaking, the Act does not oblige the data controller to seek consent, it is good practice to do so. The third party may have a good reason to object, perhaps because he has been physically threatened, or the information is covered by legal professional privilege because the worker is suing the employer and the data stem from a communication between a lawyer and occupational health. Where there is no such reason, the OH professional will have to make a decision as to whether it is reasonable to disclose without consent. In making that decision he must take into account any duty of confidentiality to the third party, any steps taken to seek consent, whether the third party is capable of giving consent, and whether the third party has expressly refused consent. Note that the decision whether to release information does not depend on the reasonableness of the third party's refusal. In *Durant* v. *Financial Services Authority* (2003), the only case so far which has reached the courts, Durant was asking for access to the records of an investigation by the FSA into his complaint against Barclays Bank:

'There are two basic points to make about the scheme [of the Act] for balancing the interests of the data subject and those of the individual who may be identified in such data. The first is that the balancing exercise only arises if the information relating to the other person forms part of the 'personal data' of the data subject ... The second is that the provisions appear to create a presumption or starting point that the information relating to that other, including his identity, should not be disclosed without his consent. The presumption may, however, be rebutted if the data controller considers that it is reasonable in all the circumstances ... to disclose it without consent.'

The FSA had withheld the identity of some employees, including one who had been abused by Mr Durant over the phone. The court held that it had power only to review the decision of the FSA as being within a range of reasonable responses, not to substitute its own decision. Where the third party is the recipient of information who might act on the data to the data subject's disadvantage, or where he is the source of the information and the data subject needs to take some action to correct a damaging inaccuracy, the data subject's right to information weighs heavily in the balance. It is submitted that information from a manager in an occupational health file is likely to fall within one or other of these categories. A decision by an OH professional to release information about allegations made by a manager in the worker's file (as, for example, that his sickness absence is caused by drug abuse) would be likely to be held to fall within a band of reasonableness. It is therefore advisable that managers should be warned that any letters or communications from or to management in the OH health records may have to be disclosed to the worker.

Suppose that the source of the 'sensitive' information is another health professional? A hospital consultant writes to a GP that in his view a patient is suffering from paranoia, but that this information must not be released to the patient. When the OH physician writes to the GP asking for information about the patient, the worker declines to exercise his right to see the GP report before it is sent. Later, he asks for a copy of the occupational health record. The consultant is strongly opposed to his opinion being given to the patient either by the GP or by the occupational physician, but this would not justify withholding it. The regulations are quite clear on this point. Only if in the occupational physician's opinion revelation would cause damage to the patient's physical or mental health or condition, or that of another person, may it be concealed. Doctors who complain that this rule runs counter to their medical etiquette should remember that the patient is asking for his own information and that it is *his* confidence that the rules of law and ethics seek to protect, not that of another doctor.

Who is empowered to decide whether medical records should be released to the patient? The obligation to disclose is on the data controller. Assuming that occupational health records are under the control of OH doctors and nurses, they will have to make the decision within the regulations. The same applies to general practitioner records since the GP will be the data controller of his patient's health records. Hospital records are under the control of the NHS Trusts. The regulations provide that, in the case of a data controller who is not a health professional, data shall not be revealed without consulting the health professional who is currently or was most recently responsible for the clinical care of the patient, or, if such a person is not available, a suitable professional with the qualifications and experience to advise. The duty is to consult, not necessarily to obey. The regulations envisage that medical records may have to be censored by removing the sensitive information and disclosing the rest. From the patient's point of view, it will be virtually impossible to challenge a decision to withhold data, because he will not be aware that anything is being kept from him.

Personal data processed only for research purposes are covered by section 33. This provides that personal data which are processed only for research purposes are exempt from subject access if processed in compliance with relevant conditions and the results of the research or any resulting statistics are not made available in a form which identifies the data subjects. The relevant conditions are that the data are not processed to support measures or decisions with respect to particular individuals, and that they are not processed in such a way that substantial damage or substantial distress is, or is likely to be, caused to any data subject.

Research data can be kept indefinitely. Research includes statistical or historical purposes.

This section permits a data controller to process for research purposes data which have been obtained for clinical or other purposes. However, there is a general obligation under the DPA to inform data subjects of the use to which their data may be put at the time it is collected. NHS Trusts should give information to the general public that their records may be used by researchers and give reassurance that results will only be published anonymously (see the section on consent earlier in this chapter).

Personal data held for the prevention or detection of crime, the apprehension or prosecution of offenders, or for tax purposes are also exempt from the subject access provisions. Confidential references given by the data controller about the education or employment of the data subject, records of the intentions of the data controller in relation to negotiations with the data subject and data covered by legal professional privilege are all exempt from the duty to make disclosure to the subject of the data.

(4)   *The duty not to disclose personal data to third parties.* This is virtually the same as the common law duty relating to manual records. The Act specifically exempts from the non-disclosure principles disclosure required by statute or by order of court or made for the purpose of obtaining legal advice or in the course of legal proceedings.

(5)   *A duty not to act on personal data without giving the data subject an opportunity to justify or refute them.* A new provision (section 12) forbids the making of a decision which significantly affects a data subject solely in reliance on computer data which relate to his performance at work, his creditworthiness, his reliability or his conduct. A complex provision, this in effect obliges employers, for example, to permit an employee to make representations about the reasons for his poor sickness record before making him redundant simply on the basis of the computer printout. The court can order the employer to reconsider the decision or to take another decision on a different basis.

An individual who suffers damage by reason of any contravention by a data controller of any of the requirements of the Act is entitled to compensation from the data controller for the damage. Action may be brought in the High Court, County Court, Court of Session or Sheriff Court. It will be a defence for the controller to show that he had taken reasonable care to comply with the Act. The Commissioner has power to investigate alleged violations and to issue an enforcement notice demanding compliance. It is a criminal offence to fail to comply with a notice. There is an appeal to the Data Protection Tribunal.

3.17   Information Commissioner's Employment Practices Data Protection Code: Information about Workers' Health

The Code is intended to assist employers in complying with the Act and to establish good practice for handling personal data in the workplace. It covers information collected by employers about job applicants, employees, agency workers, casual workers and contract workers. The legal requirement on employers is to comply with the Act itself. The benchmarks in the Code are the Information Commissioner's recommendations as to how the legal requirements of the Act can be met. The Code would be cited by the Information Commissioner in connection with any enforcement action and is likely to be taken into account by courts and tribunals in interpreting the Act.

The Code is designed in four parts: Recruitment and Selection, Employment Records, Monitoring at Work, and Information about Workers' Health. Part 4, which is most relevant to occupational health, is at the time of writing only in draft. It is accompanied by Supplementary Guidance and Guidance for Small Businesses which are not themselves part of the Code, though likely to be regarded as authoritative.

The following are core principles for dealing with health information:

(1) It will be intrusive and may be highly intrusive to obtain information about your workers' health.
(2) Workers have legitimate expectations that they can keep their personal health information private and that employers will respect this privacy.
(3) If employers wish to collect and hold information on their workers' health, they should be clear about the purpose and satisfied that this is justified by real benefits that will be delivered.
(4) One of the sensitive data conditions must be satisfied.
(5) Workers should be aware when information about their health is collected, of the nature and extent of the information held and the reasons for which it is held.
(6) Assessment of the implications of a worker's health on his or her fitness for work should normally be left to a suitably qualified health professional. 'Leave the interpretation of health information to those who are qualified to do this.'

In general, employers should only collect health information where it is necessary for the protection of health and safety, to prevent discrimination on the grounds of disability or if each worker affected has given his/her explicit consent. If consent is to be relied on, it must be freely given. That means that a worker must be able to say 'no' without penalty and must be able to withdraw consent once given. (Employers may nevertheless be able to draw adverse inferences from a refusal, if denied the opportunity, for example, to test for the presence of illegal drugs.) The Commissioner recommends that employers should consider conducting an impact assessment (this might be a proper function for occupational health).

Supplementary Guidance sets out how to carry out an impact assessment. You should consider how intrusive the obtaining of health data would be, and whether there are alternatives. Could health questionnaires rather than tests be used to obtain information, could changes in the workplace obviate the need for health surveillance, could medical testing be targeted only at a few individuals, rather than at all workers, could access to health information be confined to those with a duty of confidence? Is the collection of health information justified? What benefits will it confer? What do the workers or their representatives think?

The Supplementary Guidance reflects good OH practice. Unless unavoidable, only health professionals should have access to information on medical conditions. In general, managers should be given only a statement of a worker's current or likely future fitness to work. 'In some cases it may be necessary for managers to know about a worker's state of health in order to protect that worker or others.' Health questionnaires should be designed and reviewed by health professionals. Workers should not be asked to consent to the disclosure of their entire general practitioner records or other comprehensive care and treatment records such as those held by a hospital. The general practitioner should be asked specific relevant questions to elicit the information needed by the employer. The worker's consent will be needed before the GP can release such information.

Information should be provided to workers who are part of an occupational health scheme by giving them clear written guidance about what health information will be collected, who will have access to it and in what circumstances. An OH adviser should hold medical information about a worker, telling the manager whether or not there is a legitimate reason for the worker's absence from work, thus avoiding the disclosure of clinical details. 'It is difficult to see how the disclosure to the employer about the health of a worker's family members can be justified.'

> 'Compliance with the Guidelines on Ethics for Occupational Physicians, while not guaranteeing compliance with the Data Protection Act 1998, is in most cases likely to ensure its requirements are satisfied.'

The Code states that medical testing of job applicants should only be conducted where there is an intention to appoint them and the employer is satisfied that the testing is a necessary and justified measure to:

(1)   determine whether the potential worker is fit or likely to remain fit for the particular employment; or
(2)   meet any legal requirements for testing; or
(3)   determine the terms on which a potential worker is eligible to join a pension or insurance scheme.

The employer should only conduct a medical examination or medical testing of current workers if he is satisfied that it is a necessary and justified measure to:

(1)   prevent a significant risk to the health and safety of the worker, or others; or
(2)   determine the worker's fitness for continued employment; or
(3)   determine the worker's entitlement to health related benefits, e.g. sick pay; or
(4)   prevent discrimination against workers on the ground of disability.

The Code then goes on to deal with drug and alcohol testing, and genetic testing, which will be dealt with in Chapter 4.

Misuse of a computer may constitute a criminal offence under the Computer

Misuse Act 1990. Deliberate unauthorised access to computer material ('hacking') and unauthorised modification of the contents of a computer (deliberate erasure or modification of programs or data, or the deliberate introduction of a virus into the computer) are both punishable with fines or imprisonment. The scrutiny of data without any interaction with the computer (as, for example, the reading of data already displayed on a screen) does not fall within the Act. However, unauthorised dealing with computer data, or damaging the computer, will amount in most cases to gross misconduct, justifying summary dismissal (Chapter 8). In *Denco* v. *Joinson* (1991) a shop steward deliberately used an unauthorised password to enter a computer known to contain information to which he was not entitled. The Employment Appeal Tribunal held that such action is 'an extremely serious industrial offence'.

3.18 Human Rights Act and Privacy

In the General Introduction to this book an account was given of the Human Rights Act 1998 and it was pointed out that Article 8 of the Convention, giving a right to respect for private and family life, home and correspondence, has strengthened the law of confidentiality. The European Court of Human Rights in Strasbourg has confirmed on at least two occasions that private life includes information about physical and mental health. In *Z* v. *Finland* (1997) Z was a Swedish national married to X. During an investigation of X for a number of sexual offences, it was discovered that he was HIV positive. He was tried for attempted manslaughter. A relevant matter was at what date X first knew of his medical condition. His wife was asked to give evidence, but declined, as she had a right to do under Finnish law. The court ordered doctors treating both X and Z to give evidence, and seized their medical records. X was convicted, and in the judgment, which was a public document, the court referred to Z by name and also disclosed her medical details. The court faxed a copy of its decision to Finland's largest newspaper. The European Court held that there had been interference with Z's private life, but then considered whether this was justified by Article 8 (2). It concluded that the investigation into X's medical condition was justified by the prevention of crime and the protection of the rights and freedoms of others, and that the same argument extended to the seizure of Z's records and the interrogation of her doctor, but that, although the use of her medical data in the criminal trial was justified, the publication of her name and medical details was not.

> 'Respecting the confidentiality of health data is a vital principle in the legal system of all the Contracting Parties to the Convention. It is crucial not only to respect the sense of privacy of a patient but also to preserve his or her confidence in the medical profession and in the health service in general.'

In *MS* v. *Sweden* (1997) MS was a Swedish citizen who suffered from spondylolisthesis, a condition affecting the spine which causes back pain. She slipped and fell at work. She made a claim for compensation under the Swedish Industrial

Injury Insurance Act. The Social Insurance Office without consent (as Swedish law permitted) obtained medical records from a clinic containing information on treatment she had received for her back, but failing to mention an industrial accident. These revealed that she had at one stage asked for an abortion. It was held that the disclosure of the data by the clinic to the Office entailed an interference with her Article 8 rights. The European Court held this was justified by the need to protect the economic well-being of the country, to prevent dishonest claimants from claiming from the public purse.

When the Human Rights Act first came into force it was mooted that it would create a freestanding right of privacy in English law, but this has not proved to be the case. There have so far been no examples of conduct held unlawful under Article 8 which would not also have fallen foul of the law of confidence or that of data protection.

The Convention has, however, been influential in regulating surveillance by employers of workers' telephone calls and emails. It led to the passing of the Regulation of Investigatory Powers Act 2000. While most of its provisions are aimed directly at the security services and the State, the sections on the interception of communications have a more general application. The Act creates a new tort of unlawful interception of communications on a private network. This includes emails, telephone calls, faxes, video-conferencing, voice mail and Internet access. It relates to a private telecommunication system linked to a public system. Only the person in control of the system or someone acting with his authority can lawfully intercept. Monitoring can be done either with the consent of each individual employee or under the Telecommunications (Lawful Business Practice) Regulations 2000. Businesses can monitor or record communications without consent for the following purposes:

(1) to establish the existence of facts relevant to the business, e.g. to record a telephone conversation concerning a contract;
(2) to ascertain compliance with regulatory guidelines, e.g. whether employees are observing instructions about answering queries from customers;
(3) to ascertain or demonstrate standards which are or ought to be achieved by persons using the system;
(4) to protect national security;
(5) to prevent or detect crime;
(6) to investigate unauthorised use of the system, e.g. employees surfing the net for pornography;
(7) to ensure the effective operation of the system, e.g. monitoring for viruses.

In addition, the business can monitor but not record communications for the purpose of:

(1) determining whether or not the communications are relevant to the business, e.g. chats to mother on the office phone;
(2) monitoring communications to a free confidential anonymous counselling or support helpline (a surprising provision which arguably conflicts with Article 8) .

The system controller must make all reasonable efforts to inform every person who may use the system that interception may take place, hence the irritating preface to many public helplines. It is important for employers to create a policy and make sure that all employees are fully aware of it.

Video surveillance may be regarded as a breach of Article 8, unless it is justified by the need to prevent crime or to ensure that health and safety precautions are observed. Even then, workers should be made aware of surveillance, and surveillance of changing rooms or toilet facilities may be regarded as unacceptable in any event.

Once personal information is obtained by these means it falls within the controls in the Data Protection Act. The Information Commissioner in the Draft Employment Practices Data Protection Code (part 4) advises that sensitive data about health should not be subject to monitoring by persons who are not under a duty of confidence, such as the information technology department.

'If workers are allowed to use telephone or email for confidential communication with their occupational health service, do not compromise this confidentiality by monitoring the contents of these communications.'

The same would apply to communications between OH professionals and outside doctors, like GPs.

3.19   *Freedom of Information Act 2000*

The Data Protection Act 1998 (DPA) is concerned with the protection of personal data relating to individuals, and gives a right of access to the subject of the data, whether the data are held by a public or private body or individual. The Freedom of Information Act (FOIA) makes provision for the disclosure of information held by public authorities to any member of the public. The Act was passed in 2000 but came fully into force only on 1 January 2005. The Information Commissioner is charged with the supervision of both the data protection and freedom of information legislation, as well as the Environmental Information Regulations 2004. The Data Protection Act, which stems from a European Directive, applies throughout the United Kingdom. Scotland has its own Freedom of Information (Scotland) Act and Environmental Information (Scotland) Regulations, which are overseen by a separate regulator, the Scottish Information Commissioner's Office. The purpose of the FOIA is to promote a culture of openness and accountability among public authorities, giving better public understanding of how they carry out their duties and make decisions.

The FOIA creates two principal obligations for a public authority. The first is to adopt and maintain a publication scheme, approved by the Information Commissioner, setting out details of information it will routinely make available, how the information can be obtained, and whether there is any charge for it. The second is to comply with requests to know whether information of a certain description is held, and, if that is the case, to have that information communicated, unless an exemption from disclosure applies. Disclosure must normally be within 20 working days of a request, which must be in writing by a named applicant who provides an address for correspondence. It is intended that fees will not normally be charged.

There are a large number of exemptions from the duty of disclosure. In broad terms these are absolute exemptions and qualified exemptions. If an exemption is absolute the right to know is wholly disapplied, for instance information held by bodies dealing with national security or information covered by parliamentary privilege. Qualified exemptions require the public authority to consider whether there is a greater public interest in confirming or denying the existence of the information requested and providing that information to the applicant or in maintaining the exemption. The public interest is served where access to the information would:

(1) further the understanding of, and participation in, the debate of issues of the day;
(2) facilitate the accountability and transparency of public authorities for decisions taken by them;
(3) facilitate accountability and transparency in the spending of public money;
(4) allow individuals to understand decisions made by public authorities affecting their lives and, in some cases, assist individuals in challenging those decisions;
(5) bring to light information affecting public safety.

'Information should be disclosed if the only likely harm would be embarrassment to the authority although if disclosure might discourage openness in the expression of opinions, that might be a reason for withholding it.'

A report of a committee meeting should give an account of the committee members present, the issues raised, the discussion and the decisions reached, but it is usually unnecessary to identify which member expressed which view.

Section 40 of FOIA states that personal data of which the applicant is the data subject are exempt. A request for personal data of some other person is not exempt unless disclosure would contravene one of the data protection principles. If I ask an NHS Trust (a public authority) for my own medical records there is no obligation to disclose them under FOIA. However, this request automatically becomes a subject access request under DPA and must be treated as such. In most cases I have a right of access to my own medical records (exceptions are discussed in an earlier section). If I ask the NHS Trust for disclosure of my adult son's medical records, I would not normally be entitled to medical information about my son unless he has given explicit consent, since otherwise the data would be processed unlawfully, in breach of confidence.

The Information Commissioner advises that 'third party data', for example information about someone employed by a public authority acting in an official or work capacity, should normally be provided on request unless there is some risk to the individual concerned. 'The exemption should not be used, for instance, as a means of sparing officials' embarrassment over poor administrative decisions.' Disclosure should normally be made of the names of officials and their grades, but not of their home addresses or bank accounts. Information about salaries should be disclosed because there is a strong public interest in how public money is spent.

Occasionally, there may be a need to protect an individual's identity, for example where threats have been made. Employers are advised to develop a policy as to what information will be routinely disclosed about staff and what might be withheld.

Section 41 FOIA deals specifically with information subject to the duty of confidence. Information is exempt if it was obtained by the public authority from any other person and the disclosure of the information to the public would constitute an actionable breach of confidence. Even a confirmation or denial that information is held may constitute an actionable breach of confidence. For instance, a financial regulator might decline to confirm or deny that it is in possession of a confidential report on a company, since confirmation would indicate that the company has been investigated and is therefore suspect. The Information Commissioner advises that the law of confidence is a common law concept, and depends on the relationship between the confider and the confidant and the nature of the information. The common law of confidence was discussed earlier in this chapter. The Commissioner is of the view that protective markings on documents (e.g. restricted, top secret) should not be regarded as conclusive. Documents may have been sensitive at the time of creation, but no longer be so. Documents marked 'Commercial in Confidence' must not be permitted to impose restrictions beyond those permitted by the Act.

Information is exempt information if it constitutes a trade secret (though the authority must always confirm or deny whether it holds that information), or if its disclosure under the Act would prejudice the commercial interests of any person (including the public authority holding it). Trade secrets may be secret formulae or recipes, but also lists of customers and pricing structures. This is a qualified exemption. The bias is in favour of disclosure and there will be occasions where it is in the public interest to disclose despite the damage to commercial interests. Unauthorised disclosures of trade secrets may result in legal action being taken against public authorities, so the Information Commissioner advises caution. Very often the commercial interests exemption will overlap with that relating to information provided in confidence. It is, of course, a defence to the release of confidential information that it was in the public interest to do so, but the court's view of the public interest may differ from that of the public authority, and damages for commercial loss could be high.

When deciding whether the release of information would be likely to harm someone's commercial interests the individual circumstances of each request will need to be considered. The price submitted by a contractor will be sensitive during the tendering process but less likely to be so once the contract has been awarded. Information that a company is considering relocation may have repercussions on labour relations and therefore do commercial damage if revealed. In order to assess the impact of a revelation of commercial information, public authorities may wish to consult with the parties likely to be affected, and it may be advisable to do this in general terms with major suppliers and contractors, since the time scale on receiving a request is short. Care should be taken not to allow the contractor to dictate what can and cannot be revealed. The Lord Chancellor has prepared a Code of Practice that sets out the standards public authorities are expected to meet to comply with their obligations.

The public interest may justify releasing information even if it does commercial damage:

> 'In the course of its role as a regulator, a public authority may hold information on the quality of products or on the conduct of private companies. There would be strong public interest arguments in allowing access to information which would help protect the public from unsafe products or unscrupulous practices even though this might involve revealing a trade secret or other information whose disclosure might harm the commercial interests of a company.'

Public consultation has been undertaken by the Health and Safety Executive about possible changes to section 28 of the Health and Safety at Work Act (Chapter 5). The section forbade the disclosure of relevant information by the Health and Safety Commission without the consent of the person by whom it was furnished, other than to the Health and Safety Executive, a Government Department, the Environment Commission, a local authority or the police. Disclosure of information obtained by an inspector is permitted to allow workers or safety representatives to be informed about matters affecting their safety, health and welfare, and to furnish to a person likely to be a party to civil proceedings relevant facts observed in the course of an inspection. The section will be amended in line with the general rules and exemptions in FOIA. Thus, the HSC and the HSE will still be precluded from revealing confidential information about an individual and sensitive commercial information, as well as information relating to investigations of possible offences and criminal prosecutions, and information the disclosure of which might prejudice the prevention or detection of crime or the apprehension or prosecution of offenders. Any information which would be likely to prejudice a public authority's exercise of its functions for the purpose of securing the health, safety and welfare of persons at work, or persons other than those at work against risk to health and safety arising out of the actions of persons at work, is also exempt (section 31). This exemption extends to the confirmation or denial of whether information is held.

Information is exempt if its disclosure would be likely to endanger the physical or mental health of any individual, or endanger the safety of any individual. The duty to confirm or deny whether information is held does not arise in the event that there is such a risk.

The Environmental Information Regulations 1992 have been replaced by new regulations made in 2004 that came into force on 1 January 2005. Where a request has been made for environmental information, it should be considered under these regulations, rather than the FOIA. Public authorities have a duty progressively to make information available to the public by electronic means which are easily accessible and to make information available on request on payment of a reasonable fee, normally within 20 working days. There are exceptions, similar to those in the FOIA, and the public interest is paramount. One exception is where disclosure would in itself damage the environment, as where it relates to the site of a rare plant or the nest of a rare bird.

Enforcement of the FOIA is through the Information Commissioner to whom a complaint should be addressed. The Commissioner may order disclosure by issuing an enforcement notice. There is an appeal to the Information Tribunal. Failure to comply with an enforcement notice is a contempt of court and is punishable as a criminal offence. No civil action for damages may be brought for breach of the FOIA. A similar procedure applies to the Environmental Information Regulations.

3.20 *The employer's confidence*

It is not only the medical and nursing professions who are obliged to keep secrets: a contract of employment contains implied terms imposing duties of trust and confidence on both employer and employee. These obligations are automatically implied into every employment contract; there is no need to obtain an express undertaking. Many cases have been taken to court in which an organisation has tried to obtain an injunction to prevent its servant (or former servant) from revealing trade secrets to its competitors, or, when the secrets are already out, has sued for damages for the commercial loss caused by his revelations. If the secrets have been used to make large profits, the employer may choose instead to sue for an 'account of profits' to recover all the ill-gotten gains, as did the British Government when a sergeant in the British Army abused his position of trust to assist smugglers in Egypt where he was stationed, making a profit of £20,000 which he was ordered to pay to the Crown, his employer (*Reading* v. *Attorney-General* (1942)). The duty of trust extends to independent contractors who acquire confidential information from their privileged position, like a solicitor to a trust who makes a large profit in a takeover bid of a family company owned by the trust by using his inside knowledge. As with medical confidence, the public interest may justify disclosure. The employee who discovers that his employer is illegally threatening the health of his workers or unlawfully discriminating on the ground of sex or race may report the matter to the appropriate agencies, or even the media, as in *Lion Laboratories* v. *Evans* (1984) (above).

How does all this apply to the OH department? It may be that in the course of his employment the doctor or nurse may acquire information which is commercially valuable. He may be consulted about the health risks of a new process, or be given details of a new substance not yet on the market. The competitors of the organisation employing him would be very interested in this information but, needless to say, he should keep it as secret as he does his patients' records. But very occasionally the doctor or nurse may feel that he must speak out without his employer's permission in the interest of the employees or the public outside the factory gates. This is obviously not a step to be lightly taken. Except in an emergency, there should first be consultation with management and with senior health professionals in confidence. Management may be reminded that they have statutory duties under the Health and Safety at Work Act towards both their employees and persons not in their employment. If the doctor or nurse feels that the only way to protect others is to expose a danger this must be done, but he or she should be careful to check the facts and to give the information to those who can best investigate it, probably the HSE, who have a right to inspect the premises at any time, take samples for analysis, etc.

Attempts by NHS authorities to impose contractual obligations on their staff not to speak to the media about NHS authority matters led to many protests from professional groups. A 1992 circular from the Secretary of State for Health upheld the ultimate freedom of speech of NHS workers, but the dismissal of Graham Pink, a Stockport nurse who was publicly critical of understaffing in a geriatric ward, and a report published in 1993 which found that half the 31 professionals studied who had made allegations of fraud, malpractice or inadequate care or abuse of patients had either lost their jobs or been put under pressure to resign, gave cause for concern. The Public Interest (Disclosure) Act became law in 1998 and is now incorporated into the Employment Rights Act 1996. The Faculty of Occupational Medicine's *Guidance on Ethics* (1993) says this:

> 'Increasingly, occupational physicians are involved not only with the health of the workforce, but with the effect of a company's products, processes and practices on the health of the general public, and on the environment. Conflicts of interest may arise if the information provided by the company is not soundly based, accurate and openly available when required. The physician's responsibilities as an employee may clash with concern for public health, and it may be valuable to seek the counsel of professional colleagues in such circumstances, particularly before entering public debate. Physicians may find themselves drawn into debate on television or radio on such issues and will need to be properly prepared. Any information given should be limited to scientifically based facts and the health of named individuals should not be discussed in such circumstances.'

The Act protects workers, including the self-employed, who, in good faith and on reasonable grounds, disclose information relating to crimes, breaches of a legal obligation, miscarriages of justice, dangers to health and safety or the environment, and the concealing of evidence relating to any of these. An employee who makes a disclosure to an external body (like a newspaper or the HSE) will also have to prove that he was not motivated by personal gain and reasonably believed the information to be true. In most cases, the employer must have been approached first. Remedies are available through the employment tribunals to those penalised by the employer (Chapter 8).

An instructive case was *Tracey Cooke* v. *West Yorkshire Probation Board* (2004). Tracey Cooke was an OH nurse employed by the West Yorkshire Probation Board. She reviewed the confidential health questionnaire of Ms X, a job applicant, and reported that there was no medical reason why she should not be employed. The personnel manager noticed that a referee had stated that Ms X's sickness absence was greater than she had revealed in her application form. She asked Ms Cooke to disclose the confidential health questionnaire, but Ms Cooke explained that she could not do so without consent. While Ms Cooke was away from the office at a conference, the personnel manager removed the questionnaire from her files. Ms X had stated in the questionnaire that she had had no substantial periods of absence in the preceding two years, which was not true. The manager concluded that Ms X lacked probity vital to the post and withdrew the job offer. In addition, the manager became aware that Ms X was a carrier of hepatitis B.

Ms Cooke complained to the employer and to the Royal College of Nursing. The employer met with the representative of the RCN, who explained the ethical position, but a month later dismissed Ms Cooke because the relationship of trust and confidence had broken down. 'This was evidenced by the different view that you hold about the way the Occupation [sic] Health Service should work within the organisation.' At the date of dismissal Ms Cooke had not worked for a full year, and was not covered by the general law of unfair dismissal. She claimed, however, that she was protected as a 'whistleblower' under Section 103A of the Employment Rights Act 1996 (inserted by the Public Interest Disclosure Act 1998). She complained to the Leeds employment tribunal that she was dismissed for making a 'protected disclosure' to her employer that it was failing or was likely to fail to comply with a legal obligation to which it was subject (the duty of confidence) and that this was the principal reason for her dismissal. The one-year qualifying period does not apply to dismissal for a protected disclosure. The employer accepted that there was a duty of confidence but argued that a breach was justifiable in this case because it was in the public interest to exclude from employment in the Probation Service a job applicant who had been untruthful in her application. The tribunal found that the public interest was a matter which Ms Cooke should have been asked to consider, and should have been given the opportunity to discuss with Ms X, and that it was wrong to have removed the questionnaire before this could take place. It was held that Tracey Cooke had been unfairly dismissed for making a protected disclosure.

As discussed in Chapter 9, it is questionable whether an employer is entitled to dismiss for dishonesty in such a case, where the medical evidence is that the worker is fit for the job. It seems unduly harsh on those who suffer from conditions that are stigmatised to punish them for being wary about declaring their condition to a prospective employer (*O'Brien* v. *Prudential Assurance Co. Ltd* (1979)).

3.21   *Official secrets*

Any person who obtains information 'owing to his position as a person who holds or has held office under Her Majesty' is bound not to communicate it to unauthorised persons, on pain of conviction of a criminal offence. The Official Secrets Act binds all Crown servants and anyone who receives information from them knowing or having reasonable cause to believe that it is given in contravention of the Act. The fact that someone has or has not 'signed the Official Secrets Act' is legally irrelevant. Doctors and nurses who are employed by the Crown or who work in organisations with Government contracts should be aware of their responsibilities.

The Official Secrets Act 1989 names six kinds of information as needing protection: defence, security and intelligence, international relations, information received in confidence from other governments, information useful to criminals and the interception of telephone calls and mail. It is a defence that the defendant did not know or have reasonable cause to believe that disclosure would be damaging.

3.22   *Defamation*

An action for breach of confidence is almost always a complaint about the release of a truth which the claimant wanted to conceal. Defamation concerns lying statements which have damaged the claimant's reputation. A statement proved true cannot give rise to an action in defamation. The burden of proving a statement true is on the defendant.

To sue in defamation, the claimant must show that a defamatory statement has been made about him, that is a statement likely to bring him into 'hatred, ridicule or contempt'. If the remark is made in a permanent form (writing, film or broadcast), it is libel, if by the spoken word, slander. Untrue allegations that someone is an alcoholic, a drug addict, a homosexual, mentally ill or suffering from a sexually transmitted disease or AIDS are all defamatory. It would also probably be actionable to allege that a manager was careless of the safety of the workforce. For a statement to be actionable, it must be made to at least one person other than the object of it. A discussion between a doctor and a nurse in a private office during which one says to the other that he is incompetent would not give rise to an action in slander, but if the same remark is made in the presence of a secretary an action could be brought (unless proved to be true!).

The law recognises that sometimes allegations have to be made. Proceedings in Parliament and in a court of law are absolutely privileged; this means that no action can be brought for anything said there. In other situations there is qualified privilege: the statement may be made with impunity as long as the maker honestly believed it to be true and confined it to those who had a moral, legal or social interest in receiving it. A doctor is asked to report to the human resources department on a particular employee, with the employee's consent. He writes in confidence that the man is a liar and a malingerer. No action in defamation is possible as long as the belief was honest, even if the accusations were untrue, but if the doctor was acting from motives of spite he may be liable. Where the doctor was negligent in preparing the report, he might be held liable either to employer or employee (whoever suffers loss) in the tort of negligence (Chapter 2).

Chapter 4
Pre-employment Screening and Health Surveillance

4.1 The purpose of 'medical assessment'

This chapter is concerned with all forms of 'medical assessment', of prospective employees or those already in employment, which are designed to give an indication of either the effects of work on the individual or the suitability of the individual to do particular work. When I consult a doctor or nurse, it is normally because I am suffering from a particular symptom and need advice on how, if possible, it can be alleviated. The health professional and I are in a therapeutic relationship. But occasionally I ask the doctor or nurse for reassurance that I am in rude health. My apparent hypochondria is the result of my need, or that of my employer or prospective employer or the community at large, to detect any adverse indications before they become a problem to me or to others.

There are many methods of assessment: the administration of a simple questionnaire, an interview with an OH nurse, a selective clinical examination, e.g. of vision, physiological or biological tests and a full clinical examination by a medical practitioner. Using the terminology of specialists in occupational medicine, the following broad categories may be discerned:

(1) the routine medical examination, e.g. pre-employment, or regular routine examinations of vehicle drivers or senior executives;
(2) special examination of workers identified as exposed to a particular hazard, e.g. audiometric tests, urine tests for workers exposed to carcinogens affecting the urinary tract, blood tests for workers exposed to lead;
(3) screening tests, i.e. 'sorting through a group or population to identify a relatively small number with a certain characteristic' such as colour blindness, cancer of the cervix, hypertension, diabetes;
(4) biological testing, used to identify workers whose performance is or may be affected by the consumption of drugs or alcohol.

The Gregson Report concluded that the main purpose of an occupational health (OH) service is to prevent occupational disease or injury. It has been suggested that there are two kinds of preventive measure: primary and secondary. Primary prevention seeks to break the chain between the risk from exposure to a hazard and its effect on the worker. It includes the complete prohibition of certain highly toxic substances, engineering controls to reduce exposure to less hazardous agents, the provision of personal protective equipment, the monitoring of the environment to ensure that it complies with established standards, the biological monitoring of the worker to assess exposure and the exclusion of workers with a particular susceptibility to the hazard. Secondary prevention is the detection of harmful effects before the worker starts to show symptoms; he may then be removed from the danger before, it is hoped, real harm is done. A third type of preventive measure, in the form of an epidemiological survey, seeks to identify hazards by analysing data from a large number of workers, but once statistical effects cast suspicion on a substance or process, harm has already been done and the prevention of further harm can only be directed at the workers who come after. Medical assessment has, therefore, the following goals:

(1)   the early pre-symptomatic detection of disease;
(2)   the evaluation of the effectiveness of engineering controls and personal protection;
(3)   the detection of health effects previously unknown and unsuspected;
(4)   suitable job placement.

These scientific aims cannot be criticised; it is the methods employed and the use made of the information obtained by the scientists which gives rise to controversy. Kahn-Freund, in his important work, *Labour and the Law*, wrote: 'Any approach to the relations between management and labour is fruitless unless the divergency of their interests is plainly recognised and articulated', or as an American judge put it: 'The war between the profit-maker and the wage-earner is always with us'. Management is concerned with production in the most cost-effective manner. On the whole, young and healthy workers produce more than the old and disabled, so there is always an underlying prejudice against the employment of those whose health is poor. Workers need employment to live and support their families. Many are willing to work in an unhealthy environment as long as they need the money. Men worked in coal mines knowing that they would suffer respiratory problems because there was no other work. The Welfare State provides a cushion for the sick and disabled but it is a thin and uncomfortable one.

The earliest protective legislation was in the field of health and safety because whenever workers entered into bargaining negotiations with employers they were compelled by economics to throw in their physical security as part of the bargain. Employers may consider that medical and biological tests are for the welfare of the employees, but the employees may believe that they are an excuse to make workers redundant. The State explains to workers showing harmful effects that it is for their own good to be excluded from the damaging process, but they may reject this paternalism. Employers argue that they must be able to choose a worker who fits the job they have available. Employees reply that the job should be adjusted to the worker, not the worker to the job. If some workers are particularly susceptible to a substance, why should the solution be to dismiss them and employ a substitute? Why should the law not compel the employer to take precautions to make his process safe for everyone?

Should health professionals accept any kind of assessment, or should they refuse to take part in procedures which may be regarded as an unnecessary invasion of the privacy of the individual? Should they participate in the

administration of a questionnaire which asks about lifestyle and sexual preference? Is an employer entitled to demand information about all aspects of an
applicant's medical history, and that of his parents and grandparents, as the price
of a job?

The OH doctor or nurse is in a very delicate position when it comes to
examining the workers. It is important to ensure that the doctor or nurse are not
perceived as assisting management to reject unwanted staff on spurious medical
grounds. For this reason, the ethics of medical assessment are as important as the
law. All matters of ethics are open to debate, but it is suggested that the following
principles would receive general acceptance:

(1)   A programme of assessment should only be undertaken if the results will be
      of substantial benefit, either to individuals affected by disease or other
      workers who may be assisted to avoid it. The discovery that asbestos causes
      cancer did not benefit those unfortunates who died of lung cancer or
      mesothelioma but it enabled thousands of others to avoid exposure. The
      examination should be designed to detect specific effects. Routine exam-
      inations of general health may bring a false sense of security and take time
      and money that could be better used.
(2)   The methods used must be reliable. Too many false positives or negatives
      make any form of testing unacceptable. Tests must be both sensitive (giving
      positive results in the presence of disease) and specific (giving negative
      results in the absence of disease). Sensitivity is more important than speci-
      ficity, because positive results will be investigated but negative results will
      not. Audiometry tests must be able to test permanent hearing loss, not just
      whether a worker is suffering from a bad cold, so that the numbers and
      timing of tests must be scientifically determined. Doctors have propounded
      the theory that routine examinations for cancer of the bladder, which takes
      years to develop, should not be given to workers in the early years but only
      after a substantial period of exposure, otherwise the statistics will falsely
      reassure that workers are not being exposed to dangerous levels.
(3)   The methods of assessment must not in themselves create a hazard to the
      worker which outweighs their preventive value. One million low back
      radiography tests are done every year in the USA, although their effective-
      ness has not been established and they are estimated to result in sixteen
      leukaemia cases every year through radiation exposure.
(4)   Routine examinations should not be used as an alternative to engineering
      controls or environmental monitoring but in addition to them.
(5)   Personnel must be adequately trained to conduct and interpret the results of
      physiological or biological tests.
(6)   Individuals must consent to be examined or tested and must be told the
      results of any tests which should not normally be released to third parties
      without the subject's consent.

The Health and Safety Executive in 1999 published the second edition of *Health
Surveillance at Work* (the first edition was published in 1990), the purpose of which
is to help all those responsible for and concerned with the control of occupational

health risks to decide when surveillance of those exposed to such risks should be
introduced and what form it should take.

In 1996 Honey, Hillage, Patch and Morris from the Institute for Employment
Studies published a comprehensive research report, *Health Surveillance in Great
Britain* (HSE Research Report 121/1996). The research found that surveillance was
most common in larger organisations and the manufacturing sector. The main
reasons were to protect employees from risks, to comply with health and safety
law and to check the effectiveness of control measures. Practice varied as to
whether health surveillance was compulsory or optional. Only 69 per cent of
employers undertaking surveillance maintained health records. There was considerable confusion about what is meant by health surveillance. It should be
distinguished from general health screening i.e. aspects of the employees' health
not related to the working environment, but which still affect the health and fitness of the workforce.

4.2   Pre-employment health screening

Twenty years ago the Health and Safety Executive (HSE) (*Guidance Note MS 20*
(1982)) advised that routine pre-employment health screening of general health in
an unselective manner is a waste of time and money, other than a self-
administered questionnaire which can be examined by a doctor or nurse. It
recommended that a more complex procedure be undertaken only in the following circumstances:

(1)   The job requires the worker to enter a hazardous environment to which he
      has not previously been exposed (e.g. compressed air, deep sea diving,
      ionising radiations, lead).
(2)   The work contains specific hazards to the community at large (e.g. transport,
      health care or catering).
(3)   The work demands high standards of physical or mental fitness (e.g. police,
      fire services).
(4)   Industries where there is a statutory obligation to examine workers before
      they commence employment (e.g. work with compressed air, work involving
      exposure to ionising radiations and lead).

Pre-employment examinations involve an assessment of (i) the applicant and
(ii) the job. As well as specifically job-related defects (previous high exposure to
a dangerous substance, allergy to a substance, genetic disposition to adverse
reaction, etc.), many employers are reluctant to employ an applicant if his general health is such that he is likely to be off sick for substantial periods. They
accept that established employees may fall ill, but they do not want to take on
'bad risks'. The introduction of the Disability Discrimination Act has created
significant legal controls over the pre-employment assessment. Where a job
applicant's physical or mental health problem constitutes a disability under the
Act (Chapter 9) care must be taken to explore whether a reasonable adjustment
to the job could enable the person with a disability to be employed. Reliance on

health and safety law to justify discrimination must be based on evidence, not prejudice.

The OH professional should not be party to the exclusion of job applicants unless there is clear evidence that the job carries specific health risks and also that certain individuals are likely to be more affected than the general population. In its original guidance the HSE gave two examples: candidates for work with lung allergens who have a history of asthma should not be automatically excluded (though an individual medical assessment may be appropriate), but those who wish to work in regular contact with irritants and who have a firm diagnosis of eczema should. If the employer is concerned that the asthmatic whose condition is aggravated by the lung allergen will sue him for negligence, the opinion of experts who can demonstrate that it would be necessary to exclude many job applicants in order to be sure of rejecting the one susceptible individual can be sought. It can then be argued that the employer, and his OH personnel, have taken reasonable care. The following statutes impose duties not to discriminate.

4.3   *Human Rights Act 1998*

An outline of the Act may be found in the General Introduction, at the beginning of the book.

Article 8 of the European Convention on Human Rights, now incorporated into UK law by means of the 1998 Act, provides as follows:

(1)   Everyone has the right to respect for his private and family life, his home and his correspondence.
(2)   There shall be no interference by a public authority with the exercise of this right except such as is in accordance with law and is necessary in a democratic society in the interests of national security, public safety or the economic well-being of the country, for the protection of health or morals, or for the protection of the rights and freedoms of others.

Any medical or health screening, even asking questions about someone's physical or mental health or condition, is an invasion of privacy. It must therefore be justified. Although a direct action for breach of the Convention can be brought only against a public authority employer (civil service, local authority, NHS Trust, police force, etc.), since courts and tribunals are public authorities they must interpret legislation and develop the common law so as to uphold Convention principles, as far as possible. In many cases health screening is justified either by public safety or the protection of health.

To comply with Article 8, screening must be 'in accordance with law'. In my view, this requires either a specific statutory provision, as in the COSHH Regulations, discussed later in this chapter, or an obligation imposed by the contract of employment. It must also be justified by one of the interests set out in Article 8(2).

In *Peters* v. *Netherlands* (1994) the European Court of Human Rights held that the taking of compulsory urine samples for prison drug testing was contrary to Article 8. The 'other' European Court, the European Court of Justice in Luxembourg, applied Article 8 in X v. *Commission of the European Communities* (1995). A candidate for an administrative post in the Commission agreed to undergo a routine medical examination pre-employment but refused to be specifically screened for HIV antibodies. A blood test revealed a low-level T-cell count, from which the Commission's medical officer concluded that the applicant had full-blown AIDS. He was refused employment on the ground that he was physically unfit. The court held that the test had been performed without consent, and that this was contrary to Article 8. The right to respect for private life includes a person's right to keep his or her state of health secret. This was a Delphic victory. The court also held: 'If the person concerned, after being properly informed, withholds his consent to a test which the medical officer considers necessary to evaluate his suitability for the post for which he has applied, the [employer] cannot be obliged to take the risk of recruiting him.' Of course, not all tests will be justified. The employer will have to show that the tests are necessary in relation to the post for which the job applicant has applied. The Commission job involved residence in a country where there was only limited access to medical care. Although the now defunct European Commission of Human Rights held that a contract of employment can exclude Convention rights (*Rommelfanger* v. *Federal Republic of Germany* (1989)), this will still have to be justified under Article 8(2). Employers cannot put obligations to submit to health surveillance or random drug tests into contracts unless they can show a reason falling within Article 8. In my view, a requirement that an employee should be seen by occupational health after a specified period of absence is justifiable, partly because the employee's health may be a cause for concern, partly because he may be suffering from a condition which might create a risk to others, and partly because the employer can balance its own commercial and property rights or those of its customers against the employee's right to privacy. The same arguments justify pre-employment health screening. The employer cannot *force* anyone to have tests, but he can 'draw adverse inferences' from their refusal.

4.4   *Disability Discrimination Act 1995*

This has been of particular concern to the OH profession, and for that reason it is necessary to give a full account, which is found in Chapter 9: Equal Opportunities.

The Act repeals the Disabled Persons (Employment) Acts 1944 and 1958. Registered disabled holders of green cards were given disabled status for three years, but after that they have had to prove their disabled status in the same way as everyone else. The registration system has been abandoned, and able-bodied workers may work as car park attendants and lift attendants. There is no longer any obligation on an employer to maintain a quota of disabled workers. From 1 October 2004 the Act applies to all employers, other than the Crown in respect of the armed forces.

The Act is accompanied by a Code of Practice and Guidance which can be taken into account by employment tribunals in deciding cases. It makes it unlawful for an employer to discriminate against a disabled person on the grounds of disability both pre-employment, while the employment continues, and on termination of employment. It is therefore very relevant to pre-employment screening. By the

Companies (Directors' Report) (Employment of Disabled Persons) Regulations 1980, companies which employ on average more than 250 employees must report annually on company policy regarding the employment, training, career development and promotion of disabled people.

4.5 *Sex Discrimination Acts 1975 and 1986*

Employers are not permitted to discriminate against a job applicant on the ground of sex or, in the case of a married person, of marital status. Assumptions based on sex stereotypes cannot be made about the physical or mental abilities of a candidate. Thus, an employer who turns down a female applicant because the job is a heavy one and 'a woman couldn't cope' will be acting unlawfully. However, if the employer can prove that this particular job requires qualities which this particular applicant cannot fulfil he is not acting unlawfully if he rejects the application. He is then denying the applicant the job on grounds of suitability, not sex. Mrs Thorn applied for a job which involved radial drilling. She was refused it because she was short and slight and might therefore injure herself. The employers were able to convince the tribunal that had the application come from a short slight man they would also have refused him the job (*Thorn* v. *Meggitt Engineering* (1976)). This was not an act of sex discrimination, but a genuine assessment of the candidate's qualifications. If the employer rejects an applicant on such grounds he is in a much better position to defend himself if the applicant has been interviewed and assessed *before* the decision to reject the application (see Chapter 9).

The employer must not discriminate against a job applicant on the ground that she is pregnant, or might become pregnant. This is automatic direct discrimination on grounds of sex, since men cannot become pregnant, and is discussed in greater detail in Chapter 9.

It is common for employers to ask female job applicants to give answers to a pre-employment questionnaire which asks them about specifically female problems such as painful periods or premenstrual syndrome. Should the (probably rare) applicant who honestly admits that she regularly has to take one or two days off at the time of her period be excluded? The justification for this apparent sex discrimination would be that a male applicant who admitted to such regular absences for a health reason would also be classified as unfit. OH personnel are advised that this is a sensitive issue which may give rise to resentment and mistrust and that the question should probably only be asked if it is made clear that the purpose is to assist employees with a health problem, not discrimination. This is especially the case where the job is one predominantly done by males, because it may be seen as an excuse to keep women out. It is interesting to note that an employment tribunal in Bury St Edmunds has held that a woman who was virtually housebound at the time of her periods was disabled within the Disability Discrimination Act (*Mitchell* v. *Genchem Holdings Ltd* (2003)).

The HSE (*Surveillance of people exposed to health risks at work* (1990)) recommended that the more stringent statutory limits on exposure and absorption for women of reproductive capacity because of risks to the foetus (for instance from lead or ionising radiations) should not be used as a basis for discrimination against the recruitment of women. This advice does not appear in the second edition: *Health Surveillance at Work* (1999).

A difficult question which has yet to be answered by the judges concerns employers who demand compulsory blood tests for all prospective employees with the intention of rejecting anyone who is carrying the AIDS virus (HIV). Because, at present, most of those affected are males, such testing is a form of indirect discrimination against men. The employer will therefore have to justify it by showing that there is a good reason for exclusion other than that of sex. Possible justification might be the danger to others. British Airways has already decided to screen all candidates for pilots' jobs for HIV antibodies, lest loss of memory and intellectual function create a risk to passengers, but in most jobs there is no such excuse. I would argue that the prejudice of other workers is insufficient justification, because unlawful discrimination is not excused by the equal prejudice of others. If the job is one in which the employer has to invest in the worker by giving him expensive training, the prediction that he will not be able to give any length of service could be economic justification. The Department of Health has invited consultation on a proposal that all health professionals new to the NHS, and all students in training, who are likely to perform exposure-prone procedures should submit to an HIV test (see Chapter 2). The justification for this would be that an HIV-positive health care worker is prohibited from performing such procedures because of the small risk of transmission of the virus. Where an employee is to be sent to a country like Saudi Arabia, which demands an HIV test as part of immigration control, that also would justify testing. Doctors and nurses who carry out HIV testing have an ethical duty to provide pre-test counselling, and to make provision for further counselling should the test prove positive.

Employers might also be reminded of the 'window', the period between exposure and the appearance of antibodies in the blood during which the test would show a false negative, and of the ever present possibility that someone who tested negative yesterday may be in contact with the virus tomorrow.

Infection with HIV does not attract the protection of the Disability Discrimination Act until symptoms, however slight, begin to appear. The Government has indicated its intention to change the law to cover those diagnosed as HIV positive from date of diagnosis (Draft Disability Discrimination Bill (2003)) (see Chapter 9).

4.6   *Race Relations Act 1976*

This prohibits discrimination on grounds of colour, race or ethnic or national origins. It is, however, permissible to discriminate indirectly if it can be shown that there is a good reason other than race (see Chapter 9). Care must be taken with the questions asked of job applicants. An occupational physician in the West Midlands who asked black candidates whether they used cannabis, but did not ask the same question of white and Asian candidates, was accused of racial discrimination. It is permissible to ask applicants if they drink or smoke or take drugs, but all applicants should be asked the same questions. Note that you can be held to have discriminated unlawfully if the *effect* of what you do is discriminatory, whatever your *motive* may have been.

There are special legal rules about nationals of other EC countries. Every citizen of any Member State in principle has the same right to employment on the same terms as a national of the 'home state', assuming that he has the necessary qualifications. The same applies to social security provision.

Scientists are beginning to claim that they can predict which members of the population will be more susceptible to certain substances by genetic screening. For example, sickle cell trait increases susceptibility to hypoxia, and alpha-1 antitrypsin deficiency predisposes to the development of emphysema in some circumstances, as after exposure to cadmium fume. Molecular biology may soon enable us to detect sensitivity to occupational carcinogens. If inherited traits are found more often in one racial group, the workers may conclude that these techniques are a disguised form of racial discrimination. The law permits the use of this kind of test in selection for employment as long as the employer can prove that it is justified by the need to protect the workers. He would have to show that the test was reliable and the risk of serious harm to susceptible workers substantial. Genetic screening is discussed later in this chapter.

It is arguable that the exclusion of hepatitis B and hepatitis C carriers from employment involving exposure-prone procedures in the NHS is racially discriminatory, since the incidence of hepatitis in Asia and sub-Saharan Africa is higher than in Europe (the same applies to HIV). If it is, and I believe that to be the case, it is justifiable by the need to protect patients (see Chapter 2).

The Race Relations Act 1976 (Amendment) Regulations 2003 were introduced to implement the European Race Directive 2000. The European Union now outlaws racial discrimination of all kinds, not just discrimination against EU nationals, as before.

In 2003 regulations prohibiting religious discrimination came into force in England and Wales and Scotland. Prior to this, religious discrimination had been prohibited only in Northern Ireland (see Chapter 9).

4.7   Rehabilitation of Offenders Act 1974

The Act provides that, if a person convicted of a criminal offence completes a specified period (which varies with the sentence imposed – ten years for a sentence of imprisonment of more than six months but not exceeding thirty months, seven years for six months or less etc.) without reoffending, he can, in effect, forget the conviction, which is described as spent, when he is applying for a job. Most of the 'caring' professions – doctor, nurse, social worker, teacher – have been excluded, as well as the administration of justice, betting, insurance, finance and work with explosives. A conviction which has become spent or any failure to disclose it is not a proper ground for excluding a person from any office, profession, occupation or employment. The Act does not provide for any remedy for the person excluded, but the courts might be willing to create an action for damage for breach of statutory duty. It would be an unfair dismissal to sack an employee because he had kept a spent conviction from his employer.

Legislation has now been passed to allow employers to demand the criminal records of prospective employees. A full vetting check (including spent convictions

and police cautions) is available from the Criminal Records Bureau for jobs
involving work with children and vulnerable adults. They will in due course be
available for professions in health, pharmacy and law and senior managers in
banking and financial services. Criminal conviction certificates (which will not
contain spent convictions) for other employees will also eventually be available
(Police Act 1997). Difficulties in the introduction of a computerised system, and the
need to check all those working with children, following a series of child sex abuse
and murder cases causing great public disquiet, have meant that the legislation is
not yet fully in force.

4.8   Does the job applicant have to answer the employer's questions?

Apart from statutory restrictions, the employer is virtually free to require any
questions or examinations he likes. Since there is no legal obligation on a job
applicant to volunteer information about himself, unlike an applicant for insurance, the employer is well advised to ask specific questions if the matter is
material to him. The job applicant is free to refuse to answer, a hollow freedom
when he does not get the job. On the other hand, managers have obligations to
employees and to the public as well as shareholders: it is understandable that they
are unwilling to take risks.

   This dilemma is well illustrated by the case of *O'Brien* v. *Prudential Assurance
Co.* (1979). O'Brien applied for a job with the Prudential as a district agent visiting people in their homes. He had a history of mental illness, including periods
in hospital. However, at the time of his application, he had not had to consult a
doctor for other than minor complaints for four years. When he applied for the
job he was required to fill in a form which asked whether he had ever suffered
from a serious illness and was also medically examined by a medical referee
who asked whether he had ever consulted a psychiatrist or suffered from nervous or mental disorder. O'Brien deliberately lied in answer to these questions
because he knew that he would not get the job if he told the truth (this was
later confirmed by the employers). Having obtained employment, he proved to
be completely satisfactory and colleagues and superiors spoke highly of him,
but in the following year he applied for life assurance with the company and
gave consent for his GP to give a medical report. Thus, the whole of his previous medical history was disclosed. The junior manager recommended to his
senior that a report be obtained from a consultant psychiatrist, but the senior
manager instead referred the case to the Company's Principal Medical Adviser.
He recommended that O'Brien be dismissed and this was done without further
medical evidence being obtained. The reason given was the previous medical
history which had not been disclosed in the job application.

   Consultant psychiatrists gave evidence at the industrial tribunal where O'Brien
was complaining of unfair dismissal that there was no reason why he was currently unsuitable for employment and it was argued that a consultant's report to
that effect should have been solicited by management before reaching a decision.
The tribunal determined that the reason for the dismissal was not his conduct or

capability in employment but his past medical history. They held that employers are entitled to lay down qualifications for candidates and to specify as a policy that they would not employ someone to visit customers in their private homes who had a history of mental illness. Medical evidence from consultants would not have made any difference to the decision, because it was based on the past not the present state of O'Brien's mental health.

When the case went on appeal to the Employment Appeal Tribunal it was decided that past medical history was in a sense a qualification for a job, so that an applicant with a history of ill-health could be regarded as lacking an essential requirement. However, 'it must depend on the facts of the case as to whether for a particular employment the employer behaves reasonably in stipulating the conditions which he seeks to establish'. Was it reasonable for the Prudential to exclude someone from this particular job who had been in a mental hospital? The judge said that it was reasonable not only to impose such a condition at the beginning but also to enforce it in the case of someone who had misled them as to facts which they regarded as important:

> 'It is necessary to stress that this practice or policy is, it appears, one limited to appointment as a district agent, with the particular features of the employment to which we have referred. What the position would be in relation to some other category of employment, where a person had a history of mental illness, is a different question and would always need to be looked at on the particular facts of the case.'

As to the failure to obtain medical evidence other than from the GP and the occupational physician, the Appeal Tribunal considered that it would have been better to obtain consultant advice, but that they would accept the tribunal's finding that it would not have made any difference, because neither consultant who gave evidence was able to guarantee that there would be no recurrence of the illness. The House of Lords decision in *Polkey* v. *Dayton Services* (1987), which emphasises the importance of following a fair procedure, probably means that it is now advisable to obtain such a report.

The *O'Brien* decision must now be reviewed in the light of the disability discrimination legislation (Chapter 9). O'Brien would almost certainly now qualify as a disabled person, since past disabilities are included under the protection of the Act. The revised Code of Practice (2004), paragraph 8.21 says this:

> 'The Act does not prevent a disabled person keeping a disability confidential from the employer. But keeping a disability confidential is likely to mean that unless the employer could reasonably be expected to know about it anyway, the employer will not be under a duty to make a reasonable adjustment. If a disabled person expects an employer to make a reasonable adjustment, he will need to provide the employer – or, as the case may be, someone acting on the employer's behalf – with sufficient information to carry out that adjustment.'

In O'Brien's case, he was asked a specific question and told a lie. This is more than a failure to disclose, it is a misrepresentation. If made knowingly, it is a fraudulent misrepresentation. In my view, the vital question is whether the employer would have acted lawfully in rejecting O'Brien's job application had he been honest about his history of mental illness. The employer must show that this would have been a justified response because of the nature of the illness and the nature of the job. The employer cannot rely on the mere fact of the dishonesty, because the dismissal was 'for a reason related to the disabled person's disability', that is a lie about the disability. If I am wrong about this, those who have a disability are in the invidious position of risking rejection if they tell the truth, but risking dismissal if they are found to have lied, whether or not the disability in itself justifies rejection. The argument that the disabled person has obtained the employment by fraud, and therefore should not benefit by his wrongdoing, is answered by submitting that the lie is only the reason for obtaining the job if the employer would have been justified in rejecting the job applicant had he been informed of the true state of affairs. Otherwise, it makes no difference.

The case of Beverly Allitt, the nurse suffering from Münchausen's syndrome by proxy, who murdered several children in her charge, has led to calls to exclude anyone with a history of psychiatric illness from the caring professions. It is important that the understandably horrified reaction of the public to the facts of that case does not lead to a witch-hunt. The nursing profession advocated the setting of national selection criteria for those seeking employment as a nurse, a sensible method of ensuring that such criteria are properly debated and scientifically justified. An audit of selection criteria in the NHS was instituted. Ultimately, it will be in the discretion of the OH professional conducting the confidential pre-employment procedure as to whether he or she classifies the job applicant as unfit (clinical details should not, of course, be revealed without the applicant's consent). NHS employers have become even more sensitive to these issues following the conviction of Amanda Jenkinson, a nurse jailed for five years for assaulting a patient after tampering with life-support machinery in order to discredit a colleague.

The Report of the Allitt Inquiry was published in 1994 by HMSO. The inquiry was commissioned by the Secretary of State for Health and was chaired by a former Ombudsman, Sir Cecil Clothier. The report of the inquiry into the Jenkinson case was published in 1997. It was commissioned by North Nottinghamshire Health Authority and chaired by Richard Bullock. Both reports recommend that in the pre-employment stage a prospective employee might be required to obtain confirmation from her GP that there is nothing in her medical history which might make her unsuitable. The Clothier Report recommends that records of sickness absence in previous employment should be obtained from job applicants. For some time it has been the practice to reject applicants for nursing training or jobs who have a history of conditions like anorexia during the previous two years. This has been rejected by the NHS and is probably a breach of the Disability Discrimination Act 1995.

The Bullock Report goes further. It is critical of OH personnel who 'should be reminded of their duty not only to the employee or potential employee to whom they render professional services, but also to that employee's patients or colleagues'. The underlying message is that the OH department should be more willing to release sensitive information to line managers. In my view, this should be strongly resisted. Line managers are not usually qualified to make medical assessments. They must accept that this is the proper function of OH professionals. Mistakes will occasionally be made, but the need to maintain trust is more important. As Sir Cecil Clothier put it: 'Civilised society has very little defence against the aimless malice of a deranged mind'.

The Disability Discrimination Act (Chapter 9) does not oblige anyone to reveal any existing or prior disability, but it protects against unjustifiable discrimination on the grounds of the disability. Would the decision in *O'Brien* v. *Prudential Assurance* be different in 2004? Is a history of mental illness justification for excluding a disabled person from a job? Is it not a reflection of the prejudices of society which a generation ago led to patients being confined to secure hospitals to keep them away from the rest of us? I would argue that OH doctors and nurses are better able to assess job applicants than are managers. Adolescents suffer from eating disorders, students have exam nerves, mothers have post-natal depression, workers suffer depression through marital break-up, bullying at work, redundancy and all the 'slings and arrows of outrageous fortune'. None of these is likely to commit offences of violence.

When a prospective employee conceals disabilities from the employer because he fears that otherwise he will not be appointed, he puts himself and others at risk. In one case a man who suffered from epileptic fits kept this fact from the employer. While on a working platform 23 feet above the ground he had an epileptic fit, fell off the platform and was killed. It was held that as the employer could not be expected to know of the employee's disability he was not negligent in allowing him to work at a height (*Cork* v. *Kirby Maclean* (1952)). The employee also deprives himself of the right to ask the employer for reasonable adjustments to allow him to work, since under the Disability Discrimination Act that right arises only where the employer knows, or ought to know, of the disability.

4.9   *Examination for entry to the pension scheme*

The OH physician may frequently fulfil a dual role, examining the prospective employee both for suitability for the job and as a candidate for a pension. In the first instance he is usually reporting to the employer and in the second to the trustees of the pension fund. This is particularly important in the public sector, where generous ill-health retirement pensions have to be financed from current income, as in the police forces, and government policy is to try to reduce the numbers of ill-health retirements. Now that the Disability Discrimination Act applies to the police, prison officers and firefighters, OH personnel in those fields will be asked to estimate whether it is more likely than not that the recruit will be able to work until normal retirement age. Where it is less than 50 per cent likely, typically the recruit will not be admitted to ill-health retirement benefits but will pay reduced pension contributions to allow for this (Disability Discrimination Act (Pensions) Regulations 2003).

4.10   *Surveillance of the existing workforce*

More legal constraints are imposed on the employer who has accepted the worker into his organisation. For this reason, personnel departments are concentrating increasingly on the pre-employment stage, hoping to weed out the potential problem cases at the outset. Once the agreement has been made, the worker, employee or independent contractor, has the protection of the law of contract, and after one year's continuous service employees can complain to an employment tribunal that they have been unfairly dismissed (see Chapter 8). It is common for an offer of employment to be made subject to a satisfactory medical examination. This allows the employer to escape from the contract in the event of an unsatis-factory report. Where the employee is allowed to start work before the medical can be arranged, it should be made clear that this is subject to a condition that, should he or she fail the medical, the contract will automatically terminate. This will not be effective to exclude liability under the Disability Discrimination Act, but will protect the employer against an action for breach of contract.

A contract is concluded and becomes legally binding once there is an agree-ment; there is in general no necessity in law for the agreement to be in writing, though written evidence is better than oral in the event of a dispute. If an employer desires the inclusion in the contract of a particular obligation he is well advised to spell it out clearly in writing. In consequence, an employer who has decided that he wants his employees to undergo medical examinations or tests, either at random or at regular intervals, must specify this as a term of the contract at the time the worker is hired. If this has not been done, it will be a breach of contract for the employer to try to insist on testing at a later date unless he can show that there was an *implied* term to that effect or he can persuade the individual workers to agree to its introduction (trade union officials have no power to give a group consent to a change in the terms of a contract), or there is an overriding statutory duty to undergo testing.

The leading case on this point concerned no less a person than a consultant orthopaedic surgeon, Mr Bliss. Complaints had been made about his alleged intemperate behaviour to the Regional Medical Officer (RMO) who had referred the matter to a committee of three consultants (the 'Three Wise Men'). They concluded that Bliss was sane and that it was the orthopaedic department which had suffered the breakdown. After this the RMO asked Bliss to undergo a psy-chiatric examination by a consultant nominated by the health authority. When Bliss refused, he was suspended on full pay from his post as a consultant and denied access to the hospital. The Court of Appeal decided that there was no legal obligation on a consultant to submit to a medical examination when asked, unless the employer had reasonable grounds for believing that he might be suffering from physical or mental disability which might cause harm to patients or adversely affect the quality of the treatment of patients, when there would be an implied term in the contract. There were no reasonable grounds here, because the Wise Men had already investigated the case and found him sane. In consequence, the health authority were in breach of contract and must pay compensation for the earnings from private patients which Bliss had lost, though not for injury to his dignity and feelings, because that is not a recognised head of damages for breach of contract (*Bliss* v. *SE Thames RHA* (1985)). There was no action for defamation because the allegations about mental instability had been confined to those covered by qualified privilege; if a statement had been made to the press or the matter gossiped about at the golf club, Bliss could have claimed for loss of reputation (see Chapter 3).

Clearly, the courts are ready to accept that in the case of some employees there is an implied term in the contract of employment that they will submit to a medical examination when reasonably requested. Which employees? The answer seems to be those like health professionals whose illness could constitute a risk to others. Terms will not be implied if the reason for the tests is to protect the employees themselves or to ensure that the employer is not sued for negligence. Does this mean that an employer can lawfully introduce HIV or alcohol or drugs testing for all without the consent of his employees? Only if he can show that there is a real risk to others if the problem remains undetected. In the case of HIV this will be confined to a very few jobs.

Fear of AIDS has led to pressure on the Government to introduce compulsory testing of health professionals for HIV. Health professionals have responded with a call for the compulsory testing of patients. Department of Health guidelines and professional bodies prefer to place the responsibility on the health professional to volunteer for a test if he or she thinks there may be a risk. This has already been discussed in Chapter 2.

All health care workers in the NHS who perform exposure-prone procedures (where there is a risk that injury to the worker may result in exposure of the patient's open tissues to the blood of the worker) and all medical, dental, nursing and midwifery students are now immunised against hepatitis B, unless immunity as a result of natural infection or previous exposure has been documented. Their responses to the vaccine should be subsequently checked. Staff whose work involves exposure-prone procedures (surgery and dentistry are particularly high risk areas) and who fail to respond to the vaccine should be permitted to continue in their work provided they are not e-antigen (HBeAg) positive carriers of the virus nor have a high viral load of surface antigen (see Chapter 2). Otherwise, employers should make every effort to provide alternative employment. It is recommended that all matters arising from and relating to the employment of hepatitis B positive health care workers are co-ordinated through a consultant in occupational medicine. The same advice applies to carriers of hepatitis C, though as yet tests are not compulsory.

Since this is only advice, and does not have the force of law, legal problems may surface where an existing employee refuses immunisation or subsequent monitoring. The employer will have to argue that there is an implied duty in the health care worker's contract of employment to agree to these procedures. There is less difficulty where the employee is entering employment, because his new contract can and should include an express term. Where an existing employee falls within the guidelines, and no satisfactory alternative post can be found, it may be necessary for the employee to take early retirement or be dismissed. The employer would probably succeed in the defence that the employee has become unfit to do the job, in the same way as if he had succumbed to a crippling disease. The Faculty of Occupational Medicine recommends that clear procedures should be in place in advance to deal with cases where the test result indicates a change of duties, and where the employee or student declines to be tested or immunised. Viral hepatitis is a prescribed disease for health care workers and benefits are available under either the NHS Injury Benefits Scheme or the Industrial Injuries Scheme (see Chapter 6).

What is the importance of establishing that the employee is in breach of contract if he refuses the test or the immunisation? It allows the employer to dismiss him without a breach of contract on the employer's part, because it is then the employee who has destroyed the relationship and not the employer. It also makes it more likely that the dismissal will be upheld as fair in an employment tribunal. Sensible employers negotiate with their workers to include an express term in every contract, pointing out the benefit to fellow workers as well as to the public. It is not sufficient, though common, to impose a compulsory medical only after a period of absence from work; those suffering from severe psychiatric illness may not take time off, insisting that there is nothing wrong with them.

Of course, no health professional will wish to be associated with oppression of the workforce, and the industrial relations implications of medical examinations or biological tests must be taken into account. In such a sensitive area the role of the OH professional is as an expert to be able to present the available scientific information to both sides impartially and to stand by the ethical rules of his or her profession in consultation with other professionals.

All examinations and tests may only be performed with the consent of the individual. The exception is the police who, when investigating a serious crime, have power to take intimate samples without consent, though police surgeons refuse to carry out intimate body searches without consent. However, an employee who is contractually bound to undergo an examination is not in a strong legal position if he is disciplined or dismissed for refusing. It is a moot point whether an employee can be prosecuted under section 7 HSWA, which imposes on him an obligation to co-operate with the employer in performing the employer's statutory duties, for refusing to submit to a test where there is no specific statutory or contractual duty on him to do so. I think that our courts would be very unwilling to make a worker criminally liable for an omission to do something for which neither his contract nor Parliament has provided, especially in the light of the Human Rights Act 1998. The section was principally intended to impose on the employee a duty to wear personal protection and make use of safety precautions provided by the employer.

4.11   Levels of routine health surveillance

Occupational health hazards vary from industry to industry and job to job. Employers must be flexible in both the levels of health surveillance and the personnel employed to carry it out. For example, although a doctor might be in overall charge of biological or physiological tests, the tests themselves can be performed by nurses or other trained personnel. A doctor is not needed if hazards are low and there are easily recognisable and specific symptoms, e.g. a rash, as long as workers manifesting those symptoms are immediately sent for medical advice. In the case of greater risk, health professionals will be needed. The following levels are possible:

(1) *Screening tests.* These are designed to identify specific biological or physiological changes in workers known to be at risk. They include blood and urine tests, lung function and audiometry. They should be carried out by personnel specially trained in standard procedures and the results compared with approved reference levels. OH nurses, occupational hygienists and technicians are suitable to undertake testing. Where tests are required by statute the relevant Regulations and Approved Codes of Practice will have to be followed.
(2) *Review of records.* This can be employed in cases where there is a known risk but no agreed method of monitoring its effects on workers, e.g. substances creating mood changes. A member of the occupational health team can compare records of sickness absence with environmental records showing degrees of exposure, hours worked and so on.
(3) *Clinical examination by a doctor.* This includes both initial and periodic examinations and is probably supplemented by tests. These can take place at regular intervals, e.g. airline pilots, or if the results of tests or a review of records so indicate.

4.12 Legal duty to provide health surveillance

Employers can be held civilly liable at common law for failing to introduce health surveillance even in the absence of specific statutory regulation. In *Wright v. Dunlop Rubber Co.* (1972) the employers used an anti-oxidant called Nonox S in their process. ICI, the manufacturers, then discovered that it contained free beta-naphthylamine, a known carcinogen and now a prohibited substance, and withdrew it. In 1960 a circular from the Rubber Manufacturers Employers' Association warned that all employees who had been exposed should be screened and tested for bladder cancer, a disease with a long latency period which can be successfully treated if caught in the early stage. Dunlop stopped using Nonox in 1949 but did not introduce urine tests for workers who had been exposed until 1965. Only then was it discovered that the plaintiff had cancer of the bladder (hundreds of other cases subsequently came to light). It was held that in addition to the liability of the manufacturer the employer was liable in negligence for failing to institute tests quickly enough. This should have been done in 1960. At that time there was no statutory obligation (it was later introduced by the COSHH Regulations 1988).

There is now a specific statutory provision applying to all employees other than those working on sea-going ships. This is Regulation 5 of the Management of Health and Safety at Work Regulations 1992:

'Every employer shall ensure that his employees are provided with such health surveillance as is appropriate having regard to the risks to their health and safety which are identified by the assessment.'

Where a risk has been well documented and established, eventually the State may intervene and demand that the employer introduce a health surveillance programme regulated by inspectors with statutory powers. The provisions of such legislation will, of course, vary with each set of regulations, but common factors can be discerned. If a specific problem arises, reference must be made to the relevant regulations, but the following general comments may be helpful:

(1) Health surveillance strictly speaking is a response to a risk to the health of workers created by continued exposure to a dangerous substance, e.g. lead or ionising radiation. Medical examinations as a means of ensuring that an individual who may constitute a risk to the public, e.g. a public service driver, is fit to do the job are in a different category. The protection of the public is often achieved by a system of licensing under which an applicant must pass a medical test to be given a licence or have it renewed.

(2) In both cases it is usually necessary to examine the worker at the hiring stage so that a 'baseline' can be established. Sometimes, pre-employment screening may reveal defects which lead to the rejection of the job applicant.

(3) The statutory obligation is usually placed on both employer and employee. For example, the Control of Lead at Work Regulations 2002 provide that an employer shall secure that each of his employees employed on work which exposes that employee to lead is under medical surveillance by an Employment Medical Adviser (EMA) or Appointed Doctor (AD) if either the exposure to lead is significant or the doctor has certified that the employee must be under medical surveillance. It goes on to state that every employee who is exposed to lead at work shall, when required by the employer, present himself, during his normal working hours, for such medical examination or biological tests as may be required to allow the employer to carry out his statutory duty. There is, therefore, no need to include a contractual term, because the employee is in breach of the statute and in theory can be prosecuted if he declines to be tested. The Ionising Radiations Regulations 1999 oblige the employee not only to present himself for a medical examination and tests but also to furnish the EMA or AD with such information concerning his health as the doctor may reasonably require. An employer would clearly be justified in sacking a worker who refused these statutory tests, because he would be in contravention of the criminal law (see Chapter 8). The following statutory regulations place a duty on the employee to present himself for health surveillance: Control of Lead at Work Regulations 2002, Ionising Radiations Regulations 1999, Control of Asbestos at Work Regulations 2002, COSHH Regulations 2002, Work in Compressed Air Regulations 1996. The latter not only impose a duty of medical surveillance, but also require the provision of adequate facilities for medical treatment.

(4) The EMA or AD commonly has a statutory power in effect to stop the worker working by certifying him as unfit if the results of the medical surveillance warrant it. Employers are responsible for taking the necessary action to remove the employee from exposure and remedy an unsatisfactory working environment.

Sometimes this will only lead to a brief suspension by the employer, but if the employee is in danger of losing his livelihood, statutory regulations may give the worker a right of appeal against the medical opinion. Regulation 24 of the Ionising Radiations Regulations, for example, allows an employee aggrieved by a decision recorded in the health record by an EMA or AD to apply for the decision to be reviewed. The application must be made to the HSE within three months.

(5) There is little point in regular examination if no proper record of the result is kept. Efficient record-keeping is a vital component of medical surveillance, statutory or voluntary. It is also important evidence for the epidemiologist. The Employment Medical Advisory Service (EMAS) must be notified of the statutory examinations which have been carried out and of those workers certified unfit. Health records must be kept for at least 40 years, and in some regulations 50 years.

4.13 Control of Substances Hazardous to Health (COSHH) Regulations

The COSHH Regulations are designed to protect all workers whose job brings them into contact with a substance hazardous to health, whatever the nature of the job or the nature of the substance. The duty to provide adequate ventilation, personal protection, hygiene, health surveillance, etc. is no longer confined to specified places of work like factories, or specified substances like asbestos.

The need for the comprehensive approach is supported by statistics. The Department of Work and Pensions reports a large number of claims for social security in respect of diseases attributable to occupational exposure to substances. As the figures relate only to clearly established cases of prescribed diseases, they are acknowledged to be incomplete. Many people suffer from chronic bronchitis and asthma but no-one knows how many cases are occupationally linked. There were on average 150,000 deaths per annum from cancer in Great Britain between 1996 and 2000; it is thought that approximately 4 per cent could be occupationally linked.

In a Consultative Document issued by the Health and Safety Commission (HSC) in 1984 the objectives of the new laws were set down as:

(1)   to provide one set of regulations covering hazardous substances, including substances not yet covered by specific regulations, and all exposed employees whether or not they work in a factory;
(2)   to set out in the regulations principles of occupational medicine and hygiene;
(3)   to make provision for any future discoveries which may lead to changes in standards of control and improved techniques for the control of exposure;
(4)   to be able to implement the EC Directive on the protection of workers from risks related to exposure to chemical, physical and biological agents at work (1980) and future Directives;
(5)   to enable the Government to ratify the ILO Convention No. 139 on carcinogenic substances;
(6)   to simplify and update the law.

The Regulations have been regularly updated. The principal regulations are now the COSHH Regulations 2002. There is an Approved Code of Practice (2002) which has been extended with an appendix on control of substances that cause occupational asthma.

The core of COSHH Regulations is a duty on every employer to carry out an assessment before starting work which may involve exposure to a substance hazardous to health. This is intended to identify the nature and degree of risk. After the risk has been assessed the employer must then determine the precautions needed to protect the workers. There are basically three types of prevention: control of exposure, using engineering controls or personal protective equipment, monitoring of the environment to check that control limits are not being exceeded and health surveillance to detect the early signs of disease and assess the efficiency of the control system. The first is the province of the engineer, the second of the hygienist and the third of the health professional.

'Substance' is defined by the regulations as 'any natural or artificial substance, whether in solid or liquid form or in the form of a gas or vapour (including micro-organisms)'. 'Micro-organism' means a microbiological entity, cellular or non-cellular, which is capable of replication or of transferring genetic material. A substance hazardous to health means any substance (including any preparation) which is:

(1) any substance listed in Part I of the approved supply list as dangerous for supply within the meaning of the Chemicals (Hazard Information and Packaging for Supply) Regulations 2002 for which the classification is specified as very toxic, toxic, harmful, corrosive or irritant;
(2) any substance for which the HSC has approved a maximum exposure limit or an occupational exposure standard;
(3) a biological agent;
(4) dust of any kind, when present at a substantial concentration in air;
(5) a substance, other than those already included, which creates a risk to health because of its chemical or toxicological properties and the way it is used or is present in the workplace.

The COSHH Code advises that a substance should be regarded as hazardous to health if it is hazardous in the form in which it occurs in the work activity, whether or not its mode of causing injury to health is known, and whether or not the active constituent has been identified. Also included are mixtures of compounds, micro-organisms, allergens, etc. The regulations do not apply to substances already covered by the Control of Asbestos at Work Regulations 2002, the Control of Lead at Work Regulations 2002, or the Coal Mines (Respirable Dust) Regulations 1975 (under review). They do not extend to exposure to a substance hazardous only because of its radioactive, explosive or flammable properties, or solely because it is at a high or low temperature or at a high pressure. The Dangerous Substances and Explosive Atmospheres Regulations 2002 supplement the COSHH Regulations. If a substance is administered to a person in the course of his medical or dental examination or treatment (including research) performed under the direction of a registered medical or dental practitioner or an appropriate practitioner under section 58 of the Medicines Act 1968, the regulations do not apply.

COSHH applies to exposure which is related to work, not that which is incidental. Regulation 2 states that any reference to an employee being exposed is a reference to the exposure of that employee to a hazardous substance *arising out of or in connection with work at the workplace*. Thus, the exposure of a nurse to hepatitis B infection while nursing a patient is within the regulations, but not the possibility that a clerical worker might be infected through social contact with other employees. It may be argued that cigarette smoke falls within the regulations because it arises in connection with the work of barmen, waiters, cinema attendants and so on. The contrary argument is that it is incidental to the work and therefore not within the regulations, though covered by section 2 HSWA.

Certain substances are prohibited from use. These are listed in Schedule 2 and include 2-naphthylamine, benzidine, 4-aminodiphenyl, 4-nitro-diphenyl, their salts and any substance containing any of these compounds in a total concentration exceeding one per cent. All these substances, and matches made with white phosphorus, are prohibited from importation into the UK. Other substances are prohibited in certain processes as, for example, sand or other substances containing free silica for use in blasting.

Regulation 3 lays down the scope of the employer's duty. The employer is always responsible to those directly employed, his employees, but he is in general also under a like duty, so far as is reasonably practicable, to any other person, whether at work or not, who may be affected by work carried on by him (i.e. under his control). This will extend the employer's duty of care under the regulations to subcontractors and members of the public, both on and off the employer's premises (see Chapter 5). Not all the statutory obligations are owed to this wider group. In particular, the health surveillance provisions under Regulation 11: the employer is only obliged to provide suitable health surveillance for his own *employees*. Regulation 11 states that where it is appropriate for the protection of the health of employees who are, or are liable to be, exposed to a substance hazardous to health, the employer *shall* ensure that such employees are under suitable health surveillance (a term which includes biological monitoring). Contractors must keep their own health records for their employees, and self-employed persons working on site are not covered by this part of the law, though the protection of their health is within its scope.

When is health surveillance appropriate? When *either* the employee is exposed to a substance and engaged in a process specified in Schedule 6, unless the exposure is not significant, *or* the exposure of the employee to a substance hazardous to health is such that an identifiable disease or adverse health effect may be related to the exposure, there is a reasonable likelihood that the disease or effect may occur under the particular conditions of his work, there are valid techniques for detecting indications of the disease or the effect, and the technique of investigation is of low risk to the employee.

It has been decided as a policy matter by the HSE that the degree of significant exposure will not in the future be automatically tied to occupational exposure standards or maximum exposure levels set by the legislation. Each employer will have to determine significance, acting on expert advice. MELs and OESs will be replaced with Workplace Exposure Limits.

The following substances and processes are listed in Schedule 6: vinyl chloride monomer (manufacture, production, reclamation, storage, discharge, transport, use or polymerisation); nitro or amino derivatives of phenol and of benzene or its homologues (manufacture of nitro or amino derivatives of phenol and of benzene or its homologues and the making of explosives with the use of any of these substances); potassium or sodium chromate or dichromate (in manufacture); orthotolidine and its salts, dianisidine and its salts, dichlorbenzidine and its salts (in manufacture, formation or use of these substances); auramine, magenta (in manufacture); carbon disulphide, disulphur dichloride, benzene, including benzol, carbon tetrachloride, trichlorethylene (processes in which these substances are used, or given off as vapour, in the manufacture of india rubber or of articles or goods made wholly or partially of india rubber); pitch (in the manufacture of blocks of fuel consisting of coal, coal dust, coke or slurry with pitch as a binding substance).

The purposes of health surveillance are set out in the COSHH Approved Code of Practice as:

(1) the protection of the health of individual employees by the detection at as early a stage as possible of adverse changes which may be attributed to exposure to hazardous substances;
(2) assisting in the evaluation of measures taken to control exposure;
(3) the collection, maintenance and use of data for the detection and evaluation of hazards to health;
(4) assessing in relation to specific work activities involving biological agents, the immunity of employees.

What is suitable health surveillance? As an absolute minimum, where the regulations apply, the employer must keep an individual health record, containing the particulars set out in the Approved Code of Practice, including personnel details, a historical record of jobs involving exposure to substances requiring health surveillance and dates and conclusions of all other health surveillance procedures. These records or a copy thereof must be retained for at least 40 years from the date of the last entry. If the employer ceases to trade he must offer them to the HSE. The employer must allow each employee to see his own health record if he asks for it. It is clear that the intention behind the regulations is that the health record is to be kept separately from confidential clinical records. It must be held in a form capable of being linked with the records of the monitoring of exposure, and thus in practice it will have to be made available to hygienists and others outside the occupational health department. It can be foreseen that this may cause conflict, because health professionals will be reluctant to give detailed results of, for example, biological tests, which they regard as clinical data, to others without the written consent of the workers concerned. The Code of Practice advises that clinical data should not be included in the health record, in which only the *conclusions* of all health surveillance procedures and the date on which and by whom they were carried out should appear. These should be expressed in terms of the employee's fitness for work and, where appropriate, will record the decisions of the doctor, nurse or responsible person, *but not confidential clinical data*. The health professional or other responsible person should explain to employees undergoing health surveillance that he will have to notify their employer of his conclusions as to their fitness to work, for entry in the health record.

The Approved Code of Practice contains more detailed recommendations. It envisages at least seven levels of surveillance:

(1) The keeping of an individual health record. This is necessary for *all* employees exposed to a substance hazardous to health.
(2) Biological monitoring, i.e. the measurement and assessment of workplace agents or their metabolites either in tissues, secreta, excreta or expired air, or any combination of these in exposed workers.
(3) Biological effect monitoring, i.e. the measurement and assessment of early biological effects in exposed workers.
(4) Inspection by a 'responsible person' (e.g. a supervisor or manager). A responsible person is someone appointed by the employer, trained to know what to look for, and charged with reporting to the employer. An example given in the Code is a regular inspection by a supervisor of the skin of electroplating workers using chromium compounds.
(5) Enquiries about symptoms, inspection or examination by a 'suitably qualified person' (a qualified OH nurse is given as an example but it is not made clear what other qualification is suitable). An example might be regular inspections of skin by an OH nurse of those working with known or suspected skin carcinogens (e.g. arsenic, pitch, coal tar, shale oil).
(6) Medical surveillance by a doctor, who must be an EMA or an AD where the employee has been exposed to a substance listed in Schedule 6, or any registered medical practitioner in any other case. This may include clinical examinations and measurements of physiological and psychological effects of exposure to hazardous substances in the workplace, as indicated by alterations in body function or constituents.
(7) A review of records and occupational history during and after exposure should be used by management to check the correctness of their assessment of the risk.

'The aim should be to evolve health surveillance procedures which are easy to perform, preferably non-invasive and acceptable to employees.' Procedures should be safe, that is of low risk to workers. Valid techniques of high sensitivity and specificity must be used. It may be necessary to establish normal values and action levels. The results of health surveillance should lead to some action which will be of benefit to the health of employees. Methods of surveillance, options and criteria for action should be established *before* undertaking a programme. The procedures are not mutually exclusive. The results of biological monitoring may indicate the need for a medical examination. The keeping of records is often the only form of surveillance required for those working with carcinogens other than those specified in Schedule 6 and skin carcinogens. This is because of the usually long latent period between exposure to a carcinogenic substance and any health effect. This means that there is no specific statutory obligation on the employer to examine those workers in any way or to employ any personnel to monitor their health. The general duties under the Health and Safety at Work Act and the common law, of course, oblige him to do that which is reasonable in all the circumstances.

Employees exposed to a Schedule 6 substance and process must be regularly under medical surveillance supervised by an EMA or AD at least every 12 months, or more frequently if the doctor requires it. Medical surveillance includes clinical examinations and measurements of the physiological and psychological effects of exposure in the workplace; the exact nature of the examination is at the doctor's discretion. However, as has already been stated, the obligation on the employer to undertake and on the employee to undergo health surveillance is not confined to Schedule 6 substances. The employee who works in *any* job where it is appropriate within the regulations to perform tests or examinations on him has a duty to present himself during working hours for such health surveillance procedures as may be required by the employer. In addition, an employee subject to medical surveillance in connection with a Schedule 6 substance and process must give the doctor information about his health if reasonably required to do so. Since these obligations are imposed by statute, the employee will not be able to refuse to undergo health surveillance without being in breach of his statutory duty and therefore open to criminal prosecution and disciplinary action by the employer.

The EMA or AD (known as the relevant doctor) has power to certify in the health record that in his professional opinion the employee is unfit to work with a Schedule 6 substance, or to place conditions on his continued employment. An employee suspended by the EMA or the AD will be entitled to medical suspension pay (Chapter 8). The employer will be committing an offence if he ignores the doctor's finding. Also, the doctor will be able to certify in the health record that the employee must continue under surveillance after his exposure to the dangerous substance has ceased. The employer will be committing an offence if he fails to provide for this as long as the employee continues in his employment. The employee has a right to appeal against the doctor's decision to suspend him; he should write to the HSE within 28 days of being notified of it. The doctor must be allowed to inspect the workplace or the health records if he requires it.

Where, as a result of health surveillance, an employee is found to have an identifiable disease or adverse health effect which is considered by a relevant doctor *or other occupational health professional* to be the result of exposure to a substance hazardous to health the employer of that employee shall:

(1) ensure that a suitably qualified person informs the employee accordingly and provides the employee with information and advice regarding further health surveillance;
(2) review the risk assessment;
(3) review any measure taken to prevent or control exposure taking into account any advice given by a relevant doctor, occupational health professional or by the HSE;
(4) consider assigning the employee to do alternative work where there is no risk of further exposure to that substance, taking into account any advice given by a relevant doctor or occupational health professional; and
(5) provide for a review of the health of any other employee who has been

similarly exposed, including a medical examination where such an examination is recommended by a relevant doctor, occupational health professional or by the HSE.

Although the regulations make detailed provision for regular medical examination of those employees exposed to a substance listed in Schedule 6, they are
less specific about other substances. Health surveillance, including medical surveillance, may be required, but the necessity for medical surveillance by an EMA
or AD only attaches to Schedule 6 cases. Also, the statutory right of appeal to the
HSE against medical suspension outlined in the preceding paragraph and the
right to medical suspension pay from the employer for up to 26 weeks are
restricted to a decision of an EMA or AD. The position of the OH professional
undertaking routine surveillance for a non-Schedule 6 substance is unclear.
Suppose an employee refuses to allow him to report that he is unfit? Would it be a
breach of confidence to make a report without consent? Since the employee has a
statutory duty to submit to health surveillance, it is probably the law that the
doctor or nurse can report on simple fitness or unfitness for work (but not the
clinical details) without consent. Employers who voluntarily provide some
compensation for employees suspended or dismissed in these circumstances are
likely to achieve greater co-operation from the workforce.

4.14 Management of Health and Safety at Work Regulations 1992 and ACOP

Regulation 6 extends the obligation to provide health surveillance to all
employees, other than those employed on sea-going ships. It is such surveillance
as is appropriate having regard to the risks to the employees' health and safety
identified in the employer's assessment. The Approved Code of Practice adopts
the following criteria:

(1) There is an identifiable disease or adverse health condition related to the
    work concerned.
(2) Valid techniques are available to detect indications of the disease or con-
    dition.
(3) There is a reasonable likelihood that the disease or condition may occur
    under the particular conditions of work.
(4) Surveillance is likely to further the protection of the health of the employees
    to be covered.

The Code of Practice indicates that the primary benefit of surveillance is to detect
adverse health effects at an early stage, but that secondary gains are checking the
effectiveness of control measures, providing feedback on the accuracy of the risk
assessment and identifying and protecting individuals at increased risk. The forms
of surveillance are those already set out in the COSHH Approved Code of Practice
and discussed in the previous section of this chapter. The Management Approved
Code of Practice places emphasis on the participation of the workforce. The

employees concerned should be given an opportunity to comment on the proposed frequency of health surveillance procedures and should have access to an appropriately qualified practitioner for advice on surveillance.

This regulation has the potential for the introduction into UK law by the back door of a mandatory obligation on all employers to provide an occupational health service of some kind. Everything depends on how it is interpreted in practice. Breach of the Management Regulations now gives rise to a potential civil action for breach of statutory duty by an employee (Chapter 7). Thus, an employer who does not provide health surveillance as required by the Management Regulations may be sued for damages if his breach leads to the employee suffering harm, for example failing to discover a cancer while it is treatable.

But the obligation is only to *provide* surveillance: the employees are under no general duty to accept it, other than under the regulations which specifically impose such a duty, like the COSHH Regulations. It is interesting to note that the draft Regulations on the Control of Vibration at Work (likely to come into force in 2005), in providing for health surveillance in Regulation 7, include an obligation on employees to present themselves during working hours for health surveillance procedures required by the employer. Difficulty may arise if workers perceive surveillance as a method of excluding the less fit for the benefit of management rather than the protection of the employees. The primary duty on the employer is to care for all his workers, not to try to achieve a workforce of supermen and superwomen. In *Health Surveillance at Work*, there is this statement:

> 'Health surveillance can fail where employees have not been told what its purpose is, how it will be carried out and what it means for them as individuals. Employees might suspect that programmes are introduced, not to protect them, but as a threat to their jobs. Overcome this by involving employees and, where appropriate, their representatives, early on.'

4.15   Drugs and alcohol testing

Although these two topics are often linked, they present different dilemmas for the employer. Drug tests are usually concerned with the detection of consumption of illegal drugs, whereas, apart from driving jobs, the ingestion of large quantities of alcohol is not a crime. Alcohol moves quickly through the body, whereas some drugs may still be present up to a month after they have been consumed.

It is not for an employer to make judgments about the lifestyle of an employee; his only concern should be the effect which the employee's conduct has on his job. This principle has been reinforced by the incorporation in the Human Rights Act 1998 of the European Convention on Human Rights into UK law. Article 8 of the Convention has been discussed earlier in this chapter. Requiring an employee or job applicant to submit to a physical test to detect alcohol or drugs is an invasion of privacy. For it to be justified, a public authority employer must prove it acted in accordance with the law and that one of the reservations in Article 8 (2) applies. The courts and tribunals are likely to apply similar criteria to employers in the private sector.

When will a drugs or alcohol test be 'in accordance with the law'? My answer is that it must be imposed either in the contract of employment or by statute, and must be with the informed consent of the individual. In this respect it is similar to health surveillance testing discussed earlier in this chapter. Where the worker refuses a test, this cannot give rise to disciplinary proceedings without some contractual or statutory duty. The employer can never use force, but where there is a legal obligation to co-operate he can punish the employee for refusing a lawful order.

There are statutes which deal with drink and drugs at work, including the general provisions of the road traffic laws which extend to all drivers on the public highway (Road Traffic Act 1988). The Transport and Works Act 1992 introduced compulsory testing by the police (including the railway police) of railway employees in 'safety sensitive' positions. The Act applies to drivers, guards, conductors, signalmen, maintenance staff, supervisors of maintenance staff and look-outs. Where a constable in uniform has reasonable cause to suspect that a person is or has been working with alcohol in his body, he may require that person to undergo a breath test. There is a similar power where there has been an accident or dangerous incident and the act or omission of the person tested may have been the cause of the accident or incident. A constable may also require a person suspected of working on a railway when he is unfit, to give a specimen of blood or urine if a doctor advises him that the condition of the suspect might be due to a drug. Failure to provide a specimen without reasonable excuse is an offence. These criminal provisions do not allow for random testing, but it is open to the employer to introduce such testing in the contract of employment and since 1992 railway companies and London Transport have introduced random and 'for cause' testing for all employees.

Similar provisions apply to aviation and shipping under Part 5 of the Railways and Transport Safety Act 2003.

The possession, or worse, the distribution of controlled drugs on the employer's premises is a crime, (Misuse of Drugs Act 1971) for which the employer might be prosecuted if he knew of it. Tribunals are unsympathetic to employees who bring illegal drugs to work, as in *Mathewson* v. *Wilson Dental Laboratory* (1988), discussed in Chapter 8.

The employer's concern is whether the employee is fit for work. This is important both to protect his other employees and in some cases the general public. It will in many cases also be of commercial importance. Where the bank manager is drunk for most of the day his judgment will be flawed and he will not give a good impression to customers. It is arguable that drugs or alcohol tests at the workplace are permitted by Article 8 (2) for one or more of these reasons. However, the test of proportionality must also be satisfied. Is this a real problem, or is the employer over-reacting?

Tests fall into three categories: pre-employment, 'for cause' testing at work and random testing at work. The job applicant who is aware of pre-employment tests will take care not to indulge before the test. Where he or she is discovered to have physical signs of excessive use of alcohol, or to have illegal drugs still in the body, the employer must decide what policy he will follow. Many employers automatically exclude those with evidence of drug or alcohol abuse. In *Walton* v. *TAC*

Construction Materials (1981), a prospective employee was interviewed by an OH nurse and was asked if he suffered from any serious illnesses. He replied that he did not. In reality he was injecting himself with heroin. Soon afterwards Walton, of his own volition, consulted a GP who treated him and substituted oral diconal for intravenous heroin. The employers found another employee who was taking heroin and this led to the discovery that Walton was a registered drug addict and was being treated for it. Management sought advice from the occupational physician who stated that had he known of Walton's addiction he would not have recommended him for employment and that he could not advise the company to retain a drug addict in employment. The doctor considered him to be a potential danger to himself and others, that the incidence of relapse was high, and that if he were kept on he would have to be supervised. The employers decided to dismiss without consulting the GP. Note that the decision was not based on the nature of Walton's job or the particular facts of the case but on a general policy (this was a construction company). The tribunal held that the dismissal was fair and the Employment Appeal Tribunal upheld the decision. It was within a range of reasonable responses for an employer to decide that the risks attendant on employing a drug addict in his business precluded him from so doing. Latterly, views more sympathetic to the addict have gained support, because this kind of policy deters him from going for treatment. Had Walton never approached his doctor his problem might have remained uncovered and he might have retained his habit and his job.

The increase in the numbers of people using 'soft' drugs like cannabis raises the question whether job applicants found to have consumed such substances recreationally should be barred from employment. This must depend on evidence as to how reliable such workers are likely to be in employment. OH professionals will be able to advise the employer on recent research. A further difficulty is how to deal with people who are taking prescription or OTC (over the counter) drugs. It may be important that the employer is notified of these in case there are hazards, for example drowsiness while operating machinery. It is permissible to ask job applicants in a pre-employment questionnaire what drugs they are taking, and this will often alert the OH nurse or doctor to a medical condition. Care must be taken not to discriminate unlawfully against a job applicant who has a disability that falls within the Disability Discrimination Act. Addiction to a substance is not a disability unless it is medically prescribed, but the effects of an addiction may be. Severe depression, psychosis and cirrhosis of the liver are all potential disabilities.

The Information Commissioner in the draft Part 4 of the Code of Practice on the Use of Personal Data in Employer/Employee Relationships, discussed in Chapter 3, deals with drug testing at length. This is of concern to him because information about such matters is 'sensitive personal data' within the Data Protection Act 1998. It is of particular interest that the Commissioner suggests that the only justification for such testing is a health and safety risk. Employers should not be concerned with what the worker does off duty, but on whether he or she is safe and fit for work. Employers should not test merely to find evidence of the use of illegal drugs. The Code suggests that less invasive methods than testing of blood or urine can be employed. In the United States NASA uses task performance tests of hand-eye co-ordination and response time to determine whether astronauts and pilots are unfit for work, for whatever reason. Failing the test may be caused by fatigue, physical illness or substance abuse: the aim is to detect the unreliable worker rather than to mete out punishment.

Where blood, breath, hair, urine or mouth swab tests are employed they must comply with necessary standards:

(1) Drug testing, when used as a basis for decisions affecting a person's employability or continued employment, must be of the highest technical quality and subject to rigorous quality control procedures. Many employers now use outside laboratories which specialise in the field.

(2) The testing must be conducted and interpreted under the direction of a medically qualified person competent in the field.

(3) There should be two samples taken, one of which should be given to the worker, and there should be a right of appeal, since results are not completely reliable. One poppy seed lodged in the teeth of a worker who has recently consumed a bread roll can give a false positive.

In *Sutherland* v. *Sonat Offshore Inc* (1993) the employee returned to the mainland after two weeks on an oil rig. A drug test revealed the presence of cannabis in his urine. The result was confirmed in further tests and the employee was dismissed by letter. The tests were conducted by a specialist contractor. It was held that the employee had, as it were, been caught red-handed, given that illegal drugs and alcohol are strictly forbidden on an oil rig. The employer was entitled to take the view that to hold a formal disciplinary hearing would serve no useful purpose. The dismissal was fair.

(4) Tests may reveal the presence of other conditions, like pregnancy. This information must not be used by the employer, unless the employee has freely consented.

Employers must also decide what they will do if a positive result is obtained. It is important to have a drugs and alcohol policy which is communicated to the workforce. In order to persuade workers with a problem to come forward voluntarily, many policies provide that in that event the worker will not be disciplined but will be required to pursue medical or rehabilitation treatment as a condition of continuing employment. The employer may decide that such employees cannot be retained in safety sensitive jobs, at least until they are passed as reliable by occupational health.

Should occupational health be involved in testing? The Faculty of Occupational Medicine advises that it is neither necessary nor appropriate for medical or nursing staff to be involved in procedures such as breath analysis for alcohol where these are undertaken as part of a company programme.

'The involvement of health staff in "policing" procedures may undermine their role as confidential medical advisers and any possible confusion should be avoided.'

Where OH staff are unavoidably involved they should not give medical advice, because they should make it clear that they are acting as the employer's agent. Scrupulous care must be taken in handling samples and transmission to the laboratory. More detailed advice is given in *Guidelines on testing for drugs of abuse in the workplace* (Faculty of Occupational Medicine 1994).

In 2004 the Independent Inquiry into Drug Testing at Work published a report: *Drug Testing in the Workplace*. This concludes that the law in this area is unclear, and calls on the Government to produce clear and definitive guidance on legal and other issues around drug testing at work.

4.16   *Genetic testing*

Thus far, genetic screening of workers is virtually unknown in the United Kingdom. An exception is screening of pilots and deep sea divers for sickle cell trait because of the risk of hypoxia. But will we inexorably move towards designer workers, as some couples desire designer babies? The nightmare of Huxley's *Brave New World* may be approaching. The Nuffield Council on Bioethics in 1993 expressed the view that genetic screening could only be regarded as ethical if there is strong evidence of a clear connection between the working environment and the development of the condition for which the screening is conducted, where the condition in question is one which seriously endangers the health of the employee, or where the employee is likely to present a serious danger to third parties, and it is one for which the dangers cannot be eliminated or significantly reduced by reasonable measures taken by the employer to modify or respond to the environmental risks. This has been supported by an international conference of occupational experts in Helsinki in 1998 and by the Employment Working Group of the Human Genetics Advisory Commission in 1999. The Commission was recreated as the Human Genetics Commission in 2000.

The 1999 Report, *The Implications of Genetic Testing for Employment*, recommended that the following policy principles should be observed:

(1)   An individual should not be required to take a genetic test for employment purposes.
(2)   An individual should not be required to disclose the results of a previous genetic test unless there is clear evidence that the information it provides is needed to assess either their current ability to perform a job safely or their susceptibility to harm from doing a certain job.
(3)   Employers should offer a genetic test (where available) if it is known that a specific working environment or practice, while meeting health and safety requirements, might pose specific risks to individuals with particular genetic variations. For certain jobs where issues of public safety arise, an employer should be able to refuse to employ a person who refuses to take a genetic test.
(4)   Any genetic test used for employment purposes must be subject to assured levels of accuracy and reliability.
(5)   The Health and Safety Commission should be responsible for monitoring and advising on genetic testing in employment.

(6)   The handling of genetic test results, which are sensitive personal data, should meet the standards set by the Data Protection Act.

The Genetic and Insurance Committee (GAIC) aims to ensure that any use of genetic testing is based on sound scientific and actuarial evidence. It develops criteria for the review of specific genetic tests and their reliability and relevance in awarding or denying insurance cover. Insurers have agreed to a voluntary scheme whereby they must apply for permission to use the results of specific tests and each case is independently assessed according to the GAIC criteria. While people cannot be forced into taking tests, they can be asked to reveal the results of tests already taken for medical reasons. A five-year moratorium was agreed with the insurance industry in 2001 on the use of genetic test results for life insurance policies up to a value of £500,000. In 2000 GAIC granted its first approval of genetic tests which may be used in assessing insurance above the financial limits of the moratorium. These were two tests for Huntington's disease.

If an employer attempted to institute a policy of genetic screening of job applicants or employees it would be likely to fall foul of the Human Rights Act 1998, except with regard to the specific conditions outlined in the Nuffield Report. It might also be a breach of the Race Relations Act where a defective gene is more common in some races than others. It would not be a breach of the Disability Discrimination Act, as a gene carrying a susceptibility to a disease is not a disability until it causes physical or mental impairments.

In 2002 the Human Genetics Commission produced a report on the use of personal genetic data: *Inside Information*. It defined personal genetic information as any information about the genetic make-up of an identifiable person, whether it comes from DNA testing or from any other source (including the details of a person's family history). It concluded that private genetic information should not be obtained or held without a person's consent, that it should be treated as confidential and that no-one should be unfairly discriminated against on the basis of his or her genetic characteristics. There will be exceptions, for example where public safety issues are involved. The Commission recommended that the UK Government should ratify the Council of Europe Convention on Human Rights and Biomedicine (1994).

The UK Government replied to the Commission report in a White Paper: *Our Inheritance, Our Future* in 2003. It has undertaken to introduce legislation, making it an offence to test a person's DNA without their knowledge and consent, except as part of their medical treatment where consent is impossible to obtain, and use by the police and the courts. The Government will consider the evidence of unfair discrimination against people on the basis of their genetic characteristics and the appropriate means of addressing any concerns in this area.

In the United States, the Senate in 2003 approved legislation to outlaw genetic discrimination. Genetic tests are defined as 'the analysis of human DNA, RNA, chromosomes, proteins and metabolites, that detect genotypes, mutations, or chromosomal changes'. Employers are prohibited from asking for or using genetic information in decisions about recruitment, employment conditions and privileges, or promotion and dismissal. There is one exception: an employer can use a selection criterion that might tend to exclude people on genetic grounds if it can show that the criterion is directly related to the specific job and consistent with business necessity.

The Information Commissioner's draft Code of Practice, Part 4, deals briefly with genetic testing. It states that genetic screening for susceptibility to workplace environmental hazards clearly has some precautionary relevance, but in many cases the link between a particular genetic status and susceptibility to a particular hazard has only a theoretical base at present. The validity of a genetic test would require demonstration of its relevance to the health protection of workers, the reliability and reproducibility of the test and the level of predictive value. At present there are very few tests available that could validly be used in the context of decisions concerning employment.

Chapter 5
Health and Safety at Work: the Criminal Law

5.1 *Criminal sanctions*

The movement of workers from their rural homes to factories in industrial towns had by the beginning of the nineteenth century created such horrific conditions as to agitate reformers like the Earl of Shaftesbury to promote legislation to force manufacturers to improve conditions at work. The first such measure was the Health and Morals of Apprentices Act of 1802, but the first statute to set up an inspectorate to enforce the new laws was the Factory Act 1833.

From the beginning, the law concentrated on establishing and supporting criminal sanctions. The purpose of the legislation was to deter employers from creating unhealthy and dangerous working practices. The development of a legal right to money compensation for those killed and injured followed only 60 years later. The theory that criminal penalties are a more effective deterrent than the duty to compensate has often been debated. Where the defendant to criminal proceedings is a corporation, it cannot be sent to prison. Fines for health and safety offences are low, especially in the magistrates' courts. The maximum fine available to the magistrates was raised from £2000 to £20,000 in 1992. The Crown Court has never had an upper limit on the amount of fines. In the prosecution which followed the Southall rail crash, Great Western Trains was fined £1.5 million plus £680,000 costs, a record for a single offence under health and safety legislation. Such 'white-collar' crimes do not carry the stigma of, for instance, theft or criminal assault, probably because they are not often deliberate. Cynically, the Zeebrugge disaster was a commercial tragedy for Townsend-Thoresen because customers as well as employees were killed. Where the tragedy strikes the workers alone, the commercial damage is far less acute.

A series of disasters has made the public more aware of potential risks. The *Herald of Free Enterprise* capsize at Zeebrugge, the King's Cross Underground fire, several fatal railway accidents, the *Piper Alpha* explosion in the North Sea and the many deaths at the Hillsborough football ground have led to public demand that enterprises be punished more effectively for endangering human life in the cause of profit. However, at the same time, industry has wholeheartedly espoused the philosophy of performance-related pay and individual appraisal of managers. There has been a move away from national collective bargaining in favour of decentralisation. A manager under constant pressure to cut costs and reduce the wages bill will be likely to employ more temporary and part-time workers, who are less well-trained and more at risk. He will also be encouraged to bring in subcontractors who will be unfamiliar with the day-to-day operations of his business. The Report of the Chief Inspector of Factories in 1985 showed that several companies had reduced the numbers of their in-house safety personnel.

'The current trend towards decentralisation within large corporations seems then to carry a real risk that decisions regarding health and safety issues will increasingly be the subject of narrow, short-term, cost-benefit considerations.' (James, 1992)

Since most would agree that the main aim of the law should be to prevent accidents, not to punish offenders, how can this best be achieved? The Robens Committee on Safety and Health at Work Report (1972), which expounded the philosophy that health and safety was a matter of common interest between management and workers, laid stress on the need to involve the workers in their own safety:

'We believe that if workpeople are to accept their full share of responsibility ... they must be able to participate fully in the making and monitoring of arrangements for safety and health at their place of work.'

To enable them to fulfil this role, they must have access to information. Also, in Sweden and the Australian State of Victoria, but not the UK, worker representatives have the power to order the employer to interrupt production while the situation is investigated by Government inspectors. In fact, there has been a decline in the militancy of British workers, often because of the fear of unemployment. The Chief Inspector of Factories gave an example of this:

'The extent of the fear of the loss of one's job may perhaps be gauged by the parents who offered to pay for damage to a conveyor when their 17-year-old son jammed his shovel into it to stop it after his arm became trapped at the tail drum. They offered to waive their claim for compensation if only their son could continue to work.' (*HSE Annual Report for the Manufacturing and Service Industries* (1983))

The enforcement agencies, the Health and Safety Executive (HSE) and the local authorities, and the trade unions complain that there are not enough inspectors. Numbers of inspectors have in recent years been increasing and in 1998 the Government made some £63 million available to the Health and Safety Commission (HSC). Since the publication of the Department of Trade and Industry strategy statement *Revitalising health and safety* in 2000 there has been an increase in regulatory contacts made and enforcement notices issued, but a drop in the number of preventive inspections undertaken by inspectors in the field. Furthermore, there seems a real danger that the HSE's activities will reduce noticeably in the next few years due to a cut in budgets.

The most recent statistics (2002/3) show a fall in the numbers of fatalities. However, there has been a rise in the number of reported major injuries. Deaths from mesothelioma continue to rise. Cases of occupational asthma indicate a possible decrease but musculoskeletal disorders remain the same, the most common reason for absence from work. Public administration and defence, health and social work and education had high rates for depression, stress and anxiety. Doll and Peto (1981) estimated that some 4 per cent of cancer mortality was attributable to occupational risks. It has been suggested that up to 30 per cent of disease is work-related (Discher *et al.* 1975).

The fall in the number of fatal injuries reflects the decline of heavy industry in favour of the less hazardous service industries (since 1986 employment in coal mining has more than halved). The current fatal injury rate for employees in the construction sector is the highest of the employment sectors, five times higher than in manufacturing. Agriculture is also a high risk industry. The benign influence of legal regulation can be demonstrated by the fall in the number of head injuries on construction sites (by at least a quarter) after the coming into force in April 1990 of the Construction (Head Protection) Regulations 1989.

The Annual Reports of the Health and Safety Executive contain recent statistics of occupational ill-health. The HSE points out the potential elasticity of the term, encompassing as it does conditions which are unequivocally work-related (lead poisoning, asbestosis) and conditions with multiple causes, some of which are occupational in origin (lung cancer in asbestos workers, 'sick building' syndrome). The latter can only be linked to the occupation by statistical means, demonstrating that the prevalence of the condition is higher among those exposed to the occupational factor. The most commonly reported diseases caused by work in Great Britain are general musculoskeletal conditions, stress/depression, and lower respiratory disease. All these conditions, as well as circulatory disease, are exacerbated by work in the case of thousands of workers.

If occupational health provision is poor and GPs are untrained in the diagnosis of work-related illness, many cases of occupational disease will never be identified. In practice, it is often difficult to draw a line between occupational and non-occupational disease. Diseases with long latent periods may escape detection if the worker has had several jobs over a number of years. The proliferation of new chemicals and combinations of chemicals may even now be causing harm. The International Labour Office estimates that it will take 80 years to assess the toxic properties of about 40,000 new chemical substances using current toxicological research methods.

The importance of statistics in this field makes it imperative that there be accurate reporting. The 1990 Labour Force Survey indicated that only about 30 per cent of non-fatal injuries were being reported to the HSE. The Reporting of Injuries, Diseases and Dangerous Occurrences Regulations were updated in 1995. The list of reportable diseases or medical conditions has been expanded from 28 conditions to 47, reflecting the prescribed diseases conferring eligibility to industrial injuries benefit and the European Schedule of Industrial Diseases. The definition of accident now includes acts of violence and suicides. Railways and the offshore industry have been brought within the scope of RIDDOR. Nevertheless, it is generally admitted that RIDDOR statistics substantially underestimate the incidence of accident and disease, and the system is under review.

Another source of data is the figures for compensated industrial disease (Chapter 6), which show a rise in the number of claims for asbestosis, mesothelioma and vibration white finger. It must be emphasised that changes in compensation rules and benefit rates must be allowed for when examining trends.

From 1989 the Epidemiological Research Unit at the London Chest Hospital, in collaboration with the British Thoracic Society and the Society of Occupational Medicine and funded by the HSE, operated a reporting system for cases of occupationally related respiratory disease seen for the first time by occupational and chest physicians throughout the UK. It bore the acronym SWORD (Surveillance of Work-related and Occupational Respiratory Disease). The success of the scheme has led to the introduction of a comprehensive scheme for reporting all kinds of occupational disease which is now administered by the Occupational and Environmental Health Department of the University of Manchester (The Health and Occupation Reporting Network, currently known as THOR). This covers work-related mental health, hearing loss, musculoskeletal disorders and infections, and respiratory and skin disorders.

Since the foundation of the European Agency for Health and Safety at Work there are now European social statistics on accidents at work and work-related health problems, compiled by Eurostat. There is a European Commission scheme to harmonise data on health and safety at work, known as ESAW (European Statistics on Accidents at Work).

Evidence from all sources shows that it is in the small organisations that the worker is most at risk. The rate of major injuries is 50 per cent higher in firms employing fewer than 100 people than in large establishments. The rapid rise in the numbers of small businesses has exacerbated the problems of the inspectorate. Although it is important that new enterprises are not strangled with red tape soon after birth, it is obviously necessary to ensure that the law is obeyed throughout industry. To give inspectors more time to visit small businesses, the HSE in 1983 agreed an experimental policy of self-regulation with some of the large organisations in the construction industry. The Health and Safety Commission (HSC) proposed in 1985 (*Plan of Work for 1985–86 and Onwards*) that the HSE should withdraw from day-to-day inspection of common hazards and concentrate on areas of high risk. Self-regulation and control by private insurance companies should take its place. This move towards self-regulation reflected the policy of the Robens Committee, which was that the function of health and safety law is to provide a regulatory framework within which those in industry can themselves undertake responsibility for safety at work:

'The primary responsibility for doing something about the present levels of occupational accidents and disease lies with those who create the risk and those who work with them ... Our present system encourages rather too much reliance on state regulation and rather too little on responsibility and voluntary self-generating effect ... There is a role for government action. But those roles should be predominantly concerned with influencing attitudes and creating a framework for better health and safety organisation and action by industry itself.'

The philosophy of the Conservative Government of the 1980s and 1990s was to place more and more emphasis on self-regulation and deregulation. It conflicted with the dominant school of thought in the European Union which regarded legislation as the most effective method of protecting the workforce. As a result, the call from the UK Government to abandon many technical and outmoded laws confronted the need to enact European directives, more and more numerous as the years went on.

In 1993 the government invited the Health and Safety Commission to review by 1994 all the legislation for which it was responsible. The review, advised by seven industrial Task Groups, was asked to examine whether there are burdens arising for business which are not offset by benefits and which could be eased without endangering necessary health and safety standards. The Health and Safety Commission produced *Review of Health and Safety Regulation – Main Report* in 1994.

'The *Review* found widespread support for retaining the overall architecture of regulation... Moreover ... even though the current structure had its imperfections, there was concern about the disruption and costs of further major upheaval.'

The Task Force reported in 1995 and 1996. It recommended that alternatives to legal regulation, like insurance, should be explored.

In addition, there was movement in the European Union towards a more consistent approach to the enforcement of EC legislation by Member States. The Senior Labour Inspectors' Committee is discussing how common principles of inspection could be developed across the European Union.

The philosophy of self-regulation was adopted in the recommendations of the public inquiry into the *Piper Alpha* disaster (*Cullen Report* (1990)). Operators of offshore installations should be required to submit to the HSE a safety case in respect of each of their installations. This should set out the safety objectives of the organisation, the safety management system, performance standards to be met and the means by which performance is to be monitored. The safety cases should be regularly updated and there should be periodic audits. The recommendations were enacted in the Offshore Installations (Safety Case) Regulations 1992. Self-regulation was extended to the newly privatised railways in the Railways (Safety Case) Regulations 1994.

Failure to conform with the procedures specified in a safety case will be a criminal offence, unless the owner or operator can show that in the circumstances it was not in the best interests of the health and safety of persons to follow those procedures, or that the commission of the offence was due to a contravention by another company of its duty under the regulations to co-operate, and that the accused had taken all reasonable steps and exercised all due diligence to ensure that the procedures were followed.

The move towards deregulation in the UK was strengthened by the passage of the Deregulation and Contracting Out Act 1994 giving Ministers a power to repeal redundant legislation by an expedited procedure. This measure thus far has had little effect on health and safety law, though it did succeed in freeing British industry of the burdens of the Home Work (Lampshades) Order 1929 and the Horizontal Milling Machines (Amendment) Regulations 1934. The idea of deregulation also spread to the European Union as a result of the report of a group of independent experts under the chairmanship of Dr Bernhard Molitor (1995). The Report recommended that existing directives should be reviewed and codified. Meanwhile, there should be a presumption against the introduction of new regulations. The European Parliament has been critical of the findings in the Molitor Report.

The most extensive research so far undertaken on the operation of safety legislation (S. Dawson *et al.*, *Safety at Work: the Limits of Self-regulation* (1988)) suggests that self-regulation unsupported by external enforcement is not as effective as the Robens Committee once supposed. Although in the long term it is in the interest of the employer to care for his workers, managers tend to be short-sighted when it comes to devoting resources to health and safety, especially in a period of economic recession.

A report, *Revitalising health and safety* (2000), was produced jointly by the Department for the Environment, Transport and the Regions, the Health and Safety Commission and the Department of Trade and Industry. It was intended to inject a new impetus into the health and safety agenda. It set four targets for improvement:

(1)   to reduce the number of working days lost by 30 per cent by 2010;
(2)   to reduce the incidence of fatal and major injury accidents by 10 per cent by 2010;
(3)   to reduce the incidence of work-related ill-health by 20 per cent by 2010;
(4)   to achieve half the improvement under each of the above targets by 2004.

Statistics published in 2003 did not demonstrate any significant change. In fact, there is evidence that the number of working days lost as a result of work-related ill-health is worsening (James & Walters, 2004).

The strategy for achieving these reductions included:

(1)   motivation of employers through insurance incentives;
(2)   more partnerships with workers on health and safety issues;
(3)   introduction of a new occupational health strategy;
(4)   increase in maximum fines and extension of the range of offences which may be subject to custodial sentences.

The Health and Safety Commission responded to the Revitalising Health and Safety strategy by producing its own document: *A Strategy for Workplace Health and Safety in Great Britain to 2010 and Beyond* (2004).

'Since 1974, the workplace and the world have changed significantly. There are fewer large firms and far more small ones – over 90 per cent of the 3.5 million or so businesses employ fewer than 10 people but nearly half the workforce are employed in large organisations. Part-time working has risen and women now constitute half the workforce. The manufacturing sector is exposed to intense international competition. The service sector has become more important. Public attitudes to risk and redress, and blame and compensation have changed. The new challenges in health and safety are almost all health rather than safety but, crucially, the rate of improvement in safety has now slowed.'

The aims of the HSC are:

(1)   To work with and through others, including the local authorities. In the field of OH the HSC intends to develop innovative partnerships in the public and private sectors to develop the provision of occupational health support locally, regionally and by sector according to need. There will be a much greater emphasis on rehabilitation.
(2)   To make health and safety and its benefits more widely understood, especially by involving the workforce, and providing accessible advice and support. 'We want to develop channels of support and advice that can be accessed without fear of enforcement action while allowing the regulators to continue to be tough on those who wilfully disregard the law.'
(3)   To be clear about priorities. Resources will be concentrated into issues where the risks are of high significance. 'We do not see new regulation as the automatic response to new issues or changing circumstances but we will continue to press for higher fines, a new law on corporate killing and the removal of Crown immunity.'
(4)   To communicate effectively. 'Our goal is not to have a risk free society but one where risk is properly appreciated, understood and managed.'

Should more attention be paid to the responsibility of the individual manager and worker? The Chernobyl disaster led to prison sentences for the managers in charge. Up to now, prison sentences for breaches of the Health and Safety at Work Act are few although immediate custodial sentences have been imposed. In *R v. Hill* (1996) the defendant was sentenced to three months' imprisonment for breaches of the asbestos regulations committed in the course of demolishing a building. In previous cases, the sentences were suspended. Prosecutions for breaches of the health and safety laws can only be brought by the enforcement agencies, except with the consent of the Director of Public Prosecutions. Since 1996 a number of directors of small businesses have served prison sentences for manslaughter and health and safety offences. A private member's bill to increase fines in the magistrates court and to make imprisonment an option for most health and safety offences was introduced in 2003, but failed to become law.

Inspectors find themselves in an invidious position. On the one hand, they desire to build a good relationship with employers; on the other, they are feared because of their powers of enforcement. An employer may be deterred from asking for the HSE's advice, realising that he may be forced to introduce expensive safety measures. In most cases the HSE does not prosecute offenders. It regards its main tasks as inspecting, advising and warning. The HSC has produced a revised *Enforcement Policy Statement* (2002), which sets out the principles of enforcement. The HSE must have regard to proportionality ('the punishment fits the crime'), consistency, transparency (i.e. making clear what the law requires and how the inspectorate will act), targeting (i.e. concentrating inspections on those whose activities give rise to the most serious risks) and accountability (enforcing authorities must have policies and standards against which they are judged and an effective and easily accessible mechanism for dealing with comments and handling complaints). Prosecution will be considered where it would act as a deterrent, where the harm caused or potentially caused by the breach was considerable or where the offender has been guilty of persistent law-breaking, despite warnings. The HSC expects that enforcing authorities should normally prosecute where one or more of the following circumstances apply:

(1) death was a result of a breach of the legislation;
(2) the gravity of the alleged offence warrants it;
(3) there has been reckless disregard of health and safety requirements;
(4) there have been repeated significant breaches of the law;
(5) work has been carried out in serious non-compliance with a licence or safety case;
(6) the duty holder's standard of managing health and safety is far below that required by the law;
(7) there has been a failure to comply with an improvement or prohibition notice; or a repetition of a breach that was subject to a formal caution;
(8) false information has been supplied wilfully, or there has been an attempt to deceive;
(9) inspectors have been intentionally obstructed in the lawful course of their duties.

Research has shown that approximately one per cent of accident investigations by the factory inspectorate lead to prosecutions and, as might be expected, are more likely to follow from the investigation of an accident than from a routine inspection visit (Hutter & Lloyd-Bostock, 1990). Most prosecutions are brought in the magistrates courts, where legal costs are lower, but the sentencing powers of magistrates (up to £20,000 fine or imprisonment for six months) are paltry compared with the Crown Court. The chosen defendant in nearly all cases is the employing organisation; the number of prosecutions brought against individuals is small.

One sanction available against an individual is disqualification of a director of a company for up to two years for a breach of the health and safety laws (Company Directors' Disqualification Act 1986). The first such disqualification was imposed in 1992. Companies can purchase insurance for their directors to pay for the legal costs and expenses of defending a criminal prosecution, though not to pay any fines (Companies Act 1989, section 137). The Court of Appeal in *R v. F. Howe and Son (Engineers)* (1999) gave advice to courts about the level of fines for health and safety offences. A small company employing 12 people had annual profits of about £30,000. These were always ploughed back into the business. One of the employees was electrocuted by a dangerous vacuum machine. The circuit breaker had been deliberately interfered with in a way that made it inoperable. The company pleaded guilty to offences under the HSWA and was fined £48,000 plus £7500 costs. It was held that, though the level of fines for health and safety offences is generally too low, they should reflect not only the gravity of the offence but also the means of the offender. However, the Court of Appeal specifically made clear that the size and resources of the company and its ability to provide safety measures or to employ in-house safety advisers were not mitigating factors: the legislation imparts the same standard of care irrespective of the size of the organisation. The fine was reduced to £15,000.

It may be questioned whether this adequately reflected the gravity of the offence. The court found that the electrical state of the equipment was appalling, and the judge commented on a flagrant disregard for the safety of the company's employees, which had led to the death of a young man of 20. Further guidance was given by the Court of Appeal in *R* v. *Rollco Screw and Rivet Co Ltd* (1999), where it indicated that in appropriate circumstances fines may be made payable in instalments over a number of years, so that a company may be ordered to pay an amount reflecting the gravity of the offence without at the same time being driven out of business, thus imposing suffering on innocent employees who lose their jobs. In the latter case, both the company and two of its directors who were principal shareholders were fined. The court stated that fines should be imposed which made it clear that there is a personal responsibility on directors, but where in a small company the directors are also the shareholders, the court must be alert to ensure that it is not in effect imposing a double punishment.

The relevant factors to be taken into account in fixing the amount of a fine include the means of the offender, the gravity of the offence, whether there was a failure to heed warnings and whether the defendant deliberately ran a risk in order to save money. Mitigating features include a prompt admission of responsibility, a plea of guilty, steps to remedy deficiencies and a good safety record. 'There may be cases where the offences are so serious that the defendant ought not to be in business.'

In *R* v. *Friskies Petcare UK Ltd* (2000) the Court of Appeal advised that the prosecution should set before the court the factors which might influence the sentence (known as a 'Friskies schedule').

Where there has been a fatal accident, the Crown Prosecution Service (Procurator Fiscal in Scotland) may decide to prosecute for the common law crime of manslaughter. A private prosecution is also possible. Both the corporate body and the individual responsible for the death may be found guilty of this crime, the essence of which is gross carelessness, more culpable than run-of-the-mill negligence. Much will depend on the view the jury takes of the defendant's behaviour. The prosecution of the owners of the *Herald of Free Enterprise*, P&O, and seven of its employees, in respect of the Zeebrugge disaster, failed because the judge ruled that there was not enough evidence against the company and its five senior personnel (*R* v. *P&O Ferries (Dover)* (1991)). The prosecution decided not to proceed against the other employees, the bosun and the captain. The company could have been convicted only if very senior employees, those who decided company policy, were guilty, because they were the 'directing mind' of the company.

There have been a number of prosecutions for manslaughter. In *R* v. *OLL, R* v. *Kyte* (1994) four teenagers were drowned in a canoeing accident in Lyme Bay while on an adventure training course. Kyte, the managing director, was convicted of manslaughter and sentenced to three years' imprisonment (reduced to two on appeal). Because he was the 'directing mind' of the company, the company was also convicted. In *R* v. *Jackson Transport (Ossett) Ltd, R* v. *Jackson* (1994) one of the defendant company's employees was killed while cleaning chemical residue from a tanker. Jackson, the managing director, was sent to prison for 12 months, and the company was fined £15,000 for corporate manslaughter. The Law Commission has recommended (Law Commission No. 237) that a new statutory crime of corporate killing should be created. This would allow the prosecution to aggregate the cumulative faults of a number of company employees, senior and junior, in order to make the company liable. The law at present renders a small company run by one manager more vulnerable to a charge of corporate manslaughter than a large company like P&O with a complex management structure. The offence of corporate killing would consist of a management failure by the corporation which fell far below what could reasonably be expected of the corporation in the circumstances.

Although the Government has declared its intention to legislate, especially after a series of fatal rail crashes where it proved impossible to secure convictions for manslaughter against train operating companies, at the time of writing no statute has as yet been enacted. A proposed Involuntary Homicide Bill seeks to create a new offence of 'corporate killing' where (1) a management failure by the corporation is the cause or one of the causes of a person's death; and (2) that failure constitutes conduct falling far below what can be reasonably expected of the corporation in the circumstances. Since a corporation has no physical body, and cannot be sent to prison, it is difficult to see how this suggested new offence will be a greater deterrent than existing offences. The Crown Court already has the power to impose unlimited fines for breach of the health and safety legislation.

It is submitted that the proposed creation of a new offence of 'killing by gross carelessness', imposing criminal liability on an individual whose conduct falls below what can reasonably be expected of him in the circumstances, where a risk that his conduct will cause death or serious injury would be obvious to a reasonable person in his position and he is capable of appreciating that risk at the material time, is more likely to deter individual directors and managers than the liability of the employing company would. However, it would still be necessary to prove that the death was caused by the carelessness of the individual. In 2001 Lord Cullen's report on the Ladbroke Grove rail crash declined to blame the driver of one of the trains which collided for passing a signal at red. The fault, he found, was in the 'poor siting' of the signal, the responsibility of management.

The HSC recommends that health and safety is made a boardroom priority. Both private and public sector organisations should appoint a board-level director for health and safety. Research has shown that one in three organisations is still failing to do this. The creation of new criminal offences will be a deterrent to those at the top of organisations who are unwilling to assume responsibility for potential breaches of the law.

The House of Lords has given guidance on the degree of negligence which needs to be proved to a jury at present in order that it may return a verdict of manslaughter. In a medical case, an anaesthetist assisting at an eye operation failed to notice the disconnection for six minutes of the tube from the ventilator supplying oxygen. The patient suffered a cardiac arrest, from which he subsequently died. Expert witnesses described the conduct of the defendant as abysmal and a gross dereliction of care. The House of Lords held that he had been rightly convicted of manslaughter, approving the analysis of the Court of Appeal. Proof of the following states of mind in the defendant can properly lead the jury to make a finding of gross negligence:

(1)   indifference to an obvious risk of injury to health;
(2)   actual foresight of the risk coupled with the determination nevertheless to run it;
(3)   an appreciation of the risk coupled with an intention to avoid it but with such a high degree of negligence in the attempted avoidance that the jury considers it justifies conviction;
(4)   inattention or failure to advert to a serious risk, which goes beyond mere inadvertence, in respect of an obvious and important matter which the defendant's duty demands he should address (as with the supply of oxygen to the patient). (*R. v. Adomako* (1995))

In a second case an inexperienced houseman injected vincristine into the spine of a patient suffering from leukaemia, not realising that it should have been injected intravenously. Another junior doctor was supervising, but mistakenly believed that he was only supervising a lumbar puncture and did not need to check the drugs. The cytotoxic trolley was not in use, so the data chart was not available, and the senior nurse was not present. The patient died. The health authority, the doctors' employer, was clearly liable to pay compensation under the civil law, but it was held that the doctors were not guilty of manslaughter, because there were a number of excuses and mitigating circumstances which had to be taken into account (*R. v. Prentice and Sullman* (1993)).

At present, prosecutions for manslaughter must be brought by the Crown Prosecution Service, which in practice liaises with the Health and Safety Executive (Work Related Deaths Protocol (2003)). Since 1999 the Health and Safety Executive has published the names of firms and individuals convicted of health and safety offences on a 'name and shame' website. A parallel local authority report of convictions can also be accessed through the HSE website.

5.2   Health and Safety Commission and Health and Safety Executive

The Robens Committee in 1972 reported that the multiplicity of different agencies and inspectorates was an inefficient use of resources. They recommended a more unified and integrated system. The HSWA set up the HSC to undertake the functions *inter alia* of encouraging and organising research, making proposals for new legislation, setting and reviewing standards, approving Codes of Practice and generally laying down policy guidelines for the inspectorates. In the 1990s the growing pre-eminence of the European Union in matters of health and safety at work means that the Commission must be active in representing the United Kingdom's interests in EU negotiations and in advising on legislation to implement European directives. The HSC consists of a chairman and not more than nine other members. Three represent employers, three employees and the remainder are from bodies such as local authorities and consumer organisations. Members of the HSC are part-time.

The HSE is responsible to the HSC for the enforcement of the safety laws. After the *Piper Alpha* disaster in the North Sea in 1988 the HSE became the regulatory agency for the offshore oil and gas industry, taking over from the Department of Energy in April 1991. The Railway Inspectorate transferred to HSE from the Department of Transport in December 1990. The local authority environmental health officers police offices, shops and catering establishments. Their spheres of influence are set out in the Health and Safety (Enforcing Authority) Regulations 1998. The forum for co-operation between HSE and local authorities is the HSE/Local Authority Enforcement Liaison Committee (HELA).

Following a White Paper on the Civil Service, the HSE has been reorganised. It is now split into the following directorates: Field Operations Directorate, Nuclear Safety Directorate, Hazardous Installations Directorate, Railway Inspectorate, Operational Policy Division, Strategy and Intelligence Division, Policy Group, Communications Directorate, Corporate Science and Analytical Services Directorate. There is also a Solicitor's Office and a Health and Safety Laboratory.

The Health and Safety at Work (N. Ireland) Order 1978 enacts similar provisions to the HSWA for Northern Ireland, where enforcement is through the Health and Safety Agency.

The HSC and HSE were transferred to the Department of Work and Pensions in 2002.

5.3　Health and safety statutes

The criminal law of health and safety is virtually all in the form of statute. It is not the purpose of this book to list all the detailed regulations. The legislation pre-1974 was created piece-meal and dealt only with specific places of work. Because of this, some workplaces, like universities, fell outside any statutory regulation. The Health and Safety at Work Act 1974 (HSWA) for the first time created a legal regime which applied to all places of work. For 20 years, the old legislation and the new existed side by side. The repeal of most of the pre-1974 legislation came only in the 1990s when regulations made under HSWA gradually replaced it.

The drafting of the old and new laws follows a different pattern. Traditionally, safety legislation spelled out legal requirements in some detail. Particular safety precautions were specified (scaffolding, crawling boards and so on) and temperatures and heights were laid down to the degree and the inch. The scope for lawyers to help their clients to avoid the legislation by interpretation was considerable.

'We seem always to have been incapable even of taking a general view of the subject we were legislating upon. Each successive statute aimed at remedying a single ascertained evil. It was in vain that objectors urged that other evils, no more defensible, existed in other trades or among other classes, or with persons of ages other than those to which the particular Bill applied.' (Webb, 1910)

The HSWA in its central provisions appears simple in contrast. Section 2 obliges the employer to ensure, *so far as is reasonably practicable*, the health, safety and welfare at work of all his employees. Section 3 places a duty on the employer to conduct his undertaking in such a way as to ensure, so far as is reasonably practicable, that people not employed by him who may be affected are not exposed to risks to their health or safety.

5.4 Reasonable practicability

The employer's duty under the general sections of the HSWA is to do that which is reasonably practicable. This is very similar to the duty to take reasonable care in the tort of negligence, discussed in Chapter 7. One difference is that section 40 HSWA provides that it is for the *defendant* to prove that it was not reasonably practicable to do more than he did, whereas the burden of proof in the civil law is on the claimant to show that the defendant was negligent. In a sense, the unspecific nature of the duty increases the power of the inspector who has more flexibility in identifying unacceptable hazards.

After the incorporation of the European Convention on Human Rights into UK law, this shifting of the burden of proof was challenged in the courts as violating Convention rights. Article 6(2) of the Convention provides:

'Everyone charged with a criminal offence shall be presumed innocent until proved guilty according to law.'

David Davies operated a plant hire business with three self-employed sub-contractors, one of whom was Mr Gardner. Davies told one of his employees to park a JCB next to a dumper truck. In so doing the employee reversed with limited visibility and killed Gardner. Davies was prosecuted and charged with failing to do that which was reasonably practicable. He should have ensured that Gardner was safely out of the way and guided the JCB into the parking spot himself. Davies was convicted by a jury in the Crown Court for a breach of section 3 HSWA. He appealed that the placing of the burden of proof that he had acted reasonably on him was a breach of the Human Rights Act 1998. The Court of Appeal held that the imposition of a reverse burden of proof in section 40 HSWA is justified, necessary and proportionate. 'In this case the jury might not have been sure that it was reasonably practicable for the appellant [employer] to do more, but convicted him because he had not satisfied them that he could not have done more.'

The health and safety legislation is regulatory, rather than prescriptive. Breach of the laws does not imply moral blameworthiness in the same manner as criminal fault. The employer did not face the risk of imprisonment for the offences in question (he was not charged with manslaughter, where the burden of proof would have been on the prosecution). For these reasons, it was held justifiable to shift the burden on to the defendant to prove that he had done all that was reasonably practicable. Mr Davies was fined £15,000, with £22,500 costs (*Davies* v. *HSE* (2002)).

How can the employer discover what the law requires of him? Everyone has his own ideas of reasonableness, but even judges disagree. First, he can consult test cases to identify the factors which the courts will consider material. Cost–benefit analysis plays an important part. In *Bellhaven Brewery Co Ltd* v. *McLean* (1975) the employer was served with an improvement notice requiring secure fencing on transmission machinery. An appeal was lodged on the ground that the modifications were too costly. It was argued that minor changes would be enough because the operators were skilled and careful. The tribunal dismissed the appeal. The risk was a significant one and justified the cost.

Are standards of reasonableness lower for small companies than for multi-nationals? A truly objective standard would apply the same criteria to all, whatever their financial position. There is, however, surprisingly little judicial guidance on this point. The following definition is a paraphrase of a dictum of Lord Justice Asquith in *Edwards* v. *NCB* (1949):

'"Reasonably practicable" is a narrower term than "physically possible" and implies that a computation must be made in which the quantum of risk is placed in one scale and the sacrifice, whether in money, time or trouble, involved in the measures necessary to avert the risk is placed on the other; and that, if it be shown that there is a gross disproportion between them, the risk being insignificant in relation to the sacrifice, the person on whom the duty is laid discharges the burden of proving that compliance was not reasonably practicable. This computation falls to be made at a point of time anterior to the happening of the incident complained of.'

This fails to address the issue of whether the small employer can plead his poverty as a material factor in measuring the degree of sacrifice. My view is that lack of resources should not be a defence, because employees of small businesses would then have even less protection than they enjoy at present. In *R* v. *Howe* (1999) (above) the Court of Appeal confirmed that this analysis was correct.

In some important areas, the employer is given detailed guidance as to what is reasonable in the form of an Approved Code of Practice. The Codes are drawn up after extensive consultation with the government and both sides of industry and must be approved by the HSC. Breach of an Approved Code is not in itself a crime, but the failure on the part of any person to observe the Code is *prima facie* evidence of guilt, so that in practice it will be difficult to avoid a conviction if the recommendations in the Code have not been followed. Only Codes officially approved by the HSC have this special status. Additional guidance provided by the HSE does not count as an Approved Code, but is likely to be treated as persuasive by courts of law. The Health and Safety Commission instituted a review of Approved Codes of Practice. It announced that it will use Approved Codes more selectively than in the past. The Codes are for the purpose of giving practical guidance on methods of compliance and will be issued only when such guidance is necessary and of use (*The Role and Status of Approved Codes of Practice* (1995)).

The duty under health and safety statutes is not always to do that which is 'reasonably practicable'. A more onerous duty is to do that which is 'practicable'. It is practicable to take a precaution which is possible in the light of current knowledge, even though the cost far outweighs the risk. Occasionally, the obligation is 'strict': liability is imposed for conduct which is neither negligent, nor deliberate, nor reckless (see Chapter 7).

English lawyers have become familiar with the concept of reasonable practicability which is closely allied with the common law idea of the reasonable man. Legislation emanating from the European Community employs different expressions. English courts have interpreted phrases like 'Every employer shall ensure that the exposure of his employees to a substance hazardous to health is either prevented, or where this is not reasonably practicable, adequately controlled' (Regulation 7(1) COSHH Regulations 2002) as imposing strict liability, that is liability without proof of negligence. In practice, this is proving more important in the civil than in the criminal law, and is discussed in Chapter 7. There are defences in the criminal law which are not available in civil actions. An important example is Regulation 21 of the COSHH Regulations 2002, which states that in any proceedings for an offence consisting of a contravention of the Regulations, it is a defence for any person to prove that he took all reasonable precautions and exercised all due diligence to avoid the commission of the offence. This 'due diligence' defence, which is found in a number of regulations, is not available to defendants in civil actions for breach of statutory duty. Thus, Singleton Hospital, Swansea, which had provided latex gloves to a nurse, could not have been successfully prosecuted, since at the relevant time the risk of sensitisation leading to anaphylaxis was not known. Nevertheless, the nurse, who became sensitised and had to give up her nursing career after two incidents of anaphylaxis, was successful in a civil action for breach of statutory duty (*Dugmore* v. *Swansea NHS Trust* (2003)) (see Chapter 7).

5.5 Civil liability

The action for breach of statutory duty is discussed at length in Chapter 7. It is necessary, however, to note here that the courts have in general construed the pre-HSWA legislation as giving a right to sue for damages in the civil courts to any person injured by breach of the statute. The obligations in sections 2–8 HSWA do not give rise to such a civil action (section 47). However, breach of a duty imposed by health and safety *regulations* is actionable in the civil law except in so far as the regulations otherwise provide. A civil action may be brought, for example, for a breach of the Manual Handling Operations Regulations 1992 or the COSHH Regulations 2002, but not for most of the regulations in the Construction (Design and Management) Regulations 1994. A civil action for breach of the Management Regulations 1999 has been available to employees since 2003 (Management of Health and Safety at Work and Fire Precautions (Workplace) Amendment Regulations 2003).

Someone injured by an employer's failure to take reasonable precautions may be involved in both criminal and civil proceedings. More frequently, the inspectorate decides against a criminal prosecution, leaving the victim to pursue an action in the civil courts, as in the case of the Abbeystead pumping station explosion in 1984. In the rare case where a criminal conviction is secured, the victim will be able to rely on the findings of the criminal court as proof of negligence. No sensible insurance company would fight a claim for compensation by a worker whose employer had just been convicted of failing to do that which was reasonably practicable. Even an investigation by the inspectorate into the causes of an accident is advantageous to victims, because public funds will pay for the costs of procuring technical evidence, on which individuals may rely, assuming that it is made available to them. Section 28(9) HSWA permits an enforcing authority at its discretion to furnish to any person who appears to be likely to be a party to any civil proceedings arising out of any accident or occurrence a written statement of relevant facts observed in the course of exercising statutory powers. If the discretion is not exercised, a claimant could apply to the courts for an order to disclose, as described in Chapter 3. Only if the enforcing authority could show that it would not be in the public interest to reveal information (e.g. because it concerned technical details about a nuclear submarine) would it be able to resist a court order. The coming into force of the Freedom of Information Act 2000 has led to the HSE changing its practice to give the general public increased access to information; changes are likely to be introduced in January 2005. Section 28 powers will be used to keep a person informed about matters related to health and safety, for example giving information to bereaved relatives and to workers about a previous employer. The new rules will not apply where disclosure would prejudice a fair trial or law enforcement, or reveal the identity of a 'whistleblower'.

The Criminal Injuries Compensation Board is empowered to pay damages out of public funds to the victims of crime. It is now governed by the Criminal Justice Act 1988. The scheme is not normally relevant in cases of work-related disease or injury, because it is confined to crimes where it is necessary for the prosecution to prove that the defendant either intended to cause personal injury to another or was reckless as to whether death or personal injury were caused. None of the crimes established by health and safety statutes come within this category. If, however, injury has been suffered or death caused because of someone's intentional act or gross negligence, the Crown Prosecution Service or a private individual might be able to prosecute for an offence under the Offences against the Person Act 1861, or for manslaughter, in which event the victim or his dependants would have a claim against the fund. Also, workers like nurses, social workers or security staff who have been attacked in the course of their work would be entitled to compensation from the fund. The Criminal Injuries Compensation Board can make a payment whether or not a criminal prosecution has in fact been brought. There are now upper limits on the compensation which can be awarded, introduced in 1994. Assaults committed by those who cannot be convicted of a crime because their mental state or age precludes it nonetheless fall within the scheme.

The not insubstantial numbers of train drivers who suffer nervous shock when suicidal persons throw themselves on to the track in front of the train have been given the right to compensation. In a consultation paper issued in 2004 by the Home Office, it is suggested that other workers who suffer trauma when they witness a suicide should also be able to claim. The Act extends to UK territorial waters, British ships and aircraft, and to oil rigs etc. within the Continental Shelf Act 1964.

The Home Office consultation paper suggests that larger employers should compensate their employees for criminal injury, because they are better placed to mitigate the risks to their employees. This would not be extended to employers of fewer than 250 staff. (*Compensation and support for victims of crime* (2004).)

5.6   *The powers of the inspectorate*

The HSWA substantially increased the legal powers of the inspectorate in respect of the enforcement of all the safety legislation, old and new. Section 20 gives the power:

(1)   to enter premises without the permission of the occupier (if necessary, accompanied by a police officer);
(2)   to make such examination and investigation as may be necessary;
(3)   to direct that premises or any part of them be left undisturbed for as long as is reasonably necessary for the purpose of any examination or investigation;
(4)   to take measurements, photographs and recordings;
(5)   to take samples of articles, substances and of the atmosphere and to take them away for examination;
(6)   to require any person whom he has reasonable cause to believe to be able to give any relevant information to answer such questions as the inspector thinks fit to ask, and to sign a declaration of the truth of his answers (though this will not be admissible in any proceedings against the person making the statement);
(7)   to inspect and take copies of any books or documents which by virtue of any relevant statutory provision are required to be kept and any other books or documents which it is necessary for him to see for the purposes of any examination or investigation;
(8)   to require any person to afford him such facilities and assistance as are necessary to enable him to exercise his powers;
(9)   any other power which is necessary.

There is no exemption in this section for health professionals or confidential medical records. Only lawyers' confidential files are exempt from inspection and seizure. Where criminal proceedings against an individual are in contemplation, the inspector will usually exercise his evidence-gathering powers under the Police and Criminal Evidence Act 1984, so that a statement will be admissible in criminal proceedings. There are strict legal controls of such interviews. There must be a prior caution and the interview must be recorded.

Where the inspector in the course of his inspection finds what appears to him to be a contravention of a safety statute, or comes upon a state of affairs which he considers highly dangerous, he may issue an improvement or a prohibition notice. These powers, conferred by the HSWA, have proved popular with inspectors, if not with employers. In 1998 it was held that an inspector cannot be made liable in negligence for economic damage caused to a business by notices (*Harris* v. *Evans*).

An improvement notice must specify an alleged contravention of a relevant statutory provision. It orders the recipient to take remedial steps, such as to guard a machine, within a specified period. Informal consultation between inspectors and employers before issuing a notice is recommended by the HSC (1998) in order to allow the employer to remedy any defects without the need for an improvement notice. A prohibition notice orders the discontinuance of an activity if the inspector states that, in his opinion, it does or will involve a risk of serious personal injury, whether or not accompanied by a contravention of a relevant statutory provision. In cases of imminent danger, the notice may be of immediate effect. Thus, the inspector has power to halt production.

In 2001/2 there were 17,042 enforcement notices issued, a 1 per cent increase on the previous year. This is considerably fewer than in 1993/94 when the number was 31,249. One explanation for this is that it is generally conceded that the performance of local authority enforcing authorities is poor, because it is regarded as a low priority in local government. The HSC is reviewing the role of local authorities, with the possibility that all enforcement powers might be transferred to the HSE.

The employer who feels that the inspector is being high-handed and demanding excessive precautions may appeal against either notice to an employment tribunal, which has power to cancel, affirm or modify the notice. Pending the hearing of the appeal, all except immediate prohibition notices are suspended. Unlike other proceedings before employment tribunals, costs are normally awarded against the loser to the party who wins the case. Tribunals are reluctant to overturn improvement notices issued for failure to implement specific statutory requirements. In *Harrison (Newcastle-under-Lyme)* v. *Ramsey* (1976), a notice that an employer should comply with his obligation under the Factories Act to paint his walls was upheld, despite the absence of any danger to health and the company's financial difficulties. There is more scope for argument when the employer is obliged to do that which is reasonably practicable and there is no Approved Code of Practice. In *West Bromwich Building Society* v. *Townsend* (1983), an environmental health officer served an improvement notice alleging that a building society was in breach of its duty to do what was reasonably practicable to protect its employees against robbers. It was ordered to fit anti-bandit screens. The tribunal in confirming the notice disregarded evidence that there was a difference of professional opinion about the value of such screens. On appeal to the High Court, the improvement notice was quashed.

The employer who fails to exercise his right of appeal to the tribunal may be prosecuted for failing to comply with the notice. At this stage, it is too late to argue that the issue of the notice was unjustified.

Prosecutions for offences under the health and safety statutes can only be brought by an inspector or by or with the consent of the Director of Public Prosecutions (in Scotland, prosecutions are brought by the Procurator Fiscal). Trade unions or individual employees or their families cannot bring private prosecutions except with the consent of the DPP. Prosecutions are reserved by the inspectorate for offences of a flagrant, wilful or reckless nature. In 2002/3 the number of prosecutions brought by HSE was 1688, of which 75 per cent resulted in a conviction – 1260. The average fine was £8234, including six fines in excess of £100,000. The latest figures for local authority prosecutions relate to 2001/2. There were 325 prosecutions, of which 94 per cent led to a conviction. The average fine was £3134.

Some offences under the Acts are triable only in the magistrates' courts, but most are triable either way, i.e. before the Crown Court or the magistrates. If the inspector chooses to prosecute in the Crown Court, this is because the offence is regarded as particularly serious. The Crown Court has power to order the payment of an unlimited fine and, in the case of a few offences like contravention of a prohibition or improvement notice, to send the offender to prison for up to two years. The magistrates can fine up to £20,000 for breach of section 2–6 HSWA, breach of an improvement or prohibition notice or court remedy order, and imprison for up to six months for breach of an improvement or prohibition notice or court remedy order. In respect of other offences the maximum fine available to the magistrates is £5000. Magistrates are advised by appeal courts to decline jurisdiction in serious cases where they feel that the range of penalties available to them is inadequate.

Most prosecutions are brought against a corporate body. In a series of important test cases, the appeal courts have examined the liability of a company for the acts of its employees and contractors in criminal law. *R v. Gateway Foodmarkets Ltd* (1997) concerned a supermarket store which employed a firm of contractors to maintain its lifts. At one store, the lift jammed regularly and it became the practice of the managerial staff to go to the control room and unjam it. The company's head office knew nothing of this practice, and would not have approved it if they had. On the morning following routine maintenance by the contractors the lift jammed again and the duty manager went to release it. He did not see that a trap-door in the control room had been left open. He was killed when he fell into the lift shaft. The company was convicted under section 2(1) HSWA 1974 in that it had failed to take reasonable precautions to protect its employees. It was responsible in law not just for the failings of senior management in head office, but also for those of the management 'on the ground' in its stores. The defendant was fined £10,000.

In *R v. Associated Octel Co. Ltd* (1996) the defendant employed contractors to repair the lining of a tank within a chlorine plant during the annual shut-down. The defendant's plant was designated a major hazard site. An employee of the contractors retrieved an old bucket from a refuse bin and placed acetone in it. He was working inside the tank by the light of an electric light bulb attached to a lead when the bulb broke and a flash fire ensued in which he was badly burned. The House of Lords held that the company was guilty of an offence under section 3 HSWA 1974 in failing to conduct its undertaking in such a way as to ensure, so far as was reasonably practicable, that persons not in its employment who might be affected thereby were not exposed to risks to their health and safety. It was the company's tank which was being cleaned. Though there was a permit to work system it had been operated in a perfunctory manner. Octel did not supply a special air lamp or a closed container for the acetone or forced air extraction for the tank. They had not therefore done that which was reasonably practicable.

These cases demonstrate that the employer may be held responsible in criminal law for the acts both of senior and junior employees and even of independent contractors. The only defence is to show that the company did that which was reasonably practicable to avoid the risk. The reader should compare these decisions with those on corporate manslaughter where the company can only be responsible if a senior manager ('the directing mind') of the company is at fault.

The ability of English judges to make the statute mean 'what I say that it means' must elicit admiration.

In recent years, a growing number of larger companies, local authorities and other public bodies have created formalised procedures for checking the health and safety standards of contractors wishing to work for them. The importance of 'supply chain' pressure is stressed in the *Revitalising Health and Safety* document and the HSC strategy document.

The liability of the individual manager was considered in *R v. Boal* (1992). Francis Boal was employed by Foyles as assistant general manager of its bookshop, but had been given no training in management or health and safety at work. On a day when he was in charge of the shop serious breaches of the Fire Precautions Act were discovered. Both he and his employer were prosecuted in the Crown Court. The Court of Appeal quashed his conviction (he had pleaded guilty on bad legal advice). These Acts intend to fix with criminal liability only individuals who are in a position of real authority, who have both the power and the responsibility to decide corporate policy, not those who have charge of the day-to-day running of the business. The conviction of Foyles was upheld.

On the other hand, the employer will not be held criminally responsible for all the careless acts of employees where the employer has done everything reasonably practicable to create a safe environment. In *R v. Nelson Group Services (Maintenance) Ltd* (1999) the employer was a large company engaged in the installation and servicing of gas appliances. A gas filter failed to cap the end of a gas pipe in the home of a customer, thus exposing the householder to danger. The employer argued that it had done all that was reasonably practicable to train employees, to lay down a safe system of work and to provide supervision and safe equipment. The Court of Appeal held that the fact that the employee in question omitted to take a precaution which should have been taken did not preclude the employer from establishing a defence of reasonable practicability. The fitter could have been the subject of a prosecution in this case under section 7 HSWA.

> 'It is not necessary for the adequate protection of the public that the employer should be held criminally liable even for an isolated act of negligence by the employee performing the work. Such persons are themselves liable to criminal sanctions under the Act and under the Regulations. Moreover it is a sufficient obligation to place on the employer in order to protect the public to require the employer to show that everything practicable has been done to see that a person doing the work has the appropriate skill and instruction, has had laid down for him safe systems of doing the work, has been subject to adequate supervision, and has been provided with safe plant and equipment for the proper performance of the work.'

Of course, there is no doubt that the employer was vicariously liable in the civil law (Chapter 7).

5.7 Crown immunity

There is a common law rule that Acts of Parliament do not bind the Crown (the central government and bodies acting on its behalf) unless the Crown is included either by an express provision or by necessary implication. Because Parliament is sovereign, it always has the power to extend the effects of legislation to the Crown, but many criminal statutes have not been so extended. This has allowed the employers of many thousands of workers, like the civil service and the health authorities, to escape the full effects of legislation. In the civil law, the ancient common law rules relating to the immunity of the Crown from actions for compensation were abolished by the Crown Proceedings Act 1947. This had the effect that in general an individual injured by the negligence of a Crown servant could claim compensation from the Crown in the civil courts, with a few exceptions, principally actions by members of the armed forces. The latter exception has now been removed for cases of injury occurring after the Crown Proceedings (Armed Forces) Act 1987 came into force.

It has been held that the fact that this Act is not retrospective is not a breach of the right to a fair trial conferred by Article 6 of the European Convention on Human Rights (see Chapter 7). The existence of pension arrangements for those injured in Crown service before 1987 was held to justify their exclusion from the civil action (*Matthews* v. *Ministry of Defence* (2003)).

Local government authorities have no such special status and can be held liable in criminal or civil proceedings in the same way as a company in the private sector.

In the field of statutes relating to health and safety at work, the Factories Act 1961 but not all the provisions of the HSWA 1974 applied to the Crown. The duties imposed by the HSWA, and by regulations made thereunder, bind the Crown, but not the sections giving power to inspectors to inspect, issue improvement or prohibition notices, and prosecute. The exclusion from the enforcement provisions of large employers like health authorities and Government Ministries caused much criticism. A system of Crown Enforcement Notices was introduced as a compromise in 1978. HSE inspectors could serve these on Crown bodies in circumstances where a statutory improvement or prohibition notice would have been served, but they were in reality only advisory. An administrative procedure of Crown censures permits the HSE to reprimand a Crown body. Health authorities lost their Crown immunity in the National Health Service and Community Care Act 1990. Other Crown bodies, however, still enjoy Crown immunity, though individual managers and employees, like occupational health personnel employed in Crown establishments, can be prosecuted for their own breaches of duty. Thus, the Home Office could not be prosecuted for an unsafe system of work in one of HM Prisons, but the prison doctor could be prosecuted if he had personally failed to take such precautions as were reasonably practicable to protect the staff or prisoners from risk to their health. The Health and Safety Commission has indicated that it is in favour of the complete removal of Crown immunity.

5.8 General duties under the Health and Safety at Work Act 1974

The old legislation placed duties for the most part on the occupier of premises. The HSWA spreads its net more widely. The following is a brief summary of the general duties imposed by the Act.

Section 2 makes it the duty of every employer to ensure so far as is reasonably practicable, the health, safety and welfare at work of his employees. 'Employees' includes persons who work under a contract of employment or apprenticeship. The Health and Safety (Training for Employment) Regulations 1990 provide that trainees are to be treated as employees at work, except those receiving training at an educational establishment. Students in schools and colleges will have to rely on the provisions of the Act which require the employer to take precautions to protect those not employed by him who may be affected by his activities. Homeworkers will only be covered by section 2 if they are classed as employees.

The health of the employees includes both physical and mental health. The statistics indicate that stress-related ill-health is the second most common reason for sickness absence, costing industry many millions of pounds. The Health and Safety Executive has financed research to identify the sources of stress at work, and has mounted a programme to make employers more aware of the hazards and more proactive in dealing with them. There are no 'Stress Regulations', nor an Approved Code of Practice. The difficulty of framing rules specific enough to be enforced by the courts has thus far militated against legislation. However, the general duties in the HSWA and the Management of Health and Safety at Work Regulations 1999 may be used by the HSE to try to raise standards. In 2003 the HSE served an improvement notice on the West Dorset General Hospitals NHS Trust, requiring it to make an assessment of the stress-related risks to 1100 staff and to implement a work-related stress policy.

The HSE has developed standards against which management can measure its performance, launched in 2004. It has identified major stressors as:

(1)   support – includes the encouragement, sponsorship and resources provided by the organisation, line management and colleagues;
(2)   control – how much say the person has in the way they do their work;
(3)   demands – includes issues like workload, work patterns, and the work environment;
(4)   relationships – includes promoting positive working to avoid conflict and dealing with unacceptable behaviour;
(5)   role – whether people understand their role within the organisation and whether the organisation ensures that the person does not have conflicting roles;
(6)   change – how organisational change (large or small) is managed and communicated in the organisation.

These are guidance only, but may be taken into account by courts. In fact, there have been no criminal prosecutions but many actions in civil courts against employers for stress-related illness. This is discussed in Chapter 7. It is significant that the HSE is requiring employers to be proactive and seek out those potentially vulnerable, whereas the civil courts have ruled that the employer is entitled to assume that employees are coping well with work unless they inform him to the contrary. This is not as inconsistent as it may at first appear, since the HSE's guidance relates to the workforce as a whole, whereas the civil courts are dealing with isolated complaints by individuals.

The employer is obliged to provide and maintain so far as is reasonably practicable safe plant and equipment. This extends to work done away from the employer's premises, if the employer could be reasonably expected to exercise control over it. Any place of work under the employer's control must be maintained in a reasonably safe condition. The employer must also maintain reasonably safe systems of work. This may impose an obligation on an employer in charge of a site on which a number of different contractors are working to co-ordinate their activities. This duty is now made express in the Management of Health and Safety Regulations 1999, Regulation 11.

In *R* v. *Swan Hunter* (1981), a fire killed eight men working on a ship in the Swan Hunter shipyard. The fire was caused by a welder who, without any negligence on his part, ignited leaking oxygen with a welding torch. An employee of a subcontractor, Telemeter Installations, had failed to turn off the oxygen supply in a confined space when he left work on the previous evening. Swan Hunter had taken reasonable care to inform and train their own employees as to the dangers of oxygen, but they had not concerned themselves with the instruction or training of those not employed by them but working on their site. The Court of Appeal upheld the convictions of both Swan Hunter and Telemeter for breaches of section 2 HSWA:

'If the provision of a safe system of work for the benefit of his own employees involves information and instruction as to potential dangers being given to persons other than the employer's own employees, then the employer is under a duty to provide such information and instruction, so far as is reasonably practicable.'

The Construction (Design and Management) Regulations 1994 require employers or project supervisors to appoint health and safety co-ordinators at all construction sites and to prepare a construction plan. The principal contractor, as he is termed, will be responsible for co-ordinating the activities of all the contractors on the site and also the provision and use of shared work equipment. These measures do not absolve the individual contractor from responsibility. The importance of 'supply chain' pressure has been highlighted both by the Government and the HSC, in relation to construction and more widely.

The duty to provide safe plant does not depend on whether the plant is in use. In *Bolton MBC* v. *Malrod Installations* (1993) a contractor engaged to strip asbestos had installed a decontamination unit. The day before he started work an inspector found electrical faults. It was held that the defendant was under a duty to ensure that the decontamination unit would be safe when the employees came to use it and he was convicted of an offence under the HSWA.

The employer must also make arrangements for ensuring, so far as is reasonably practicable, safety and absence of risks to health in connection with the use, handling, storage and transport of articles and substances. He must provide such information, instruction, training and supervision as is necessary to ensure, so far as is reasonably practicable, the health and safety at work of his employees. He must maintain and provide a working environment for his employees that is, so far as is reasonably practicable, safe, without risks to health, and adequate as regards facilities and arrangements for their welfare at work. It is arguable that this could oblige the employer to provide medical or nursing services in a particular case. The civil courts have held that an employer who failed to institute regular examinations of his workers who had been exposed to carcinogenic substances failed in his common law duty to take reasonable care, despite the lack of any specific statutory obligation (*Wright* v. *Dunlop Rubber Co.* (1972), Chapter 4).

Is the employer permitted to employ people in jobs which are very hazardous, or can it be argued that some tasks are so risky that they should be banned? After all, certain substances are banned by the COSHH Regulations. In *Canterbury City Council* v. *Howletts and Port Lympne Estates Ltd* (1997) the defendant company operated a zoo which specialised in breeding endangered species with the aim of releasing some of them into the wild. One of its most important philosophies was to encourage 'bonding' between animal and keeper by close contact. A keeper, Mr Smith, was killed by a tiger when he entered its enclosure for cleaning purposes. An HSE inspector issued a prohibition notice which stated that the company was in breach of section 2 HSWA and forbade the employer to continue with the previous practice of 'bonding'. The High Court judge, on appeal from an industrial tribunal, held that the HSWA was not intended to outlaw work activities merely because they were dangerous, therefore the Act did not seek to legislate what work could or could not be performed but rather the manner of its doing.

It is difficult to follow his argument. If tigers were dangerous, but could be cared for by confining them to one side of the enclosure while the other side was cleaned, was this not a reasonably practicable method of avoiding the hazard? On the other hand, if workers are to be prohibited from performing dangerous tasks, would we be deprived of firefighters, police officers and tight-rope walkers? It is, perhaps, important for occupational health specialists to accept that not all hazards can be avoided. The legislation attempts to create a balance. The social utility of the task to be performed is one factor to be considered. It may also be relevant that those engaging in the activity are aware of the risks and willingly accept them, though this can never excuse a negligent failure to take reasonable precautions. Sky-divers injured because of defective parachutes can justifiably complain, but what if the accident is caused by, for example, freak weather conditions? Should the State be able to ban all hazardous activities?

It was held in *R* v. *East Sussex County Council ex parte A* (2003) that care assistants might be required by their employer to lift patients in their homes where hoists were unavailable or impracticable, despite the risks of injury to their backs, because the rights of the patients had to be balanced against those of the employees.

The medical and nursing professions must themselves accept some hazards in the course of treating patients, because it would be both unethical and unlawful to decline to care for patients who constituted a danger. The continued employment of HIV-positive health professionals in non exposure-prone procedures carries no risk to patients, but some risk to the HIV-positive doctor or nurse because of a reduced ability to fight infection. On the other hand, the importance of allowing such people to work, and the advantage of employing them, if they wish, to treat HIV-positive patients in my view balances out the hazards.

Section 3 obliges both employers and self-employed persons to do what is reasonably practicable to protect persons not employed by them who may be affected by their activities. Thus, a place of work and work activities should be made reasonably safe for employees of contractors, other visitors, and members of the public in the vicinity (the duty is not confined to those present on premises occupied by the employer). When a passer-by was killed by the collapse of a building in the course of demolition into the street, the company in control of the site was convicted of an offence under section 3 HSWA, as was the BBC after a member of the public who had volunteered to take part in a stunt for a TV programme was killed when a safety rope failed.

In *R* v. *Mara* (1987), a small cleaning company agreed to clean the premises of International Stores in Solihull. John Mara was a director of the company, of which the only other director was his wife. His company provided a polisher/scrubber which was left on the premises for the use of Mara's cleaners. It was agreed that the employees of International Stores could also use this machine. An employee of International Stores was electrocuted while using the machine which was seriously defective. Mara was prosecuted and convicted in the Crown Court of an offence of consenting or conniving to a breach by his company of section 3 HSWA. He was fined £200.

Prosecutions under section 3 have been brought where the defendant is accused of spreading the bacterium *legionella pneumophila* (LP) in such a way as to cause risk to the general public. One illustrative case was *R* v. *Board of Trustees of the Science Museum* (1993). An inspection disclosed that these bacteria existed in the water in the air cooling system at the Science Museum. The trustees of the museum were convicted in the Crown Court of a section 3 offence, in that they failed to institute and maintain a regular regime of cleansing and disinfection, failed to maintain in operation an efficient chemical water treatment regime and failed to monitor the efficacy of the regime, so that members of the general public were exposed to risks to their health from exposure to the bacteria. They appealed, arguing that there was no proof that members of the public inhaled LP, or even that LP had escaped into the atmosphere to be inhaled. The appeal was dismissed. There was a risk to the public, whether or not it could be proved to have materialised. The primary purpose of the HSWA was preventive, in comparison with the civil law which provides compensation only where the claimant can prove damage (Chapter 7). The defendants were fined £500 and ordered to pay prosecution costs of £35,000.

Section 3 imposes a duty on self-employed persons. An independent safety consultant, Mr Glen, was asked by a demolition contractor to draw up a method statement. He eventually undertook the daily supervision of the demolition site. Because of his inadequate supervision his method statement was not observed, and employees of the contractor were exposed to high levels of lead and asbestos. Glen was convicted of an offence, fined £2000 and ordered to pay £5000 towards prosecution costs (*R* v. *Glen* (1994)). Presumably, he found it difficult to obtain further commissions. An occupational health specialist acting as a consultant runs the risk of a similar prosecution in a case of serious incompetence. There has already been a successful prosecution of an occupational hygienist whose incompetence led to unlawful exposure of employees to high levels of wood dust (*R* v. *Lockwood* (2001)).

Section 4 relates not to employers but to 'controllers' of premises who make available non-domestic premises as a place of work to those who are not employed by them. It is the duty of the person in control of such premises to take such measures as it is reasonable for a person in his position to take to ensure, so far as is reasonably practicable, that the premises and means of access and egress thereto are safe and without risks to health. A lift in a block of flats, which needed repair by electricians, has been held to fall within this section (*Westminster CC* v. *Select Management* (1985)).

Section 6 has been strengthened by amendments in the Consumer Protection Act 1987. Duties are imposed upon any person who designs, manufactures, imports, supplies, erects or instals any article, plant, machinery, equipment or appliances for use at work, or manufactures, imports or supplies a substance for use at work. This part of the 1987 Act is aimed at the protection of workers, not consumers, unlike Part I which deals with product liability, discussed in Chapter 7. 'Substance' includes a micro-organism. The safety requirements concern the safety of goods and substances in use, and in the course of setting, cleaning, maintenance, dismantling and disposal (goods) and handling, processing, storing and transporting (substances), by a person at work.

The duty is to do that which is reasonably practicable, whether by information, advice or otherwise. Risks to health and safety which could not have been reasonably foreseen are to be disregarded in deciding whether there is a breach of the statute. Reasonable testing and examination should be undertaken. Manufacturers of articles or substances must carry out or arrange for the carrying out of research necessary to discover any risks and to minimise or eliminate them. The manufacturer, importer, designer and supplier have a duty to take such steps as are necessary to warn of risks to health and safety, the results of relevant tests, and of any conditions necessary to ensure that the article or substance will be safe. They must also take such steps as are reasonably practicable actively to communicate relevant revisions of information, when it becomes known after the product has been supplied that there is a serious risk to health and safety.

In *R* v. *Bristol Magistrates Court ex parte Junttan Oy* (2004) a company designed and manufactured piling rigs. A hammer on one of the rigs was accidentally released, killing a worker. The HSE prosecuted for a breach of section 6 HSWA in respect of the supply of the rig (the design and manufacture had taken place in Finland, so the English court had no jurisdiction over those). The House of Lords held that it was not necessary to bring a prosecution under the Supply of Machinery (Safety) Regulations 1992 where the potential fine is much lower than under the HSWA. The general provisions of HSWA were also available.

Section 6 allows the designer, manufacturer, importer or supplier of an article to obtain a written undertaking from the person to whom the article is supplied that the latter will take specified steps to ensure its safety (as, for example, that he will only use a machine after a guard has been fitted or after it has been repaired). This undertaking relieves the supplier from the obligation to ensure that the article is safe when it leaves his hands, as long as it was reasonable to rely on it.

The Supply of Machinery (Safety) Regulations 1992 as amended 1994 oblige manufacturers who supply work equipment covered by the regulations to comply with European Community safety standards from 1 January 1995. The Chemicals (Hazard Information and Packaging for Supply) Regulations 2002, known as CHIP, require suppliers of chemicals to identify the hazards of the chemicals they supply, to give information to those to whom the substances are supplied and to package the chemicals safely. There is a positive duty on suppliers to assess and classify. The duty is to exercise due diligence. It is not sufficient to take the manufacturer's classification on trust, but if you deal with him regularly and use your experience and commonsense simple checks in a reference book will be enough. Safety data sheets will need to be provided for dangerous chemicals which are to be used in connection with work.

Section 7 states that it is the duty of every employee while at work:

(1) to take reasonable care for the health and safety of himself and of other persons who may be affected by his acts or omissions at work; and
(2) as regards any duty or requirement imposed on his employer or any other person by relevant statutory provisions, to co-operate with him so far as is necessary to enable that duty or requirement to be performed or complied with.

Note that this section imposes a duty on the employee to look after himself as well as his fellow employees. Employees may be prosecuted as well as or instead of their employer. Prosecutions are few. More often, an employer uses the sanction of dismissal for gross misconduct in a case of deliberate flouting of safety rules. Assuming he has followed a fair procedure, this is likely to be upheld as a fair dismissal by an employment tribunal (see Chapter 8).

An example of a prosecution for a breach of section 7 was *R. v. Farr* where a manager had used a forklift truck to gain access to a roof in order to check some repair work, thereby putting his own safety at risk.

Section 8 makes it a criminal offence for any person intentionally or recklessly to interfere with safety arrangements. This is something more than mere careless-ness: the prosecution must prove that the defendant showed a wanton disregard for the safety of others.

Section 9 prohibits any employer from charging his employees for any safety equipment provided in respect of any *specific* statutory requirement. Now that the Personal Protective Equipment Regulations 1992 oblige employers to provide personal protective equipment (PPE) wherever necessary, the employer will never be permitted to levy a charge when a risk assessment has identified a need for PPE.

5.9 Safety representatives and safety committees

Although in the early part of the nineteenth century workers tacitly accepted poor conditions, concentrating their efforts on the improvement of pay and working hours, by 1871 the improvement of working conditions had become a definite part of trade union policy. The earliest safety statutes were the product of what Sidney and Beatrice Webb described as 'middle class sentiment' (Webb, 1897) but trade unions eventually supported the need for legislation to lay down minimum standards, backed by a powerful inspectorate. Workers with weak bargaining power would be protected, and there would be no opportunity for employers to entice workers to work in unsafe conditions for extra pay.

Participation by employees in the policing of safety legislation has a long history in the mining industry. Since 1872, coalminers have had a statutory right to appoint representatives to inspect mines on their behalf. The voluntary establishment in manufacturing industry of joint safety committees, with representatives of management and workers, grew during the 1960s. The influence of Heinrich, who in 1931 first postulated the thesis that accident prevention should be based on prediction, rather than 'shutting the stable door after the horse has bolted', by the 1970s had led to the development of more systematic approaches to accident prevention by some large organisations, involving the setting of positive safety policies and objectives in consultation with the workers. The Robens Committee in 1972 wrote:

'There is no legitimate scope for "bargaining" on health and safety issues, but much scope for constructive discussion, joint inspection and participation in working out solutions.'

The Committee recommended that worker participation in health and safety be put on a statutory basis so that all, not just enlightened, employers would be compelled to involve the workforce. A fundamental political debate then arose. Should the new health and safety legislation provide for management to consult with trade unions representing workers, or with employee representatives elected by all the workers, not just those who were members of the union? The Health and Safety at Work Act finally became law after the election of a Labour Government. The Act (section 2(4)) provides that regulations may provide for the appointment by recognised trade unions of safety representatives from among the employees, and that those representatives shall represent the employees in consultation with the employers. The Safety Representatives and Safety Committees Regulations and Approved Code of Practice 1977 finally came into force in 1978. Employers who do not recognise trade unions were, therefore, permitted to avoid the mandatory involvement of safety representatives.

New general provisions were added to the 1977 regulations by a Schedule to the Management of Health and Safety at Work Regulations 1992. Every employer must consult safety representatives in good time about the introduction of changes in the workplace, health and safety information, training and so on. He must also provide them with such facilities and assistance as they may reasonably require. The employer must not dismiss or discriminate against a safety representative who is doing his job in good faith. Statutory protection is conferred by the Employment Rights Act 1996 (see Chapter 8).

In the 1980s and 1990s, recognition of trade unions became less and less common. Some employers went so far as to 'de-recognise'. The powers of trade unions to take industrial action were limited by a series of statutes in the 1980s. Membership fell to an unprecedentedly low level. Workers in some of the most hazardous industries had no safety representative to support them, because there was no recognised trade union. Change was brought about by two occurrences. The disastrous fire on the *Piper Alpha* oil rig in the North Sea exposed the vulnerability of off-shore workers in an industry largely non-unionised.

The obligation to appoint and recognise worker representatives was extended to the offshore oil and gas industry by the Offshore Installations (Safety Representatives and Safety Committees) Regulations 1989). Election of safety representatives is done by the entire workforce. The installation manager must establish a system of constituencies of about 40 workers, each constituency to elect one representative.

The European Court held that a law which imposed an obligation to consult workers, but excluded a large percentage of the workforce, was contrary to European law (*Commission of the European Communities* v. *United Kingdom* (1994)). The Health and Safety (Consultation with Employees) Regulations 1996 now provide that where there are employees who are not represented by safety representatives, the employer shall consult those employees in good time on matters of health and safety, either directly or through elected representatives for each group. The employer has the choice whether to consult employees directly or through an elected representative. Elected representatives must be consulted, given information and provided with training in the same way as trade union representatives. It is debateable how effective employee representatives can be without the backing of a trade union. Confronting the employer on matters of health and safety when production is at stake has always required courage. The protection against victimisation in the Employment Rights Act 1996 (Chapter 8) may give some reassurance. However, the non-union safety representatives have no legal right to require the establishment of a safety committee, investigate potential hazards or accidents or carry out inspections of the workplace or inspect relevant documents, although employers can, voluntarily, arrange for the elected representatives to carry out these functions.

Safety representatives should normally be employees with at least two years' service. Numbers will depend on the nature of the workplace and the levels of risk. It is the duty of the employer to consult them on matters of health and safety. They have a right to reasonable time off with pay for training (see Chapter 8).

As well as consultation with the employer, the union-appointed safety representatives have the power to investigate potential hazards and dangerous occurrences at the workplace. They have the right routinely to inspect the workplace or part of it on giving reasonable notice in writing to the employer of their intention to do so, usually every three months, but more often if there have been substantial changes in working conditions, or new information from the HSC/HSE. In the event of a notifiable accident or disease, they have the right to inspect the scene as long as it is safe to do so.

The 1977 and 1996 regulations provide that a safety representative, although liable to prosecution as an employee under sections 7 and 8 HSWA, shall not be under any additional legal duty by virtue of exercising his functions as a safety representative. A representative who forgot to mention to the manager dangerous fumes reported to him by an employee would not be legally liable for that failure. A safety officer would have no such immunity.

Every employer, if requested in writing to do so by at least two union-appointed safety representatives, must establish a safety committee. Safety committees should be concerned with all relevant aspects of health, safety and welfare of persons at work in relation to the working environment. An HSE Guidance Note advises that the functions of a safety committee could include:

(1) the study of accidents, diseases, statistics and trends, so that reports can be made to management with recommendations for improvement;
(2) consideration of reports from the inspectorates and liaison with them;
(3) consideration of reports from safety representatives;
(4) assistance in the development of works safety rules and safe systems of work;
(5) a watch on the effectiveness of safety training;
(6) a watch on the adequacy of safety and health communications in the workplace.

The safety committee should be small, with at least as many worker representatives as management representatives. Occupational health physicians, industrial hygienists and safety officers should be *ex officio* members.

The trade unions would like the powers of safety representatives to be increased. They advocate that the safety committee should appoint occupational health personnel and control occupational health and safety services. The safety representatives should be given the power to issue a prohibition notice where they believe there is an imminent risk of serious injury or harm.

The Health and Safety Commission in 2002 supported a pilot scheme to appoint through the HSE worker safety advisers (WSAs) or roving safety representatives. A team of nine worked with employers in small non-unionised workplaces in automotive engineering, construction, hospitality and the voluntary sector. These WSAs were drawn from people who had gained their skills and experience through trade union health and safety activities, temporarily seconded to the project, and funded through the Department of Work and Pensions. The success of the pilot has resulted in the creation of a WSA Challenge Fund of £3 million.

There are, however, a number of problems which arise from the appointment of roving safety representatives. First, it is obviously vital that they should have adequate qualifications and experience, probably of the level of the TUC Certificate in Occupational Health and Safety. Secondly, some employers are concerned that the introduction of a trade union official into a non-unionised workplace may lead to union recruitment and industrial relations problems. This did not arise during the pilot, because it was agreed that the WSAs would not involve themselves in recruitment, but it remains to be seen whether unions would be content to devote significant resource to non-unionised workplaces without at least the opportunity to try to recruit new members.

Thirdly, the WSAs are not at present protected by the Safety Representatives Regulations, and therefore have to be given professional indemnity insurance. Fourthly, it will have to be made clear that there is a distinction between the WSA role and that of the HSE inspectors, otherwise employers will not co-operate. It would seem advisable that an independent board of management with both trade union, employer and HSE representation should run the scheme were it to become permanent. It is unlikely that individual businesses will need a WSA as a permanent fixture: he or she will rather act as a catalyst in the creation of good practice in the workplace. (Shaw and Turner (2003): *The worker safety advisers' pilot* (HSE).)

In 1998 the Government asked the HSC to seek ideas for promoting and encouraging greater worker involvement and consultation. The HSC in 1999 published a document, *Employee consultation and involvement in health and safety*, for discussion, with the intention of making proposals to harmonise the 1977 and 1996 Regulations. They also asked for comments on roving safety representatives, a system established in Sweden for 25 years. The most politically sensitive section of the document relates to Provisional Improvement Notices (PINs). In two of the Australian States safety representatives have legal powers to issue their employers with a PIN requiring an alleged breach of the law to be remedied within a specific period. If the enforcing authority agrees that there has been a breach of the law it can issue a formal improvement notice. Another possibility would be to give legal protection to safety representatives who recommend workers to leave the place of work in circumstances of serious, imminent and unavoidable danger. There might be a need to consider whether a system would be justified which could recompense employers where financial and other loss resulted from an erroneous use of such powers (HSE inspectors are not liable for economic loss caused by negligent advice: *Harris* v. *Evans* (1998)). In 2001 the HSC published proposals on harmonised regulations, but found it impossible to obtain substantial consensus. In July 2003 the HSC indicated that, as producing draft consultative regulatory proposals supported by both businesses and trade unions was 'some way off', non-regulatory initiatives such as the Worker Safety Adviser Challenge Fund would be pursued.

In 2004 the HSC issued a collective declaration on worker involvement:

'A universally involved and consulted workforce would be a major achievement and contribute to getting health and safety recognised as a cornerstone of a civilised society.'

The declaration has been criticised as a retreat from regulation.

5.10 Access to information

There was no general principle of freedom of information enshrined in the laws of this country until the Freedom of Information Act 2000 was passed. On the whole, therefore, industry has no duty to give warning either to workers or to the general public of hazards created by the enterprise. There are at least three possible routes whereby the disclosure of such information may, exceptionally, be required:

(1)   The management of the enterprise may be placed under a statutory duty to notify a public authority which may then disseminate the information.

(2)   Management or the inspectorates may be required by statute to notify workers directly or through their representatives.

(3)   A court may order disclosure of information relevant to legal proceedings.

Disclosure to a public authority is required by various legal regulations. The Reporting of Injuries, Diseases and Dangerous Occurrences Regulations 1995 (RIDDOR) have already been discussed in Chapter 3. They are currently under review. The Notification of New Substances Regulations 1993 oblige manufacturers or importers of new chemical substances to notify the HSE of technical details. The Dangerous Substances (Notification and Marking of Sites) Regulations 1990 require notification to the fire authority and the HSE and marking of sites where there are 25 tonnes or more of dangerous substances present.

Membership of the European Community has brought with it obligations in connection with major hazards. After the Seveso chemicals disaster in Italy, a Directive was agreed which was incorporated into UK law as the Control of Industrial Major Accident Regulations 1984, amended in 1990. The Regulations were updated in 1999 following the adoption of a Directive on the Control of Major Accident Hazards by the European Council of Ministers in 1996. These apply to industrial activities involving very toxic, flammable or explosive substances, and to the isolated storage of quantities of such substances. Operators that have control of such activities must identify major accident hazards and take adequate steps to prevent accidents, limit their consequences, and provide persons working on the site with the information, training and equipment necessary to ensure their safety. Where a major accident occurs, the operator must notify the HSE, which in its turn must notify the European Commission. In addition, the operator must in any event give information to the competent authority (the HSE and the Environment Agency have joint responsibility but the HSE is the primary contact) about the dangerous substance, a description of process or storage arrangements, a map of the site, and details of the workforce on the site, emergency procedures, and even prevailing meteorological conditions in the vicinity. The operator must also approach the local authority with a view to informing persons outside the site of possible risks. Operators of top-tier (especially hazardous) sites must also produce a safety report to show that they have taken all necessary measures to prevent major accidents, and an on-site emergency plan. The local authority of the area where the top-tier establishment is located must prepare an off-site emergency plan. Radiation hazards are dealt with by the Radiation (Emergency Preparedness and Public Information) Regulations 2001.

All these laws, however, limit the disclosure of information to third parties without the consent of the organisation to which it relates. Section 28 HSWA forbids the disclosure of information obtained under section 27 or furnished in pursuance of a statutory requirement. Certain exceptions are set out in section 28, notably disclosure to a local authority, water authority or to the police. The Freedom of Information Act 2000 creates a general right of access to information held by public authorities, but allows information to be withheld on grounds of breach of confidence, national security, legal professional privilege, the prevention or detection of crime or prejudice to commercial interests. It would seem that the HSE is likely to be somewhat more flexible in releasing information under its powers in section 28(8) (see below), but that section 28 is unlikely to be repealed.

Inspectors exercising powers of inspection may not as a general rule disclose any information obtained by them other than for the purpose of legal proceedings, except that they are expressly authorised by section 28 (8) to disclose information to employees or their representatives, as well as to the employer, if it is necessary for the purpose of keeping them adequately informed about matters affecting their health, safety or welfare. This may be either factual information obtained as to the premises or anything done therein, or information with respect to action taken or to be taken by the inspectorate. The Environment and Safety Information Act 1988 compels the inspectorates to make a list of improvement and prohibition notices available to the general public.

Section 2 HSWA imposes a duty on the employer to provide such information to his employees as is necessary to ensure, so far as is reasonably practicable, their health and safety at work. The Health and Safety (Safety Signs and Signals) Regulations 1996 impose requirements about safety signs and signals, and at the same time introduce a standard format with which signs must comply (e.g. 'no smoking' is a black pictogram on a white background within a round shape with a red edging and a diagonal red line across a smoking cigarette). The Health and Safety (Information for Employees) Regulations 1989 oblige an employer to display posters at work (or distribute leaflets) about the Health and Safety at Work Act. These posters are published by the HSE. The Management of Health and Safety at Work Regulations 1999 oblige the employer to tell his employees of any special health risks involved in their work. Section 6 HSWA obliges manufacturers, importers, suppliers, etc. of an article or substance to give adequate information about any conditions necessary to ensure that it will be safe and without risks to health when properly used. The Chemicals (Hazard Information and Packaging) (CHIP) Regulations 2002 regulate suppliers of dangerous chemicals. These chemicals must be labelled with their particular hazard (e.g. toxic, corrosive, highly flammable), safety precautions, and the name of the substance and its supplier or manufacturer. Dangerous substances must be accompanied by a safety data sheet. Standard symbols are to be adopted (e.g. the skull and cross-bones for very toxic chemicals).

The Management Regulations 1999 state that every employer shall provide his employees with comprehensible and relevant information on the risks to their health and safety identified by the risk assessment and the preventive and protective measures.

The Safety Representatives Regulations 1977 and the Health and Safety (Consultation with Employees) Regulations 1996 require the employer to make available to safety representatives information necessary to enable them to carry out their functions. There are a number of exceptions, including a document consisting of or relating to any health record of an identifiable individual. The Approved Code of Practice particularises the kinds of information which should be made available to safety representatives by the employer. It includes plans about proposed changes, technical information about plant, equipment and substances, information kept by the employer to comply with RIDDOR, and any other information specifically related to matters affecting the health and safety at work of his employees, including the result of any measurements taken by the employer or persons acting on his behalf in the course of checking the effectiveness of his health and safety arrangements.

In practice, if the employer and the inspectorate stubbornly refuse to disclose information, the only method of obtaining it is for an individual to bring a civil action for damages in the courts and apply for discovery of documents (see Chapter 3). Where no actual damage has been suffered by any individual, this option will not be available.

In 2004 the Secretary of State for Trade and Industry announced proposals for the new statutory Operating and Financial Review procedures for companies, to include information for shareholders on the company's environmental and health and safety performance.

5.11   The control of substances hazardous to health

Much of the work of health professionals in British industry has from the nineteenth century onwards been concerned with the prevention of disease caused by exposure to dangerous substances. Lead poisoning in the pottery trades, necrosis of the jaw caused by working with phosphorus in the match factories, mercury poisoning in the process of silvering mirrors and, of course, the effects of the inhalation of dust of various kinds, were well-known and documented long before the eventual creation of statutory controls. 'Phossy-jaw' was mentioned in Parliamentary Reports of 1843. Legislation prohibiting the use of white phosphorus was finally passed only in 1908.

The development of the chemical and pharmaceutical industries and the discovery of nuclear power in the twentieth century have greatly added to the potential risks faced by the workers. The horror of this kind of danger is that irreparable damage may be suffered before the risk is identified, because the symptoms may only appear years after exposure. Even today, legislation may be slow in gestation. The Health and Safety Commission is a tripartite body. It has to reconcile the interests of commercial industry and agriculture and the trade unions. Research has to be commissioned. In the 1990s the control of dangerous substances was seen as an international problem and laws increasingly originated from Brussels rather than London. Control of dangerous substances at work was linked with pollution control to protect the public and the environment.

Up to now, legislation has been passed on a substance by substance basis. The principal regulations which in practice will most concern OH professionals are as follows:

(1)   Coal Mines (Respirable Dust) Regulations 1975 and 1978 (under review);
(2)   The Control of Lead at Work Regulations 2002;
(3)   The Control of Asbestos at Work Regulations 2002.

Just as the HSWA introduced a new philosophy by providing general rules for all places of work, the Control of Substances Hazardous to Health (COSHH) Regulations and Approved Code of Practice (the latest regulations came into force in 2002) extend to all hazardous substances whether or not specifically named.

First, they require the employer to assess the risk. Secondly, he must introduce engineering controls to reduce exposure to the lowest level which is reasonably practicable. Upper limits may be set by the regulations themselves. Where necessary, personal protective equipment must be provided as a 'back-up', but never as a replacement for proper engineering. Thirdly, the premises and perhaps also the workers must be monitored to check that controls are effective. Fourthly, where exposure may cause harm to health, health surveillance procedures, ranging from keeping a health record of exposure to regular checks by a doctor, must be instituted. Some regulations, like the Control of Lead at Work (2002), Ionising Radiations (1999) and Control of Asbestos at Work (2002) direct that employees who will be exposed to the dangerous substance shall be medically examined before or soon after the beginning of their employment in order to provide a base-line for later tests. This is not specifically mentioned in the COSHH Regulations, but may be advisable in some cases.

The 'one-substance' regulations have by definition already identified the hazardous substance. One of the revolutionary aspects of the COSHH Regulations is that it is to some extent up to the employer to assess the danger. He can no longer wait for an official Government warning. Regulation 6 provides that an employer shall not carry out any work which is liable to expose any employees to any substance hazardous to health unless he has made a 'suitable and sufficient' assessment of the risks created by that work to their health and of the steps needed to meet the requirements laid down in the Regulations. The employer is not left completely on his own. The Regulations list a number of substances defined as hazardous to health. They have already been referred to in Chapter 4. They include any substance classified as being very toxic, toxic, harmful, corrosive or irritant under the Chemicals (Hazard Information and Packaging for Supply) Regulations 2002, any biological agent, dust of any kind, when present at a substantial concentration in air, and those substances which have a maximum exposure limit (MEL), or an occupational exposure standard (OES) approved by the HSC. (A MEL is the maximum limit of exposure considered safe which should never be exceeded; an OES is the acceptable limit within which the employer should aim to stay as a general rule.) The proposed wholesale withdrawal of most occupational exposure limits as part of the revision of the regulations will now not take place. In the new regulations, which are likely to come into force in 2005, MELs and OESs will be replaced by WELs (workplace exposure limits). There will be two kinds of WEL, the first where the substance is so hazardous that the law will continue to require exposure to be as low as reasonably practicable (including carcinogens, mutagens and asthmagens), even below a WEL, and the second where the employer will comply with the law if he reduces exposure to below the WEL.

This is not, however, the end of the list, for employers will have to ask themselves whether their workers are exposed to any *other* substance which might be harmful. The HSC advises that the following questions should be answered:

(1) *What hazardous substances are there?*
     In most cases, the employer will not need to commission his own research, but will be able to rely on information from the supplier, including labels

attached to the containers, trade and technical literature, HSE Guidance Notes and data sheets, and past experience. In the case of research laboratories themselves, new and unknown substances will have to be treated with great caution until their properties become known.

(2)   *What are the harmful effects?*
      The effect will partly depend on the form of the substance and partly on the way it acts on the body. Answers will be obtained from the same sources as in (1) above. The possibility of dangers arising from a mixture of substances should be considered.

(3)   *Where will the hazardous substance be likely to be present?*

(4)   *Who may be affected?*

(5)   *How great is the degree and length of exposure likely to be?*
      The employer must enquire into working practices and experience. All routes must be considered – inhalation, and contamination of skin, clothing, food, drink and smoking materials. Exposure sampling may be necessary. This may be an examination of the working environment or of the employees themselves, or both. The Code of Practice states that 'Employers must ensure that whoever carries out monitoring of exposure is competent to do so.'

(6)   *How do the exposure data compare with recognised standards?*

(7)   *What action should be taken in response to the assessment?*
      Control is the most important message. Perhaps the substance can be eliminated from the process, or replaced. Efficient engineering controls are the next consideration. In all cases, control should be achieved by measures other than personal protective equipment, if reasonably practicable. To ensure that everything is going according to plan, routine monitoring of the environment, or health surveillance may be necessary. Assessments should be recorded and made available to the employees. They should be reviewed if there is a change in the work, or new information comes to light.

The trade unions argue that substances should no longer be regarded as 'innocent until proven guilty':

'The cost of giving inanimate substances the benefit of a criminal court's defence has been unacceptably high, with 2000 asbestos deaths a year standing as a tragic testament to this traditional approach. The histories of mineral oil, silica, coal dusts, gas retort fumes and chemicals in the rubber and dyestuffs industries provide similar examples of the high human and community costs of giving substances, not workers, the benefit of the doubt.' (General, Municipal, Boilermakers and Allied Trades Union (1987))

The duties imposed on the employer by the Regulations are owed in the first instance to his own employees and they are strict: he *must comply* with the Regulations, not merely to do that which is reasonably practicable, though the use of wording like 'suitable and sufficient assessment' and 'suitable health surveillance' allows inspectors and judges flexibility in interpretation. Also, Regulation 21 states that in any proceedings for an offence consisting of a contravention of the Regulations it shall be a defence for any person to prove that he took all reasonable precautions and exercised all due diligence to avoid the commission of the offence. In other words, the burden of showing that reasonable care was taken is on the employer, not the prosecutor. As the Regulations do not exclude a civil action for breach of statutory duty, they have given rise to a number of claims for damages for breach of statutory duty as well as criminal prosecutions. There is an important distinction between civil and criminal proceedings. Section 47(3) HSWA states that no defence made available by health and safety regulations in respect of criminal proceedings shall afford a defence in civil proceedings, unless specifically extended to civil liability. The 'due diligence' defence in Regulation 21 does not apply to civil actions for breach of statutory duty, therefore the civil liability of the employer under several of the Regulations, at least to his employees, is strict.

The employer also has obligations under the Regulations to non-employees. The duties to assess risks (Regulation 6), prevent or control exposure (Regulation 7) and use control measures, and maintain, examine and test control measures (Regulations 8 and 9) are owed both to non-employees on the employer's premises (e.g. contractors, students) and other persons likely to be affected by the employer's work (e.g. members of the public living nearby). The employer is only obliged to take care for these persons so far as is reasonably practicable (he would still have the burden of proving that it was not reasonably practicable to do more than was in fact done (section 40 HSWA)).

The duty to monitor exposure at the workplace (Regulation 10) and to provide information and training (Regulation 12) is owed to employees and non-employees on the employer's premises, but not to persons off the premises. Again, the duty to non-employees is only to do that which is reasonably practicable. The duty of health surveillance (Regulation 11) is owed *only to employees* (see Chapter 4).

Take a typical scenario of a factory manufacturing hazardous chemicals oper-ated by Company X. Several different categories of people are affected by X's activities. On the factory premises, there are:

(1) X's own employees;
(2) employees of Company Y, which has a contract with X to instal new electrical wiring;
(3) students from the nearby university who are visiting the factory;
(4) firemen, who have been summoned to deal with a small fire caused by defective wiring.

As well, the factory is near several other factories and a motorway.

Company X's management must comply with all the regulations in respect of their own employees. Also, they will have to do that which is reasonably prac-ticable to assess the risk and control exposure to hazardous substances of all those in the area, both on and off their premises, but there is no obligation to monitor any exposure outside the factory. Reasonable information needs to be given to the employees of Company Y and the students, as well as to the firefighters, but not to the public off the premises. A health record, and other health surveillance pro-cedures, will be required only for those directly employed by X.

What are the obligations of Company Y to its electricians, who are its employees? Of course, it has general duties under the HSWA itself to give training and take reasonable precautions against foreseeable dangers. Regulation 2 (2) provides that any reference in the Regulations to an employee being exposed to a substance hazardous to health is a reference to the exposure of that employee to such a substance *arising out of or in connection with work at the workplace*. Company Y owes the same duties to its own employees as any other employer. Thus, the employees of subcontractors can rely on the obligations placed by the regulations both on their own employers and on the main contractor. As regards health surveillance, the duty will be on the subcontractor. This is also the legal position in respect of agency workers. Where a worker is employed by an agency, the agency owes the duty of health surveillance. In practice, it may agree with the main contractor that the latter will perform that function. Co-operation and collaboration between employers will be necessary and this is now the subject of regulation by the Management Regulations 1999 (Regulation 11).

Regulation 3 states that the Regulations shall apply to self-employed persons, but not to the master or crew of a sea-going ship or the employer of such persons, in relation to normal ship-board activities. They do not cover lead, coal dust or asbestos where regulations are already in force. Nothing in the Regulations shall be taken to prejudice any requirement imposed by public health or environmental protection legislation. Although the Regulations cover exposure to micro-organisms, this is merely when the risks of exposure are work-related, not incidental (Regulation 2 (2), Chapter 4). If I am exposed to a dangerous substance in the course of having it administered to me as part of my medical or dental treatment, or as part of a research study, the Regulations do not apply, unless there is also a risk to the health professional caring for me.

Regulation 7 provides that employers must either prevent the exposure of their employees to hazardous substances, or, where not reasonably practicable, adequately control it. So far as is reasonably practicable, except in the case of carcinogens and biological agents, this should be secured without relying on protective equipment, but if this is not possible (e.g. routine maintenance, plant failure, lack of technical feasibility), the employer must provide suitable personal protection in addition to reasonably practicable engineering controls. Items of protective equipment should comply with the requirements of the European standards, where they exist. Where there is exposure to a substance for which an MEL is fixed, the control of exposure is adequate, so far as the inhalation of that substance is concerned, only if the level of exposure is reduced at least to below the MEL, and even lower if reasonably practicable. Where exposure is to a substance for which an OES has been approved by the HSC, the control of exposure is adequate, so far as the inhalation of that substance is concerned, if either the OES is not exceeded, or where it is exceeded, the employer identifies the reasons and takes appropriate action to remedy the situation as soon as is reasonably practicable.

The MEL is the maximum concentration of an airborne substance, averaged over a reference period, to which employees may be exposed by inhalation under any circumstances. Control to the OES, or below it, can always be regarded as adequate, so far as exposure from inhalation is concerned. The absence of a substance from the lists of MELs and OESs does not indicate that it is safe. Some substances are hazardous by routes other than inhalation, and lists will always need updating. Where a substance has not been listed, the employer should control exposure to a level to which the bulk of the population could be regularly exposed without injury.

In 2004 the system of exposure limits is under review and is likely to change to bring the UK into line with Europe in 2005. Workplace Exposure Limits will take the place of MELs and OESs.

All kinds of control measures should be considered, ranging from totally enclosed process and handling systems to the provision of ventilation and adequate facilities for washing and laundering clothing. Control measures must be regularly examined, maintained and tested, and records must be kept. Regulation 8 obliges the employer to take all reasonable steps to ensure that control measures and personal protective equipment are properly used and applied. Employees also have a responsibility to themselves.

'Every employee shall make full and proper use of any control measure, personal protective equipment or other thing or facility provided pursuant to the Regulations and, if he discovers any defect therein, he shall report it forthwith to his employer.'

The employee who contravenes this Regulation is committing a crime. Also, his employer may decide to treat a bad case as a disciplinary matter.

Regulation 10 concerns the monitoring of exposure at the workplace. Monitoring means 'the use of valid and suitable occupational hygiene techniques to derive a quantitative estimate of the exposure of employees to substances hazardous to health'. It is, in general, needed:

(1)	when failure or deterioration of control could result in a serious health effect;
(2)	when measurement is necessary so as to be sure that a MEL or OES, or any self-imposed working standard, is not exceeded; or
(3)	as an additional check on the effectiveness of any control, and always in the case of a substance specified in Schedule 5 (vinyl chloride monomer and vapour or spray given off from vessels in which an electrolytic chromium process is carried on, except trivalent chromium).

The HSE provides guidance on suitable sampling techniques and methods of analysis. A further source mentioned in the Code of Practice is occupational health text books.

Records must be kept. Where the record represents the personal exposure of identifiable employees, it should be kept for 40 years, and in any other case for at least five years. The records should be kept in such a way that the results can be compared with any health records under Regulation 11, which has already been dealt with in Chapter 4.

Regulation 12 directs an employer who undertakes work which may expose any of his employees to hazardous substances to provide suitable and sufficient information, instruction and training to enable such employees to know:

(1) the nature and degree of the risks to health, including any factors which may influence it, e.g. smoking, and
(2) the precautions which should be taken, including the role of health surveillance.

In particular, the employer has a specific statutory obligation to give to his employees and to safety representatives information on the results of any monitoring of exposure at the workplace and of any case where the MEL was exceeded. He must also give information on the collective results (without any individual being identified) of any health surveillance undertaken in accordance with Regulation 11. The HSE can request copies of an employee's personal health record.

Regulation 13 imposes duties on employers to ensure that procedures to deal with accidents, incidents and emergencies are in place. These include first-aid facilities and safety drills. Information must be given to employees about emergency arrangements. An employee shall report forthwith, to his employer or a safety officer, any accident or incident which has or may have resulted in the release of a biological agent which could cause severe human disease.

Regulation 14 and Schedule 9 require the employer in some circumstances to notify public officials, like a harbour authority or the police, of intended fumigations with hydrogen cyanide, phosphine or methyl bromide. Suitable warning notices must also be placed at all points of reasonable access to the premises to be fumigated. The regulation does not apply to fumigations carried out for research.

Schedule 3 contains special provisions relating to biological agents. The HSC maintains a list of biological agents which are classified within one of four groups. Group 1 covers agents unlikely to cause human disease, Group 2 those which can cause human disease and may be a hazard to employees, but are unlikely to spread to the community, Group 3 those which can cause serious human disease and may be a serious hazard to employees, with a possibility of spread to the community, Group 4 those which cause severe human disease, may be a serious hazard to employees, are likely to spread to the community and for which there is no effective prophylaxis or treatment available. Groups 2 and 3 include agents for which there is effective treatment available. There is a duty to notify the HSE of the storage or use of Group 2, 3 or 4 biological agents.

5.12   *Noise at Work Regulations 1989*

Noise-induced hearing loss has been well known for over a century, but only recently has legislation been enacted. The mushrooming of claims against employers for occupational deafness has made them more conscious of the risks and more inclined to introduce regular audiometric testing, though as yet there is no legal obligation on the employer to provide such tests. The European Commission argues that in failing to provide for compulsory testing the UK has not implemented the EC noise directive.

By the 1989 Regulations employers are required to make a formal noise assessment where employees are likely to be exposed to 85 decibels (dB) (first action level) or above, or to peak action level (200 pascals) or above. Records must be kept. Every employer shall reduce the risk of damage to the hearing of his employees from exposure to noise to the lowest level reasonably practicable (Regulation 6). Where the employee is likely to be exposed to the second action level (90 dB) or above or to the peak action level or above, the employer must reduce exposure so far as is reasonably practicable by methods other than the provision of personal ear protectors. These are appropriate between 85–90 dB and should be provided at the employee's request, but can also be used at higher levels to reduce the exposure to below 90 dB. Ear protection zones should be established with signs indicating that hearing protection should be worn.

A comprehensive review of the 1989 Regulations after the agreement of a new European Directive on Noise has led to draft regulations, which will come into force in 2006 (except for the music and entertainment sectors, where the implementation date is 2008). The regulations reduce by 5 decibels the exposure levels at which action must be taken, i.e. to 80 decibels. There will be two action values:

(1)   lower exposure action value – a daily or weekly noise exposure of level of 80 decibels and a peak sound pressure of 135 decibels;
(2)   upper exposure action value – a daily or weekly noise exposure of 85 decibels and a peak sound pressure level of 137 decibels.

Employers will have to make a risk assessment of work where exposure to noise is likely to be above the lower action value. Hearing protection will only be acceptable as a last resort where all other measures have been taken, or as interim protection during the implementation of noise controls.

The assessment of risks is not restricted to noise induced hearing loss. Other risks include not being able to hear an audible warning and interaction with some drugs (for example streptomycin). The emphasis of the new legislation will be on getting employers to control noise rather than just measuring it.

5.13   The 1992 Regulations

The changes in Europe brought about by the Single European Act gave considerable impetus to health and safety law. A framework directive and five 'daughter' directives were agreed in 1989 and 1990 and these were enacted into UK law as regulations made under the Health and Safety at Work Act. They were the Management of Health and Safety at Work Regulations 1992, the Workplace (Health, Safety and Welfare) Regulations 1992, the Provision and Use of Work Equipment Regulations (PUWER) 1992, the Personal Protective Equipment Regulations 1992, the Manual Handling Operations Regulations 1992 and the Display Screen Equipment Regulations 1992.

All these provisions came into force to some extent on 1 January 1993, but transitional provisions caused considerable confusion for some years. For example, the new regulations about display screen equipment applied immediately to workstations put into service after 1 January 1993, but not to pre-existing workstations. The latter needed only to comply with the regulations from 31

December 1996. If new display screen equipment was put into a pre-1993 work-station it became a new workstation, but changing a chair or desk did not activate the regulations, except with regard to the new piece of furniture. This is not to say that 'old' workstations were outside the law. The employer had to comply with the general duty to do that which is reasonably practicable to protect his employees against injury, and he was bound immediately by the Management Regulations to assess and record risks to the health and safety of employees and others who work with display screen equipment.

For lawyers, these regulations represent a major revision, because they repeal many sections of such legislation as the Factories Act, the Offices, Shops and Railway Premises Act, the Abrasive Wheels Regulations, the Protection of Eyes Regulations and the Woodworking Machines Regulations. Transitional pro-visions provided that these laws would remain in force side by side with the new regulations for a number of years.

Since all the regulations now give rise to civil liability, the action for damages for breach of statutory duty has been significantly affected. The increase in the numbers of regulations, Approved Codes of Practice and HSE Guidance assists employee claimants in their search to make employers liable.

Since the new laws enact EC directives, the courts in interpreting them must strive to implement the intentions of the Council of Ministers. Also, it may be possible to argue that the regulations are out of line with the directive in some particular respect, thus allowing a possible appeal to the European Court.

Since 1992 further important regulations have been enacted to comply with EC directives. The old Construction Regulations have been replaced by the Con-struction (Health, Safety and Welfare) Regulations 1996. The management of construction sites has been revolutionised by the Construction (Design and Management) Regulations 1994. New regulations relating to work in compressed air came into force in September 1996 (Work in Compressed Air Regulations 1996). Comprehensive safety laws covering the newly privatised railway industry have been enacted: Railways (Safety Critical Work) Regulations 1994, Railways (Safety Case) Regulations 2000 and Railway Safety (Miscellaneous Provisions) Regulations 1997.

The regulations are regularly reviewed and where necessary updated. The latest Management Regulations date from 1999, the Provision and Use of Work Equipment Regulations from 1998, and the Railway Safety Regulations from 1999.

5.14   *Management of Health and Safety at Work Regulations 1999 and ACOP*

The original regulations came into force on 1 January 1993 and were of immediate application. The latest version dates from 1999. They lay down broad general principles which apply to virtually all places of work except sea-going ships. From 2003 an action for breach of statutory duty lies in respect of these regulations. The central provision is Regulation 3. Every employer shall make a suitable and suf-ficient assessment of (a) the risks to the health and safety of his employees to which they are exposed while they are at work; and (b) the risks to the health and safety of persons not in his employment arising out of or in connection with the conduct by him of his undertaking, for the purposes of identifying the measures he needs to take to comply with the requirements and prohibitions imposed upon him by or under the relevant statutory provisions. An employer who employs five or more employees must record (this can be computerised) the significant findings of the assessment and any group of his employees identified by it as being especially at risk.

Risk assessment may already be familiar from compliance with the COSHH Regulations. There are no fixed rules about how it should be undertaken. Paragraph 18 of the Approved Code of Practice sets out the most important factors. A risk assessment should:

(1) ensure that all relevant risks and hazards are addressed (they should not be obscured by an excess of information or by concentrating on trivial risks);
(2) address what actually happens in the workplace or during the work activity (remembering that what happens in practice may differ from the works manual and not forgetting the non-routine operations such as maintenance);
(3) ensure that all groups of employees and others who might be affected are considered (not forgetting cleaners, security staff, visitors, etc.);
(4) identify workers who might be particularly at risk, such as young workers, disabled staff, etc.;
(5) take account of existing protective and precautionary measures.

Every employer shall make and give effect to such arrangements as are appropriate, having regard to the nature of his activities and the size of his undertaking, for the effective planning, organisation, control, monitoring, and review of preventive and protective measures (Regulation 5). Every employer shall ensure that his employees are provided with such health surveillance as is appropriate having regard to the risks to their health and safety which are identified by the assessment (Regulation 6).

The employer must appoint one or more competent persons to assist him (Regulation 7). This provision puts more pressure than before on employers to appoint safety advisers and occupational health personnel with recognised specialist qualifications (though there is still no statutory requirement). Employers must establish procedures to cope with emergency situations (e.g. fire drills) (Regulation 8). Every employer shall provide his employees with comprehensible and relevant information (Regulation 10). There is now a statutory duty on the employer to tell the employees about any special health risks involved in their work.

Where two or more employers share a workplace each employer has a duty to co-operate with the other and to co-ordinate the measures he takes with those the other employers are taking (Regulation 11). An employer in control of a site must give health and safety information to the employees of contractors (Regulation 11). Where there is no controlling employer, the employers and self-employed persons present should agree such joint arrangements, such as appointing a health and safety co-ordinator, as are needed to comply with the regulations.

Employees must be provided with adequate health and safety training during working hours (Regulation 13). Employees must obey the employer's instructions as to the use of equipment, safety devices, etc. and must inform the employer of any work situation which they would reasonably consider a serious and immediate danger and any matter which they would reasonably consider represented a shortcoming in the employer's protection arrangements (Regulation 14). Regulation 15 deals with temporary workers (defined as those working under a fixed term contract). It obliges the employer to provide information about any special occupational qualifications or skills needed to do the job safely and also any health surveillance required by statute. Regulation 16 requires risk assessments for women of child-bearing age who may become pregnant (Chapter 9). Regulation 19 deals with the protection of young persons (Chapter 9).

5.15   *Workplace (Health, Safety and Welfare) Regulations 1992 and ACOP*

These came into force on 1 January 1993 as respects new workplaces or new parts of workplaces. They supersede many provisions of the Factories Act and the Offices, Shops and Railway Premises Act, but existing workplaces fell within scope from 1 January 1996. The exception is Regulation 17 which imposed an immediate obligation to provide traffic (including pedestrian) routes in all workplaces which are, so far as is reasonably practicable, suitable for the persons using them, sufficient in number, in suitable positions and of sufficient size.

   These regulations affect all places of work except ships, building operations and works of engineering construction and workplaces undertaking exploration or extraction of mineral resources (mines, quarries, oil rigs). Regulations already exist in relation to those places of work. Moving vehicles are covered while stationary inside the workplace (e.g. while being unloaded). They include provisions about ventilation, temperature, lighting, cleanliness, floors, windows, doors, lavatories and washing facilities. The Approved Code of Practice states that the minimum acceptable temperature at the workstation is 16°C. Separate lavatories must be provided for men and women except where the convenience is in a separate room which can be locked from the inside. An amendment to the regulations states that rest areas and rest rooms should be arranged to enable employees to use them without experiencing discomfort from tobacco smoke. Methods of achieving this include the provision of separate rooms or areas for smokers and non-smokers, or the prohibition of smoking in rest areas and rest rooms.

5.16   *Provision and Use of Work Equipment Regulations (PUWER) 1998*

The original regulations came into force on 1 January 1993 as respects work equipment first provided for use in the workplace after that date and were updated in 1998. Existing equipment was not affected until 1 January 1997. It is the date of supply to the employee which is important, not the date of manufacture. An employer who on 2 January 1993 for the first time provided a second-hand van for his employee to use at work must observe the regulations. The same applied to equipment hired or leased after the due date. But an employer who moved existing equipment from one site to another did not have to comply immediately, nor would equipment which was delivered to the place of work before the due date, but only put into use after it, be affected by the new laws.

Equipment means 'any machinery, appliance, apparatus or tool, and any installation for use at work (whether exclusively or not)', e.g. combine harvester, automatic car wash, computer, crane, hammer, linear accelerator. It does not include livestock, substances, structural items, or privately owned vehicles. Only workers on sea-going ships are excluded. The Regulations cover not only the situation where the employer provides work equipment for his employee, but also apply to equipment provided by the employee for use at work (other than a private car).

Every employer shall ensure that work equipment is so constructed or adapted as to be suitable for the purpose for which it is used or provided (Regulation 4). 'Suitable' means suitable in any respect which it is reasonably foreseeable will affect the health or safety of any person. Every employer shall ensure that work equipment is maintained in an efficient state, in efficient working order and in good repair (Regulation 5). The HSE Guidance indicates that efficient means in relation to health and safety, not productivity. Every employer shall ensure that all persons who use work equipment have available to them adequate health and safety information and, where appropriate, written instructions pertaining to the use of the work equipment (Regulation 8). Every employer shall ensure that all persons who use work equipment have received adequate training for purposes of health and safety (Regulation 9).

Work equipment has to comply with EU product standards (Regulation 10). This part of the legislation applied to brand-new equipment provided after 31 December 1992 (second-hand equipment was included only if imported from outside the EU). There is a growing number of EC directives setting out essential safety requirements which manufacturers must meet before putting the goods on to the market. Compliance with the EU standard is demonstrated by affixing a CE mark to the goods. At present not all work equipment is covered by a product directive, but one of the most significant relevant directives is the Machinery Directive, enacted here as the Supply of Machinery (Safety) Regulations 1992, amended in 1994. The enforcement of the regulations in respect of machinery used at work is in the hands of the HSE. The manufacturer had the option of complying with the EU standards or the national standards until 1 January 1995, when the EU standards became mandatory.

PUWER repeals section 14 Factories Act 1961 which made it an offence of strict liability to fail to guard dangerous machinery. The new law is Regulation 11. Every employer shall ensure that measures are taken which are effective to prevent access to any dangerous part of machinery or to any rotating stock bar or to stop the movement of any dangerous part before any part of a person enters the danger zone. This is to be done by the provision of guards where it is practicable (a higher standard than reasonably practicable, but not as high as strict liability) to do so. Further regulations cover high and low temperatures, controls, isolation from sources of energy, lighting, maintenance and warnings.

5.17   Personal Protective Equipment at Work Regulations 1992

These regulations, which came into force on 1 January 1993, repeal the Protection of Eyes Regulations 1974. There are no transitional provisions. Where there is already specific legislation, e.g. lead, asbestos, noise, the regulations will not apply. Personal protective equipment (PPE) means all equipment (including clothing affording protection against the weather) which is intended to be worn or held by a person at work and which protects him against one or more risks to his health or safety, and any addition or accessory designed to meet that objective. It does not include uniforms, offensive weapons, signalling devices, seat belts and crash helmets worn on the public highway, sports equipment.

Every employer shall ensure that suitable PPE is provided to his employees who may be exposed to a risk to their health or safety while at work except where and to the extent that such risk has been adequately controlled by other means which are equally or more effective (Regulation 4). The HSE Guidance indicates that PPE is always to be regarded as a last resort: engineering controls should be considered first. Since there is a specific requirement to provide PPE for any work where it is necessary, the employer cannot levy any charge on the employee (section 9 HSWA 1974). The equipment provided must comply with EC standards (Personal Protective Equipment Regulations 2002). It must be regularly checked and maintained, and employees must be given instruction and training in its use. Employees must use PPE provided and must report any loss of or obvious defect in the equipment. Amendments to the regulations require that PPE should be appropriate for the risk or risks involved, the conditions and place where exposure to risk may occur, and the period for which it is worn. It should take account of ergonomic requirements, the state of health of the person or persons who may wear it, and of the characteristics of the workstation of each such person.

5.18   Manual Handling Operations Regulations 1992

These came into force on 1 January 1993. They repeal section 72 of the Factories Act 1961. Manual handling means any transporting or supporting of a load (including the lifting, putting down, pushing, pulling, carrying or moving thereof) by hand or by bodily force. A load includes an animal or a human being. The core provision is Regulation 4. Each employer shall, so far as is reasonably practicable, avoid the need for his employees to undertake any manual handling operations at work which involve a risk of their being injured. If this is not possible, the employer must make a suitable and sufficient assessment and reduce the risk of injury to the lowest extent which is reasonably practicable. There are four main factors: the load, the working environment, the task and individual capability. More than a quarter of reported industrial accidents are associated with manual handling, most commonly a strain of the back. The HSE Guidance stresses an ergonomic approach – in other words, fitting the job to the worker and not the worker to the job. Amendments to the regulations specify that in determining for the purposes of this regulation whether manual handling operations at work involve a risk of injury and the appropriate steps to reduce that risk, regard shall be had to the physical suitability of the employee to carry out the operations, the clothing, footwear or other personal effects he is wearing, his knowledge and training, the results of any risk assessment, whether the employee is within a group of employees identified by the risk assessment as being especially at risk, and the results of any health surveillance.

The regulations do not specify maximum weights, nor is there any emphasis on the relative strengths of men and women, young and old. Occupational health nurses are specifically mentioned in the Guidance as having the skills both to assess the worker's capabilities and to identify high risk activities. Allowance should be made for pregnancy where the employer can reasonably be expected to be aware of it. Hormonal changes can affect the ligaments and postural problems may increase as the pregnancy progresses. Particular care should also be taken for women lifting loads within three months of giving birth. Medical advice should be sought where an employee's health problem may make him or her particularly vulnerable.

Each employee while at work shall make full and proper use of any system of work provided by his employer in compliance with the regulations (Regulation 5).

These regulations have given rise to important civil litigation about the relationship between the duty of the employer to his employees and his duty to his clients and customers. In *R* v. *East Sussex County Council ex parte A* (2003) A and her sister B were young women who both suffered from profound physical and learning disabilities. They lived in the family home, which had been specially adapted for them, where they were cared for by their mother and stepfather. They both suffered from greatly impaired mobility and even the most simple movements, like getting out of bed, required them to be lifted by carers. The County Council provided carers in its capacity as the local authority. Their policy was not to permit care staff to lift patients manually, in order to prevent injury to their backs. In the case of A and B this meant that on occasion they were left sitting in their chairs because care staff refused to move them.

The judge referred to the European Convention on Human Rights in holding that the duty of the employer to do that which was reasonably practicable to prevent harm to carers had to be balanced against the rights of the patients to have their welfare and dignity respected. It was held that the employees could be required to undergo some risks, though these should be reduced to the minimum possible. In other words, no activity is completely without risk, and employees may have to accept some level of risk in the interest of doing a good job, especially where their employment is socially valuable, as with public service and the caring professions.

5.19 Health and Safety (Display Screen Equipment Regulations) 1992

These regulations came into force on 1 January 1993, but did not apply to existing workstations in service prior to that date until 31 December 1996. This is the first legislation in this growing area of employment. The main hazards so far identified are stress, eye strain and upper limb disorders. There is no evidence to substantiate fears of over-exposure to radiation or higher levels of miscarriage and birth defect. The regulations only cover those who habitually use display screen equipment as a significant part of normal work. This is a question of fact and degree. There are two categories of workers protected: users (employees) and operators (self-employed persons). Employees who work at home are included, whether or not the workstation has been provided by the employer, as are those who work at another employer's workstation.

Every employer shall perform a suitable and sufficient analysis of workstations for the purpose of assessing risks to health and safety (Regulation 2). Workstations must comply with the detailed requirements of the regulations (Regulation 3). Every employer shall so plan the activities of users at work in his undertaking that their daily work on display screen equipment is periodically interrupted by breaks and changes of activity (Regulation 4). The employer must provide training for employees and information for employees and self-employed (Regulations 6 and 7).

The OH professional is likely to become involved with eye and eyesight testing. Only users, i.e. employees, are entitled to tests by competent persons which must be provided free by the employer on request. Both registered ophthalmic opticians and registered medical practitioners with suitable qualifications are competent to undertake these tests. Vision screening tests may also be offered. Tests may be requested at the beginning of employment and thereafter should be repeated as the doctor or optometrist advises. Any evidence of injury or disease should be referred to the general practitioner, with the employee's consent.

If it is found that the user needs special glasses, because normal spectacles or contact lenses will not serve, the employer must provide these free of charge. Less than 10 per cent of the population will need special corrective appliances for display screen work.

A review of the regulations has led to new guidance from the HSE, published in 2003. This points out that the regulations extend to televisual display screens, like CCTV, as well as computers. There is extensive guidance on the use of laptops. Where the worker is employed by an employment agency, the host employer is responsible for the workstation, but the agency is responsible for the eye tests, if requested, and health and safety training and information. The agency must check that the host employer has carried out its duties under the Regulations.

5.20   *Control of Vibration at Work Regulations*

These regulations are, at the time of writing, in draft and are due to come into force in 2005. They implement the European Physical Agents Directive of 2002. They set maximum limits for exposure to both hand-arm and whole-body vibration.

Employers must make a suitable and sufficient risk assessment where they carry out work which is liable to expose any employees to risk from vibration. The employer shall ensure that risk from the exposure of his employees to vibration is either eliminated at source or, where this is not reasonably practicable, reduced to a minimum. If the risk assessment indicates that there is a risk to the health of his employees who are, or are liable to be, exposed to vibration, the employer shall ensure that such employees are under suitable health surveillance. Where, as a result of health surveillance, an employee is found to have an identifiable disease or adverse health effect which is considered by a doctor or other occupational health professional to be the result of exposure to vibration, the employer of that employee shall:

(1) ensure that a suitably qualified person informs the employee accordingly and provides the employee with information and advice regarding further health surveillance, including any health surveillance which he should undergo following the end of exposure;
(2) ensure that he is informed of any significant findings from the employee's health surveillance, taking into account any medical confidentiality;
(3) review the risk assessment;
(4) review any measure taken to comply with the regulations, taking into account any advice given by a doctor, occupational health professional, or by the HSE;
(5) consider assigning the employee to alternative work where there is no risk of further exposure to vibration, taking into account any advice given by a doctor or occupational health professional; and
(6) provide for a review of the health of any other employee who has been similarly exposed, including a medical examination where such an examination is recommended by a doctor, occupational health professional or by the HSE.

An employee to whom this regulation applies shall, when required by his employer and at the cost of his employer, present himself during his working hours for such health surveillance procedures as may be required. Health surveillance is recommended where employees are regularly exposed above the exposure action value (EAV), where they are only occasionally exposed but the frequency and severity of the exposure may pose a risk, or where employees have symptoms of hand-arm vibration syndrome.

5.21 Protection of the environment

The OH professional and the Health and Safety Executive have up to now been seen as the protectors of the workers. In the last decade of the twentieth century there was a growing awareness of the need to protect the environment and the public outside the factory gates. The White Paper, *This Common Inheritance*, published in 1990, was the first comprehensive statement by the British Government of its policy on issues affecting the environment. The Secretary of State for the Environment, Transport and the Regions has general responsibility for co-ordinating the work of the Government on environmental pollution. In addition, local authorities and a wide range of voluntary organisations are involved in environmental protection.

In England and Wales the Environment Agency (in Scotland the Scottish

Environment Protection Agency) has an important role in the control of releases to land, air and water from certain industrial processes through the mechanism of integrated pollution control. It is the successor of the Inspectorate of Pollution, formed in 1987 by the merger of three existing Inspectorates: the Industrial Air Pollution Inspectorate (formerly part of the Health and Safety Executive), the Hazardous Waste Inspectorate and the Radiochemical Inspectorate, together with a new Water Pollution Inspectorate. Its main function is to implement the environmental protection legislation through the authorisation and monitoring of prescribed processes. It has power to prosecute operators of processes which breach release limits set in their permits and, by analogy with the Health and Safety at Work Act, to issue enforcement notices (where the operator is in breach of his authorisation) and prohibition notices (where there is an imminent risk of serious pollution of the environment). Environmental health officers of local authorities have similar powers.

The Environmental Protection Act 1990 was repealed by the Pollution Prevention and Control Act 1999. The concept of integrated pollution prevention and control (IPPC) was introduced into Europe by the directive bearing that name in 1996; the 1999 Act implements the directive. The aim is to eliminate pollution at the source, through the careful use of natural resources. The legislation covers emissions to air, land and water, as well as heat. It covers noise, vibration, energy efficiency, environmental accidents, site protection and many processes, including energy, metal production, mineral production, chemical production, waste management and other processes like slaughterhouses and paper manufacture.

In order to obtain a permit operators will have to use best available techniques (BATs) not entailing excessive cost. If there is one technology which reduces emission of polluting substances by 90 per cent and another which reduces the emissions by 95 per cent, but at four times the cost, it may be a proper judgment to hold that because of the small benefit and the great cost the second technology would entail excessive cost. If, on the other hand, the emissions are particularly dangerous, it may be proper to judge that the additional cost is not excessive. Applications for permits must show that installations use best available techniques, minimise and, if possible, recycle waste, conserve energy, prevent accidents and return the site to a satisfactory state after operations cease.

Enforcing authorities must establish and maintain a public register of applications for permits, permits, enforcement and prohibition notices and criminal convictions.

Apart from the considerable legislative activity in Europe and elsewhere, English courts have succeeded in using the common law in order to give remedies to those affected by pollution. J.W. Roberts owned a factory in the 1930s in the middle of a densely populated suburb in Leeds. They produced asbestos products. The factory was constantly filled with asbestos dust which was extracted by ventilators and exhausted into the neighbouring streets. Bales of asbestos were left on loading bays, and local children were known to play on them. Arthur Margereson and June Hancock as children had lived in the immediate vicinity of the factory, and had played in the loading bays. Arthur was born in 1925, June in 1936. In the 1990s both were dying from mesothelioma, cancer of the pleura, the only known cause of which is exposure to asbestos.

Neither had ever been employed by J.W. Roberts. Nevertheless, it was held that Roberts was liable to pay compensation to both plaintiffs. A duty of care was owed to those within the foreseeable area of risk. Asbestos had been condemned as a hazard as early as 1898. Specific Asbestos Industry Regulations had been enacted in 1931. There was evidence that engineering technology existed in the 1930s which could have reduced the dust by 85 per cent. The defendants were negligent, and they should have taken care not only of their employees, but also of surrounding residents (*Margereson and Hancock* v. *J.W. Roberts* (1996)). It is, of course, too late to save thousands of workers who have already suffered through exposure to asbestos. The strict legal regulation of asbestos dates only from the 1980s.

Chapter 6
The Law of Compensation: Welfare Benefits

6.1   The purposes of a system of compensation

The direct enforcement of safety regulations is in the hands of the various inspectorates who in the last resort can ask for the imposition of criminal sanctions by the magistrates or the Crown Court. Where no-one has suffered injury from a breach of the law, that will be the end of the matter, but for an individual injured by an accident at work or suffering from an industrial disease compensation is probably far more important. Parliament has for nearly a century provided for a system of no-fault compensation for employees injured at work. The introduction of this system in 1897 had a dramatic effect in reducing the number of factory accidents, because employers became aware of the cost of accidents and the fact that often it was cheaper to take safety precautions. In addition, it is arguable that the fear of legal liability to pay damages in the civil courts, especially if numbers of employees are involved, operates as another inducement to the employer to take care. Of course, it is not the employer but the Department of Work and Pensions or his private insurance company who actually pays the compensation. The Robens Committee in 1972 examined the interplay between compensation and accident prevention. It was represented to them that insurance is basically inimical to accident prevention because the careful employer is subsidising the negligent organisation. They recommended that the statutory industrial injuries scheme should provide for differential rates of employers' contributions based on claims experience, as in France and Germany, but this has never been implemented.

As for the tort-based action for damages, because this in most cases requires the injured plaintiff to establish negligence – a failure to take reasonable care by the employer – the right to compensation depends partly on luck and having a good lawyer. It is also very expensive to administer, though changes in civil procedure have in recent years reduced the costs of litigation. The fear of legal liability may make it difficult to investigate an incident and take steps to prevent its recurrence, because no-one will talk freely. Employers are obliged by law to insure with private insurance companies against liability for injury to their employees (Employers' Liability (Compulsory Insurance) Act 1969), and although the insurance companies exercise some control, as by inspecting fire precautions and equipment, the careless employer does not suffer the direct cost of compensating his employee. 'High risk' employers have to pay higher premiums than others, but these will be based as much on the general experience of the industry as on the safety record of that company.

If the system of compensation cannot be justified by its preventive effects, the only rationale for its existence is to provide the worker who has been injured in the cause of furthering his employer's business with enough money to make up to him for the less comfortable life he is now living, or to his family for the loss of their breadwinner. Social justice demands that a worker who has undertaken risks for the economic benefit of the community should be cushioned against the consequences of industrial accidents and disease. The fact that many workers pay for their own insurance by reduced wages is an unavoidable consequence of the relative economic strengths of employer and employee.

The Workmen's Compensation Act of 1897 was designed to secure that compensation for industrial accidents should be based on the principle that any employee injured by an 'accident arising out of and in the course of employment' would have an automatic claim against his employer. In 1906, the scheme was extended to disabilities caused by a work-related disease which had been prescribed for that particular employment. The no-fault element is still the major difference between the industrial injuries insurance scheme and the tort-based system of damages. In the former the employee does not have to prove that his injury was caused by anyone's fault: it is enough that he has suffered, whereas in the latter he must establish some fault on the part of a defendant, usually his employer. Until 1946 workmen's compensation was financed in the main by employers paying premiums to private insurance companies. However, the growth from 1911 onwards of a national insurance scheme financed through contributions levied by central government and administered by civil servants meant that those who had not suffered industrial injury but were unable to work because of illness which was not job-related had also become entitled to some benefits.

Beveridge, the architect of the new Welfare State, thought that there were weighty arguments in favour of the merger of the two systems:

'If a workman loses his leg in an accident, his needs are the same whether the accident occurred in a factory or the street; if he is killed, the needs of his widow and other dependants are the same, however the death occurred.'

He was persuaded, however that the industrial preference should continue. First, many industries vital to the community were dangerous, yet workers must not be deterred from entering them. Secondly, he felt that a man disabled during the course of his employment had, like a soldier, been disabled while working under orders. Thirdly, he thought that the only justification for limiting the employer's common law liability to damage caused by negligence was that there was a parallel system of no-fault compensation.

A separate and more favourable industrial injuries scheme was retained in the National Insurance (Industrial Injuries) Act 1946, though it was now removed from the private insurance companies and administered by the State. Since then, industrial injuries benefits have gradually been reduced and other social security benefits increased, so that now the industrial preference has been eroded but not abandoned. Consolidation of all the principal social security statutes took place in 1992 in the Social Security Contributions and Benefits Act and the Social Security Administration Act. Changes in the system of adjudication of the right to benefits were brought about by the Social Security Act 1998.

6.2   *An outline of the scheme*

'Employed earners' are covered from their first day at work, because this is not a benefit which depends on contributions by the employee. The statutory definition of an employed earner is 'a person who is gainfully employed in Great Britain either under a contract of service, or in an office with emoluments chargeable to income tax under Schedule E'. A trade union shop steward who sustained an injury at a college where he was attending a training course was an office-holder. Most self-employed workers are outside the industrial injuries scheme, and this can be a serious disadvantage for, for example, construction workers 'on the lump'.

The regulations extend the benefit of industrial injuries insurance to apprentices.

Employees working in the National Health Service are also protected by the parallel and more generous NHS Injury Benefits Scheme. This provides temporary or permanent benefits for all NHS employees who lose remuneration because of an injury or disease attributable to their NHS employment. The scheme is also available to medical and dental practitioners. It must be established that the injury or disease was acquired during the course of work. An employee who suffers a needle-stick injury is advised to have a serum sample taken at the time of injury and follow-up samples at appropriate intervals in case of infection by, for example, hepatitis B. For those having to give up their employment, the scheme provides a guaranteed income of 85 per cent of pre-injury NHS earnings. There is also a right to a lump sum and dependants' benefits where death occurs. The scheme is administered within the NHS.

Workers on British ships and aircraft and on offshore oil rigs are covered, as during their first year abroad are workers employed in a foreign country by an employer with a place of business here. Reciprocal agreements with foreign countries often qualify those who work abroad for protection under the foreign system.

They can claim if they either:

(1)   suffer a personal injury caused by accident arising out of or in the course of employment; or
(2)   suffer from a 'prescribed disease', that is one designated by the Secretary of State, usually after consultation with the Industrial Injuries Advisory Council (IIAC), as a special risk for particular occupations, e.g. viral hepatitis for those working in contact with human blood or human blood products, or tenosynovitis for manual labourers or those in jobs involving frequent or repeated movements of the hand or wrist.

It is presumed that the disease was in fact caused by the performance of the prescribed occupation, unless the decision maker proves to the contrary. So far, the Government has not accepted the proposal of the IIAC that claims should be allowed where the claimant is able to show that his disease was caused by his work even though not yet prescribed for it by the Secretary of State (often called a case of 'individual proof'). However, in 1991 occupational asthma was prescribed not only for jobs involving contact with such well-established sensitisers as isocyanates and laboratory animals but also for work with 'any other sensitising agent'. Claimants must name the suspected substance and must be examined by a doctor. In the first year of operation 129 claims were successful under this head. Substances found guilty of causing occupational asthma included resins, chrome and nickel.

The Industrial Injuries Advisory Council includes representatives of employers and unions and doctors, epidemiologists, toxicologists and lawyers. The suspect disease must be proved with reasonable certainty to be attributable to work and not a risk common to all persons. IIAC adopts the 'twice as likely' principle, that is that a worker in a particular process must be shown to double the risk of contracting a disease compared with a member of the general population. This is relatively simple where there is only one cause of a disease (as with mesothelioma), but far more difficult where there are a number of causes (as with lung cancer). Epidemiological evidence is therefore of great importance. There are four categories of occupational disease:

(1)   physical (e.g. cramp of the hand or forearm due to repetitive movements);
(2)   biological (e.g. viral hepatitis, Q fever);
(3)   chemical (e.g. lead poisoning, certain cancers caused by exposure to chemicals);
(4)   miscellaneous conditions (e.g. pneumoconiosis, mesothelioma, non-infective dermatitis).

In recent years an 'intermediate' form of prescription has been adopted, whereby a disease is listed subject to certain conditions. For example, compensation for occupational deafness will only be paid if the claimant can show hearing loss of at least 50 dB in each ear, being the average of hearing losses at 1, 2 and 3 kHz frequencies, and being due in the case of at least one ear to occupational noise. The claimant must have been employed for a minimum aggregate of 10 years in one or more of the qualifying occupations, the claim must be made within five years of the claimant last working in one of the qualifying occupations and the claimant must show that the hearing loss in at least one ear is due to noise at work.

'Noisy hobbies such as musketry and listening to amplified pop music should not be overlooked.' (*DSS Industrial Injuries Handbook for Adjudicating Medical Authorities*)

An amendment in 1989 removed the requirement that hearing loss should be measured by pure tone audiometry as opposed to evoked response audiometry or any other test.

Vibration white finger was not prescribed until 1985. Three or more fingers must be affected throughout the year for a claim to be made. In 2005 prescription has been extended to sensorineural effects as well as blanching. In 1993 carpal tunnel syndrome became a prescribed disease for work using hand-held vibrating tools. Chronic bronchitis and emphysema were in 1993 prescribed for miners after many years of debate.

6.3   The benefits available

When a worker is first struck down by accident or disease, he needs a guaranteed income to pay his household expenses, mortgage and so on. Here there is now no industrial preference. All employees are entitled to statutory sick pay from their employer, whatever the cause of their absence from work. If the worker is self-employed and not entitled to statutory sick pay he can claim incapacity benefit. The majority will also be entitled to additional contractual benefits depending on the terms of the contract of employment, which may be more generous to those absent through industrial disease or injury. After 90 days, industrial benefits will be payable.

The Social Security Act 1986 abolished the death benefit whereby dependants of a worker killed by a work-related disease or injury could claim benefit. What is left is a scheme to provide for disablement. It is argued that disabled people should receive similar benefits whatever the cause of their disability, but the IIAC's opinion is that 'the only acceptable reason for, and method of, abolishing the industrial preference would be by extending industrial injuries-type benefits to all disabled people'.

The Government in the late 1980s was faced with the alternative either of levelling down industrial injuries benefits or extending them to all disabled people at a cost of over £3000 million. The abolition of the reduced earnings allowance for those disabled after 1990 was a further step in the reduction of industrial benefits. The Social Security Contributions and Benefits Act 1992 contains separate regimes for the disabled and the industrially disabled. Appeals by the non-industrially disabled are referred to Disability Appeal Tribunals.

Another important change brought about by the 1986 Act was the abolition of lump sum payments for small handicaps. The philosophy behind the scheme is now to maintain the living standards of those injured at work rather than to give an award of 'damages', as in the days of workmen's compensation. If the employee wishes to obtain a lump sum he will have to pursue a civil action against the person allegedly responsible for his injury.

There is now only one benefit: a disablement benefit. The additional reduced earnings allowance (known as special hardship allowance up to 1986) has been abolished in respect of losses of faculty resulting from an accident or the onset of a prescribed disease on or after 1 October 1990. Reduced earnings allowance is still being paid to those disabled before October 1990 up to the date they reach pensionable age. All payments under the scheme are tax-free.

The disablement pension compensates for injury to the employee's physical or mental health caused by work-related accident or disease. It is a regular payment which continues as long as the disablement lasts, in many cases up to the claimant's death. The pension is payable whether or not the claimant is employed and whether or not his earnings are reduced. To receive a pension, the claimant must be assessed by a medical panel as at least 14 per cent disabled, except in the case of those suffering from pneumoconiosis, byssinosis or diffuse mesothelioma. The amount of the pension depends on the degree of disablement. Total loss of hearing or amputation of both hands can amount to 100 per cent disablement: it is not necessary for the worker to be completely bedridden. The assessment of the degree of disability is made by doctors, but there are guidelines laid down in regulations: e.g. loss of whole index finger – 14 per cent; loss of thumb – 30 per cent; loss of both hands – 100 per cent. Supplements are payable to those who are 100 per cent disabled and need constant care. These are known as the constant attendance allowance and exceptionally severe disablement allowance.

Sweeping changes in national insurance benefits paid during incapacity for work to those unable to work for any reason, other than industrial injury, were introduced in the Social Security (Incapacity for Work) Act 1994 and the Social Security (Incapacity for Work) (General) Regulations 1995. The employee has to supply information and evidence of sickness and be prepared to undergo a medical examination to decide whether he is fit to work. If he has worked for more than eight weeks in the 21 weeks immediately preceding the first day of sickness, he will be tested on his capacity to do work which he could reasonably be expected to do in the course of his occupation. This criterion continues up to the 197th day of incapacity. After that, the employee will be required to be more flexible in the work he applies for. An 'all work' test is applied. This is administered through self-assessment, a GP's report and a report of a DWP doctor. The medical effects of the condition are measured by a points system. In each functional activity (walking, lifting and carrying, etc.) a level of impairment is designated as the threshold for incapacity for work. It is necessary to acquire 15 points (or 10 on the mental descriptors) to qualify for benefit. The problem is that some people will be able to walk several yards because they refuse to surrender to pain, while others will be less stoic. 'Functional ability or disability is a continuum; only the decisions are bipolar.' (Mashaw, 1996). Certain people are deemed incapable of work because of their condition (e.g. the terminally ill, registered blind, those suffering from chronic renal failure and receiving regular dialysis). The DSS published a booklet: *The Medical Assessment for Incapacity Benefit* (1994). Claimants are allowed to earn a small amount while on incapacity benefit if the work is done on a doctor's advice.

6.4 Making a claim

A new and greatly simplified system of adjudication of claims was introduced by the Social Security Act 1998, with the vesting of all first instance decision making in the Secretary of State. At the second stage a generic appeal tribunal has been constituted, comprising one, two or three members, depending on the type of case involved. At the apex of the system are the Social Security Commissioners, whose decisions may be appealed to the Court of Appeal and the House of Lords. The claim is first made to a decision maker, a civil servant from the Department of Work and Pensions, who decides solely on the documents including medical reports. Claimants are told of the decision in writing and of their right to appeal to a tribunal. A written statement of reasons must be given on request. A decision may be revised or superseded if made in ignorance of a material fact, or if the facts have changed (for example there is a new medical report).

There is a right of appeal to a unified appeal tribunal, which includes one lawyer member. Other panel members may be doctors, accountants or people with experience of dealing with disabled clients or as voluntary workers. Legal aid is not available. A lawyer and two doctor members are assigned to hear industrial injuries appeals. An oral hearing is held. The tribunal may carry out a physical examination of the appellant where the assessment of disablement or diagnosis in an industrial injuries case is in issue. The only ground of appeal from a tribunal to the Social Security Commissioners is on a point of law, and leave to appeal must be given. There will be an oral hearing. A final appeal may be taken to the Court of Appeal, House of Lords and/or the European Court of Justice where a point of European law arises.

6.5   *Review of decisions*

Sometimes, the claimant wants his case to be looked at again rather than appealed to a higher level. He may argue that the authorities have made a mistake of fact or that fresh evidence is now available. The new evidence must be such that it could not be obtained with reasonable diligence for use at the original assessment. The claimant may ask for a review of his assessment on the ground that sequelae have now become apparent, under the heading of unforeseen aggravation. The decision maker may supersede an earlier decision on the ground that there has been a relevant change in circumstances (for example, a change in the claimant's condition evidenced by a fresh medical report). But supersession on the basis of a change in circumstances is not available where a claim is correctly disallowed in the first instance and the claimant's situation later changes. The remedy in such a case is to make a fresh claim.

6.6   *Compensation for accidents*

The claimant must show:

(1)   personal injury;
(2)   which has been caused by accident;
(3)   which has arisen out of and in the course of employment.

An accident, a word notoriously difficult to define, is an unexpected event, and in industrial injury cases may even include the murder of a schoolteacher by his pupils in the playground (*Trim School* v. *Kelly* (1914)). Accident includes a slipped disc caused by heavy lifting, even if the claimant realised at the time that his back might suffer. It differs from a disease in that it occurs over a short period and not by a continuous process, but this may be a fine distinction in practice. Silicosis caused by exposure to dust over many years is not an accidental injury, nor is deafness gradually induced by the noise of a mechanical saw used for cutting up meat, whereas a psychoneurotic illness caused by irregular explosive reports from a machine has been held to be accidental on the argument that each separate explosion was an accident. In 1986 a Scottish civil servant who had been off work for 19 months claimed industrial injury benefit on the basis that he had developed acute anxiety tension due to various strains at work, including diminishing prospects of promotion and transfers to different departments. It was held by the Social Security Commissioner that strain arising from uncongenial working conditions could not be described as caused by an accident (*Fraser* v. *Secretary of State for Social Services*). However, it was subsequently held by the English courts that a civil servant who had suffered a mental breakdown through overwork was entitled to benefits under the special and more generous terms of the civil service pension scheme which includes 'injury or disease attributable to or caused by' his work, but only if he could establish by medical evidence that the illness was caused by the pressure of work combined with his personality (*R* v. *Minister for the Civil Service, ex parte Petch* (1987)).

The leading authority is now *Chief Adjudication Officer* v. *Faulds* (2000). A senior fire officer suffering from post traumatic stress disorder was discharged from the service. The basis of his claim was that his condition had been brought on by his attendance at a series of horrific fatal accidents, including road traffic accidents and aircraft crashes. The House of Lords held that it was essential to identify the relevant incident or incidents which had caused the injury. The event itself was not an accident in the required sense.

> 'What has to be identified is not the occurrence of some or other accident in general, but an accident to a claimant, an accident suffered by him.'

On the available evidence, the court doubted whether it could be demonstrated that the aetiology of the claimant's disorder could be identified with the particular incidents that occurred to him. However, in another case a senior prison officer who developed a stress-related illness following a specific confrontation with a disruptive prisoner, who was known to be violent, was entitled to benefit.

A health professional who contracts the HIV virus through a sudden event, for example a needle-stick injury or a violent attack from a patient, would be able to claim compensation for accidental injury, despite the absence of AIDS from the list of prescribed diseases. In *Clay* v. *Social Security Commissioner* (1990) the claimant, an asthmatic, from time to time suffered painful attacks of nausea, breathlessness and headaches through passive exposure to cigarette smoke at work. It was held that she was entitled to benefit for personal injury caused by accident.

The accident must cause personal injury to either physical or mental health. Damage to property is excluded (even to false teeth or a wooden leg). It is very important that a potential claimant should be certain that a record is kept of industrial accidents, as proof of what occurred. One of the best ways of giving notice is to enter the details in the accident book. The Social Security (Claims and Payments) Regulations 1979 oblige an employed earner who suffers an accident at work to give either oral or written notice to the employer. This must be recorded either by the worker or the employer in the accident book. In the case of accidents or diseases within the RIDDOR Regulations, notice must also be given by the employer to the Health and Safety Executive (HSE) or local authority (see Chapter 3).

If the cause of the claimant's injury is outside his employment he will not be entitled to industrial injury benefit. Thus, an employee who suffers from a pre-existing heart condition cannot claim because his heart attack occurs by chance when he is at work. But if the work causes or contributes to the injury in any material degree a claim can be made, so that if there is evidence that the attack was brought on by the employee having to lift a heavy cupboard at work he will be covered. It is irrelevant that an average employee would have had no problems with the cupboard. In addition, if the employee collapses at work and injures himself on his employer's building or machinery, that injury will be deemed an industrial accident.

Difficulties arise over the interpretation of the words 'arising out of and in the course of employment'. They are not confined to the employer's premises during strict working hours, but have to be given a broad common sense interpretation. An accident which occurs in the course of employment is presumed to arise out of it unless it can be proved to the contrary. The Social Security Act specifically provides that accidents which occur in the course of employment and are caused by another person's misconduct, skylarking or negligence, or the behaviour or presence of an animal (including a bird, fish or insect), or are caused by or consist in the employee being struck by any object or by lightning, are to be treated as arising out of employment.

In *Chief Adjudication Officer* v. *Rhodes* (1999) an employee of the Benefits Agency, at home on sick leave, was physically assaulted in her own driveway by a neighbour whom she had previously reported for working while claiming income support. This undoubtedly arose 'out of' her employment, but could it be said to have taken place 'in the course of' that employment? The Court of Appeal decided that she could not claim benefit. At the time she was attacked she was not working or doing anything connected with her work. Had she been assaulted in the office the decision would of course have been different.

6.7   Accidents on the way to work

'Commuter' accidents are not included in the scheme, unlike in France, Australia, Germany and Sweden, and contrary to the recommendation of the Pearson Commission. Normally a person's employment begins when he arrives at his place of work and ends when the person leaves it. If, however, the travel from one place to another is part of the job, as with a lorry driver or commercial traveller, benefit will be payable. What about the journey from home to the first call of the day and the return home from the last job? If the 'travelling' employee's home is his base from which he works these will be covered. It has been held that a local authority home help injured on her way to her first house of the day was not entitled to claim because the nature of the job is not to travel. The home help travels to duty, not on duty. Contrast with this *Nancollas* v. *Insurance Officer* (1985) in which a disablement resettlement officer employed by the Department of Employment was involved in a road accident on the way from his home to an employment office at which he had arranged to interview a disabled person. He was based at an office in Worthing and made many visits to job centres and private houses in the course of his work. Many of his journeys commenced and terminated at the Worthing office, but in this case, because the appointment was early in the morning, he started from home. The

Court of Appeal decided that Nancollas could claim industrial injury benefit because on a common sense reading of the situation he was acting in the course of his employment as he drove to his appointment. This decision shows the unpredictability of the law in this area. The claimant was not based at home, but he was covered on the way to his first appointment because he was regarded as an employee with no precisely definable place of work. Unlike the home help, he travelled to many different destinations.

The law provides that an employee injured in an accident on the way to or from his place of work while a passenger in a vehicle operated by or on behalf of his employer or by arrangement with his employer, not being a public transport service, shall be entitled to industrial injuries benefit. Such travel must be with the express or implied permission of the employer.

6.8   Accidents during breaks from work

Normal and reasonable breaks in work are included in the course of employment as long as the employee remains on his employer's premises. Accidents in the canteen or the toilets are covered as incidental to the employment. But if the employee leaves his place of work, he will not usually be protected, unless he is employed to travel, like a lorry driver stopping at a motorway service station. An employee who disobeys instructions may exclude himself from protection. A dock labourer who used an unattended forklift truck to move an obstacle was denied benefit (*R* v. *Albuquerque ex parte Bresnahan* (1966)). In *R* v. *Industrial Injuries Commissioner ex parte AEU* (1966) an employee waited outside a booth provided by the employer in the factory so that workers could safely smoke during breaks. Because the booth was full, he remained there for five minutes after the tea-break had ended and was hit by a fork-lift truck. The court, somewhat harshly, denied him benefit because he had taken himself outside his employment by overstaying his break. Workers who were injured using occupational health facilities provided by the employer have made successful claims, as did an employee hurt on the way to a mobile X-ray unit parked on his employer's premises.

If the employee arrives early or stays late he will still be covered as long as his presence is reasonably incidental to his employment, but not if it is simply to suit his own convenience.

Employees who are injured away from their employer's premises may claim if acting in the course of employment. Apprentices on day release at a college of education will be covered, and a school teacher injured in Switzerland while accompanying a school party was held entitled to claim. Spare time activities are not included: a policeman injured in a rugby game having volunteered to represent his county force lost his appeal (*R* v. *National Insurance Commissioner ex parte Michael* (1977)).

6.9   Emergencies

If the employee is injured while trying to save people or property in an emergency connected with his job he will usually be covered. A driver who deviated from his journey to obtain medical assistance for a fellow employee made a successful claim. When a dockyard policeman was injured outside the docks in rescuing a child in a runaway pram he received benefit, but an ordinary member of the public acting in the same way would not have been protected, because it would not have been incidental to his employment.

6.10   *Compensation for prescribed diseases*

An injury caused by a gradual process does not fall within the definition of an accident. The legislation provides that those who gradually over a period contract one of a number of work-related diseases specifically prescribed for particular occupations by the Secretary of State in regulations can also claim benefit. A claimant who is able to prove that his injury has been caused by his job, but cannot bring himself within either the accident or the prescribed disease provisions, will be denied industrial injury benefit. Sometimes claimants try to establish that a non-prescribed disease has been caused by an accident in order to bring it within the 'accident' rules. Infective illnesses may occasionally be included within the category of accident in that there must have been a moment of time in which, in non-medical language, the infection entered the body. Post-traumatic stress disorder caused by one horrific incident may be an accident.

A disease will only be prescribed if:

(1)   the disease ought to be treated, having regard to its causes and incidence and any other relevant considerations, as a risk of occupations and not as a risk common to all persons; and
(2)   it is such that, in the absence of special circumstances, the attribution of particular cases to the nature of the employment can be established or presumed with reasonable certainty.

The claimant must prove:

(1)   employment in an occupation listed in relation to the disease;
(2)   that the disease is prescribed;
(3)   that the disease was caused by the job;
(4)   that he has suffered loss of physical or mental faculty.

There is a general presumption that a prescribed disease is caused by the relevant occupation if the employee worked in it at any time within one month preceding the date of development of the disease. This is varied in the following cases:

(1)   *Occupational deafness.* The claimant must have been employed for an aggregate of at least 10 years in a relevant occupation and have worked in such an occupation within the five years preceding the claim.
(2)   *Tuberculosis.* The claimant must have worked for at least six weeks in the relevant occupation and have done so within two years before the development of the disease.

(3) *Pneumoconiosis*. The claimant must have worked for at least two years in aggregate in a relevant occupation; 20 years service is required for coal miners suffering from chronic bronchitis or emphysema.

(4) *Byssinosis*. The presumption applies to any employee who has worked in a relevant occupation for any period.

(5) *Inflammation of the nose, throat or mouth, and non-infective dermatitis*. There is no presumption. The employee must prove that his injury is job-related in every case.

(6) *Occupational asthma caused by 'any other sensitising agent'*. The claimant will have to identify the agent and prove that the asthma is job-related. The claim must be made within 10 years.

(7) *Carpal tunnel syndrome*. There is no presumption.

To rebut these presumptions, the decision maker will have to prove that the claimant's illness has some other cause, like his living conditions or personal habits. The job does not have to be proved to be the only cause of the disease as long as it is a substantial cause.

6.11   Sequelae

A claimant who contracts a prescribed disease may develop another non-listed condition as a result. This sequela will be treated as an industrial injury even though not prescribed. For example, tenosynovitis may lead to carpal tunnel syndrome and insanity may be a sequela of poisoning by mercury or methyl bromide. Obviously, medical opinion is very important in these cases and the DSS published a booklet: *Notes on the Diagnosis of Prescribed Diseases*.

6.12   Recrudescence

Where a claimant has suffered from more than one attack of the same illness and that illness is not a chronic one like byssinosis or deafness from which no-one can be expected to recover completely, it will be necessary to decide whether this is the old disease flaring up (recrudescence) or a fresh attack. Dermatitis causes much difficulty. A new attack must give rise to a new claim; recrudescence will be taken into account in reviewing any previous assessment and will also 'back-date' the onset of the disease. There is a rebuttable presumption that an attack occurring during the period of an existing assessment of disablement is a recrudescence of the old disease.

6.13   Pneumoconiosis

There are special rules applying to this disease, involving permanent damage to the lung due to inhalation of mineral dust, and including silicosis and asbestosis. There is a presumption that anyone showing typical symptoms who worked in one of the scheduled occupations for at least two years is entitled to benefit. Most claimants have worked in coal mines or with asbestos. Diagnosis and disablement decisions are made by specialist doctors appointed by the Secretary of State. A pension is payable as long as the disability is assessed as at least one per cent, and since the Social Security Act provides that a person found to be suffering from pneumoconiosis shall be deemed to be suffering from loss of faculty of at least one per cent, every case diagnosed is entitled to a payment which in administrative practice is assessed as 10 per cent because of the difficulties of calculation. Appeal lies to an Appeal Tribunal.

When a doctor makes a diagnosis of pneumoconiosis he notifies the claimant of whether it is safe to continue at work and, if so, what kind of work. If the claimant gives his consent, the doctor writes to the employer and asks him to provide the claimant with suitable working conditions. The doctor also notifies the claimant's GP.

In addition to the statutory scheme, British Coal made a private no-fault compensation agreement with the mining unions, introduced in 1974, now Government-administered. This makes lump sum payments on top of industrial injury benefit to coal miners who are in receipt of a DWP disablement pension for pneumoconiosis, or to dependants where the miner has died. Anyone who receives a payment under the scheme must agree to relinquish any right to sue for civil damages at common law. British Nuclear Fuels operate a similar scheme for radiation-induced cancer. The Pneumoconiosis etc. (Workers Compensation) Act 1979 gives workers with specified lung diseases a right to a lump sum from the State, where they cannot recover damages from the employer because he is no longer in business. Mesothelioma is now included in the scheme.

6.14   Assessment of disablement

The determination of this question decides whether the claimant is entitled to benefit and, if so, how much. The decision matter must decide:

(1)   whether the accident or disease has resulted in a loss of faculty;
(2)   at what percentage the extent of disablement resulting from the loss of faculty is to be assessed and for what period.

6.15   Loss of faculty

The basic pension is to compensate the claimant for the fact that his bodily or mental condition has deteriorated as a result of his industrial injury; he is not the man he once was. It is irrelevant that he has not lost earning capacity. The assessment is to be made, unlike common law damages, without reference to the claimant's personal circumstances, other than age, sex and physical and mental condition. A rich, sedentary restaurant manager receives the same disablement pension for the loss of his hand as a poor waiter who was a keen amateur footballer. However, age and sex are relevant. A physical disfigurement may be assessed more highly in the case of a woman claimant. Stiffness in the joints may not be loss of faculty in a worker of 60, where it would be in one of 18. The claimant must establish on a balance of reasonable probabilities that the loss of faculty resulted from the industrial accident or prescribed disease.

6.16 Disablement

This may or may not flow from a loss of faculty. A small scar in an inconspicuous place is not disabling; an ugly disfigurement of the face causing psychological problems can be a serious disability. In any event, since the abolition of a right to benefit for most disabilities of less than 14 per cent, many minor disabilities fall outside the scheme. A disability has been defined as an 'inability to do something which persons of the same age and sex and normal physical and mental powers can do'.

The decision makers are given considerable flexibility, but for some injuries they are guided by the statutory tariff. All assessments must be expressed in percentage terms. The assessment is made for the period during which the claimant has suffered and may be expected to suffer from the loss of faculty. If the claimant's condition is such as not to allow of a final assessment, because of possible changes, a provisional assessment is made which can be later reviewed. Loss of a hand and a foot counts as 100 per cent disablement, loss of a thumb 30 per cent.

6.17 Multiple disabilities

If a man already blind in one eye suffers an injury to his other eye at work, the injury is more disabling than for a fully sighted worker. The two eye injuries are connected conditions because the combination of the two is more disabling than if they were treated in isolation and the percentage disablement will be increased. The regulations provide that the doctors should first assess the combined disability (blindness in one eye plus injury to the other) and then deduct from that figure a percentage to cover the degree of disablement had the industrial accident not occurred (blindness in one eye only). The decision maker has a discretion not to reduce an assessment if satisfied that in the circumstances 100 per cent is a reasonable assessment of the extent of disablement from the relevant loss of faculty.

Where the claimant suffers a non-industrial accident after the industrial injury, as for example where a man blinded in one eye at work then suffers an injury to the other eye in a domestic accident, regulations of such complexity that they have been the subject of judicial criticism provide in effect that the combined figure of the two disabilities should be taken together minus the percentage for the non-industrial injury, but only if the industrial injury on its own is assessed at more than 10 per cent disablement. Thus, if the industrial injury counts as 60 per cent, the domestic injury alone as 30 per cent and the connected industrial and non-industrial injuries together as 100 per cent, the claimant's disablement is assessed as 100 minus 30, that is 70 per cent.

Pre-existing conditions which might never have become apparent had the industrial injury not occurred are not to be treated as existing disabilities and are therefore not deductible. The industrial injuries scheme adopts the common law principle that you 'take your victim as you find him'. Thus, in a case in 1981 where a Medical Appeal Tribunal reduced benefit because they found that at the time of the industrial injury the claimant was in any event liable to develop multiple sclerosis, the Commissioner held that no deduction should have been made. In addition, since the claimant is to be compared with an average healthy person of the same age, the percentage disablement should not be reduced because the claimant is already showing signs of normal ageing. A middle-aged worker claiming for a serious back injury should not have his pension reduced because 'at your age you must expect problems with your back'.

6.18   Reduced earnings allowance (REA)

This was formerly known as special hardship allowance. It may be additional to the disablement pension. It was payable only if the industrial injury had caused the claimant to lose wages. It has been abolished in respect of injury caused by accidents occurring or the onset of prescribed disease on or after 1 October 1990. In 2001 there were still 152,000 recipients of the allowance.

The claimant must prove:

(1)   that he was entitled to a disablement pension, or had been assessed as not less than one per cent disabled;
(2)   that as a result of the relevant loss of faculty, he was either permanently or temporarily incapable of following his regular occupation and also incapable of following employment of an equivalent standard which was suitable in his case.

6.19   Incapacity for work

The following sections apply only to applications for reduced earnings allowance.

Incapacity means that the claimant must show (in cases of pneumoconiosis the burden is on the decision maker to show that the claimant is capable) that there is no work which he can reasonably be expected to do. Medical evidence is obviously of prime importance. The decision maker is likely to ask the DWP's doctors for their opinion, as well as the claimant's own doctor. He may also ask the claimant's employer for a report on the nature of the claimant's normal work and the disablement employment adviser for an assessment of the claimant's capabilities. If the claimant has returned to work this is good evidence that he is capable, but it is not conclusive. The claimant who finds that he cannot work for as many hours as his contract requires (disregarding voluntary overtime), or perform a task essential to his job, will be incapable.

Where the claimant is found to be only intermittently incapable, he will not be entitled to reduced earnings allowance. The doctors will be asked to decide whether the claimant is likely to remain permanently incapable of following his normal job: if so, he will receive the allowance for as long as he is also incapable of suitable alternative employment. If not (and doctors are reluctant to certify permanent incapacity) the claimant must show that he has been *continuously* incapable of doing his job or a suitable alternative since the end of the 15-week period after the accident or onset of disease. Thus, an employee who returns to work and then finds it is too much for him may have put himself at a disadvantage if he cannot show that he is permanently incapable. To alleviate this potential hardship, the regulations provide that the claimant can return to work 'for the purpose of rehabilitation or training or of ascertaining whether he had recovered from the effects of the relevant injury' and not lose benefit, but only in restricted circumstances. These are that the work is with the approval of the Secretary of State or on the advice of a medical practitioner and that it does not amount in aggregate to more than six months. The claimant's doctor should have sanctioned the return to work; the fact that he did not advise against return may be insufficient.

If the claimant returns to work pending surgical treatment for the effects of his industrial injury, this period may also be discounted under the regulations, as long as a medical practitioner has previously advised surgery, or the claimant while at work was in the process of obtaining such advice (as where he was attending hospital as an outpatient). It is necessary for the claimant to prove that he used reasonable zeal and expedition in trying to secure surgical treatment.

Sometimes the claimant is incapable of work because of some psychological illness. If this has been caused by the industrial injury, as where the employee suffers from claustrophobia as a result of being trapped at work, the phobia is in itself a loss of faculty and should be so diagnosed by the medical authorities. It is irrelevant that the fear is unreasonable. Where the claimant is not suffering from any psychiatric condition, but refuses to return to work or undergo medical treatment which will assist him to do so because he is afraid, he will be denied the allowance unless his fear is found to be reasonable, for example because the suggested treatment carries significant risk of failure.

It is presumed that a claimant who is receiving a disablement pension in respect of pneumoconiosis and who changes his job after having been advised by the doctors that he should not follow his regular occupation unless he complies with special restrictions relating to the conditions in which he works, will be entitled to REA if he suffers a drop in wages. The presumption may be rebutted if, for example, the claimant was nearing retirement or likely to be made redundant at the time he made the change.

6.20 The regular occupation

What is the claimant's regular occupation? Suppose that the claimant changed his job before the consequences of the industrial disease manifested themselves? Since the REA depends on a comparison between what the claimant would have earned in his regular employment and what he now earns, how can the system cope with a job which has disappeared? A flexible approach has been adopted. As the Commissioner said in a case in 1975:

> '[A] fair and realistic view must be taken in the light of the work which the claimant was doing and was required to do and all other circumstances including the claimant's reasons for doing the work he was doing and his intentions for the future.'

In one case, a bus driver agreed to take a job as a storekeeper to see whether he liked it; he then had an industrial accident. It was held that his regular occupation was to drive a bus. But if he had made a definite change in his job, his regular occupation would have been that of storekeeper however short his period of employment in that position. Regulations provide for an exception if the employee has been forced to change his job by the symptoms of industrial disease, though before the official date of onset; here, the regular occupation is that done at the time the symptoms necessitated a change of job.

Sometimes, an employee will be injured at a very young age and will claim benefit for many years. It will be difficult to continue to assess how much the claimant would have been earning if he had not suffered the loss of faculty; if the job has completely disappeared it may be virtually impossible. The Social Security Act 1986 now assists the DWP by providing that after the first assessment of loss of remuneration, all subsequent assessments may be determined by reference to scales of earnings in the relevant industry – that is, they will be index-linked. The regulations also allow for the possibility that the claimant would have gained promotion to a higher grade, as long as he can demonstrate that in general persons in his position are normally promoted. Thus, an injured apprentice can claim on the basis that he would have become a skilled worker.

6.21   Alternative employment

If the claimant cannot do his normal job but is able to undertake another recognised occupation which is of an equivalent standard of remuneration, he will not receive REA, because this benefit is for loss of earning capacity, not loss of a particular job. The alternative employment must be suitable for the claimant in question, taking into account his age, capabilities, education and so on. A job in a different part of the country which would require the claimant to move house is not usually treated as suitable.

6.22   Subsequent ill-health

Lump sum awards of damages at common law allow for the possibility that the claimant might not have lived his normal span untouched by accident or disease. REA is regularly reviewed because it is granted only for a period fixed by the authorities. If it is shown that the claimant has become incapable because of an illness unconnected with work, REA will not be renewed.

In *R* v. *National Insurance Commissioner ex parte Steel* (1978), Henry Steel was a miner who was diagnosed as suffering from pneumoconiosis in 1959. The medical board told him that he could continue to work in mining as long as he confined his work to approved dust conditions and had regular checks. They continued to give him this advice until 1975 when he gave up work because of breathlessness. This was subsequently diagnosed as caused by hypertension. He was incapable of following his regular occupation, but capable, apart from the hypertension, of following employment of an equivalent standard under approved dust conditions. He was denied special hardship allowance.

Chapter 7
The Law of Compensation: Civil Liability

7.1 The tort action

In 1987, Graham Cook, a man in his thirties, was awarded damages of £850,000 for catastrophic injury suffered when in the course of his employment he placed a batch of scrap batteries in a bath of water and then added nitric acid to extract silver. The batteries had been contaminated with iron pyrites, so that they gave off hydrogen sulphide, a highly toxic gas, when immersed. Mr Cook was totally paralysed, save for some slight movement in his head. He lost the power of speech, but not his intellect, so that he was a conscious prisoner in a useless body, only able to communicate by means of a computer. To obtain his damages, he had pursued a civil action in tort in the High Court in the course of which he had been required to prove that someone had caused his disablement by negligence, a failure to take reasonable care: it was eventually held that his employer was not negligent but that the company which had sent the scrap to be treated was solely responsible, because they should have warned Cook's employers of its contamination (*Cook* v. *Engelhard Industries*). The accident happened in 1982, but judgment was given in 1987. Even then, it would have been possible for the defendant's insurance company to have taken the case on appeal to the higher courts which would have added to the delay and to the legal costs, and might have meant the reversal of the High Court's decision.

From the standpoint of the injured employee, a more unsatisfactory system of obtaining compensation cannot be imagined. However, Mr Cook was in one sense exceptionally fortunate, in that he was one of the approximately 10 per cent of those injured at work who are successful in a claim for damages for common law negligence. (This was the estimate of the Pearson Commission in 1977.) He would already have been in receipt of social security disablement and reduced earnings benefits. At the time, only half of these payments over five years would have been deductible but now, by the Social Security Administration Act 1992, anyone paying a compensation payment must first pay to the Department of Work and Pensions the amount of social security payments made to the plaintiff over five years from the accident or onset of the disease, but these sums may only be deducted from compensation for loss of earnings, not from general damages for pain and suffering and loss of amenity (Social Security (Recovery of Benefits) Act 1997).

How does the tort system differ from the industrial injuries scheme? One very significant difference is that damages in tort have always in the past been paid as a lump sum, rather than as a regular payment. High Court judges have had up to now to guess what the future holds, whereas social security tribunals can make provisional assessments and make subsequent variations if circumstances change.

The inadequacy of the rough and ready method of the tort system has been accepted by the judges in their increasing willingness to approve structured settlements in tort actions. The first such case was *Kelly* v. *Dawes* (1990). The structured settlement permits the defendant to pay the bulk of the damages by purchasing an annuity. The Inland Revenue has agreed to treat the annuity payments to the claimant as tax-exempt payments of capital. Thus, the amount the defendant has to pay will be reduced, and the claimant is assured of a reasonable tax-free income for as long as he or she may live.

In the Courts Act 2003 there is now a general power to award periodical payments instead of a lump sum of damages for personal injury, but the court may only do this where the continuity of payments is reasonably guaranteed, as by a financial scheme in the form laid down in the Act. This is unnecessary where the payment is to be made by a government or health service body.

Another important point is that the family of a deceased worker can no longer claim for his death under the social security scheme, while those relatives who were financially dependent on him can claim for loss of their breadwinner under the tort system. Tort in most cases requires proof of negligence: this is unnecessary in the no-fault social security system. Claims in tort are referred to the slow, expensive and highly technical County Courts and High Court (though legal aid is at the time of writing sometimes available to the less well-off); social security tribunals are quicker, more informal and cheaper (but not covered by legal aid and it cannot be said that the law they administer is free of technicality). Industrial injury compensation is paid from State funds; workers who seek tort damages must establish a case against a defendant who is either wealthy enough to pay or is sufficiently insured against liability. In the end both damages and social security payments are paid from money contributed by the public at large, because all employers, except local authorities, health authorities and certain others exempted by regulations, are required by law (Employers' Liability (Compulsory Insurance) Act 1969) to insure against actions by their employees for work-related injury: they recoup the cost of this insurance from the prices charged for goods and services. If the employer has not complied with this law, the employee cannot sue the directors for failure to do so, though they can be prosecuted (*Richardson* v. *Pitt-Stanley* (1995)). Thus, the employee is left without a remedy. There is no duty to insure the employee against risks of employment outside Great Britain (*Reid* v. *Rush and Tompkins Group PLC* (1989)).

A comprehensive review of Employers' Liability Insurance has been undertaken by the Government, leading to the publication of a First Stage Report in 2003 and a Second Stage Report in 2004. These concluded that there had been no general market failure, despite a substantial rise in premiums in 2002/3. The Government has indicated that any pricing interventions in the market on its part would be unwise and short-sighted. Work is being done to encourage underwriting to be more risk-based, to improve health and safety and occupational health and to encourage rehabilitation, thus reducing overall costs (Department of Work and Pensions (2004)). Insurance companies are encouraged to pay for treatment, rather than lump sum payments. The role of insurance in the prevention of ill-health can only be limited. A research report by Wright and Marsden notes that working practices that might give rise to compensation claims in the distant future ('long tail') are unlikely to affect, or be affected by, the levels of current insurance premiums (*Changing business behaviour – would bearing the true cost of poor health and safety performance make a difference?* HSE (2002)). Small firms were found to be the least likely to be motivated by insurance costs to change their occupational health and safety practice.

In 1978 the report of the Royal Commission on Civil Liability and Compensation for Personal Injury (Pearson Commission) examined the effectiveness of the system of compensation for work-related injury. The members of the Commission were impressed by the range and levels of benefits available under the social security system. They thought that the existence of the no-fault scheme prompted serious consideration of the abolition of the tort action. The potential risk of civil liability often made it difficult to investigate the causes of an accident, and potential defendants feared that the introduction of new safety measures might be inter-preted as an admission that previous practices were defective. On the other hand, the fear of being sued was an incentive to maintain standards of accident pre-vention. Only Professor Schilling, an eminent professor of occupational health, thought that the tort action should be abolished. He argued that accident pre-vention is best secured by strong and effective criminal laws and that compensation should be left to the social security system.

The relative value to the injured worker of the two types of compensation has been assessed by Richard Lewis (Lewis 1987). He writes that the industrial scheme annually compensates three times as many people as the common law, if those who are regularly in receipt of disablement benefit are included. He also points out that the value to an individual of industrial injury benefits is greater than many suppose, because the benefits are tax-free income and are regularly updated in line with inflation. Damages are in general awarded as a lump sum tax-free payment of capital, but income tax must be paid on the interest. In addition, judges do not take future inflation into account in assessing the amount of the award.

The defects of the tort action have to some extent been remedied by sweeping changes in civil procedure introduced on the recommendation of a committee chaired by Lord Woolf. The new Civil Procedure Rules came into effect in April 1999. They have led to a 500 per cent decrease in claims being commenced in the Queen's Bench Division of the High Court. One reason for this is the sharp decline in the availability of public funding for litigation, but another is greater resort to pre-action negotiation leading to settlement, encouraged by the rules. Parties who refuse to negotiate may be penalised in costs. In most cases of negligence a single expert witness will be instructed rather than each party using separate experts. The new arrangements include a fast track system for personal injury claims up to a value of £15,000.

7.2 *The employer's duty of care*

In cases of industrial injury the claimant usually attempts to prove that his employer was at fault under two headings:

(1)   common law negligence; and
(2)   breach of statutory duty.

Common law negligence has been created and developed by the judges who have ruled in a series of precedents that an employer must take reasonable care to protect his employee, or any other person within the area of foreseeable risk. Where Parliament has imposed duties on an employer in the criminal law, the judges have in the case of some statutes implied a right in the person for whose benefit the duty was imposed to bring a civil action for damages in addition to the possible criminal prosecution brought by the public authority. Not all safety statutes will give rise to such a civil action. The Health and Safety at Work Act (HSWA) specifically provides (section 47) that no civil proceedings shall lie for failure to carry out the duties in sections 2–8 of the Act. A civil action may, however, be brought for breach of statutory regulations made under the HSWA. By the Management of Health and Safety at Work and Fire Precautions (Workplace) Amendment Regulations 2003 a civil action for breach of statutory duty was for the first time created for a breach of the Management and Fire Precautions Regulations. This, however, extends only to persons in employment. In the lay term this may have important consequences for the injured employee because, as discussed below, the employer's duty under the regulations may be more onerous than under the common law of negligence. Most of the leading cases on the interpretation of provisions in health and safety regulations are decisions of civil courts.

7.3   What is negligence?

Negligence is a failure to take reasonable care which causes foreseeable damage. In the context of the employment relationship, the employer has a three-fold duty, to provide safe plant and equipment, safe personnel and a safe system of work. What is reasonable depends on the facts of each case. As with the criminal law, the courts may balance the risk against the cost of avoiding it. In *Latimer* v. *AEC* (1953), a factory floor was flooded by exceptionally heavy rainfall. When the water subsided the floor became slippery from oil which usually ran in a channel in the floor. The employers could have closed the factory, but they decided to continue production after spreading sawdust. Latimer slipped and was injured. It was held that on the facts the employer had acted reasonably and was not liable.

If the employer is aware of a special vulnerability in one of his employees, his duty of care rises. In one case in 1951 (*Paris* v. *Stepney Borough Council*) an employer knew that his employee was blind in one eye. The man was working on a job which involved the slight risk of a chip of metal entering the eye. Other workers were not provided with goggles because the risk was small, but the House of Lords held that the employer was negligent in not giving Paris goggles, because the risk of blindness, though not of accident, in his case was greater (he was blinded when a piece of metal entered his good eye). On the other hand, an employer cannot be reasonably expected to take care if he is not aware of his employee's disability, as in the case of the worker who concealed his epilepsy from his employer, had been warned by his doctor not to work at a height, but fell to his death when he had a fit while working 20 feet above ground; it was held that the worker was 50 per cent to blame for his own death even though the employer was also at fault in not providing full safety equipment (*Cork* v. *Kirby Maclean* (1952)).

There are special rules about defective tools and equipment. Where an employer provides defective equipment to his employee for use in the course of the employer's business and the employee is injured or killed, he or his dependants can sue the employer whether or not the employer has been negligent, as long as there has been fault on the part of a third party, usually the manufacturer of the equipment. The fault of the third party is attributed to the employer for policy reasons: the employee would find it difficult to pursue the manufacturer, often in a foreign jurisdiction, so Parliament has placed that burden on the employer who is better able to bear it. Of course, the employee may also choose, if he wishes, to sue the manufacturer, and the imposition on the manufacturer or importer of strict liability for goods by the Consumer Protection Act 1987, discussed later in this chapter, has made this easier. An example of the operation of the Employer's Liability (Defective Equipment) Act 1969 concerned seamen drowned when their ship sank off the coast of Japan. The House of Lords held that a ship was 'equipment' within the Act, so that the shipowners were liable without negligence on their part for defects in it caused by the negligence of the builder (*Coltman* v. *Bibby Tankers* (1987)). The Act includes any plant or machinery, vehicle, aircraft or clothing and any disease or physical or mental illness. But note that the employer is only liable under this legislation to his own employees and for equipment which he himself provides. Liability to the employees of sub-contractors or to the self-employed will still depend on proof of negligence on his part.

Many cases are brought for a failure to provide a safe system of work. It is not enough to see that the premises are safe and that safety equipment is available: the employer must take reasonable care to see that workers are properly trained and supervised. When a worker was blinded because he was not wearing goggles, it was not enough to show that goggles were provided: the employer should have issued orders that they were to be used and the foreman should have supervised the workers to see that instructions were obeyed (*Bux* v. *Slough Metals* (1974)). Though the employer is entitled to expect the workers to take care for their own safety to some degree, it is especially important to warn of latent dangers. In *Pape* v. *Cumbria County Council* (1991) the employee was a cleaner who contracted severe dermatitis through contact with household chemicals. She was provided with gloves, but it had not been explained to her why it was important to wear them. She was awarded £22,000 damages:

'The danger of dermatitis or acute eczema from the sustained exposure of unprotected skin to chemical cleansing agents is well known, well known enough to make it the duty of a reasonable employer to appreciate the risks it presents to members of his cleaning staff, but at the same time not so well known as to make it obvious to his staff without any necessity for warning and instruction.'

What can reasonably be expected from the employer depends on a number of different factors. The standard is only that of the average, not of the pioneer. Therefore, it is usually sufficient to follow a practice generally established.

An important test case in the early 1980s raised the issue of the duty of care of employers in noisy industries to take precautions against hearing loss. Albert Thompson was employed as a labourer in a ship-repairing yard for about 40 years. It had been known for over a century that excessive noise caused deafness, but no protection was provided by employers until the early 1970s. By the time Thompson was made redundant in 1983, aged 61, he needed to wear a hearing aid and suffered from a continuous buzzing in the ears. The High Court accepted that his employer was negligent in not providing him with ear protectors at an earlier date, but then had to fix the material date. Suitable devices had been developed by the RAF during World War II and were mentioned in medical journals from about 1951, but the first official guidance came with the report of the Wilson Committee in 1963. Thereafter, a Ministry of Labour pamphlet gave advice and in 1972 the Department of Employment issued a Code of Practice. The judge held that an employer cannot be expected to be much in advance of general practice in the industry. 'The employer must keep up to date, but the court must be slow to blame him for not ploughing a lone furrow.' He concluded that 1963 'marked the dividing line between a reasonable (if not consciously adopted) policy of following the same line of inaction as other employers in the trade, and a failure to be sufficiently alert and active ...'. Sadly for Thompson, the medical evidence was that most of his hearing loss had occurred before 1963. He was awarded damages of £1350 (*Thompson* v. *Smiths Shiprepairers* (1984)).

This decision is but one illustration of the stress placed by judges on official pronouncements. Employers are expected to be aware of statements from the Health and Safety Executive and other official bodies and ignore them at their peril. It is vital to have an efficient method of receiving and taking note of relevant publications. This may be considered a suitable role for the larger occupational health department.

The Northern Ireland Court of Appeal differed from the ruling of the English judge in the Thompson case. They held that even before the publication of *Noise and the Worker* in 1963 there was sufficient medical, scientific and legal knowledge available to shipyard employers to have warned them of the nature and extent of the problem and that some kind of protection was required (*Baxter* v. *Harland and Wolff* (1990)). Northern Irish shipyard workers were awarded damages for hearing loss in respect of exposure back to 1954, the cut-off date fixed by the Limitation Acts (*Arnold* v. *CEGB* (1988)).

Where an employee worked for a succession of negligent employers it is the practice to apportion liability between offending employers (or rather their insurers).

Since the late 1980s there has been a notable rise in the numbers of claims for work-related ill-health, reflecting the increased awareness of the workers both of the hazards and the availability of compensation. The duty to educate and train the employees makes it more likely that they will connect symptoms with their work.

Hand-arm vibration syndrome

Vibration white finger (VWF), or hand-arm vibration syndrome, gives rise to many civil actions. It is caused by exposure to vibration and progresses from intermittent tingling in the hands to extensive blanching, tingling and numbness. The condition has been a prescribed industrial disease since 1981. Hugh Bowman worked in the Northern Ireland shipyards for many years, for 16 years with vibrating tools (caulking hammers). He often worked in the open, in cold and wet conditions. It was argued that the employer, once he became aware of the risks, should have reduced the hours of work with the hammers, should have provided the workers with specially designed protective gloves and should have given warnings and instituted medical examinations and monitoring, none of which had been done. The Northern Ireland High Court had to determine the date at which a reasonable employer should have become aware of VWF and begun to take precautions. It was held that by 1973 when the condition had been examined in a large number of medical publications, and had been the subject of two reports from the Industrial Injuries Advisory Council,

> 'a sensible and reasonably well informed safety officer and factory doctor would between them have reached the conclusion that there was something of which they should take note and to which they should alert the management.'

Mr Bowman was awarded £2500 for a Stage 3 condition (on the Taylor-Pelmear scale published in 1982) (*Bowman* v. *Harland and Wolff* (1992)). The judge stated that the modern occupational physician should regularly read the *British Journal of Industrial Medicine* and have access to and consult *Hunter's Diseases of Occupation*. Failure to do so might constitute negligence. See also *Armstrong* v. *British Coal Corporation* (1996), another VWF case, where failure to undertake pre-employment and routine examinations and to give warnings was held to be negligent. The English Court of Appeal fixed the relevant date at 1976 for the coal industry. Dr Milne, deputy area medical officer for North Yorkshire, had produced a report about VWF in 1968. This should have put the employer on notice, and should, it was held, have given rise to an epidemiological investigation which would have uncovered the problems. Making allowance for the time this would have taken, British Coal should have instituted the necessary precautions from 1976 onwards. After this the Government set up a compensation scheme for miners affected by VWF. Regulations, stemming from a European directive, are in draft and are likely to come into force in 2005 (Control of Vibration at Work Regulations) (see Chapter 5). It is now more common to use the Stockholm scale to assess the severity of VWF.

It was held in the test case of *Griffiths* v. *British Coal* (1998) that British Coal was also liable in negligence to miners for chronic obstructive pulmonary disease (COPD) caused by exposure to coal dust which from 1949 could have been suppressed by techniques then available. The liability of British Coal passed to the Department of Trade and Industry, and many thousands of compensation payments have been made both for VWF and COPD.

Work-related upper limb disorders

In the 1990s work-related upper limb disorders, often called repetitive strain injury (RSI), achieved prominence. There are two kinds of work which carry this risk: the 'white collar cases' – mainly work with word processors, and the 'blue collar cases' – manual work involving repeated movements of the hand or arm. Despite a statement of Judge Prosser in the High Court in 1993 that the term RSI is 'meaningless' and 'has no place in the medical dictionary', there have been several cases in which employees have been awarded substantial damages against their employers in respect of these conditions, some of which are now prescribed diseases. In 1991 a court awarded two British Telecom computer operators £6000 each in respect of musculoskeletal injuries sustained while using a keyboard. It was held that in 1981–2 the state of developing knowledge was such that BT could not have been expected to know the full causal link between RSI and keyboard work, but that they should have known of the importance of seating and posture for those engaged in intensive repetitive keyboard work (*McSherry* v. *British Telecom*). The judge dismissed BT's claim that the occupational health department had no means of knowing that there was a problem because no complaint had been made. It was the duty of the department to inform managers of the need to provide proper workstations and seating. In fact, the Chief Medical Officer of BT, who was not called as a witness, was an acknowledged expert on tenosynovitis.

The retiring Chairman of the Health and Safety Commission stated in November 1993 that the Commission had no doubt that RSI exists and can be avoided or minimised by employer action. However, most cases in the courts were decided in favour of employers until *Pickford* v. *ICI* (1998). A secretary whose typing work increased over the years to about 75 per cent of her working time had not been identified as an intensive user of the word processor and had not been warned about the dangers of work-related upper limb disorder. She developed such severe pain in her hands that she was unable to continue as a secretary and was ultimately dismissed. Miss Pickford was denied a remedy by the House of Lords who held that the employer did not need to give warning of the need to take breaks. Typing took up only 75 per cent of her time, and a person of her intelligence and experience could be expected to take rest breaks on her own initiative. There was also doubt about whether her condition was psychogenic. The House of Lords decided against this particular claimant, but effectively held that RSI (or work-related upper limb disorders) did exist. The dam was breached and in subsequent cases claimants were successful. One example was *Alexander* v. *Midland Bank* (1999). The claimants were employed part-time as encoders. Their sole function was the rapid recording of the details of each cheque or voucher transaction. The average keying rate was 12,700 depressions an hour. There was a 10-minute tea break every two hours and employees were monitored. They were prohibited from talking. A number of encoders began to experience pain in their necks and right arms and eventually had to give up work. Two rheumatologists gave evidence that they had suffered a physical injury, though the precise aetiology of the condition was not known. The employer argued that the condition was psychogenic. It was held that their workstations were ergonomically of unsound design and that the claimants had established on a balance of probabilities that their symptoms had a physical cause.

> 'Simply because the precise pathological, physiological and anatomical explanation of a condition cannot be explained by existing techniques does not mean that the condition must be all in the mind.'

Work-related stress

We are seeing an increase in claims for stress-related disease or injury, especially mental health problems caused or exacerbated by work. Mental illness is as common as heart disease and three times as common as cancer. In 2001/2 563,000 cases of stress-related illness by work were reported. The HSE published guidance *Stress at Work – a Guide for Employers* in 1995. The courts have held that the employer has a duty to take care to protect his employees against unreasonably high levels of stress and to provide support to those whose work is inherently stressful. A junior doctor alleged that long working hours were damaging his health. The Court of Appeal held that this was capable of being a breach of contract by the employing health authority who had a duty to care for the welfare of its employees. To the extent that the contract provided for excessive hours it was arguably void (*Johnstone* v. *Bloomsbury Health Authority* (1991)). Junior doctor contracts were subsequently varied. And in *Petch* v. *Customs and Excise Commissioners* (1993), it was accepted by the Court of Appeal that employers owe their employees a duty to take reasonable care of both their physical and mental health, subject to the caveat that foreseeability and causation are likely to be more difficult issues in mental injury cases.

John Walker was an area social services officer employed by Northumberland County Council. He was responsible for four teams of field workers in an area where suspected child abuse was prevalent. The volume of work increased considerably, without extra staff being appointed. In 1986 Mr Walker suffered a nervous breakdown. He was off work for three months. He had no previous history of mental disorder. He returned to work with the promise that more support would be provided, but this failed to materialise. In September 1987 he suffered a second breakdown and was dismissed by the council on the grounds of permanent ill-health. He was awarded damages against his employer for psychiatric injury caused by negligence. The employer knew that the work was stressful, that Walker was vulnerable, and yet failed to take reasonable care to provide additional staff. The defendants stated that, as a local authority, they had insufficient financial resources, but this was not considered a valid defence on the facts. It was, however, regarded as vital that the employer knew of Walker's susceptibility to stress after his first breakdown. It was also important that he had a stable family life and had never before succumbed to stress. If he had had serious problems in his home life, it would have cast doubt on his allegation that his illness was caused by his work (*Walker* v. *Northumberland County Council* (1995)).

In these cases we are dealing with psychiatric injury, rather than upset, distress or injury to feelings. 'Stress' is not an illness, and a reasonable amount of stress can be beneficial. It is when the demands become too great for the individual to bear that conditions such as depression or anxiety neurosis may arise. Some individuals are more vulnerable than others, either in general or at certain periods in their lives when they are also subjected to pressures from outside work.

After the *Walker* decision was announced, solicitors for the defendants stated that in future they would advise employers not to reinstate employees who had had a breakdown. This could be bad advice if they run foul of the law of unfair dismissal (Chapter 8) or the Disability Discrimination Act 1995 (Chapter 9).

The importance of stress-related illness in British industry is reflected in two major developments since the third edition of this book was published in 1998. The first is significant research commissioned by the Health and Safety Executive, leading to a determined effort to lay down minimum standards and to persuade employers to take hazards to the mental health of their employees as seriously as those to physical health. A number of factors have been identified as potentially causing unreasonably high levels of stress at work and gave rise to official guidance in 2004. These are as follows:

(1)   the culture of the employer's organisation;
(2)   the demand placed on employees;
(3)   the amount of control employees have over the manner in which they perform their work;
(4)   relationships at work – in particular where bullying and harassment occur;
(5)   the manner in which change is managed and communicated;
(6)   an employee's understanding of his or her role;
(7)   support, training and factors relating to the individual employee.

The Health and Safety Commission published a draft Code of Practice in 1999 in respect of stress at work, but decided not to proceed with it on the basis that there was a lack of agreed standards against which an employer's performance with regard to the prevention of stress at work could be judged. The Health and Safety Executive created a questionnaire to be used by employers on a voluntary basis to assess stress levels in the workplace. They advised that 85 per cent of employees should state that they can cope with the demands of the job, that they have an adequate say over how they carry out their work, and that they believe that they are given adequate support from colleagues and superiors; 65 per cent should state that they are not subjected to unacceptable behaviour like bullying, that they understand their roles and responsibilities and that they are involved in organisational changes.

The HSE has issued improvement notices against employers who have failed to address the issue of hazards to mental health, but as yet there has been no prosecution in the criminal courts. In contrast, the civil courts have been dealing with a number of actions for damages in the steps of *Walker*, to the extent that the Court of Appeal laid down guidelines in 2002 in *Sutherland* v. *Hatton*. These are:

(1)   Claims by employees against their employers for damages for psychiatric illness caused by stress at work fall to be determined according to the ordinary principles of employer liability.

(2)   Unless he knows of some particular problem or vulnerability, an employer is usually entitled to assume that the employee can withstand the normal pressures of the job and he is generally entitled to take what he is told by or on behalf of the employee at face value. The employer generally does not have to make searching enquiries of the employee or seek permission to obtain further information from his medical advisers.

(3)   To trigger the duty on an employer to take steps to safeguard an employee from impending harm to health, the indications must be plain enough for any reasonable employer to realise that he should do something about it. The test is whether a harmful reaction to the pressures of the workplace is reasonably foreseeable in the individual concerned.

(4)   The answer to the foreseeability question depends on the inter-relationship between the particular employee concerned and the particular demands cast upon him. 'There are no occupations which should be regarded as intrinsically dangerous to mental health.'

(5)   Once the risk of harm to health from stresses in the workplace is foreseeable, it is essential to consider whether and in what respect the employer has broken his duty of care. The employer is only in breach if he has failed to take the steps which are reasonable in the circumstances. Steps which might be suggested include giving the employee a sabbatical; transferring him to other work; redistributing the work; giving him some extra help for a while; arranging treatment or counselling; or providing 'buddying' or mentoring schemes to encourage confidence. Whether it is reasonable to expect the employer to take such steps depends on size, resources and other demands, including those of other employees. 'It may not be reasonable to expect the employer to rearrange the work for the sake of one employee in a way which prejudices the others.'

(6)   An employer who provides a confidential advice service, with access to counselling and treatment services, is unlikely to be found in breach of duty 'except where he has been placing totally unreasonable demands upon an individual in circumstances where the risk of harm was clear'.

(7)   If the only reasonable and effective way of safeguarding the employee would be to demote or dismiss him, the employer will not be in breach of duty in allowing a willing employee to continue in the job. 'It has to be for the employee to decide whether or not to carry on in the same employment and take the risk of a breakdown in his health, or whether to leave that employment and look for work elsewhere before he becomes unemployable.'

One of the cases reported under the heading of *Sutherland* v. *Hatton* was appealed to the House of Lords. Alan Barber was a schoolteacher who took early retirement after suffering a mental breakdown. His serious depressive illness meant that, in his fifties, he was able to do only undemanding part-time work. He was the head of mathematics in an unpopular comprehensive school and, because of falling rolls, was forced to take on extra responsibilities to maintain his salary level. He worked long hours, up to 70 a week. The head teacher was autocratic and bullying. Mr Barber began to suffer from stress, lost weight and had difficulty sleeping. He mentioned work overload to the Deputy Head. There was an Ofsted inspection in the offing and in May 1996 he saw his GP and was signed off work for three weeks with stress/depression. The sick notes recorded this as the reason for absence. Nothing was done on his return to work. He asked for a meeting with the Head in June. She was unsympathetic and told him that all the staff were under stress. Further meetings with the other Deputy Head led to nothing being done to help. In September the situation worsened until Mr Barber, previously a reliable and conscientious teacher with an excellent record, lost control of himself at work and started shaking a pupil. He never returned to work (*Barber* v. *Somerset County Council* (2004)).

The Law Lords gave their approval to the guidelines laid down in *Sutherland* v. *Hatton*, but disagreed with the Court of Appeal ruling in the *Barber* case on the facts. They held that the employer knew sufficient to make it foreseeable that Barber was becoming ill and should have investigated and seen what could be done to help. Even a sympathetic appreciation of his problems might have assisted him, and there might have been the possibility of engaging a supply teacher or sending him for counselling.

There are significant differences in the approach of the HSE as compared to the judges in the civil courts. First, the judges rule that it is for the employee to notify his employer of his difficulties, whereas the HSE emphasises the requirement to undertake a risk assessment, a far more proactive procedure. It is, of course, true that many employees will be reluctant to disclose mental health problems for fear of discrimination. Secondly, the civil courts expressly state that there is no job inherently more stressful than others, whereas the HSE's research demonstrates that certain kinds of employment are more likely to throw up mental health problems, such as the emergency services, the NHS and teachers in inner city schools, often jobs where the worker is at risk of violent attack. In addition, the HSE would advise an employer to remove an employee from a stressful job which is causing ill-health in the interests of protecting his health and safety, whereas the civil courts are of the view that this is paternalistic and that it should be left to the stressed employee to decide whether or not to leave the job.

It is surprising that in neither the *Sutherland* nor the *Barber* decision is there any consideration of the Health and Safety at Work Act or the Management of Health and Safety at Work Regulations. There is no discussion of the employer's duty to conduct a risk assessment, which is mentioned only in passing. It must be remembered that the employee can now sue his employer for breach of statutory duty for a failure to comply with the duties in the Management Regulations. In future cases employees may be successful in claims against the employer by taking this route, rather than by relying on the common law of negligence.

Another area where there are many claims pending against the employer is damage caused by passive smoking. Since Mrs Veronica Bland, an employee of Stockport MBC, received £15,000 in an out-of-court settlement in 1993, the floodgates have opened in the sense that large numbers of claims are now being pursued. Proof of causation will be a major problem, but less so now that there is more scientific evidence of the dangers of second-hand cigarette smoke, classified by the US Environmental Protection Agency as a first class carcinogen. Several actions are also proceeding against cigarette companies, who are likely to argue that smokers' injuries are self-inflicted. 'No smoking' policies have been adopted by many employers in order to avoid the possibility of legal action and consideration is being given by the Health and Safety Commission to legislative controls. It may be argued that these already exist in the Health and Safety at Work Act and the Control of Substances Hazardous to Health Regulations.

7.4   Breach of statutory duty

'Old' safety legislation dating from before the Health and Safety at Work Act 1974, like the Factories Acts, invariably provided only criminal sanctions by way of enforcement. Judges in the nineteenth century felt that those injured by acts declared criminal by these statutes should be given a right to compensation, which the common law at that time failed to provide (the tort of negligence only grew to its present stature in the twentieth century). They therefore implied into Parliament's express words an implied right to civil damages for breach of statutory duty. The essence of this tort is that a duty imposed by statute has been infringed, so that only if the case falls within the wording of the statute can the victim sue for compensation. In addition, not all statutory duties give rise to civil actions. Sometimes, the statute expressly confers or denies such an action, but more often it is left to the judges to read the mind of Parliament. With the development of negligence, statutory duty is not now the vital source of compensation that it once was. It is, however, still valuable to claimants, especially in the following respects:

(1) The statutory regulations spell out the employer's duty in detail, whereas the common law is expressed in vague terms of reasonableness. It is easier to prove that goggles or a crawling board were not provided than that the employer failed to take reasonable care. This is both a strength and a weakness. Complex technical legislation gives rise to much detailed case law with decisions based on literal interpretation rather than abstract justice. In *Close* v. *Steel Co. of Wales* (1962) it was held that section 14 of the Factories Act 1961, which at that time imposed a duty on the occupier of a factory to fence every dangerous part of any machinery, only applied to an accident caused by the machine operator being caught in the machine, not by parts of it flying out and striking him. Close also failed to win damages for common law negligence, because the likelihood of a bit on an electric drill shattering and ejecting fragments which flew far enough to damage a worker's eye was so remote that it could not be said that the employer was negligent. Section 14 has now been repealed.

(2) Most statutory obligations demand that the employer or occupier must do that which is reasonably practicable, but sometimes Parliament will impose a duty which is strict or absolute, that is not dependent on proof of negligence. A provision in the Factories Act 1961, section 5, that effective provision shall be made for securing and maintaining sufficient and suitable lighting was construed as imposing liability even in a case where a light bulb had unexpectedly failed without fault on the employer's part (*Davies* v. *Massey Ferguson* (1986)). The existence of such obligations in the pre-1974 legislation reflects its basically criminal character. The rationale of imposing criminal liability without fault, as is frequently done in statutes designed to protect the public, is that it induces an organisation to aim at ever higher standards. Proof that a defendant took all possible steps to avoid damage can be taken into account at the stage of imposing sentence after the commission of the crime has been established, by fixing only a nominal penalty. But if the statute is held also to create a civil action for breach of statutory duty, it is not possible to reduce damages because a defendant was not at fault. Judges, unwilling to order a careful defendant to pay large sums in damages, used their power of interpretation to avoid strict liability, as in the *Close* case above. The Health and Safety at Work Act contains no offences of strict liability in the parent Act, which in any event expressly excludes any civil action for breach of statutory duty in respect of sections 2–8, though regulations made under the Act may impose strict liability.

In Chapter 5 there is a detailed account of the 1992 Regulations made under the HSWA in order to implement the European Framework Directive and the five daughter directives. This legislation departs from the language of reasonable practicability with which English lawyers are familiar. It uses expressions like 'efficient', 'adequate', 'appropriate'. When judges have been required to interpret these provisions, they have leaned in favour of imposing strict liability if the words of the regulations, read literally, bear that meaning. Thus, there is a whole new area of health and safety law where the employer can be liable to pay damages even though he was not negligent.

One Court of Appeal decision concerned a postman who was provided by his employer with a bicycle with which to make his deliveries. When he was riding it, part of the front brake broke in two and lodged in the front wheel. He was catapulted over the handlebars and suffered serious injury. There was evidence that no inspection, however careful, could have detected the metal fatigue which caused the accident. The Post Office had regularly inspected the bike and repaired it when it was necessary. Regulation 6(1) of the Provision and Use of Work Regulations 1992 reads as follows:

'Every employer shall ensure that work equipment is maintained in an efficient state, in efficient working order and in good repair.'

The Court decided that the words 'shall ensure' imputed strict liability. The regulations did not oblige the employer to do that which was reasonably practicable, but to make certain that the bike was in good repair. It was not (though they were not at fault) and therefore they were liable to pay compensation for breach of statutory duty (*Stark* v. *Post Office* (1999)).

An even more striking example of strict liability arose in *Dugmore* v. *Swansea NHS Trust* (2003). Alison Dugmore was employed as a nurse at Singleton Hospital, Swansea, from 1990 to 1996. Whilst there, she developed a type 1 allergy to latex protein as a result of using powdered latex gloves in the course of her work, probably in 1993/4. In June 1996 she suffered a serious reaction leading to treatment in the accident and emergency department. Following her return, she was supplied with vinyl gloves instead of latex ones. In January 1997 Miss Dugmore moved to the Morrison Hospital. She told the OH department of her allergy and was supplied with vinyl gloves. However, the extent of her sensitivity was such that in December 1997, when picking up an empty box which had contained latex gloves, she had an anaphylactic attack and, since then, has been unable to return to her work as a nurse.

Regulation 7(1) of the COSHH Regulations requires that:

'Every employer shall ensure that the exposure of his employees to a substance hazardous to health is either prevented or, where this is not reasonably practicable, adequately controlled.'

Miss Dugmore brought a civil action for breach of statutory duty against the Singleton Hospital. It was held that at the time she became sensitised to latex the employer was not negligent, since in 1993/4 a reasonable employer could not have been expected to be aware of the risk. Latex allergy was not fully recognised in the UK until the publication of a bulletin by the Medical Devices Agency in April 1996. The judge found that since it would take some months to introduce a new policy, employers could not be expected to guard against this hazard until January 1997 at the earliest. In the absence of negligence, was the Singleton Hospital liable for breach of statutory duty? Regulation 7 said that the employer 'shall ensure' that exposure is either prevented or adequately controlled. 'Adequate' is defined as meaning 'adequate having regard only to the nature of the substance and the nature and degree of exposure to substances hazardous to health'. There is nothing in this definition about reasonable foreseeability of harm. The facts were that latex had not been adequately controlled as far as Miss Dugmore was concerned. It was not reasonably practicable to remove latex completely from a hospital environment but the duty of adequate control was not dependent on proof of negligence. Singleton Hospital was liable on the basis of strict liability. The Trust should have provided Miss Dugmore with vinyl gloves before she become sensitised to latex protein. She was awarded damages of £354,000. As a result, all health care workers who became sensitised to latex even prior to 1997 are able to claim damages from the employer for a breach of the COSHH Regulations.

A similar result was reached by a Scottish court in *Williams* v. *Farne Salmon and Trout Ltd* (1998) where the pursuer alleged that he had developed occupational asthma as a result of exposure to micro-organisms in salmon. The judge held that the employer was in breach of the COSHH Regulations even though it was unaware of the hazard and could not reasonably be expected to be aware of it. No negligence, but liability was strict.

In *Fytche* v. *Wincanton Logistics* (2004) the House of Lords decided that strict liability was not absolute. Fytche was the driver of a milk tanker who got stuck on an icy country road in December 1999. He spent three hours digging the tanker out in sub-zero temperatures. He was wearing boots (supplied by his employer) with steel toecaps in case something heavy fell on his foot. One of the boots had a tiny hole next to the toe through which water leaked. As a result, he suffered mild frostbite which led to him being off work for several months. Fytche sued his employer for a breach of the Personal Protective Equipment Regulations 1992, Regulation 7. This imposed a strict duty on the employer to provide boots in good repair. The House of Lords held that strict liability only covered a defect which impaired the PPE in the specific protective function for which it was provided. There was no negligence, because the employer neither knew nor ought to have known of the hole and in any case could have not foreseen the incident. Fytche lost the case.

(3) The existence of a statutory duty reinforces an allegation of negligence (conversely the absence of such a duty helps to negative an assertion of negligence).

'The reasonable employer is entitled to assume *prima facie* that the dangers which occur to a reasonable man have occurred to Parliament.' (Lord Justice Somervell in *England* v. *NCB* (1953))

However, it is possible for an employer to be liable under the statute but not at common law (as in cases of strict liability), and liable at common law but not under the statute (where the words of the statute do not apply to this particular case, as, for example, where there are no specific statutory regulations, but there is a failure to take reasonable care). In *Chipchase* v. *British Titan Products* (1956), statutory regulations obliged the employer to provide employees working six and a half feet or more above the ground with working platforms at least 34 inches wide. Chipchase was working at six feet and fell off a platform only nine inches wide. There could be no breach of the statute for that must be literally interpreted, but it could still be held that the employer had failed to take reasonable care and was negligent at common law.

7.5 Liability for the negligence of others

In the civil law, an employer is liable for the negligence of all his employees when acting in the course of their employment. This principle of vicarious liability is founded on the idea that the employer profits from the activities of his employees and in justice should pay for any harm perpetrated by them. An employer may be held liable even though he took every possible precaution. Employers have had to pay damages for the carelessness of an employee contrary to the employer's specific instruction, and even for criminal acts. Only if the employee was 'on a frolic of his own' will the employer be exempt. As with industrial injuries benefit, the employee is not normally acting in the course of his employment when on his way to or from work unless travel is part of the job. However, in case law, the courts have shown increasingly flexibility. In *Smith* v. *Stages* (1989), two workers were employed at a power station in Burton-on-Trent; they were asked to go to Pembroke for a week to work there. The employer paid their expenses *and wages* for the period while they were travelling. While driving back from Wales to his home in Burton in his own car, one employee drove negligently, causing the other's death. The House of Lords held that the employer was vicariously liable.

The scope of vicarious liability has been extended by the ruling of the Law Lords in *Lister* v. *Hesley Hall Ltd* (2001). The claimants were residents at a school for boys with emotional and behavioural difficulties. Unknown to the employers they were sexually abused by the warden of the boarding annexe. Was this conduct committed 'in the course of employment'? It was strongly argued that it was not part of the warden's job to abuse the children in his charge. The House of Lords laid down a new test. When determining whether an employer is vicariously liable for an employee's wrongful act, it is necessary to concentrate on the relative closeness of the connection between the nature of the employment and the particular tort, taking a broad approach to the nature of the employment by asking what was the job on which the employee was engaged for his employer. The defendants had undertaken to care for the boys and had employed the warden to assist them. They were vicariously liable for his wrongful acts.

Disobedience to instructions does not necessarily take the employee out of the scope of his employment. In *Century Insurance Co. v. N. Ireland Road Transport Board* (1942), an employee delivering petrol from a tanker lit a cigarette and caused a conflagration. He knew that smoking was strictly prohibited by the employer. Nonetheless, the employer was held vicariously responsible.

Several cases deal with accidents caused by a practical joker. In general, an employer will not be responsible for dangerous tricks perpetrated by an employee, because that cannot be said to be part of the job. In a case in 1987, a young woman was in the washroom at work when a fellow employee as a joke rocked one of the wash basins which was known to be slightly unstable in her direction. The plaintiff turned quickly and strained her back. The Court of Appeal applied the following test:

> '... a master is responsible not merely for what he authorises his servant to do, but also for the way in which he does it. If a servant does negligently that which he was authorised to do carefully, or if he does fraudulently that which he was authorised to do honestly, or if he does mistakenly that which he was authorised to do correctly, his master will answer for that negligence, fraud or mistake.'

It was held that, although visiting the washroom was within the scope of employment, pushing the wash basin was outside employment and thus the employer was not liable (*Aldred v. Nacanco* (1987)).

On the other hand, the employer will always be liable for his own negligence. When he knows that a particular employee is a danger to others his duty of care dictates that he should warn him, or in a bad case dismiss him. Had the school authorities in the *Lister* case failed to check on the warden's background and references, they would have been liable for their own primary negligence. And in the case of the washbasin, the employer would have been liable if there had been evidence that its instability made it hazardous if properly used.

Before 1948, English law applied a principle known as the doctrine of common employment. This held that no employee could hold his employer vicariously liable for an act of negligence of a fellow worker in the same employment. Judges tried to avoid this doctrine by stressing the primary duties of the employer which, they held, could not be delegated to anyone else. If an employee was injured by the negligence of someone to whom the employer had delegated the performance of one of his primary duties, the employer would still be liable, for this would be a breach of a duty placed directly on the employer, not an example of vicarious liability. The leading case (*Wilson's and Clyde Coal Co.* v. *English* (1938)) concerned an employer who entrusted the task of providing a safe system of work to a reliable and competent employee. Because of an uncharacteristic act of carelessness on the latter's part, a fellow employee was injured. The employer could not be held vicariously liable because of common employment, nor was he negligent himself because care had been taken in selecting a delegate. The House of Lords held the employer liable for breach of a *personal* duty to see that care was taken by the person whom he appointed.

The abolition of common employment by the Law Reform (Personal Injuries) Act in 1948 pushed this idea of non-delegable duty into the background, whence it has been resurrected in cases involving a different problem: liability for the negligence of contractors. Vicarious liability in general makes the employer responsible for employees, but not for independent contractors. It would seem that, at least in some situations, the employer can be held responsible to his employee for the negligence of a contractor, as in *McDermid* v. *Nash Dredging* (1987), where an employer 'lent' his employee to another employer who negligently failed to provide a safe system of work. Lord Brandon said this:

'The essential characteristic [of the employer's duty of care] is that, if it is not performed, it is no defence for the employer to show that he delegated its performance to a person, whether his servant or not his servant, whom he reasonably believed to be competent to perform it.'

For example, where an employer has delegated to an occupational health department the performance of his duty of care towards his employees, like the duty to provide appropriate health surveillance, it may be argued that it makes no difference whether he employs his own in-house staff, or buys in the services of an independent contractor. If the doctor or nurse is negligent, the employer will be vicariously liable. One example might be a case where the employer had delegated his duty of health surveillance.

This principle will apply as a general rule only where the contractor works in close conjunction with the defendant employer and it does not make the employer automatically responsible for a contractor's defective premises. In *Cook* v. *Square D. Ltd* (1992) the employee was an electronics engineer who was sent on assignment to Saudi Arabia to work on a contractor's site. There, he tripped on an unguarded hole in the flooring and sustained injury. It was held that his employer was not liable for the state of contractors' premises over which it had no control. However, one judge was of the opinion that where a number of employees are going to work on a foreign site, or where one or two employees are called on to work there for a very considerable period, an employer may be required to inspect the site and satisfy himself that the occupiers are conscious of their obligations concerning the safety of people working there. The following *dictum* was cited:

'The master's own premises are under his control: if they are dangerously in need of repair he can and must rectify the fault at once if he is to escape the censure of negligence. But if a master sends his plumber to mend a leak in a respectable private house, no one could hold him negligent for not visiting the house himself to see if the carpet in the hall creates a trap. Between these extremes are countless possible examples in which the court may have to decide the question of fact: did the master take reasonable care so to carry out his operations as not to subject those employed by him to unnecessary risk? (Lord Justice Pearce in *Wilson* v. *Tyneside Window Cleaning Co.* (1958)).

7.6   Causation

The claimant must prove negligence and/or breach of statutory duty and he must show that he suffered damage as a result. He must prove that, on a balance of reasonable probability ('more likely than not'), his injury was caused by the defendant's fault. In *McGhee* v. *NCB* (1972), a labourer cleaned out brick kilns. Although he was exposed to clouds of brick dust, the employers did not provide showers and McGhee had to cycle home daily caked with sweat and grime. He contracted dermatitis after five days in these conditions. The court found that the employers were not negligent in requiring him to work in dusty conditions, but failed in their duty in not supplying adequate washing facilities. The problem was that the doctors could not state with confidence that he would certainly not have contracted dermatitis if the employers' plumbing had been first class, though willing to give evidence that the failure to provide showers materially increased the chance that dermatitis might set in.

In this case the employers were held liable, but the McGhee decision has been questioned in a subsequent action for medical negligence outside the field of health and safety at work (*Wilsher* v. *Essex AHA* (1988)). A premature baby was given too much oxygen soon after his birth, allegedly because of the negligence of his doctors. He was eventually found to be suffering from retrolental fibroplasia, a condition which might or might not have been caused by the excess oxygen. Other possibilities were hypercarbia, intraventricular haemorrhage, apnoea or patent ductus arteriosus. The House of Lords held that is for the plaintiff to satisfy the court that the negligence of the defendant materially contributed to the plaintiff's injury (even if not the sole cause). The judge must not assume that the labourer's dermatitis or the child's blindness was caused by the defendant's negligence, but must ask for evidence that this was a likely cause. The House of Lords was satisfied that such evidence existed in the *McGhee* case, but sent the *Wilsher* case back for a retrial.

Similar issues arose in *Bryce* v. *Swan Hunter* (1988). Bryce had been employed by the defendants for only part of his working life. It was established that during these periods the defendants had negligently and in breach of statutory duty exposed him to excessive amounts of asbestos dust. Bryce contracted mesothelioma, a cancer caused by exposure to asbestos dust and proved to be dose-related, though the medical profession does not know precisely why an increase in exposure adds to the risk of contracting the disease which is caused by one fibre entering the pleura. It may be that increased exposure merely increases the statistical risk. Did the fatal fibre which caused the cancer arise from the defendants' negligence, or was it a fibre for which they were not responsible, one of those inhaled when he was working for another employer or within the acceptable level of exposure at the time? It was, of course, impossible ever to identify the source of the rogue fibre and if the law demanded that degree of proof the plaintiff would be bound to fail. The judge held that it was sufficient to show that the defendants' negligence materially increased the risk that the plaintiff would contract mesothelioma, so the plaintiff won his action.

This decision was upheld by the House of Lords in a case which received much publicity, *Fairchild* v. *Glenhaven Funeral Services Ltd* (2002). Arthur Fairchild had a number of jobs in his working life which involved his being exposed to asbestos. He was able to prove that he had been exposed to negligently high levels of asbestos dust by three employers. He died of mesothelioma. His widow was unable to establish which employer was responsible for the fibre or fibres which had caused the cancer. It was decided that the conventional test of causation in claims for damages for negligence – that a claimant must prove that, but for the defendant's wrongful conduct, he would not have sustained the harm in question – can be departed from in special circumstances where justice so requires. In these cases it is enough that the employer's breach of duty materially increased the risk of the claimant contracting the disease. Fairchild was entitled to recover damages against any one of his negligent employers or all of them (any employer held liable to pay the full compensation would be able to seek contribution from the others). This was the principle established in *McGhee* v. *NCB* (above) and it is applied wherever the limitations of medical knowledge make it impossible to prove exactly how the condition occurred.

Epidemiological evidence may be important. In *McPherson* v. *Alexander Stephen and Sons Ltd* (1990) the plaintiff was exposed to excessive levels of asbestos dust through his employer's negligence. He neither smoked nor drank heavily. He contracted cancer of the larynx. The Scottish court heard evidence that there was an increased occupational risk of 1.3 to 2.0 on a 95 per cent confidence basis of cancer of the larynx from asbestos. The court was satisfied that the plaintiff had established causation.

The law of tort in most cases imposes liability only for damage which the defendant could foresee. If a reasonable man could not have appreciated that his acts or omissions would cause harm, he cannot be held liable for his failure to take precautions. Thus, a failure by a doctor to appreciate that ampoules in which a spinal anaesthetic was stored in a solution of phenol had developed cracks so fine that they could not be seen or felt, but which allowed the phenol to contaminate the drug, was not tortious because this danger was unknown to the medical profession at that time (*Roe* v. *Minister of Health* (1954)).

If, however, the defendant was negligent, he is liable for all the damage which results, however unforeseeable in its extent. The best known example of this principle is the maxim: 'The wrongdoer must take his victim as he finds him'. In *Smith* v. *Leech Brain Co.* (1962), a workman while working with molten metal was burned on his lip from a fleck of metal splashed on to it. His employer was negligent in not providing a shield. The wound later became malignant and the employee died of cancer, a result totally unforeseen at the time of the accident. The employer was liable for the death, because his negligence had caused the burn: his ignorance of the employee's predisposition to cancer was irrelevant. In *Bradford* v.

Robinson Rentals (1967), a lorry driver contracted frost-bite when he had to drive his employer's unheated lorry in bad weather for a long distance. Despite the unusual severity of his reaction to an English winter, he was able to recover full compensation from his employer. The principle also applies when the physical extent of damage was unforeseeable, so that a defendant will be responsible for a catastrophic fire if he could have foreseen a small one.

Care must be taken with this principle. Where the employee has a particular condition unknown to his employer, the employer cannot be held liable if he fails to protect his employee against harm. Where, for example, he does not know that his employee is subject to stress, he is not liable for employing him in a post with heavy responsibilities and long hours (*Petch* v. *Customs and Excise Commissioners* (1993) (above)). But if he can foresee *some* damage he is liable for damage more extensive than could have been foreseen. In *Page* v. *Smith* (1995) the plaintiff was involved in a relatively minor road accident caused by the defendant's negligent driving. Although not physically injured, he suffered from a severe recrudescence of ME (myalgic encephalomyelitis) brought on by the shock of the accident. The House of Lords held that since the plaintiff was a primary victim directly involved in the accident (and not a mere bystander or observer), the test was whether the defendant should have reasonably foreseen some injury resulting from his conduct. Since the defendant might have expected some physical injury resulting from the accident, he was liable for the unforeseeable psychiatric injury. No distinction could be drawn between physical and mental illness. But if the defendant had been driving with reasonable care, and could not therefore have foreseen any injury, he would not have been liable. Thus, an employer who takes reasonable care of his employees cannot be held responsible in negligence for, for example, an unforeseeable allergic reaction to a normally benign substance.

Negligence in itself does not give rise to civil liability: damage must result. Thus, a doctor who negligently gave an injured employee the full dose of ATS, an anti-tetanus injection, without waiting for half an hour to test his sensitivity, was not liable for his resulting encephalitis, since that developed more than a week after the injection. The employer whose carelessness had caused the original wound was held liable for all the damage because he had to take his victim as he found him, with a special susceptibility to the vaccine (*Robinson* v. *Post Office* (1974)). If the encephalitis had developed soon after the injection, the doctor would have been liable for the encephalitis and the employer only for the wound, because the doctor's negligence would in effect have broken the chain of causation, being what lawyers term a *novus actus interveniens* (a new intervening event).

Courts occasionally assume that there has been negligence if an injury has been suffered in circumstances where there should have been no risk. The patient who leaves the operating theatre with a surgical instrument in her abdomen will argue that there must have been negligence: the thing speaks for itself (*res ipsa loquitur*).

7.7 Liability of the employer to non-employees

The law of negligence imposes a duty of care in many situations towards anyone within the foreseeable area of risk. A factory owner has to consider his own employees, employees of contractors, visitors to the premises and members of the public both on his premises and within the vicinity. In *Haley* v. *London Electricity Board* (1965), the Board was held liable to an unaccompanied blind man who fell into a hole in a public pavement because it was insufficiently guarded. The House of Lords held that the Board's employees should have foreseen that blind persons were in the community and taken special precautions for their benefit.

The duty of care of an occupier of land in respect of premises has been enacted in the Occupiers' Liability Acts 1957 and 1984. The occupier may be the owner of the premises or a contractor in control of a site. The first statute deals with liability to *visitors*, those with express or implied permission to be on the premises, the second with liability to *trespassers*, those who enter the premises without the permission of the occupier. A common duty of care is owed to all visitors, a duty to take reasonable care in all the circumstances of the case. Relevant considerations are that an occupier must be prepared for children to be less careful than adults and that he is entitled to expect that someone who enters his premises to do a job will appreciate and guard against the usual risks of the job. A warning of a danger does not exonerate an occupier unless it is sufficient to enable the visitor to be reasonably safe and the Unfair Contract Terms Act 1977 makes ineffective a notice excluding liability for death or personal injury in respect of business premises.

The occupier is not liable for the negligence of an independent contractor, but he will be responsible for his own negligence in choosing a contractor who he should have known was unreliable, or failing to exercise reasonable supervision. In the case of *Ferguson* v. *Welsh* (1988), Ferguson was injured when working on a site occupied by a local authority. He was employed by a demolition sub-contractor who had been brought in by the main contractor and who had adopted a thoroughly unsafe system of demolishing a building from the bottom up. It was held that the council were not liable under the Occupiers' Liability Act. They were unaware that the main contractor had employed a 'cowboy' contractor (it had been done without their permission) and it is not normally reasonable to expect an occupier of premises to supervise the contractor's activities unless he has reason to suspect that the contractor is adopting an unsafe system of work.

The 1984 Act imposes a duty towards trespassers, but an occupier is only liable if he knows, or has reasonable grounds to believe, that a danger exists and that trespassers may come into its vicinity. The plaintiff must also prove that the risk was one against which the occupier can reasonably be expected to provide protection. The Act is designed to give statutory force to cases like *British Rail* v. *Herrington* (1972), where damages were awarded to a small child who was injured on a live rail to which he had gained access through a gap in the defendants' fence of which they knew.

7.8 Duty to the unborn child

First, it must be remembered that a woman with child is, in effect, two people, both of whom may wish to seek compensation. The tragedy of the thalidomide children made the community conscious of the vulnerability of the child in its mother's womb. At the time, lawyers were uncertain whether an action could be brought by a child for damage sustained before birth. Parliament clarified the law in the Congenital Disabilities (Civil Liability) Act 1976 and since then the court in *Burton* v. *Islington Health Authority* (1993) has held that children born before 1976 have a cause of action at common law. An action only lies under the Act if the child is injured by an act or omission which is also actionable by one or other of the child's parents. The child must be born alive. A foetus killed in the womb has no rights under this Act, but the *mother* has a right of action at common law if she miscarries because of another's negligence, as where she can prove that exposure to a substance or process has caused a spontaneous abortion. Damage to the reproductive capacity of a male worker through radiation or toxic chemicals, if it can be proved, may also give rise to an action for damages.

The legislation is not limited to an injury to a child after conception, but extends to an occurrence which affects either parent in his or her ability to bear a normal healthy infant and which leads to the birth of a disabled child, *unless at the time of conception either parent knew of the risk of disablement*. Again, the parents can also sue at common law for negligence which affects their ability to have children.

The mother cannot be legally liable to her own baby if her conduct (drinking, smoking, taking drugs, etc.) causes its disability (except that a woman driving a motor vehicle when she knows or ought to know herself to be pregnant is under a duty of care towards her unborn child – the policy behind this being that the insurance company will bear the loss). The father has no such immunity and is liable in all circumstances for negligent or criminal conduct that causes harm to his unborn child.

In the employment situation, therefore, the employer will have to consider the health of father, mother and child. If, through his negligence, a woman worker loses her baby or is advised to have an abortion, the mother will be able to claim damages. If his negligence causes a deformity in the child of either a male or female worker, both child and parent will be able to sue, the child for his disability and the parent for psychological distress. English courts have refused to give damages for 'wrongful life' to a child whose complaint was that her mother's doctor was negligent in not informing her that the foetus was defective so that she could have aborted her (*McKay* v. *Essex AHA* (1982)).

The 1976 Act includes a special section for health professionals:

'The defendant is not answerable to the child, for anything he did or omitted to do when responsible in a professional capacity for treating or advising the parent, if he took reasonable care having due regard to the then received professional opinion applicable to the particular class of case; but this does not mean that he is answerable only because he departed from received opinion.'

This sounds very like the standard of reasonable care discussed in Chapter 2.

A report by Professor Martin Gardner in 1990 explaining the higher than average incidence of childhood leukaemia and Hodgkin's disease in children born to fathers who had worked at the Sellafield nuclear processing plant as caused by pre-paternal irradiation was relied upon by two plaintiffs in an action against

British Nuclear Fuels in 1993 (*Hope and Reay* v. *BNFL*). The High Court rejected the claim, finding insufficient proof of causation on the facts.

7.9 Post traumatic stress disorder

No damages will be paid for mental suffering alone, but if as a result of fear or terror the claimant becomes ill, compensation can be given for that illness. It must be shown that the defendant's negligence caused a shock which was reasonably foreseeable in an average phlegmatic individual. Doctors have developed better understanding of post traumatic stress disorder, and this has been reflected in an increase in the numbers of claims under this head.

The law on nervous shock was reviewed by the House of Lords in *Alcock* v. *Chief Constable of the South Yorkshire Police* (1991), one of the cases arising out of the disaster at the Hillsborough football stadium. Due to the negligence of the police in controlling the crowd too many spectators were admitted to the enclosure and some were crushed to death. The events were broadcast on radio and television as they occurred and were seen and heard by many relatives and friends of the deceased. Others were eye-witnesses at the ground or identified bodies in the mortuary.

The House of Lords decided that the mere fact that nervous shock to the claimant was reasonably foreseeable did not give rise to a duty of care, because of the multitudinous claims which might result. The law had to limit the remedy to those 'proximate' to the accident, either close relatives present at the scene, described as 'secondary victims', or those directly involved in the events, like rescuers. Those who saw the incident on television or heard it on radio could not be included, nor those who saw the victims some hours later and not in the immediate aftermath. A subsequent action was brought by police officers who assisted the victims shortly after the accident. The Court of Appeal decided that because there was already a master/servant relationship between the policemen and their employing force they were in a different position from the relatives of the victims and granted them damages for nervous shock. The House of Lords reversed the decision of the Court of Appeal. In *White* v. *Chief Constable of the South Yorkshire Police* (1999) it was held that police officers were not entitled to recover damages from the Chief Constable for psychiatric injury suffered as a result of assisting with the aftermath of the disaster. Only where they had either themselves been at physical risk of injury or reasonably believed that to be the case were they sufficiently proximate. For example, in *Young* v. *Charles Church (Southern) Ltd* (1998) an employee who suffered psychiatric injury when he saw a colleague working close by electrocuted, recovered damages because he himself was in similar danger and was fortunate to escape.

Where the employee is put in fear for his own safety, he is a primary victim and can recover damages. David Donachie was a police officer required in the course of his duty to attach a tagging device to the underside of a car believed to belong to a gang of criminals. The car was parked in a Manchester street outside the pub where the criminals were drinking. Because the battery in the device had failed, he had to make nine trips from the car to the tracking van and back before he succeeded in making the device work. This was very stressful, since he was in constant fear that the suspects would return to the car. There was an established history of problems with these devices. Because of this incident, Donachie's hypertension was aggravated and he suffered an acute rise in blood pressure which caused a stroke. This was the evidence of the consultant cardiologists called as expert witnesses. The Court of Appeal held that the Chief Constable was negligent, in that the device should have been tested before Donachie was supplied with it. Donachie was in fear for his own safety, thus he was a primary, not a secondary victim. It was therefore irrelevant that the Chief Constable did not know of Donachie's pre-existing hypertension ('you take your victim as you find him'). The employer was liable (*Donachie* v. *Chief Constable of Greater Manchester* (2004)).

These rulings do not interfere with the authority of prior cases like that of a crane driver who, without any fault on his part, injured a fellow worker while operating a defective crane and suffered a psychiatric illness. He recovered damages from those responsible for the defect (*Carlin* v. *Helical Bar* (1970)). Damage to property may give rise to nervous shock as in the case of the lady whose house burned down because of the negligence of British Gas and who recovered damages for the nervous illness caused by the spectacle of the conflagration (*Attia* v. *British Gas* (1987)). Both these plaintiffs were more than spectators: they were themselves directly involved, described by the courts as 'primary victims'. Compare these with *McFarlane* v. *E. E. Caledonia* (1994) where a painter on a support vessel suffered psychiatric illness after he witnessed the explosion and fire on the *Piper Alpha* oil rig, though not in danger himself. He lost his action for compensation.

Where the claimant suffers a physical injury due to the defendant's negligence and in consequence suffers a psychiatric illness, both physical and mental effects are compensable. In *Pigney* v. *Pointer's Services* (1957), the negligence of the defendants caused head injuries to the plaintiff's husband, which induced depression. He eventually committed suicide and it was held that the defendants were liable for his death.

In *Sykes* v. *Ministry of Defence* (1984), the plaintiff had been employed in the dockyards all his working life. Due to his employer's negligence, he had been exposed to excessive amounts of asbestos dust. He was told by his doctors that his X-rays showed calcified pleural plaques, but no asbestosis or cancer. The plaques gave rise to no symptoms, but were evidence of his exposure to asbestos. The judge gave damages of £1500 for the physiological damage and the plaintiff's anxiety that he might develop more serious illness at a later date.

7.10   *Assumption of risk and the fault of the claimant*

Tort liability being dependent on fault, the carelessness of the claimant for his own safety will sometimes reduce, sometimes preclude damages. As we have seen, it will not usually deny him no-fault industrial injury benefit unless his actions take him out of the scope of his employment. *Volenti non fit injuria* is a Latin maxim which means that no-one can sue if a risk, willingly assumed, materialises. A participant in a sport cannot sue the player who tackles him according to the rules of a game, just as a patient cannot sue a doctor for performing an operation to which the patient consented. Yet neither the player nor the patient has assumed the risk of play or treatment outside the rules and thus could sue for an unlawful tackle or a negligent performance of the operation.

Rarely does the law deny a remedy to an injured worker on the basis that he has voluntarily assumed the risk of injury, because it appreciates that one in an inferior economic position is not free to choose. The labourer who worked under a crane loaded with stones was able to recover damages when a stone fell on him: his knowledge of the risk did not mean that he had accepted it (*Smith* v. *Baker* (1891)). A health professional is deemed to have accepted the risk that he may contract an infection through contact with patients, but not if this is the fault of the employer who has been negligent in not supplying proper equipment, sufficient qualified staff or a safe system of work. If the risk is significant, as with some workers in potential contact with hepatitis B, the employer will be negligent in not providing vaccination.

The defence of assumption of risk cannot apply where the employer is in breach of his statutory duty unless the employer has done everything within his power to comply with the statute, when he may escape responsibility if an injury is caused solely by the employee's failure to take precautions in breach of the employee's own statutory duty. In *ICI* v. *Shatwell* (1965), the brothers Shatwell, both of whom were trained and experienced shotfirers, disobeyed all their instructions in carrying out an electrical circuit test in the open without taking cover. They were both injured. The employers had provided safety equipment and safety training: there was nothing more that could have been done by them. The employees' conduct constituted a breach of statutory duty placed on them by regulations made under the Mines and Quarries Act. It was held that neither brother could recover damages. Where an accident is caused solely by the carelessness of the injured employee himself and the employer is not at fault, courts are unwilling to impose civil liability.

Far more common is the reduction of the amount of the claimant's damages for contributory negligence (Law Reform (Contributory Negligence) Act 1945). Where any person suffers damage as a result partly of his own fault and partly of the fault of any other person, his damages are reduced to such extent as the court thinks just and equitable. In *O'Connell* v. *Jackson* (1972), the defendant was wholly to blame for colliding with the plaintiff on his moped, but paid only 85 per cent of the damages, because the plaintiff's failure to wear a helmet had made his injury more severe. The plaintiff is guilty of contributory negligence if he has failed to exercise reasonable prudence. One employee who contracted dermatitis because he failed to use the protective cream provided by his employer was held only 5 per cent to blame, because the employer had not insisted on its use (*Clifford* v. *Challen* (1951)). A foundry worker who had been provided with safety goggles, but not instructed that he must wear them nor reprimanded for not wearing them, was held 40 per cent to blame when his eyes were damaged by molten metal (*Bux* v. *Slough Metals* (1974)). A miner who was told that he must bring down an unsafe roof before working under it and disobeyed instructions so that he was killed when the roof collapsed on to him was held 80 per cent responsible (*Stapley* v.

Gypsum Mines (1953)). In such cases, the court assesses the full amount of the damages and then reduces them by the appropriate percentage.

7.11 Paternalism

Though the employer cannot escape liability for negligence by submitting that his employee freely accepted the risk, where the risk is relatively minor and the employee accepts the job with full knowledge of it the employer may be held *not to be negligent*. The civil courts have in a number of cases held that the decision whether or not to remain in a job which carries some risk to health is for the worker, not for a paternalistic employer.

In *White* v. *Holbrook Precision Castings* (1985) there was evidence that it was well known to grinders that they would suffer from Raynaud's phenomenon, a numbness of the fingers causing minor discomfort and minor inconvenience. It was held that the employer was not liable for continuing to allow them to work. In *Withers* v. *Perry Chain* (1961) an employee after five years in the same job had to stop work because of dermatitis. The employers had taken all possible precautions, but the employee developed an allergy. There was no over-exposure to any substance, merely the development of an abnormal sensitivity in the employee. The employers moved her to a different job, but the dermatitis returned. She sued the employer for permitting her to continue in the second job. The Court of Appeal held that there was no duty to dismiss or refuse to employ an adult employee who wished to do a job because of a slight risk of which the employee was fully aware, and which the employer had taken reasonable steps to guard against. Employers, concerned about legal liability, may sometimes be too paternalistic. Every job carries some risks, but if the employer has done everything he reasonably can to protect the employee he is not negligent.

This principle has been expanded in a series of recent decisions of civil courts, but has caused consternation among those whose duty is to enforce the criminal law, like the Health and Safety Executive. For example, in *Dugmore* v. *Swansea NHS Trust* (above) a nurse sued two hospitals in which she had been employed, the first for causing her to become hypersensitive to latex, the second for employing her in a job where it was impossible for her to avoid contact with latex completely. She wore vinyl gloves, but suffered an anaphylactic shock when she picked up an empty box which had contained latex gloves. As regards the liability of the second hospital, the Court of Appeal held that the claimant was so anxious to continue her career in nursing that, even if the problem of latex allergy had been better recognised, the probability is that she would still have been working in the intensive care unit when she had her attack.

> 'There is no duty at common law to sack an employee with a particular sensitivity who wants to take the risk of carrying on working in what for others is a reasonably safe environment.'

A similar ruling is found in *Sutherland* v. *Hatton* (above) which was approved by the House of Lords in *Barber* v. *Somerset County Council*. Where an employee decides to continue in a stressful job despite medical evidence that this is damaging to health the employer has no duty to move him or her to a different post, or to dismiss if that is not practicable. And in *Coxall* v. *Goodyear (Great Britain) Ltd* (2002) the Court of Appeal decided that the principle established in *Withers* v. *Perry Chain* that there is no legal duty on an employer to dismiss an employee who wants to go on working merely because there may be some risk to the employee in doing the work, and that the employee is free to decide what risks he or she will run, was still good law. *Coxall* involved an employee who had developed a particular sensitivity to a new paint, although other employees were not affected. He was diagnosed with occupational asthma. The court cited this dictum of Lord Justice Devlin in the *Withers* case:

> 'The relationship between employer and employee is not that of schoolmaster and pupil ... the employee is free to decide for herself what risks she will run ... if the common law were to be otherwise it would be oppressive to the employee by limiting his ability to find work, rather than beneficial to him.'

OH professionals sometimes meet with workers whose work is actually or potentially damaging their health and their instinct is to remove them from the job, if necessary by advising the employer that they should not continue. Where there is no alternative employment this may lead to dismissal. Is the doctor or nurse entitled to breach confidence, not to protect third parties, but to protect the worker against himself? Is the employer entitled to dismiss such an employee, or would a dismissal be unfair? My view would be that the duty of OH is to give full information and warnings to the worker, but let him or her make the decision whether to inform management. It is advisable to keep a full note of everything said, in case the worker at a later date alleges that he was not told of the risk.

There are, however, two caveats to be made to this advice. The first is that the Court of Appeal in *Coxall* stated that cases would undoubtedly arise when, despite the employee's desire to remain at work notwithstanding the recognition of the risk he runs, the employer will nevertheless be under a duty in law to dismiss him for his own good so as to protect him from physical danger. 'For example, it could not be right to find that an employer was immune from liability if an employee known to suffer intermittently from vertigo or epileptic fits was allowed to continue working as a spiderman.' But is not permitting a nurse who is hypersensitive to latex to continue working in an environment from which latex cannot be excluded highly dangerous? Miss Dugmore could have died from the anaphylactic shock.

Secondly, there are now many statutory regulations which impose duties on employers to engage in health surveillance, which will occasionally lead to a decision that the worker is not fit. The COSHH Regulations, for example, provide for regular health surveillance in some circumstances (Chapter 4). My view is that where a serious adverse health effect is discovered in the course of such surveillance, the OH professional would be entitled to report to the employer that the worker is unfit, without giving clinical information. It is significant that in all the cases discussed above the main issue for the court was whether the employer was liable in common law negligence, not breach of statutory duty.

This dilemma of autonomy versus paternalism has been considered by the Supreme Court of the United States in *Echazabal* v. *Chevron USA Inc.* (2002). An oil refinery worker underwent a pre-employment medical which showed that he was infected with hepatitis C. Chevron decided that exposure to hazardous chemicals and solvents at the plant would increase the risk of damage to his liver, and refused to employ him. By the Americans with Disabilities Act 1990 (but not by the UK Disability Discrimination Act) Echazabal was disabled. It was argued that there was no threat to the health and safety of anyone other than Echazabal and that if he were willing to take the risk he should be allowed to do so. The Supreme Court ruled in favour of the employer.

Were this scenario to arise in the UK, it is important to note that the employer would have to demonstrate that he had either eliminated or reduced exposure to hazardous substances as far as was practicable. This might reduce the risk to all workers to the extent that a disabled person could be employed. On the other hand, in cases like *Coxall, Withers* and *Dugmore* the workers in question had a special sensitivity not shared by their colleagues. The employers had done everything reasonable to protect the bulk of the workforce. It is submitted that workers should be free to accept a 'residual risk' if they do so with full knowledge of what it entails. If this happens (and it should be documented) the employer will not be liable to pay compensation if the risk materialises. But when is a risk residual and when more serious? We await further guidance from the courts.

In addition, there are situations where a threat to the disabled person also involves the safety of others. For example, where a wheelchair user refuses to use emergency evacuation equipment in a fire, others may risk their own safety in trying to carry her out of the building.

The most recent case which has examined this issue is an employment law case, where a warehouseman suffered a disabling psoriasis, such that he could not wear the boots supplied to him by his employer as personal protective equipment. He was willing to accept the risk of injury (which was relatively minor), but the employer decided that his health and safety obligations could not be waived and dismissed him. The Employment Appeal Tribunal determined that this was a justifiable discrimination under the Disability Discrimination Act 1995. It can be argued that the employee should have a choice whether to wear safety equipment or not if the risk is to him alone. Clearly, this would not be reasonable where the risk is substantial, or it is a risk of death or serious injury. On the other hand, the employer's decision was understandable, given that he was acting on the advice of an inspector, who threatened to serve an improvement notice if the employee were found to be continuing without PPE. In addition, there are many employees who forget or refuse to wear PPE who do not have the reason which this applicant had and are not given the right to choose. This employer had acted reasonably in that he had suspended the employee on full pay while searching without success for suitable protective footwear (*Lane Group plc* v. *Farmiloe* (2004)).

This decision holds that the *Withers* v. *Perry Chain* principle cannot apply where there is a specific statutory provision obliging the employer not to allow the employee to work in certain situations. The PPE Regulations impose a strict liability to provide PPE where the risk cannot be adequately controlled by other means.

7.12 Several potential defendants

Very often a claimant will have a possible right to compensation from more than one defendant. A worker injured in an accident caused partly by the negligence of his employer and partly by that of a third party may sue either or both. Each defendant has the right to a contribution from the other: the amount of contribution is such proportion as is just and equitable, having regard to the extent of each party's responsibility for the damage in question (Civil Liability (Contribution) Act 1978). The claimant is, however, entitled to his full damages, so that if one defendant has no money the other will have to pay the full amount.

Until 1990 it was the practice for health authorities sued as employers of negligent doctors to recover all or part of the damages by way of contribution from the doctors' defence organisations. This practice has now been abandoned under a system known as 'Crown indemnity', whereby the NHS Trust takes full responsibility for defending the action and paying any compensation agreed or awarded.

7.13 Attempts to exclude liability

In these days when actions for negligence are increasing, potential defendants try to protect themselves with notices and contract clauses excluding liability. 'Visitors enter these premises at their own risk.' 'The company does not accept responsibility for the employees of subcontractors.' 'Employees should take note that the employer accepts no liability for loss of or damage to their personal effects brought on to the employer's premises.'

English law in general does not permit anyone to exclude liability for negligence causing death or personal injury, except in his private and family relationships. The Law Reform (Personal Injuries) Act 1948 renders void any provision in a contract excluding or limiting the liability of an employer for personal injuries caused to an employee or apprentice by the negligence of persons in common employment with him. The Unfair Contract Terms Act 1977 makes void any contract term, or any notice given to persons generally or to particular persons, which attempts to exclude or restrict liability for death or personal injury resulting from negligence committed in the course of a business or arising from the occupation of premises used for business purposes. Business includes a profession and the activities of any government department or local or public authority. In *Johnstone* v. *Bloomsbury HA* (above) it was said that a contract with a junior doctor was void to the extent that it required him to work hours so long that his health was damaged. The Act also provides that, in the case of other loss or damage, namely to property, a person cannot so exclude or restrict his liability for negligence except in so far as the term or notice satisfies the requirement of reasonableness. Note that the statute is inappropriately named, for it extends to attempts to exclude liability by notice where there may be no contractual relationship, like a notice in an NHS doctor's surgery, or a DWP office.

What is a reasonable exemption clause in a case of damage to property is left to the courts, guided by section 11 of the Act, which states that it is for those alleging that a provision is reasonable to prove it.

Exclusion and exemption clauses should not be confused with warning notices. If an employer warns an employee that he should not use a particular vehicle, because the brakes are defective, he will escape liability if the worker disobeys him. But a notice pinned to the notice board, or included with the pay slip, stating that the employer is not liable for loss or injury caused by his negligence, will be totally ineffective.

7.14   *Product liability*

We have seen that the Health and Safety at Work Act imposes criminal law duties on designers, manufacturers, importers and suppliers of goods. We now turn to the liability of these persons in the civil law. The *fons et origo* of the modern law of negligence was the decision of the House of Lords in *Donoghue* v. *Stevenson* (1932). In that case, it was held that a manufacturer of goods owed a duty of care not just to the person who purchased the goods directly from him, with whom he had a contract, but also to the ultimate consumer of those goods in the law of tort. However, there was a vitally important difference between the duty in tort and that in contract. In tort, the consumer must prove that the manufacturer failed to take reasonable care and thereby caused foreseeable damage, but where there is a contract for the sale of goods, the Sale of Goods Act 1979 and previous legislation imposes a duty on the seller of goods in the course of a business to provide goods of satisfactory quality, a duty which is strict in the sense that it is not merely to take reasonable care. If I buy a bottle of aspirin tablets from my local pharmacist and suffer damage because the tablets have been carelessly manufactured, I can recover damages from the pharmacist whether or not I am able to prove that he should have known of the defect. We have a contract and he is strictly liable. He may then in his turn be able to sue his supplier under a similar principle, so that the manufacturer may end up paying the bill. But if I want to sue the manufacturer, with whom I have no contract, directly, English law until 1988 demanded that I prove negligence, a hurdle at which many claimants, like the thalidomide children and the Opren claimants, have stumbled over the years. In addition, if drugs are dispensed under the NHS, there is no contract with the pharmacist and negligence must be proved to render him liable, and only the purchaser of the goods can sue in contract: his family and other third parties must sue in tort.

The problems of consumers in attempting to obtain compensation led American judges to create a form of strict liability imposed on manufacturers with regard to the ultimate purchasers of their goods. This came to be known as product liability. The European Community took up this idea and agreed that it be introduced into the laws of all the Member States. The Consumer Protection Act 1987 was the UK's response to the European Product Liability Directive and came into force in March 1988. The Act does not destroy the old rules of sale of goods and negligence but creates additional remedies for consumers. It is inflationary in effect in the sense that manufacturers increase their insurance cover (though insurance is not compulsory) and pass on the costs of the higher premiums by raising their prices.

The Act only applies to goods and electricity. It has no effect on the law relating to the provision of services, although the European Community has proposed the introduction of legislation similar to that on product liability. 'Goods' includes substances (any natural or artificial solid, vaporous or liquid substance) and ships, aircraft and vehicles. In *A v. National Blood Authority* (2001) it was held to apply to transfused blood and blood products infected with hepatitis C. This made the defendant liable, though not negligent, because at the time of the transfusions there was no known method of obviating the risk, since the virus had not been discovered or identified and, at a later stage, was undetectable through a screening test in any individual case. 'Goods' does not extend to land or buildings, though products used in the erection of buildings like bricks or cement are covered. The UK has also taken the option provided in the directive of excluding primary agricultural products and game. Strict liability is imposed in respect of industrially processed food, like tinned meat, but not for the fresh joint of beef on the butcher's slab. Injury or damage arising from nuclear accident is excluded: in the UK this is already covered by the Nuclear Installations Act 1965.

Liability is imposed where any damage is caused wholly or partly by a defect in a product. Anyone injured by defective goods may claim. If a vehicle is sold with defective brakes and causes an accident in which the owner, his passenger and a passer-by are injured all three can sue the manufacturer. Damage means death or personal injury or any loss or damage to property (including land), but only if that property is both of a kind ordinarily intended for private use, occupation or consumption and was in fact intended by the person suffering the damage mainly for his own private use. The Act is designed to protect the private consumer against personal loss, not the business against commercial loss. Very small losses are excluded. If the claimant is suing for damage to property under the Act, he must show that his total damages (including any for personal injury) would exceed £275. But remember that anyone injured by defective goods still has the option of suing for negligence or a breach of the Sale of Goods Act, if applicable.

Not all injury caused by goods attracts strict liability. Knives cut fingers as well as carrots, people fall off safe ladders, whisky kills alcoholics, but it does not follow that those products are necessarily defective. The consumer will no longer have to prove negligence, but the burden will be on him to show a defect in the goods. According to the Act, there is a defect in goods if the safety of the product is not such as the public is entitled to expect, taking into account the way the product has been presented and marketed, including any instructions or warnings attached to the goods. The courts should also consider whether the goods have been used in a manner which could reasonably be anticipated (the manufacturer of surgical scissors would not expect them to be given to small children for cutting out pictures) and the time at which the product was first put onto the market (a car without rear safety belts is not defective if, at the time it was first supplied, they were not mandatory). The introduction of the legislation has led manufacturers to attach more warnings to their goods. Cigarettes and plastic bags are already labelled. Sainsbury's were labelling houseplants in 1997: 'Houseplants are for ornamental use and should not be consumed' and Boots sold an insect-repellent cream labelled 'harmful to fish'. In 2004 a beer manufacturer sold bottles with the message that over-consumption leads to inebriation.

Who is liable for defective goods? The Consumer Protection Act identifies four classes of potential defendant:

(1)   the producer;
(2)   the 'own-brander' who, by attaching his name or trade mark to goods, holds himself out as the producer;
(3)   the importer who brings goods into the EC and supplies them in the course of a business;
(4)   the supplier.

Producers include manufacturers, processors of natural products, and suppliers of component parts and raw materials incorporated in manufactured or industrially processed products. Where Manufacturer A produces a defective tyre which is then built into a car by Manufacturer B, the tyre and the car are both defective, so that, if the car causes an accident, both A and B would be liable. No doubt, the contract between them would provide for an apportionment of liability in such a case. If the supplier of the component or raw material can show that the defect in the finished product was due solely to the design or specifications of the producer of the finished product, he will have a defence. Suppliers (often retailers) are only liable if they cannot identify to the consumer the producer or importer of the goods. If they can do this, their liability under the Act ceases, though they may still have obligations under the Sale of Goods Act.

It is important to note that the strict liability imposed by this legislation only attaches to goods after they are put on the market, unlike in the United States. Therefore, if an employee of a manufacturer is injured by goods in the course of their manufacture or testing by his own employer, he will have to prove negligence in order to obtain compensation. But if an employee is injured by a defect in tools, equipment, vehicles, food and so on supplied to him or his employer by another manufacturer or importer, he will be able to sue that supplier under the Consumer Protection Act.

The Act provides a number of possible defences. One which still causes considerable debate is the development risks defence. The producer of defective goods will be strictly liable for damage caused by those goods *unless he can prove that the state of scientific and technical knowledge at the time the goods were supplied was not such that a producer of products of that kind might be expected to have discovered the defect.* The manufacturers of thalidomide would have had a defence under this provision if they could have proved that medical science was not aware of the risk to the foetus at the time the drug was marketed. The UK has included this defence in its legislation (it is optional and other Member States have excluded it) because of pressure from the insurance industry, fearful of open-ended liability especially in the pharmaceutical industry. The European Commission protested that the wording of the 1987 Act is too widely drawn and is in breach of the directive because it alludes to the knowledge of a reasonable producer rather than a reasonable research scientist. An action in the European Court against the UK Government was unsuccessful (*European Commission v. UK* (1997)).

Critics protest that British consumers have been shabbily treated. A drugs company with a new drug to try may choose to sell first in the UK to take the benefit of the defence. Note that, even with the defence, the consumer is in a better position than before the Act, in that the burden of proof has been shifted to the defendant.

Other possible defences are that the producer was complying with a statutory requirement, that the defect did not exist in the goods when they were supplied but was caused by the way they were subsequently treated, and contributory negligence. An action must normally be commenced within three years of the damage complained of, unless the delay was caused by the consumer's ignorance of material facts. In any case, no action can be brought more than ten years after the date when the product was first put into circulation. Potential defendants are precluded from limiting or excluding their liability by contract or notice.

7.15 *Damages*

In the tort system, damages are usually given as a lump sum payment calculated to provide, when properly invested, for the relevant period, and taking into account that tax will have to be paid on the income. Our courts do not, however, make any attempt to predict future inflation. When the victim survives, he may need income support for the rest of his life, and when he has been killed, his surviving family who were formerly dependent on him will need another source of income.

The parties, on the other hand, may agree a settlement whereby the claimant receives an annuity backed by insurance. The Inland Revenue has agreed to treat these annuity payments as tax-free payments of capital. 'Structured settlements' as they are familiarly known have been approved by judges in several cases. The principal advantage for the claimant is that he will be provided for throughout his life, for the defendant that he usually ends up paying less. The Courts Act 2003 gives the court power to make an order that a defendant pay periodical payments, rather than a lump sum, in limited circumstances.

It is possible for courts to make a provisional award of damages, allowing the claimant to return for more at a later date if his medical condition deteriorates (Supreme Court Act 1981). The reason for this power is to try to settle compensation at an earlier date. Suppose an employee is injured in an accident at work. He seems to have fully recovered after a year, but his doctor writes that there is a possibility of epilepsy developing at a later date. Formerly, his lawyers might advise him that he should wait until his medical condition became clearer, but now he can safely accept a settlement approved by the court, reserving the right to come back if his health deteriorates in the specified manner. This option has little effect in most cases, because they are settled out of court by insurance companies who aim for finality in their agreements.

The tort system involves the use of a crystal ball in two respects. First, the judge must guess what would have happened had the damage not occurred. Would the victim have been promoted? How long would he have lived? Secondly, estimates will have to be made of what the future now holds. Will he make a complete recovery? Will he continue to suffer pain? If the victim is now retraining for a different job, how likely is it that he will be successful, and what sort of earnings will he be likely to be able to command? Formerly, judges used to estimate how likely it was that the grieving widow would be able to attract another husband, but this is now forbidden by statute. Even if the widow has remarried the court cannot take this into account in assessing her damages, though it can reduce her children's compensation because they have a new father. The dependent widower has no similar protection.

7.16   The living claimant

He is entitled to *restitutio in integrum* (full compensation). In 1979, a senior registrar aged 36, soon probably to be promoted to consultant, who suffered irreparable brain damage while undergoing a minor operation due to the negligence of staff employed by a health authority, was awarded £250,000, though barely sentient and without dependants (*Lim Poh Choo* v. *Camden and Islington HA* (1979)). Damages are awarded for financial loss, like loss of earnings, both up to the date of judgment and prospective (including those for the years which he will not now live because of his likely premature death), loss of earning capacity in a competitive job market (*Smith* v. *Manchester Corporation* (1974)), and also for injury less easy to quantify, like pain and suffering and loss of amenity (in the industrial deafness cases this included watching TV, chatting with friends and hearing the birds sing). The victim of negligence is entitled to seek private medical treatment if he wishes; the possibility of using the NHS is to be disregarded (Law Reform (Personal Injuries) Act 1948). On the other hand, the claimant is under a duty to mitigate his loss if possible by, for instance, undergoing medical care which would improve his condition or seeking alternative employment. This does not oblige an injured person to submit to an operation which carries some substantial risk. If the claimant is or is likely in the future to be maintained at the public expense in a hospital or other institution, that will be taken into account.

In assessing damages for non-pecuniary loss, the courts have to put a money figure on the loss of a hand or a leg, in the same way as in the social security system the medical panels must assess the degree of disablement. It is important for there to be consistency in the level of awards, both because equality of treatment is just and because insurance companies need some kind of tariff to be able to negotiate settlements. The exclusion of juries in personal injury cases means that the judges have been able to work out a reasonably consistent scheme. Guidelines are now published by the Judicial Studies Board. This is not to ignore the arbitrary nature of undertaking an assessment of the value of pain and suffering or loss of a limb. The level of tort damages is not linked to disability pensions under the industrial injury system. Further, tort damages are tailored to the circumstances of the individual claimant. A worker who loses his hand obtains higher damages if he was an enthusiastic amateur artist in his spare time than if he did nothing but work and watch television. In the social security system, as we have seen, the assessment is made objectively, only taking into account age and sex.

The Pearson Commission recommended that claimants should not be compensated twice, by the defendant and by social security payments. The Social Security Administration Act 1992 amended in 1997 (Social Security (Recovery of Benefits) Act) provides that virtually all benefits payable for disability and unemployment (including disablement pensions, income support, disability living and working allowance, and jobseekers' allowance) for five years from the onset of disease or injury shall be deducted from the damages for loss of earnings paid to the claimant. The Act excludes damages for fatal accidents, compensation paid by the DTI under the Pneumoconiosis Compensation Scheme, payments in respect of sensorineural hearing loss where the loss is less than 50 dB in one or both ears, and any payment made under the NHS (Injury Benefit) Regulations 1995. The defendant does not gain: he has to pay to the Secretary of State the amount of benefit received by the claimant.

It is now proposed that defendant employers should compensate the National Health Service for the costs of medical care caused by their negligence. This will increase employers' liability insurance premiums to an even higher level.

Public policy considerations cast a different light on the deduction of benefits from private insurance policies. If the employee has taken out his own insurance it is thought wrong to punish his prudence by deducting the insurance money from his damages. Why should his negligent employer benefit from his premiums? The same applies if the claimant receives a payment from a charity or a disaster fund or some other charitable third party, like his trade union. In *Parry* v. *Cleaver* (1970), the House of Lords held that an occupational disability pension is not deductible. In *Gaca* v. *Pirelli General plc* (2004) however, the proceeds of a personal accident policy taken out by the employers for all their employees and financed by the employers were held deductible. Contractual sick pay must be deducted from damages for loss of earnings.

7.17   Fatal accidents

Relatives of the deceased worker can claim for the loss of their breadwinner caused by the defendant's negligence or breach of statutory duty if dependent on him at the date of death (Fatal Accidents Act 1976). Spouses, former spouses, children, parents, grandparents, grandchildren and siblings, step-parents and children, uncles and aunts and their issue, and adopted and illegitimate children are all included, as is any person who has lived in the same household as husband or wife of the deceased for at least two years before the death. The action is for financial loss caused by the death, not for grief and sorrow, except that spouses and parents of unmarried children under 18 are entitled to £7500 for bereavement. The introduction of this head of damages by the Administration of Justice Act 1982 has caused resentment and misunderstanding in cases where young children have died, because the parents have had the impression that their child is being valued as worth only the statutory amount. It is a truism that it is cheaper to kill than to maim: no damages need be paid to compensate a dead claimant for the years of life or earnings lost, other than to the extent that others would have been financially dependent on him.

In assessing damages, no account is taken of any property inherited from the deceased, nor of any insurance monies. Social security benefits received by the dependants are not deducted. No reduction will be made in a widow's damages for wages she can earn; if she was not working during her husband's life she can claim full loss of dependency.

7.18   Exemplary damages

In the United States, damages for personal injuries are much higher than in the UK, partly because juries and not judges fix the amounts, but also through the availability of exemplary (punitive) damages. In English and Scottish law, the purpose of damages in most cases is to compensate, not to punish. The latter is the function of the criminal law. Exemplary damages are rarely awarded, and never in claims for personal injury. In many American jurisdictions, the employer who negligently exposes his workforce to some dangerous substance will have to pay not just for their loss of earnings, medical expenses, etc. Damages will be increased by a substantial amount to demonstrate the jury's disapproval of the employer's conduct. In our philosophy, it is wrong to use damages as a means of punishment when it is not the wrongdoer but his insurance company who pays, but there may be an element of hypocrisy here since we do give damages for non-pecuniary loss like pain and suffering, which many regard as a concealed penalty.

In *AB* v. *South West Water Services* (1993) the plaintiffs suffered ill-effects as the result of drinking contaminated water polluted by the introduction of 20 tonnes of aluminium sulphate into the system at a water treatment works. It was held that only compensatory, not exemplary, damages would be awarded.

7.19   Limitation of actions

In the civil law, a person who wishes to claim a remedy from the courts must start his action within a period of time fixed by statute. There are a number of reasons for this. The memories of witnesses will fade with time, the defendant and his insurance company must be allowed after a reasonable period to proceed with their business on the assumption that the claimant is not going to pursue the case, and it is in the general public interest to limit litigation.

Different periods are specified for different purposes. In unfair dismissal, the dismissed employee has three months from dismissal to start proceedings in an employment tribunal, whereas a claimant suing for property damage caused by a breach of a contract made by deed has 12 years from the date of the breach. Where such an action is based on the breach of a simple contract, the claimant has six years from the breach. Time stops running against the claimant on the day his claim is issued. There is then usually a very substantial delay before the case comes to trial, if indeed it ever does, for most actions are settled out of court. The court has power to prevent a claimant from continuing with his action if he is unreasonably dilatory in proceeding with it.

In actions for breach of contract or tort in respect of personal injury (including disease or impairment of physical or mental condition), the limitation period is normally three years from the date on which the cause of action accrued, that is, in contract the date of the breach and in tort when the damage was suffered (Limitation Act 1980).

In most cases, this is a simple matter to determine, because the claimant knows only too well the date on which he was injured. However, if the claimant has contracted a disease which only manifests itself years after his exposure to some dangerous substance, his three years may pass long before the symptoms appear. For example, if a claimant had contracted pneumoconiosis after years of exposure to noxious dust, but had not been exposed during the period immediately before the illness was diagnosed, if the limitation period were strictly applied, it would be too late to bring an action for compensation against the employer who had negligently exposed him to the dust. To do justice in this type of case, Parliament provided that in a personal injury case the claimant has an alternative of bringing the action within three years of the date of his 'knowledge'.

The knowledge in question is actual or constructive knowledge of all the following facts:

(1)   that the injury in question was significant;
(2)   that the injury was caused in whole or in part by the act or omission alleged to be wrongful;
(3)   the identity of the defendant (or of a person for whom the defendant is alleged to be liable).

Thus, an employee who did not know the name of the company employing him because it was one of a group of companies all with similar names and he had been given the wrong one was able to bring his action within three years of discovering his employer's name (*Simpson* v. *Norwest Holst* (1980)).

If the claimant does not know these facts because he turns a blind eye, as where he refuses to see a doctor about obvious symptoms, he will be deemed to have that knowledge which he would have acquired had he sought expert advice. Suppose that he does seek medical help and the doctor negligently fails to diagnose his true condition? The Act states that he is not deemed to know what the expert should have told him but did not, so he will not be legally prejudiced by his doctor's negligence in such circumstances.

Since it is knowledge of facts and not law which is important, a claimant who knows that he is ill, knows the cause, and knows the name of the person who probably caused the damage, will lose his right of action after three years if he does not issue a claim because he is ignorant of the law. This is so even in a case where he has received bad advice from a lawyer. He can sue the lawyer for negligent advice but a lawyer, like a doctor, is not necessarily negligent just because he is wrong. However, the court has an overriding discretion to allow an action to proceed notwithstanding the expiry of the limitation period if it considers it equitable to do so. It must take into account the length of and the reason for the delay, the perishability of the evidence, the conduct of the defendant after the cause of action arose, including his response to the claimant's request for information, the duration of any disability of the claimant arising after the cause of action, the extent to which the claimant acted promptly and reasonably once he knew the facts, and the steps taken by the claimant to obtain medical, legal or other expert advice and the nature of any advice received. Judges tend to be sympathetic to those who refrain from suing at first because they want to continue working.

In *Brooks* v. *J. and P. Coates* (1984), the plaintiff worked in the defendants' cotton spinning mills in Bolton from 1935 until 1965. In the course of his employment he was exposed to large quantities of fine cotton dust. During that period fine cotton dust was not regarded by the experts as dangerous to health. Brooks, who smoked 10–20 cigarettes a day, left his employer in 1965 because of breathlessness and bronchitis which he and his doctor thought was exacerbated by the dusty conditions at work. In 1979, by chance, he had a talk with a friend who had worked in a quarry and had been granted a disablement pension for silicosis. The plaintiff applied to the DHSS for a similar pension and was diagnosed for the first time as suffering from byssinosis. His disability was assessed as 40 per cent. In 1980, the plaintiff issued a writ against his former employers claiming breach of statutory duty and negligence.

Obviously, the plaintiff's action was *prima facie* out of time. He had had full knowledge of all the relevant facts since at least 1965. He may not have known the name of his illness but he knew that he had symptoms and that these might be caused by cotton dust. The plaintiff therefore asked the court to exercise its discretion in his favour. The judge decided that Brooks was not blameworthy in not realising sooner that he had a legal claim and that, despite the disadvantage to the defendants of having to find evidence (both the mills where Brooks had worked had closed ten years before, records had gone and the workforce had dispersed), the prejudice to the plaintiff of being denied the right to litigate outweighed the prejudice to the defendants. The judge went on to decide that on the evidence Brooks' chest problems were caused at least in part by cotton dust. This was somewhat surprising, considering the evidence that fine cotton dust rarely causes byssinosis and because the diagnosis of byssinosis depends on the plaintiff's history, particularly his own account of increased breathlessness on Mondays after the weekend absence, so that there is always a possibility of invention. It was held that the employers were not negligent because they could not have foreseen byssinosis in a fine cotton mill. They were, however, in breach of statutory duty under the Factories Act 1961 which obliged them to take 'all practicable measures' to render harmless all fumes, dust and other impurities as might be injurious to health (section 4) and to protect against the inhalation of 'any substantial quantity of dust of any kind' (section 63). It was practicable (defined as 'a precaution which could be taken or undertaken without practical difficulty') to control the dust by use of a vacuum process. The employers were held liable to the plaintiff, but his damages were reduced by 50 per cent for his cigarette smoking.

Where an employer has gone into liquidation before the employee brings his action the Companies Act 1989 permits the revival of the employing company in order that the employee may be able to claim on the employer's liability insurance policy.

These provisions in respect of latent damage were for a long time only applicable to actions for personal injury. After a series of test cases involving defective buildings which were discovered to have been negligently constructed years after completion, similar rules have now been introduced for negligence causing loss of or damage to property by the Latent Damage Act 1986. The claimant has six years from the date the damage occurred or three years from the date he has knowledge of all the relevant facts. There is, however, a long-stop period of 15 years from the date of the last act of negligence to which the damage in respect of which compensation is claimed is alleged to be attributable.

If the claimant is under 18 or of unsound mind when the right of action accrues, time does not start to run against him until he becomes an adult or recovers his sanity. This does not mean that no action may be brought meanwhile: procedures exist to allow minors and insane persons to bring actions through representatives.

7.20 Alternatives to the tort-based system

The increase in the numbers of civil actions for medical negligence has led the medical profession to call for the introduction of a no-fault system of compensation, similar to those in Sweden and New Zealand. They are not alone. Accountants, architects, designers and solicitors are appalled at their potential liability and the costs of professional liability insurance. There is confusion about the exact definition of a no-fault system. It contains two central concepts:

(1) liability for damage without the necessity of proving negligence (often termed strict or absolute liability);
(2) a guarantee to the person injured that he will receive the compensation to which he is entitled because the money comes, not directly from the wrongdoer, but from a central fund.

In the field of industrial injuries, of course, we already have a no-fault system. It is based on a relatively simple administrative process. In 1980 the DSS estimated that the costs of running the scheme were only 13.3 per cent of the combined total of compensation and operating costs. The Pearson Commission in 1978 estimated that each pound in tort damages took at least 85p in costs to obtain. *Atiyah's Accidents, Compensation and the Law* (Cane 1993) says:

> 'It is hard to believe that anyone could make a dispassionate review of the tort system and the industrial injury system, without coming to the firm conclusion that on almost every count the latter is a superior and more up to date model of a compensation system.'

Proposals to extend the industrial injury scheme to, for example, commuting accidents or individual cases of disease proved to have an occupational cause, are increasingly countered by the objection that it is fundamentally unjust to discriminate by paying more to the industrially disabled than to those disabled by non-industrial illness or injury. However, the introduction of the Criminal Injuries Compensation scheme, discussed in Chapter 5, compensation for damage caused by mass vaccination of children (Vaccine Damage Payments Act 1979), compensation for haemophiliacs who contracted HIV from contaminated blood products, all three financed by the State, and strict liability on the producer of defective products (Consumer Protection Act 1987), show that governments are conscious of the disadvantages of a negligence-based system, though the Pearson Commission's recommendation of a trial scheme for road accidents, financed by a special levy on the price of petrol, has never been implemented. Would a system of liability without fault not be preferable in all cases of personal injury?

One misconception easily dispelled is that no-fault liability does away with the need for lawyers. Strict liability for vaccine damage still obliges the claimant to prove that brain damage was *caused* by the whooping cough vaccine. Under the Consumer Protection Act, it is still for the claimant to prove that the product was *defective* and to find some defendant who is responsible. If costs are to be kept in check, any system of no-fault compensation for medical injury would probably have to distinguish between the consequences of 'natural' ageing and disease, and injuries which should not have occurred in the normal course of events.

Who would benefit from the general introduction of a no-fault system? All those potential claimants who now fail to recover damages in tort because they are unable to prove negligence and those who now cannot obtain compensation because the person responsible for their injury has neither money nor insurance.

Should the tort system run parallel with the no-fault system, as at present in the field of industrial injury, or should it be superseded? An advantage of retention might be that the tort system could be used to top up a basic State level of compensation. Changes in procedure have made the tort system more cost-effective The Pearson Commission thought that tort was a method of holding wrongdoers personally responsible and was therefore a deterrent, but it can be argued that the criminal law and professional disciplinary bodies like the General Medical Council and the Nursing and Midwifery Council are sufficient and potentially more effective in this respect.

Finally, how should any new system be financed? The industrial injuries scheme is administered by the Government and paid for through the Consolidated Fund. Product liability is in the hands of individual producers and their insurance companies. It is possible that the Government would consider a system based on private insurance. An important issue is whether there should be varying premium rates based on the degree of risk, unlike the industrial injuries scheme, but similar to employers' liability insurance. The theory of general deterrence developed in the United States by Calabresi and others holds that:

'If we can determine the costs of accidents and allocate them to the activities which cause them, the prices of activities will reflect their accident costs, and people in deciding whether or not to engage in particular activities will be influenced by the accident costs each activity involves.'

In other words, an employer will be deterred from using a dangerous process because the costs of insurance put up his operating costs and result in less profit. The evidence from many countries is that the introduction of workmen's compensation laws dramatically reduces the numbers of industrial accidents. It is submitted, however, that market forces are not the only relevant considerations. Obstetricians and orthopaedic surgeons are more likely to be sued for negligence than any other doctors, but this is not an argument for more Caesarian sections and fewer hip replacements. Even in commercial industry, the idea that if the profit is high enough a risk becomes acceptable has a decidedly nineteenth century ring about it.

Chapter 8
Employment Law

8.1 Introduction

The law relating to employment is concerned with the relationship between the employer, his employee and the employee's trade union. As with the law of industrial injuries, the sanctions provided for breach of the rules are in the form of money compensation, but there is also the possibility of court orders protecting property rights or ordering a return to legality. An injunction is a powerful remedy, obtained from a High Court or County Court judge, disobedience to which is a contempt of court for which the contemnor can be fined or sent to prison.

Employment rights are regulated partly by the law of contract and partly by statute, of which the most important is the Employment Rights Act 1996 (ERA). Other legislation is comprised in the anti-discrimination laws enacted in the Equal Pay Act 1970 (EPA), the Sex Discrimination Acts 1975 and 1986 (SDA), the Race Relations Act 1976 and the Disability Discrimination Act 1995 (DDA). European law has been of particular significance in the employment field, as explained in the General Introduction of the book. In the field of discrimination law legislation stemming from a European directive in 2003 made discrimination on grounds of religion or belief and sexual orientation unlawful (Employment Equality (Religion or Belief) Regulations 2003, Employment Equality (Sexual Orientation) Regulations 2003). Regulations against age discrimination are in the pipeline. Actions for breach of contract must be pursued in the High Court or County Court, where it is usually necessary to be represented by a lawyer and legal aid is sometimes available, whereas the statutes confer jurisdiction on the employment tribunals (formerly known as industrial tribunals), informal courts chaired by a lawyer who sits with two lay persons, one representing employers and the other employees. Legal aid cannot be obtained to take a case to an employment tribunal, but it is not necessary to be represented by a lawyer, and trade union officials and human resources managers regularly appear. Frequently the claimant represents him or herself. The loser before the tribunal does not have to pay the winner's costs (unlike in the High Court and County Court) unless he has brought or defended the case unreasonably. Appeal lies from the tribunals only on a point of law to the Employment Appeal Tribunal, which sits in London and Glasgow and which is composed of a legally qualified judge and two lay representatives from both sides of industry. Legal aid is available in this court. Further appeals may be taken to the Court of Appeal and the House of Lords.

If an employee is dissatisfied with his employer's behaviour but wants to stay in his job, he may sue for breach of contract of employment in the County Court. The alternative, when the employee can tolerate no more, is to resign and claim constructive dismissal before an employment tribunal. This has the major disadvantage that there is an upper limit to compensation for unfair dismissal in the employment tribunal (in 2004 £55,000), the average level of damages awarded is far lower than this, many tribunals reduce damages by a percentage because of the employee's contributory fault, and the success rate of applicants to employment tribunals is less than 30 per cent. Tribunals have power to recommend reinstatement, but cannot force an employer to re-employ a worker who has been dismissed. Since 1994, employment tribunals have had the power to award compensation for breach of contract on termination of the agreement, up to £25,000. This has the advantage of a quicker, cheaper procedure, but the disadvantage of an upper limit on the amount of damages, and the absence of legal aid. In 2004 the House of Lords decided that compensation for unfair dismissal is limited to financial loss. Nothing can be given for injury to feelings, or psychiatric harm (*Dunnachie* v. *Kingston on Hull City Council*).

A very important institution in the employment field is ACAS, the Advisory, Conciliation and Arbitration Service. Although paid for by taxation, this body is independent of Government, having its own Council with representatives from both sides of industry and independent members. When an application is made to an employment tribunal ACAS will offer its services to both parties to try to conciliate. The majority of applications are dropped before they reach the tribunal partly because of the effectiveness of this procedure. ACAS also gives advice about industrial relations both to companies and individuals and arranges arbitrations in industrial disputes by agreement of both parties. The award of the arbitrator is not usually legally binding, though it is open to both parties to make it binding by agreement in writing. A 'pendulum' arbitration is one in which the parties have directed the arbitrator to decide either for one side or the other, but not to split the difference between them. In 1998, the Employment Rights (Dispute Resolution) Act made a number of changes to the employment tribunal system, and introduced binding arbitration as an alternative to an application to a tribunal, with the agreement of both parties. This procedure has not up to now been popular, and only a few applications have been received. Employers, in particular, are unwilling to put themselves at risk of a legally enforceable award made by a single arbitrator without any opportunity to appeal if the decision goes against them. With all their perceived faults, the employment tribunals are at least subject to the control of the Employment Appeal Tribunal.

The bulk of the work of employment tribunals is concerned with allegations of unfair dismissal. The introduction of the unfair dismissal law by the Industrial Relations Act 1971 has had significant effects on the conduct of industry. Now that an employer who dismisses an employee must give a reason and be prepared to defend it at a tribunal, employers have refined their disciplinary procedures and created new ones. Justice demands that the employee be allowed to speak in his own defence before action is taken against him, and that he should not be dismissed for misconduct (other than gross misconduct), incapability, redundancy or ill-health, unless he has previously been warned that this is a likely outcome if there is no improvement. Employers have rewritten their disciplinary rules and agreed new procedures for dealing with conflict, providing for a system of informal and formal warnings, and appeals to a higher level of management. Employers feel that unmeritorious claimants use the tribunals for their nuisance value. A possible deterrent is the pre-hearing review which can be initiated by either party or by the tribunal. Written representations may be presented to try to show that either party has no chance of success. If the tribunal agrees, it may order the party who is unlikely to win to make a deposit of up to £500 as a condition of allowing the case to proceed. The case will then be heard by a second tribunal, who may order the unmeritorious party to forfeit the deposit and pay additional costs if he loses.

In 2004 regulations brought into force provisions of the Employment Act 2002 relating to dispute resolution in the workplace. Litigation to resolve employment disputes is costly and can often weaken employment relations and the employability of claimant workers. The provisions of the Act aim to encourage parties to avoid litigation by resolving differences through the proper use of internal procedures. They, in effect, require all employers to have minimum procedures and give incentives to both employers and employees to use them. The Act creates statutory dismissal and disciplinary procedures, and grievance procedures. Where the employer fails to implement at least a minimum dismissal procedure the dismissal will be automatically unfair. Where the employee fails to use a minimum grievance procedure he or she will be barred from taking a case to a tribunal. The details of this legislation are outside the scope of this book, and any questions should be referred to human resources or ACAS, but OH professionals should be aware that the new procedures apply to ill-health dismissals as well as dismissals for alleged misconduct.

Occasionally, the High Court or County Court procedure is used to try to obtain an injunction. The employee who has been dismissed in breach of the agreed procedure may ask to be reinstated while his appeal is heard. An employer may ask the court for an injunction prohibiting the employee from publishing confidential information belonging to the employer. Such remedies can never be obtained from an employment tribunal.

The occupational health professional may be asked to give evidence before a court or tribunal. His duty of confidentiality directs him to refuse to give clinical information about the employee without the employee's consent to ACAS or at an internal interview or appeal, unless there is some overriding public interest, though he can be compelled to answer at a court or tribunal. Sometimes, his care for his patient will conflict with the employer's wish to dispense with an unsatisfactory employee. In such circumstances, he must seek as an expert to give information to both sides without himself trying to make the decision about the employee's future.

8.2 The contract of employment

A contract is made when one party makes an offer to another and he accepts. This need only exceptionally be evidenced by writing (e.g. contracts of apprenticeship). Contracts of employment must be distinguished from other legal relationships. As has been explained in Chapter 2, the employment relationship is marked by the employee's subjection to his employer's control and participation in his business organisation, rather than being in business on his own account.

It is often hard to identify the terms of a contract of employment. Express terms may be found in letters of appointment, written contracts or remarks made at an interview, for example, but many contract terms are never put into words but are included by implication. Often, parties do not express their intentions because they assume that they are obvious. In one case a steel erector working for a civil engineering company refused to move to a site too far from his home to allow him to live there in the week. The court held that the nature of the business was such that employees impliedly agreed to be mobile (*Stevenson* v. *Teesside Engineering Ltd* (1971)). In 1963 an Act of Parliament was passed with the intention of protecting the employee by imposing a legal obligation on his employer to put the terms of the contract into writing and give him a copy so that he knew where he stood. Because that statute was called the 'Contracts of Employment Act', these statements are universally known as contracts of employment but this is a misnomer. The written statement is evidence of what the employer says was agreed, but it can be challenged as inaccurate. In practice, it usually goes uncontradicted and is important evidence when a dispute arises, sometimes years later. The signature of the employee makes no difference to its binding force unless the employee has signed an express agreement that the statement incorporates his terms and conditions of employment. The statutory obligation, now to be found in the Employment Rights Act 1996, is to give a written statement within eight weeks of the employee starting work. It does not extend to all the terms of the agreement, but to pay, hours, holidays, absence due to sickness or injury, sick pay, pensions, notice, job title, place of work and details of disciplinary and grievance procedures. The statement should inform the employee of any collective agreements which directly affect his contract. The employer must update the statement within one month of any change in the contract taking effect. If the employer fails to deliver the statement the employee can complain to an employment tribunal which can remedy the defect.

Many employees have their contractual terms regulated by negotiations between trade unions and employers in the process called collective bargaining. The collective agreement between union and employer is not legally binding on those parties unless it expressly states in writing that it is intended to be so (Trade Union and Labour Relations (Consolidation) Act 1992). There are a few single union agreements which incorporate such a clause, but they are very much in the minority. But even a non-binding collective agreement becomes legally enforceable if it is incorporated into the individual contract between employer and employee. Thus, if an employee is notified that in the event of sickness absence the collective agreement for the industry entitles him to up to six months full pay, he can sue the employer for breach of contract when he does not comply.

English law was in the past remarkable for the degree to which it left regulation of the employment relationship to the agreement of the parties, but in recent years there has been considerably more statutory regulation, much of it originating in Europe. There was no minimum wage fixed by law after the Wages Councils were abolished in 1993, though a national minimum wage was introduced in the National Minimum Wage Act 1998. There was no minimum holiday provision before the Working Time Directive was incorporated into UK law by the Working Time Regulations 1998. Such a system has allowed the judges scope for judicial engineering in the erection of a structure of implied terms. The duty of trust and confidence has been discussed in Chapters 2 and 3. In *Scally* v. *Southern Health and Social Services Board* (1991) employees of the Northern Ireland health boards were required to make contributions to a statutory superannuation scheme. Full benefits depended on the completion of 40 years' service. Regulations were introduced in 1974 allowing employees to purchase extra years of service in order to make up the 40 years' contribution, but this right had to be exercised within 12 months of the coming into force of the regulations. Four doctors failed to take up the option in the regulations because their employer had never brought it to their attention. The House of Lords held that there is an implied obligation on the employer to take reasonable steps to publicise this kind of contractual benefit in order that the employee may take advantage of it. Substantial damages were awarded. Since this case was decided, subsequent case law has established that the facts were somewhat exceptional, and that there is in general no duty on employers to give advice about pensions. In *University of Nottingham* v. *Eyett* (1999) an employee retired one month too early to qualify for an enhanced pension. He sued the employer for negligently failing to give him adequate information and lost. The court held that the employer had neither a contractual duty, nor a duty of care, to advise him on his pension rights.

The concept of the implied term has permitted courts to impose duties on employers which cannot be found in writing, and in some cases may come as something of a surprise to both employer and employee. In *Aspden* v. *Webbs Poultry and Meat Group (Holdings) Ltd* (1996) it was held that, where an employee was covered by a permanent health insurance scheme during his employment, there was an implied term that prevented the employer from dismissing him while he was off sick. This was explained in later cases as not excluding the employer's right to dismiss for redundancy or gross misconduct (*Briscoe* v. *Lubrizol Ltd* (2002)). In 1990 Mr Briscoe began a long period of sickness absence. The terms of his employment included benefits under a long-term disability scheme, where the employee was unfit for his normal occupation. Payments continued until the disablement ceased or the employee reached normal retirement age. The employers continued to pay Briscoe in the expectation that the insurance company would reimburse them, but in 1991 the insurance company rejected the claim on the ground that the employee was not medically unfit. The employers continued to support him, but sent him to the company doctor who referred him to a specialist. The specialist's report did not support Mr Briscoe's claim that he was unfit for his normal occupation. Briscoe continued to be absent from work, supported by his GP, and refused to meet his employers and to answer their telephone calls. He was dismissed for gross misconduct in not complying with his employer's reasonable requests and instructions. This was held to be a fair dismissal which effectively terminated any right Briscoe had to insurance benefits.

In 1997 the Employment Appeal Tribunal held that there is an implied contractual term that an employer will provide and monitor, so far as is reasonably practicable, a working environment suitable for the performance of employees' contractual duties. The employer, who had failed to provide a smoke-free atmosphere for his secretary, who did not smoke, was held to be in breach of this term (*Waltons and Morse* v. *Dorrington*).

There is, however, no implied term that the employer will provide personal accident insurance for an employee who works abroad, or advise the employee on the need to take out his own insurance (*Reid* v. *Rush and Tompkins Group* (1989)).

There is an implied term in every contract of employment that the employer will take reasonable care to protect his employee's safety and health while he is acting in the course of his employment. Many examples could be given. One is that of Mrs Austin who worked for BAC in a job where she had to wear protective eye-wear. She asked a manager on a number of occasions whether it would be possible to provide her with protective glasses made up to her own prescription because she found it cumbersome to wear the protective spectacles over her own glasses. The manager brusquely rejected her complaint and refused to investigate the matter. It was held to be a breach of contract by the employer not at least to investigate reasonable safety requests (but not frivolous complaints) (*BAC* v. *Austin* (1978)). Mr Justice Phillips said this in the course of his judgment:

'It seems to us that it is plainly the case that employers ... are under an obligation under the terms of the contract of employment to act reasonably in dealing with matters of safety, or complaints of lack of safety, which are drawn to their attention by employees ...'

Another case concerned Mrs Firth (*Oxley Steel Tools* v. *Firth* (1980)). She had to endure working for several months in intolerably cold conditions: a breach of contract by the employer as well as a breach of the employer's statutory duty under the Factories Act.

Where an employee is subjected to unreasonable stress by the employer such that the employee is made ill, the employer may be held liable for breach of the contractual duty of trust and confidence. In *Gogay* v. *Hertfordshire County Council* (2000) a care worker was suspended pending an inquiry into an allegation of sexual abuse against a child in her care. The employee had previously told her superiors that the child was engaging in inappropriate behaviour and that she did not wish to be left alone with her. The suspension inevitably led to gossip about the employee; she suffered from a depressive illness and was unable to return to work, even when the inquiry found that she was not at fault. It was held by the Court of Appeal that the suspension was a 'knee-jerk reaction' and unnecessary in the circumstances. The employee could have been moved, sent on a training course or given a period of leave. There was a breach of the duty of trust and confidence and the employee was entitled to damages for breach of contract. But it was further held by the House of Lords in *Johnson* v. *Unisys* (2001) that this principle did not apply to a dismissal. This somewhat confusing ruling has given rise to much criticism, but was upheld by the House of Lords in *Eastwood* v. *Magnox* (2004).

The importance of implied terms leads to the question of how they may be identified. There are basically three kinds. The first is established by custom and practice in the industry. This must be 'reasonable, certain and notorious', so well known that everyone in the field takes it as read. The second is created by the previous behaviour of the parties. If Joe Bloggs has worked for the same employer for three years and has throughout that time accepted that he will work an extra hour each Friday it is likely that this will have become contractually binding. The third is created by the judges from the employment relationship. The courts have held that schoolteachers are under an implied duty to fill in for colleagues off sick (*Sim* v. *Rotherham MBC* (1986)).

Express terms cannot in general be contradicted by implied terms. If you want the position to be clear you should make an express agreement, preferably in writing. Even then, the court may use its power of interpretation to vary the effect of the term. In *United Bank* v. *Akhtar* (1989) there was an express clause allowing the employer to move the employee to any branch of the bank in the UK. The employer ordered Akhtar to move from Leeds to Birmingham at only six days' notice, refusing to consider his personal circumstances. The Employment Appeal Tribunal decided that the employer was in breach of an implied term in the contract to show trust and respect to his employee.

Neither party to a contract of employment may unilaterally change its terms without the other's agreement. However severe the employer's financial difficulty, he cannot reduce wages without consent. Confusion sometimes arises between the specific contractual duties of the employee and his general implied obligation to obey his employer's lawful instructions. Contract terms cannot be changed by the employer alone, but managerial prerogative can decide on working rules and practices.

Can management lawfully introduce a no smoking rule and impose it on employees without their consent? The answer is that the employer's duty to protect his employees and the employee's duty to co-operate entitle the employer to introduce new health and safety rules without agreement, just as he can unilaterally change disciplinary rules. Ms Dryden was employed as a nursing auxiliary in the theatre section of the Western Infirmary, Glasgow. She was accustomed to smoking 30 cigarettes a day. Her job was such that she was unable to leave the premises during the course of the day but, until 1991, areas were set aside within the employer's premises in which smoking was permitted. The employers decided to prohibit smoking in all general and maternity hospitals. During 1991, all employees were issued with letters giving notice of the change with offers of advice and counselling. The policy was implemented in July 1991 and 12 days later the employee resigned, claiming constructive dismissal. The Employment Appeal Tribunal held that the employers were not in breach of contract. There was no implied term that the employee would be permitted to smoke at work. Ms Dryden lost her case (*Dryden* v. *Greater Glasgow Health Board* (1992)).

To comply with the law of unfair dismissal and, more important, to be likely to achieve general acceptance, the imposition of a ban on smoking should usually be enforced only after consultation with the workers and consideration of what is reasonable. The employer must be able to prove that he has a good reason for the change. He may be able to point to a fire risk or the dangers of passive smoking to non-smokers. Here, the health education role of the OH professional will come to the fore. It is possible that the medical evidence about passive smoking now *obliges* the employer to ban smoking in order to comply with the statutory duties under the Health and Safety at Work Act (Chapter 5). The provision of a smokers' room, if feasible, should be considered. The ban must be clearly communicated to the workforce individually (not merely through the trade union), together with the consequences of breach. In most cases advance notice should be given, because a reasonable manager recognises that a smoking habit is not easy to relinquish. In a tribunal case, the employers introduced a ban on smoking after a fire, notified each employee individually and posted notices in the no smoking areas. An employee was dismissed when found smoking in the toilets, where smoking was forbidden. The tribunal decided that the dismissal was fair (*Martin* v. *Selective Print* (1987)).

In *Waltons and Morse* v. *Dorrington* (above) an employer who failed to provide a smoke-free environment for his secretary was held to have constructively dismissed her. The Employment Appeal Tribunal emphasised the employer's duty to provide for the *welfare* of his employees, as well as health and safety.

In contrast, because of the principle of inviolability of the person, I think it unlikely that English courts would imply an obligation to submit to body searches, random testing for drugs or alcohol, other biological testing or medical examination without the employee's agreement, unless the special nature of the job allowed the implication of such a term. Health professionals may have a term implied in their contracts that they will undergo medical examination if patients may be at risk (*Bliss* v. *SE Thames RHA* (1985)) (see Chapter 4).

In any event, developments in the law of unfair dismissal discussed later in this chapter mean that an employer may be held to have fairly dismissed an employee who refuses to agree to a change in the terms of his contract if the employer can show a good reason (like the protection of other employees from passive smoking) for imposing the change.

8.3 Contractual sick pay

The importance of making clear the terms of a contract can be illustrated from the legal rules about the employee's right to payment when he is absent through ill-health. Originally, the rule was 'no work – no pay'. Then, the Welfare State provided social security benefits for those who could not work because of ill-health, financed by contributions from employers and workers. Trade unions on behalf of their members negotiated collective agreements with employers whereby they agreed to 'top up' sickness benefits to provide normal earning levels for at least a period (some 80 per cent of workers were covered by such schemes by 1975). These were incorporated into contracts of employment and became express contractual terms. What of those who did not have the benefit of an occupational sick pay scheme? One such was Mr Mears, a security guard, working for a small family business. There was no provision in his written statement about sick pay and nothing had been said. There was evidence that it was not the practice of the company to pay employees when they were off sick and that this was well known to them. It was held that the employer was not bound by an implied term to pay contractual sick pay (*Mears* v. *Safecar Security* (1982)).

An interesting decision was that in *Beveridge* v. *KLM UK Ltd* (2000). An employee informed her employers that, after a long period of absence through sickness during which she had exhausted her right to sick pay, she was fit to return to work. They refused to allow her to return, however, until their own doctor had certified her fit. This took six weeks during which she was unable to work and to earn wages. She complained that the employer had made an unlawful deduction from her salary. The court found that since she was able to prove that she was fit and willing to work throughout the six weeks she was entitled to be paid. However, if her contract had given the employer the right to demand medical clearance as a condition of allowing a return to work, she would not have been able to claim her six weeks' wages. This might be a provision which the occupational health department should suggest could be inserted in contracts of employment.

In *Meikle* v. *Nottinghamshire County Council* (2004) the Court of Appeal held that the duty to make reasonable adjustments for a disabled person under the Disability Discrimination Act may oblige the employer to pay the disabled person sick pay when on long-term sick leave for a longer period than he allows other employees.

8.4   Statutory sick pay (SSP)

Soon after the *Mears* case was decided, an Act of Parliament transferred the obligation to provide income support during short periods of sickness from the DSS to the employer under the Statutory Sick Pay scheme, now to be found in the Social Security Contributions and Benefits Act 1992. Now, the employee is entitled to payment of at least part of his wages by his employer for up to 28 weeks. The costs of administering the scheme fall mainly on the employer who is responsible for all short-term sickness benefit. An employer can recover SSP paid in a tax month where it exceeds 13 per cent of the employer's national insurance contributions liability in the same tax month. The excess amount of SSP can be deducted from the national insurance contributions due in that month (Statutory Sick Pay Percentage Threshold Order 1995).

Much of the enforcement of the SSP Regulations has now been transferred to the Inland Revenue.

The employee is liable to pay income tax on sick pay. SSP will not give the employee the whole of his wages during sickness: he will have to prove a contractual obligation on his employer to make the amount up to full pay. Note that the same rules apply whether a worker is unable to work because of a work-related accident or industrial disease or because of an illness totally unconnected with his work. No statutory payment is due for the first three days, but many employers are contractually bound to make payment for that period. Part-time employees are included, and there is no qualifying period of employment, but employees over 65, and those with average earnings of less than the lower earnings limit for National Insurance liability are excluded. Self-employed workers are excluded.

Incapacity for work, entitling the employee to SSP, includes absence from work for precautionary reasons on the recommendation of a doctor (for example a pregnant woman working in a place where there is an outbreak of German measles), convalescence on the advice of a doctor, and absence from work by the carrier of an infectious disease on the advice of the Medical Officer for Environmental Health.

8.5 Proof of sickness

Before 1982, an employee who was off work for more than three days needed a medical certificate from his GP to claim sickness benefit. The same certificate was used to claim contractual sick pay from the employer. This system was notoriously unscientific. In 1982 the (then) DHSS adopted a procedure of self-certification for the first seven days of illness and the GPs' contracts with the (then) Family Health Services Authorities were changed so that they were no longer obliged to give a free medical certificate for an absence from work of less than seven days. In practice, therefore, most employers now rely on self-certification for the first seven days for all purposes. The SSP rules provide that an employer is not entitled to ask for a doctor's statement for the first seven days of a spell of sickness.

In 2003 there was a move towards removing the responsibility for certifying longer term sickness from the GP to other health professionals. Where the employer has an occupational health department this might obviously become an important function for OH. The proposed General Medical Services contract describes pilot schemes to evaluate the effectiveness of in-house OH services as an alternative to using general practice for certification. The dangers of OH being perceived by employees as less than objective and 'on the company's side' are obvious. In addition, the GP will continue to be responsible for the worker's clinical care, so that it will be important for there to be a good liaison and understanding between the OH professional and the GP.

The Green Paper *Pathways to Work: Helping People into Employment* (2002) also considers the possible transfer of the responsibility for providing sick notes to other health professionals such as practice nurses and physiotherapists. At the time of writing the results of pilot schemes are unknown. The view of many OH professionals is that it is important to clarify the role of the GP in sickness absence certification. The statutory certificate (FMed 3) is issued for the purpose of access to State benefits, not for the purpose of assisting employers to manage their attendance issues. It is accepted that the current arrangements are unsatisfactory, because doctors do not in most cases have the time or the evidence to challenge what the patient tells them, but it is important not to replace one unsatisfactory system with another that is equally unsatisfactory. Statutory certification for benefit purposes is not directly related to assessment of fitness for work, including rehabilitation following illness or injury. In addition, most of the working population do not have access to OH services, and there is a national shortage of qualified OH professionals. A system of self-certification, perhaps with spot checks, might be a better solution than the present system of medical certification.

8.6   *The control of absenteeism*

This is a problem which affects contractual sick pay, SSP and may also be relevant in disciplinary proceedings. It is a management not a medical problem with which each employer must deal for himself in consultation with worker representatives. Employers are advised not to challenge a doctor's note unless they have clear evidence to the contrary. In *Hutchinson* v. *Enfield Rolling Mills* (1981), the employee, a maintenance electrician, was diagnosed by his GP as suffering from sciatica and signed off for seven days. Two days later, he was seen by one of the directors taking part in a union demonstration in Brighton. He was dismissed for gross misconduct after consultation with the company's doctor. The Employment Appeal Tribunal disagreed with the industrial tribunal's refusal to go behind a sick note:

> 'The employer is concerned to see that his employees are working, when fit to do so, and if they are doing things away from the business which suggest that they are fit to work, then that is a matter which concerns him.'

This does not mean that an employee while off sick must remain at home in bed at all times. It might well be that an employee convalescing from a serious illness, but still unfit to work, could without any misconduct be sunning himself on the front at Brighton.

Those suspected of abuse of self-certification may be refused SSP; they may then appeal to the Inland Revenue which, together with the Department of Work and Pensions (DWP), has a contract with Corporate Medical Services, the independent service whose main job is to give advice on the medical aspects of claims for state benefits. Medical advice may also be sought from the occupational health service or the GP, but the employee's consent will be necessary. It is advisable for employers to anticipate these matters in the contract of employment and include contractual obligations to submit medical reports after periods of absence. If an employee has self-certified himself four times within a year, the Inland Revenue suggests that the suspicious employer may refuse to pay SSP on the fifth occasion and send him to the Medical Services for medical checks. If the employer can prove that the employee lied on the certificate, this may be treated as misconduct and give rise to disciplinary action, but action of this kind based on mere suspicion without proper investigation can amount to a constructive dismissal. A self-certification case was *Bailey* v. *BP* (1980). Bailey, a rigger at an oil refinery, went on holiday to Majorca and, on return, certified that he had been suffering from a 'gastric stomach'. Unfortunately for him, he had been seen in Majorca by the assistant maintenance engineer. His summary dismissal was upheld as fair by the Court of Appeal.

It is important that employers keep full records of sickness absence. Patterns of ill-heath are often the best way to identify an employee with a drink problem ('the Monday morning syndrome') who may be persuaded to undertake treatment at an early stage. Many employers set absence norms for the workforce and provide that any employee who exceeds the norm will be investigated, possibly including an interview with the company doctor or nurse.

Medical advice may also be indicated if an employee has been continuously absent for some weeks. These procedures should be communicated to each employee and incorporated into individual contracts of employment. An employer with an OH service is at an advantage, because he will have expert knowledge not just of medical aspects but also of the nature of the work. As the ACAS Advisory Booklet, *Absence and Labour Turnover*, puts it:

'The organisation's doctor becomes familiar with the kind of work done, and the typical stresses caused by it. The doctor is better able to judge whether someone who is sick or 'off colour' can safely be allowed to continue to work, or should be sent home to avoid accident or more prolonged illness. Serious illness may be spotted at an early stage.'

The Audit Commission published a report *Managing Sickness Absence in London* (1990) which exposed excessively high levels of sickness absence in local authorities in the capital. They identified five key principles important to successful management: commitment by senior management, clear responsibilities, appropriate information, suitably trained managers and attention to staff welfare. A follow-up report published in 1993 demonstrated that setting targets for reduction in sickness absence, instituting automatic return to work interviews, maintaining computer records of absence levels, with regular reporting to senior management, and improvements in the occupational health service had led to significant improvements. 'Five authorities referred to improvements in their occupational health service as being one of the factors that had the greatest impact on managing sickness absence.' There has now been considerable research on the problem of reducing sickness absence. In 1998 the Cabinet Office issued a report on sickness absence in the civil service. The government set targets to reduce public sector sickness absence by 20 per cent by 2001 and 30 per cent by 2003. Statistics show that improvements in absence are nowhere near those called for. A literature review and analysis by Dr Anne Spurgeon (*Managing attendance at work: an evidence-based review* (2003)) reached the following broad conclusions:

(1) All policies depend on accurate and detailed monitoring of absence statistics.
(2) Before implementing attendance management policies, organisations must be clear about their objectives; for example, with regard to target groups and figures identified through analysis of absence statistics.
(3) Attendance management policies often lead to unpredictable results (trigger points linked to disciplinary warnings in one organisation led to a reduction in one or two-day absences but an increase in long-term spells).
(4) Attendance management policies tend to be most effective in reducing absence among those with poor attendance records.
(5) There is some evidence that early contact with individuals can be effective in reducing the duration of absence.
(6) Trigger points are commonly used, but there is little information and agreement on which strategies are effective.
(7) There is, as yet, insufficient research data on the impact of return-to-work interviews and on the content and effectiveness of management training.

In May 2004 Tesco announced that it would henceforth not pay employees for the first three days of sickness absence, to try to reduce the numbers of 'sickies'. In return, bonuses will be given to employees with good attendance records. However, care must be taken in employing attendance management policies not to contravene the Disability Discrimination Act (Chapter 9).

8.7   Notification to the employer

Well-drafted company rules will impose on the employee the duty personally and as early as possible to let the employer know by telephone that he is unable to come to work. This may be made a contractual obligation, breach of which may lead to disciplinary action. The SSP rules allow an employer to withhold SSP as a penalty for late notification, but only within limits laid down in the regulations:

(1)   Notification cannot be required by a specific time on the first qualifying day. Any time during that day is sufficient.
(2)   The employer must accept notification by some other person.
(3)   The employer cannot demand a medical certificate as notification and he cannot require notification more frequently than once a week during the sickness.

The employer does not have to change his company rules about notification of sickness, but if they are strict he may find that a notification late by company standards and thus constituting a breach of discipline is in time for SSP. It is important to give employees full information about what notice he requires.

8.8   The employer's right to suspend

Sometimes, the employee is willing to work but is prevented by the employer. Can the employee demand compensation for being deprived of the opportunity to earn his wages? It depends on the nature of the contract and the reason for the suspension. As a general rule the employer has a contractual duty to pay wages while the contract of employment subsists. The secretary who comes to work and is given nothing to do must still be paid. As long as the employer pays wages he is usually not obliged to provide the employee with work, so suspension on full pay at least for a short period is lawful. There may, however, be either express or implied terms in the contract which allow the employer to suspend without pay. In some companies, suspension without pay is used as a method of discipline according to a disciplinary code. This is lawful if the code has been properly notified to the employees, usually when they are given their written statements at commencement of their employment. In some industries, like construction or ship-building, there is an express or implied term in the employees' contracts that the employer can lay the workers off temporarily because of bad weather or lack of orders but he is then often bound by collective agreements to pay a guaranteed minimum. There is also a limited statutory right to guarantee payments in the

Employment Rights Act (up to 20 days a year), and job seekers' allowance under the social security system, but job seekers' allowance is not payable for any day for which the employee receives a guarantee payment.

8.9 *Medical suspension*

Health and safety legislation which provides for medical surveillance of those working with hazardous substances like lead or ionising radiations, those substances specifically mentioned in Schedule 6 of the COSHH Regulations, or with compressed air gives EMAS or the Appointed Doctor the power in effect to direct the suspension of an employee on medical grounds. If the employee is suspended because he is incapable of work by reason of disease or bodily or mental disablement he will only have the right to SSP, unless in addition he has a contractual right to sick pay. If, however, he is suspended as a preventive measure so that he does not fall ill, he will be entitled to remuneration under section 64 of the Employment Rights Act, amounting to full pay for up to 26 weeks. The employee must have been employed for at least one month at the time of the suspension and if he unreasonably refuses suitable alternative work offered by the employer, whether or not it is his usual job, he will lose his right to remuneration.

In a 1987 case, two men worked for a company manufacturing batteries, of which lead is an important component. They were subject to regular medical surveillance under the Control of Lead at Work Regulations 1980 (updated in 2002), which stipulated that if the blood lead concentration rose to 80 μg per 100 ml or above the Appointed Doctor or Employment Medical Adviser must in most cases certify the employee as unfit to work with lead, except where he had worked with lead for 20 years or at least ten years if he was over 40, in which case the AD or EMA had a discretion. Mr Appleton fell into a skip containing lead paste. His blood lead level was over the statutory level for a while, but even when it fell below that level, the GP did not consider that Appleton was fit for work. Another employee, Mr Hopkinson, was also kept off work by his GP because of high blood lead levels, but neither man had a certificate from an AD or EMA. Both men felt so unwell that they were unable to do any alternative work. The Employment Appeal Tribunal held that neither employee was entitled to medical suspension pay, though they could claim SSP. They were unable to do *any* job: medical suspension pay is intended for workers who are moved from a job carrying a particular risk to another, not those who are unable to work at all because of ill-health (*Stallite Batteries* v. *Appleton and Hopkinson* (1987)).

It is important to note that in a case where an employee complains that he has been unfairly dismissed for a reason which could lead to medical suspension, the minimum qualifying period of employment is one month, instead of the usual two years.

There are special rules relating to the medical suspension of new or expectant mothers whose work constitutes a risk to the mother or the child (see Chapter 9). There is no minimum qualifying period of employment, and the right to be paid lasts for as long as is necessary to protect pregnant employees, those who have given birth within the preceding six months and those who are breast feeding.

8.10   Changes in contractual terms

Once a contract is made, neither party can unilaterally alter its terms without the other's agreement. Management cannot introduce new working hours or payment systems or HIV tests without the consent of each individual employee. Trade union officials have no power to give consent by proxy. The effects of this rule have been blunted by two legal developments. The first is the use by the judiciary of the implied term. An employee refuses to move from one site to another but is held to have impliedly agreed to be mobile. Another objects to the introduction of a new disciplinary code and finds that he has impliedly agreed to obey his employer's reasonable commands. Miss Glitz was appointed as a 'copy typist/ general clerical duties clerk' in a small office. Two years later she was told that she would have to operate the duplicator which she had not done before. She found that the vapour from the machine gave her headaches, though it was in good working order. The Employment Appeal Tribunal held that the operation of the duplicator was impliedly part of her job and that it was fair to dismiss her because of her incapability, since there was no other suitable job available (*Glitz* v. *Watford Electric Co. Ltd* (1979)).

The second is the fact that an employer almost invariably has the contractual right to terminate a contract of employment by giving an agreed period of notice. The courts have held that an employer who dismisses an employee with notice because he refuses to accept a change in his contract is not liable for unfair dismissal if he has a good business reason for making the change. A health authority wished to close down a small unit and move the employee to a different post in a larger one. This was a change in the employee's contract and he refused to move. The tribunal held that the employer had acted reasonably and was not liable for unfair dismissal (*Genower* v. *Ealing and Hounslow AHA* (1980)). Good industrial relations practice, of course, dictates that an employer must make every attempt at persuasion before reaching this stage. If the employee agrees to a change in his terms, the contract is varied by consent.

Not all documents issued by employers constitute legally binding employment terms. Codes of practice, policy statements and advice about compliance with health and safety rules may usually be changed unilaterally without the agreement of employees (often because of legal changes or updated advice from official bodies). Thus, in *Wandsworth London Borough Council* v. *D'Silva* (1998) the local authority announced its intention to change its policy on staff sickness to introduce more frequent checks on sickness absence. The Court of Appeal held that the code was advisory only and was not contractually binding. Also, in *Dryden* v. *Greater Glasgow Health Board* (1992) the employer's introduction of a ban on smoking did not constitute a breach of contract. Employers are entitled to make rules for the conduct of employees in their place of work within the scope of their duty to protect health and safety, and the consent of the employees is not required.

8.11   Transfer of undertakings

At common law, an employee whose employer transferred the business to another company was effectively dismissed. Now, because of legislation originating in

Europe, employees are automatically transferred with the business and have the right to the same terms and conditions of employment from the transferee employer as they enjoyed with the transferor. The regulations are the Transfer of Undertakings (Protection of Employment) Regulations 1981, universally known as TUPE. Acquisition of control of a company by share purchase lies outside the regulations, because the identity of the company does not change. Where it is necessary for economic, technical or organisational reasons for the transferee employer to make transferred employees redundant, he may lawfully do so as long as he follows a fair procedure and pays redundancy compensation. The regulations do not require the transfer of an occupational pension scheme. This is likely to change when the Pensions Bill 2003 becomes law.

In 2004 the European Court held that contractual provisions for early retirement compensation were transferable under TUPE (*Martin* v. *South Bank University*). Where an employee of the transferor has a claim for damages for personal injury against the transferor employer this will pass to the transferee employer, along with the transferor's employer's liability insurance (*Bernadone* v. *Pall Mall Services Group* (2000)).

8.12   The right to dismiss

Employers' freedom of action is limited by the law of contract and the law of unfair dismissal. Dismissal in breach of contract is known by lawyers as wrongful dismissal. Actions for wrongful dismissal may be brought in the County Court or in the High Court. An employment tribunal has jurisdiction to award up to £25,000 for wrongful dismissal. A dismissal is wrongful if the employer has broken a term of the agreement. Thus, if a company has agreed to employ a consultant for a fixed term of three years and dismisses him after six months it will have to compensate him for the loss of two and a half years' employment, minus what he can reasonably be expected to earn elsewhere. However, if the employee commits a serious breach of his side of the bargain the employer can treat the relationship as terminated without further obligation on his part: this is known as summary dismissal. Dishonesty usually justifies summary dismissal, whereas mere carelessness does not, even if the consequences are expensive.

The Employment Rights Act imposes minimum periods of notice on all employers who are free to agree longer but not shorter periods. Employees who have been employed for up to two years are entitled to be given at least one week's notice, and each extra year of employment gives the right to one more week's notice, up to twelve weeks. The employee must give a minimum of one week's notice, however long he has been employed. Wages in lieu of notice are permitted. Employees on fixed term contracts in which the employer has guaranteed employment for a set period cannot be dismissed by being given notice. Everything depends on the terms of the contract and it is advisable to make an express agreement in writing before the employment starts.

The employee who is dismissed with the agreed period of notice cannot usually complain that he has been wrongfully dismissed, unless he can show that a disciplinary procedure has been incorporated into his contract and that the employer has not observed it. The motive for the dismissal is irrelevant in the law of contract. For this reason Parliament in 1971 created the additional remedy of unfair dismissal which is concerned not solely with procedure, as is the law of contract, but with the reason for the dismissal. For the first time, the employer had to give the employee a reason and justify it as fair before an employment tribunal if required by the employee to do so. Only employees under retirement age with a minimum continuous service of one year at the date of dismissal can complain to the tribunal. Part-time employees were at one time excluded from the protection of the legislation, but this was changed in 1995 because the House of Lords had decided that discrimination against part-timers was an indirect form of discrimination against women, and therefore contrary to European law. There are now special regulations to protect part-timers: Part-Time Workers (Prevention of Less Favourable Treatment) Regulations 2000.

There are also regulations to protect employees on fixed term contracts (Fixed-Term Employees (Prevention of Less Favourable Treatment) Regulations 2002). These cover only employees directly employed and do not extend to independent contractors. Agency workers are excluded. The employer must not discriminate against fixed-term employees engaged in the same or broadly similar work as permanent staff. The Court of Appeal, interpreting a similar provision in the Part-Time Workers Regulations, held in 2004 that retained firefighters were not entitled to a pension (*Matthews* v. *Kent and Medway Towns Fire Authority* (2004)) because they did not do the same or broadly similar work as full-time firefighters. Discrimination may be objectively justified, including the provision of a 'total package' which is not as good as that given to the other employees. An example would be an exclusion from a pension scheme compensated by additional pay. It will be unfair to make a fixed-term employee or part-time worker redundant simply because of his status, unless there is an objective justification.

An application to the employment tribunal must normally be made within three months of the date of dismissal, that is, where notice has been given, three months from the date of the expiry of the notice, and where dismissal was without notice, three months from the date the employee left. The fact that an employee has been given proper notice does not prevent him from complaining that he was unfairly treated. Conversely, it is possible for a tribunal to hold that an employee sacked without proper notice was treated fairly in all the circumstances of the case (though this is less likely).

Where a dismissal is for trade union membership or activities, or because the employee belongs or refuses to belong to a trade union, or is an act of unlawful discrimination, no minimum length of qualifying service is needed by an employee who wishes to complain to a tribunal. A dismissal for a reason which could lead to medical suspension requires only one month's employment at the date of dismissal for the tribunal to have jurisdiction. Certain kinds of dismissal are classified as for an inadmissable reason and are automatically unfair. There is no minimum qualifying period for inadmissable dismissals – which include dismissals connected with pregnancy or childbirth, paternity, maternity or adoption leave, and time off to look after dependants – dismissals connected with complaints about health and safety and dismissals for making a protected disclosure (whistle-blowing). All these are discussed in greater detail in other parts of the chapter.

The introduction of unfair dismissal reduced the importance of wrongful dismissal, but actions for breach of contract are still brought in cases of high-earning employees because there is an upper limit on damages for unfair dismissal but not for breach of contract. Also, in exceptional cases, the High Court has power to order reinstatement, whereas the employment tribunals cannot force the employer to take back the dismissed employee.

8.13 The concept of dismissal

An employee may be dismissed in any one of three ways. He may be told to go, with or without notice, he may be informed that the fixed term contract on which he is employed will not be renewed when it expires, or he may be the subject of 'constructive' dismissal. The employer dismisses constructively when he behaves in a way which constitutes such a breach of his side of the contract of employment that the employee is justified in terminating the relationship. An employer constructively dismisses an employee when he puts the employee's health or safety at risk so that the employee resigns. A manager of a shoe shop who failed to introduce any safety precautions, even to instal a telephone, after the shop had been robbed twice was held to have constructively dismissed one of the assistants who left after the second robbery (*Keys* v. *Shoefayre Ltd* (1978)). It is, of course, often a matter of debate as to whether the employer's conduct is bad enough to constitute a breach of contract on his part. The cases show that employers who fail to investigate complaints and show a complete lack of concern for the workers are likely to be held to have constructively dismissed. Mr Lynn, a manager who was the victim of such intemperate criticism by one of the directors of Weatherall's that he eventually resigned and succumbed to a nervous breakdown, was held to have been the victim of a constructive dismissal (*Weatherall Ltd* v. *Lynn* (1978)).

The courts have over the last 15 years developed an implied term in the contract of employment that the employer is under a duty of 'trust and confidence'. This is potentially very wide-ranging. In *Hilton International Hotels* v. *Protopapa* (1990) an employee who had been absent from work for a short time because of toothache was subjected to a rebuke from her line manager that was humiliating, intimidating and degrading. This was held to be a breach of the implied term of mutual trust and confidence and a constructive dismissal.

In *Reed* v. *Stedman* (1997) Reed was sexually harassing Stedman who did not lodge a formal grievance, but complained privately to colleagues. Management became aware of the situation, but did nothing to investigate, even though Stedman's health was beginning to suffer. The Employment Appeal Tribunal held that the employer's failure to intervene constituted a fundamental breach of its duty of trust and confidence. This will apply in cases of bullying without a sexual, racial, religious, homophobic or disability context. Where there is an element of discrimination, it is likely that a complaint will be brought for harassment under one of the anti-discrimination statutes, since there is no upper limit on compensation, and damages can be given for injury to feelings. Alternatively an action may be brought in the High Court where there is also no upper limit on damages. In *Horkulak* v. *Cantor Fitzgerald International* (2003) it was held that the use of foul language by a male managing director to a male subordinate, despite the lack of any element of discrimination, was capable of being a breach of the duty of trust and confidence. Damages of nearly £1 million were awarded by the High Court for wrongful dismissal.

At this stage it is important to emphasise a point which many misunderstand: a constructive dismissal, like dismissal with notice or summary dismissal, is not necessarily an unfair dismissal. A supervisor of a packing department who had been off sick was told that he would have to move to the job of production foreman. He refused because, he said, it would damage his health, but he would not agree to a medical examination to assess his suitability and he resigned. He had been constructively dismissed because the employer had no contractual right to move him to another job without his consent, but the employer had acted reasonably and was not liable for unfair dismissal (*Savoia* v. *Chiltern Herb Farms* (1982)).

If the employee voluntarily resigns from his job other than in response to his employer's unlawful behaviour, he is not dismissed and cannot claim any of the statutory rights dependent on dismissal, like compensation for unfair dismissal and statutory redundancy compensation. 'Voluntary' means what it says: an employee who is told that he will not be sacked if he agrees to go quietly is dismissed. Those who volunteer to be made redundant are usually held to be dismissed in law, but in a case concerned with the Universities' Premature Retirement Scheme the Court of Appeal decided that employees who accepted the generous compensation had terminated their contracts by agreement and had not been sacked. They were thus excluded from claiming redundancy payments (*Birch* v. *University of Liverpool* (1985)). Sometimes, it is in the worker's interest to wait to be told to go. A pregnant woman who gives up her job because she feels that the job is too much for her will run the risk of losing her statutory maternity rights, but if she is dismissed by the employer because she is unwell all her rights are preserved.

From time to time human resources managers make use of a legal doctrine quaintly known as 'frustration of contract'. The law provides that a contract automatically ceases, so that neither side has any further obligation under it, if it is overtaken by a supervening event that destroys its whole purpose. Frustration may be applied to the contract of employment in two separate situations: the employee's supervening illness or his incarceration for a criminal offence. The performance of the contract must have become impossible (as where the employee dies) or something radically different from what the parties contemplated when they entered into it. The principles to be applied by tribunals in an ill-health case were laid down in 1976 (*Egg Stores* v. *Leibovici*). Where illness or accident is relied upon as bringing about frustration, the employer must ask whether a time has arrived when he can say that matters have gone on so long and the prospects for future employment are so poor that it is no longer practical to regard the contract as still subsisting. Among the matters to be taken into account are:

(1)　the length of the previous employment;
(2)　how long it had been expected that the employment would continue;

(3) the nature of the job (the employment of key workers is more easily frustrated);
(4) the nature, length and effect of the illness and the medical prognosis;
(5) the employer's need to appoint a replacement or to make a temporary replacement permanent;
(6) whether wages or sick pay have continued to be paid.

However, in *Williams* v. *Watsons Luxury Coaches Ltd* (1990) Mr Justice Wood said that the court should guard against too easy an application of the doctrine of frustration, especially where there is a redundancy situation, or a dismissal by reason of a disability. The protection of the Disability Discrimination Act may be avoided if the tribunal holds that the disabled employee's employment has been terminated by operation of law.

The use of the doctrine in such cases is infrequent because of the effects on the employee. Imagine a worker who has just been seriously injured in a road accident or has had a crippling stroke. The employer writes to him telling him that, as he is unlikely to be able to work for at least a year, his contract is frustrated and he will receive nothing more from the employer, neither sick pay, nor wages in lieu of notice, nor compensation for the loss of his job. But the Court of Appeal in 1986 confirmed that the doctrine is still available to employers who wish to use it. Derek Notcutt had worked for a small company as a milling machine operator for 27 years. His contract of employment expressly provided that he had no right to sick pay (he would now be entitled to up to 28 weeks' statutory sick pay from the employer). When he was 63 he suffered a coronary infarction. When he had been off work for six months, the employers asked for a medical report from his GP. The latter wrote that he doubted whether Notcutt would be able to work again. The employers then gave him 12 weeks' notice, as they were advised was obligatory under the Employment Protection (Consolidation) Act 1978 (now re-enacted as the Employment Rights Act 1996). The Act gave employees during the statutory periods of notice the right to full wages or to full sick pay even though if they were not under notice they would have no right to sick pay, so Notcutt claimed 12 weeks' sick pay. It was held that the heart attack had frustrated the contract of employment such that Notcutt's contract had automatically terminated. He was entitled to neither notice nor to pay (*Notcutt* v. *Universal Equipment* (1986)).

The inclusion of sick pay benefits in the contract of employment may have effects on the doctrine of frustration. In *James* v. *Greytree Trust* (1995) a cleaner in a care home had been off sick for four months with 'tennis elbow'. She then handed in a sick note from her GP for a further six months and was told that her contract was frustrated. The contract provided for sick pay for up to a year. Ms James had worked in the home for 18 years and had been expected to continue working until retirement. It was held that the contract was not frustrated. Ms James' work could have been done by a temporary replacement and the fact that the contract provided for lengthy sickness absence demonstrated that this was not an event which rendered the contract radically different from what the parties contemplated.

A contract of employment cannot be frustrated by the possibility that an employee's health may deteriorate. A manager employed as works director in a company in Darwen had a heart attack in April. He returned to work part-time in June and was told by a consultant that he would be able to resume full-time at the end of July. The employers felt that the job of works director would be too great a strain, so they offered him an alternative job at a lower salary which he refused. He was then given notice. The employers' decision was based not on any medical report, either from the employee's doctor or the company's own doctor, but on the statistical possibility that there might be a second heart attack. They said that the contract had been frustrated. It was held that frustration is brought about by events, not the risk of such events. There was a dismissal and it was unfair because it was not based on medical evidence about the employee (*Converfoam* v. *Bell* (1981)).

An alternative to dismissal of an employee who has had a long period of absence due to ill-health, and is unlikely to return in the near future, is to 'suspend' his contract, with his agreement. He is transferred to a 'holding department' until his return to work or his retirement, whichever is the earlier. The advantage of this scheme is that the employee, though not obliged to work and not in receipt of salary, maintains continuity of employment, because he has not technically been dismissed. Depending on the rules of the pension scheme, he may be able to accrue further pensionable service. Care should be taken to consult with the employee, and to obtain his agreement to this course of action, otherwise it could be regarded as a constructive dismissal.

8.14   The reason for the dismissal

The employee has to prove that he has been dismissed. If he does so, the burden shifts to the employer to give a reason; the tribunal then decides whether in all the circumstances he acted justly and equitably in treating it as justifying dismissal. If the case goes to an employment tribunal they only require to be convinced that the employer acted within a range of reasonable responses, not necessarily that the members of the tribunal would have reached the same decision. Only if the employer has made a decision so unreasonable that no reasonable employer could have made it can he be held liable for unfair dismissal. This has been upheld by the Court of Appeal in recent cases, including *Post Office* v. *Foley* (2000).

The Employment Rights Act lists five possible groups of fair reasons:

(1)   capability or qualifications, capability being assessed by reference to skill, aptitude, health or any other physical or mental quality;
(2)   misconduct;
(3)   redundancy, that is that the employee's job will disappear;
(4)   that the employer cannot continue to employ the employee without contravention of a statute;
(5)   some other substantial reason.

In addition, the tribunal has to ask whether on the facts the employer acted justly. For example, an employer may give it as a reason for dismissal that the employee is dishonest, but if he has no evidence on which to base his suspicions he will be held to have acted unfairly. The Act provides that the size and administrative resources of the employer's undertaking are to be taken into account in deciding what was reasonable.

Where the tribunal in an unfair dismissal action finds that an employee has caused or contributed to his own dismissal by a culpable act it can reduce the compensation by a percentage of up to 100 per cent. Dismissal on grounds of ill-health will normally not raise the issue of contributory fault, but the Employment Appeal Tribunal said in *Slaughter* v. *Brewer* (1990) that a blatant and persistent refusal to obtain medical reports or undergo a medical examination could lead to a reduction in damages. Contributory fault cannot, of course, be relevant where the allegation is one of unlawful discrimination.

8.15   Dismissal for incompetence

The employer is not expected to continue to employ indefinitely someone whose performance in the job is poor. As there is a one year qualifying period for unfair dismissal, employers are advised to review all their employees after six months or so. Where the employee has worked for more than one year, the employer will have to be able to produce evidence of unsatisfactory work and to demonstrate that the employee has been made aware of his shortcomings and given time and, if necessary, further guidance or training to help him to improve. It is important to keep a record of interviews at which the employee was counselled and warned that improvement was necessary if the employee were to continue in employment.

8.16   Ill-health dismissals

This is a difficult area in practice because the employee may have to lose his job for something which is not his fault. Any member of a profession whose main purpose is to care for an individual will find it hard to be associated in any way with depriving a patient of his opportunity to work. On the opposite side of the coin are those who are suspected of malingering. If the employer asks the doctor or nurse to act as detective and prosecuting counsel, the confidence of the workforce in his impartiality is at risk. Only if the occupational health service is known to be both competent and fair will respect be maintained.

The leading case on dismissal for ill-health is *East Lindsey District Council* v. *Daubney* (1977). There, a surveyor employed by the Council was dismissed after long periods of absence due to 'anxiety and general debility'. The personnel director had sought medical advice from the district community physician, who wrote that the employee was unfit to carry out his duties and should be retired on the ground of permanent ill-health, and acted on it without indicating to the employee that his job might be at risk or allowing him to obtain his own doctor's report. The dismissal was held unfair. Tribunals must consider whether the employer acted reasonably in reaching a decision that he could no longer continue with the employee in an unfit state. Obviously, the two most important factors are the nature of the job and the nature of the employee's illness. The size of the employer's business is a relevant factor: it is easier for British Telecom to hold a job open for a year than it is for a small company. As a general rule it will be necessary to obtain medical evidence before making a decision, both to assess the potential for return to work and the likely capability of the employee if he is allowed to return. It is also advisable for a manager to interview the employee in person, or at least communicate with him by post, to ask how he feels about coming back and warn him that the employer is considering dismissal. It is not true that employers are prohibited from dismissing before the employee's entitlement to sick pay expires, nor should they automatically dismiss as soon as that period is over. If it can be shown that an employer's main reason for ending his employee's contract was to avoid paying statutory sick pay, he is legally required to go on paying until his liability ends for some other reason, and the employee might well be able to claim unfair dismissal in such circumstances.

One employer had a contract with employees which provided that a worker's absence for ill health or injury of 225 or more working days in the preceding 12 months entitled the company to give notice of dismissal. An employee, Brookes, had suffered from a recurrent depressive illness for 20 years. At the time he was eventually dismissed, he had not been absent for 225 days. The Employment Appeal Tribunal held, nonetheless, that the dismissal was capable of being fair, depending on the medical evidence and all the other facts of his case (*Smith's Industries* v. *Brookes* (1986)). Equally, a dismissal after an absence of more than 225 days could have been held unfair.

The purpose of consultation with the employee is partly to enable the true medical condition to be ascertained. It is also to allow the whole employment situation to be assessed and to consider whether the employee could be offered ill-health retirement or a different job more suited to his condition. The fair employer should at least consider the availability of other posts, but it has been held that he is not obliged artificially to create work for a sick employee, however deserving his case. In *Garrick's Ltd* v. *Nolan* (1980) a maintenance fitter working shifts had a heart attack. He wished to return but was told that he could not because the job involved shift-working, which his doctor had advised him to avoid, and heavy lifting and he was dismissed. The evidence was that he could have done a day job and that the heavy lifting was an excuse – it was minimal and someone else could have done it. The dismissal was held unfair on the facts. However, there are few rigid rules in the law of unfair dismissal because everything depends on what is considered reasonable in the particular instance. Mr McInally worked as a barman at a BP workers' camp at Sullom Voe, in an isolated community. He consulted his own GP who diagnosed that he was suffering from asthenia. Later, he was interviewed by Dr Macaulay, one of BP's OH physicians, who concluded that he had a depressive illness caused by the unusual environmental conditions; he told McInally's employers, a catering firm, that he was medically unfit for that kind of work. The GP agreed. The employee was dismissed and claimed that he had been unfairly treated because he had not been consulted. The Scottish Employment Appeal Tribunal decided that consultation was not necessary in this case because it would have made no difference. There was no job suitable for the employee at Sullom Voe and he had been specifically recruited to work there (*Taylorplan Catering (Scotland)* v. *McInally* (1980)).

Where the ill-health may have been caused by the fault of the employer, the employer has a duty to try to remedy the situation, rather than removing the employee from the job. In *Jagdeo* v. *Smiths Industries Ltd* (1982) the employee became allergic to solder fumes. An HSE inspector suggested that an extractor fan might assist. The Employment Appeal Tribunal held that the employers should investigate this suggestion, and would act unfairly if they dismissed the employee without doing so.

The Disability Discrimination Act 1995 has made significant changes to the law relating to the dismissal of employees for long-term sickness absence. The employer has a duty to make reasonable adjustments for employees disabled within the meaning of the Act, and failure to do so may make the dismissal unlawful discrimination (Chapter 9).

Intermittent sickness absence for a variety of different complaints is discussed in 8.21 below.

8.17   *Medical reports*

Occupational physicians in general do not give the employer clinical details, but confine themselves to a bald statement that the worker is fit or unfit for work. Where the worker has been off sick for a long period, this is insufficient to enable management to make decisions about the worker's future. In such cases, it is necessary that the physician gives a summary of the employee's medical problem and the likely prognosis *with the employee's consent.*

'There are occasions when the employee is seen subject to a formal process, such as part of a sickness absence or substance abuse policy, and this may be on the instruction of line management or a personnel department. In these circumstances the occupational physician should take particular care to explain precisely the purpose of the assessment, make it clear to the individual that the physician is acting as an impartial medical adviser, and ensure that the employee agrees to the assessment. A misunderstanding is less likely when the purpose of such a referral has been defined in a company policy agreed between management and the workforce.' (Faculty of Occupational Medicine: *Guidance on Ethics for Occupational Physicians* (1993))

The courts have emphasised that the decision to dismiss is a management one. Medical evidence should be available, but it is not for the doctor to decide: he is asked only for an expert opinion. In practice, however, where a doctor advises that an employee is unfit the employer may have little discretion, because continued employment of that person may involve him in legal liability to that employee or to others. Sometimes, the doctors do not agree. In a case in 1980, *Harper* v. *National Coal Board*, an employee, a known epileptic, had worked for a number of years without incident as a dust mask cleaner in a lamp cabin. Then he had three fits within a period of two years during which he displayed violence to other employees. The local OH physician recommended that he be retired on grounds of ill-health, but the Area Medical Officer advised that adjustments in the employee's medication had made further incidents unlikely. The colliery managers preferred the advice of the local doctor and dismissed. The tribunal obviously shared the fears of the managers and upheld the dismissal in a decision which has been criticised for its apparent approval of prejudice:

'Where the belief [that the employee was a danger] is one which is genuinely held, and particularly one which most employers would be expected to adopt, it may be a substantial reason even where modern sophisticated opinion can be adduced to show that it has no scientific foundation.'

The decision might now be different, following the enactment of the Disability Discrimination Act 1995 (Chapter 9).

In that case the doctors who differed were both specialist OH physicians, but more frequently any disagreement is between an outside doctor and an OH specialist. Such a case was *Jefferies* v. *BP Tanker Co. Ltd* (1979), which concerned a radio officer on an oil tanker who had two attacks of myocardial infarction in one year. BP's Chief Medical Officer advised that he was permanently unfit for duties at sea and there was no shore-based post available, so he was dismissed. A consultant cardiologist paid by the employee's union then advised that there was no reason whatsoever from the medical point of view why the employee should not continue to do the job. An industrial tribunal held the dismissal fair:

'Were they [the employers] to be criticised because they accepted the advice of their own medical officer, who was qualified in occupational medicine ...?'

It is submitted that managers when deciding whether to dismiss on grounds of ill-health are faced with two issues:

(1) What is the state of the employee's health?
(2) Is he fit to do the job he is employed to do or some other job which might be available?

Very few patients will have medical conditions so clear-cut that a doctor can say either that they are definitely fit or definitely unfit. Therefore, he may be obliged (with, of course, the employee's consent) to give some account of the case, for example that the man has had a serious heart attack, has made a good recovery, but that there is a risk of a further attack. He can say from his knowledge of the job that the risk is increased by the long hours, stress and environmental conditions, but in the end it is the manager who, having been made aware of the risk, has to decide if he is willing to take it.

The manager is entitled to take the doctor's opinion as authoritative with regard to the first question, because he is the undoubted expert. Human resources departments are not expected to have medical textbooks on their shelves:

'We do not think that an employer, faced with a medical opinion, unless it is plainly erroneous as to the facts in some way, or plainly contains an indication that no proper examination of any sort has taken place, is required to evaluate it as a layman in terms of medical expertise.' (*Liverpool AHA* v. *Edwards* (1977))

One case where a medical opinion was inadequate was *Scott* v. *Secretary of State for Scotland* (1988). The employee, having suffered a neck injury at work, was absent for 668 days over a five-year period. Eventually, management asked for the advice of the OH physician who, without examining or interviewing the employee, reported that he was not optimistic about the employee being able to resume satisfactory working. It was held to be an unfair dismissal to sack the employee in reliance on such an inadequate report, based only on the employee's personnel file.

The nature of the employment and possible alternatives are, however, matters where medical opinion, though important, is only one factor to take into account. This is bad news for some managers who prefer to be able to shelter behind a bald statement that the employee 'failed the medical'. Also, there is a growing demand from workers to be given the right of appeal to an independent consultant against the OH physician's report. Increasingly, the OH physician's advice will not be final, because the 'medical' part of it can be appealed to another doctor, and the 'job-related' section can be challenged.

The *Jefferies* case was a decision only of a local tribunal and it therefore has no authority as a binding precedent. A different approach prevailed in *Milk Marketing Board* v. *Grimes* (1986), a decision of the Employment Appeal Tribunal. Mr Grimes was a milk salesman employed by the Milk Marketing Board who had taken over a small company. His duties included driving a milk float. After a month the new employers realised that he was so deaf that the only way he could communicate with others was in writing. The personnel department took the employee off the road until he had had tests and seen their OH doctor, Dr Burgess. The latter concluded that he was unfit for driving duties. A copy of Dr Burgess's report and the audiometry findings were sent to Grimes's GP, who agreed that the deafness was not materially assisted by a hearing aid. Grimes was dismissed with notice. Afterwards, he consulted an ENT surgeon who advised that use of a hearing aid would restore his threshold to a tolerable level and also pointed out that there were many drivers on the road with levels of hearing worse than Grimes. He drew attention to the fact that the employee had a record of 34 years' accident-free motoring in his private car and that he continued to drive it after the dismissal. Grimes also had an accident-free record of several years of driving the milk float. The employers had a disciplinary procedure concerned with dismissals but it only covered dismissals for misconduct, not capability. They stated, however, that they would have allowed him to appeal against his dismissal if he had asked.

The tribunal criticised the employers for not expressly inviting Grimes to obtain his own medical report if he wished. They held that the employee did not have a proper opportunity to challenge Dr Burgess's findings and had therefore been unfairly treated. Two contested issues arose in the Grimes case. One concerned the degree of his deafness and whether it could be improved with a hearing aid, the other whether a profoundly deaf individual is fit to drive on the public highway. Medical evidence must be conclusive on the first, but management should have reviewed the doctor's opinion on the second. The willingness of the tribunal to interfere is probably partly to be explained by the very 'ordinariness' of the employee's job. Employment tribunals are prepared to accept that an OH physician has special knowledge about working on an oil tanker, but they are more critical of his views on milk float propulsion. There was also the difficulty of communication in Grimes's case which meant that the employers should have taken care to allow him the opportunity to protest. Grimes would now fall within the protection of the Disability Discrimination Act (Chapter 9).

It is important to identify two separate strands in the case law. One well-established line of decisions requires employers not to act solely on the advice of their medical adviser but to allow the employee to commission his own medical report. There is, however, little judicial guidance thus far for the manager who receives two conflicting medical reports. Suppose that Grimes procures medical evidence in his favour? Must the employer automatically accept it and reject the report of the occupational health specialist? Considering the disastrous consequences of a poor medical report on the employee's livelihood, it may be thought fair to institute a procedure whereby the employee may be allowed the right to 'appeal' against the occupational physician's opinion to a *third* doctor, a consultant who is independent of both parties. Some large employers now incorporate this final appeal into their procedures, in the event of two conflicting medical reports. As the employer will be paying for this opinion, it is likely that he will wish to nominate the consultant, though it is preferable for the parties to agree on the identity of the 'arbitrator'.

Recent developments in the law of disability discrimination have been to uphold management decisions based on a competent risk assessment performed by an OH professional based on sufficient evidence and not irrational (*Jones* v. *Post Office* (2001)). A full account appears in Chapter 9. Lawyers in subsequent cases have attacked the competence of the OH professional by arguing that he or she should have obtained specialist advice before making a decision (*Marshall* v. *Surrey Police* (2002)). In my experience, it may be necessary to explain to a tribunal that OH is a specialism in its own right and that in many cases it is unnecessary to obtain a second opinion. It is advisable to obtain a GP report, and, where the worker has been seeing a specialist, also a report from the specialist, before making a recommendation that a disabled person is unfit to do a job, even with reasonable adjustments.

The employee who is invited to submit medical evidence on his own behalf, and refuses, cannot complain if a decision is made on evidence which is available. One case involved an engineer working overseas who, after five years, suffered a nervous breakdown and was treated for anxiety. After examination by the company doctor, he was allowed to return to work, but his behaviour gave cause for concern. He refused to be examined by the company doctor or an independent specialist, and refused to make available a report from his own doctor. His dismissal was upheld as fair, since the employer had acted reasonably in the circumstances (*McIntosh* v. *John Brown Engineering Ltd* (1990)). A similar decision was reached in 2004 in *O'Donoghue* v. *Elonbridge Housing Trust*.

The OH doctor should submit a clear report. In *WM Computer Services Ltd* v. *Passmore* (1987) an accounts controller was off work for some weeks suffering from depressive illness. He attempted suicide and was being treated by a psychiatrist. The employers asked him to see their OH physician, Dr Johnson. The latter wrote both a report and a covering letter. The report stated that the employee was anxious to return, but was unlikely to be able to perform at 'peak level' for some time to come. The letter said that the doctor was 'rather gloomy' in his prognosis, and that the employee was aware that if he did return it might be only for a short period. The doctor admitted in evidence in the tribunal that he was trying 'to sit on the fence'. The employers construed his opinion as an indication that the employee was unfit and decided to dismiss him. They asked Dr Johnson how they should do this and he advised by letter rather than interview. It was held that the employers had acted unfairly. The proper mode of termination was an employment not a medical matter and the employee should have been consulted (presumably he should have been sent a letter inviting him for interview if he wished to come). The employers had 'misconstrued' the doctor's letter, and they should have considered the possibility of alternative employment.

Compare the Scottish case of *Eclipse Blinds* v. *Wright* (1992). Ms Wright was a registered disabled person who had been employed as a receptionist since 1978. Between 1985 and 1987 her health deteriorated and she was frequently off work. After some improvement she became ill again in March 1989, and was absent for several months. The employers contacted her own doctor, with her permission. He indicated that the ultimate prognosis was not good. Ms Wright herself believed that her health was improving and that she would soon return to work. The employers did not wish to engage in a conversation with Ms Wright in which they might have to disclose the gloomy news, so they dismissed her by letter. The Employment Appeal Tribunal upheld the decision of the tribunal that in the exceptional circumstances it was not unfair to fail to consult the employee. Each case rests on its own facts. In the *Wright* case the employee was unlikely ever to work again, whereas in the *Passmore* case the tribunal members were of the opinion that there was hope of the employee continuing to hold down a job if he could weather the current crisis. Unemployment is not the best medicine for clinical depression.

The Faculty of Occupational Medicine advises that statements in medical reports such as 'fit for light duties' should be avoided:

> 'The physician should bear in mind that it is the employer who is responsible for allocating duties even though the decision should take account of constructive professional advice wherever practicable.'

The doctor's job is to assess the capabilities of the worker, not to decide whether he should be dismissed. Sympathy for an employee and the knowledge that the loss of his job may well affect his health must be balanced against the need for the employer to be able to trust in the doctor's objectivity in the interests of the rest of the workforce.

There is a further discussion of medical reports in relation to allegations of disability discrimination in Chapter 9.

8.18 'No illness' agreements

These stem from a decision of the Scottish courts in *Leonard v. Fergus and Haynes* (1979). The employee was a steel fixer who entered into a contract of employment with contractors supplying labour for the construction of a concrete oil platform. Conditions were arduous and it was vital that all the employees were in rude health. A written contract provided that any man absent for two shifts in 14 days would be dismissed as unsuitable for North Sea related work. Leonard was absent for some time because, he alleged, of an industrial injury. The employers dismissed him without consultation and without a medical report; the dismissal was held to be fair. However, employers who put such terms into contracts with all their employees are likely to be disappointed. It was the special nature of the work, not the way the contract was drafted, which led to the decision in favour of the employer. Also, the Court of Appeal has regarded with disfavour contracts providing for automatic termination if the employee does not come to work, holding that they are void as an attempt to exclude the protection of the statute (*Igbo v. Johnson Matthey Chemicals* (1986)).

8.19 Disabled workers

Care must now be taken not to fall foul of the Disability Discrimination Act 1995. Any dismissal of an employee with a serious and longstanding disability, whether acquired pre-employment or in the course of employment, must be measured against the provisions of the Act. A full account is given in Chapter 9: Equal Opportunities. Remember that the Act defines as disabled many who have no obvious medical problem, for example a well-controlled diabetic or someone who many years ago suffered from serious depression, but has since recovered.

8.20 Dismissal for misconduct

The ACAS Code of Practice, *Disciplinary and Grievance Procedures* (2004), stresses the need for all employers to have disciplinary rules which should be communicated clearly to all employees. Rules should cover issues like timekeeping, absence (including the need to notify the employer of ill-health and the need for medical certification), health and safety matters (like prohibitions on smoking, drink and drugs), use of company facilities, and the attitude of the employer to racial or sexual abuse. The employer should make it clear which offences are regarded as constituting gross misconduct which could lead to summary dismissal. In one case, because of problems of absenteeism after the staff Christmas party in the previous year, the company and the union agreed the following December that, if as a result of the Christmas party an employee so indulged himself that he was unable to attend for work the next day, he would be summarily dismissed. Mr Skinner, who was dismissed in pursuance of this rule, was successful in a claim for unfair dismissal because the company had not communicated it to the employees in writing or given sufficient warning (*Brooks* v. *Skinner* (1984)).

It is also important to have disciplinary procedures. These should be in writing, specify the levels of management authorised to take disciplinary action, and provide for individuals to be informed of the complaints against them and to be given an opportunity to state their case, accompanied by a trade union representative or fellow employee, before decisions are reached. Except in cases of gross misconduct, no employee should be dismissed for a first breach of discipline. No disciplinary action should be taken until the case has been carefully investigated. There should be a right of appeal to a higher level of management.

Minimum requirements for dismissal and disciplinary procedures (DDP) have been introduced by regulations which came into force in 2004. These lay down steps which must be taken by the employer if he is to be able to defend a complaint of unfair dismissal. The employer must give a written statement of the allegations against the employee, must allow him or her to put his or her case at a meeting and must give a right to an appeal (Employment Act 2002 (Dispute Resolution) Regulations 2004). Without these procedures a dismissal will be automatically unfair.

In the case of minor offences, the individual should be given a formal oral warning, and a note should be kept. In the case of more serious offences or an accumulation of minor offences the employee should be given a formal written warning and, if this is ignored, eventually a final written warning stating that any further infringements will lead to dismissal. Many procedures provide that these warnings will be expunged from the record after a period of satisfactory conduct, but this is for the employer and the union to agree. Only in cases of gross misconduct will this procedure be inapplicable.

The House of Lords held in *Polkey* v. *A.F. Dayton Services Ltd* (1988) that, however justifiable the employer's reason for dismissal, a failure to follow a fair procedure could in itself render a dismissal unfair. The Employment Act 2002 modifies this to some extent. If the employer can prove that, even though he has failed to follow a fair procedure (other than the mandatory DDP) in relation to the dismissal of an employee, he would have decided in any event to dismiss the employee (for example, because of strong evidence that the employee was guilty of gross misconduct) he will not be liable for unfair dismissal. To summarise: if an employer dismisses an employee without the correct statutory DDP the dismissal will be automatically unfair. If the employer has followed the DDP but has not otherwise conducted a fair procedure (which may, for example, be set out in the company's own handbook or in the ACAS Code of Practice) this does not make the dismissal necessarily unfair, as under *Polkey*. The issue is whether the employer's decision to dismiss fell within a band of reasonable management responses in all the circumstances of the case. The new procedures do not affect claims for unlawful discrimination.

The employee who puts himself or others at risk by flouting safety rules is clearly guilty of misconduct. In a serious case this may amount to gross misconduct justifying summary dismissal; in other situations it may be enough to give a warning. In *Martin* v. *Yorkshire Imperial Metals* (1978), the employee was dismissed after it was discovered that he had tied down with a piece of wire the left hand lever on the automatic lathe that he operated. This in effect removed the safety device whereby the machine could be operated only if the operator used both hands, thus excluding them from the area of danger. It was held that the dismissal was fair. What of the worker who is a danger but not deliberately careless? One such case which reached the Court of Appeal concerned an airline pilot whose carelessness and incompetence caused a plane crash. He was held to have been fairly dismissed. His job was too responsible to risk another mishap (*Taylor* v. *Alidair* (1978)).

Industrial misconduct depends to a large extent on the nature of the industry. Smoking one cigarette in a mine is a criminal act as well as justifying summary dismissal, but in an office it may not even be a disciplinary offence, unless there is a no-smoking rule. A school teacher who is convicted of a homosexual offence unconnected with his employment may lose his job, while a labourer convicted of the same offence would be unfairly treated if he were to be dismissed.

8.21   Ill-health and misconduct

It is sometimes difficult to distinguish a case of ill-health from one of misconduct. To be absent from work through illness is not misconduct, but failure to turn up for work with no good reason is. Disciplinary procedures are inappropriate in genuine ill-health cases, but where the employee has a series of short-term absences all ostensibly for medical reasons (flu, back-ache, gastritis, nervous debility and so on) and is never absent for long enough to need a doctor's note, managers may use procedures analogous to the disciplinary code. First, they may institute a series of warnings. If the employee is ill it may be thought illogical to threaten him with the sack if his health does not improve, because that is presumably a matter outside his control, but in *International Sports Co* v. *Thomson* (1980), it was decided that where the employee has an unacceptable level of absences due to minor ailments (in that case 25 per cent of working days lost during 18 months) the employer should interview the employee and, if not satisfied, give appropriate warnings that if there is no improvement in the attendance record the employee will be dismissed. The justification for this is that the employer cannot reasonably be expected to continue employing an unreliable employee, whatever the reason for his unreliability. The need for warnings reflects, as in the redundancy cases, the philosophy that no-one should lose his job unexpectedly without an opportunity to prepare for the eventuality. If, of course, the manager can prove that the employee is malingering, he can dismiss for misconduct, but in most cases this is impossible to establish.

Further guidance on intermittent sickness absence was given by the Employment Appeal Tribunal in *Lynock* v. *Cereal Packaging* (1988). In determining whether to dismiss an employee with a poor record of intermittent sickness absence, an employer's approach should be based on sympathy, understanding and compassion. A disciplinary approach involving warnings is not appropriate but the employee should be cautioned that the stage has been reached when it has become impossible to continue with the employment. Factors which may prove important include the nature of the illness; the likelihood of it recurring or of some other illness arising; the length of the various absences and the periods of good health between them; the need of the employer to have done the work of the employee; the impact of the absences on those who work with him; the adoption and carrying out of the policy; the emphasis on a personal assessment in the ultimate decision; and the extent to which the difficulty of the situation and the position of the employer have been explained to the employee. There is no principle in such cases that the fact that the employee is fit at the time of dismissal makes the dismissal unfair. In *Wilson* v. *Post Office* (2000) the Court of Appeal held that dismissal for intermittent sickness absence after warnings is not dismissal for misconduct or incapability but for 'some other substantial reason'. The good health of the employee at the date of dismissal and the absence of an underlying medical condition did not carry as much weight as they would in a capability dismissal.

ACAS recommends that where there is no medical advice to support frequent self-certified absences, the employee should be asked to consult a doctor to establish whether medical treatment is necessary and whether the underlying reason for absence is work-related. If the employee is suffering from alcoholism or psychological stress, or diabetes or glandular fever, or other disorders, these may manifest themselves in a series of minor ailments. It may even be the case that the employee has a recurrent medical condition which constitutes a disability. In all cases the employee should be told what improvement in attendance is expected and warned of the likely consequences if this does not happen. In the case of workers addicted to drugs or alcohol the employer may agree to continue to employ them on condition they submit to treatment, but warn that if the treatment is rejected or proves unsuccessful he will have to consider dismissal. If the unreliable attendance continues, despite warnings, the employer may decide to dismiss. In contrast to cases of dismissal for long-term absence through ill-health, medical evidence is not so vital where there have been frequent absences for minor complaints, because of the variety and fleeting nature of the employee's illnesses.

What if the employee has been told by his doctors that he must take certain precautions which he then proceeds to ignore? A diabetic is instructed that he must monitor his insulin levels and eat at regular intervals, but he is careless. It is submitted that such a case is analogous to a failure to use safety equipment and that it is misconduct justifying dismissal if the employee has been warned that the employer will not tolerate such carelessness, because it mars job performance and carries risk to the diabetic and others. People with diabetes are suffering with a disability and may now be protected by the Disability Discrimination Act 1995 (Chapter 9).

Company rules frequently provide that anyone found drunk at work will be summarily dismissed, but employers may also have a policy that alcoholics should not be sacked if they agree to treatment. Brown, who for the first time in his life is drunk at work because his wife has had a baby, is dismissed for gross misconduct, but Green, who has been drinking heavily for years, is sent to a nursing home. A case in point was *Chamberlain Vinyl Products* v. *Patel* (1996). The employee was found at work by his departmental manager unsteady on his feet. The manager formed the view that he was drunk. The employee became argumentative and grabbed at the manager's throat. When interviewed by the works manager, the employee explained that he was seeing a psychiatrist. The employee was suspended, and the works manager made 12 attempts to contact either the employee's GP or the psychiatrist without success. Eventually, the employee contacted the doctor and the GP wrote stating that he suffered from 'recurrent depression' and was on medication. The works manager interviewed Patel again and dismissed him for gross misconduct (being drunk at work). It was held that the dismissal was unfair. The manager should have made further enquiries about the employee's health, and should have involved the company doctor. Sick employees must be treated with understanding, but if they are in a job which carries a risk to others they will have to be suspended from it until they can again be relied upon. Employers, to show consistency and fairness, should have a policy for drink and drugs at work which is made known to the workforce. As with all disciplinary rules, they must be clearly communicated, as must the consequences of a breach.

Though the Health and Safety Executive advocates the setting up of drug policies providing support in confidence for workers who seek help with drug addiction, courts tend to be unsympathetic to those involved with prohibited drugs. One Scottish dental technician who purchased a small amount of cannabis during his lunch break for personal consumption at home was summarily dismissed when he was convicted of a criminal offence. The dismissal was held to be fair (*Mathewson* v. *Wilson Dental Laboratory* (1988)).

8.22 *Selection for redundancy*

Redundancy in law means that the job, not the worker, has gone. It is caused either by the employer closing down the business where the employee was employed, or by the cessation or diminution of the requirements of the business for employees to carry out work of a particular kind. It is not designed to support the employee while he is unemployed, but to compensate him for the loss of a job, so it is payable even when the redundant employee obtains a better position elsewhere. If the employer genuinely has no further need for the employee's services, it will be fair to make him redundant, but there is a statutory obligation to make a redundancy payment based on the employee's age and length of service to employees who have worked for the employer for at least two years at the date of dismissal. Many employers agree by contract to pay more than the statutory minimum as an incentive to workers to leave. Redundancy money must be paid in full by the employer: the redundancy rebates system to which all employers had to contribute and which was administered by the Department of Employment has been abolished. This has made it easier for employer and employee together to agree a redundancy. An employee who volunteers for redundancy or early retirement will not thereby lose his right to jobseekers' allowance (Social Security Contributions and Benefits Act 1992). The employer may avoid making a redundancy payment if he offers suitable alternative employment which the employee unreasonably refuses. It is usually reasonable for an employee to refuse a new job which carries lower wages, lower status, or involves substantially more travel and inconvenience.

Employees who have been made redundant sometimes take a case to an employment tribunal to complain that their dismissal is unfair. Often, this is on the ground that they have been selected for redundancy before someone else who is more suitable. The criteria for selection for redundancy should be as objective as possible. The principle of 'last in, first out' is no longer popular, because it leaves the employer with the older employees, who may not have up-to-date skills. Most employers these days adopt a points system, assessing skills, efficiency and job performance. It may be fair to take an employee's attendance record into account in deciding to choose him for redundancy, but where the employee's poor health is due to a disability, the employer may have to beware of the Disability Discrimination Act. In *Clare* v. *County Durham Health Authority* (1997), an employment tribunal case, the employee was absent from work for a long period because of a brain haemorrhage. His attendance before his illness had been excellent. He was made redundant after his return to work. The tribunal found that the selection criteria, which included attendance records, were inherently discriminatory and this was not justified because no proper account had been taken of the employee's abilities when he was fit. In other cases, the employee objects to the procedure by which he has been dismissed. He says that he was not consulted or given any prior warning, or that he was not considered for alternative employment which he knows was available. All these factors may make a dismissal unfair. If the employee establishes that his redundancy was unfair, he will obtain extra compensation in addition to his redundancy payment.

Where an employer intends to dismiss as redundant 20 or more employees at one establishment within a period of 90 days or less he must consult either a recognised trade union or, where there is none, employee representatives elected by the workers from among their number. If the employer fails to consult he may be ordered to make a protective award of extra wages to the redundant employees.

An occupational health department often becomes involved in a case of redundancy or early retirement because these are seen as relatively humane ways of getting rid of an employee whose performance is unsatisfactory because he is unwell. The pension fund rules probably demand evidence that the employee is permanently incapable of doing the job to allow him to take ill-health retirement. 'Redundancy' may be a face-saving formula, but care should be taken to obtain the employee's full agreement, otherwise he may later allege that the redundancy was not genuine and complain of unfair dismissal.

8.23 Contravention of a statute

It is a potentially fair reason for dismissal that the employee could not continue to work in his job without contravention (either on his part or on that of the employer) of a duty or restriction imposed by a statute. Thus, it is fair to dismiss a doctor or nurse who has been removed from the register because he can no longer be lawfully employed in a professional capacity.

8.24   *Some other substantial reason for dismissal*

This fifth potentially fair reason covers a wide spectrum. If an employer wishes to introduce a change in his employees' terms of employment, such as hours, location or pay structure, for a good business reason and they refuse to agree, their non-cooperation may amount to a fair reason for dismissal, even though the law of contract does not allow him to force the new terms on them against their will (a somewhat hollow reassurance). A refusal by an important customer to accept an employee may justify dismissal, but the employer has to establish that he had no alternative. In *Grootcon* v. *Keld* (1984) a plater on an oil rig owned by BP sustained a knee injury in the course of his work and was sent home three days early. BP sent a telex to Grootcon, his employer, stating that he was not to be allowed to return until cleared by BP's medical officer. Keld was then dismissed. The Employment Appeal Tribunal decided that an ultimatum from BP that the employee should be removed from the rig might have justified his dismissal. On the evidence presented to the tribunal, however, there was no such demand and the dismissal was unfair.

Even prejudice within the community has sometimes sufficed, as in *Saunders* v. *Scottish National Camps* (1980) where the employee, who worked in a children's holiday camp, was held fairly dismissed only because he was discovered to be homosexual. Legislation to render discrimination on grounds of sexual orientation unlawful came into force in October 2003. Despite an express provision in the Employment Rights Act that a threat by other employees of industrial action if an employee is not dismissed cannot be used by the employer as a defence, it seems that extreme antisocial behaviour (strong body odour, frequent discussion of intimate matters and so on), found objectionable by other workers and not yielding to warnings, can be a fair reason to dismiss.

The Trade Union Reform and Employment Rights Act 1993 created a new class of unfair dismissal: victimisation. An employee dismissed for bringing proceedings or making a complaint in good faith against the employer to enforce any of his rights under various provisions now specified in the Employments Rights Act 1996 and the trade union rights conferred by the Trade Union and Labour Relations (Consolidation) Act 1992, will automatically be entitled to compensation for unfair dismissal. There is no minimum qualifying period of employment.

8.25   *The importance of procedure*

This discussion began with a statement that in unfair dismissal it was the reason, not the procedure, which was important. However, a fair person does not have a good reason for dismissing an employee unless he has undertaken a reasonable investigation and acts on evidence rather than prejudice. On the whole, procedure is most important in misconduct cases and this is reflected by the creation in 1977 by ACAS of a special advisory Code of Practice for dismissals for misconduct. This has been amended in 2004 to take into account changes in the Employment Act 2002. The House of Lords held in an important test case concerning a dismissal for redundancy that a failure to follow a fair procedure, as dismissing without first hearing the employee's side of the case, refusing to allow him to be accompanied by a trade union official or fellow employee, denying him an internal appeal and so on, is capable of in itself rendering a dismissal unfair, whether or not the employer has a good reason (*Polkey* v. *Dayton Services* (1987)). Managers should never, therefore, act on the spur of the moment. Even in cases of gross misconduct, the employee should be suspended for a few days and then interviewed with his trade union representative or fellow worker before a decision is reached. If the employee is genuinely redundant he should be given notice of his impending dismissal and the opportunity to make suggestions about suitable alternative employment or other strategies for avoiding redundancy. In an ill-health case, the employee should be consulted and allowed to produce medical evidence, and possible alternative jobs should be considered.

From 1 October 2004 the employer must provide the minimum procedural steps laid down in the Employment Act 2002 (Dispute Resolution) Regulations 2004, or be automatically held liable for unfair dismissal.

8.26 The right to refuse to work in unsafe conditions

Collective action by groups of employees is subject to different rules from those governing the individual employer/employee relationship. Because employers have a duty to take reasonable care of their employees, a worker who is asked to work in unreasonably uncomfortable or dangerous conditions is not acting in breach of contract if he refuses. There may be debate between the parties about the degree of risk. In *Lindsay* v. *Dunlop Ltd* (1980), the employee refused to work in an area where he was exposed to hot rubber fumes after a preliminary report from the HSE that they might be carcinogenic. The concentration of fumes in Dunlop's factory exceeded the threshold limit recommended by the British Rubber Manufacturers' Association. The trade union and the rest of the workforce agreed to use masks as a temporary measure pending a full report; the masks made the job even hotter and more unpleasant than before. Lindsay refused to work, arguing that the employers were under a duty to provide an expensive new ventilation system. The Employment Appeal Tribunal held that it was not their job to investigate whether there had been a breach of the criminal law, but to decide whether the employer had done what was reasonable. The employers had responded to complaints by providing masks and were willing to continue to monitor the situation. It was held that Lindsay had been fairly dismissed.

If the trade union in similar circumstances had called on all the workers to down tools the legal rules about collective action would have come into play. As a general rule, an employer who dismisses all those taking strike or other industrial action while the action is in progress and does not reinstate any within three months is immune from proceedings in an employment tribunal. An employer faced with unofficial action can choose which of the strikers he will punish, but in a case of action officially supported by the union he must dismiss all or none. The rationale for this approach is the reluctance of Parliament to subject the rights and wrongs of industrial conflict to the scrutiny of the courts. The definition of 'industrial action' is much wider than might be supposed. To take a hypothetical example, an employer insists that his employees work with a hazardous substance without any of the advised precautions. The trade union calls on its members to refuse to work until proper protection is provided. This is industrial action however much it is the employer who is in the wrong. Because of the need to protect workers who take industrial action in good faith to protest against unsafe and unhealthy working conditions, the Trade Union and Labour Relations (Consolidation) Act 1992 makes it unlawful to dismiss either official or unofficial strikers whose action is protected by the provisions set out in the next paragraph.

The need to support workers who act in good faith to preserve their health and safety has led to legislation. The Trade Union Reform and Employment Rights Act 1993 (TURERA) (now the Employment Rights Act 1996, section 100) gave employees the right not to be subjected to any detriment by their employer (including, of course, dismissal) on the ground that:

(a)   having been designated by the employer to carry out activities in connection with preventing or reducing risks to the health and safety of employees at work (this would embrace occupational health professionals as well as safety officers and hygienists), he carried out or proposed to carry out any such activities;

(b)   he performed or proposed to perform his functions as a safety representative, appointed by a recognised trade union, or elected by the workforce where there is no recognised trade union, or as a member of a safety committee;

(c)   being an employee at a place *where there was no safety representative or safety committee or it was not reasonably practicable for him to raise the matter through the safety representative or safety committee*, the employee brought to the employer's attention, by reasonable means, circumstances connected with his work which he reasonably believed were harmful or potentially harmful to health and safety;

(d)   he left or proposed to leave his work in circumstances of danger which he reasonably believed was serious and imminent and which he could not reasonably be expected to avert; or

(e)   he took or proposed to take appropriate steps to protect himself or other persons from danger in circumstances of danger which he reasonably believed to be serious and imminent, but not if those steps were so negligent that the employer acted reasonably in disciplining him.

This leaves a great deal to the judgment of the employment tribunal to which any complaint must be made. Serious and imminent danger is to be judged from the perspective of the reasonable belief of an employee of normal fortitude. There is no minimum qualifying period of employment. Unlimited damages may be awarded for breach of this section. It protects police officers, who cannot because of their special status normally claim for unfair dismissal.

One case (*Goodwin* v. *Cabletel UK Ltd* (1998)) concerned a construction manager whose duties included ensuring that sub-contractors complied with the requirements of health and safety legislation. The safety record of one particular firm caused him some concern, and he wanted to take a strong line. His employers favoured a more conciliatory approach and eventually demoted him to a position where he did not have to deal with sub-contractors. At no time did they question the genuineness of his complaints, merely his manner of dealing with them. The manager resigned and claimed constructive dismissal contrary to section 100. The Employment Appeal Tribunal directed that the issue was whether the manager was carrying out activities in connection with preventing or reducing risks to health and safety. If he had behaved in a very intemperate or malicious fashion he might have exceeded his authority, but the mere fact that he was outspoken and undiplomatic did not remove him from the statutory protection. Sometimes it is necessary to be firm to convey the message.

Where an individual employee raises a health and safety matter with the employer directly, not through a safety representative, he must prove the following in order to have the protection of the statute: that he reasonably believed that the circumstances connected with the work were harmful or potentially harmful; that it was not reasonably practicable for the employee to raise the matter through a representative or safety committee; that the employee had raised the matter by reasonable means; and the fact that the employee had raised the health and safety question was the reason or principal reason for the dismissal (*Tedeschi v. Hosiden Besson Ltd* (1995)).

In *Kerr v. Nathan's Wastesavers Ltd* (1995) the employee was dismissed because he refused to drive a vehicle which, in his opinion, might have become overloaded by the end of the working day. The employers had a procedure whereby employees could either return to the depot or telephone in to arrange for a second vehicle to meet them. It was held that Kerr did not have reasonable grounds for his belief that there was a potential danger and thus was fairly dismissed. A belief that third parties may be put at risk is covered by the section. An ambulance driver's concerns for the safety of patients following a reduction in the quality of the escort service was a concern which could be protected by the health and safety provisions of section 100 (*Barton v. Wandsworth Council* (1994)). And in *Masiak v. City Restaurants UK Ltd* (1999) a chef left the restaurant premises after refusing to cook food which he considered was a potential hazard to public health (chicken that was not properly thawed). He was held protected by section 100(1)(e). In *Balfour Kilpatrick v. Acheson* (2003) the Employment Appeal Tribunal decided that building workers who were unhappy with working conditions on a rat-infested flooded site did not lose the protection of section 100 because they had complained to management through their shop steward rather than a safety representative.

The employer is prohibited from taking disciplinary action against trade union representatives who complain of unfair or unhealthy conditions. This protection covers safety representatives, under the Employment Rights Act 1996, and others acting on behalf of the union, like a shop steward, under the Trade Union and Labour Relations (Consolidation) Act 1992. The protection does not extend to rank and file members acting unofficially on behalf of fellow workers. In *Chant v. Aquaboats* (1978) a union member (not a safety representative) complained about safety standards at work and organised a petition of other employees which was vetted by the local union branch. When he was dismissed soon after, he claimed that the real reason was his petition. Chant had not been employed long enough at the date of dismissal to be able to complain of unfair dismissal unless the reason was participation in union activities for which there is no qualifying period of employment. The Employment Appeal Tribunal held that the activities were not those of a trade union but of a trade unionist, so Chant lost his case. The activity must be with union authority rather than as an individual. It follows that a shop steward who acts against union policy is not participating in the activities of the union. Chant might now be protected by the Employment Rights Act 1996 (above) in that in good faith he took reasonable steps to bring a perceived hazard to the employer's attention, but only if there was no safety representative or it was not reasonably practicable to ask for his help.

Safety representatives are protected only when performing their proper functions. In *Shillito* v. *van Leer (UK) Ltd* (1997) a safety representative was disciplined and suspended without pay for taking action following complaints about an odour given off by a chemical solvent in an area of the factory for which he was not the designated representative. The Employment Appeal Tribunal held that he was motivated by personal considerations, and that he had exceeded his duties, so that he was not protected by section 100 Employment Rights Act 1996.

The law does not protect safety representatives against properly conducted redundancy. A safety representative selected for redundancy on the basis of a points system relating to performance at work was held to have been fairly dismissed. He had no right to special treatment because of his position as safety representative (*Smith Industries Aerospace and Defence Systems* v. *Rawlings* (1996)).

In *Harvest Press Ltd* v. *McCaffrey* (1999) an employee left work because he felt he was in danger of being attacked by another employee who was abusive and aggressive. His dismissal for leaving work was held to be unfair because it fell within section 100: he reasonably believed that danger was serious and imminent, and there was nothing in the circumstances which he could reasonably be expected to do to avert it. This was even though the danger was caused by the behaviour of fellow employees, not by the workplace itself.

8.27   Whistleblowers

Protection of those who report the wrongdoing of an employer has now been enacted, following a number of cases where the public only became aware of a serious cause for concern through the actions of an employee (as, for example, in the case of the Bristol hospital where the failure rate of paediatric heart surgery was considerably higher than the national average). Such employees are protected from victimisation by sections 47B and 103A of the Employment Rights Act 1996 if they make 'qualifying disclosures'. A qualifying disclosure is any disclosure of information which, in the reasonable belief of the worker making the disclosure, tends to show one or more of the following:

(1)   that a criminal offence has been committed, is being committed or is likely to be committed;
(2)   that a person has failed, is failing or is likely to fail to comply with any legal obligation to which he is subject;
(3)   that a miscarriage of justice has occurred, is occurring or is likely to occur;

(4)   that the health and safety of any individual has been, is being or is likely to be damaged;

(5)   that the environment has been, is being or is likely to be damaged; or

(6)   that information tending to show any matter falling within any one of the preceding paragraphs has been, or is likely to be deliberately concealed.

Information should normally be given first to the employer and then to the proper authorities, like the Health and Safety Executive or the Environment Agency, except where the matter is 'exceptionally serious', or where the proper authorities have failed to act. Disclosure to the media as a last resort may be protected, but only where the worker acts in good faith, reasonably believes that the information is true and does not make the disclosure for purposes of personal gain. This law protects police officers, who normally cannot complain of unfair dismissal because of their special status.

8.28   *Time off for trade union activities*

Special consideration is given by the Trade Union and Labour Relations (Consolidation) Act 1992 to members and officials of unions recognised by the employer. Recognition means that the employer regularly negotiates with the union and allows it to represent employees in grievance and disciplinary matters. An employer is obliged by the Act to allow an official (including shop stewards) of a recognised independent trade union who is in his employment to have reasonable time off *with pay* for the purpose of enabling him

(1)   to carry out
  (a)   any duties of his, as such an official, which are concerned with negotiations with the employer on industrial relations matters such as terms and conditions of employment, or
  (b)   any other duties of his, as such an official, which are concerned with the performance of any functions connected with those matters which the employer has agreed may be performed by the union, or

(2)   to undergo training in aspects of industrial relations which are relevant to the carrying out of those duties and which have been approved by the TUC or by his union.

An ACAS Code of Practice: *Time off for Trade Union Duties and Activities* (1998) gives guidance on the operation of the legislation.

Reasonable time off without pay should be given to members of recognised trade unions to attend union meetings, vote in union elections and so on.

Safety representatives are entitled to time off with pay to carry out their duties and to undergo such training as is reasonable. The Health and Safety Commission has issued an Approved Code of Practice as guidance. The approval by the TUC or the union of a training course is not a legal requirement for safety training courses. Thus, an employer who refused his employee time off to attend a course at a college because he provided what, in his opinion, was a perfectly satisfactory course on his own premises, though not approved by the union and lacking any guidance on representing members with a grievance, was not necessarily in breach of the law; it depended on whether the tribunal thought he had acted reasonably (*White* v. *Pressed Steel Fisher* (1980)).

8.29   *Working Time Regulations*

The European Court of Justice held that the Working Time Directive should have been transposed into UK law in November 1996 and it was eventually enacted in the Working Time Regulations 1998, which came into force in October 1998. Amendments which extend the regulations to junior doctors and non-mobile workers in the transport industry were made by the Working Time (Amendment) Regulations 2003 and came into force in 2004. All road transport workers will have to be covered by the legislation by 2005 (self-employed drivers will not be covered until 2009). In addition, Member States can derogate from some of the provisions if they so wish. The UK Government excluded civil protection services, dock workers, agricultural workers and workers 'where there is a foreseeable surge of tourism'. Managing executives and those working in a family business are also exempt from the 48-hour working week, but are entitled to paid leave. But even if certain workers are exempted they must be given alternative protection by the employer so that their health and safety does not suffer.

Regulation 4 provides that the period of weekly working time should be limited such that the average working time for each seven-day period, including over-time, does not exceed 48 hours. The regulation provides that an employer shall have the option of not observing this rule as long as:

(1)   The employer has obtained the employee's agreement in writing to work more than 48 hours.
(2)   The employee is not penalised if he refuses to agree.
(3)   The employer keeps up-to-date records of workers who work more than 48 hours.
(4)   The records are made available to the Health and Safety Executive, who may intervene to protect workers.

The UK legislation allows individuals the choice of volunteering to work more than 48 hours, and permits employers to make collective agreements with independent trade unions to the same effect. This right to opt out of one of the main planks of the directive is controversial, and is under review by the European Council of Ministers. Tony Blair, the Prime Minister, is known to be determined to keep the right to opt out of the 48-hour maximum week, but the European Commission has already indicated that it wishes to remove the opportunity of opting out from the directive. Whether or not a worker has opted out, he must still be protected from damage to his health and safety. Overlong working hours may be a breach of the Health and Safety at Work Act 1974 and may constitute neg-ligence in the civil law (*Johnstone* v. *Bloomsbury HA* (1992)).

Workers must be given at least one day off a week, and at least four weeks' annual paid leave. Night workers must receive special protection, including a free health assessment at regular intervals. They should be transferred to day work if suffering from health problems caused by working nights. There must be minimum daily rest periods of at least 11 consecutive hours in each 24-hour period. Workers should receive rest breaks after working six hours.

> 'Member States shall take the measures necessary to ensure that an employer who intends to organise work according to a certain pattern takes account of the general principle of adapting work to the worker, with a view, in particular, to alleviating monotonous work and work at a pre-determined work rate, depending on the type of activity, and of safety and health requirements, especially as regards breaks during working time.'

The Regulations are enforced partly through the health and safety enforcement authorities, and partly through employment tribunals (the holiday provisions).

Occupational health professionals are concerned mainly with the protection of night workers. A night worker cannot normally be required to work more than an average of eight hours in each 24, calculated over a standard 17-week reference period. Where night work involves special hazards or heavy physical or mental strain, a worker's working hours must not exceed eight in any 24-hour period during which he or she performs night work. A night worker is one who regularly works at least three hours of his or her daily working time between 11pm and 6am (this may be varied by agreement, but must include the period between midnight and 5 am). In *R* v. *Attorney General for Northern Ireland ex parte Burns* (1999) it was held that a worker who worked on a night shift throughout one week in every three was a night worker.

Regulation 7 obliges an employer to give an adult worker an opportunity of a free health assessment before assigning him or her to night work, unless a previous assessment has been made which the employer has no reason to believe to be no longer valid. The worker should not have to lose wages or incur expenses as a result of undergoing a health assessment. The assessments must be repeated as is appropriate to each case, depending on the judgment of a health care professional. Repeat questionnaires should normally be completed annually. Regulatory Guidance published by the Department of Trade and Industry sets out the following, non-exhaustive, list of conditions which may in some cases be made worse by night work: diabetes (particularly where treatment with insulin injections on a strict timetable is required); some heart and circulatory disorders, particularly where physical stamina is affected; stomach or intestinal disorders, such as ulcers, and conditions where the timing of a meal is particularly important; chronic chest disorders where night-time symptoms may be particularly troublesome; other medical conditions requiring regular medication on a strict timetable.

The Regulations do not specify what form the health assessments should take. The UK Government's view is that they do not necessarily have to be carried out by a doctor. The Regulatory Guidance recommends that as a minimum the employer should construct a screening questionnaire for workers to complete, compiled with guidance from a qualified health professional. In the case of any doubt as to the worker's fitness for night work, there should be a referral for a medical examination. Health assessments are subject to the principle of medical confidentiality. They cannot be disclosed without the worker's written consent. However, this does not preclude disclosure of a simple statement that the worker is fit or unfit to carry out night work.

Where a registered medical practitioner classifies a worker as unfit for night work, the worker is entitled to be transferred, if possible, to suitable day work. If such work cannot be found, the employer may be entitled to fairly dismiss, but in the case of a worker suffering from a disability under the Disability Discrimination Act, the employer will have to consider whether reasonable adjustments might assist the worker to continue with the job. Medical evidence and appropriate consultation with the worker would be, as always, important factors in determining whether the employer has acted fairly.

The Working Time (Amendment) Regulations 2002 lay down special rules for young workers, i.e. those over compulsory school age but under 18. The restricted period is between 11 pm and 7 am. Young workers must be given the opportunity of a free assessment not merely of health but also of physical and mental capacities.

Chapter 9
Equal Opportunities

9.1 The concept of discrimination

Until 2003 discrimination was only unlawful if it was on grounds of sex, race, colour or ethnic or national origins, marital status or disability. Religious discrimination was not prohibited (except in Northern Ireland). Discrimination against transsexuals was held to be discrimination on the grounds of sex by the European Court (*P* v. *S* (1996)) but the European Court in 1998 held that discrimination against homosexuals was not a form of sex discrimination (*Grant* v. *South West Trains* (1998)). Dismissal on grounds of sexual orientation was not unlawful under the Sex Discrimination Act. Discrimination against Sikhs was held to be racial rather than religious, against Moslems and Rastafarians religious rather than racial.

The Disability Discrimination Act in 1995 extended the anti-discrimination laws to protect the disabled, but the most significant changes since the 1970s have been brought about by the European Union's adoption of an Equal Treatment Framework Directive in 2000, expanding the classes of people protected against discrimination to include homosexuals, those discriminated against because of their religion and those discriminated against because of their age. Directives also for the first time extend European law to cover discrimination on grounds of race and disability, and make changes to the law of sex discrimination. All of these provisions must be incorporated into UK law. Important changes have been introduced by the Employment Equality (Religion or Belief) Regulations 2003 and the Employment Equality (Sexual Orientation) Regulations 2003. There is now specific legislation relating to discrimination against transsexuals (Sex Discrimination (Gender Reassignment) Regulations 1999). The Disability Discrimination (Amendment) Regulations 2003 widen the scope of the 1995 Act from October 2004. Age discrimination will become unlawful from 2006. The Race Relations Act (Amendment) Regulations 2003 make important changes to the Race Relations Act, implementing the European Race Directive 2000.

The legislation protects all workers, male and female, black and white, and is not confined to employees: it embraces contract workers, young persons working on a job training scheme, members of trade unions and partners in a business. The Equal Opportunities Commission (EOC), the Commission for Racial Equality (CRE) and the Disability Rights Commission (DRC) monitor the legislation, issue guidance which may be in the form of Codes of Practice, and assist complainants to take cases to court. They also have power to conduct their own investigations, at the end of which they may issue a non-discrimination notice, ultimately enforceable through the courts. The Government plans to create a unified Commission for Equality and Human Rights bringing together all the Commissions into one body. Employment tribunals have power to hear complaints of discrimination in employment and can award damages, including compensation for injury to feelings. One vital point to grasp about this legislation is that it is not concerned with motives and that it is possible to act unlawfully if the *effect* of what you do is discriminatory despite the manager's good intentions.

The Fair Employment and Treatment (Northern Ireland) Order 1998 prohibits discrimination on religious grounds in Northern Ireland. The Fair Employment Commission (now combined with the Equal Opportunities Commission, the Commission for Racial Equality for Northern Ireland, and the Northern Ireland Disability Council to form the Equality Commission) has wide powers. Quotas may be set, and all employers must monitor the religious composition of the workforce. The Fair Employment Tribunal can award damages. Religious discrimination became unlawful in the rest of the United Kingdom in December 2003 when the Employment Equality (Religion or Belief) Regulations 2003 came into force.

The concept of discrimination is a highly technical and complex one. The law prohibits conduct of four kinds:

(1)   direct discrimination;
(2)   harassment;
(3)   indirect discrimination;
(4)   victimisation.

The employer must not discriminate against either job applicants or existing employees. Failure to interview a candidate, rejection of a job application, failure to promote, the provision of adverse working conditions and dismissal on sexist or racial grounds or on grounds of disability are all unlawful. The legislation deals with discrimination in a number of different fields, but this discussion will be confined to employment. There is no qualifying period of employment, nor minimum number of hours.

In matters of sex, race, religion and sexual orientation, positive discrimination is just as unlawful as negative discrimination ('We must have a coloured supervisor or else we shall be accused of discrimination'). The only exception is the provision of training courses for one sex or racial group to try to give them increased opportunity. This is not true of disability discrimination, which requires employers to take positive action to assist disabled people to work, within the bounds of reasonable practicability and reasonable cost. In fact, the Disability Discrimination Act 1995 differs in many important respects from the other legislation.

In a case of direct discrimination, the employer treats an employee worse on prohibited grounds than he would someone of a different sex, race, religion, sexual orientation or on grounds of that person's disability. It is not a defence that the employer has a reason for discrimination. The following excuses are not accepted by the law:

'It can be proved that women have more time off than men.'
'My workers/customers would reject a black supervisor.'
'Women haven't got the stamina for this job.'
'Gay teachers are less acceptable to parents than heterosexuals.'
'I can't employ someone with epilepsy because if he has a fit it will frighten other employees.'

In *Ministry of Defence* v. *Jeremiah* (1979), a man employed in an ordnance factory protested that the unpleasant job of making colour-bursting shells was confined to male employees because the women found it dirty and were excused. The Court of Appeal held that this was unlawful direct discrimination on grounds of sex. Exceptionally, the employer may discriminate against one sex if the job falls within one of those listed in the statute where sex is a 'genuine occupational qualification'. Examples are actors, models, and welfare and educational jobs where it is more effective for pupils or clients to be cared for by someone of a particular sex. There is also a particular exception for ministers of religion.

Harassment is a free standing act of unlawful discrimination per se. The new legislation includes a standard definition of harassment taken from the European Directive. For example, racial harassment is committed when a person subjects another person:

(1)   on grounds of race or ethnic or natural origins;
(2)   to unwanted conduct;
(3)   which has the purpose or effect of:
      (a)   violating his dignity; or
      (b)   creating an intimidating, hostile, degrading, humiliating or offensive environment.

Conduct will be regarded as having the effect in (a) or (b) above if, having regard to all the circumstances, including in particular the perception of the victim, it should reasonably be considered as having that effect. Where someone is hypersensitive a remark not intended to be offensive may be regarded as acceptable, as where, in a sex discrimination case, a male worker remarked to a female colleague who was eating some melon: 'You've got some lovely melons there,' realised the double entendre and apologised. When the woman complained that she had been offended, because the remark could refer to her breasts, it was held that she was over-sensitive (*Smith* v. *Vodafone* (2001)).

In *Porcelli* v. *Strathclyde Regional Council* (1986) a woman was subjected by male colleagues to suggestive remarks, unwanted physical contact and a display of pictures of half-clothed women. She was awarded compensation against her employer who had failed to take reasonable steps to protect her from this kind of annoyance.

Indirect discrimination is more subtle. It consists of the application of a provision, criterion or practice with which the proportion of members of one group who can comply is considerably smaller than the proportion of members of another group, and which is to the disadvantage of the former. The following are examples of indirect discrimination:

'Part-time workers will be made redundant before full-time workers.' (Women find it more difficult to work full-time.)
'Applicants must have GCSE English.' (Those whose native language is not English will be less likely to be able to comply.)
'Applicants must be under the age of 35.' (In practice, even today women find it more difficult to be active in the job market in their 20s and 30s.)
'Employees must work on Saturdays. (Jews are prohibited by their religious laws from working on Saturdays.)
'The post involves a lot of travelling.' (A disabled person may find this difficult.')

Indirect discrimination is permitted if the employer can show that the requirement or condition is *justifiable*, that is based on some objective job-related requirement unconnected with the qualities of the worker. The new legislation defines justification in terms of a 'proportionate means of achieving a legitimate aim'. Note that the test of justification in the Disability Discrimination Act is more restricted; the employer must show a 'material and substantial reason'. Part-time workers may be economically less valuable to the company, GCSE English may be needed for workers whose job requires communication skills and the age profile of the department may be such that younger members are needed (*University of Manchester* v. *Jones* (1993)). The job may be in a small shop or hairdressers where Saturday is the busiest day and the need for travel may be an essential part of the duties (e.g. of a commercial traveller).

The exclusion of male Sikhs because of their religious requirement to wear a turban has been held justifiable if safety or hygiene are at risk. Statutory regulations give Sikhs exemption from the need to wear hard hats on construction sites, but the employer will not be liable to a Sikh who incurs injury which would have been avoided had he been wearing a hard hat (Construction (Head Protection) Regulations 1989). These regulations do not apply to workplaces other than construction sites: there, the employer will continue to be free to exclude Sikhs without hard hats if that is a necessary safety precaution. It has been held that employers who operate rules prohibiting the wearing of beards by employees in a food factory are justified by hygiene in discriminating against Sikhs (*Panesar* v. *Nestlé* (1980)). The introduction into England, Wales and Scotland of a law prohibiting religious discrimination is likely to lead to a number of applications to tribunals in respect of dress codes. Company rules imposed for health and safety reasons or to protect their image with customers are likely to be justifiable. Organisations should try to be as flexible as possible to enable staff to dress in accordance with their beliefs but still meet the organisation's requirements.

Victimisation is committed when the employer 'punishes' his employee for complaining in good faith about alleged discrimination or supporting someone else's complaint.

The murder of Stephen Lawrence and the findings of the MacPherson report criticising the police investigation into his death led to the Race Relations (Amendment) Act 2000 which places a general statutory duty on all public bodies to promote racial equality. This expects that they will take the lead in promoting equality of opportunity and good race relations, and preventing unlawful discrimination. This will include producing new policies, monitoring them for effectiveness, publishing the results of monitoring, ensuring public access to information and services and training staff. The Commission for Racial Equality has produced a Code of Practice on the Duty to Promote Race Equality (2002). A Draft Disability Bill published in 2003 proposes the imposition of a similar duty on public authorities to promote equality for disabled people.

There is no upper limit on the amount of compensation which may be awarded by an employment tribunal for an unlawful act of discrimination. Damages in recent cases have been substantial, especially awards for injury to feelings. In one case involving an 18-month campaign of racial harassment against a prison officer by fellow officers which had not been properly investigated by the prison governor, the applicant was awarded £20,000 for injury to feelings and £7500 aggravated damages (*Prison Service* v. *Johnson* (1997)). The Court of Appeal has indicated that the minimum award for injury to feelings should be £500 and the maximum £25,000 (*Vento* v. *Chief Constable of West Yorkshire Police* (2003)).

Employment tribunals have the power to give damages for personal injury (a physical or mental illness) caused by discrimination. *Essa* v. *Laing* (2004) involved a Welshman of Somali ancestry. He was working on the construction of the Millennium Stadium in Cardiff when his foreman in front of a gang of men said: 'Make sure that black c... doesn't wander off'. He claimed compensation for the clinical depression which he said this incident had caused him. The Court of Appeal held that he was entitled to damages for personal injury if he could prove with medical evidence that the incident had caused the depression, even if it was not foreseeable. This test differs from that applied in the County and High Courts and might be a reason for bringing the case in the tribunal rather than the civil courts, although in other respects it is advisable to sue in the civil courts for stress-related illness (*Sutherland* v. *Hatton*, Chapter 7).

Employers are responsible in law for the acts of their employees on the principle of vicarious liability, that is when the employees are acting in the course of their employment. Where it is a manager or supervisor who has been guilty of discrimination towards a junior employee, it is relatively easy to conclude that the supervisor has acted in the course of employment. More difficult is the situation of discrimination by employees on the same level. Raymondo Jones was a 16-year-old youth of mixed ethnic origin. He was employed as an operative in a shoe factory. Fellow operatives burnt his arm with a screwdriver, whipped him on the legs, threw metal bolts at him and called him 'chimp', 'monkey' and 'baboon'. He understandably gave notice. It was held that on a broad commonsense interpretation of the Race Relations Act the employees had acted in the course of employment and the employer was liable (*Jones* v. *Tower Boot Co. Ltd* (1997)). On the other hand, in *Waters* v. *Commissioner of Police of the Metropolis* (2000) a woman police constable was sexually assaulted by a male policeman in her home while both were off duty. It was held that this could not be regarded as in the course of employment, because it was not connected with work. However, it was also held that the Commissioner of Police owed a duty of care to Ms Waters to protect her against alleged victimisation, bullying and harassment by fellow officers who resented her making a complaint about her colleague. And in *Chief Constable of Lincolnshire Police* v. *Stubbs* (1999) the employer was held liable for acts of sexual harassment perpetrated by a police officer on a female colleague when they were both socialising with other colleagues outside work. Such social events are connected to work and are 'an extension of employment'. Since many similar acts are committed at Christmas parties and the like, when some have had too much to drink, employers should be careful to include such events in their harassment policies.

In order for the employer to avoid liability in cases of discrimination in the course of employment, it is necessary for him to take such steps as were reasonably practicable to prevent the act of discrimination. If the employer in *Jones* v. *Tower Boot Co.* had made a clear equal opportunities policy, had given all his employees notice of it, had created a grievance procedure so that Jones could have complained about his treatment to a senior manager, had investigated any complaints, and had taken disciplinary proceedings against anyone accused of breaking the rules, he would have been able to avoid legal responsibility for the acts of Jones's colleagues.

In some situations the employee may have been harassed by third parties not directly connected with the employer. The employer of a nurse cannot be held legally responsible for the wolf whistles of contractors engaged on building work at the hospital. In *Pearce* v. *Governing Body of Mayfield Secondary School* (2003) the House of Lords observed that a school cannot be held vicariously responsible for a campaign of abuse against a teacher mounted by her pupils, since the pupils are not employees. Only where the school authorities failed to protect the teacher against the abuse because they also discriminated on prohibited grounds would this constitute unlawful discrimination. Nevertheless, it might constitute a failure to take reasonable care, giving rise to a claim in negligence for stress-related illness.

Harassment has proved difficult to define. Harassment related to sex, race, religion, disability or sexual orientation is contrary to European, as well as UK law. The European Commission promulgated a Recommendation in 1992 'on the protection of the dignity of women and men at work'. Harassment was defined as 'unwanted, unreasonable and offensive to the recipient'. Accompanying the Recommendation is a Code of Practice. Employees are advised to make it clear that they regard conduct as offensive, because it is for each individual to determine what behaviour is acceptable to them and what they regard as offensive. 'It is the unwanted nature of the conduct which distinguishes sexual harassment from friendly behaviour, which is welcome and mutual.'

The Code recommends that employers:

(1) create a policy statement;
(2) communicate the policy;
(3) impose a duty on managers to ensure that sexual harassment does not occur;
(4) introduce training;
(5) develop clear procedures to deal with sexual harassment, including the provision of confidential counsellors who may assist to resolve matters informally. There should be a complaints procedure, adequate investigation and appropriate disciplinary sanctions.

Changes in the anti-discrimination statutes as a result of the implementation of the Framework Directive have led to a new definition of harassment, discussed earlier in this section. It is important to remember that the law now condemns all forms of discriminatory harassment, including racial, religious, homophobic and disability harassment. Harassment policies should cover all kinds of unacceptable behaviour, including bullying, without a discriminatory element. For example, in *Moores* v. *Bude-Stratton Town Council* (2000) a councillor had been hostile to a council employee for three years and had made various unjustified allegations of dishonesty and abuse of position against him. The last straw was when she subjected Moores to abuse in front of other staff, calling him a 'lying toe-rag' and accusing him of running a protection racket. Moores resigned and successfully claimed that he had been constructively dismissed. The implied term that the employer must provide a tolerable working environment applies to this kind of behaviour. It is interesting to note that the Council was held liable for the acts of the councillor, though she was not its employee.

Of course, harassment may be so severe that it causes damage to the physical or mental health of the employee. In such a case, a civil action might be brought against the employer for negligence, and there is also the possibility of a criminal prosecution by the HSE under the Health and Safety at Work Act. The Protection from Harassment Act 1997 makes severe forms of harassment, like 'stalking', both a criminal and civil wrong. The Public Order Act 1986 makes it a criminal offence to incite racial hatred.

9.2 Special laws protecting women workers

'The Victorian idea of woman was as a wife and mother, centre of the family, consequently the guardian of all Christian and domestic virtues' (Equal Opportunities Commission Report on Health and Safety Legislation (1979)). The conditions in factories in the nineteenth century were abominable for men, women and children, but the plight of women and children most aroused public sympathy. In contrast, the Victorians on the whole did not object to working class women being exploited in domestic service, laundries and dressmaking, which were regarded as their proper place. Male workers resented women working in factories, fearing that women would take jobs from men. The first laws protecting women workers were the Factory Acts 1844 and 1847 which reduced working hours for adult women and forbade the employment of women underground in mines. They were in fact the first victories in the campaign to limit working hours for all employees, both male and female, but they began the industrial segregation of the sexes. Women objected to the restriction of employment opportunity. Some women even dressed as men to work down the pit:

> 'Protective legislation was both a cause and effect of the emergence of the housewife as the dominant mature female role, whether or not a woman worked outside the home. Thus it became possible for employers to employ women on terms that would have been unacceptable to men. It followed that women were effectively excluded from many jobs and skills, and restricted to "women's work".' (Equal Opportunities Commission (1979))

The hypocrisy of the system became obvious in the twentieth century during both World Wars when restrictions were suspended to allow women to do all kinds of work for which they were supposed to be unfitted by their sex. But women workers themselves by this time mostly supported protective legislation, because they also had to carry the burden of domestic chores. The Equal Opportunities Commission has argued that as long as women have to be treated differently the employer has an excuse for refusing equality of opportunity but, to some extent, the move towards the abolition of these laws giving special treatment to women workers, strongly influenced by the policy-makers in the EC, has been against the wishes of the average British woman on the shop floor.

The new philosophy holds that there are in principle no tasks which a woman is constitutionally unable to perform. Strong women, like strong men, can work down a mine and do heavy manual work. The unique quality of women workers is not that they are frail creatures unable to tolerate harsh physical conditions and bad language, but that they are capable of giving birth. Therefore, special legislation is only justified where it is necessary to protect the mother or the unborn child. All legislation should be examined objectively to determine:

(1) whether it is really needed – for example, do women need the separate provision of lavatories?
(2) whether protection should be extended to *both* sexes – for example against dangerous machinery or inessential night work.

The Sex Discrimination Act 1986 has abolished many restrictions on women's hours of work. The general obligations under the Health and Safety at Work Act which remain state that the employer must do that which is reasonably practicable to ensure the health and safety of all his employees, both male and female, so that it will be unlawful to impose long hours or fail to provide rest breaks if this causes ill-health or accidents caused by fatigue. Statutory rules prohibiting the employment of women on the night shift (subject to the grant of exemption by the Health and Safety Executive) were finally repealed in February 1988.

The Treaty of Rome (the treaty which created the European Economic Community) provided in Article 119 for equal pay for men and women doing equal work. This legislation is now found in Article 141 of the Treaty of Amsterdam. This principle has been developed in a series of directives agreed by the Council of Ministers. The Equal Treatment Directive 1976 provides that:

> '... the principle of equal treatment shall mean that there shall be no discrimination whatsoever on grounds of sex either directly or indirectly ... without prejudice to provisions concerning the protection of women, particularly as regards pregnancy and maternity.'

After Miss Marshall, an employee of the Southampton Health Authority, successfully took a case to the European Court, claiming that, by forcing her to retire at 60 when men were allowed to continue to 65, her employer was in breach of this directive (*Marshall* v. *Southampton AHA* (1986)), the UK Parliament passed the Sex Discrimination Act 1986 making it unlawful for an employer to discriminate in the age of retirement. Four years later, the European Court held in the landmark case of *Barber* v. *Guardian Royal Exchange Assurance Group* (1990) that benefits paid under a contracted-out, private occupational pension scheme must be available to men and women at the same age. This decision was not to be retrospective, but to apply to pensions paid after 17 May 1990. This Delphic ruling was clarified in a protocol to the Maastricht treaty which declares that only service after the relevant date will be affected by the judgment. A differential State retirement age is impossible to maintain in these circumstances, and the UK Government announced late in 1993 that this should become 65 for both men and women workers. Because of financial problems in providing occupational pensions caused by poor performance of investments, in 2004 the Government is considering raising the age of retirement to 70 and encouraging those who are fit to continue working until that age.

The interpretation of European Community law is ultimately for the Court of Justice of the European Communities in Luxembourg. Conflict between the law of a Member State and European law may occasionally arise. If the European Court decides that European law is directly applicable, the courts of the Member States will have to implement that decision in preference to their own rules. One illustration is the case of Mrs Johnston. She was a policewoman employed in the Royal Ulster Constabulary in Northern Ireland. A policy decision was made by the Chief Constable to arm all male police officers in the regular course of their duties, but that women would not carry firearms. This meant that women officers were unable to perform many routine operations, and Mrs Johnston was told that her contract would not be renewed. UK law allowed the Secretary of State to authorise an act of discrimination by issuing a certificate that it was for the purpose of safeguarding national security and protecting public safety and order, and he had done so in this case. This certificate was by statute to be treated as conclusive. Mrs Johnston, realising that her action in the UK courts was bound to fail, appealed to the Luxembourg court that the Chief Constable's decision contravened European law. They ruled that it was contrary to Community law to try to remove any issue from the jurisdiction of the courts, so that the Secretary of State's certificate should have been reviewed. They also decided that the ban on women carrying guns could only be justified if it could be proved that women were under an inherently greater danger than men because of their sex, which could not be established. A chivalrous desire to protect women as 'the weaker sex' was insufficient (*Johnston* v. *RUC* (1986)).

The Employment Act 1989 repealed all protective legislation, other than that imposed for biological reasons. There is little justification for sex-based discrimination against women working underground in a mine or cleaning machinery in a factory, but there are good medical reasons for special protection for women working with ionising radiations, because of risks to a possible fetus. The Act allows all employers to continue to take special precautions in regard to women of child-bearing potential, whether or not the job is governed by specific regulations, as long as there is scientific evidence of risk. The Sex Discrimination Act 1975 provides that no account shall be taken of special treatment afforded to women in connection with pregnancy or childbirth (though it does not explicitly cover *potential* reproductive capacity). The Employment Act 1989 states that compliance with legislation prior to the Sex Discrimination Acts (like the Health and Safety at Work Act) shall not be an automatic defence to an allegation of unlawful sex discrimination. However, nothing shall render unlawful any act done by a person in relation to a woman if it was *necessary* (not merely advisable) to comply with an existing statutory provision protecting women as regards pregnancy or maternity or other circumstances giving rise to risks specifically affecting women. Certain protective laws were preserved by name in the new provisions. They included regulations limiting the exposure of women workers to lead, regulations excluding pregnant women from work with ionising radiations and regulations excluding pregnant women in some circumstances from working on a sea-going vessel or as flight crew in an aircraft. Restrictions preventing women from being employed underground in a mine or cleaning machinery in a factory were repealed.

The European Court has held that employers cannot rely on these health and safety provisions to refuse a woman a job or dismiss her from her employment. In *Habermann-Belterman* v. *Arbeiterwohlfahrt, Bezirksverband Ndb/Opf eV* (1994) and *Mahlburg* v. *Land Mecklenburg-Vorpommern* (2000) it was held that employers could not rely on German health and safety laws, prohibiting pregnant women from performing night work or being employed in posts where they might be exposed to dangerous substances, to deny jobs to pregnant job applicants. It is not permissible for an employer to refuse to take on a pregnant woman on the ground that a prohibition on employment would prevent her from working from the outset and for the duration of pregnancy in a post of unlimited duration. In *Busch* v. *Klinikum Neustadt GMBH* (2003) the fact that a pregnant nurse would have been unable to perform certain aspects of her duties did not permit the employer to prevent her returning early from a career break (and therefore receiving full pay throughout her pregnancy, though absent from work).

An EC directive on the Protection of Pregnant Women at Work was agreed by the Council of Ministers by a majority in 1992, the UK Government abstaining. The main points of the directive are that:

(1) A specific regime must be established for the review of health and safety risks to pregnant women.
(2) Women should not be obliged to work on night work during their pregnancy and for a period following childbirth.
(3) Protected workers are entitled to a minimum of 14 weeks' continuous maternity leave, including at least two weeks' compulsory leave before and after childbirth.
(4) Workers are entitled to time off without loss of pay for ante-natal examinations.
(5) Dismissal of workers during the period beginning with conception and ending with the end of their maternity leave is prohibited, save in exceptional circumstances unconnected with the pregnancy. If a worker is dismissed during this period the employer must provide written reasons for the dismissal.
(6) Rights under workers' contracts of employment should be preserved during maternity leave. Pay should not be less than she would receive if she were absent for a sickness related reason.

The directive was enacted into UK law and is now to be found in the Employment Rights Act 1996 and the Management Regulations 1999.

Further laws to protect new and expectant mothers are enacted in the Management Regulations 1999. Employers must carry out an assessment of the specific risks posed to the health and safety of pregnant women and new mothers in the workplace and then take steps to ensure those risks are avoided. Risks include those to the unborn child or child of a woman who is still breastfeeding – not just risks to the mother. In *Day* v. *T. Pickles Farms Ltd* (1999) the Employment Appeal Tribunal held that the risk assessment should be done when employing a woman of childbearing age even if she is not pregnant. Certainly as soon as she notifies her employer of her pregnancy a risk assessment is vital. A failure to do so has been held to be an act of sex discrimination (*Hardman* v. *Mallon* (2002)). The main hazards to be avoided are physical agents (shocks, vibrations, handling of loads, noise, non-ionising radiation, extremes of heat and cold), biological agents (listeria, rubella, chickenpox, toxoplasma, cytomegalovirus, hepatitis B and HIV), chemical agents (mercury, antimiotic drugs, carbon monoxide and various chemical agents) and working conditions (mining, work with VDUs). The employer must take preventive action, as by temporarily altering working conditions or hours of work. If this is not possible, suitable alternative work should be found. Where these options are not viable, the woman must be suspended on full pay for as long as is necessary to protect her health and that of her child (HSE: *New and expectant mothers at work, a guide for employers* (2002)).

Where a new or expectant mother works at night and has been issued with a certificate from a doctor or midwife stating that night work would affect her health and safety, the employer must offer her suitable alternative day work, and if not available suspend her on full pay. The obligation to alter working conditions or suspend only arises when the woman notifies the employer in writing that she is pregnant, has given birth within the previous six months or is breastfeeding. However, the general duty under the Health and Safety at Work Act to protect her health and safety applies even without a written notification.

A number of cases have now gone to employment tribunals about duties to pregnant employees. An example of a careful risk assessment is reported in *Bruce* v. *Saffronland Homes* (1998). A support worker in a residential home gave notice of her pregnancy. The employer concluded that the Special Needs Unit, which housed potentially violent clients, was unsuitable. The alternative was the regular care unit for physically disabled persons. Though there was considerable manual handling, the premises were equipped with lifting hoists and there was adequate staffing to ensure that the pregnant employee would not have to undertake too much physical work. The tribunal found this careful and fair risk assessment to comply with the regulations. When the employee refused the alternative post and then went off sick having obtained a sick note from a GP, the employer paid Statutory Sick Pay. The employee claimed Maternity Suspension Pay (MSP). It was held that she was not entitled to MSP. She had unreasonably refused an offer of suitable alternative work and her absence was due to sickness, not the unsuitability of the job for a pregnant worker.

In *British Airways* v. *Moore* (1999) two female cabin crew were removed from flying duties, under the terms of a relevant collective agreement, after their 16th week of pregnancy. They continued to be employed as ground crew, but were no longer entitled to the special flying allowances paid to staff engaged on flying duties. It was held that they had been suspended by reason of maternity and should be paid the equivalent of their normal remuneration.

In *Day* v. *T. Pickles Farms Ltd* (1999) Mrs Day told her employer that she was pregnant and provided medical certificates from her GP stating that she suffered from morning sickness and hyperemesis grandarum (severe vomiting associated with pregnancy). The employer also knew she was attending an ante-natal clinic. Mrs Day was employed as a counter assistant in a sandwich shop and also had to roast chickens in an oven. The constant smell of food made her feel nauseous and her GP certified her as unfit for work. The Employment Appeal Tribunal condemned the employer for not undertaking a risk assessment. They also decided that the knowledge of the employer of Mrs Day's condition plus the written sick notes from the GP constituted written notification of pregnancy. Thus, the employer was under a duty to consider alternative work or, if not available, Maternity Suspension Pay.

There has already been debate about whether it is necessary to impose controls on the employment of all women, when many are unlikely to be pregnant, through age, sterilisation, or contraception. The Euratom Directive of 1980, revised in 1984, imposed specially low limits on the exposure of 'women of reproductive capacity' to ionising radiation, but it did not define who should be included in the definition. Germany applies the standard to all females under the age of 45, whereas the UK Ionising Radiations Regulations and Approved Code of Practice (2002) give a discretion to the doctor monitoring the individual worker. The employer is obliged to inform women employees engaged in work with ionising radiation of the possible hazard to the fetus in early pregnancy and of the importance of informing the employer as soon as they discover that they have become pregnant. The Control of Lead at Work Regulations 2002 and Approved Code of Practice also protect pregnant women and those of child-bearing potential, as defined by EMAS or an Appointed Doctor, by excluding them or limiting the permitted exposure. The 2002 Lead Regulations permit a woman worker or her employer to appeal against the decision of the doctor undertaking health surveillance that she is or is not of reproductive capacity.

The Equal Opportunities Commission has pointed out on a number of occasions that levels of exposure to dangerous substances should be reduced for all workers, male and female. There is evidence that men's exposure to hazards may also affect reproductive capacity (Fletcher 1985). It may not be sufficient to abolish special laws protecting women if both sexes are then exposed to unacceptable risks. Troup and Edwards in their HSE paper *Manual Handling* (1985) conclude that neither sex nor age are reliable predictors or criteria for ability to handle loads. It does not therefore follow that all laws relating to heavy lifting should be abolished, but that employers should be prohibited from requiring any employee, male or female, to handle loads likely to injure. Each employee should be assessed as an individual. This principle is now incorporated in the Manual Handling Regulations 1992 (see Chapter 5). The Code of Practice advises that allowance should be made for pregnancy because it has significant implications for the risk of manual handling injury. Hormonal change can affect the ligaments, increasing the susceptibility to injury; and postural problems may increase as the pregnancy progresses. Particular care should be taken for women who handle loads during the three months following a return to work after childbirth.

Doctors and nurses are apprehensive that they may be caught between Scylla and Charybdis. On the one hand they are told that they may not discriminate against women, on the other that they will be liable to compensate any child born disabled through their negligence in failing to protect it in the womb (Congenital Disabilities (Civil Liability) Act 1976 (Chapter 7)). They may be reassured that if they act according to the findings of scientific research and the generally recognised standards of their profession they will steer a safe course. If, however, they either exclude women because of prejudice unsupported by science, or fail to guard them against risks where there is published evidence to show a danger to health, they may come to grief.

The laws against sex discrimination permit the employer to demand strength from a worker if the job requires it, but not to assume that all women are weak and all men like Hercules. A good example was *Shields* v. *Coomes* (1978). A male counterhand in a betting shop was paid more than the women with whom he worked on the assumption that as a man he would bear the responsibility of dealing with any violent disturbance. The employer could only justify unequal pay if he could prove that there was a genuine material difference between the man's job and the women's (Equal Pay Act 1970). Lord Denning said this in deciding that the women were entitled to equal pay:

'It would be otherwise if the difference was based on any special personal qualification that he had; as, for instance, if he was a fierce and formidable figure, trained to tackle intruders ... But no such special personal qualification is suggested ... He may have been a small and nervous man, who could not say boo to a goose. She may have been as fierce and formidable as a battle-axe.'

The Equal Pay Act and Article 141 of the Treaty of Amsterdam allow an employee to claim equal pay with a comparator of the opposite sex who is employed by the same employer at the same establishment if he or she can show that he or she is doing the same job or a job of equal value. An employment tribunal can be asked to appoint an independent job evaluation expert to decide whether jobs are of equal value. The employer may defend the claim if he can show a material difference other than sex between the man and woman, like additional qualifications, seniority, or the need to attract employees with particular skills in short supply.

If the employer sets up his own job evaluation exercise, he will not be permitted to weight it unfairly in favour of either sex by artificially giving more points for manual strength or dexterity. In *Rummler* v. *Dato-Druck* (1987), a woman printer argued that she should be placed in a higher pay grade because the work was, for her, heavy physical work. The same work, she said, did not require so much effort from a man. The European Court rightly held that it would be discriminatory to use values which differed from sex to sex. Women cannot be given more points for doing heavy manual work than men doing the same work. Nevertheless, it is difficult to design a job evaluation scheme which is totally objective, since it will always to some extent reflect the values of the designer. If society undervalues caring skills, seeing them as a natural attribute of the female and not requiring any particular effort, it may not give a high score to a job like nurse or home help.

9.3   Pregnancy dismissals and maternity leave

The Employment Protection (Consolidation) Act (EPCA) provided in 1978 that dismissal for pregnancy or a pregnancy-related illness was automatically unfair. For a woman to claim the benefit of this provision, she had to have worked full-time for at least two years at the date of dismissal. Later cases managed to avoid the need to establish this qualifying period of service by showing that dismissal for pregnancy is a form of sex discrimination, and holding an employer liable if it could be proved that he would not have dismissed a man who was off sick for a lengthy period (there is no minimum period of employment under the Sex Discrimination Act). The European Court eventually decided that discrimination against a woman because of pregnancy is always direct discrimination on grounds of sex, since only a woman can become pregnant. There should be no comparison with the 'sick man'.

The UK was forced to expand protection for pregnant employees in line with the EC Pregnancy Directive (see above). The new laws are to be found in the Employment Rights Act 1996 and the Maternity and Parental Leave Regulations 1999. Dismissal of an employee is automatically unfair if the reason or principal reason for the dismissal is connected with (inter alia):

(1)   the pregnancy of the employee;
(2)   the fact that the employee has given birth to a child;
(3)   the fact that she is subject to medical suspension from her job;
(4)   the fact that she took ordinary or additional maternity leave, or sought to take it.

A pregnant employee has the right under the Employment Rights Act 1996 to be given reasonable time off work to attend ante-natal care recommended by a doctor, midwife or health visitor. She is entitled to time off with pay. After the first visit, the employee may be required to produce a certificate that she is pregnant and a record of the appointments made for her.

The identification of a pregnancy-related reason for dismissal has caused problems of interpretation. In *Webb* v. *EMO* (1995) an employer advertised for a substitute for an employee who was about to go off on maternity leave. The substitute discovered soon after beginning work that she too was pregnant and was dismissed. The House of Lords held that the reason for the dismissal was not the pregnancy so much as the inability of the substitute employee to fulfil her contract. A man who announced that he would have to be absent for several weeks in similar circumstances would have been treated the same. The European Court disagreed. It was unlawful discrimination to dismiss her because of her pregnancy. The European Court decided in two subsequent cases (*Tele Danmark A/S* v. *Handels-og Kontorfunktionaerernes Forbund i Danmark (HK)* (2001) and *Jimenez*

Melgar v. *Ayuntiamento de Los Barrios* (2001)) that the rule in *Webb* v. *EMO* also applies to fixed term contracts. In the *Tele-Danmark* case a woman had been recruited to perform a six-month contract from July to December. At the time she was recruited she knew she was pregnant but kept this from the employer. She expected to give birth in November and would be entitled to take maternity leave from 11 September. When she told her employer about her pregnancy she was dismissed with effect from 30 September. The employer argued that she had acted in bad faith, because when recruited she knew that she would not be able to perform a substantial part of the contract. It was held that the employer was guilty of unlawful sex discrimination.

In *Abbey National plc* v. *Formoso* (1999) an employee was alleged to have spread false rumours at work that her manager had suggested that they spend the night together in a hotel. On the day she was confronted by the manager she discovered she was pregnant. Her GP gave her a sick note certifying her unfit for work due to anxiety and pregnancy. A disciplinary hearing was held which Ms Formoso did not attend because the doctor said she was emotionally unfit. She was dismissed in her absence. It was held that the dismissal of an employee who was unable to attend a disciplinary hearing for a pregnancy-related reason was an act of sex discrimination and unfair.

Employers are not permitted to discriminate against pregnant employees because of ideas of morality. In *O'Neill* v. *Governors of St Thomas More School* (1997) a religious studies teacher in a Roman Catholic school was not allowed to return to work after giving birth to a child whose father was a priest. The case attracted considerable publicity. The employer argued that her immorality rendered the teacher unfit to be employed in a church school. It was held that the reason for the dismissal was pregnancy and thus that the dismissal was unfair.

The financial support of the pregnant woman is, like sick pay, dependent partly on contract, partly on statute. Many employers pay employees all or a proportion of their normal wages during maternity leave. Where this is not agreed in the contract, most women have the right to Statutory Maternity Pay (see below). Where a woman is suspended from work because of a risk to her or her unborn child, she will be entitled to medical suspension pay. This is her full salary, but she will not receive it if her employer offers her suitable alternative work which she unreasonably refuses. The right to medical suspension pay is not available to a woman who is off sick because of a pregnancy-related illness. It is confined to women who work in a job which in itself carries a risk, either as defined by the Management Regulations, or in any recommendation contained in an Approved Code of Practice. It is a criminal offence to employ a woman during the period of two weeks commencing with the day of childbirth.

Central to the new provisions is the concept of maternity leave. An employee has a right to 26 weeks' maternity leave during which all her contractual rights must be preserved as though she had not been absent, except that the employer does not have to pay her her normal wages unless obliged to do so by her contract of employment. Maternity leave starts on the date which the employee notifies to the employer at least 21 days before that date or as soon as is reasonably practicable. The earliest it may do so is the eleventh week before the expected week of the birth. If she is absent from work for a pregnancy related reason at any time after the beginning of the sixth week before the birth the maternity leave is triggered by the first day of absence. The rights of pregnant employees who have worked full-time for the employer for 26 weeks at the fourteenth week before the baby is due are more extensive. The employer must allow them additional maternity leave up to a further 26 weeks. There is no law which compels the employee to stop working at any stage before the birth. In *ILEA* v. *Nash* (1979), the employee was a school teacher whose baby was due at the end of September. She chose to resign with effect from the beginning of September, realising that she would be on holiday during August. It was held that the employers could not force her to leave at the end of the summer term: the decision was hers.

The pregnant employee must give the employer written notification before she goes on maternity leave of her expected week of childbirth and the date she intends to start maternity leave. The employer must then write to the employee within 28 days, setting out her return date. The employee can change this date if she gives her employer 28 days' notice.

Where the woman is unable to return to work at the end of maternity leave she should be treated like any other employee absent through ill-health (*Handelsog Kontorfunktionaernes Forbund i Danmark (acting for Larsson* v. *Dansk Handel Service* (1997)). This is even though her illness may relate to her pregnancy. She will be entitled to normal sick pay. If the employer considers dismissal, he must ignore the maternity leave period itself and any periods of absence before the birth connected with the pregnancy when considering the employee's absence record (*Brown* v. *Rentokil* (1998)).

The returning mother must normally be restored to a post in the same grade and capacity as before, unless the employer shows that this is not reasonably practicable and offers her suitable alternative work which she unreasonably refuses. Employers with five or fewer employees are not obliged to allow her to return if it is not reasonably practicable because there is no work for her to do. Otherwise, failure to reinstate as required by the statute is unfair dismissal. As with all statutory rights, the employer can agree better terms with his employees, but he cannot fall below the statutory minimum. Temporary replacements may be fairly dismissed when the permanent employee returns as long as they were initially notified in writing that this would happen.

The right to return under the Employment Rights Act is a right to return to full-time working: the employer is not obliged to allow the new mother to work part-time. However, in one case, *Home Office* v. *Holmes* (1984), a woman successfully used the sex discrimination laws to establish that a requirement to work full-time is one which discriminates indirectly against women because a smaller proportion of them can work full-time because of family commitments. The Home Office was unable to justify its insistence that she work full-time after the birth of her second child. The Kemp-Jones Report had stated that the civil service was losing valuable trained personnel when they left to start families and that in some departments efficiency increased with the introduction of part-timers. In *Greater Glasgow Health Board* v. *Carey* (1987), in contrast, the Employment Appeal Tribunal decided that a requirement that a health visitor work a five-day week, though discriminatory, was justifiable by the need for continuity of attendance on mothers on a daily basis. What happened at weekends?

9.4 Maternity pay

Employees are entitled in some circumstances to Statutory Maternity Pay (SMP). The qualifying conditions are that the employee must have been employed for at least 26 weeks up to and into the fifteenth week before the expected week of confinement, that she must normally give 28 days' notice by the end of the fifteenth week of the date she intends to start maternity leave, that she must have been earning on average more than the NI lower earnings limit, that she must provide medical evidence of pregnancy or birth and that she must have stopped work. The right to SMP does not depend on the woman's intention to return to work. Self-employed or non-employed women do not qualify for SMP but can claim maternity allowance from the DWP. There are two rates of SMP: the higher rate which is payable for the first six weeks only, and the lower rate. The higher rate is 90 per cent of average weekly earnings. SMP is paid for a maximum of 26 weeks. It is subject to income tax. The employer can claim reimbursement of SMP by deducting the money from his National Insurance contributions.

Small employers (those whose total National Insurance liability for the previous tax year was less than £20,000) are entitled to 100 per cent reimbursement, plus a handling charge of 5 per cent; all others can claim 92 per cent of the payments made.

A woman who does not qualify for SMP may be entitled to maternity allowance, for up to 26 weeks.

Since the contract of employment continues throughout the ordinary maternity leave period, the employer must continue to provide her with the normal contractual benefits, e.g. accrued holiday pay, pension rights, private health insurance and her company car unless strictly reserved for business purposes. Where the woman chooses to take additional maternity leave (AML) she has the right to return, but AML does not count towards seniority or pension rights (though her rights are only suspended during the period; they are preserved exactly as they were at the beginning of the AML period).

9.5 Parental leave and time off for dependants

In 1997 the UK government agreed to accede to the Social Chapter of the Maastricht Treaty. This involved, *inter alia*, the acceptance of the Parental Leave Directive which had already been adopted in the other Member States. The provisions were incorporated into UK law and are now found in the Paternity and Adoption Leave Regulations 2002. Fathers have the right to up to two weeks' paid leave at the time of the birth of a child (or within 56 days of the birth). They must show that they have or expect to have responsibility for the child's upbringing, are the biological father of the child or the mother's husband or partner and have worked continuously for their employer for 26 weeks ending with the fifteenth week before the baby is due. Both parents have the right to an unpaid period of 13 weeks' leave which can be taken up to the child's fifth birthday, but only after consultation with the employer.

Adoption leave and pay are available to individuals who adopt and one member of a couple where a couple adopt jointly (the couple must choose which partner takes adoption leave). Adopters are entitled to up to 26 weeks' ordinary adoption leave (with Statutory Adoption Pay) followed immediately by up to 26 weeks' additional adoption leave. To qualify, the adopter must have worked continuously for his or her employer for 26 weeks ending with the week in which he or she was notified of being matched with a child for adoption.

Employees are entitled to take a reasonable amount of unpaid time off during working hours in order to deal with emergencies involving dependants, e.g. a sick child or elderly relative taken to hospital. There is no maximum period; each case depends on its facts. This does not allow the employee to take unlimited time off to care for a dependant in person, only to make alternative arrangements like a child-minder or carer. Disruption or inconvenience caused to an employer's business are irrelevant. There is no qualifying period of employment. Parents of children under five may ask the employer to permit flexible working. If he refuses, he must give a good reason, for example cost, problems with reorganisation of work among existing staff, or detrimental impact on performance.

9.6   Children and young persons

It was the plight of young children in the factories which inspired the first protective laws at the beginning of the nineteenth century. Soon after, similar legislation was passed to protect children in mines. Gradually, an intricate patchwork of statutes and regulations developed. That was in an era when children became adult wage-earners at a very early age after only rudimentary schooling. When children left school at 16 and achieved full adult status at 18 much of the old law had become obsolete. There remains a need for legislation to protect those under the school-leaving age who engage in part-time jobs. No person under 13 may be lawfully employed in any capacity, and from 13–16 only outside school hours and not for more than two hours a day. These restrictions do not apply to approved work experience for children in their last year of school (Education (Work Experience) Act 1973). The Health and Safety (Training for Employment) Regulations 1990 deem children on work experience to be employees for the purposes of health and safety legislation. New regulations based on an EC Directive were introduced in the Children (Protection at Work) Regulations 1998 and 2000.

There is evidence that people under 25 are more accident-prone than older citizens, but none to show that under-18s are more at risk than the 18–25s. Young people's stamina in the face of long hours, shift work or night work is no less than that of their elders. However, where a young person is not yet fully developed physically, a few occupations may be especially hazardous for teenagers, and the untrained and inexperienced are always at increased risk. Comprehensive measures have been enacted to ensure the health and safety of all employees. The employer owes a duty to do that which is reasonably practicable to protect them, as by giving instruction and training, providing a safe working environment, and fixing hours and meal-breaks in order to avoid risks to health (Health and Safety at Work Act, Chapter 5).

Most of the outdated restrictions on young people's employment and hours of work were repealed by the Employment Act 1989. A European directive on the protection of young people at work was implemented by the Health and Safety (Young Persons) Regulations 1997 which introduced new requirements into the Management of Health and Safety at Work Regulations 1999. The special needs of young workers have been addressed by the following legal obligations on the employer:

(1)   A duty to assess risks to young people, under 18, before they start work.
(2)   A duty to take into account their inexperience, lack of awareness of existing or potential risks, and immaturity.
(3)   A duty to provide information to parents of school-age children about the risk and the control measures introduced.
(4)   A duty to consider whether a young person should be prohibited from certain work activities, except where they are over minimum school-leaving age, the work is necessary for their training, risks are reduced so far as is reasonably practicable, and proper supervision is provided by a competent person.

Employers are prohibited in general from employing young persons for work which is beyond their physical or psychological capacity; involves harmful exposure to agents which are toxic, carcinogenic, cause heritable genetic damage or harm to the unborn child, or which in any other way chronically affect human health; involves harmful exposure to radiation; involves a risk of accidents which it may reasonably be assumed cannot be recognised or avoided by young persons owing to their insufficient attention to safety or lack of experience or training; or presents a risk to health from extreme cold or heat, noise or vibration.

The Working Time Regulations 1998 entitle workers under 18 to a health and capacities assessment if working at nights, an uninterrupted period of 12 hours' rest in each 24 hour period during which they work, two days' rest in each week and a rest break of 30 minutes where daily working time is more than $4\frac{1}{2}$ hours. There is some latitude if unusual or unforeseeable circumstances have arisen.

9.7   Workers with a disability

Continuing pressure on politicians to enact legislation protecting the disabled finally bore fruit in the Disability Discrimination Act 1995 (DDA). The Act is not restricted to employment, but it is outside the scope of this book to cover any but the employment provisions, which came into force on 2 December 1996. The Act repealed the previous legislation relating to disabled persons, the Disabled Persons (Employment) Acts 1944 and 1958, which were universally acknowledged to be of little practical effect. Those Acts obliged employers to employ a quota of registered disabled ('green card' holders). There were insufficient registered disabled to enable employers to meet the quota. Many employees preferred not to register and enforcement procedures were lax. The Code of Good Practice on the Employment of Disabled People 1984 was advisory only.

It was argued that UK legislation should be based on that in the United States, but the DDA gives significantly less protection. One major criticism was the failure to set up a quango to assist with enforcement, similar to the Equal Opportunities Commission and the Commission for Racial Equality. The new Labour government announced in 1997 that this would be remedied and the Disability Rights Commission was created in 1999. The Act is accompanied by a Code of Practice, and Guidance on matters to be taken into account in determining questions relating to the definition of disability. At first, it did not apply to employers with fewer than 20 employees but this was later reduced to 15. From 1 October 2004 the Act applies to all employers, except for the armed services. The Disability Discrimination (Meaning of Disability) Regulations 1996 and the Disability (Employment) Regulations 1996 deal with matters of detail. The Act applies to both Great Britain and Northern Ireland.

It may be dangerous to compare the DDA with other anti-discrimination statutes because the pattern of the DDA differs in some respects. The DDA encourages positive discrimination in favour of disabled workers, whereas the other legislation makes most positive discrimination unlawful. In many other areas, however, there are similarities with other statutes, as, for example, in the definition of harassment.

The Government was urged to define disability in terms of stigma, but it decided to adopt a strictly medical model. The DDA defines 'disabled person' as a person with 'a physical or mental impairment which has a substantial and long-term adverse effect on his ability to carry out normal day-to-day activities'. Anyone who was registered as a disabled person under the 1944 Act and whose name appeared on the register on 12 January 1995 and on 2 December 1996 was treated as having a disability for the purposes of the DDA during a period of three years starting on 2 December 1996. He was then treated as having had a disability in the past, whether or not he continued to be disabled under the new definition.

Although the definition of disability in the DDA may be different from that in other legislation, the fact that the applicant is receiving disablement benefit under the Industrial Injuries Scheme, or has a blue badge as a result of limited mobility, or is registered as disabled with social services, or attended special school may all be taken into account by the employment tribunal.

Physical impairment includes sensory impairments such as those affecting sight or hearing. Mental impairment includes learning difficulties and any mental illness as long as it is clinically well-recognised, i.e. recognised by a responsible body of medical opinion. Employment tribunals have held that ME (chronic fatigue syndrome) is such an illness. In 2004 the Government announced that it would remove the requirement that a mental illness be clinically well-recognised. The diagnosis of mental illness has proved to be one of the most challenging problems in the interpretation of the legislation. It is established that it is for the applicant to prove that he or she has the status of a disabled person, and that this must be done by adducing medical evidence. In *Morgan* v. *Staffordshire University* (2002) the Employment Appeal Tribunal held that simple references to 'anxiety', 'stress' and 'depression' in an applicant's medical notes did not amount to proof of a mental impairment under the DDA. There must be a report from a doctor (who may be a GP or a specialist) identifying a mental illness included in the World Health Organisation's Classification of Diseases or some other classification of very wide professional acceptance, such as the American Diagnostic and Statistical Manual of Mental Disorders. The tribunal cannot ignore uncontested medical evidence, unless it rejects the evidence on the basis of which the medical opinion has been formed (for example a ten-minute interview) or where it is clear that the medical witness has misunderstood that evidence. The tribunal should not make any judgment on whether an applicant has a mental impairment from the way he or she gives evidence on the day.

Where the applicant is suffering from physical symptoms through a psychological problem ('functional overlay') this will be regarded as a physical impairment, though resulting from a psychological cause. In *College of Ripon and York St John* v. *Hobbs* (2002) the applicant claimed to have experienced muscle weakness and wasting, though there was no sign of any organic disease. This was held to be a physical impairment. It may be argued that obesity which impairs mobility is a physical impairment, even if the cause is overeating resulting from emotional problems. Anorexia, also, may lead to substantial physical impairment, though also classified as a mental illness.

A substantial adverse effect is one which is more than minor or trivial. Long-term means having lasted 12 months or more, likely to last 12 months or more, or terminal. Normal day-to-day activities are:

- mobility;
- manual dexterity;
- physical co-ordination;
- continence;
- ability to lift, carry or otherwise move everyday objects;
- speech, hearing or eyesight;
- memory, or ability to concentrate, learn or understand;
- perception of the risk of physical danger.

The courts have emphasised that it is a question of what the applicant cannot do, rather than what he can do. Disabled people avoid tasks they find difficult, and develop coping mechanisms.

> 'What the Act is concerned with is an impairment in the person's *ability* to carry out activities. The fact that a person can carry out such activities does not mean that his ability to carry them out has not been impaired...' (*Goodwin* v. *Patent Office* (1999))

They have also held that the doctor's advice on whether there is a substantial impairment is not conclusive. This is a commonsense decision to be made by the tribunal. Thus, the OH professional's opinion on whether there is a physical or mental impairment is more authoritative than his assessment of interference with normal day-to-day activities. For this reason it is preferable for the medical report to state that it is likely or unlikely that the worker is disabled within the DDA, rather than making a definite ruling (*Abadeh* v. *British Telecommunications plc* (2001)).

The fact that the worker finds work difficult is not the issue: the tribunal must

look at normal day-to-day activities common to the general population, like getting on and off a bus, climbing stairs, cleaning, shopping, cooking a meal. A
professional violinist's playing may be impaired by slight damage to a finger
which does not affect normal day-to-day activities. An international rugby player
may have to give up the game because of damage to his back which does not
interfere with his ordinary everyday life. What is normal does not depend on
whether a majority of people do it. In *Ekpe* v. *Commissioner of the Police for the
Metropolis* (2001) the applicant claimed that she found difficulty in putting curlers
in her hair. The tribunal held that, since only women engage in this activity, it is
not normal day-to-day, but the Employment Appeal Tribunal disagreed. I hardly
ever travel on a bus, but this remains a normal day-to-day activity for a substantial
proportion of the population, as does air travel. There is more doubt about horse
riding. I would not classify hang-gliding as a normal day-to-day activity.
Nevertheless, some work activities are relevant to the assessment of whether a
worker is disabled because they are not special to work. Use of a word processor
or a spanner are obvious examples. In *Cruickshank* v. *VAW Motorcast Ltd* (2002) a
worker suffered from asthma which was exacerbated by exposure to fumes at
work. The employer was advised by occupational health to move him out of the
foundry into the offices or the yard, but the employer decided there were no
vacancies and dismissed him. The medical evidence was that his condition
improved, as might be expected, when he was off sick at home, but worsened on
his return to work. It was held that the tribunal should assess the worker's ability
to lead his normal life both when he was at work and absent from work. In order
to determine whether the physical impairment amounted to a disability, the tribunal should ask whether there was a substantial and long-term effect while the
employee was still in employment. Of course, it may well be that in this case the
employer could justify discrimination if no reasonable adjustment was available
at the place of work.

The Disability Rights Commission argues that the list of normal day-to-day
activities is incomplete. For example, a woman suffering from bulimia or anorexia
may be aware that she is endangering her health, but unable to cease her
destructive behaviour. Also, those with certain mental illnesses may find it difficult to communicate with others, or to socialise (Asperger's syndrome is one
example). The Secretary of State has power to add activities to the list. However, it
must be noted that people with bulimia and autism have been held by tribunals to
be disabled within the Act on the medical evidence available to them. (In *Hewlett*
v. *Motorola Ltd* (2004) an autistic applicant was held to be disabled.)

Pain and fatigue may be taken into account, e.g. where a person has a mental
illness, such as depression, account may be taken of that person's inability in
practice to perform tasks for which he is physically competent. If walking is very
painful, this may constitute a substantial impairment of mobility. The Act provides that a condition counts as a disability even though it is being treated or
corrected by means of drugs or a prosthesis or other aid. The condition is to be
assessed without their assistance, e.g. a diabetic without drugs, an epileptic
without drugs, a deaf person without a hearing aid, or an asthmatic without an
inhaler. The one exception is sight impairments which are corrected by spectacles
or contact lenses. It has been held that counselling sessions with a consultant

clinical psychologist constitute an aid (*Kapadia* v. *London Borough of Lambeth* (2000)). Only continuing (and not concluded) treatment is relevant (*Abadeh* v. *British Telecom* (2001)). The assessment of the likely effect on the person's capability if the aid or treatment is withdrawn ('deduced effect') is essential in these cases. The Disability Discrimination (Blind and Partially Sighted) Regulations 2003 provide that a person either (1) certified as blind or partially sighted by a consultant ophthalmologist or (2) registered as blind or partially sighted in a local authority register is deemed to be a disabled person within the DDA.

Progressive conditions are those which are likely to change and develop over time. The Act gives the examples of cancer, multiple sclerosis, muscular dystrophy and HIV infection. Where a person has a progressive condition, he or she will be treated as having an impairment which is substantial from the moment the condition has *some* effect on ability to carry out normal day-to-day activities. Thus, a medical diagnosis of MS or HIV infection does not render the person disabled, but once he or she begins to stumble, or to suffer from opportunistic infections, the definition of disabled will apply. It is proposed that asymptomatic HIV infection, MS and cancer should be brought within the definition of disability from date of diagnosis (Draft Disability Discrimination Bill 2003). Presumably, a person who suffers a disabling depression on the discovery of the progressive condition would be able to establish an impairment. The Act states that those suffering remission in a condition having a substantial effect on ability to carry out normal day-to-day activities will be treated as having a continuing disability if the substantial adverse effect is likely to recur. Seasonal allergic rhinitis is specifically excluded. An example given in the Guidance is of a person with rheumatoid arthritis whose symptoms 'come and go'. If the effects are likely to recur beyond 12 months after the first occurrence, they are to be treated as long-term. However, the person will be expected to take reasonable precautions, e.g. if he knows that he is allergic to products containing wheat he will be expected to avoid them. It is for the claimant to produce medical evidence that the substantial adverse effects are more likely than not to recur.

Severe disfigurements, though not interfering with normal day-to-day activities, are to be treated as amounting to a disability. This includes scars, birthmarks, diseases of the skin and congenital abnormalities, but not self-inflicted blemishes like tattoos. This is an example of a 'stigma' disability being protected. Other conditions giving rise to a stigma, like asymptomatic HIV infection, are at present excluded.

The Act was extended in the late stages of its passage through Parliament to cover discrimination on account of past disability, i.e. one from which the person has now recovered, and is unlikely to recur. This is particularly important to those who have in the past suffered from a mental illness (another condition where a stigma remains). The past disability must have been long-term. If a person broke a leg five years ago and was in plaster for six weeks, their mobility was severely impaired, but if there are no lasting effects the disability was not long-term.

Though the Guidance does not specifically mention it, I would submit that a disability caused by a reaction to drugs which are being taken to alleviate a medical condition, if sufficiently substantial and long-term, falls within the Act, since it is (if only indirectly) caused by the disability. The Guidance states that indirect effects should be taken into account.

Certain 'anti-social' conditions are excluded from the Act. These are:

- a tendency to set fires;
- a tendency to steal;
- a tendency to physical or sexual abuse of other persons;
- exhibitionism;
- voyeurism.

Perhaps more common, addiction to alcohol, nicotine or any other substance (except medically prescribed drugs or other medical treatment) does not count as a disability. However, the *effects* of the addiction may bring the person within the Act, e.g. liver disease caused by alcohol addiction.

An interesting case was *Murray* v. *Newham Citizens Advice Bureau Ltd* (2003). Edward Murray applied to work as a volunteer and when interviewed disclosed that he had been diagnosed as a paranoid schizophrenic while in prison for having stabbed a neighbour with a knife. The CAB argued that it was not his mental illness which led to his rejection, but his violence. The Employment Appeal Tribunal decided that the physical abuse of his neighbour was a consequence of his disability, namely schizophrenia, and that discrimination for a tendency to violence was on the grounds of disability and had to be justified. When the case went back to the employment tribunal they held that the acts of the CAB were justified on the facts. This was a Bureau where clients had in the past became abusive and aggressive. It was also held that it was unnecessary to seek medical advice from Mr Murray's GP and psychiatrist. Although it is in most cases wrong to assume that schizophrenia will result in violent acts, it would seem that, where a serious assault has occurred, tribunals are likely to hold that the employer is justified in rejecting a job applicant, even though the medical advice may be that the chances of recurrence are small, at least where the job involves direct contact with potentially aggressive members of the public. As a postscript, in another case it was held by the Employment Appeal Tribunal that the Act does not protect volunteer workers (*South East Sheffield CAB* v. *Grayson* (2004)).

Certain professions were originally excluded. They were:

- the armed forces;
- prison officers;
- firefighters;
- police officers;
- members of the Ministry of Defence Police, the British Transport Police, the Royal Parks Constabulary or the UK Atomic Energy Constabulary;
- employment on a ship, aircraft or hovercraft;
- admission as a partner to partnerships.

By the Disability Discrimination Act 1995 (Amendment) Regulations 2003 all these groups, other than the armed forces, were brought within the ambit of the legislation from 1 October 2004. The Act applies to employees, apprentices, self-employed people who contract personally to do any work, contract workers, and office-holders.

The 1995 Act made unlawful discrimination which related to a person's disability, that is discrimination because of a consequence of disability, such as excessive sickness absence or inability to perform essential tasks. The Amendment Regulations 2003 (in force from 1 October 2004) created a new concept of *direct* discrimination, that is less favourable treatment because of the fact of disability itself. 'This post is not open to insulin-dependent diabetics (or those with epilepsy or a history of mental illness).' Here, the employer is making a judgment about the suitability of the disabled person on the basis of a blanket assumption about the nature of his condition, rather than an investigation of the particular individual's medical history and capabilities. Direct discrimination is unlawful, and cannot be justified.

Indirect discrimination, referred to as disability-related in the revised Code of Practice, occurs where the employer discriminates against the disabled person for a reason which relates to that person's disability, for example will employ those with epilepsy in office jobs but not working at a height, will employ those with manic depression but not in a high stress job working unsocial hours without supervision, will employ a wheelchair user in an office but not as a firefighter. Indirect discrimination can be justified if the employer has a material and substantial reason.

Where two job applicants apply for a secretarial post and both have difficulty typing, one because she has arthritis, the other because she has never been taught to type, and both are rejected for lack of qualifications, there is no discrimination since both have been treated the same. If the non-disabled applicant is appointed and the disabled applicant rejected just because of her disability, without further investigation, this will be direct discrimination and cannot be justified. But if the employer obtains medical evidence about the disabled job applicant, considers possible reasonable adjustments, but still turns her down because of her poor sickness absence record, this may be justified indirect discrimination.

The comparator in an allegation of direct discrimination is a non-disabled person, or someone with a different disability, with the same abilities as the disabled person. Indirect discrimination requires a comparison with someone to whom the reason related to the disability does not apply. Thus, in *Clark* v. *Novacold* (1999) Darren Clark was employed as a process operator in manual and physically demanding jobs. He suffered a back injury at work and after four months' sickness absence the employer obtained a report from his GP which indicated that he was unlikely to return to work within the near future. A second report from an orthopaedic consultant stated that it was likely that the injury would improve over a period of 12 months from when it occurred, but could not give an exact date for return to work. The employer dismissed Clark. It was accepted that he was disabled, because he would have substantial problems with mobility for 12 months or more. Why had he been dismissed? Because of his sickness absence, a reason related to his disability. The employer argued that it would have dismissed a non-disabled employee who had been off sick for four months with no likely date of return, but the Court of Appeal held that the appropriate comparator was not an absent non-disabled person but a non-disabled person who was not off sick, that is was at work. The reason for the discrimination was sickness absence and thus the comparison must be with someone who was not absent. The Court of Appeal, however, indicated that the dismissal might have been justified, pointing to what is now paragraph 8.24 of the Code of Practice:

'It would be justifiable to terminate the employment of an employee whose disability makes it impossible for him any longer to perform the main functions of his job, if an adjustment such as a move to a vacant post elsewhere in the business is not practicable or otherwise not reasonable for the employer to make.'

It is likely that the tribunal would demand evidence that there was no possibility of rehabilitation within a reasonable time, and that the employer needed to replace Clark. In cases involving public authorities and large companies, tribunals have expected employers to wait longer than four months.

An important decision was *Heinz* v. *Kenrick* (2000). Kenrick had been employed for seven years when he went off sick at the end of May 1996. He consulted many doctors but his condition was never satisfactorily identified, though he told the company's OH physician that he thought he had chronic fatigue syndrome (ME). In February 1997 he was warned that he was at risk of being dismissed if there was no indication of a likely date for his return. His GP reported that he did not know how long it would take him to get back to normality. He was dismissed in April 1997 after he had been off sick for nearly a year, when the OH physician advised the employer that he was still not fit for work, though Kenrick asked the employer to wait until he had seen an immunologist before acting. Three weeks after his dismissal a diagnosis of ME was confirmed. The employer acknowledged that he had ME at the date of dismissal and that this was a disability within the Act, but argued that neither it nor its OH physician knew this at the relevant time. The Employment Appeal Tribunal held that it was not necessary to prove that the employer knew of the disability. The employee had been dismissed for a reason related to disability, his sickness absence, and this was enough to establish discrimination. It was held that the dismissal was not justified, because a large employer like Heinz could have explored the possibility of part-time work and lighter duties, and also could have waited three weeks for the immunologist's report.

The DDA outlaws discrimination in every aspect of employment, from recruitment to dismissal (including constructive dismissal). A disabled person has no right to a job for which he is not properly qualified simply because of his disability. If there are two applicants for a job, one with superior qualifications and experience, but no disability, and the other with a disability, the employer may choose the better qualified applicant as long as he does not reject the other simply because of his disability.

Selection for redundancy because of a disability will be unlawful, as will a decision not to give promotion to an employee because he has a disability. Disability harassment is a form of discrimination, and the employer has a duty to try to protect disabled workers against abuse, practical jokes and bullying.

Where the person with a disability has proved discrimination, the burden shifts to the employer to show that the discrimination was justified. Justification is a reason which is both material to the circumstances of the case and substantial. To give an obvious example, an employer could justifiably reject a blind applicant for the job of lorry driver. The disability makes it impossible for the applicant to perform the duties of the post. Less obvious cases will have to be left to commonsense, medical opinion, and the judgment of the tribunal. The courts have held that the threshold for justification of a disability-related less favourable treatment is a low one. The test is very different from the objective justification test which applies in sex and race discrimination cases. 'Material' means relevant and 'substantial' means more than minor or trivial.

It is likely that tribunals will construe the word substantial in the light of their views on what is reasonable. However, in *Jones* v. *Post Office* (2001) it was held that the tribunal only has power to decide whether the employer acted within a range of reasonable management responses, not to substitute its own views for those of the employer. An example given in the Code of Practice (Paragraph 7.8) is of a worker with a mental illness who is rejected because the employer assumes he will have poor attendance. The employer should check that individual's probable attendance, otherwise he will have unlawfully discriminated against him.

The need to justify discrimination will invariably require the employer to act on proper medical evidence, and not on a stereotype. For this reason, OH specialists should always be asked for advice when making decisions about the hiring or firing of a person with a disability. It is important that the professionals agree on the principles. It will bring the profession into disrepute if one physician invariably rejects job applicants with epilepsy, while others accept their competence in at least some jobs. Where a person is known to suffer from a disability he should be considered as an individual. An example given in the Code of Practice (Paragraph 4.8) is of someone who is blind and not shortlisted for a job involving computers because the employer thinks blind people cannot use them. The employer should look at individual circumstances. *This* job applicant may have the necessary competence. This is an example of direct discrimination which cannot be justified.

The most important decision on justification to date is *Jones* v. *Post Office* (2001). Jones was a long-serving employee who drove a mail delivery van in a rural area. In 1997 he was removed from driving duties because he had become an insulin-dependent diabetic. After a review by OH he was allowed to drive only two hours a day, and required to have regular medical assessments every six months. He was unhappy about the limitation of his driving and complained that he had been discriminated against on grounds of disability. He submitted that the DVLA did not restrict the numbers of hours he could drive his own private car. The employer accepted that Jones was disabled and that the reduction in driving was discrimination related to his disability, but argued that the discrimination was justified on safety grounds, since there was a small risk that the employee might suffer a hypoglycaemic attack which would render him unconscious. The employment tribunal heard evidence from two occupational physicians employed by the Post Office, and for the applicant from a consultant physician who gave evidence of recent research. It preferred the evidence of the consultant who stated that the Post Office had been over-cautious and that there was no reason why Jones could not continue with full-time driving. In effect the tribunal made its own risk assessment.

The Court of Appeal decided that the tribunal had been in error.

'Where a properly conducted risk assessment provides a reason which is on its face both material and substantial, and is not irrational, the tribunal cannot substitute its own appraisal. The employment tribunal must consider whether the reason meets the statutory criteria; it does not have the more general power to make its own appraisal of the medical evidence and conclude that the evidence from admittedly competent medical witnesses [the OH physicians] was incorrect or make its own risk assessment.'

This ruling of the Court of Appeal is an important one for occupational health. As long as a risk assessment is 'properly conducted, based on the properly formed opinion of suitably qualified doctors and produces an answer which is not irrational' the employment tribunal has no power to substitute its own decision for that of the employer. Lady Justice Arden said this:

'Employers are not obliged to search for the Holy Grail. It is sufficient if their conclusion is one which on critical examination is found to have substance.'

Lord Justice Kay's view was that where new medical evidence arises which casts doubt on an employer's decision, it is open to the employee with a disability to submit the new evidence and ask the employer to reconsider his treatment. The employer should then ask its medical experts to consider contrary medical opinion and, if it fails to do so, the continued discriminatory treatment might cease to be justified.

In what circumstances can the tribunal interfere with the employer's risk assessment? When it is not properly conducted, or is not based on the properly formed opinion of suitably qualified doctors, or produces an irrational answer. In *Marshall* v. *Surrey Police* (2002) Rachel Marshall applied for a job with Surrey Police as a fingerprints recognition officer (a civilian post). She disclosed that she had bipolar affective disorder (manic depression) for which she had been hospitalised on three occasions in 1996 and 1997. She was interviewed and offered the post, subject to medical clearance. She was then informed that the Force Medical Officer, who had vocational training in psychiatry, had decided that she did not meet the required medical standard. She was particularly concerned that Miss Marshall had stopped taking the normal medication for her condition, lithium. The tribunal decided that the employer had not obtained a suitably qualified and expert medical opinion about the applicant's condition. The OH physician had not obtained a report from her consultant, but had made the decision on the basis of a letter from a GP who had never met Marshall. The request for a report said nothing about the requirements of the job. A consultant psychiatrist with a special interest in occupational medicine, Dr Lipsedge, gave evidence that on the report from the GP it was reasonable for the OH physician to reach a decision that Miss Marshall was likely to be unreliable. The issue before the Employment Appeal Tribunal was whether the tribunal should have excluded the consultant's evidence, following *Jones* v. *Post Office*. The Appeal Tribunal was concerned at the finding that the Force Medical Officer was not suitably qualified. She was a Doctor of Medicine, an Associate of the Faculty of Occupational Medicine and had an MSc in Occupational Health. She had been a specialist in occupational medicine for more than ten years and was now senior occupational physician for the Metropolitan Police. The judge said this:

> '... there is a real danger, if tribunals set too high a requirement for medical advice as to justification, that employers will be deterred from offering jobs because of the expense, delay and difficulty in obtaining the correct experts to report.'

The Appeal Tribunal held that it was a matter of expert medical opinion as to whether an adequate occupational medicine decision could reasonably have been made on the information available to the Force Medical Officer without her meeting Miss Marshall or obtaining a report from her psychiatrist. The expert evidence before the tribunal was that it could, and should have been taken into account. The evidence was admissible on the issue of the competence of the risk assessment, though not on the question of whether Miss Marshall was fit for the job. This case highlights the importance of explaining to employment tribunals the role of OH, the qualifications of OH professionals and the need, or absence of it, for further medical advice. It may be worth calling expert medical evidence, as in this case, as to the competence of OH professionals.

Can an employer justify discrimination by appealing to the prejudices of others – customers or fellow-employees? 'I can't employ John in the shop because his face is hideously disfigured by a burn and no-one would buy from him.' 'I have nothing against Mary, but the other secretaries know she is schizophrenic and they won't work with her, especially when she talks to herself.' As a general rule, the bigotry of others cannot justify unlawful discrimination. The first edition of the Code of Practice advised that it would be justifiable if an applicant for a job involving modelling cosmetics is turned down because she suffers from psoriasis. However, it is likely that disfigurement cannot be taken into account in 'ordinary' jobs like receptionist, hairdresser, shop assistant, school teacher (paragraph 4.16). The fact remains that human beings, and especially children, can find disfigurements repellent, and even amusing. Discrimination is unlawful, but OH professionals may be able to assist management in enlightening at least fellow-employees. Fear is often the result of ignorance.

Often, the employee's disability will make it impossible to do the job unless special adjustments are made. A wheelchair user needs a ramp up to the door, a lift to reach his office on the fourth floor and a specially adapted toilet. A partially deaf person needs a 'loop' system. Someone suffering from multiple sclerosis cannot work a full day, but has to have regular rest breaks. A person with diabetes has to have meals at regular intervals. The DDA does not permit an employer to reject any of these because the facilities are not available. He has a positive duty to explore whether adjustments can be made either to the physical environment or to working practices which would enable disabled people to undertake employment.

This is not an absolute duty. It is a duty to make a reasonable adjustment.

Reasonableness depends on practicability and cost. The Act says that, in determining what is reasonable, regard shall be had, in particular, to:

(a)   the extent to which taking the step would prevent the effect in question;
(b)   the extent to which it is practicable for the employer to take the step;
(c)   the financial and other costs which would be incurred by the employer in
      taking the step and the extent to which taking it would disrupt any of his
      activities;
(d)   the extent of the employer's financial and other resources;
(e)   the availability to the employer of financial or other assistance with respect to
      taking the step;
(f)   the nature of his activities and the size of his undertaking;
(g)   where the step would be taken in relation to a private household, the extent
      to which taking it would –
      (a)   disrupt that household, or
      (b)   disturb any person residing there.

The duty of reasonable adjustment has given rise to more litigation under the
DDA than any other issue. It is important to note that it only applies when the
employer either knows, or can reasonably be expected to know, that a job
applicant or potential applicant, or person in employment, has a disability. The
test is an objective one: did the employer take such steps as it was reasonable in all
the circumstances for him to have to take in order to prevent the arrangements he
made from placing the disabled person at a substantial disadvantage in comparison with those who were not disabled (*British Gas Services* v. *McCaull* (2001))?
An important decision is *Mid Staffordshire General Hospitals NHS Trust* v. *Cambridge*
(2003). Mrs Cambridge worked as a receptionist in a hospital. She became ill after
being exposed to dust at work when a wall was demolished. She was diagnosed
with bowing of the vocal cords and tracheitis. Management was informed by
occupational health that it would be at least 12 months before she was likely to
make a full recovery. They made the decision that she would have to be dismissed, even though she still had six months of half-pay to run. They decided (for
no obvious reason) to use the disciplinary procedure, which caused the applicant
great distress. Eventually, she was dismissed on grounds of ill-health after more
than a year's absence. The employer had taken no steps to consider how her job
and place of work might be modified to allow her to return, although there had
been a proposal to move her to a smaller department, which she had rejected.

The Employment Appeal Tribunal approved the employment tribunal's decision that the employer was in breach of the DDA in not commissioning an
assessment to enable it to decide what steps would be reasonable to prevent the
applicant from being at a disadvantage. This would include medical evidence of
her condition, and the prognosis, the effect of her disability on her, possible
modifications to her workplace and working arrangements, and possible alternative employment. The failure to undertake the assessment was in itself a breach
of the duty of reasonable adjustment under the DDA. The message is that
employers should not dismiss disabled people without first obtaining a comprehensive written report, probably from occupational health, about the matters
referred to above.

The revised Code of Practice emphasises the duty to make a risk assessment. In paragraph 6.9 it states that when an employer has reason to think that the effects of a person's disability may give rise to an issue about health and safety, it is prudent for it to have a risk assessment carried out by a suitably qualified person, both to avoid an accusation of direct discrimination and to provide justification for any discriminatory action.

'A pilot develops a heart condition, and his employer asks him to undertake a risk assessment to be carried out by an appropriate consultant. This is likely to be justifiable.'

To be carried out properly, a risk assessment should be conducted by reference to individual circumstances, and must also consider whether reasonable adjustments may remove or reduce health and safety risks related to a person's disability.

Other illustrative decisions on reasonable adjustment include *Beart* v. *H.M. Prison Service* (2003). Mrs Beart was an administrative officer who had an angry exchange of words at work with her line manager. She went off sick and was diagnosed as suffering from depression. After eight months' absence a medical report from an OH consultant stated that suitable redeployment to another prison was advisable. This recommendation was never acted upon. The tribunal held that on the facts employment was available at different prisons and that the employer should have explored the possibility of implementing the OH consultant's recommendation. This was despite the fact that Mrs Beart was still on sick leave. The Court of Appeal upheld the tribunal's decision that the employer had unlawfully discriminated against Mrs Beart.

Contrast *Callagan* v. *Glasgow City Council* (2001). A residential social worker went off sick with stress after two assaults by inmates of the home where he worked. Thereafter the sickness record of Mr Callagan seriously deteriorated. His employer tried to set up meetings with him to discuss this, but he refused to co-operate. He was warned for not complying with absence reporting procedures. Medical evidence was that he was suffering from depression and was unfit for work. There was no date when he might be likely to return to work. He was dismissed after three years of this unsatisfactory state of affairs. It was held that Callagan was disabled within the DDA. It was decided that his dismissal was justified and that there was no duty on the employers to offer part-time work as a reasonable adjustment in circumstances where he had not requested it, where he had refused to discuss his problems with the employer, where his sickness and absence record were so poor, and at the date of dismissal there was no indication of when, if ever, he would be fit for any form of work.

The case law indicates that it is important for employers to try to keep in touch with employees on long-term sickness absence, to obtain regular occupational health reports and to seek to find ways in which an employee may be assisted to return to work. However, employees are expected to act reasonably in co-operating with the employer and, where there is evidence that there are no adjustments which would in fact assist, the employer's duty is discharged.

The Act lists examples of possible adjustments:

(a)   making adjustments to premises;
(b)   allocating some of the disabled person's duties to another person;
(c)   transferring him to fill an existing vacancy;
(d)   altering his hours of working or training;
(e)   assigning him to a different place of work or training;
(f)   allowing him to be absent during working or training hours for rehabilita-
      tion, assessment or treatment;
(g)   giving him, or arranging for, training or mentoring (whether for the disabled
      person or any other person);
(h)   acquiring or modifying equipment;
(i)   modifying instructions or reference manuals;
(j)   modifying procedures for testing or assessment;
(k)   providing a reader or interpreter;
(l)   providing supervision or other support.

Note that the Act does not oblige employers to make adjustments for hypothetical employees, merely those who are already in employment and those who have made, or are likely to make, a job application. Also, the revised Code of Practice indicates (paragraph 5.6) that more extensive duties to make reasonable adjustments are owed to employees than to people who are merely thinking about applying for a job. Sometimes, disabled people are deterred from applying for a job because of the way in which the advertisement is framed. The Disability Rights Commission can make a complaint to an employment tribunal about a discriminatory advertisement. It is important that employers make public their positive attitude towards applicants with a disability. The Jobcentre Plus Service encourages them to become disability symbol users (the disability symbol is two ticks surrounded by the words 'Positive about Disabled People'). To be qualified to display this logo, employers must agree to guarantee to interview all applicants with a disability who meet the minimum criteria for a job vacancy and to consider them on their abilities, to ask disabled employees at least once a year what the employer can do to make sure that they can develop and use their abilities at work, to make every effort when employees become disabled to make sure that they stay in employment, to take action to ensure that key employees develop the awareness of disability needed to make the employer's commitments work, and, each year, to review these commitments and what has been achieved, plan ways to improve on them and let all employees know about progress and future plans. Further information about the symbol may be obtained from the Disability Employment Adviser.

The OH professional will assess the individual worker in relation to a particular job, but the employer may be reluctant to 'take a chance' on the disabled person. The Access to Work scheme, accessible through Access to Work Advisers based in Access to Work Business Centres, may cover up to 100 per cent of approved costs where an unemployed disabled person is newly recruited. If a disabled worker is already employed, the scheme pays up to 80 per cent of approved costs between £300 and £10,000, and 100 per cent of approved costs between £10,000 and the actual cost. Workstep enables people with more complex employment barriers to work effectively with the right support alongside non-disabled colleagues. Access to Work can give grants of up to 100 per cent to pay for an interpreter to remove barriers to communication at interview, provide a support worker, for example to read to a visually impaired person or help a person with care needs, provide special aids to help a disabled person function in the workplace, pay for a disabled person's fares to work and generally give advice about the employment of people with disabilities.

The Job Introduction Scheme enables the employer to take on someone with a disability for a trial period, by providing him with a contribution towards wages for the first few weeks (up to a maximum of 13 weeks). The job must be expected to last for at least six months; it must be genuine and not specially created to take advantage of JIS. Supported placements for severely disabled people are sponsored by voluntary organisations like Mencap or Scope or local authorities, who pay the disabled person's wages, with the host company providing an agreed amount for the employee's services. The sponsor pays National Insurance contributions and deducts tax.

Occasionally, able bodied employees object to what they see as preferential treatment for the person with a disability. This is not a justification for refusing to make the adjustment (Code of Practice, Paragraph 5.22). The Code of Practice advises that it is more likely to be reasonable for an employer with a substantial number of staff to have to make certain adjustments, than for a smaller employer (Paragraph 5.37). The disabled person is expected to co-operate. The Code of Practice gives this example (Paragraph 5.42):

'An employee with a mobility impairment works in a team located on an upper floor to which there is no access by lift. Getting there is very tiring for the employee, and the employer could easily make a more accessible location available for him (though the whole team could not be relocated). If, after a workplace assessment, it was decided that this was the only reasonable adjustment the employer could make, but the employee refused to work there, then the employer would not have to make any adjustment.'

The first decision of the House of Lords on the interpretation of the Disability Discrimination Act is *Archibald* v. *Fife Council* (2004). Mrs Archibald was employed by Fife Council as a road sweeper. After an operation she became virtually unable to walk. It was not disputed that she was disabled under the Act. She could do sedentary work and was keen to do so. The council arranged for her to undertake a number of computer and administration courses to equip her with appropriate skills. The assessment was positive and recommended that she was more than capable of carrying out skills in an office environment. Over the next few months she applied for over 100 posts within the council, all at a slightly higher grade than the manual grade on which she was previously employed. She was compelled to undertake competitive interviews because of the council's redeployment policy. Having failed to obtain any of these posts, Mrs Archibald complained of disability discrimination. She was eventually dismissed on grounds of incapacity and brought tribunal proceedings. She argued that the employer's duty of reasonable adjustment obliged it to transfer her to another available post, even at a higher grade. The employer argued that this was only the case where the alternative job was in the same grade. Section 7 of the Local Government and Housing Act 1989 requires all staff engaged by a local authority to be appointed on merit, so that they submitted that they were compelled to make Mrs Archibald compete with other job applicants.

The House of Lords held that the duty of reasonable adjustment meant that the employer had to consider whether Mrs Archibald could be transferred to the higher grade, without a competitive interview.

> 'There is no law against discriminating against people with a background in manual work, but it might be reasonable for an employer to have to take that difficulty into account, when considering the transfer of a disabled worker who could no longer do that kind of work. I only say "might" because it depends on the circumstances of the case.'

The 1989 Act was subject to the duty to make reasonable adjustments in the Disability Discrimination Act.

The case was sent back to the employment tribunal for a ruling on whether it was reasonable to expect the employer to transfer Mrs Archibald to an office job without making her compete with other job applicants. It might be reasonable to expect a small modification to policy either in general or in the particular case to meet the needs of a well-qualified and well-motivated employee who had become disabled. On the other hand, paragraph 8.16 of the Code states that where no reasonable adjustment enables the disabled person to continue with similar terms and conditions, it might be reasonable for the employer to have to offer a disabled employee a lower-paying job, applying the rate of pay that would apply to such a position under his usual pay practices.

The employer is not obliged to create a job for an employee who has become disabled, for example as a result of an accident at work. He is, however, required to ask whether the worker could continue with his old job if reasonable adjustments were made. Perhaps a minor part of his duties could be done by someone else, or he could work flexi-time, or he could be provided with special equipment. If this is not feasible, the employer should consider whether suitable alternative employment could be made available. It may be necessary for the employee to be provided with training. The Code of Practice advises (Paragraph 6.14) that the employer is entitled to ask whether the employee will remain in the job for long enough to justify the costs of training.

Changes in the duty of reasonable adjustment were made by the Amendment Regulations from 1 October 2004. The obligation of the employer is now to make adjustments in 'any provision, criterion or practice applied by or on behalf of an employer, or any physical feature of premises occupied by the employer.' This may extend the duty to such matters as permitting the employee to work part-time instead of full-time and providing support workers to care for the disabled person's personal needs as well as the requirements of the job. An important change is that an employer who fails to provide an adjustment deemed to be reasonable cannot then plead a defence of justification. If it is reasonable there is a duty to make it.

Where a reasonable adjustment leads to the employee working fewer hours or being less productive he is likely to receive less pay. The Disability Discrimination (Employment) Regulations 1996 provide that a system of performance-related pay, if applied equally to all employees, justifies a lower wage to the disabled person who performs less well. Paragraph 8.6 of the Code of Practice states that an employer should consider whether there might be reasonable adjustments which could help the worker be more productive, e.g. by providing different equipment. Paragraph 5.20 suggests that a disabled woman who is paid purely on her output but who needs frequent short additional breaks (for example to go to the lavatory) to which her employer has agreed, might be entitled to be paid at her average hourly rate for these breaks, as a reasonable adjustment.

When the employer is forced to make some workers redundant, he may assess all the workers in terms of skills, experience, attendance records and productivity. Is it unlawful to make an employee with a disability redundant because he scores less than his colleagues? I would submit that, as so often with employment law, much will depend on procedures. The employer should investigate the disabled person's attendance record and the reasons for absence, whether his poor attendance and productivity have been caused by failure to make reasonable adjustments, whether the disabled person is being considered for redundancy because reasonable adjustments cost the employer money (e.g. allowing him to have regular time off for hospital appointments). But if, having made these investigations, the employer identifies the employee with a disability as objectively less valuable to his enterprise, it is likely that a tribunal would uphold a decision to make him redundant. Note that the revised Code of Practice, paragraph 8.25, states that it is likely to be a reasonable adjustment to discount disability related sickness absence when assessing attendance as part of a redundancy selection scheme. My view would be that the degree of latitude depends on the amount of absence. Since there is nothing in law to prevent the employer giving the disabled employee preferential treatment, it is likely that many employers will err on the side of caution and retain the employee with a disability.

In *Morse* v. *Wiltshire County Council* (1998) the Council needed to reduce its workforce for financial reasons. Peter Morse was employed as a road worker and, after a road accident, had been left with a 20 per cent disability which meant that he could not drive a vehicle. A redundancy exercise awarded points on a number of criteria, including ability to drive, which was deemed important so that workers could be flexible. Morse was made redundant. The tribunal had not considered whether there was any reasonable adjustment which the employer could have made which would have enabled Morse to avoid redundancy. For that reason the case was remitted to a fresh tribunal to investigate that matter. Was it practicable to allocate the driving duties to another worker so that Morse could continue to work? In *Meikle* v. *Nottinghamshire County Council* (2004) the Court of Appeal held that contractual sick pay was subject to the duty of reasonable adjustment. A partially-sighted schoolteacher asked for better lighting and large print documents, and went off sick with stress when these were not provided. It was held that the employer had acted unreasonably and must pay her full pay for the year she was absent until she resigned. It is unlikely that this means that the disabled are entitled to unlimited sick pay in every situation.

Section 59 of the DDA provides that nothing in the Act makes unlawful any act done 'in pursuance of any enactment'. Therefore, an employer carrying out his statutory duties under the HSWA and regulations made thereunder can claim exemption from the DDA. Care will have to be taken with this section. It is always possible for an employer to argue that a very slight risk justifies the rejection of a disabled employee, but most health and safety legislation imposes a standard of 'reasonable practicability', not an absolute duty. Where regulations or a Code of Practice impose strict liability, section 59 will apply. In *Lane Group plc* v. *Farmiloe* (2004) a disabled employee with psoriasis could not wear safety boots as required by the Personal Protective Equipment Regulations. It was held that the employer, who had tried to find suitable footwear but failed, was justified in dismissing him. In other cases, the employer, with expert occupational health advice, will have to balance the risks against the rights of the person with a disability. Research undertaken jointly by the Health and Safety Executive and the Disability Rights Commission has indicated that at least some employers use health and safety as a 'false excuse' to justify not employing people with a disability (HSE Research Report 167: *The extent of use of health and safety requirements as a false excuse for not employing disabled persons*). In almost 30 per cent of the cases where employers used health and safety as a justification for discrimination they failed to convince the employment tribunal. In some of those cases the employer was at fault in making an assessment with inexperienced staff, relying on assumptions and general-isations, ignoring the disabled person's coping mechanisms, failing to seek OH advice or misunderstanding medical evidence.

In the context of disability discrimination, an employee's disability will not justify exclusion by itself. A thorough assessment must be made of the medical condition of the employee, the duties of his job, and the likelihood of injury. This should be done by an expert and based on scientific principles, not on prejudice. It may be that reasonable adjustment will avoid health and safety problems. The original Code of Practice gave this example:

> 'If a particular adjustment would breach health and safety or fire legislation then an employer would not have to make it. However, the employer would still have to consider whether he was required to make any other adjustment which would not breach any legislation. For instance, if someone in a wheel-chair could not use emergency evacuation arrangements such as a fire escape on a particular floor, it might be reasonable for the employer to have to relocate that person's job to an office where that problem did not arise.'

Occupational pension schemes and insurance provided by the employer are subject to the Act. However, the increased risk of employing someone with a disability may justify discrimination. Regulations permit discrimination in elig-ibility conditions (Disability Discrimination (Employment) Regulations 1996). The original Code of Practice gave the example of an employer who receives medical advice that an employee with MS is likely to retire early on health grounds. Actuarial advice is obtained that the cost of providing early retirement benefit would be substantially greater than for the average employee and so the individual is refused access to the ill-health retirement section of the pension scheme. This is justified. It may be that the employee is entitled to the job, but not the pension, so that employers will have to give them separate consideration. But an employer who denies a newly recruited disabled person access to ill-health retirement benefits without any consideration of whether he will be able to work for as many years as other employees, will be acting unlawfully. This will be direct discrimination which will not be justifiable. The duty of reasonable adjustment now applies to the provision of benefits under an occupational pension scheme or any other benefit in respect of termination of service, retirement, old age or death, or accident, injury, sickness or invalidity (Disability Discrimination Act (Pensions) Regulations 2003). The employer will be able to exclude a disabled person who is likely to be unable to work until normal retirement age from the ill-health retirement pension, but should then reduce the contributions to the pension scheme generally or, if non-contributory, pay extra wages. Police officers, who are after 1 October 2004 excluded from an ill-health retirement pension because of a medical condition which makes it more than 50 per cent likely that they will not work until retirement, are to be paid 3.5 per cent extra salary. The employer's insurance cover may be affected by the employment of a person with a disability. An example is of an employee with Parkinson's disease working in an antiques business. What if the insurance company withdraws cover for fear that the employee will drop the priceless Sèvres porcelain? It is likely that the employer would be justified in barring that person from contact with fragile items.

The non-discrimination rules as regards pensions apply not only to employers but also to trustees or managers of occupational pension schemes, including the duty of reasonable adjustment. The duty of employers, managers and trustees to make reasonable adjustments only applies to benefits in respect of periods of service after 1 October 2004. Applications alleging disability discrimination in an occupational pension scheme should be made to an employment tribunal.

As regards group insurance schemes, like medical insurance, the employer's role is often limited to explaining the availability of the scheme and proposing employees to the insurer for cover. The insurance company is permitted to treat the employee in the same way as it would treat a member of the public applying for insurance, that is, if there is actuarial justification for increasing a premium or even refusing medical insurance because of a health condition, neither the employer nor the insurance company will be liable under the DDA.

Where the employer rents premises from a landlord, he will not be able to make structural alterations without the landlord's permission. The DDA gives the disabled worker a right to make a claim against a landlord who unreasonably refuses permission. If the employer owns the premises he may need planning consent to make adjustments. An employer does not have to make an adjustment if it requires a statutory consent which has not been given. Modern buildings are likely to conform with regulations which take into account access and facilities for disabled people. The employer is not excused from the duty to make reasonable adjustments by the fact that the design and construction of a building meet the requirements of the Building Regulations.

9.8   *Occupational health and the DDA*

It should be noted that section 3A(1) of the DDA states that unlawful indirect discrimination is less favourable treatment *'for a reason related to the disabled person's disability'* (not 'on grounds of' disability, as in the sex and race discrimination legislation). There is no provision in the DDA obliging the employee to notify the employer of disability in order to receive the protection of section 3A(1). Section 4A, however, which imposes a duty to make reasonable adjustments, clearly states that there is no such duty on the employer who does not know, and cannot reasonably be expected to know of the disability.

Since the employer will be deemed to know whatever occupational health knows, it is good practice to select the best person for the job taking into account qualifications and experience before asking for medical clearance. It is then easier to justify the rejection of a disabled person before the question of medical fitness has been raised with job applicants.

Job applicants are, of course, in a dilemma. If they notify the employer of a disability they may not be interviewed; if they do not, he has no obligation to explore reasonable adjustments. The best advice is to wait until the interview before disclosing the problem, unless special facilities will be needed at the interview itself. A good employer will give applicants the opportunity of indicating any relevant effects of a disability and suggesting adjustments when he invites them to apply. In *Fozard* v. *Greater Manchester Police Authority* (1997), the applicant suffered from congenital myotonic dystrophy which caused learning difficulties and reduced manual dexterity. She applied for a job as a word processor operator. GMPA had agreed to grant an interview to any disabled job applicant with the basic qualifications for the job. On her application form Ms Fozard stated that she had a disability, but gave no details. She also stated that she did not have any special needs which needed special provision. The application form was poorly written with many mistakes of spelling and grammar. Since it was essential to be able to produce accurate written work, she was not shortlisted for interview. The tribunal decided that the employer's decision was for a reason relating to disability, but was justified by evidence that the applicant was not qualified for the job. It was not necessary for the employer to investigate the nature of the disability, because the applicant had been given the opportunity of giving that information on her application form. In *Coles* v. *Somerset County Council* (1997) the tribunal refused to draw an inference of discrimination merely from the fact that Coles stated on his application form that he had a disability (unspecified) and was not short-listed. They accepted the employer's submission that the reason was his lack of relevant experience, as disclosed on the form.

Occupational health professionals are already involved in pre-employment screening of job applicants. It is to the OH department that the employer is likely to turn for advice about the implications of the DDA. The first step will be to review any standard questionnaire. Such a document should contain a statement by the employer on the lines of the employer's commitment both to health and safety laws and the DDA, as well as an indication that clinical information is confidential to the OH department. It should also tell the applicant that the employer is not obliged to make adjustments for those with a disability if he does not know of it, and that it may be in the applicant's interest to make disclosure. It is permissible to use standard questions, for example: 'Do you suffer from diabetes?', 'Have you ever suffered from depression or other psychiatric illness?', 'Have you ever suffered from a back injury?', 'Are you taking any prescribed medication?', as long as all job applicants are asked the same questions. It is, in my view, justifiable to ask for the applicant's attendance record in recent employment. This was recommended by the Clothier Report on the Allitt case (Chapter 4) for NHS employers, as flagging up possible cause for concern.

The revised Code of Practice (paragraph 7.31) deals with medical examinations. It states that an employer will probably be acting unlawfully if, without justification, he insists on a medical check for a disabled person but not for others.

> 'An employer issues a health questionnaire to all job applicants and requires any successful job applicant who states that they are disabled to undergo a medical examination. This is unlikely to be justified.'

But the Code advises that a medical examination is justified if the job applicant discloses a condition, such as a disabling heart condition, which may be relevant to the job or the working environment. An OH nurse told me at a conference that in her organisation (an NHS Trust), where the doctor only came in once a week, human resources were unwilling to wait for a medical examination for the candidate who had been chosen as the best but disclosed a medical condition, and therefore appointed the next most suitable candidate. I advised that this was a clear breach of the DDA.

The revised Code emphasises that the OH professional must have the appropriate knowledge and expertise if his/her advice is to be relied on by the employer (Paragraph 6.15). Paragraph 6.16 continues:

> 'In any event, although medical evidence may generally be considered as an "expert contribution" it should not ordinarily be the sole factor influencing an employer's decision on employment related matters. The views of the disabled person (about his own capabilities and possible adjustments) should be sought. In addition, and subject to the considerations about confidentiality, other contributions should come from the disabled person's line manager (about the nature of the job and possible adjustments). It may also be possible to seek help from disability organisations or from JobCentre Plus, who have staff who are trained to advise about disability issues in the workplace. Ultimately, it is for the employer – and not the medical adviser – to take decisions as to whether, for example, to reject a job applicant or to maintain a disabled person's employment.'

Advice from an occupational health expert stating simply that an employee is 'unfit for work' would not mean that the employer's duty to make a reasonable adjustment was waived.

Having made the assessment, the OH professional will have to decide whether to approve the application, approve it with a recommendation for adjustment, or disapprove it. 'The buck stops here.' This is a professional judgment which must be made by the specialist in the field. It is then up to the manager to make the decision whether to appoint or not.

An illustrative case was *Paul* v. *National Probation Service* (2003). Paul applied for a job as a part-time Community Service Supervisor. At the interview he informed the manager about his impairment (chronic depression) and that he had previously taken time off as a result. He was offered the post subject to a satisfactory OH report. The OH nurse who completed the assessment was provided with a questionnaire filled in by Paul and asked to assess his suitability. She also obtained a very brief GP report that merely stated that he was likely to be on medication for the foreseeable future, but which did not comment on his ability to do the job. The nurse did not examine Paul, did not obtain a report from his consultant psychiatrist, did not speak to the consultant or the GP, and did not allow Paul to provide her with further information as he requested. He was refused the post.

Paul then contacted the nurse. He informed her that his psychiatrist supported him and that the GP who wrote the report was new, did not know him and had hardly seen him. He also asked to present a further report from his psychiatrist. The nurse told him it was not her decision and that he needed to talk to Personnel. Personnel told him that they were relying on the nurse's view that he was unfit.

The Employment Appeal Tribunal decided that this was a case of unlawful discrimination which was not justified. The GP's report did not address Paul's fitness for the post and the nurse did not take on board Paul's comments. More importantly, the nurse did not consider adjustments that might be made to the job to minimise the effects of his impairment.

Section 57 provides that a person who knowingly aids another person to do an act made unlawful by the DDA is to be treated as himself doing the same kind of unlawful act. In *London Borough of Hammersmith and Fulham* v. *Farnsworth* (2000) it was held that an occupational health professional might be held liable under this section. In this case a job applicant applied for a post with Hammersmith as a residential social worker. She was interviewed and given a provisional job offer, but was referred to the council's OH physician for medical clearance. The physician consulted her GP and hospital doctor. Miss Farnsworth had a history of depression, requiring hospital admission on more than one occasion. Despite this she had obtained a degree and had gained both voluntary and paid work experience in the social work field. It was held that the applicant was suffering from a disability under the DDA and had been discriminated against unlawfully. The discrimination was not justified. Both the employer and the OH physician were held liable.

There were two major issues in the case. The first was whether the employer knew or ought to have known of the disability. It was held that since the OH physician was an agent of, though not directly employed by, the borough, she was part of the 'decision-making team', and thus the employer, through her, had knowledge of the applicant's disability. The second point was that the OH physician had followed good ethical practice by not revealing any clinical details about Miss Farnsworth, simply stating that there was evidence of ill-health over a number of years, such that the physician was concerned that she might be liable to further recurrences affecting her performance and attendance at work. The Employment Appeal Tribunal pointed to the heading to the health questionnaire completed by Miss Farnsworth in which she revealed her disability: 'London

Borough of Hammersmith and Fulham, Health Questionnaire. All information will be treated as strictly confidential.' They decided that this meant that the applicant had consented to her answers being seen by the personnel department as well as occupational health, since the questionnaire did not specify that it was confidential to OH.

This finding reflects the general lack of knowledge of occupational health issues among the tribunals. It may be criticised on the basis that Miss Farnsworth was unlikely to have given informed consent to the disclosure of all her medical information to any manager in the London borough. Some employers have taken this decision as indicating that OH professionals are entitled to give clinical information to the personnel department, but it definitely does not decide this. It is confined to situations where the job applicant consents to the health questionnaire being sent to the personnel department, a practice which most OH professionals deplore, and which conflicts with the guidance of the Information Commissioner on the Data Protection Act (see Chapter 3).

As regards the personal liability of the OH physician, this was abandoned on appeal on a technicality, but there is no doubt that she was potentially liable under section 57. The Employment Appeal Tribunal held that the discrimination by the employer was not justifiable. Miss Farnsworth had held two part-time positions without any problems for over a year and her GP reported that her health had been good. The OH physician turned her down because of her medical history alone without considering any adjustments which might have been made. Tribunals are sympathetic to those who have suffered ill-health problems in the past but are trying to put the past behind them. The message from the tribunals is that disabled people should be given a chance to prove themselves, though the employer may insist on reasonable safeguards, such as regular monitoring, measures to reduce stress, or supervision.

The employer is liable for the acts of his employees in the same way as under the other discrimination legislation, subject to the defence that he took reasonably practicable steps to prevent the employee from doing the unlawful act. The employers of OH professionals might be held liable under these provisions. In addition, there may be potential liability for negligence if there is a failure to take reasonable care (Chapter 2). Employment tribunals may make recommendations or make an award of compensation. In cases of disability discrimination there is no upper limit on the level of damages, and damages can be awarded for injury to feelings, including aggravated damages for particularly reprehensible behaviour. The claimant does not have to establish a minimum length of service, as with the complaint of unfair dismissal. Many complaints have been made claiming compensation both for unfair dismissal and disability discrimination, but tribunals will not award double compensation.

Is the job applicant or employee obliged by law to reveal a disability to the employer? As has been discussed in Chapter 4, there is no duty to reveal information about one's own faults and shortcomings. The person with a disability must weigh the pros and cons. If he reveals information he may not get the job; if he does not, he has no right to reasonable adjustments under the DDA, and his employer has no extra duty of care to him to take account of his disability, as in *Cork* v. *Kirby MacLean* (1952) where a worker with epilepsy fell from a height when he had a fit. The employer was held not to be negligent, because he did not know of the epilepsy. In addition, the worker who puts others at risk because he does not reveal his medical condition, as, for example, Dr Ngosa, the HIV-positive gynaecologist and Dr Gaud, the hepatitis B e-antigen positive surgeon, may be both criminally and civilly liable (Chapter 2).

What if the job applicant or employee tells the OH doctor or nurse of his disability, but forbids him to repeat that information to anyone else? *Prima facie*, the ethical duty of confidence dictates silence unless there is a serious risk of harm to others. The DDA Code of Practice gives advice which at first sight seems to challenge this. It states (Paragraph 5.15) that if an employer's agent or employee (for example an occupational health officer, a personnel officer or line manager) knows in that capacity of an employee's disability then the employer cannot claim that he does not know of that person's disability and that he is therefore excluded from the obligation to make reasonable adjustment. The Code of Practice concludes that it will be necessary to set up confidential channels whereby managers will be able to receive the necessary information. I strongly disagree. In my opinion, the doctor or nurse is entitled to reveal information to managers without consent only if it is in the public interest to do so. Of course, in most cases, the worker, having been advised that adjustments would be necessary to enable him to work, will agree to disclosure. If not, my advice would be to convey to management that the worker is fit, with adjustments, without revealing clinical details. A compromise to which most workers will agree is to report the adjustments considered necessary, without giving the reason why they are advised. The Code of Practice accepts this: 'It might even be necessary for the line manager to implement adjustments without knowing precisely why he has to do so.' The Society of Occupational Medicine's Working Group on the DDA gives the example of someone with Crohn's disease who has problems with diarrhoea and may not be able to tolerate travelling during the rush hour. The occupational physician could advise management that the employee should be allowed to work different working hours without informing them of the employee's condition (*Disability Discrimination Act 1995: a Guidance for Occupational Physicians*).

Sometimes, it may be advisable for those working with the disabled person to know of his disability. A consultant anaesthetist with insulin dependent diabetes could be asked to consent to other health professionals being made aware of his condition so as to obtain prompt treatment in the event of a hypoglycaemic event.

> 'An office worker with cancer says that he does not want colleagues to know of his condition. As an adjustment he needs extra time away from work to receive treatment and to rest. Neither his colleagues nor the line manager need be told the precise reasons for the extra leave but the latter will need to know that the adjustment is required in order to implement it effectively.' (*Code of Practice*, paragraph 8.22)

Such information should never be revealed to other employees without consent, though it may be that if consent is not forthcoming reasonable adjustment is deemed impossible (*Code of Practice*, paragraph 8.23).

There is no legal authority for the proposition that confidential information in someone's personnel file can be communicated to other members of the workforce without consent. It is a breach of the employer's duty of trust and confidence.

The Code of Practice is confusing in its definition of employers' agents or employees. It states that a company would be imputed with knowledge acquired by an 'occupational health officer' (Paragraph 5.16), but not that gained by 'a person providing services to employees independently of the employer', even if the employer has arranged for those services to be provided.

> 'An employer contracts with an agency to provide an independent counselling service to employees. The contract says that the counsellors are not acting on the employer's behalf while in the counselling role. Any information about a person's disability obtained by a counsellor during such counselling would not be imputed to the employer and so would not trigger the employer's duty to make reasonable adjustments'. (Paragraph 5.16)

Why not? The counselling service is the agent of the employer. Would the same argument apply to a company like BUPA providing executive medical examinations of physical and mental health? Would an employer who uses an in-house employed occupational health service to undertake counselling services be imputed with knowledge, but not one who buys in a service from a private organisation or an NHS Trust? Could it not be argued that the special relationship of OH professional and worker carrying the obligation of confidentiality separates the OH service from management to the extent that confidential information imparted to a doctor or nurse is not in law imputed to the employer? Only test cases can give a clear answer. There are likely to be few volunteers to provide them.

In Chapter 4 there is a discussion of the (frequent) occurrence of a job applicant lying in his answers to a health questionnaire. The case of *O'Brien* v. *Prudential Assurance* (1979) found the Employment Appeal Tribunal upholding the dismissal of an employee with a history of mental illness who denied it in order to get the job. It was important that the history of ill-health was material to the particular post which involved visiting customers in their own homes. Would the result be the same under the DDA? Past illness qualifies as a disability, if it otherwise falls within the statutory definition. The employer would, no doubt, argue that he was dismissing for dishonesty, rather than disability, but a lie about a disability could be regarded as a reason related to the disability. My advice to an employer who discovers a lie is that he must undertake the same process of assessment as if he had been told the truth from the beginning. What is the likelihood of relapse? Is the employee likely to be a danger? Is an adjustment possible, e.g. a move to different duties not dealing directly with the public, or being accompanied by another employee? The fact that, as in O'Brien's case, the employee has performed in an exemplary fashion for some time, would be relevant to the assessment. The dishonesty would not to me be decisive, because disabled people, even after the DDA, are understandably nervous of the possibility of prejudice. O'Brien had applied truthfully for many jobs before he lied to the Prudential. It was only the Prudential who offered him work.

The other side of this coin is the job applicant or employee who claims to have a disability but appears to be in the best of health. There is nothing to prevent the employer from asking for medical evidence. There can also be a problem where the employee is asking for early retirement, but the employer's view is that, with rehabilitation and reasonable adjustment, the disabled person can continue in employment. The employer who acts on specialist OH medical advice, possibly backed by an independent consultant, is unlikely to be held liable under the DDA.

There are 6.9 million disabled people in the United Kingdom. The disabled make up 19 per cent of people of working age, and about 50 per cent are in employment (DWP 2002).

Since the DDA came into force, hundreds of claims have been brought to employment tribunals; a few of these have reached the Court of Appeal, and one the House of Lords. A Disability Rights Commission has been created and the result of European legislation has been to extend the protection of the Act to many employees previously excluded. Provisions relating to education and those providing goods and services have come into effect.

The Department of Work and Pensions has in recent years emphasised the importance of rehabilitation and the need for better OH and vocational rehabilitation services in the UK (*Pathways to Work – Helping People into Employment* (2003)). In a paper *Concepts of Rehabilitation for the Management of Common Health Problems* (Waddell and Burton 2004), it is stated that whilst illness, disability and incapacity are clearly related, the link between them and any objective medical condition is weaker than many patients, health professionals and employers assume.

> 'The first assumption is that work might be harmful – but current evidence suggests that, on balance, work is good for physical and mental health while long-term worklessness is detrimental. The second assumption is that rest from work is part of treatment – but modern approaches to clinical management stress the importance of continuing ordinary activities and early return to work. Finally, there is the belief that it is not possible or advisable to return to work until symptoms are completely "cured" – but modern clinical and OH management stress that return to work as early as possible is an essential part of treatment and that work itself is the best form of rehabilitation.'

A *Framework Work Document on Vocational Rehabilitation* was published by the DWP in October 2004.

Though the Act has caused great concern among OH professionals, it has also given them an increased role. The history of the Americans with Disabilities Act in the USA has been to generate considerable research into objective evaluation of risk to health, 'evidence-based medicine'. In AD 172 Galen wrote: 'Employment is nature's best physician and is essential to human happiness'. It is for the occupational health profession to seek to provide a balance between the needs of workers for employment, and the needs of the employer for reliable, safe and productive employees.

Appendix A
Reporting of Injuries, Diseases and Dangerous Occurrences Regulations 1995

Schedule 3 *Reportable diseases*

PART I OCCUPATIONAL DISEASES
(Guidance is given at Paragraph 159 on those items marked with an asterisk)

Column 1 Diseases	Column 2 Activities
Conditions due to physical agents and the physical demands of work	
1* Inflammation, ulceration or malignant disease of the skin due to ionising radiation.	Work with ionising radiation.
2* Malignant disease of the bones due to ionising radiation	
3* Blood dyscrasia due to ionising radiation.	
4* Cataract due to electromagnetic radiation.	Work involving exposure to electromagnetic radiation (including radiant heat).
5* Decompression illness.	Work involving breathing gases at increased pressure (including diving).
6 Barotrauma resulting in lung or other organ damage.	
7 Dysbaric osteonecrosis.	
8* Cramp of the hand or forearm due to repetitive movement.	Work involving prolonged periods of handwriting, typing or other repetitive movements of the fingers, hand or arm.
9 Subcutaneous cullulitis of the hand (beat hand).	Physically demanding work causing severe or prolonged friction or pressure on the hand.
10 Bursitis or subcutaneous cellulitis arising at or about the knee due to severe or prolonged external friction or pressure at or about the knee (beat knee).	Physically demanding work causing severe or prolonged friction or pressure at or about the knee.
11 Bursitis or subcutaneous cellulitis arising at or about the elbow due to severe or prolonged external friction or pressure at or about the elbow (beat elbow).	Physically demanding work causing severe or prolonged friction or pressure at or about the elbow.

Column 1 Diseases	Column 2 Activities
12 Traumatic inflammation of the tendons of the hand or forearm or of the associated tendon sheaths.	Physically demanding work, frequent or repeated movements, constrained postures or extremes of extension or flexion of the hand or wrist.
13 Carpal tunnel syndrome.	Work involving the use of hand-held vibrating tools.
14* Hand-arm vibration syndrome.	Work involving: (a) the use of chain saws, brush cutters or hand-held or hand-fed circular saws in forestry or woodworking; (b) the use of hand-held rotary tools in grinding material or in sanding or polishing metal; (c) the holding of material being ground or metal being sanded or polished by rotary tools; (d) the use of hand-held percussive metal-working tools or the holding of metal being worked upon by percussive tools in connection with riveting, caulking, chipping, hammering, fettling or swaging; (e) the use of hand-held powered percussive drills or hand-held powered percussive hammers in mining, quarrying or demolition, or on roads or footpaths (including road construction); or (f) the holding of material being worked upon by pounding machines in shoe manufacture.

Infections due to biological agents

Column 1 Diseases	Column 2 Activities
15 Anthrax.	(a) Work involving handling infected animals, their products or packaging containing infected material; or (b) work on infected sites.
16 Brucellosis.	Work involving contact with: (a) animals or their carcasses (including any parts thereof) infected by brucella or the untreated products of same; or (b) laboratory specimens or vaccines of or containing brucella.
17 (a) Avian chlamydiosis.	Work involving contact with birds infected with chlamydia psittaci, or the remains or untreated products of such birds.
(b) Ovine chlamydiosis.	Work involving contact with sheep infected with chlamydia psittaci or the remains or untreated products of such sheep.
18* Hepatitis.	Work involving contact with: (a) human blood or human blood products; or (b) any source of viral hepatitis.
19 Legionellosis.	Work on or near cooling systems which are located in the workplace and use water; or work on hot water service systems located in the workplace which are likely to be a source of contamination.

Column 1 Diseases	Column 2 Activities
20 Leptospirosis.	(a) Work in places which are or are liable to be infested by rats, fieldmice, voles or other small mammals; (b) work at dog kennels or involving the care or handling of dogs; or (c) work involving contact with bovine animals or their meat products or pigs or their meat products.
21 Lyme disease.	Work involving exposure to ticks (including in particular work by forestry workers, rangers, dairy farmers, game keepers and other persons engaged in countryside management).
22 Q fever.	Work involving contact with animals, their remains or their untreated products.
23 Rabies.	Work involving handling or contact with infected animals.
24 Streptococcus suis.	Work involving contact with pigs infected with streptococcus suis, or with the carcasses, products or residues of pigs so affected.
25 Tetanus.	Work involving contact with soil likely to be contaminated by animals.
26 Tuberculosis.	Work with persons, animals, human or animal remains or any other material which might be a source of infection.
27* Any infection reliably attributable to the performance of the work specified in the entry opposite hereto.	Work with micro-organisms; work with live or dead human beings in the course of providing any treatment or service or in conducting any investigation involving exposure to blood or body fluids; work with animals or any potentially infected material derived from any of the above.

Conditions due to substances

28 Poisonings by any of the following:	Any activity.

    (a) acrylamide monomer;
    (b) arsenic or one of its compounds;
    (c) benzene or a homologue of benzene;
    (d) beryllium or one of its compounds;
    (e) cadmium or one of its compounds;
    (f) carbon disulphide;
    (g) diethylene dioxide (dioxan);
    (h) ethylene oxide;
    (i) lead or one of its compounds;
    (j) manganese or one of its compounds;
    (k) mercury or one of its compounds;
    (l) methyl bromide;
    (m) nitrochlorobenzene, or a nitro- or amino- or chloro-derivative of benzene or of a homologue of benzene;
    (n) oxides of nitrogen
    (o) phosphorus or one of its compounds.

Column 1 Diseases	Column 2 Activities
29 Cancer of a bronchus or lung.	(a) Work in or about a building where nickel is produced by decomposition of a gaseous nickel compound or where any industrial process which is ancillary or incidental to that process is carried on; or (b) work involving exposure to bis (chloromethyl) ether or any electrolytic chromium processes (excluding passivation) which involve hexavalent chromium compounds, chromate production or zinc chromate pigment manufacture.
30 Primary carcinoma of the lung where there is accompanying evidence of silicosis.	Any occupation in: (a) glass manufacture; (b) sandstone tunnelling or quarrying; (c) the pottery industry; (d) metal ore mining; (e) slate quarrying or slate production; (f) clay mining; (g) the use of siliceous materials as abrasives; (h) foundry work; (i) granite tunnelling or quarrying; or (j) stone cutting or masonry.
31 Cancer of the urinary tract.	1 Work involving exposure to any of the following substances: (a) beta-naphthylamine or methylene-bis-orthochloroaniline; (b) diphenyl substituted by at least one nitro or primary amino group or by at least one nitro and primary amino group (including benzidine); (c) any of the substances mentioned in sub-paragraph (b) above if further ring substituted by halogeno, methyl or methoxy groups; but not by other groups; or (d) the salts of any of the substances mentioned in sub-paragraphs (a) to (c) above. 2 The manufacture of auramine or magenta.
32 Bladder cancer.	Work involving exposure to aluminium smelting using the Soderberg process.
33 Angiosarcoma of the liver.	(a) Work in or about machinery or apparatus used for the polymerisation of vinyl chloride monomer, a process which, for the purposes of this sub-paragraph, comprises all operations up to and including the drying of the slurry produced by the polymerisation and the packaging of the dried product; or (b) work in a building or structure in which any part of the process referred to in the foregoing sub-paragraph takes place.

Column 1 Diseases	Column 2 Activities
34 Peripheral neuropathy.	Work involving the use or handling of or exposure to the fumes of or vapour containing n-hexane or methyl n-butyl ketone.
35 Chrome ulceration of: (a) the nose or throat; or (b) the skin of the hands or forearm.	Work involving exposure to chromic acid or to any other chromium compound.
36 Folliculitis. 37 Acne. 38 Skin cancer.	Work involving exposure to mineral oil, tar, pitch or arsenic.

39 Pneumoconiosis (excluding asbestosis).

  1 (a) The mining, quarrying, or working of silica rock or the working of dried quartzose sand, any dry deposit or residue of silica or any dry admixture containing such materials (including any activity in which any of the aforesaid operations are carried out incidentally to the mining or quarrying of other minerals or to the manufacture of articles containing crushed or ground silica rock); or

     (b) the handling of any of the materials specified in the foregoing sub-paragraph in or incidentally to any of the operations mentioned therein or substantial exposure to the dust arising from such operations.

  2 The breaking, crushing or grinding of flint, the working or handling of broken, crushed or ground flint or materials containing such flint or substantial exposure to the dust arising from any of such operations.

  3 Sand blasting by means of compressed air with the use of quartzose sand or crushed silica rock or flint or substantial exposure to the dust arising from such sand blasting.

  4 Work in a foundry or the performance of, or substantial exposure to the dust arising from, any of the following operations:

     (a) the freeing of steel castings from adherent siliceous substance; or

     (b) the freeing of metal castings from adherent siliceous substance:

        (i) by blasting with an abrasive propelled by compressed air, steam or a wheel, or

        (ii) by the use of power-driven tools.

  5 The manufacture of china or earthenware (including sanitary earthenware, electrical earthenware and earthenware tiles) and any activity involving substantial exposure to the dust arising therefrom.

Column 1 Diseases	Column 2 Activities
	6 The grinding of mineral graphite or substantial exposure to the dust arising from such grinding. 7 The dressing of granite or any igneous rock by masons, the crushing of such materials or substantial exposure to the dust arising from such operations. 8 The use or preparation for use of an abrasive wheel or substantial exposure to the dust arising therefrom.
	9 (a) Work underground in any mine in which one of the objects of the mining operations is the getting of any material; (b) the working or handling above ground at any coal or tin mine of any materials extracted therefrom or any operation incidental thereto; (c) the trimming of coal in any ship, barge, lighter, dock or harbour or at any wharf or quay; or (d) the sawing, splitting or dressing of slate or any operation incidental thereto.
	10 The manufacture or work incidental to the manufacture of carbon electrodes by an industrial undertaking for use in the electrolytic extraction of aluminium from aluminium oxide and any activity involving substantial exposure to the dust therefrom. 11 Boiler scaling or substantial exposure to the dust arising therefrom.
40 Byssinosis.	The spinning or manipulation of raw or waste cotton or flax or the weaving of cotton or flax, carried out in each case in a room in a factory, together with any other work carried out in such a room.
41 Mesothelioma. 42 Lung cancer. 43 Asbestosis.	(a) The working or handling of asbestos or any admixture of asbestos; (b) the manufacture or repair of asbestos textiles or other articles containing or composed of asbestos; (c) The cleaning of any machinery or plant used in any of the foregoing operations and of any chambers, fixtures and appliances for the collection of asbestos dust; or (d) substantial exposure to the dust arising from any of the foregoing operations.
44 Cancer of the nasal cavity or associated air sinuses.	1 (a) Work in or about a building where wooden furniture is manufactured; (b) work in a building used for the manufacture of footwear or components of footwear made wholly or partly of leather or fibre board; or (c) work at a place wholly or mainly for the repair of footwear made wholly or partly of leather or fibre board.

Column 1 Diseases	Column 2 Activities
	2 Work in or about a factory building where nickel is produced by decomposition of a gaseous nickel compound or in any process which is ancillary or incidental thereto.
45* Occupational dermatitis.	Work involving exposure to any of the following agents: (a) epoxy resin systems; (b) formaldehyde and its resins; (c) metalworking fluids; (d) chromate (hexavalent and derived from trivalent chromium); (e) cement, plaster or concrete; (f) acrylates and methacrylates; (g) colophony (rosin) and its modified products; (h) glutaraldehyde; (i) mercaptobenzothiazole, thiurams, substituted paraphenylene-diamines and related rubber processing chemicals; (j) biocides, anti-bacterials, preservatives or disinfectants; (k) organic solvents; (l) antibiotics and other pharmaceuticals and therapeutic agents; (m) strong acids, strong alkalis, strong solutions (e.g. brine) and oxidising agents including domestic bleach or reducing agents; (n) hairdressing products including in particular dyes, shampoos, bleaches and permanent waving solutions; (o) soaps and detergents; (p) plants and plant-derived material including in particular especially the daffodil, tulip and chrysanthemum families, the parsley family (carrots, parsnips, parsley and celery), garlic and onion, hardwoods and the pine family; (q) fish, shell-fish or meat; (r) sugar or flour; or (s) any other known irritant or sensitising agent including in particular any chemical bearing the warning 'may cause sensitisation by skin contact' or 'irritating to the skin'.
46 Extrinsic alveolitis (including farmer's lung).	Exposure to moulds, fungal spores or heterologous proteins during work in: (a) agriculture, horticulture, forestry, cultivation of edible fungi or malt-working; (b) loading, unloading or handling mouldy vegetable matter or edible fungi whilst same is being stored; (c) caring for or handling birds; or (d) handling bagasse.
47* Occupational asthma.	Work involving exposure to any of the following agents: (a) isocyanates; (b) platinum salts;

Column 1	Column 2
Diseases	Activities

(c) fumes or dust arising from the manufacture, transport or use of hardening agents (including epoxy resin curing agents) based on phthalic anhydride, tetrachlorophthalic anhydride, trimellitic anhydride or triethylene-tetramine;

(d) fumes arising from the use of rosin as a soldering flux;

(e) proteolytic enzymes;

(f) animals including insects and other arthropods used for the purposes of research or education or in laboratories;

(g) dusts arising from the sowing, cultivation, harvesting, drying, handling, milling, transport or storage of barley, oats, rye, wheat or maize or the handling, milling, transport or storage of meal or flour made therefrom;

(h) antibiotics;

(i) cimetidine;

(j) wood dust;

(k) ispaghula;

(l) castor bean dust;

(m) ipecacuanha;

(n) azodicarbonamide;

(o) animals including insects and other arthropods (whether in their larval forms or not) used for the purposes of pest control or fruit cultivation or the larval forms of animals used for the purposes of research or education or in laboratories;

(p) glutaraldehyde;

(q) persulphate salts or henna;

(r) crustaceans or fish or products arising from these in the food processing industry;

(s) reactive dyes;

(t) soya bean;

(u) tea dust;

(v) green coffee bean dust;

(w) fumes from stainless steel welding;

(x) any other sensitising agent, including in particular any chemical bearing the warning 'may cause sensitisation by inhalation'.

Guidance on diseases/conditions in Schedule 3, Part I

159   The following table gives notes on those diseases in Schedule 3, Part 1 which have been highlighted with an asterisk.

Disease/condition	Schedule 3, Part 1, Item No	Guidance
Inflammation, ulceration or malignant disease of the skin due to ionising radiation	1	The following conditions should always be reported under this heading: • erythema, primary or secondary radiation burns; • subsequent acute or chronic ulcers.

Disease/condition	Schedule 3, Part 1, Item No	Guidance
		Non melanoma skin cancer is common in the general population. It need only be reported if the history of exposure or the features of the condition suggest an association with ionising radiation. This would be the case in respect of: • squamous cell carcinoma occurring after high-dose exposure or at the site of past ulceration; • basal cell carcinoma where features such as multiple lesions suggest a possible relationship with ionising radiation.
Malignant disease of the bones due to ionising radiation	2	Sarcoma of the bone is reportable. Secondary malignant disease of the bone is not reportable.
Blood dyscrasia due to ionising radiation	3	The following conditions are reportable: • acute changes in the blood picture, e.g. reduction in the number of small lymphocytes where no other clinical causes are established and there is reason to believe that this is the result of acute exposure to ionising radiation; • acute leukaemias; • chronic myeloid leukaemia; • Non-Hodgkins lymphoma; • aplastic anaemia. Polycythaemia rubra vera is not reportable.
Cataract due to electromagnetic radiation	4	Cataracts are common in the general population. They need not be reported where there is good reason to believe that they were not caused at work by exposure to electromagnetic radiation (e.g. ionising radiation, microwaves). Cataracts resulting from exposure to ionising radiations or to radiant heat typically occur at the posterior pole of the lens. Intense exposure to microwave radiation may result in anterior or posterior subcapsular opacities.
Decompression illness	5	Decompression illness is defined as any signs or symptoms arising from the presence of gas within tissues or vessels of the body following a reduction in ambient pressure.
Cramp of the hand or forearm due to repetitive movements	8	Cramp is reportable where it is a chronic condition linked to repetitive work movements. The condition is usually characterised by the inability to carry out a sequence of what were previously well co-ordinated movements. An acute incident of cramp which may occur in the course of work is not reportable.

Disease/condition	Schedule 3, Part 1, Item No	Guidance
Hand-arm vibration syndrome (HAVS)	14	Workers whose hands are regularly exposed to high vibration, for example in industries where vibratory tools and machines are used, may suffer from several kinds of injury to the hands and arm including impaired blood circulation and damage to the nerves and muscles. The injuries collectively are known as 'hand-arm vibration syndrome'. Other names used in industry include – vibration white finger, dead finger, dead hand and white finger. The severity of the vascular and neurological effects is indicated using an agreed classification system, the Stockholm Workshop Scales. More information on this and HAVS is contained in HSE guidance *Hand-arm vibration*.
Hepatitis	18	The likely sources of hepatitis are:
		Hepatitis A and E – human excreta and objects and consumables contaminated principally by excreta from people infected with hepatitis A or E virus.
		Hepatitis B, C and D – human blood and body fluids from people infected with hepatitis viruses B, C and D*, objects contaminated by blood and body fluids, particularly sharp objects such as used hypodermic needles, contaminated broken glassware and other items where these penetrate the skin or otherwise may act as a vehicle for transmission of infection.
		Other, as yet uncharacterised, forms of viral hepatitis are known to exist.
		* hepatitis D virus is only infectious in the presence of concomitant or pre-existing infection with hepatitis B.
Any infection reliably attributable to the performance of the work specified opposite hereto	27	Many minor infections such as those causing bouts of diarrhoea and respiratory complaints such as colds and bronchitis are common in the community and everyone is exposed to them. These minor illnesses cannot generally be attributed to infection contracted at work and they are generally not reportable. However, where there is reasonable circumstantial evidence, for example, known contact with the infectious agent in laboratory work, a report should be made.
Occupational dermatitis	45	*Item 45 (s) – any other known irritant or sensitising agent.* A list of examples of 'other known irritants or sensitising agents' is given in Appendix 1 of HSE Guidance Note MS 24, *Health Surveillance of Occupational Skin Disease,* and further guidance is available in the references provided in Appendix 3 of the document.

Disease/condition	Schedule 3, Part 1, Item No	Guidance
		Dermatitis can be caused by exposure to a range of common agents found outside the workplace. If there is good evidence that the condition has been caused solely by such exposure rather than by exposure to an agent at work it need not be reported.
Occupational asthma	47	*Item 47(x) – any other sensitising agent.* For examples of agents reported to have caused occupational asthma see *Preventing Asthma at Work – How to Control Respiratory Sensitisers.* Asthma is a common condition in the general population. If there is good evidence that the condition: • was pre-existing and/or; • has been caused solely by exposure to agents outside work; and • was neither exacerbated nor triggered by exposure at work, the condition need not be reported.

PART II   DISEASES ADDITIONALLY REPORTABLE IN RESPECT OF OFFSHORE WORKPLACES

48 Chickenpox.

49 Cholera.

50 Diptheria.

51 Dysentery (amoebic or bacillary).

52 Acute encephalitis.

53 Erysipelas.

54 Food poisoning.

55 Legionellosis.

56 Malaria.

57 Measles.

58 Meningitis.

59 Meningococcal septicaemia (without meningitis).

60 Mumps.

61 Paratyphoid fever.

62 Plague.

63 Acute poliomyelitis.

64 Rabies.

65 Rubella.

66 Scarlet fever.

67 Tetanus.

68 Tuberculosis.

69 Typhoid fever.

70 Typhus.

71 Viral haemorrhagic fevers.

72 Viral hepatitis.

Appendix B
Control of Substances Hazardous to Health Regulations 2002

Regulation 11 Health Surveillance

(1) Where it is appropriate for the protection of the health of his employees who are, or are liable to be, exposed to a substance hazardous to health, the employer shall ensure that such employees are under suitable health surveillance.

(2) Health surveillance shall be treated as being appropriate where –

(a) the employee is exposed to one of the substances specified in Column 1 of Schedule 6 and is engaged in a process specified in Column 2 of that Schedule, and there is a reasonable likelihood that an identifiable disease or adverse health effect will result from that exposure; or

(b) the exposure of the employee to a substance hazardous to health is such that –

    (i) an identifiable disease or adverse health effect may be related to the exposure,

    (ii) there is a reasonable likelihood that the disease or effect may occur under the particular conditions of his work, and

    (iii) there are valid techniques for detecting indications of the disease or effect,

and the technique of investigation is of low risk to the employee.

(3) The employer shall ensure that a health record, containing particulars approved by the Executive, in respect of each of his employees to whom paragraph (1) applies, is made and maintained and that that record or a copy thereof is kept available in a suitable form for at least 40 years from the date of the last entry made in it.

(4) The employer shall –

(a) on reasonable notice being given, allow an employee access to his personal health record;

(b) provide the Executive with copies of such health records as the Executive may require; and

(c) if he ceases to trade, notify the Executive forthwith in writing and make available to the Executive all health records kept by him.

(5) If an employee is exposed to a substance specified in Schedule 6 and is engaged in a process specified therein, the health surveillance required under paragraph (1) shall include medical surveillance under the supervision of a relevant doctor at intervals of not more than 12 months or at such shorter intervals as the relevant doctor may require.

(6) Where an employee is subject to medical surveillance in accordance with paragraph

(5) and a relevant doctor has certified by an entry in the health record of that employee that in his professional opinion that employee should not be engaged in work which exposes him to that substance or that he should only be so engaged under conditions specified in the record, the employer shall not permit the employee to be engaged in such work except in accordance with the conditions, if any, specified in the health record, unless that entry has been cancelled by a relevant doctor.

(7) Where an employee is subject to medical surveillance in accordance with paragraph (5) and a relevant doctor has certified by an entry in his health record that medical surveillance should be continued after his exposure to that substance has ceased, the employer shall ensure that the medical surveillance of that employee is continued in accordance with that entry while he is employed by the employer, unless that entry has been cancelled by a relevant doctor.

(8) An employee to whom this regulation applies shall, when required by his employer and at the cost of the employer, present himself during his working hours for such health surveillance procedures as may be required for the purposes of paragraph (1) and, in the case of an employee who is subject to medical surveillance in accordance with paragraph (5), shall furnish the relevant doctor with such information concerning his health as the relevant doctor may reasonably require.

(9) Where, as a result of health surveillance, an employee is found to have an identifiable disease or adverse health effect which is considered by a relevant doctor or other occupational health professional to be the result of exposure to a substance hazardous to health the employer of that employee shall –

(a) ensure that a suitably qualified person informs the employee accordingly and provides the employee with information and advice regarding further health surveillance;

(b) review the risk assessment;

(c) review any measure taken to comply with regulation 7, taking into account any advice given by a relevant doctor, occupational health professional or by the Executive;

(d) consider assigning the employee to alternative work where there is no risk of further exposure to that substance, taking into account any advice given by a relevant doctor or occupational health professional; and

(e) provide for a review of the health of any other employee who has been similarly exposed, including a medical examination where such an examination is recommended by a relevant doctor, occupational health professional or by the Executive.

(10) Where, for the purpose of carrying out his functions under these Regulations, a relevant doctor requires to inspect any workplace or any record kept for the purposes of these Regulations, the employer shall permit him to do so.

(11) Where an employee or an employer is aggrieved by a decision recorded in the health record by a relevant doctor to suspend an employee from work which exposes him to a substance hazardous to health (or to impose conditions on such work), he may, by an application in writing to the Executive within 28 days of the date on which he was notified of the decision, apply for that decision to be reviewed in accordance with a procedure approved for the purposes of this paragraph by the Health and Safety Commission, and the result of that review shall be notified to the employee and employer and entered in the health record in accordance with the approved procedure.

Control of Substances Hazardous to Health. Approved Code of Practice 2002

The objectives of health surveillance

211   The objectives of health surveillance are to:

(a)   protect the health of individual employees by detecting as early as possible, adverse changes which may be caused by exposure to substances hazardous to health;

(b)   help evaluate the measures taken to control exposure;

(c)   collect, keep up to date and use data and information for determining and evaluating hazards to health.

212   Assessing employees' immunity before or after vaccination will provide an indication of their fitness to work with the particular biological agent, as required by the Management of Health and Safety at Work Regulations 1999. Routine testing for antibodies or the taking of specimens to attempt to isolate infectious agents is not generally appropriate unless there is an indication that infection may have occurred. If an employee is found to be suffering from an infection or illness which is suspected to be the result of exposure at work, other employees who have been similarly exposed should be placed under suitable surveillance until it is established that they are not affected. Where there are early symptoms of disease that employees themselves may be able to recognise, an effective measure is to provide instruction and information that will enable them to do so, and systems for symptom reporting, though this is not 'health surveillance' within the strict meaning of the Regulations.

213   The results of health surveillance, and particularly any adverse results, should lead to some action which will benefit employees' health. Therefore, *before* health surveillance takes place, the employer should decide:

(a)   the options and criteria for action; and

(b)   the method of recording, analysing and interpreting the results.

Suitable health surveillance

214   Suitable health surveillance will *always* include the keeping of an individual health record (see paragraphs 232–236). There are a number of health surveillance procedures which can be used and the most suitable one chosen will depend on the particular workplace circumstances. The range of available procedures includes the following:

(a)   *biological monitoring* is the measurement and assessment of workplace agents or their metabolites (substances formed when the body converts the chemical) in exposed workers. Measurements are made either on samples of breath, urine or blood, or any combination of these. This may be appropriate where it is possible to link the results directly to an adverse health effect, e.g. mercury, cadmium;

(b)   *biological effect monitoring* is the measurement and assessment of early biological effects in exposed workers caused by absorption of chemicals;

(c)   *medical surveillance*, i.e. both surveillance under the supervision of a medical inspector of the HSE's Employment Medical Advisory Service, or an appointed doctor for the purpose of regulation 11(5) and under the supervision of a registered medical practitioner. It may include clinical examinations and measurements of physiological, e.g. lung function testing and psychological effects of exposure to hazardous substances in the workplace which may show as changes or alterations in body function;

(d) *enquiries* about symptoms, inspection or examination by a suitably qualified person, e.g. an occupational health nurse;

(e) *inspection* by a responsible person such as a supervisor or manager, e.g. for chrome ulceration;

(f) *review of records and occupational history* during and after exposure; this should check the correctness of the assessment of risks to health and indicate whether the assessment should be reviewed.

215   The different types of procedures need not be independent of each other because the results of one might indicate the need for another, e.g. the results of biological monitoring may show a need for other health surveillance procedures.

The person who carries out health surveillance procedures

216   For employees exposed to a substance specified in Schedule 6 and working in the related listed process, regulation 11(5) specifies the frequency of medical surveillance carried out under the supervision of medical inspectors or appointed doctors. This is at intervals not exceeding 12 months, or at such shorter intervals as the medical inspector or appointed doctor requires, and the exact nature of the examination is at their direction and discretion.

217   Other health surveillance procedures should be carried out either under the supervision of a registered medical practitioner or, where appropriate, by a suitably qualified person, e.g. an occupational health nurse or a responsible person. A responsible person is someone appointed by the employer who is competent, in accordance with regulation 12(4), to carry out the relevant procedure and who is charged with reporting to the employer the conclusions of the procedure.

When health surveillance is appropriate

218   Health surveillance, including medical surveillance under the supervision of a medical inspector or appointed doctor, is appropriate for employees liable to be exposed to the substances and working in the processes listed in Schedule 6 if the specific conditions laid down in regulation 11(2)(a) apply. Health surveillance, including the keeping of health records, will also be appropriate when employees are exposed to hazardous substances and the three requirements of regulation 11(2)(b) are satisfied.

219   The judgements that employers make under regulation 11(2)(a) and (b) on the likelihood that an identifiable disease or adverse health effect will result from or may be related to exposure should:

(a) relate to the type and extent of exposure;

(b) include assessment of current scientific knowledge such as:

   (i)   available epidemiology;

   (ii) information on human exposure;

(iii)   human and animal toxicological data; and

(iv)   extrapolation from information about similar substances or situations.

220   Valid health surveillance techniques need to be sufficiently sensitive and specific to detect abnormalities related to the type and level of exposure concerned. Those carrying out the health surveillance should know how to interpret data and this may mean having to identify normal values and to set action levels. The aim should be to establish health surveillance procedures which are easy to perform, preferably non-invasive and acceptable to employees. In particular, procedures should be safe, that is of low risk to workers, and none should be carried out if there is a risk of an employee's health being harmed.

221   Health surveillance procedures may need to be reviewed, modified or discontinued, as appropriate, depending on which of the criteria set out in paragraphs 219–220 can be applied to the particular work conditions and exposures concerned.

222   Table 2 gives examples where health surveillance is appropriate under the criteria in regulation 11(2) together with information on typical forms of surveillance. The list is not definitive and there will be other instances where health surveillance is required under the criteria at 11(2)(b).

Table 2 Substances for which health surveillance is appropriate under regulation 11(2)(b)

Substance/process	Typical procedure
(a) Substances of recognised systemic toxicity (i.e. substances that can be breathed in, absorbed through the skin or swallowed and that affect parts of the body other than where they enter).	Appropriate clinical or laboratory investigations. Biological effect monitoring
(b) Substances known to cause occupational asthma.	Enquiries seeking evidence of respiratory symptoms related to work.
(c) Substances known to cause severe dermatitis.	Skin inspection by a responsible person.
(d) (i) Electrolytic plating or oxidation of metal articles by use of an electrolyte containing chromic acid or other chromium compounds; (ii) Contact with chrome solutions in dyeing processes using dichromate of potassium or sodium; (iii) Contact with chrome solutions in processes of liming and tanning of raw hides and skins (including re-tanning of tanned hides or skins).	Skin inspection by a responsible person.

223   Other examples of where it is appropriate to carry out health surveillance are provided in relevant technical literature including HSE Guidance Notes.

Detection of an adverse health effect or identifiable disease

224   Where an employee is found to have an adverse health effect or identifiable disease which a medical inspector, appointed doctor or other occupational health professional considers to be the result of exposure to a substance hazardous to health, the employer must arrange for the employee concerned to be interviewed and told.

225   The employer should consult the medical inspector, appointed doctor or occupational health professional concerned to consider:

(a)   whether it is necessary to transfer the employee to other work where there is no exposure to the hazardous substance concerned;

(b)   whether a medical examination of the employee concerned should be arranged and if so, the person who should carry it out;

(c)   if a medical examination is necessary, whether all other employees who have been similarly exposed to the substance concerned as the affected employee should also be medically examined; and

(d)   if necessary, the facilities which should be provided and the arrangements which should be made.

226   Taking into account any advice received from the medical inspector etc. the employer must also ensure that the employee who has suffered the adverse health effect or identifiable disease is advised by a suitably qualified person of the:

(a)   arrangements which will be put in place for continuing health surveillance;

(b)   arrangements if any to transfer the employee to alternative employment within the workplace; and

(c)   action to be taken to re-assess the workplace controls.

227   The employee concerned should also be advised to visit their own doctor (general practitioner) to report the ill-health condition so that the doctor is aware of the work the employee does, and the adverse health effect which has resulted from exposure to the substance(s) concerned.

228   Any adverse health effects or identifiable diseases resulting from exposure to a substance hazardous to health should automatically prompt the employer to:

(a)   review the assessment of the work in accordance with regulation 11(9)(b); and

(b)   where necessary, review and revise the control measures in place to prevent a recurrence of the ill-health effect or disease.

Continuing health surveillance after exposure has ceased

229   In certain circumstances it may be appropriate for an employer to continue health surveillance of their employees (at least while they remain their employees) after exposure to a substance hazardous to health has ceased. The circumstances where this will be of benefit to workers may be those where an adverse effect on health may be anticipated after a latent period and where it is believed that the effect can be reliably detected at a sufficiently early stage. Examples might include those substances which cause cancer of the urinary tract.

Facilities for health surveillance

230   Where health surveillance procedures are carried out at the employer's premises, suitable facilities should be available. Where the nature of examinations or inspections requires it, the facilities should include a room which is:

(a)   clean, warm and well-ventilated;

(b)   suitably furnished with a table and seats;

(c)   equipped with a washbasin with hot and cold running water, soap and a clean towel. If it is not reasonably practicable to provide hot and cold running water, either a supply of warm water should be provided or the means of heating water in the room;

(d)   set aside for the exclusive purpose of health and safety when required and it should provide privacy.

231   Where a substantial number of employees is to be examined or assessed, the employer should also provide a suitable waiting area when reasonably practicable. Where employees are providing specimens for biological monitoring or biological effect monitoring, an adjacent toilet with hand-washing facilities should be available.

Health records

232   Employers must keep an up-to-date health record for each individual employee placed under health surveillance. It should contain at least the following particulars which are approved by HSE:

(a)   identifying details:

  (i)   surname;

  (ii)   forenames;

  (iii)   gender;

  (iv)   date of birth;

  (v)   permanent address and post code;

  (vi)   National Insurance number;

  (vii)   date when present employment started; and

  (viii) a historical record of jobs in this employment involving exposure to identified substances requiring health surveillance;

(b)   results of all other health surveillance procedures and the date on which and by whom they were carried out. The conclusions should relate *only* to the employer's fitness for work and will include, where appropriate:

  (i)   a record of the decisions of the medical inspector or appointed doctor; or

  (ii)   conclusions of the medical practitioner, occupational health nurse or other suitably qualified or responsible person.

233   The health record should not include confidential clinical data. In accordance with regulation 11(3), employers must keep these health records for at least 40 years. They may be kept in any format, e.g. on paper or electronically. Where records are kept electronically,

employers should ensure that they have a suitable back-up system that allows access to copies of the records in the event of a serious computer failure.

When individual health records only are required

234   In some circumstances, the only health surveillance required is the setting up and maintenance of individual health records containing the information in paragraph 232(a). Examples are:

(a)   known or suspected carcinogens except those in Schedule 6 shown in Table 2 (see paragraph 222);

(b)   machine-made mineral fibres, also known as 'man-made' mineral fibres and MMMF;

(c)   rubber manufacturing and processing giving rise to rubber process dust and rubber fume (except the entry for indiarubber in Schedule 6);

(d)   leather dust in boot and shoe manufacture, arising during preparation and finishing.

235   Where health surveillance consists only of setting up and maintaining an individual health record, the information required is that in paragraph 232(a).

236   In addition to keeping the particulars in paragraph 232, the employer should also keep an index or list of the names of people undergoing, or who have undergone, health surveillance. The record should be kept in a form compatible with and capable of being linked to those required by regulation 10 for monitoring of exposure, so that, where appropriate, the type and extent of exposure can be compared with effects. For example, where personal exposure monitoring under regulation 10 is carried out for an employee who is under health surveillance in accordance with regulation 11, the employer may keep the information required by regulations 10(6) and 11(3) on the same record.

Disposing of records when a business ceases to trade

237   When an employer or employer's representative, e.g. an appointed administrator, receiver or liquidator, decides that the business will cease trading, the employer should contact a medical inspector at the HSE area office nearest to where the business is located, and offer to provide the employees' health records (or copies of them) for safe keeping.

Access to employees' records

238   As well as allowing their employees to see their own individual health records maintained under regulation 11(3), employers may, with the employee's consent, also allow the employee's representatives to see them. Where under regulation 11(4)(b) HSE requests copies of an employee's personal health records, the employer should provide the information summarised in paragraph 232.

Control of Substances Hazardous to Health Regulations 2002

Schedule 6 Medical surveillance

Column 1 *Substances for which medical surveillance is appropriate*	Column 2 *Processes*
Vinyl chloride monomer (VCM).	In manufacture, production, reclamation, storage, discharge, transport, use or polymerisation.
Nitro or amino derivatives of phenol and of benzene or its homologues.	In the manufacture of nitro or amino derivatives of phenol and of benzene or its homologues and the making of explosives with the use of any of these substances.
Potassium or sodium chromate or dichromate.	In manufacture.
Orthotolidine and its salts. Dianisidine and its salts. Dichlorbenzidine and its salts.	In manufacture, formation or use of these substances.
Auramine. Magenta.	In manufacture.
Carbon disulphide. Disulphur dichloride. Benzene, including benzol. Carbon tetrachloride. Trichlorethylene.	Processes in which these substances are used, or given off as vapour, in the manufacture of indiarubber or of articles of goods made wholly or partially of indiarubber.
Pitch.	In manufacture of blocks of fuel consisting of coal, coal dust, coke or slurry with pitch as a binding substance.

Appendix C
Prescribed Occupational Diseases

Social Security (Industrial Injuries) (Prescribed Diseases) Regulations 1985, as amended

Disease number	Name of disease or injury	Type of job Any job involving
A Conditions due to physical agents (physical cause)		
A1	Leukemia (other than chronic lymphatic leukemia) or cancer of the bone, female breast, testis or thyroid.	Exposure to electromagnetic radiations (other than radiant heat) or to ionising particles where the dose is sufficient to double the risk of occurrence of the condition. *For example, people working in the nuclear industry and hospital X-ray departments.*
A2	Cataract.	Frequent or prolonged exposure to radiation from red-hot or white-hot material. *For example, glass and metal workers, stokers.*
A3	Dysbarism, including decompression sickness, barotrauma and osteonecrosis. *For example, the bends.*	Subjection to compressed or rarefied air or other respirable gases or gaseous mixtures. *For example, underwater or tunnel workers.*
A4	Cramps of the hand or forearm due to repetitive movements. *For example, writer's cramp.*	Prolonged periods of handwriting, typing or other repetitive movements of the fingers, hand or arm. *For example, typists, clerks and routine assemblers.*
A5	Subcutaneous cellulitis of the hand. (Beat hand).	Manual labour causing severe or prolonged friction or pressure on the hand. *For example, miners and road workers using picks and shovels.*
A6	Bursitis or subcutaneous cellulitis arising at or about the knee due to severe or prolonged external friction or pressure at or about the knee. (Beat knee). *For example, housemaid's knee.*	Manual labour causing severe or prolonged external friction or pressure at or about the knee. *For example, workers who kneel a lot.*
A7	Bursitis or subcutaneous cellulitis arising at or about the elbow due to severe or prolonged external friction or pressure at or about the elbow. (Beat elbow).	Manual labour causing severe or prolonged external friction or pressure at or about the elbow. *For example, jobs involving continuous rubbing or pressure on the elbow.*
A8	Traumatic inflammation of the tendons of the hand or forearm or of the associated tendon sheaths. *Tenosynovitis.*	Manual labour, or frequent or repeated movements of the hand or wrist. *For example, routine assembly workers.*

Disease number	Name of disease or injury)	Type of job Any job involving

Conditions due to physical agents (physical cause)

| A9 | Miner's nystagmus.
Jerky movements of the eyeballs. | Work in or about a mine. |
| A10 | Occupational deafness. Sensorineural hearing loss amounting to at least 50dB in each ear, being the average of hearing losses at 1, 2 and 3KHz frequencies, and being due in the case of at least one ear to occupational noise. | (a) The use of powered (but not hand powered) grinding tools on metal (other than sheet metal or plate metal), or work wholly or mainly in the immediate vicinity of those tools whilst they are being so used; or
(b) the use of pneumatic percussive tools on metal, or work wholly or mainly in the immediate vicinity of those tools whilst they are being so used, or
(c) the use of pneumatic percussive tools for drilling rock in quarries or underground or in mining coal or in sinking shafts for tunnelling in civil engineering works, or work wholly or mainly in the immediate vicinity of those tools whilst they are being so used; or
(ca) the use of pneumatic percussive tools on stone in quarry works, or work wholly or mainly in the immediate vicinity of those tools whilst they are being so used; or
(d) work wholly or mainly in the immediately vicinity of plant (excluding power press plant) engaged in the forging (including drop stamping) of metal by means of closed or open dies or drop hammers; or
(e) work in textile manufacturing where the work is undertaken wholly or mainly in rooms or sheds in which there are machines engaged in weaving man-made or natural (including mineral) fibres or in the high speed false twisting of fibres; or
(f) the use of, or work wholly or mainly in the immediate vicinity of machines engaged in cutting, shaping or cleaning metal nails; or
(g) the use of, or work wholly or mainly in the immediate vicinity of, plasma spray guns engaged in the deposition of metal; or
(h) the use of, or work wholly or mainly in the immediate vicinity of, any of the following machines engaged in the working of wood, that is to say: multi-cutter moulding machines, planing machines, automatic or semi-automatic lathes, multiple cross-cut machines, automatic shaping machines, double end tenoning machines, vertical spindle moulding machines (including high speed routing machines), edge banding machines, saw banding machines with a blade width of not less than 75 millimetres and circular sawing machines in the operation of which the blade is moved towards the material being cut; or |

Disease number	Name of disease or injury	Type of job Any job involving

Conditions due to physical agents (physical cause)

A10 *cont.*		(i) the use of chain saws in forestry; or (j) air arc gouging or work wholly in or mainly in the immediate vicinity of air arc gouging; or (k) the use of band saws, circular saws or cutting disks for cutting metal in the metal founding or forging industries, or work wholly or mainly in the immediate vicinity of those tools whilst they are being so used; or (l) the use of circular saws for cutting products in the manufacture of steel, or work wholly or mainly in the immediate vicinity of those tools whilst they are being so used; or (m) the use of burners or torches for cutting or dressing steel based products, or work wholly or mainly in the immediate vicinity of those tools whilst they are being so used; or (n) work wholly or mainly in the immediate vicinity of skid transfer banks; or (o) work wholly or mainly in the immediate vicinity of knock out and shake out grids in foundries; or (p) mechanical bobbin cleaning or work wholly or mainly in the immediate vicinity of mechanical bobbin cleaning; (q) the use of, or work wholly or mainly in the immediate vicinity of, vibrating metal moulding boxes in the concrete products industry; or (r) the use of, or work wholly or mainly in the immediate vicinity of, high pressure jets of water or a mixture of water and abrasive material in the water jetting industry (including work under water); or (s) work in ships' engine rooms; or (t) the use of circular saws for cutting concrete masonry blocks during manufacture, or work wholly or mainly in the immediate vicinity of those tools whilst they are being so used; or (u) burning stone in quarries by jet channelling processes, or work wholly or mainly in the immediate vicinity of such processes; or (v) work on gas turbines in connection with: (i) Performance testing on test bed; (ii) Installation testing of replacement engines in aircraft; (iii) Acceptance testing of Armed Service fixed wing combat planes; or (w) the use of, or work wholly or mainly in the immediate vicinity of:

Disease number	Name of disease or injury	Type of job Any job involving

Conditions due to physical agents (physical cause)

A10 *contd*		(i) Machines for automatic moulding, automatic blow moulding or automatic glass pressing and forming machines used in the manufacture of glass containers or hollow ware; (ii) spinning machines using compressed air to produce glass wool or mineral wool; (iii) continuous glass toughening furnaces.
A11	Episodic blanching, occurring throughout the year, affecting the middle or proximal phalanges, or in the case of a thumb the proximal phalanx, of: (a) in the case of a person with 5 fingers (including thumb) on one hand, any 3 of those fingers; or (b) in the case of a person with only 4 such fingers, any 2 of those fingers; or (c) in the case of a person with less than 4 such fingers, any one of those fingers or, as the case may be, the one remaining finger. (Vibration white finger).	(a) the use of hand-held chain saws in forestry; or (b) the use of hand-held rotary tools in grinding or in the sanding or polishing of metal, or the holding of material being ground, or metal being sanded or polished, by rotary tools; or (c) the use of hand-held percussive metalworking tools, or the holding of metal being worked upon by percussive tools, in riviting, caulking, chipping, hammering, fettling or swaging; or (d) the use of hand-held powered percussive drills or hand-held powered percussive hammers in mining, quarrying, demolition, or on roads or footpaths, including road construction; or (e) the holding of material being worked upon by pounding machines in shoe manufacture.
A12	Carpal tunnel syndrome.	The use of hand-held powered tools whose internal parts vibrate so as to transmit that vibration to the hand, but excluding those which are solely powered by hand.

B Conditions due to biological agents

B1	Anthrax.	Contact with animals infected with anthrax or the handling (including the loading or unloading or transport) of animal products or residues. *For example, glue and shaving brush makers.*
B2	Glanders.	Contact with equine animals or their carcasses. *For example, farm and slaughterhouse workers, and grooms handling horses.*
B3	Infection by leptospira. *For example, swamp fever, swineherd's disease, and Weil's disease.*	(a) Work in places which are, or are liable to be, infested by rats, field mice or voles, or other small mammals; or (b) work at dog kennels or the care of handling of dogs; or (c) contact with bovine animals or their meat products or pigs or their meat products. *For example, farm, veterinary, sewerage and slaughterhouse workers.*

Disease number	Name of disease or injury	Type of job Any job involving

Conditions due to biological agents

B4	Ancylostomiasis. *Hookworm disease, rarely found in this country.*	Work in or about a mine.
B5	Tuberculosis. *TB infection.*	Contact with a source of tuberculous infection. *For example, doctors, nurses, ambulance crews, pathology technicians and social workers.*
B6	Extrinsic allergic alveolitis (including farmer's lung).	Exposure to moulds or fungal spores or heterologous proteins by reason of employment in: (a) agriculture, horticulture, forestry, cultivation of edible fungi or malt-working; or (b) loading or unloading or handling in storage mouldy vegetable matter or edible fungi; or (c) caring for or handling birds; or (d) handling bagasse.
B7	Infection by organisms of the genus brucella. *Brucellosis.*	Contact with: (a) animals infected by brucella, or their carcasses or parts thereof, or their untreated products; or (b) laboratory specimens or vaccines of, or containing, brucella. *For example, farm, veterinary, slaughterhouse, animal laboratory workers.*
B8	Viral hepatitis. *An infection of the liver by a virus.*	Contact with (a) human blood or human blood products; or (b) a source of viral hepatitis. *For example, doctors, nurses, ambulance crews, pathology workers.*
B9	Infection by Streptococcus suis. *A very rare form of meningitis from exposure to injected pigs or pork products.*	Contact with pigs infected by Streptococcus suis, or with the carcasses, products or residues of pigs so infected. *For example, pork butchers, pig breeders, slaughterhouse workers.*
B10(a)	Avian chlamydiosis.	Contact with birds infected with chlamydia psittaci, or with the remains or untreated products of such birds. *For example, duck farm workers, feather processing workers, poultry meat inspectors, pet shop owners and assistants.*
B10(b)	Ovine chlamydiosis.	Contact with sheep infected with chlamydia psittaci, or with the remains or untreated products of such sheep. *For example, sheep farm workers, veterinary surgeons.*
B11	Q fever.	Contact with animals, their remains or their untreated products. *For example, farm workers involved in the rearing of sheep, abattoir workers, veterinary surgeons.*

Disease number	Name of disease or injury	Type of job Any job involving

Conditions due to biological agents

B12	Orf.	Contact with sheep or goats, or with the carcasses of sheep or goats. *For example, farm workers, abattoir workers, meat inspectors.*
B13	Hydatidosis	Contact with dogs. *For example, shepherds, veterinarians and people who care for dogs.*

C Conditions due to chemical agents

C1	Poisoning by lead or a compound of lead.	The use or handling of, and exposure to the fumes, dust or vapour of, lead or a compound of lead, or a substance containing lead. *For example, plumbers, painters, enamellers, pottery glazing workers.*
C2	Poisoning by manganese or a compound of manganese.	The use or handling of, or exposure to the fumes, dust or vapour of, manganese or a compound of manganese, or a substance containing manganese. *For example, dry battery, pottery glazing and soap workers.*
C3	Poisoning by phosphorus or an inorganic compound of phosphorus or poisoning due to the anticholinesterase or pseudo anticholinesterase action of organic phosphorus compounds.	The use or handling of, or exposure to the fumes, dust or vapour of, phosphorus or a compound of phosphorus, or a substance containing phosphorus. *For example, pest control, agricultural workers, workers on incendiary devices, match makers.*
C4	Poisoning by arsenic or a compound of arsenic.	The use or handling of, or exposure to the fumes, dust or vapour of, arsenic or a compound of arsenic, or a substance containing arsenic. *For example, leather, agricultural and metal pickling workers.*
C5	Poisoning by mercury or a compound of mercury.	The use or handling of, or exposure to the fumes, dust or vapour of, mercury or a compound of mercury, or a substance containing mercury. *For example, mirror/thermometer makers, market gardeners and explosive workers.*
C6	Poisoning by carbon bisulphide.	The use or handling of, or exposure to the fumes or vapour of, carbon bisulphide or a compound of carbon bisulphide, or a substance containing carbon bisulphide. *For example, artificial silk and cellophane makers.*
C7	Poisoning by benzene or a homologue of benzene. *Benzol/benzole, toluene/toluol, xylene/xylol.*	The use or handling of, or exposure to the fumes of, or vapour containing, benzene or any of its homologues. *For example, paint, dye, rubber goods and artificial leather workers.*

Disease number	Name of disease or injury	Type of job Any job involving
Conditions due to chemical agents		
C8	Poisoning by nitro- or amino- or chloro-derivative of benzene, or of a homologue of benzene, or poisoning by nitrochlorbenzene. *For example, Tri-nitrotoluene (TNT).*	The use or handling of, or exposure to the fumes of, or vapour containing, a nitro- or amino- or chloro-derivative of benzene; or of a homologue of benzene, or nitrochlorbenzene. *For example, dyeing and chemical workers, solvents, disinfectants and wood preservation makers and users.*
C9	Poisoning by dinitrophenol or a homologue of dinitrophenol or by substituted dinitrophenols or by the salts of such substances. *Di-nitro-ortho-cresol (DNOC).*	The use or handling of, or exposure to the fumes of, or vapour containing, dinitrophenol or a homologue or substituted dinitrophenols or the salts of such substances. *For example, dye and wood preservative makers and users, agricultural workers.*
C10	Poisoning by tetrachloroethane.	The use or handling of, or exposure to the fumes of, or vapour containing, tetrachloroethane. *For example, photographic film, wax polish, adhesives, safety glass workers.*
C11	Poisoning by diethylene dioxide (dioxan). *Not dioxin (2 4 5 T).*	The use or handling of, or exposure to the fumes of, or vapour containing, diethylene dioxide (dioxan). *For example, polishing compounds, cosmetics and paint stripper makers.*
C12	Poisoning by methyl bromide	The use or handling of, or exposure to the fumes of, or vapour containing, methyl bromide. *For example, pest controllers, makers and users of fire extinguishers.*
C13	Poisoning by chlorinated naphthalene.	The use or handling of, or exposure to the fumes of, or dust or vapour containing, chlorinated naphthalene. *For example, synthetic wax and insulated wire makers.*
C14	Poisoning by nickel carbonyl.	Exposure to nickel carbonyl gas. *For example, nickel refinery workers.*
C15	Poisoning by oxides of nitrogen.	Exposure to oxides of nitrogen. *For example, explosives and nitric acid workers.*
C16	Poisoning by gonioma kamassi. *(African boxwood).*	The manipulation of gonioma kamassi or any process in or incidental to the manufacture of articles therefrom. *For example, weaving shuttle makers.*
C17	Poisoning by beryllium or a compound of beryllium.	The use or handling of, or exposure to the fumes, dust or vapour of, beryllium or a compound of beryllium, or a substance containing beryllium. *Beryllium (or glucinum) is found in the manufacture of fluorescent lights, neon signs, metallic alloys, atomic energy, radio valves, crucibles and electrical porcelain.*

Disease number	Name of disease or injury	Type of job Any job involving

Conditions due to chemical agents

C18	Poisoning by cadmium.	Exposure to cadmium dust or fumes. *For example, alkaline battery, jewellery and fluorescent light makers. Nuclear reactor workers.*
C19	Poisoning by acrylamide monomer.	The use or handling of, or exposure to, acrylamide monomer. *For example, paper, adhesive, dye, artificial leather, photographic emulsion makers.*
C20	Dystrophy of the cornea (including ulceration of the corneal surface) of the eye. *Wasting and ulceration of the corneal surface of the eye.*	(a) The use or handling of, or exposure to, arsenic, tar, pitch, bitumen, mineral oil (including paraffin), soot or any compound, product or residue of any of these substances, except quinone or hydroquinone; or (b) exposure to quinone or hydroquinone during their manufacture. *For example, chemical workers.*
C21(a)	Localised new growth of the skin, papillomatous or keratotic. *Warts and scaliness.*	The use or handling of, exposure to, arsenic, tar, pitch, bitumen, mineral oil (including paraffin), soot or any compound, product or residue of any of these substances, except quinone or hydroquinone.
C21(b)	Squamous-celled carcinoma of the skin. *A form of skin cancer/chimney sweep's cancer.*	*For example, bituminous shale workers, optical lens makers, cotton mule spinners, workers exposed to tarry fumes.*
C22(a)	Carcinoma of the mucous membrane of the nose or associated air sinuses. *Cancer of the lining of the nose or air sinuses.*	Work in a factory where nickel is produced by decomposition of a gaseous nickel compound which necessitates working in or about a building or buildings where that process or any other industrial process ancillary or incidental thereto is carried on.
C22(b)	Primary carcinoma of a bronchus or of a lung. *Cancer of the lung or bronchus.*	

C23	Primary neoplasm (including papilloma, carcinoma-in-situ and invasive carcinoma) of the epithelial lining of the urinary tract (renal pelvis, ureter, bladder and urethra).
	Includes a form of cancer of the lining of the bladder or urinary tract.
		(a) Work in a building in which any of the following substances is produced for commercial purposes:
		    (i) alpha-naphthylamine, beta-naphthylamine or methylene-bis-orthochloroaniline;
		    (ii) diphenyl substituted by at least one nitro or primary amino group (including benzidine);
		    (iii) any of the substances mentioned in sub-paragraph (ii) above if further ring substituted by halogeno, methyl or methoxy groups, but not by other groups;
		    (iv) the salts of any of the substances mentioned in the sub-paragraphs (i) to (iii) above;
		    (v) auramine or magenta; or
		(b) the use or handling of any of the substances mentioned in sub-paragraph (a)(i) to (iv), or work in a process in which any such substance is used, handled or liberated; or

Disease number	Name of disease or injury	Type of job Any job involving

Conditions due to chemical agents

C23 *contd*		(c) the maintenance or cleaning of any plant or machinery used in any such process as is mentioned in sub-paragraph (b), or the cleaning of clothing used in any such building as is mentioned in sub-paragraph (a) if such clothing is cleaned within the works of which the building forms a part or in a laundry maintained and used solely in connection with such works; (d) exposure to coal tar pitch volatiles produced in aluminium smelting involving the Soderberg process (the method of producing aluminium by electrolysis in which the anode consists of a paste of petroleum coke and mineral oil which is baked in situ). *For example, gas retort workers, laboratory workers, workers in the synthetic dye, rubber, cable and chemical industries.*
C24(a)	Angiosarcoma of the liver. *A form of liver cancer.*	(a) Work in or about machinery or apparatus used for the polymerization of vinyl chloride monomer, a process which, for the purposes of this provision, comprises all operations up to and including the drying of the slurry produced by the polymerization and the packaging of the dried product; or (b) work in a building or structure in which any part of that process takes place. *For example, PVC makers.*
C24(b)	Osteolysis of the terminal phalanges of the fingers. *A condition of the bones of the fingertips.*	
C24(c)	Non-cirrhotic portal fibrosis. *A form of liver damage.*	
C25	Occupational vitiligo. *White patches on the skin.*	The use or handling of, or exposure to, para-tertiary-butylphenol, para-tertiary-butylcatechol, para-amyl-phenol, hydroquinone or the monobenzyl or monobutyl ether of hydroquinone. *For example, car, shoe or chemical workers.*
C26	Damage to the liver or kidneys due to exposure to Carbon Tetrachloride.	The use of or handling of, or exposure to the fumes of, or vapour containing Carbon Tetrachloride. *For example, workers in chemical factories.*
C27	Damage to the liver or kidneys due to exposure to Carbon Trichloromethane (Chloroform).	The use of or handling of, or exposure to the fumes of, or vapour containing Trichloromethane (Chloroform). *For example, workers in chemical factories, laboratory workers.*
C28	Central nervous system dysfunction and associated gastro-intestinal disorders due to exposure to Chloromethane (Methyl Chloride).	The use of or handling of, or exposure to the fumes of, or vapour containing Chloromethane (Methyl Chloride). *For example, workers in chemical factories, laboratory workers.*
C29	Peripheral neuropathy due to exposure to n-hexane or methyl n-butyl ketone.	The use of or handling of, or exposure to the fumes of, or vapour containing n-hexane or methyl n-butyl ketone. *For example, printers, workers exposed to fuel emissions or adhesive fumes.*

Disease number	Name of disease or injury	Type of job Any job involving

Conditions due to chemical agents

| C30 | Chrome dermatitis, or ulceration of the mucous membranes or the epidermis, resulting from exposure to chromic acid, chromates or bi-chromates. *For example, ulcers of the inside of the nose or mouth, or skin rash, dermatitis through working with chromium compounds.* | The use or handling of, or exposure to chromic acid, chromates or bi-chromates. *For example, workers in chemical factories, dye factories, photographic processors, leather tanning industry, chromium plating industry.* |

D Miscellaneous conditions

| D1 | Pneumoconiosis. *Includes silicosis and asbestosis.* | (1) (a) The mining, quarrying or working of silica rock or the working of dried quartzose sand or any dry deposit or dry residue of silica or any dry admixture containing such materials (including any occupation in which any of the aforesaid operations are carried out incidentally to the mining or quarrying of other minerals or to the manufacture of articles containing crushed or ground silica rock); (b) the handling of any of the materials specified in the foregoing subparagraph in or incidental to any of the operations mentioned therein, or substantial exposure to the dust arising from such operations. (2) The breaking, crushing or grinding of flint or the working or handling of broken, crushed or ground flint or materials containing such flint, or substantial exposure to the dust arising from any such operations. (3) Sand blasting by means of compressed air with the use of quartzone sand or crushed silica rock or flint, or substantial exposure to the dust arising from sand and blasting. (4) Work in a foundry or the performance of, or substantial exposure to the dust arising from, any of the following operations: (a) the freeing of steel castings from adherent siliceous substance; (b) the freeing of metal castings, from adherent siliceous substance: (i) by blasting with an abrasive propelled by compressed air, by steam or by a wheel, or (ii) by the use of power-driven tools (5) The manufacture of china or earthenware (including sanitary earthenware, electrical earthenware and earthenware tiles), and any occupation involving substantial exposure to the dust arising therefrom. (6) The grinding of mineral graphite, or substantial exposure to the dust arising from such grinding. |

Disease number	Name of disease or injury	Type of job Any job involving

Miscellaneous conditions

(7) The dressing of granite or any igneous rock by masons or the crushing of such materials, or substantial exposure to the dust arising from such operations.

(8) The use, or preparation for use, of a grindstone, or substantial exposure to the dust arising therefrom

(9) (a) The working or handling of asbestos or any admixture of asbestos;

(b) the manufacture or repair of asbestos textiles or other articles, containing or composed of asbestos;

(c) the cleaning of any machinery or plant used in any foregoing operations and of any chambers, fixtures and appliances for the collection of asbestos dust;

(d) substantial exposure to the dust arising from any of the foregoing operations.

(10) (a) Work underground in any mine in which one of the objects of the mining operations is the getting of any mineral;

(b) the working or handling above ground at any coal or tin mine of any minerals extracted therefrom, or any operation incidental thereto;

(c) the trimming of coal in any ship, barge, or lighter, or in any dock or harbour or at any wharf or quay;

(d) the sawing, splitting or dressing of slate, or any operation incidental thereto.

(11) The manufacture of carbon electrodes by an industrial undertaking for use in the electrolytic extraction of aluminium from aluminium oxide, and any occupation involving substantial exposure to the dust arising therefrom.

(12) Boiler scaling or substantial exposure to the dust arising therefrom.

(13) Exposure to dust if the person employed in it has never at any time worked in any of the other occupations listed.

| D2 | Byssinosis.
A respiratory condition. | Work in any room where any process up to and including the weaving process is performed in a factory in which the spinning or manipulation of raw or waste cotton or of flax, or the weaving of cotton or flax, is carried on.
For example, cotton or flax workers. |

Disease number	Name of disease or injury	Type of job Any job involving

Miscellaneous conditions

D3   Diffuse mesothelioma (primary neoplasm of the mesothelium of the pleura or of the pericardium or of the peritoneum).
A cancer starting in the covering of the lungs or the lining of the abdomen.   Exposure to asbestos, asbestos dust or any admixture of asbestos at a level above that commonly found in the environment at large.

D4   Allergic rhinitis which is due to exposure to any of the following agents:
(a) isocyanates
(b) platinum salts
(c) fumes of dusts arising from the manufacture, transport or use of hardening agents (including epoxy resin curing agents) based on phthalic anhydride, tetrachlorophthalic anhydride, trimellitic anhydride or triethylenetetramine
(d) fumes arising from the use of rosin as a soldering flux
(e) proteolytic enzymes
(f) animals including insects and other anthropods used for the purposes of research or education or in laboratories
(g) dusts arising from the sowing, cultivation, harvesting, drying, handling, milling, transport or storage of barley, oats, rye, wheat or maize, or the handling milling, transport or storage of meal or flour made therefrom
(h) antibiotics
(i) cimetidine
(j) wood dust
(k) ispaghula
(l) castor bean dust
(m) ipecacuanha
(n) azodicarbonamide
(o) animals including insects and other anthropods or their larval forms used for the purposes of pest control or fruit cultivation, or the larval forms of animals used for the purposes of research, education or in laboratories
(p) glutaraldehyde
(q) persulphate salts or henna
(r) crustaceans or fish or products arising from these in the food processing industry
(s) reactive dyes
(t) soya bean
(u) tea dust
(v) green coffee bean dust
(w) fumes from stainless steel welding.
For example, hay fever symptoms.   Exposure to any of the agents set out in column 2 of this paragraph.
Wide range of occupations, for example, metal plating industry, food processing, laboratory workers, grain processing, drug manufacture, washing powder manufacture, hair dressing, electronic industry, welders, dye, tea and coffee processing.

Disease number	Name of disease or injury	Type of job Any job involving

Miscellaneous conditions

D5	Non-infective dermatitis of external origin (excluding dermatitis due to ionising particles or electromagnetic radiations other than radiant heat). *For example, skin rash, dermatitis.*	Exposure to dust, liquid or vapour or any other external agent except chromic acid, chromates or bi-chromates, capable of irritating the skin (including friction or heat but excluding ionising particles or electromagnetic radiations other than radiant heat). *For example, any job involving exposure to a substance which can irritate the skin except for jobs involving exposure to chromium compounds (see C30) and radiation.*
D6	Carcinoma of the nasal cavity or associated air sinuses (nasal carcinoma). *Cancer of the nose.*	(a) Attendance for work in or about a building where wooden goods are manufactured or repaired; or (b) attendance for work in a building used for the manufacture of footwear or components of footwear made wholly or partly of leather or fibreboard; or (c) attendance for work at a place used wholly or mainly for the repair of footwear made wholly or partly of leather or fibreboard.
D7	Asthma which is due to exposure to any of the following agents: (a) isocyanates (b) platinum salts (c) fumes or dusts arising from the manufacture, transport or use of hardening agents (including epoxy resin curing agents) based on phthalic anhydridge, tetrachlorophthalic anhydride, trimellitic anhydride or triethylenetetramine (d) fumes arising from the use of rosin as a soldering flux (e) proteolytric enzymes (f) animals including insects and other arthropods used for the purposes of research or education or in laboratories (g) dusts arising from the sowing, cultivation, harvesting, drying, handling, milling, transport or storage of barley, oats, rye, wheat or maize, or the handling, milling, transport or storage of meal for flour made therefrom (h) antibiotics (i) cimetidine (j) wood dust (k) ispaghula (l) castor bean dust (m) ipecacuanha (n) azodicarbonamide (o) animals including insects and other arthropods or their larval forms, used for the purposes of pest control or fruit cultivation, or the larval forms of animals used for the purposes of research, education or in laboratories	Exposure to any of the agents set out in column 2 of this paragraph.

Disease number	Name of disease or injury	Type of job Any job involving

Miscellaneous conditions

D7 *contd*	(p) glutaraldehyde (q) persulphate salts or henna (r) crustaceans or fish or products arising from these in the food processing industry (s) reactive dyes (t) soya bean (u) tea dust (v) green coffee bean dust (w) fumes from stainless steel welding (x) any other sensitising agent *Occupational asthma*	

D8	Primary carcinoma of the lung where there is accompanying evidence of one or both of the following:
	(a) asbestosis
	(b) unilateral or bilateral diffuse pleural thickening extending to a thickness of 5mm or more at any point within the area affected as measured by a plain chest radiograph (not being a computerised tomography scan or other form of imaging) which:
	  (i) in the case of unilateral diffuse pleural thickening, covers 50% or more of the area of the chest wall of the lung affected; or
	  (ii) in the case of bilateral diffuse pleural thickening, covers 25% or more of the combined area of the chest wall of both lungs.
		(a) The working or handling of asbestos or any admixture of asbestos; or
		(b) the manufacture or repair of asbestos textiles or other articles containing or composed of asbestos; or
		(c) the cleaning of any machinery of plant used in any of the foregoing operations and of any chambers, fixtures and appliances for the collection of asbestos dust; or
		(d) substantial exposure to the dust arising from any of the foregoing operations.

D9	Unilateral or bilateral diffuse pleural thickening extending to a thickness of 5mm or more at any point within the area affected as measured by a plain chest radiograph (not being a computerised tomography scan or other form of imaging) which:
	  (i) in the case of unilteral diffuse pleural thickening, covers 50% or more of the area of the chest wall of the lung affected; or
	  (ii) in the case of bilateral diffuse pleural thickening, covers 25% or more of the combined area of the chest wall of both lungs.
		As D8 above.

D10	Primary carcinoma of the lung.	(a) Work underground in a tin mine; or (b) exposure to bis (chloromethyl) ether produced during the manufacture of chloromethyl methyl ether; or (c) exposure to zinc chromate, calcium chromate or strontium chromate in their pure forms.

Disease number	Name of disease or injury	Type of job Any job involving

Miscellaneous conditions

D11	Primary carcinoma of the lung where there is accompanying silicosis.	Exposure to silica dust in the course of: (a) the manufacture of glass or pottery (b) tunnelling in, or quarrying sandstone or granite (c) mining metal ores (d) slate quarrying or the manufacturing of artefacts from slate (e) mining clay (f) using siliceous materials as abrasives (g) cutting stone (h) stonemasonry (i) work in a foundry
D12	Chronic bronchitis or emphysema; or both where, with maximum effort, there is accompanying evidence of a forced expiratory volume in one second which is: (i) at least one litre below the appropriate mean value predicted, obtained from the following prediction formulae which gives the mean values predicted in litres: • For a man, where the measurement is made without back-extrapolation, $(3.62 \times \text{Height in metres})$ minus $(0.031 \times \text{Age in years})$ minus 1.41; or, where the measurement is made with back-extrapolation, $(3.71 \times \text{Height in metres})$ minus $(0.032 \times \text{Age in years})$ minus 1.44 • For a woman, where the measurement is made without back-extrapolation, $(3.29 \times \text{Height in metres})$ minus $(0.029 \times \text{Age in years})$ minus 1.42; or, where the measurement is made with back-extrapolation, $(3.37 \times \text{Height in metres})$ minus $(0.030 \times \text{Age in years})$ minus 1.46 (ii) **or** less than one litre.	Exposure to coal dust by reason of working underground in a coal mine for a period or periods amounting in the aggregate to at least 20 years (whether before or after 5 July 1948) and any such period or periods shall include a period or periods of incapacity while engaged in such an occupation.

Appendix D
Management of Health and Safety at Work Regulations 1999 and Approved Code of Practice

Regulation 6 Health Surveillance

Every employer shall ensure that his employees are provided with such health surveillance as is appropriate having regard to the risks to their health and safety which are identified by the assessment.

Approved Code of Practice

41 The risk assessment will identify circumstances in which health surveillance is required by specific health and safety regulations e.g. COSHH. Health surveillance should also be introduced where the assessment shows the following criteria to apply:

(*a*) there is an identifiable disease or adverse health condition related to the work concerned; and

(*b*) valid techniques are available to detect indications of the disease or condition; and

(*c*) there is a reasonable likelihood that the disease or condition may occur under the particular conditions of work; and

(*d*) surveillance is likely to further the protection of the health of the employees to be covered.

42 Those employees concerned and their safety or other representatives should be given an explanation of, and opportunity to comment on, the nature and proposed frequency of such health surveillance procedures and should have access to an appropriately qualified practitioner for advice on surveillance.

43 The appropriate level, frequency and procedure of health surveillance should be determined by a competent person acting within the limits of their training and experience. This could be determined on the basis of suitable general guidance (e.g. regarding skin inspection for dermal effects) but in certain circumstances this may require the assistance of a qualified medical practitioner. The minimum requirement for health surveillance is keeping a health record. Once it is decided that health surveillance is appropriate, it should be maintained throughout an employee's employment unless the risk to which the worker is exposed and associated health effects are rare and short term.

44 Where appropriate, health surveillance may also involve one or more health surveillance procedures depending on suitability in the circumstances (a non-exhaustive list of examples of diseases is included in the footnote for guidance).[10] Such procedures can include:

(a) inspection of readily detectable conditions by a responsible person acting within the limits of their training and experience;

(b) enquiries about symptoms, inspection and examination by a qualified person such as an Occupational Health Nurse;

(c) medical surveillance, which may include clinical examination and measurement of physiological or psychological effects by an appropriately qualified person;

(d) biological effect monitoring, i.e. the measurement and assessment of early biological effects such as diminished lung function in exposed workers; and

(e) biological monitoring, i.e. the measurement and assessment of workplace agents or their metabolites either in tissues, secreta, excreta, expired air or any combination of these in exposed workers.

45 The primary benefit, and therefore objective of health surveillance should be to detect adverse health effects at an early stage, thereby enabling further harm to be prevented. The results of health surveillance can provide a means of:

(a) checking the effectiveness of control measures;

(b) providing a feedback on the accuracy of the risk assessment; and

(c) identifying and protecting individuals at increased risk because of the nature of their work.

---

[10] If the worker is exposed to noise or hand-arm vibrations, health surveillance may be needed under these regulations. If the worker is exposed to hazardous substances such as chemicals, solvents, fumes, dusts, gases and vapours, aerosols, biological agents (micro-organisms), health surveillance may be needed under COSHH. If the worker is exposed to asbestos, lead, work in compressed air, medical examinations may be needed under specific regulations.

Appendix E
Disability Discrimination Act 1995: Guidance on matters to be taken into account in determining questions relating to the definition of disability

C   Normal day-to-day activities

Meaning of 'normal day-to-day activities'

C1.   The Act states that an impairment must have a long-term substantial adverse effect on normal day-to-day activities (S1).

C2.   The term 'normal day-to-day activities' is not intended to include activities which are normal only for a particular person or group of people. Therefore in deciding whether an activity is a 'normal day-to-day activity' account should be taken of how far it is normal for most people and carried out by most people on a daily or frequent and fairly regular basis.

C3.   The term 'normal day-to-day activities' does not, for example, include work of any particular form, because no particular form of work is 'normal' for most people. In any individual case, the activities carried out might be highly specialised. The same is true of playing a particular game, taking part in a particular hobby, playing a musical instrument, playing sport, or performing a highly skilled task. Impairments which affect only such an activity and have no effect on 'normal day-to-day activities' are not covered. The examples included in this section give an indication of what are to be taken as normal day-to-day activities.

C4.   The Act states that an impairment is only to be treated as affecting the person's ability to carry out *normal day-to-day activities* if it affects one of the following:

- mobility;
- manual dexterity;
- physical co-ordination;
- continence;
- ability to lift, carry or otherwise move everyday objects;
- speech, hearing or eyesight;
- memory or ability to concentrate, learn or understand; or
- perception of the risk of physical danger (Sch 1, Para 4).

C5.   In many cases an impairment will adversely affect the person's ability to carry out a range of normal day-to-day activities and it will be obvious that the overall adverse effect is substantial or the effect on at least one normal day-to-day activity is substantial. In such a case it is unnecessary to consider precisely how the person is affected in each of the respects listed in paragraph C4. For example, a person with a clinically well-recognised mental illness may experience an adverse effect on concentration which prevents the person from remembering why he or she is going somewhere; the person would not also have to demonstrate that there was an effect on, say, speech. A person with an impairment which has an adverse effect on sight might be unable to go shopping unassisted; he or she would not also have to demonstrate that there was an effect on, say, mobility.

C6.   Many impairments will, by their nature, adversely affect a person directly in one of the respects listed in C4. An impairment may also indirectly affect a person in one or more of these respects, and this should be taken into account when assessing whether the impairment falls within the definition. For example:

- medical advice: where a person has been professionally advised to change, limit or refrain from a normal day-to-day activity on account of an impairment or only do it in a certain way or under certain conditions;
- pain or fatigue: where an impairment causes pain or fatigue in performing normal day-to-day activities, so the person may have the capacity to do something but suffers pain in doing so; or the impairment might make the activity more than usually fatiguing so that the person might not be able to repeat the task over a sustained period of time.

C7.   Where a person has a mental illness such as depression account should be taken of whether, although that person has the physical ability to perform a task, he or she is, in practice, unable to sustain an activity over a reasonable period.

C8.   Effects of impairments may not be apparent in babies and young children because they are too young to have developed the ability to act in the respects listed in C4. Regulations provide that where an impairment to a child under six years old does not have an effect in any of the respects in C4, it is to be treated as having a substantial and long-term adverse effect on the ability of that child to carry out normal day-to-day activities where it would normally have a substantial and long-term adverse effect on the ability of a person aged six years or over to carry out normal day-to-day activities.

C9.   In deciding whether an effect on the ability to carry out a normal day-to-day activity is a substantial adverse effect, account should be taken of factors such as those mentioned under each heading below. The headings are exhaustive – the person must be affected in one of these respects. The lists of examples are not exhaustive; they are only meant to be illustrative. The assumption is made in each example that there is an adverse effect on the person's ability to carry out normal day-to-day activities. A person only counts as disabled if the substantial effect is adverse.

C10.   The examples below of what it would, and what it would not, be reasonable to regard as substantial adverse effects are indicators and not tests. They do not mean that if a person can do an activity listed then he or she does not experience any substantial adverse effects; the person may be inhibited in other activities, and this instead may indicate a substantial effect.

C11.   In reading examples of effects which it would not be reasonable to regard as substantial, the effect described should be thought of as if it were the only effect of the impairment. That is, if the effect listed in the example were the only effect it would not be reasonable to regard it as substantial in itself.

C12.   Examples of effects which are obviously within the definition are not included below. So for example, inability to dress oneself, inability to stand up, severe dyslexia or a severe speech impairment would clearly be covered by the definition and are not included among the examples below. The purpose of these lists is to provide help in cases where there may be doubt as to whether the effects on normal day-to-day activities are substantial.

C13.   The examples below describe the effect which would occur when the various factors described in Parts A and B above have been allowed for. This includes, for example the effects of a person making such modifications of behaviour as might reasonably be expected, or of disregarding the impact of medical or other treatment.

Mobility

C14.   This covers moving or changing position in a wide sense. Account should be taken of the extent to which, because of either a physical or a mental condition, a person is inhibited in getting around unaided or using a normal means of transport, in leaving home with or without assistance, in walking a short distance, climbing stairs, travelling in a car or completing a journey on public transport, sitting, standing, bending, or reaching, or getting around in an unfamiliar place.

Examples

It would be reasonable to regard as having a substantial adverse effect:

- inability to travel a short journey as a passenger in a vehicle;
- inability to walk other than at a slow pace or with unsteady or jerky movements;
- difficulty in going up or down steps, stairs or gradients;
- inability to use one or more forms of public transport;
- inability to go out of doors unaccompanied.

It would not be reasonable to regard as having a substantial adverse effect:

- difficulty walking unaided a distance of about 1.5 kilometres or a mile without discomfort or having to stop – the distance in question would obviously vary according to the age of the person concerned and the type of terrain;
- inability to travel in a car for a journey lasting more than two hours without discomfort.

Manual dexterity

C15.   This covers the ability to use hands and fingers with precision. Account should be taken of the extent to which a person can manipulate the fingers on each hand or co-ordinate the use of both hands together to do a task. This includes the ability to do things like pick up or manipulate small objects, operate a range of equipment manually, or communicate through writing or typing on standard machinery. Loss of function in the dominant hand would be expected to have a greater effect than equivalent loss in the non-dominant hand.

Examples

It would be reasonable to regard as having a substantial adverse effect:

- loss of function in one or both hands such that the person cannot use the hand or hands;
- inability to handle a knife and fork at the same time;

- ability to press the buttons on keyboards or keypads but only much more slowly than is normal for most people.

It would not be reasonable to regard as having a substantial adverse effect:

- inability to undertake activities requiring delicate hand movements, such as threading a small needle;
- inability to reach typing speeds standardised for secretarial work;
- inability to pick up a single small item, such as a pin.

Physical co-ordination

C16.   This covers balanced and effective interaction of body movement, including hand and eye co-ordination. In the case of a child, it is necessary to take account of the level of achievement which would be normal for a person of the particular age. In any case, account should be taken of the ability to carry out 'composite' activities such as walking and using hands at the same time.

Examples

It would be reasonable to regard as having a substantial adverse effect:

- ability to pour liquid into another vessel only with unusual slowness or concentration;
- inability to place food into one's own mouth with fork/spoon without unusual concentration or assistance.

It would not be reasonable to regard as having a substantial adverse effect:

- mere clumsiness;
- inability to catch a tennis ball.

Continence

C17.   This covers the ability to control urination and/or defecation. Account should be taken of the frequency and extent of the loss of control and the age of the individual.

Examples

It would be reasonable to regard as having a substantial adverse effect:

- even infrequent loss of control of the bowels;
- loss of control of the bladder while asleep at least once a month;
- frequent minor faecal incontinence or frequent minor leakage from the bladder.

It would not be reasonable to regard as having a substantial adverse effect:

- infrequent loss of control of the bladder while asleep;
- infrequent minor leakage from the bladder.

Ability to lift, carry or otherwise move everyday objects

C18.   Account should be taken of a person's ability to repeat such functions or, for example, to bear weights over a reasonable period of time. Everyday objects might include such items as books, a kettle of water, bags of shopping, a briefcase, an overnight bag, a chair or other piece of light furniture.

Examples

It would be reasonable to regard as having a substantial adverse effect:

- inability to pick up objects of moderate weight with one hand
- inability to carry a moderately loaded tray steadily.

It would not be reasonable to regard as having a substantial adverse effect:

- inability to carry heavy luggage without assistance;
- inability to move heavy objects without a mechanical aid.

Speech, hearing or eyesight

C19.   This covers the ability to speak, hear or see and includes face-to-face, telephone and written communication.

(i) Speech

Account should be taken of how far a person is able to speak clearly at a normal pace and rhythm and to understand someone else speaking normally in the person's native language. It is necessary to consider any effects on speech patterns or which impede the acquisition or processing of one's native language, for example by someone who has had a stroke.

Examples

It would be reasonable to regard as having a substantial adverse effect:

- inability to give clear basic instructions orally to colleagues or providers of a service;
- inability to ask specific questions to clarify instructions;
- taking significantly longer than average to say things.

It would not be reasonable to regard as having a substantial adverse effect:

- inability to articulate fluently due to a minor stutter, lisp or speech impediment;
- inability to speak in front of an audience;
- having a strong regional or foreign accent;
- inability to converse in a language which is not the speaker's native language.

(ii) Hearing

If a person uses a hearing aid or similar device, what needs to be considered is the effect that would be experienced if the person were not using the hearing aid or device. Account should be taken of effects where the level of background noise is within such a range and of such a type that most people would be able to hear adequately.

Examples

It would be reasonable to regard as having a substantial adverse effect:

- inability to hold a conversation with someone talking in a normal voice in a moderately noisy environment;
- inability to hear and understand another person speaking clearly over the voice telephone.

It would not be reasonable to regard as having a substantial adverse effect:

- inability to hold a conversation in a very noisy place, such as a factory floor;
- inability to sing in tune.

(iii) Eyesight

If a person's sight is corrected by spectacles or contact lenses, or could be corrected by them, what needs to be considered is the effect remaining while they are wearing such spectacles or lenses, in light of a level and type normally acceptable to most people for normal day-to-day activities.

Examples

It would be reasonable to regard as having a substantial adverse effect:

- inability to see to pass the eyesight test for a standard driving test;
- inability to recognise by sight a known person across a moderately-sized room;
- total inability to distinguish colours;
- inability to read ordinary newsprint;
- inability to walk safely without bumping into things.

It would not be reasonable to regard as having a substantial adverse effect:

- inability to read very small or indistinct print without the aid of a magnifying glass;
- inability to distinguish a known person across a substantial distance (e.g. playing field);
- inability to distinguish between red and green.

Memory or ability to concentrate, learn or understand

C20.   Account should be taken of the person's ability to remember, organise his or her thoughts, plan a course of action and carry it out, take in new knowledge, or understand spoken or written instructions. This includes considering whether the person learns to do things significantly more slowly than is normal. Account should be taken of whether the person has persistent and significant difficulty in reading text in standard English or straightforward numbers.

Examples

It would be reasonable to regard as having a substantial adverse effect:

- intermittent loss of consciousness and associated confused behaviour;
- persistent inability to remember the names of familiar people such as family or friends;
- inability to adapt after a reasonable period to minor change in work routine;
- inability to write a cheque without assistance;
- considerable difficulty in following a short sequence such as a simple recipe or a brief list of domestic tasks.

It would not be reasonable to regard as having a substantial adverse effect:

- occasionally forgetting the name of a familiar person, such as a colleague;
- inability to concentrate on a task requiring application over several hours;
- inability to fill in a long, detailed, technical document without assistance;
- inability to read at faster than normal speed;
- minor problems with writing or spelling.

Perception of the risk of physical danger

C21. This includes both the underestimation and overestimation of physical danger, including danger to well-being. Account should be taken, for example, of whether the person is inclined to neglect basic functions such as eating, drinking, sleeping, keeping warm or personal hygiene; reckless behaviour which puts the person or others at risk; or excessive avoidance behaviour without a good cause.

Examples

It would be reasonable to regard as having a substantial adverse effect:

- inability to operate safely properly-maintained equipment;
- persistent inability to cross a road safely;
- inability to nourish oneself (assuming nourishment is available);
- inability to tell by touch that an object is very hot or cold.

It would not be reasonable to regard as having a substantial adverse effect:

- fear of significant heights;
- underestimating the risk associated with dangerous hobbies, such as mountain climbing;
- underestimating risks – other than obvious ones – in unfamiliar workplaces.

References

Beveridge, W. (1942) *Social Services and Allied Services*. Cmnd 6404. HMSO, London.

BMA (1984) *The Occupational Physician*, 3rd edn. British Medical Association, London.

BMA (2001) *The Occupational Physician*. British Medical Association, London.

Brahams, D. (1992) Death of a remand prisoner. *Lancet*, **340**, 1462.

Bunt, Karen (1993) *Occupational Health Provision at Work*. HMSO, London.

Calabresi, G. (1970) *The Costs of Accidents*. Yale University Press, New Haven, Connecticut.

Campbell, S. (1986) *Labour Inspection in the European Community*. HMSO, London.

Cane, P. (1993) *Atiyah's Accidents, Compensation and the Law*, 5th edn. Butterworth's, London.

Commission of the European Union (1997) *Information notices on diagnosis of occupational diseases*. EUR 14768 EN, Luxembourg.

Committee of Inquiry into Industrial Health Services (Dale Committee) Report (1951). Cmnd 8170, HMSO, London.

Committee of Inquiry into Health and Safety at Work (Robens Committee) Report (1972). Cmnd 5034. HMSO, London.

Dawson, S., Willman, P., Clinton, A. & Bamford, M. (1988), *Safety at Work: the Limits of Self-Regulation*. Cambridge University Press, Cambridge.

Department of Health (1992) *The Health of the Nation*. Cm 1986. HMSO, London.

Department of Health (1994) *The Allitt Inquiry*. HMSO, London.

Department of Health (1998) *Our Healthier Nation*. Cm 3852. HMSO, London.

Department of Health (2001) *Governance Arrangements for NHS Research Ethics Committees*. Department of Health, London.

Department of Health (2003) *Confidentiality NHS Code of Practice*. Department of Health, London.

Department of Health (2003) *Our Inheritance, Our Future*. Cm 5791-II. Stationery Office, London.

Discher, D., Kleinman, G. and Foster, F.J. (1975) *Pilot Study for Development of an Occupational Disease Surveillance Method*. Publication no.75–162, National Institute for Occupational Safety and Health (NIOSH), USA.

Doll, R. & Peto, R. (1981) *The Causes of Cancer: Quantitative Estimates of Avoidable Risks of Cancer in the United States Today*. Oxford University Press, Oxford.

Dorward, A. (1993) *Managers' Perceptions of the Role and Continuing Education Needs of Occupational Health Nurses*. HSE Books, Suffolk.

DTI (1993) *Review of the implementation and enforcement of EC law in the UK*. Department of Trade and Industry, London.

DWP (2004) *Building Capacity for Work: A UK Framework for Vocational Rehabilitation*. Department of Work and Pensions, London.

English National Board for Nursing, Midwifery and Health Visiting and the Department of Health (1998) *Occupational Health Nursing*. English National Board, London.

EOC (1979) *Health and Safety Legislation: Should we distinguish between Men and Women?* Equal Opportunities Commission, Manchester.

Fletcher, A.C. (1985) *Reproductive Hazards at Work*. Equal Opportunities Commission, Manchester.

GMBATU (1987) *Hazards of Work.* General, Municipal, Boilermakers and Allied Trades Union, Esher, Surrey.

GMC (2003) *A Licence to Practise and Revalidation.* General Medical Council, London.

GMC (2004) *Confidentiality: Protecting and Providing Information.* General Medical Council, London.

Goodman, M.J. (ed.) *Encyclopaedia of Health and Safety at Work: Law and Practice.* Sweet & Maxwell, London.

Ham, C., Dingwall, R., Fenn, P. & Harris, D. (1988) *Medical Negligence: Compensation and Accountability.* King's Fund Institute, London.

Harvey, S. (1988) *Just an Occupational Hazard?* King's Fund Institute, London.

Health and Safety Commission (HSC) (1978) *Occupational Health Services: The Way Ahead.* HMSO, London.

Honey, S., Hillage, J., Patch, A. & Morris, S. (1996) *Health Surveillance in Great Britain.* HSE Books, Sudbury, Suffolk.

HSC (1986) *The International Labour Organisation Convention 161 and Recommendation 171 on Occupational Health Services.* HMSO, London.

HSC (1994) *Review of Health and Safety Regulation: Main Report.* HMSO, London.

HSC (2001) *Securing Health Together: An Occupational Health Strategy.* HSE Books, Sudbury, Suffolk.

HSE (1991) *Successful Health and Safety Management.* HSE Books, Suffolk.

HSE (1993, 2nd edn 1997) *The Cost of Accidents at Work.* HSE Books, Suffolk.

HSE (1995) *The costs to the British economy of work accidents and work-related ill-health.* HSE Books, Suffolk.

HSE (1998) *The Changing Nature of Occupational Health.* HSE Books, Sudbury, Suffolk.

House of Lords Select Committee on Science and Technology (1983) *Occupational Health and Hygiene Services (Gregson Report).* HLP 28. HMSO, London.

House of Lords Select Committee on Science and Technology (1984). *Occupational Health and Hygiene Services: the Government Response.* HLP 289. HMSO, London.

Human Genetics Commission (2002) *Inside Information.* Human Genetics Commission, London.

Hutter, B.M. & Lloyd-Bostock, S. (1990) The power of accidents: the social and psychological impact of accidents and the enforcement of safety regulations. *British Journal of Criminology* **30**, 409.

Independent Inquiry into Drug Testing at Work (2004) *Drug Testing in the Workplace.* Joseph Rowntree Foundation, York.

Industrial Injuries Advisory Council (1981) *Industrial Disease: a review of the schedule and the question of industrial proof.* Cmnd 8393. HMSO, London.

International Commission on Occupational Health (ICOH) (1992) International Code of Ethics for Occupational Health Professionals. *Bull.Med.Eth.* **82**, 7 October.

James, P. (1992) Reforming British health and safety law: a framework for discussion. *Industrial Law Journal* **21** (2), 83.

James, P. & Walters, D. (2004) Is workplace health and safety really revitalised? *Occupational Health Review* **108**, 12.

Kahn-Freund, O. (1983) *Labour and the Law* (eds P. Davies & M. Freedland), 3rd edn. Stevens, London.

Lewis, R. (1987) *Compensation for Industrial Injury.* Professional Books, Abingdon.

Mashaw, J.L. (1996) *Work and Cash Benefits.* WE Upjohn Institute for Employment Research, Kalamazoo, MI, USA.

Morgenstern, F. (1982) *Deterrence and Compensation.* International Labour Organisation, Geneva.

Occupational Health Review (1996) Occupational Health nurses: a survey.

Occupational Health Review **59**, 9–16, **60**, 21–27.

RCN (1987) *Code of Professional Practice in Occupational Health Nursing*. Royal College of Nursing, London.

RCN (1991) *Guide to Occupational Health Nursing*. Royal College of Nursing, London.

RCN (2003) *Confidentiality: RCN Guidance for Occupational Health Nurses*. Royal College of Nursing, London.

RCP (1986) *Research on healthy volunteers*. Royal College of Physicians, London.

RCP (1993) *Guidance on ethics for occupational physicians*, 4th edn. Royal College of Physicians (Faculty of Occupational Medicine), London.

RCP (1996) *Guidelines on the Practice of Ethics Committees in Medical Research*, 3rd edn., Royal College of Physicians, London.

RCP (2001) *Good Medical Practice for Occupational Physicians*. Faculty of Occupational Medicine, Royal College of Physicians, London.

Royal Commission on Civil Liability and Compensation for Personal Injury (Pearson Commission) (1978) Cmmd 7054. HMSO, London.

Samuels S.W. (1986) Medical surveillance: biological, social and ethical parameters. *J. Occup. Med.* **28**, 572–7.

Society of Occupational Health Nursing and the Association of Occupational Health Nurse Practitioners (UK) (1998) *Occupational Health Nursing: a professional perspective*.

Troup, J.D.G. & Edwards, F.C. (1985) *Manual Handling: a Review Paper*. HMSO, London.

Waddell, G. & Burton, K. (2004) *Concepts of Rehabilitation for the Management of Common Health Problems*. Stationery Office, London.

Webb, S. (1910) Preface to *A History of Factory Legislation*, 3rd edn (by B.L. Hutchins & A. Harrison). Frank Cass & Co Ltd, London.

Webb, S. & Webb, B. (1897) *Industrial Democracy*. Reprinted 2003 as part of *Webbs on Industrial Democracy* by Palgrave Macmillan Archive Collection, London.

INDEX